Visual J++ 1.0 Publishers Edition

Microsoft® Corp. Visual J++™ Publishers Edition, included on the accompanying CD, allows you to create your own Visual J++™ programs without purchasing the commercial version. The Publishers Edition does differ from the commercial version in some ways: No Database support for SQL and ODBC databases through Data Access Objects (DAO) and Remote Data Objects (RDO); no JET engine for creating programs that work with Access and other DAO databases; no Zoomin and WinDiff tools; no third-party tools and libraries that integrate with Visual J++™; no redistribution of Java virtual machine and Internet Explorer; no code samples; no Microsoft technical support; no free or discounted upgrades to later versions of Visual J++™ Professional Edition.

Microsoft Corp. Visual J++™ Publishers Edition requires the following to operate:

- Personal computer with a 486 or higher processor running MS Windows® 95 or Windows NT® Workstation version 4 or later operation system
- 8M of memory (12M recommended) if running Windows 95; 16M (20M recommended) if running Windows NT Workstation
- Hard-disk space:

  Typical installation: 20M

  Minimum installation: 14M

  CD-ROM installation (tools run from the CD): 50M
- A CD-ROM drive
- VGA or higher resolution monitor (super VGA recommended)
- Microsoft mouse or compatible point device

Tom Swan's Mastering Java with Visual J++

Tom Swan

sams
net

201 West 103rd Street
Indianapolis, Indiana 46290

To Richard and Ray.

Copyright © 1997 by Tom Swan

FIRST EDITION

International Standard Book Number: 1-57521-210-2

Library of Congress Catalog Card Number: 96-70393

2000   99   98   97   4   3   2   1

Interpretation of the printing code: the rightmost double-digit number is the year of the book's printing; the rightmost single-digit, the number of the book's printing. For example, a printing code of 97-1 shows that the first printing of the book occurred in 1997.

Composed in AGaromond and MCPdigital by Macmillan Computer Publishing

Printed in the United States of America

Trademarks

Publisher and President:	Richard K. Swadley
Publishing Manager:	Greg Wiegand
Director of Editorial Services:	Cindy Morrow
Managing Editor:	Mary Inderstrodt
Director of Marketing:	Kelli S. Spencer
Assistant Marketing Manager:	Wendy Gilbride
	Rachel Wolfe

Acquisitions Editor
Greg Wiegand

Development Editor
Anthony Amico

Software Development Specialist
Brad Myers

Production Editor
Ryan Rader

Indexer
Cheryl Dietsch

Technical Reviewers
Greg Guntle
Chris Stone

Editorial Coordinator
Katie Wise

Technical Edit Coordinator
Lynette Quinn

Editorial Assistants
Carol Ackerman
Andi Richter
Rhonda Tinch-Mize

Cover Designer
Tim Amrhein

Book Designer
Alyssa Yesh

Copy Writer
David Reichwein

Production Team Supervisors
Brad Chinn
Charlotte Clapp

Production
Georgiana Briggs
Cyndi Davis
Betsy Deeter
Ayanna Lacey

Overview

Contents

vii

Answers to Exercises

Preface

Computer programmers of all kinds, from old salts to lowly swabs, have watched the Java programming language flood the world of software development like a rogue wave born in a storm at sea. Until recently, however, using Java development systems seemed like rowing upstream in a leaky boat without a paddle. (I know because I've done both!)

Java is a cleanly implemented language, similar to C++ in many respects but without most of that language's well-known quirks. Especially if you know C++, you'll want to learn Java. But if you are just getting started in programming, you'll find Java to be an excellent first language.

As in my other books, I tried to pack as many listings as I could into these pages. There's nothing like real code running on a real computer to illustrate programming topics. I present a wide range of Java applets and applications in the book and on the CD-ROM found inside the back cover. You can use most of this book's information with any Java compiler, but some information about specific tools and compilation techniques necessarily requires Visual J++ versions 1.0 or 1.1.

I truly hope you enjoy reading this book as much as I have enjoyed writing it. Good luck!

Tom Swan
Key West, FL

Acknowledgments

Many thanks to all who helped on this book, provided encouragement, and made it possible for me to write this text, including (in alphabetical order) Tony Amico, Greg Guntle, Ryan Rader, Richard Swadley, and Greg Wiegand. Thanks also to my friends and family for your support and understanding.

About the Author

Tom Swan is an internationally popular author of more than 30 books on computer programming in C++, Pascal, and assembly language. His books are favorites in classrooms and have been translated into 10 different languages. Professional developers worldwide have cut their programming teeth on Tom Swan's best-selling books such as *Mastering Borland C++ 5.0*, *Mastering Turbo Assembler*, *Learning C++*, and *Code Secrets*. Tom Swan is a frequent contributor and former columnist of *Dr. Dobb's Journal*, *PC World*, and *PC Techniques* magazines.

Tell Us What You Think!

As a reader, you are the most important critic and commentator of our books. We value your opinion and want to know what we're doing right, what we could do better, what areas you'd like to see us publish in, and any other words of wisdom you're willing to pass our way. You can help us make strong books that meet your needs and give you the computer guidance you require.

Do you have access to CompuServe or the World Wide Web? Then check out our CompuServe forum by typing GO SAMS at any prompt. If you prefer the World Wide Web, check out our site at http://www.mcp.com.

> **NOTE**
>
> If you have a technical question about this book, call the technical support line at 317-581-3833.

As the publishing manager of the group that created this book, I welcome your comments. You can fax, e-mail, or write me directly to let me know what you did or didn't like about this book—as well as what we can do to make our books stronger. Here's the information:

Fax: 317-581-4669

E-mail: programming_mgr@sams.mcp.com

Mail: Greg Wiegand
Sams.net Publishing
201 W. 103rd Street
Indianapolis, IN 46290

Introductions

CHAPTER

1

Introducing
This Book

Microsoft's Visual J++ for Windows 95 and Windows NT is rapidly changing the scene of Java programming, not only for developing interactive Internet applets, but also for constructing full-scale applications. During the past several months, I've spent most of my waking hours (and some of my sleeping hours as well) working with and writing Java code using Visual J++. The result is this book, *Mastering Java with Visual J++*, which covers Java from soup to nuts.

This chapter explains the book's parts and pieces, and suggests ways to use the information. The next two chapters in Part I introduce the Visual J++ development system and the Java programming language.

Here's What's Here

As in my other Sams *Mastering* titles, this book is for programmers who need a focused guide for using Java and Visual J++ to write real code for the real world. This book is short on theory and long on actual programming techniques. I'll suggest some ways to configure your system and use the Visual J++ development system, but this book is not intended to replace the product's references and user guides. (For instance, I won't waste your time or mine explaining how to use the text editor in Microsoft's Developer and Visual Studio 97 development systems.)

Mastering Java with Visual J++ is a complete tutorial and advanced guide for using Java to write applets and applications. Part II presents a complete Java tutorial, suitable for programmers who know another language or for beginners just getting started. Exercises at the end of each chapter in Part II help you test your knowledge; answers for all exercises are at the end of the book. Parts III and IV cover advanced topics and explain how to use Java packages, the Microsoft SDK, converting C++ code to Java, and more.

Getting the Most Bang from Your Book

Because this book covers a wide variety of Java programming topics for a broad audience, depending on your programming skill, you can read the chapters in different ways. For example, if you are a C++ programmer, you might first want to read Chapter 20, "Java for C++ Programmers," before tackling the Java tutorials in Part II. However, most readers—especially beginners—will benefit from reading this book from start to finish. I've arranged the chapters in order of difficulty, and later chapters tend to build on the information in earlier ones. To help you find information most useful to you, consult the chapter summaries in this chapter.

I do not assume in this book that you are an expert-level programmer, but you'll find the going easier if you have at least a smattering of programming experience. Because Java resembles C++, if you know that language, you can probably scan the early chapters quickly; however, there are important differences between C++ and Java that you won't want to miss. If you are relatively new to programming, it's best to thoroughly study the Java tutorials in Part II, and do all the exercises in those chapters, before moving on to the book's more advanced subjects.

Sample Source Code

All source code files for all sample programs are included in this book and on the CD-ROM. You may use any or all of these source code files in your own compiled programs. You do not need special permission to use my code—in fact, I'll be honored if you do!

Tutorial Exercises

To help you test your growing knowledge of Java programming, the tutorial chapters in Part II end with several exercises. Try your hand at completing the suggested projects—or, if you're really in a hurry, just think about the problems and then look up the answers near the end of the book to find out if you are on target. Answers to all exercises are included, and any referenced listings are in the Answers directory on the CD-ROM.

Part and Chapter Summaries

The following summaries describe this book's parts and chapters. Use these summaries along with the Table of Contents and Index to find exactly the information you need.

Part Summaries

Mastering Java with Visual J++ is divided into four parts, each of which contains several chapters. (Part V contains the appendixes.) This layout is similar to that used in my book, *Mastering Borland C++ 5.* The four parts are as follows:

- **Part I, "Introductions."** Chapters in this part introduce this book, the Visual J++ development system, and the Java programming language. Read these chapters to get started programming with Java quickly, and for quick overviews of the information covered in the book.

- **Part II, "Java Tutorials."** Chapters in this part provide a complete tutorial to the Java programming language. Numerous sample applications fully explain how to write Java code and how to use the language's fundamental elements.

- **Part III, "Packages."** Chapters in this part demonstrate how to use most of Java's class libraries, called packages. Because Java grows almost daily, it isn't possible to cover every class, but with the information in this part, you will be able to pick up new packages easily on your own. Numerous sample listings demonstrate how to import packages and use their facilities to create applets, windows, graphics, and other types of applications. You also learn how to create your own packages.

- **Part IV, "Developer's Toolbox."** Chapters in this part introduce the Microsoft Java SDK, which provides tools and classes for advanced Java programming, and they also provide a guide to Java for C++ programmers.

Chapter Summaries

The following summaries briefly describe the content of each of the book's chapters.

Part I, "Introductions"

1. **"Introducing This Book."** This chapter, as you are discovering, explains how to get the most from this book and also summarizes its parts and chapters.

2. **"Introducing Visual J++."** This chapter introduces the Visual J++ development system and suggests ways to configure your computer.

3. **"Introducing Java Programming."** This chapter introduces Java programming and explains how to use Visual J++ to create Java applets and applications.

Part II, "Java Tutorials"

4. **"Elemental Constructions."** This chapter covers Java fundamentals such as identifiers, keywords, data types, variables, operators, expressions, and flow-control statements.

5. **"Classes and Objects."** This chapter introduces the concept of object-oriented programming using Java classes, and it shows how to program methods, use input and output, program with inheritance, initialize objects, and clean up unused objects. (Chapter 8 covers additional and advanced class and object-oriented topics.)

6. **"Strings and Characters."** This chapter explains how to use Java's String and StringBuffer classes, the char data type, string constructors, string methods, and the Character wrapper class.

7. **"Numerical Classes."** This chapter demonstrates how to use the Math class, random numbers, and object-oriented numerical wrapper classes.

8. **"More About Classes and Objects."** This chapter expands on the information introduced in Chapter 5 and provides an in-depth guide to object-oriented programming with Java objects and classes, covering advanced class concepts, abstract classes, interface classes, access specifiers, and friendly declarations.

9. **"Exceptions."** This chapter introduces the concept of exception handling for building robust applications that correctly handle error conditions, and it covers try, catch, and throw blocks; the finally statement; creating your own exception objects; and Java's class library exceptions.

10. **"Arrays and Other Containers."** This chapter explains how to create arrays, use multidimensional arrays, initialize array elements, copy arrays, handle array exceptions, use the Cloneable and Enumeration interfaces, and create storage vessels with Java's container classes.

11. **"Threads."** This chapter explains the concepts of multithreaded programming and demonstrates how to use the Thread class, implement the Runnable interface, and synchronize code for safe data access.

Part III, "Packages"

12. **"Introducing Packages."** This chapter explains how to import and use classes from Java's packages, which are analogous to class libraries in other development systems. The chapter also introduces Java's standard packages and explains how to create your own packages—a great way to organize a complex application's many classes and to share classes among applications.

13. **"Applets."** This chapter introduces techniques for writing applets using the Applet class. The chapter also explains how to use the HTML `<applet>` tag, call Applet class methods, and use other applet programming techniques.

14. **"Another Window Toolkit."** This chapter demonstrates how to design graphical applet interfaces, use the AWT classes, program with components such as buttons and scroll bars, handle events, and use component and component-container classes. (Officially, AWT stands for Abstract Window Toolkit, but it is more commonly known by the title shown here.)

15. **"Events and Layouts."** This chapter explains how to use the Event and Toolkit classes, program event handlers, configure components with the AWT's layout classes, and develop layout strategies.

16. **"Windows, Menus, and Dialogs."** This chapter shows how to program separate frame windows, and it explains the differences between windows and frames. You learn how to create a menu bar, respond to menu selections, create a dialog window, transfer data to and from dialog controls, and use the file dialog to prompt users for filenames.

17. **"Graphics, Animation, and Multimedia."** This chapter covers a variety of graphics classes, including Graphics, Color, Polygon, and Font. The chapter also explains how to load and display image files, the proper use of multithreaded code in graphics applications, how to animate a sequence of images, and how to play a sound file.

18. **"Input and Output."** This chapter reviews standard input and output techniques introduced in Part II and shows how to use the File class to access files and directories, read and write binary data, use file streams, read and write typed data files, and program random-access file applications.

Part IV, "Developer's Toolbox"

19. **"Microsoft's Java SDK."** This chapter provides an overview of the Microsoft Java SDK (Software Development Kit) and explains how to use the SDK's tools to create stand-alone Windows executable Java applications, and how to use other tools such as WJview, ClassVue, and AppletViewer. The chapter also explains the advantages and disadvantages of using the extended FontX class for displaying text using TrueType fonts. You'll find information here on creating true Windows menu bars using the SDK's extended menu classes.

20. **"Java for C++ Programmers."** This chapter compares Java and C++, and it lists numerous examples written in both languages. C++ programmers can use this chapter to learn Java quickly, or as a guide to converting C++ programs to Java.

Other Goodies

In addition to its many chapters, *Mastering Java with Visual J++* provides several appendixes and references that you might find useful. The following are brief summaries of these extra goodies:

- **Appendix A, "Operator Precedence and Associativity."** This table lists Java's operators and shows their precedence and associativity levels for creating expressions that are evaluated correctly.
- **Appendix B, "Keywords."** This table lists all of Java's reserved keywords.
- **"Answers to Exercises."** This section provides answers to all exercises in the book's tutorial chapters in Part II.
- **"Glossary."** This section defines many of the terms and phrases used in this book.
- **"Bibliography."** This section lists additional references and books on Java programming.
- **"Index."** This alphabetically arranged subject index lists most of the book's individual topics and page numbers.
- **"Installing the CD-ROM."** This page explains how to install the CD-ROM. Sample listings are in directories named the same as the program. For example, the DateDemo application explained in Part II is in the Part2\DateDemo directory. To compile and run the sample programs, copy the files to your hard drive and refer to instructions in the next two chapters and also in the chapters that list the programs.

Summary

- *Mastering Java with Visual J++* is short on theory and long on practical programming techniques using Java. It is not intended to replace the official Visual J++ references.
- If you already know another programming language, you'll find this book easier to understand, but beginners and gurus are equally welcome. Experienced programmers can skip to specific chapters. If you are just getting started, your best bet is to read the book from cover to cover.
- All source code files for all sample applets and applications are included in this book and on the accompanying CD-ROM. You may use any or all of my source code in your own compiled programs without special permission.
- This chapter lists chapter and part summaries. When searching for specific topics, remember to consult the Table of Contents and Index.

What's Next?

Continue reading the next two chapters in Part I for overviews of Visual J++ and the Java programming language.

Turn to Part II for tutorials on Java programming fundamentals.

Turn to Part III for tutorials on using Java's class libraries, known as packages.

Turn to Part IV for information on using the Microsoft Java SDK, and for comparisons between C++ and Java.

2

CHAPTER

Introducing
Visual J++

This chapter introduces Visual J++ and the Studio 97 software development system. Use this chapter to get started using Studio 97 and as a guide to compiling and running this book's sample Java applets and applications.

> **NOTE**
>
> Visual J++ 1.0 runs under Microsoft's Developer Studio. Visual J++ 1.1 runs under the newly released Studio 97. You may use either version of Visual J++ with this book. I used version 1.0 to develop the book's sample programs, which I tested using a beta copy of version 1.1.

Introduction to Visual J++

Visual J++ is a full-featured Java development system—including debugger, editor, and other tools—that runs under the umbrella of Studio 97. Figure 2.1 shows the ColorScroll sample applet from Part III loaded into Visual J++ and Studio 97. Notice the window at left, which shows the program's classes, methods, and other declarations in an outline form for fast browsing. For example, to find a specific method, simply double-click on its name in the outline, and the text editor jumps to that spot in the source code—very handy!

Figure 2.1.

The ColorScroll sample applet loaded into Visual J++ and Studio 97.

The following are some of the features you'll find in Visual J++:

- Applet Wizard for generating Java applet shells. Other wizards are provided for resources, database programming, and ActiveX components.
- Integration with Windows resources. This lets you use Studio 97 to design windows, using components such as buttons and scroll bars, and then convert the results to Java code.
- Automatic generation of multithreaded code and also animated images.

- Class browser showing classes, methods, and instance variables in an outline format. Simply double-click on any declaration to jump to that location in the source code. (Note: This is particularly useful when reading this book's descriptions of the sample applications. Use the class browser to find declarations mentioned in the text.)

- Upgraded debugger with numerous cool features. Figure 2.2 shows the debugger running the ColorScroll applet. You can display variables and objects (note the bottom left panel with Name and Value columns), and even disassemble Java programs to their compiled byte codes (click the far right button in the Debug floating toolbar). You might want to run many of this book's sample programs using the debugger; this way, you can single-step the program's statements and investigate variables while you read about the program in the text.

Figure 2.2.
The ColorScroll applet running in Studio 97's debugger.

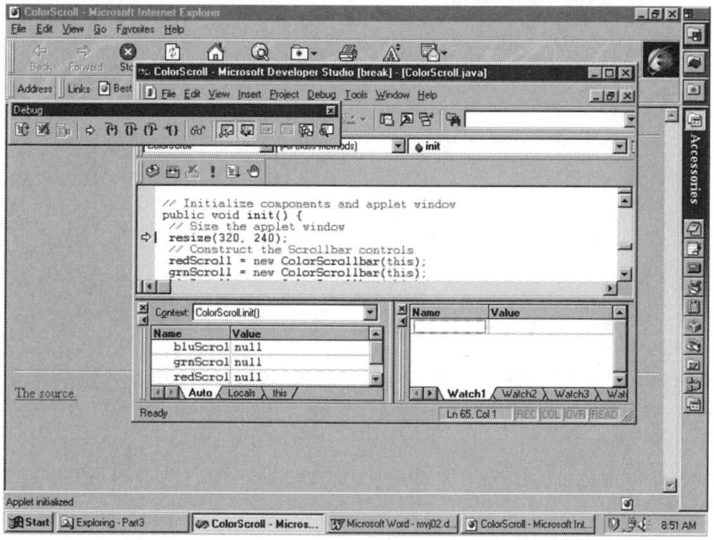

Using Studio 97

As I mentioned, I won't waste your time or mine explaining how to use Studio 97's text editor and other features. This book focuses on Java programming rather than the nuts and bolts of the development system. The following list, however, gives some of the features you will find in Studio 97. If you are using the older Developer Studio, you'll want to upgrade to the new release as soon as possible. It provides these features:

- A vastly improved interface that is more intuitive and easier to use.

- Icons in menu commands. Although this feature might seem frivolous, I find it helps me learn what toolbar icons do.

- Improved help commands and organizers. I use Studio 97 to search my Microsoft Developer Network CD-ROMs—one-stop software development at its best.

- Integration with Internet browsing through Internet Explorer, provided and installed with Visual J++.

- Floating and docking toolbars and other windows. I sometimes like to float the compiler output window to make more room for the source code window. This is especially useful on limited resolution laptops.

- Full-feature, multiwindow text editor. For all listings in this book, I turn off tab insertions and set tab indentation to 1. Normally, I use an indentation of 2, but I changed this to 1 so that longer lines would print correctly in this book without wrapping around.

- Multiple projects. Rather than close and reopen different projects as you must do in Developer Studio, you can set the active project using Studio 97's *Project\Set Active Project* command.

- Syntax highlighting. This uses colors to distinguish keywords, comments, expressions, and other constructions. The syntax highlighter is smart—it recognizes a file's type by its filename extension. (Hint: When starting a new file, before typing any text, save it so that it has a filename extension. Until you do this, syntax highlighting is disabled.)

- Studio 97 can run other Microsoft products including Visual C++ and the Developer Network of CD-ROMs. This makes it easy to switch among different languages, databases, and sample programs.

Using Command-Line Tools

Visual J++ provides command-line tools that you can run at a DOS prompt. These include the `Jvc.exe` Java compiler and the `Jview.exe` application viewer. To compile a program, open a DOS prompt window and enter a command such as

```
jvc welcome
```

The compiler automatically adds the `.java` filename extension. If successful, the compilation produces a `.class` file that contains the program's byte codes. To run that file, you must use an interpreter. For example, the following command runs the `Welcome.class` program:

```
jview welcome
```

> **NOTE**
>
> I recommend using command-line tools to compile and run the Java tutorial programs in Part II. However, you can't use this technique for all Java programs in this book. For additional instructions on compiling and running programs, see the next section.

Compiling and Running Programs

The following notes describe techniques for compiling and running this book's sample applications and applets. You may use Studio 97 to compile and run all programs, but simple applications such as those in Part II are more easily run from a DOS prompt.

Compiling Applications

An application is a Java program with a class that contains a method named main(). This is analogous to a C++ program's main() function. (More on this in Chapter 4, "Elemental Constructions," and in other chapters in Part II.)

To run an application, it is often easiest to compile the program from a DOS prompt using the Jvc.exe Java compiler. To try this now, open a DOS prompt window, and change to a copy of the CD-ROM's Part1\HelloWorld directory. Listing 2.1 shows the program's source code. If this is your first look at a Java program, don't worry about understanding its statements—we'll get to that, starting in Chapter 4.

Listing 2.1. HelloWorld.java (Demonstrates a Java application).

```
//===============================================================
// HelloWorld - Demonstrates a Java application
// Copyright (c) 1997 by Tom Swan. All rights reserved.
//===============================================================

class HelloWorld {
 public static void main(String args[]) {
  System.out.println("Hello world!");
 }
}
```

> **NOTE**
>
> All listings on the CD-ROM begin with a four-line header that identifies and describes the program and includes my copyright notice. In the interest of saving space, most listings in this book do not show this header. As I mentioned in Chapter 1, the copyright applies only to the printed text. You may use any and all programming in this book in your own compiled programs without obtaining special permission.

To make sure the Jvc.exe compiler is available, enter the command

```
jvc /?
```

at the prompt. You should see a list of compiler options. If not, you need to set your system Path to reference the directory where `Jvc.exe` is located. To compile the HelloWorld program, enter

```
jvc /verbose HelloWorld
```

Just for fun, I specified the `/verbose` option to display a running account of the compiler's activities. After compiling, run the resulting `HelloWorld.class` byte-code file by entering this command:

```
jview /p HelloWorld
```

The `/p` option is not required, but it pauses the interpreter if any errors are detected. This ensures that you'll have a chance to read error messages before Jview terminates. If the program runs successfully, you should see this message on screen:

```
Hello world!
```

You can also compile and run Java applications using Studio 97—but this takes more work. (The commands are similar for the older Developer Studio.) To try this with the HelloWorld application, start Studio now, and then follow these steps:

1. Select *File|Open...* and change to a copy of the `Part1\HelloWorld` directory from the CD-ROM.

2. If you don't see the `HelloWorld.java` file, change *Files of type:* to `Java Files (.java)`. Open the `HelloWorld.java` source code file.

3. Use the *Build* menu's *Build* command to compile the program. Alternatively, you can use the *Build* menu's *Compile HelloWorld.java* command, but this compiles only a single file. To build an application, which might be composed of multiple files, you should usually select *Build*.

4. Because no project workspace is defined for this program, a dialog asks if you want to create a default workspace. Answer Yes. (Unless you are using the command-line technique to compile applications, you must do this for all sample Java applications in this book.) You have to perform this step only once for each application.

5. When the program is finished compiling, if no errors were detected, the compilation window shows the final score: `HelloWorld -- 0 error(s), 0 warning(s)`.

6. Open the *Build* menu again, and you will see several additional commands. Select *Execute* (preceded with an exclamation-mark icon) to run the program. This brings up a dialog labeled Information for Running Class. Because this is a stand-alone application, select the *Stand-alone interpreter* button near the bottom of the window. Normally, this is `Jview.exe`.

7. All stand-alone applications need to specify a class that contains a `main()` method. For all of this book's sample applications, this is the same name as the program. *Enter the class name carefully!* Classes are case-sensitive, and if you make a mistake, you will have to start over with the original files from the CD-ROM and create a new project. In

this case, into the *Class file name:* field, enter `HelloWorld`, spelled exactly like that, and then press Enter.

8. The HelloWorld program runs in a DOS window. When the program ends, the window closes and control passes back to Studio 97.

When running applications this way, you might find that the DOS window closes before you have a chance to view its output. If this happens, there are two solutions I've found for keeping the window open:

• Run the program using the built-in debugger. Complete steps 1–5, and then select *Build\Start Debug,* which opens a nested submenu. From that menu, select *Step into.* This runs the program and pauses at its first statement. Choose the *Step into* button from the debugger's toolbar to run statements one at a time, or use the other buttons as you wish. This technique is particularly good for running this book's sample applications (and applets) and investigating the values of variables and objects.

• Here's another way to keep the DOS window open. Use the Windows Explorer to locate the `C:\Windows\Dosprmpt.pif` file (the filename extension might not be shown). Select *File\Properties...,* choose the Program tab, and clear the *Close on exit* checkbox. Select OK to close the properties window. Next, in Studio 97, after creating or opening a default project workspace, choose *Project settings...* Select the Debug tab, and change *Stand-alone interpreter:* to `C:\Windows\Dosprmpt.pif`. (You must enter the filename extension.) In the *Stand-alone interpreter arguments:* field, enter `/c jview.exe`. Click OK to close the window. You can now use the *Build* menu's *Execute* command to run the application. When it ends, the DOS window stays open so that you can inspect its output. Close the DOS window by clicking its close button.

> **NOTE**
>
> Although the preceding steps might seem complicated, they are easier after you go through the motions a few times. However, as I mentioned, for most of this book's sample applications, you'll save a lot of time and hassle by compiling and running the code from a DOS prompt using `Jvc.exe` and `Jview.exe`.

Compiling Applets

An applet is a Java program that does not have a `main()` method and is intended to run inside an Internet browser such as Internet Explorer. Applets can be, and usually are, embedded in an HTML document for downloading and running on the World Wide Web.

Listing 2.2, `WelcomeToJava.java`, is similar to the preceding `HelloWorld.java` program, but it is written as an applet. As before, don't worry about understanding the program's statements—

applet programming is covered fully in Part III.

Listing 2.2. WelcomeToJava.java (Demonstrates a Java applet).

```
//================================================================
// WelcomeToJava - Demonstrates a Java applet
// Copyright (c) 1996 by Tom Swan. All rights reserved.
//================================================================

import java.awt.Graphics;

public class WelcomeToJava extends java.applet.Applet {
 public void paint(Graphics g) {
  g.drawString("Welcome to Java Programming!", 50, 25);
 }
}
```

All sample applets in this book have associated Studio project files ending with the filename extension .mdp, and HTML files ending with the extension .html.

The simplest way to run a sample application is to open its .html file. For example, use the Windows Explorer to change to the Part1\WelcomeToJava directory—you can copy this directory to your hard drive, or use the directory on the CD-ROM—and open WelcomeToJava.html.

Several events now take place. First, Internet Explorer, or another default browser, starts running. The HTML document is loaded into the browser, and its <applet> tag causes the browser to load the applet's compiled byte code file—in this case, WelcomeToJava.class. The browser interprets these codes, runs the program, and displays "Welcome to Java Programming!" in the window. As you can see from the source code listing, this text is *painted* in the window, as are other applet graphics. Of course, I cover these and other graphical topics, and more about applet programming, at the appropriate places. (Turn to Part III if you already know Java and want to get started programming applets right away.)

Because all sample applets in this book have Studio project files, you can load them into Developer Studio or Studio 97. To try this with the sample WelcomeToJava applet, follow these steps:

1. Start Studio 97, and select the *File|Open Workspace...* command.

2. Change to the Part1\WelcomeToJava directory, and open the WelcomeToJava.mdp project file. If you don't see this file listed, be sure the Open Workspace dialog's *Files of type:* field is set to Workspaces (.dsw;.mdp). Open the project file. If you see a message about updating the file, answer yes.

3. To open the program's source code so you can read it, click the InfoViewer panel's FileView button, and select the file you want.

4. To compile the program, choose the *Build* menu's *Build* command.

5. If step 4 is successful, choose *Build|Execute* to run the applet. This transfers to Internet

Explorer or another browser, loads the applet's HTML document file, interprets the `<applet>` tag in that file, and loads and runs the compiled applet byte-code file—in this case, `WelcomeToJava.class`.

> **NOTE**
>
> If you have the Microsoft Java SDK, you can use the AppletViewer utility to run applets from a DOS command line. This is much faster than using Developer Studio or Studio 97. For example, the command
>
> `appletviewer carddemo.html`
>
> runs the CardDemo sample applet from Part III. You must type the `.html` filename. If a directory on this book's CD-ROM does not have an HTML file, then it is not an applet. In that case, use the information in this chapter under "Compiling Applications" to compile and run the program.

Summary

- Visual J++ is a full-featured Java development system that runs under the umbrella of Microsoft's Studio 97.

- You may use Visual J++ 1.0 and the older Developer Studio or Visual J++ 1.1 and the newer Studio 97 with all of this book's sample applets and applications.

- This chapter introduces some of the features of Visual J++ and Studio 97, and it explains how to compile and run the sample applets and applications on the CD-ROM.

What's Next?

To whet your appetite for this book's tutorials and sample programs, in the next chapter, I show some of the kinds of programs you will learn how to write using Java.

3

CHAPTER

Introducing Java Programming

Throughout this book, I explain all of Java's fundamental elements and I demonstrate how to use Java's standard classes to write applets and applications. In this chapter, just to whet your appetite for what's to come, I show some of the kinds of software you can write using this exciting programming language.

Welcome to Java Programming

Many programmers mistakenly believe that Java is useful only for writing Internet applets—small programs that are embedded in HTML documents and executed by a user's Web-page browser. While it's true that Java is unique in this respect, it is also a fully capable, general-purpose programming language that is more than adequate for small- to large-scale software development.

This section takes a quick glance at what Java is, and why, as a programmer, you need to learn this language.

What Is Java?

Java is an evolving language—its current implementation will undoubtedly undergo revisions in the next several years—but its success among programmers speaks well of its early design. Few other programming languages have started out having the necessary tools for writing real code.

Perhaps this is because Java's developers at Sun Microsystems constructed Java to solve real problems—primarily those troubles frequently associated with C and C++, and also with interactive programs on networks such as the Internet's World Wide Web. C++ is too complex, too tricky in its object-orientation, and too dependent on its past links to C to make it ideal for software distribution over the Internet. Something was needed—an object-oriented programming language like C++, but without its many quirks—to give programmers a practical tool for interactive network software, but one that would also be perfectly suited for other types of programming. Java is the answer.

Java is still a young language, and a new release from Sun is expected to modify some of its classes and, perhaps, its fundamental elements. Now, however, is the time to learn this language, which will undoubtedly play a major role in the development of the Web and also other kinds of network programming.

However, Java is not limited to network programming. Many programmers are using Java for application development. I know of at least one team of programmers at a major software development company who use Java for most of their internal programming. The reason, I'm told, is that Java code tends to run correctly the first time out of the starting gate, and programmers find it easier to develop robust, reliable code more quickly than with any other language.

Java is a compiled language, but its code output is interpreted. Because of this design, any computer that properly implements a Java interpreter can run your programs. This makes Java ideal for cross-development and, of course, for software distribution over the Internet. The only downside of Java's interpreted code generation is speed—native code from a C++ compiler is probably faster than the equivalent Java output. However, this is not to say that Java is slow. With modern processors beating speed records on a weekly basis, Java programs tend to run fast enough to suit even the most impatient users.

Java is object oriented. Though it supports only single inheritance, the `class` in Java is not merely an add-on, as in C++. Java's object-orientation is fundamental, and all code and data in a Java program exists within the confines of an object-oriented class. This makes Java the first, if not the only, programming language that implements objects in a practical way without interfering with the program's design.

Error handling is another of Java's jewels. Exception handling with `try`, `catch`, and `throw` statements provides the perfect solution for writing reliable code that responds to all possible error conditions. Exception handling is nearly the same in Java as in C++. The only key difference is that C++ programs can throw any type of data as an exception object. Java programs must throw objects of a specific type of class. I think this is an advantage, however, and it lends consistency to a program's error-handling code.

Some of Java's other advantages include a `String` class that does away with null-terminated, length-byte, and other types of strings that have plagued programmers over the last decade or two. String handling in Java is a dream. Arrays are also easy to use and robust. A program creates an array at runtime, and boundary errors are reported by exceptions.

Java is multithreaded. A class can easily provide code that runs concurrently with other programming—an essential ingredient for producing smooth-running programs, especially image graphics, over relatively slow networks. For example, a Java program can display an animated series of images while other code runs in separate threads.

Perhaps one of Java's prime advantages—one that surprises and might even scare some programmers—is the lack of a pointer data type. However, with this wise stroke, Java's designers not only killed off the pointer; they did away with one of the most bug-prone areas in software development—memory management. In Java, the destruction of all objects is completely automatic, and memory is organized by the Java virtual machine's (VM) garbage collector, which runs in a separate background thread and is completely transparent.

Java provides a rich class library in the form of *packages* that are easily imported into modules. Chances are good that you'll find numerous classes ready to use, which will save you much development time. You can also develop your own packages.

Finally, Java's security blanket provides a sigh of relief for those who have been bitten by network viruses, worms, and other bugaboos. Because Java code is interpreted locally on the user's system, a security manager can completely control disk access, window creation, and memory management. Java programs run in a kind of black box, to which only the user has the key.

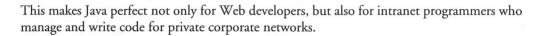

This makes Java perfect not only for Web developers, but also for intranet programmers who manage and write code for private corporate networks.

Who Needs Java?

Although it is loosely based on C and C++, Java is *not* an extension of these languages, nor is it dependent on C and C++ standard libraries. This makes Java especially attractive to C++ programmers, but you don't need to know C, C++, or another language to learn Java. If you are just getting started programming, Java is an excellent place to begin. If you are an experienced programmer, you'll find Java is easily mastered.

Many Java programmers will use the language along with one or more other languages. Java will not, I believe, replace C++ as the primary compiler at most software houses. (I continue to use C++, and have no plans to change entirely to Java.) However, for such code as applets, in-house utilities, and algorithm tests, Java is fast becoming the number one choice among many programmers. I suspect that Java will also soon be used to develop full-scale commercial applications.

In short, if you write code for today's graphical computer systems, you will benefit from knowing Java. If you are just getting started in programming, I recommend learning Java before C++. Career programmers probably need to know both languages, but you'll be operating on a half-empty tank of fuel if you know only one.

Java Appetizers

The following sections briefly describe some of Java's capabilities. I'll use sample applications from this book's chapters, but I won't go into any great detail here about the programs' source code. Of course, I'll fully explain all aspects of Java programming at the proper time and place. These sections merely introduce you to a few of Java's intriguing capabilities.

Applets

After you read Part II's Java tutorials, you'll be ready to write applets and embed them in HTML documents. Part III explains how to do this with numerous sample programs, which cover a wide variety of topics from animation, graphics, text processing, and other techniques.

For example, try the Animation applet in Part III. The easiest way to do this is to locate the `Part3\Animation` directory, and then load the `Animation.html` file into Internet Explorer or another Java-aware Web browser. The program also demonstrates how graphical (and other) software can run processes in background threads. For example, before the demonstration begins, you see a message that tells you the program is loading image files. This does not pause the program; other processes continue to run concurrently until the animation is ready. When the program is executed over the Internet, users can interact with other parts of the document until the animation begins to run. Of course, the animation is also threaded—which means that its display does not interfere with other executing code.

As you will learn when we look at the Animation.java source code, images are simply stored in an array using a declaration such as

```
private Image m_Images[];
```

To provide a separate thread in which to load the images and run the animation, the program declares an object of the Thread class:

```
Thread m_Animation = null;
```

Starting the separate process is a simple matter of constructing the object and calling its start() method. The two statements

```
m_Animation = new Thread(this);
m_Animation.start();
```

cause the program's run() method to begin to load images. (Actually, the real code is a little more complex, but more on that in Part III.) After loading the image files, the program animates the display with a simple loop:

```
while (true) {
 try {
  repaint();
  m_nCurrImage++;
  if (m_nCurrImage == NUM_IMAGES) m_nCurrImage = 0;
  Thread.sleep(50);  // Controls animation speed
 }
}
```

This loop is a typical example of multithreaded programming in Java. An exception terminates the loop, which paints the display and sleeps so that other code gets a chance to operate. Multithreading is simple and intuitive.

Graphics

Java is great for writing graphics. You can draw lines, fill shapes, paint text, and do many other kinds of graphics programming using Java. For a sample, run the GraphicsDemo application in Part III. Again, the easiest method is to load the GraphicsDemo.html file into Internet Explorer (look for it in the Part3\GraphicsDemo directory).

To spruce up your applets and applications, simply insert graphics statements into a paint() method. Java calls paint() as necessary to update the display. The method receives an object of the Graphics class, which provides graphical services and links your code to the operating system's native graphics capabilities. For example, to paint the applet's window, GraphicsDemo first obtains the window size with the statement

```
Rectangle r = bounds();
```

After this, `Graphics` class methods paint the window yellow:

```
g.setColor(Color.yellow);
g.fillRect(0, 0, r.width, r.height);
```

The program uses similar code to paint a blue shape:

```
g.setColor(Color.blue);
g.fillRoundRect(cx + 4, cy + 4, w, h, 10, 10);
```

It selects a font, like so:

```
Font f = new Font("TimesRoman", Font.BOLD + Font.ITALIC, 24);
g.setFont(f);
```

Then it draws text in the window using this statement:

```
g.drawString("Mastering Java", cx + 25, cy + 36);
```

As you will discover, graphics programming is a simple matter of drawing and painting with `Graphics` class methods. What's more, your graphics code will run on *any* computer with a Java-aware Internet browser!

Components

An exciting aspect of Java programming is the ability to provide interactive components in Internet applets. You can insert buttons, scrollbars, input fields, and other components for users to click and nudge as they wish. For example, load `ColorScroll.html` from the `Part3\ColorScroll` directory into Internet Explorer. Use the mouse to click and drag the three scrollbars and observe the resulting sample color. Or, click inside the text entry fields and enter red, green, and blue color values.

ColorScroll demonstrates how easy it is to insert and use components in applet windows. To arrange the components, Java employs a simple, yet highly effective, layout strategy. Several standard layout classes make it possible to design dialogs and other interactive windows for a wide variety of computer displays. By selecting an appropriate layout, you ensure that users will see similar results regardless of resolution and other features on their system's display.

To insert components into a window, the program simply declares component objects of standard classes, which you can extend and enhance as you wish. For example, the statement

```
ColorScrollbar redScroll, grnScroll, bluScroll;
```

declares three color scrollbars of the `ColorScrollbar` class, which the program extends from the standard `ScrollBar` class. This shows that, simply by building on existing classes, you can write software tailored to your needs. The three scrollbars are instantiated (made into objects) with the statements

```
redScroll = new ColorScrollbar(this);
grnScroll = new ColorScrollbar(this);
bluScroll = new ColorScrollbar(this);
```

This creates the actual objects in memory and associates them with the applet through the `this` reference. Painting the sample program's color square is a simple matter of interrogating the objects in a `paint()` method for their current color values:

```
g.setColor(new Color(
 redScroll.getValue(),
 grnScroll.getValue(),
 bluScroll.getValue()));
g.fillRect(0, 0, 64, 64);
```

Responding to events that are generated when users click inside the scrollbar components is equally simple. ColorScroll implements a `handleEvent()` method:

```
public boolean handleEvent(Event evt) {
switch (evt.id) {
 case Event.SCROLL_ABSOLUTE:
 case Event.SCROLL_LINE_DOWN:
 case Event.SCROLL_LINE_UP:
 case Event.SCROLL_PAGE_DOWN:
 case Event.SCROLL_PAGE_UP:
  ((ColorScrollbar)evt.target).updateText();
  repaint();
  return true;
 default:
  return super.handleEvent(evt);
 }
}
```

Event-handling for other types of component interactions is a simple matter of programming a similar `handleEvent()` method and responding to the reported events.

Windows

Java applets and applications can generate separate popup windows, which are especially handy for dialogs, data entry screens, and other chores. For an example of a separate window, load `FrameEvents.html` from the `Part3\FrameEvents` directory. Click the *Make Frame* button to display a separate popup window. (Notice that the window's status bar warns you that this is an applet window, courtesy of Java's strict security measures.) Click the Exit button to close the window; this demonstrates how separate windows can respond to their own events apart from the applet itself.

To create the frame window, the sample program extends the standard `Frame` class using this declaration:

```
class CustomFrame extends Frame {
...
}
```

Elsewhere, the program declares an object of the `CustomFrame` class:

```
CustomFrame theFrame;
```

When you click the button, the program's event handler constructs the `CustomFrame` object with the statement

```
theFrame = new CustomFrame(makeFrameButton,
  "Popup Window! " + count++);
```

To display the resulting window, the program simply calls `Show()`:

```
theFrame.show();
```

This brings up the window, which immediately begins responding to events.

Summary

- This chapter whets your appetite with descriptions of Java programming cooked up for this book.

- Java is known for its ability to create interactive Internet applets, but Java is also a full-featured, general-purpose programming language that is perfectly suitable for application development.

- Java is object oriented, and though it resembles C++, Java does not have many of that language's known deficiencies. For example, Java does not have pointers, and therefore, memory management is fully automatic. These and other features such as multithreading, exception handling, dynamic arrays, and other capabilities make Java a slick language that is ideal for creating robust code.

- Java compiled code is interpreted, which might cause applications to run slower than the equivalent native code from a C++ compiler. Given today's superfast computers, however, this isn't a tremendous disadvantage, and Java code tends to run fast enough for most users.

What's Next?

This chapter whets your appetite for the tutorials and sample programs in the coming chapters. This chapter also ends Part I. In Part II, you learn the fundamentals of the Java programming language.

Java Tutorials

CHAPTER

Elemental
Constructions

This chapter will help you discover what Java is and how easy it is to use. If you know another programming language such as C++, Visual Basic, or Pascal, so much the better. I'll assume only that you know a few basics such as what bits and bytes are, how to create and edit text files, and how to run Visual J++. If you are starting from scratch, you've come to the right place to begin.

In This Chapter

This chapter introduces the following elemental constructions in the Java programming language:

- Java source code files
- Identifiers and keywords
- Comments
- Literal values
- Data types and variables
- Operators and expressions
- Flow-control statements

Welcome to Java Programming

A Java program consists of one or more *source code files*, which are merely text files with the filename extension .java. In standard Java, source code files contain Unicode characters, but in Visual J++ running under Windows, they contain ASCII text. This means you can use any text editor, Visual J++, or even the Windows Notepad utility to create and edit Java source code files. Of course, most readers will use the text editor in the Microsoft Developer Studio that comes with Visual J++ 1.0, or the Visual Studio 97 that comes with version 1.1. Except for references to specific versions, the information in this book is compatible with both releases.

In this section, you enter, compile, and run a simple Java program. Although some of this same information appeared in the preceding chapter, the following notes suggest simple working techniques that are best for understanding this book's tutorial listings. Use these suggested methods to compile and run all of the tutorial listings in this and other chapters throughout Part II. Chapters in other Parts require different compilation techniques.

> **NOTE**
>
> C and C++ programmers will recognize a lot of information in this and other chapters in Part II. This is because Java is similar in many respects to C and C++ (especially in their fundamental elements), but there are many key differences that you might miss if you read this chapter too

quickly. Even if you are an experienced programmer, compiling and running the examples in this chapter will help you learn the differences between Java and your favorite language. You might also find it beneficial (as I do) to type in each example. If, however, you don't have the time or patience to type the listings, all are provided in full on the book's accompanying CD-ROM.

Tutorial Listings

The source code file in Listing 4.1, `Welcome.java`, shows the basic format of a Java program. Although Java programs may consist of multiple files, all of the sample tutorial listings in this and the other chapters in Part II are similarly self contained. For now, you can merely examine this listing's text; in the next section, I explain how to compile and run the program.

NOTE

You can find `Welcome.java` in the `Part2\Welcome` subdirectory either in your installation directory (`\Mvj` by default) or on the book's CD-ROM. All listings in this book are similarly organized by Part number and filename.

Listing 4.1. `Welcome.java` (Welcome to Java programming).

```
class Welcome {
 public static void main(String args[]) {
  System.out.println("Welcome to Java programming!");
 }
}
```

As `Welcome.java` shows, a basic Java program consists of a class named the same as its filename minus the `.java` extension. The class is bracketed with opening and closing braces, inside of which are various declarations and other items that make up the program. Source code lines are typically indented to show their association, but Java ignores indentation and line separations, which simply make programs more readable and understandable. (Due to space limitations, this book's listing lines are indented in multiples of one space. It's more common, however, to indent lines by two or four spaces, or to use tab characters.)

The key element in the sample program is a *class,* a construction that contains data and methods. The next chapter introduces more about classes—for now, you need to know only that a Java program exists inside at least one class such as `Welcome`. Without its content, the `Welcome` class looks like this:

```
class Welcome {
 ...
}
```

Here and elsewhere in this book, a three-dot ellipsis indicates text you are expected to supply or text that is irrelevant to the topic at hand. In this example, the Welcome class contains a method that performs the program's activity. This method is defined inside the Welcome class as

```
public static void main(String args[]) {
 System.out.println("Welcome to Java programming!");
}
```

There are numerous elements to this method, all of which you'll meet in due course. The important facts here are the method's name (main) and the statement inside the method's delimiting braces. That statement calls another method, println ("print line" in English), provided by an object named out in the System class, which is available to all Java programs.

All Java programs that run in stand-alone fashion (that is, not as applets in a Web page browser) must have one and only one main() method. The program begins running at the first statement inside main(). To distinguish them from other items, method names in this book are followed by a pair of parentheses.

I'll explain more about objects, classes, and methods as we go along. For now, you need only to realize that the result of running this program is the string Welcome to Java programming! appearing on your display. The next section explains how to make this happen.

Compiling and Running Listings

As you gain experience with Visual J++, you'll probably use the Microsoft Developer Studio or Visual Studio 97 to enter, compile, debug, and run Java programs. When learning Java (or any other computer programming language), however, it is simpler and more instructive to compile and run sample listings at a DOS command-line prompt. (You can still use Developer or Visual Studio to type in and view the listing files.)

While primitive, compiling from a DOS prompt will help you zip through the Java tutorials in this and other chapters in Part II as quickly as possible without getting hung up on Developer or Visual Studio commands and options. Another advantage is that command-line programs can use simple output statements to display their results rather than the more sophisticated techniques required to create text and graphics. Of course, I'll explain these techniques fully in this book. First, however, you need to understand Java fundamentals.

After entering or locating a listing such as Welcome.java from the preceding section, open or switch to a DOS prompt window. Enter a *change directory* (CD) command such

```
cd \MVJ\Part2\Welcome
```

This makes MVJ\Part2\Welcome the current directory. Next, type the following command to compile the Welcome.java source code file:

```
jvc welcome
```

This produces some text on screen such as the following, which comes from an early version of Visual J++ that I used while writing this book:

```
D:\TSwan\Mvj\Source\Part2\Welcome>jvc welcome
Microsoft (R) Visual J++ Compiler Version 1.00.6173
Copyright (C) Microsoft Corp 1996. All rights reserved.
```

If the compiler detects no errors in the program's source code, the result is a new file, `Welcome.class`, in the current directory. This file contains Java *byte codes,* which you can execute by feeding them to a Java *interpreter,* also sometimes called a *viewer.* Do that now by entering this command:

```
jview welcome
```

Here's what appeared on my screen when I did this (again, I was using an early version of the Microsoft Java interpreter—note that Version is misspelled):

```
D:\TSwan\Mvj\Source\Part2\Welcome>jview welcome
Microsoft (R) Visual J++ Command-line Interpreter Verion 1.00.6173
Copyright (C) Microsoft Corp 1996. All rights reserved.
Welcome to Java programming!
```

The final line shows the program's output—the string that the source code file passed to `System.out.println()`.

> **NOTE**
>
> When entering `jvc` or `jview` commands, if you receive the DOS error "Bad command or file name," check that the system path contains the directory specification `C:\MSDev\bin`, in which the Java command-line compiler (`jvc.exe`) and runtime viewer (`jview.exe`) are located. Type `PATH` at a DOS prompt to verify that your path is set correctly. If it isn't, enter and run the batch file in Listing 4.2, `Vj.bat`, to set the path. (This file is located on the CD-ROM in the `Extras` directory.) Do this each time you open a DOS prompt window. If this is bothersome, set the path when you start Windows by entering a similar `set path` statement into your system's `Autoexec.bat` file.

Listing 4.2. `Vj.bat` (Configure PATH for Microsoft Visual J++).

```
@echo off
rem
rem Vj.bat -- Configure PATH for Microsoft Visual J++
rem
set path=%path%;c:\msdev\bin
echo Configured for Microsoft Visual J++
echo type jvc to compile; jview to run
path
```

> **NOTE**
>
> Not listed here, but even more useful, is a batch file, `Mvj.bat`, which you can use to find any
> named sample program. Copy this file to `\windows\command`, and then enter a command such as
>
> `mvj nocomment`
>
> to locate a sample listing such as `NoComment.java`, one of the listings in this chapter. You might
> have to modify the path names in `Mvj.bat`, but you'll save a lot of typing by using this utility to
> find sample program directories.

Command-Line Options

The Java compiler (`jvc`) and viewer (`jview`) provide a number of command-line options. You probably won't need to use these options for the tutorial examples in this and other chapters in Part II, but you might want to view them just to know what kinds of options are available. Use the `/?` option to get a complete list. For example, enter this command:

`jvc /?`

In the resulting list, you'll find the option `/cp:o`. Use it to reveal the path where Java stores its class library, which provides numerous operations such as input and output methods. (Literally speaking, the command "outputs the class path.") To find this path, enter this command:

`jvc /cp:o`

When I did this, the compiler reported:

```
Using classpath:
        c:\windows\java\trustlib\tclasses.zip;c:\windows
\java\trustlib;c:\windows\java\classes\classes.zip;
c:\windows\java\classes;.;c:\windows\java\lib
```

This information shows that Java looks for its system classes in the indicated files and directories.

> **WARNING**
>
> Don't make the common mistake of decompressing and then deleting files such as `classes.zip`.
> The Java compiler reads its classes directly in Zip-compressed form. Decompressing the Zip
> files wastes disk space. Deleting them will cause the Java compiler to fail!

Identifiers and Keywords

The individual elements of a Java source code file are known as *tokens.* They include literals, operands, operators, separators, identifiers, and keywords.

Literals are values such as 3.14159 or strings such as "Hi there!" that you enter into a program. Other literals are symbols such as true and false that have special meanings.

An *expression* such as A + B consists of the operands A and B, and one or more operators such as +. Together, operands and operators create expressions and *statements,* which perform calculations on data and perform other actions.

Separators have special meaning in programs. They consist of spaces, semicolons, periods, colons, and other punctuation. I won't list each separator character here; you can easily learn proper separator etiquette by examining this book's listings. There's one separator, however, that you must know about—the semicolon, which is the source of a lot of confusion in Java and in other programming languages. In Java, a statement *always* ends with a semicolon, as demonstrated by the output statement from Welcome.java:

```
System.out.println("Welcome to Java programming!");
```

The reason you need to terminate a statement with a semicolon is because statements might have numerous tokens, and the compiler needs you to identify the statement's end. Not all declarations, however, need semicolons because the compiler can detect their ends from the declaration's context. For example, a class declaration ends with a closing brace—a semicolon would be superfluous (and is not allowed):

```
class {
  ...
}
```

Other Java tokens are identifiers and keywords, both of which are important enough to deserve the following special explanations.

Identifiers

Identifiers are words that you invent to describe your program's variables, methods, and classes. For example, you might identify a data object as accountBalance or a method as SwitchOff.

You may use any combination of letters, digits, underscores, and dollar signs in identifiers. An identifier, however, must begin only with a letter, underscore, or dollar sign. (Underscores and dollar signs are used internally by the Java linker, so it's best never to begin your own identifiers with these special characters.) Because spaces are not allowed in identifiers, some programmers like to use underscores to make words more readable, as in the identifier

```
speed_of_light
```

Because underscores are sometimes difficult to see on screen, I prefer to use capitalization for a similar effect:

```
speedOfLight
```

Java source code is case sensitive, which means that the three identifiers SpeedOfLight, speedoflight, and SPEEDOFLIGHT are completely different words to the compiler. All uppercase identifiers are permitted, but not recommended because they might conflict with #define text macros in code linked to C and C++ libraries. Such macros are endemic throughout the Windows SDKs (software development kits), and it's best not to use all uppercase for your own identifiers.

> **TIP**
>
> The standard Java specification states that identifiers may consist of letters a through z, and A through Z, plus Unicode characters with values greater than hexadecimal 00C0. For practical purposes, however, it's best to create readable identifiers using only the keys on your keyboard. Despite Unicode's appeal as a worldwide 16-bit character standard, strange characters have no place in well-formed identifiers.

Keywords

Keywords are identifiers that Java reserves for its own purposes. You've already seen one such keyword—class. Because this word has special meaning to the Java language, you can't use it to identify your own program elements.

Table 4.1 lists all Java reserved keywords. The keywords byvalue, const, and goto are reserved but not used. The words true, false, and null are not technically keywords, but I included them in the table because they are reserved and you cannot use them for your own identifiers.

Table 4.1. Visual J++ keywords.

abstract	int
boolean	interface
break	long
byte	native
byvalue	new
case	null
catch	package
char	private
class	protected
const	public
continue	return
default	short
do	static

double	super
else	switch
extends	synchronized
false	this
final	threadsafe
finally	throw
float	throws
for	transient
goto	true
if	try
implements	void
import	while
instanceof	

Comments about Comments

While writing this book, I made many notes on the side to remind me to expand a thought, research a fact, or insert a program listing in the text. Comments in a program are exactly like these notes. They are private messages that explain some fact about the program. The compiler completely ignores comments.

Java has three styles of comments, as explained in the next sections.

C-Style Comments

A standard Java comment, also recognized in the C language, is delimited with the two-character symbols /* and */. All text between and including these symbols is ignored. You can use this style to create single- or multiple-line comments. For example, you might enter a header like the following one at the beginning of a program file:

```
/* Title: MyProgram.java by Tom Duck */
/* Revision 2.0 -- all bugs converted to features */
/* Copyright (c) Ugly Duckling Software, Inc. */
```

The advantage of this type of comment style is that it may enclose several lines. For example, the preceding text could also be written this way:

```
/* Title: MyProgram.java by Tom Duck
   Revision 2.0 -- all bugs converted to features
   Copyright (c) Ugly Duckling Software, Inc. */
```

C++-Style Comments

For single-line comments, or for those at the ends of lines, begin the text with a double slash. For example, the compiler ignores the following line:

```
// The compiler ignores this comment.
```

This style, introduced in the C++ language (and also recognized by other languages such as Delphi's Object Pascal), starts with the double slash and extends to the end of the line. This makes the double-slash comment style ideal for adding a note to the end of a statement or declaration, as in

```
char ch;   // Input character variable
```

The preceding comment documents the use of the character variable ch. In a large program with hundreds of declarations, good comments are essential for creating understandable source code.

> **NOTE**
>
> Good code should be readable on its own, and it is far more valuable to create clear identifiers than it is merely to comment declarations. A variable WX is not as clear as widthOfDisplay. Good comments *clarify* self-documenting code.

Documentation Comments

A third type of comment is sometimes used in Java to create automatic documentation. This *documentation comment* is a C-style comment with an extra asterisk. For example, the following text documents a method named MakeItHappen():

```
/** This makes it happen */
MakeItHappen() {
 ...
}
```

The second asterisk identifies this comment as documentation for a following declaration, in this case, the MakeItHappen() method.

> **NOTE**
>
> The Microsoft Developer Studio and Visual Studio 97 automatically prepare a documented list of methods and other declarations for Java source code files, so you'll have little use for documentation comments. You might, however, see them in other published listings, and you can use them if you intend to compile your programs on other systems.

No Comment

Listing 4.3, `NoComment.java`, demonstrates the three Java comment styles.

Listing 4.3. NoComment.java (Demonstrates Java comments).

```
//===============================================================
// NoComment.java - Demonstrates Java comment styles
// Copyright (c) 1997 by Tom Swan. All rights reserved.
//===============================================================

/* This paragraph shows that C-style comments
   may extend for
   several lines. */

class NoComment {
 /** This is a documentation comment for the main method */
 public static void main(String args[]) {
  // This comment is not displayed
  System.out.println("This string is displayed");
  System.out.println( /* Embedded comment is not displayed */
   "This string is also displayed");
  /* This single-line C-style comment is not displayed */
 }
}
```

The program begins with double-slash comments that identify the filename and list my copyright notice. All listings on the CD-ROM begin similarly, but to save space, this extra header information is not printed in the book. Following the header is a three-line comment that uses the C-style double-character brackets. The program's demonstration class, named `NoComment`, contains a documentation comment above method `main()`. Following this is another double-slash comment.

The second `println()` statement shows an example of an embedded comment, which must use the C-style brackets, `/*` and `*/`. Notice that this comment is inside the `println()` statement, but nevertheless, it is ignored as are all comments. In general, embedded comments might be more confusing than helpful, but it's good to know that Java allows them.

Debugging with Comments

You might use an embedded comment to temporarily disable some items for debugging purposes. Just surround the text to disable with comment brackets as in this example:

```
System.out.println(/*"Original string"*/ "test string");
```

In that statement, the original string is commented out and a second string is entered for test purposes. You might also disable entire statements this way and run the program to observe what happens:

```
/*
System.out.println("some text"); // Display some text
System.out.println("more text");
*/
```

This disables both `println()` statements, which are easily restored to action by deleting the comment brackets. I usually place the brackets on separate lines to make them easy to find. Notice that the double-slash comment is nested inside the C-style comment.

Literal Values

A literal value is a number, a character, a string of characters, or a symbolic name such as `true` or `false` that you type directly in a program. You might use a literal value to initialize an object to hold that value—assigning 10, for example, to an integer variable:

```
int i = 10;  // Assign literal 10 to variable i
```

The following sections briefly describe literal values just to introduce their formats. The next major section, "Data Types and Variables," gives more complete examples of each value type.

Numeric Literals

Numeric literals are either integers (whole numbers) or floating point values (fractions).

Integers may be expressed in decimal (base 10), hexadecimal (base 16), or octal (base 8). Following are examples of each type of integer literal:

```
int i = 123;      // Assign decimal 123 to integer i
int j = 0x10F9;   // Assign hexadecimal 10F9 to integer j
int k = 0123;     // Assign octal 123 to integer k
```

Floating point numbers have a decimal point, or are expressed in scientific notation—following a number with the letter e or E and a positive or negative exponent:

```
double f1 = 123.45;     // Assign 123.45 to floating point f1
double f2 = 4.257e-3;   // Assign 0.004257 to floating point f2
double f3 = 4.257e2;    // Assign 425.7 to floating point f3
```

The word `double` specifies a kind of floating point variable. Unless specified otherwise, literal floating point numbers are of this type.

Any numeric literal number can be made negative by preceding it with a minus sign:

```
int q = -45;          // Assign -45 to integer q
double p = -67.8;     // Assign -67.8 to floating point p
double r = -3.41e-4;  // Assign -0.000341 to floating point r
```

Character and String Literals

All characters in Java programs are Unicode 16-bit values. Enclose single characters in single quotes. Enclose strings of zero of more characters in double quotes. Following are some examples:

```
char ch = 'X';  // Assign X to character ch
char atSign = '@';  // Assign @ to character atSign
String s = "Multiple characters";  // Assign string to s
String emptyString = "";  // Assign empty string
```

> **NOTE**
>
> When entering characters and strings, don't type opening and closing quote marks as you might in a word processing document. Type all quotes using the apostrophe and quote key immediately to the left of the Enter key on most PC keyboards.

Boolean Literals

In addition to numeric, character, and string literals, a Java program may have symbolic literal values. Most common are the predefined values `true` and `false`, which are spelled in lowercase. These are *boolean* values, used in programs to test various conditions. The following statement sets a `boolean` variable named `exitProgram` to `false`:

```
boolean exitProgram = false;  // Assign false to exitProgram
```

Data Types and Variables

Variables are named items with values that can change over the course of a program. A program can assign and manipulate variables to perform operations a specified number of times, for example, or to calculate expressions.

The key to using variables correctly is to learn as much as you can about Java's data types. When you create a variable, you must specify its type, and any operations on that variable must conform to that type. It makes no sense, for example, to multiply two strings. It also makes no sense to assign a character to a floating point variable. As you will learn, there are ways to convert values to different types—changing a string to a floating point value, for example—but you can't indiscriminately mix values of any types.

In this section, you learn more about Java's data types and how to use them to create variables in programs. First, however, we need to agree on a few terms.

A Few Good Terms

The following definitions are not rigorous (I'll leave such concerns to textbook authors), but I find them helpful in using data in programs:

- A *data type* is literally the amount of memory space that can hold a value of this specific type. When you specify a data type, you are giving a command that reserves one or more bytes of memory for this kind of value. Most important is to realize that it can take a different amount of space to hold different types of values: A floating point value, for example, might take eight bytes, while an integer might need only two. Some care is therefore needed when performing operations on variables—trying to stuff an 8-byte value into a 2-byte space is likely to have severe consequences on the health of the program! Java checks the types of expressions to ensure that you don't do this by accident, but no compiler can prevent all such mistakes. It's your responsibility to use appropriate data types for the operations you want to perform.

- A *variable* is an *instance* of a specific data type. It is called a variable because the program can change the instance's value, either by assigning to it a literal value or the value of another variable, or by performing some operation on the variable—incrementing an integer, for example.

- An *object* in this book is an instance of a class—but more on that in the next chapter. In some other books, you might see the word *object* used to describe all kinds of variables. Here, an object is always an instance of a class.

- A *value* refers to the contents of a variable or object. Values can also be literal. A value is not necessarily numeric. For example, 123 is a value, but the string `"Cockadoodledo"` is also correctly called a value.

- A *simple data type* is an integer, floating point, boolean, or character type. You may also come across the equivalent terms *built-in type* or *native type* to describe Java's simple data types. Simple variables occupy a preset amount of space.

- A *composite* data type is an array, a class, or an interface (you'll meet that term in Chapter 8, "More About Classes and Objects"). A string is also a composite type. Composite types may occupy a variable amount of space, and they typically have more complex operations than are defined for simple types. For example, you can search for a substring inside a string variable.

Declaring Variables

To store a value of a specific type, you declare a variable of that type. As with all other Java programming elements, variables are always declared inside a class. Listing 4.4, `VarDemo.java`, demonstrates how to declare and assign a value to a variable.

Listing 4.4. VarDemo.java.

```
class VarDemo {
 public static void main(String args[]) {
  int count;    // Declare a variable
  count = 10;   // Assign value to variable
  System.out.println("Count = " + count);
 }
}
```

Inside method `main()`, the program declares an integer variable, `count`, of the data type `int`. Next, the program assigns to count the value `10`. Finally, it displays count's value. When you compile and run the program, it displays

```
Count = 10
```

Notice how a plus sign appends the value of `count` to a string in the `println()` statement. Actually, this *converts* count to a string, which is appended to the literal string in quotes. You can use a similar technique to display most kinds of data values, as long as Java can convert them to strings.

Alternatively, you can declare and assign a value to a variable with one statement:

```
int count = 10;
```

This declares `count` as an `int` variable and assigns it the initial value `10`. Elsewhere, you can assign a different value to count, but you need to declare a variable only once. You can declare multiple variables on separate lines:

```
int i;  // Declare int variable i
int j;  // Declare int variable j
int k;  // Declare int variable k
```

Or, you can declare multiple variables of the same type by separating them with commas:

```
int i, j, k;  // Declare int variables i, j, and k
```

If you don't assign variables initial values, they are uninitialized and might have any value depending on the bit patterns in memory where the variables are created. It's always a good idea, therefore, to assign initial values to the variables you declare. You may do this individually, or by using a form such as

```
int i = 1, j = 2, k = 3;
```

This single line declares three `int` variables—i, j, and k—and assigns them the values 1, 2, and 3 respectively.

Integer Variables

Java defines the exact sizes of its simple data types, and these sizes are guaranteed to be the same on any computer that can run Java byte codes. This fact gives Java a tremendous advantage over other computer languages such as C, in which the sizes of data types are strictly undefined. With Java, for example, an int is 32-bits long, and an int variable can hold values in decimal ranging from –2,147,483,648 to 2,147,483,647. This fact is true regardless of the computer system on which your applications run!

> **NOTE**
>
> In this book, commas in numbers are for readability and are never entered into a program's source code.

Java supports other integer types with different memory sizes and corresponding minimum and maximum value ranges. Table 4.2 lists Java's integer data types, their sizes in bytes and bits, and their minimum and maximum ranges. All integer types are signed (that is, they can hold negative and positive values).

Table 4.2. Integer data types.

Type	Bytes	Bits	Minimum	Maximum
byte	1	8	-128	127
short	2	16	-32,768	32,767
int	4	32	-2,147,483,648	2,147,483,647
long	8	64	-9,223,372,036,854,775,808	9,223,372,036,854,775,807

You may specify integer values of any type in decimal, hexadecimal, or octal. Decimal values cannot begin with zero. Hexadecimal values are preceded with 0x or 0X (that's a zero, not a capital O). Octal values must begin with zero. Here are some sample declarations using each format and showing the equivalent values in decimal:

```
int decimalCount = 123;  // decimal 123
int hexCount = 0xF89C;   // decimal 63644
int octalCount = 037;    // decimal 31
```

Literal integer values are by default considered to be of the int data type. As long as the values are in the proper range, Java can convert them to the appropriate size. Literal 255, for example, can be converted automatically to a two-byte short value. When a program executes a statement such as

```
short shortCount = 255;
```

Java first interprets 255 as an int value, which is then downsized to the short data type for assigning to shortCount. The following, however, does not compile:

```
byte byteCount = 255;  // ???
```

That doesn't work because 255 is higher than the maximum value that a byte variable can hold, which is 127.

> **NOTE**
>
> In this book, the comment // ??? indicates a construction that either doesn't compile or that might produce faulty results.

Because literal numbers are of type int by default, you must append L to numbers larger than 2,147,483,647. This is true even when specifying values in hexadecimal. (You may use a lowercase l, but this isn't recommended because it looks too much like the digit 1.) For example, the following declares a long variable, bigNumber, and assigns it the maximum positive value a variable of this type can hold:

```
long bigNumber = 0x7FFFFFFFFFFFFFFFL;
```

Try this statement in a test program. Listing 4.5, IntDemo.java, demonstrates how to do this. From now on, I won't list similar programs for every single example statement in this book, so don't wait for me to suggest running the code examples in this book. Insert them into a program and try them out!

Listing 4.5. IntDemo.java (Demonstrates integer variables).

```
class IntDemo {
 public static void main(String args[]) {

  // Values in decimal, hex, and octal
  int decimalCount = 123; // decimal 123
  int hexCount = 0xF89C;   // decimal 63644
  int octalCount = 037;    // decimal 31

  // Display preceding variables
  System.out.println("decimalCount = " + decimalCount);
  System.out.println("hexCount     = " + hexCount);
  System.out.println("octalCount   = " + octalCount);

  // Variables of each integer data type
  byte byteCount = 0x0F;
  short shortCount = 32767;
  int intCount = 99999;
  long bigNumber = 0x7FFFFFFFFFFFFFFFL;  // Note final L

  // Display preceding variables
  System.out.println("byteCount    = " + byteCount);
  System.out.println("shortCount   = " + shortCount);
  System.out.println("intCount     = " + intCount);
  System.out.println("bigNumber    = " + bigNumber);
  }
}
```

Floating Point Variables

Java has two floating point data types, `float` and `double`. A `float` variable can hold *single-precision* values. A `double` variable can hold *double-precision* values. Table 4.3 shows Java's floating point data types, their sizes, and their value ranges. Because `float` and `double` variables can hold very small and very large values, the table expresses minimum and maximum values using scientific notation.

Table 4.3. Floating point data types.

Type	Bytes	Bits	Minimum	Maximum
float	4	32	1.4013e-045	3.40282e+038
double	8	64	2.22507e-308	1.79769e+308

When using floating point variables, keep in mind that their values may be approximate. Mathematical operations on floating point values might be rounded internally, and it is a mistake to expect the results to be completely exact. (This is true of most computer languages, by the way, not only Java.)

Use integer data types for exact quantities such as account balances and item counts. Floating point data types are more appropriate for a measurement or in a scientific formula such as a calculation of the distance between planets.

> **TIP**
>
> Use the `int` or `long` integer data types to store financial data in cents or another base denomination. Because calculations with floating point values might be only approximately accurate, the `float` and `double` data types are inappropriate for financial information.

You can specify a literal floating point value to be of the `float` or `double` data types. Append `F` to a literal value to specify it as a `float` type. Append `D` to specify the `double` type. You may do this with decimal or scientific notation values. You may also use lowercase letters `f` and `d`. Generally, Java chooses the correct data type to represent literal floating point values, but you can use this technique for extra safety. Consider these declarations:

```
double d1 = 1.55000009e-100D;  // Force double type
double d2 = 1.55000009e-100F;  // Force float type
double d3 = 1.55000009e-100;   // ??? but probably okay
```

The first assignment forces the literal value to be of type `double`, because this is the type of the variable to which the value is assigned. The second assignment forces the value to be of type `float`. Because that type is less precise than double, `d2` is not exactly equal to `d1`. The third assignment is probably okay, provided the Java interpreter is correctly programmed. For safety, however, appending a D to the literal value as in the first assignment ensures that the correct type is used.

> ### WARNING
>
> You can't use the preceding technique to force an inappropriately large or small value to fit into a smaller space. For example, the following statements do not produce the expected results:
>
> ```
> float doubleTrouble = 1.556701e-050F;  // ???
> System.out.println("doubleTrouble = " + doubleTrouble);
> ```
>
> Despite appearances, the first statement assigns zero to doubleTrouble because the literal value is outside the allowable range for the float data type. Appending F to the literal value allows the program to compile, but the results are still incorrect. The only solution in this instance is to change float to double and remove the F (or change it to D).

Boolean Variables

A boolean variable can have only one of two values, true or false. Unlike in some programming languages, Java's boolean is an actual data type, and equivalent integer values for true and false are not defined. This means you cannot mix integer and boolean values in expressions, as you can, for example, in C and C++.

Boolean variables and expressions will become more important when we examine flow control statements in this chapter, so the following statements have no practical purpose. Insert these statements into a main() method (you can use any of the sample listings presented so far):

```
boolean positive = true;   // Assign true to positive variable
boolean negative = false;  // Assign false to negative variable
System.out.println("positive = " + positive);
System.out.println("negative = " + negative);
```

The keyword boolean is lowercase (as are all Java keywords), and so are the values true and false. As the output statements show, you can display the values of boolean variables such as positive and negative. When you compile and run the preceding code, it displays these lines on screen:

```
positive = true
negative = false
```

Character Variables

A character variable can hold one 16-bit Unicode value, and thus can represent any character in all languages worldwide. Declare a character using the char data type. Try these statements in a main() method:

```
char ch = '#';
System.out.println("ch = " + ch);
```

As you probably suspect, this displays the pound-sign character, #. Internally, characters are represented as Unicode values, so you can also assign integers to char variables. Change the first line to

```
ch = 123;
```

and the program now displays an opening brace, {, the character having the Unicode value 123. You may specify any value from 0 to 65535. The following two examples assign equivalent values to ch (notice that Unicode integer values are unsigned):

```
ch = 65000;   // Assign integer Unicode value to ch
ch = 0xFDE8;  // Same as above but in hexadecimal
```

Specify control codes by using the backslash commands in Table 4.4. These special codes, also called *nonprinting characters,* represent characters that have no display symbols, or that don't appear on most keyboards. Because a backslash triggers a special control code character, you must type two backslashes to represent a single one. Also, because quotes delimit characters and strings, you must use the backslash symbols \' and \" to designate single and double quote marks respectively. All of these backslash symbols may be inserted in literal characters and strings.

Table 4.4. Nonprinting characters.

Name	Example	Result
New line	'\n'	Start new output line
Tab	'\t'	Insert tab
Backspace	'\b'	Backspace
Return	'\r'	Carriage return
Form feed	'\f'	Eject page
Backslash	'\\'	Insert backslash
Single quote	'\''	Insert single quote
Double quote	'\"'	Insert double quote
Unicode hex value	'\u0037'	Unicode digit 7
Unicode octal value	'\37'	Unicode octal 037

When you assign an integer value to a char variable, you are assigning it a *bit pattern.* This is not necessarily equivalent to a Unicode character's value. Consider these three declarations:

```
ch = '\037';    // Octal
ch = '\37';     // Octal
ch = '\u0037';  // Unicode 0037
```

The first two are equivalent; digits following a backslash in a literal character or string are always considered to be expressed in octal. Use the \u code to specify a Unicode value, which must have four digits and is expressed in hexadecimal. The Unicode character associated with 0x0037 is the digit character '7'. To verify this on your system, try these two lines in a main() method:

```
ch = '\u0037';  // Unicode 0037
System.out.println("ch = " + ch);
```

String Variables

I won't say much about strings here because we'll get into them in detail in Chapter 6, "Strings and Characters." All strings in Java are actually objects of the String or StringBuffer classes, and because classes are introduced in the next chapter, I'll avoid the subject of strings for the moment.

You already know that strings are delimited with double quotes. Although they may appear to be simply arrays of characters, internally they are sophisticated objects with a wide variety of associated methods.

Like characters, strings may include any of the nonprinting symbols in Table 4.4. One useful trick is to insert new-line codes, \n, to display blank lines. The following displays the value of count with an extra blank line above and below. This is often simpler and more efficient than inserting multiple println() statements to do the same:

```
int count = 123;
System.out.println("\nCount = " + count + '\n');
```

Operators and Expressions

Now that you know about data types and how to declare variables, you're ready to begin performing actions on data. To do that, you write expressions and statements using a wide variety of operators.

Operator Precedence

An operator is a symbol that performs some kind of action on data. For example, the plus sign + is an operator that adds two numbers or joins two strings. Operators also include some additional separation characters such as commas for listing multiple items and periods for specifying related objects, as in this statement:

```
System.out.println("Print me!");
```

The two period operators tell Java that the println() method is a member of the out object in the System class. Table 4.5 lists all Java operators, and shows their precedence level. Operators higher in the table take precedence over those on lower lines. Operators on the same row have equal precedence.

Table 4.5. Operator precedence.

()	.	[]		
++	--	!	~	instanceof
*	/	%		
+	-			
<<	>>	>>>		
<	>	<=	>=	
==	!=			
&				
^				
&&				
||				
?:				
=	op=			
,				

In expressions, operators with higher precedence are evaluated before those with lower precedence. Otherwise, expressions are evaluated from left to right. For example, the expression to the right of the equal sign in the statement

```
a = b + c * d;
```

multiplies c and d and then adds that product to b before assigning the total to a. The expression works this way because the times operator (*) has a higher precedence than +. To force a different evaluation order, use parentheses:

```
a = (b + c) * d;
```

You may also use extra parentheses to make an expression clear—encasing the entire expression ((b + c) * d), for example. Regardless of precedence, operations inside parentheses are always completed before those outside.

Notice that the equal sign is Java's *assignment operator*. In the statement

```
a = b + c + d;
```

the result of adding b, c, and d is assigned to a. I am purposely not declaring the data types of these variables—they might be integers, or they could be floating point values. As a general rule, the destination should be as large as the largest operand. For example, if b and d are type int and c is type long, then variable a must be long to hold the result of the expression. In the next several sections, I'll explain more about different types of expressions.

Unary Integer Expressions

Unary integer expressions are so-called because they have only one operator. The statement

```
a = -b;  // Assign negation of b to a
```

assigns the negation of b to a. This does not change b's value. To do that, you would have to write

```
b = -b;  // Negate b
```

Use the tilde (~) to perform a bitwise negation, turning all binary ones to zeros and vice versa:

```
a = ~b;  // Assign bitwise negation of b to a
```

Use the double character operators ++ and -- to increment and decrement operands. Unlike unary - and ~, the operators ++ and -- change the values of their operands. The expression

```
count++;
```

increments the value of count by one, and has the same result as

```
count = count + 1;
```

That's not necessarily as efficient, however, because most computers have low-level increment and decrement instructions. (There's no guarantee, however, that a specific Java interpreter will use those instructions.) Consider some more examples:

```
i = i + 1;  // Add 1 to i
i++;        // Same as above
j = j - 1;  // Subtract 1 from j
j--;        // Same as above
```

One concept that confuses many programmers on first meeting is that an expression such as i++ performs an action (incrementing i) but also has a value. In fact, all expressions have values, so this isn't a special rule. It is important here, however, because the placement of ++ and -- affects the expression's result. The statements

```
++i; // Prefix notation
i++; // Postfix notation
```

each increment the value of i. The first expression, however, equals i's incremented value because ++ comes *before* its operand. The second expression has the value of i before it is incremented because ++ comes *after* its operand. The two different placements are called prefix

and postfix notation. A few more examples will help make this concept clear. Declare variables i and j and assign 100 to i:

```
int j, i = 100;
```

Then increment i and assign the result to j:

```
j = i++;  // j = 100, i = 101
```

The comment shows the resulting values of i and j. Because postfix notation is used in the expression i++, the value of i is assigned to j *before* i is incremented. Using prefix notation produces a different result. Reassign 100 to i and then increment with ++, but this time place the operator before its operand:

```
i = 100;  // Reassign 100 to i
j = ++i;  // j = 101, i = 101
```

Because prefix ++ is applied to its operand before the expression is evaluated, the second statement sets both i and j to 101. The same prefix and postfix rules apply to the -- operator. Try these statements in a program:

```
int i, j;  // Declare integer variable i and j
i = 100;   // Initialize i to 100
j = i--;   // j = 100, i = 99
j = --i;   // j = 98, i = 98
```

Here's a hint: To display the preceding results, insert the following statement at strategic locations in the program. Notice how the + operator is used multiple times to form an output string.

```
System.out.println("j = " + j + ", i = " + i);
```

Binary Integer Expressions

Binary integer expressions—a + b, for example—are so-called because they require two operands. You may mix any types of integers—byte, short, int, and long—in a binary integer expression. Because Unicode characters are represented as 16-bit unsigned integers, you may also mix char values in binary integer expressions.

If any value, whether literal or variable, in a binary integer expression is of type long, then the results are long, even if the value of that result might fit in a smaller space. In all other cases, the results of binary integer expressions are type int, which holds true even if all operands are of shorter types.

Ignoring that fact will cause you no end of grief! For example, the following statements do not compile:

```
byte b1 = 1, b2 = 2, b3;
b3 = b1 + b2;  // ???
System.out.println("b3 = " + b3);
```

You cannot declare three `byte` variables, add two of them, and assign the result to the third because the data type of the expression `b1 + b2` is `int`, not `byte`, and you cannot assign larger `int` values to smaller bytes. (By larger and smaller, I mean the space these values occupy in memory, not their integer values.) The solution is to use a *type cast expression,* which is merely the intended type in parentheses ahead of a variable or expression:

```
b3 = (byte)(b1 + b2);
```

The program now compiles because the type cast expression tells the compiler to downsize the result of the expression to an 8-bit byte. It is your responsibility, however, to ensure that the resulting value can be represented by a byte. Otherwise, a loss of information might occur. For example, consider these statements:

```
int a, b = 1;
int c = 2147483647;
a = b + c;
System.out.println("a = " + a);
```

Because `c` equals the maximum integer value that can fit in 16 bits, the resulting value in a equals -2,147,483,648. To compute the correct result, change variables `a` and `b` to type `long`. This now sets `a` to one greater than `c`:

```
long a;
long b = 1;
int c = 2147483647;
a = b + c;
```

When the result of an expression is to be reassigned to one of its operands, you can often use shorthand expressions to save some typing, and perhaps improve the program's efficiency. For example, rather than write

```
count = count + k;
```

use the shorthand equivalent:

```
count += k;  // Assign count + k back to count
```

This adds `count` to `k` and assigns the result back to `count`. The `+=` characters form a single operator, which might seem a bit cryptic but permits you to write `count` only once. This might improve runtime performance a tad because the interpreter needs to find where `count` is in memory only once.

Table 4.6 lists Java's binary integer operators and shows their shorthand assignment forms.

Table 4.6. Binary integer operators.

Operator	Description	Assignment shorthand
*	Multiply	*=
/	Divide	/=

continues

Table 4.6. continued

Operator	Description	Assignment shorthand
+	Add	+=
–	Subtract	–=
%	Modulo	%=
&	Bitwise AND	&=
¦	Bitwise OR	¦=
^	Bitwise XOR	^=
<<	Left shift	<<=
>>	Right shift	>>=
>>>	Shift in 0 at right	>>>=

The modulo operator returns the remainder of an integer division, any fraction of which is truncated. Given the declarations

```
int a = 7, b = 2, c = 0;
```

this sets c to 3 (a divided by b):

```
c = a / b;  // c = 3
```

This sets c to 1 (the remainder of a divided by b):

```
c = a % b;  // c = 1
```

Use the bitwise logical operators, & (AND), ¦ (OR), and ^ (XOR) to perform those operations on the binary digits in integer values. If result is an int variable, the statement

```
result = result ^ 0xFFFFFFFF;
```

applies an XOR (exclusive OR) operation with each bit in result and 1, resulting in a value with all 1 bits changed to 0 and all 0 bits changed to 1. Repeating this same operation sets result back to its original value. You may use shorthand notation, as in

```
result ^= 0xFFFFFFFF;
```

Use shift operators to shift the bits in an integer variable to the left:

```
result = result << 3;  // Shift result left 3 bits
```

Or, using the alternative shorthand, shift the bits to the right:

```
result >>= 4;  // Shift result right 4 bits
```

Shift operations are signed, which might cause results to be different from what you expect (especially if you think in binary). Use the zero-fill-shift operator to perform unsigned right shifts. For example, try these statements:

```
int result = 0x80000001;
result >>= 4;    // result = 0xF8000000
```

The hexadecimal value assigned to `result` equals the negative decimal value -2,147,483,647. Shifting this value right four bits fills result with 1 bits from the left. The resulting value in hexadecimal, `0xF8000000`, or -134,217,728 in decimal, remains negative. Using the zero-fill-shift operator produces a different result:

```
int result = 0x80000001;
result >>>= 4;    // result = 0x08000000
```

This time, the resulting value in hexadecimal, `0x08000000`, equals 134,217,728 in decimal. Because zeros are shifted in at left, the negative integer becomes positive.

Floating Point Expressions

You can use arithmetic operators—*, /, +, and -—in floating point expressions. You can also combine floating point and integer values, but the result is always either `float` or `double`. If all values are of type `float` or any integer type, the result is `float`; if any value is `double`, the result is `double`. Here's an example:

```
double d1, d2;
d1 = 3.14159;
int q = 3;
d2 = d1 * q;   // d2 = 9.42477
```

The final line multiplies `double d1` by integer q, and assigns the `double` result to d2. You may also use shorthand assignment operators, as in

```
d2 *= d1;
```

That's equivalent to

```
d2 = d2 * d1;
```

Unlike in some programming languages, modulo, increment, and decrement operators are defined for floating point values. The following declares three `double` variables and applies the modulo operator:

```
double result;
double a = 3.14159, b = 3;
result = a % b;   // result = 0.14159
```

The final line sets `result` to `0.14159`, the remainder of dividing 3.14159 by 3.0.

You can also use increment ++ and decrement -- operators as you do in integer expressions. They increment and decrement the integer part of a floating point value. Examine these statements:

```
double result = 3.14159;
result++; // result = 4.14159
++result; // result = 5.14159
result--; // result = 4.14159
--result; // result = 3.14159
```

As with integer expressions, prefix notation increments or decrements its operand before evaluation; postfix increments or decrements after evaluation. If `count` is type `double`, the statement

```
result = count++;
```

sets `result` equal to `count`, and then increments `count` by one. The statement

```
result = ++count;
```

increments `count`, and then sets `result` equal to `count`'s new value.

Three types of errors might occur with floating point expressions. These are

> Overflow: Result is too large for data type
>
> Underflow: Result is too small for data type
>
> Divide by zero: Attempt to divide by zero

Unlike in some programming languages, these errors do not halt the program with an error message. Overflow sets the result to a special value, `Inf`, for Infinity. Underflow sets the result to `0` (however, some early versions of Visual J++ set the underflow result to `-1`). Dividing a floating point value by zero sets the result to `Inf`.

Type Casting

As mentioned, type casting is required to assign a value of one type to a variable of another type. Some type casting operations are safe; others may or may not cause a loss of information. For example, it is always safe to assign an `int` value to a `long` variable because the value is guaranteed to be within the `long` data type's defined minimum and maximum boundaries.

Safe type casts occur automatically. For example, the statements

```
long result;
int a = 10;
result = a;
```

assign an `int` variable to a `long`. Trying to make this assignment in the other direction is like using a shoe horn to put sneakers on a buffalo:

```
a = result;  // ???
```

This doesn't compile because the `int` data type is smaller in size than `long`. If the *value* in `result` is small enough to fit in an `int` variable, you can force the compiler to accept the statement (ignore the choking sound you hear during compilation) by using a type cast expression:

```
a = (int)result;
```

It is now your responsibility to ensure that the value can safely fit inside `a`. If not, bits are lost and the resulting value may not be what you want.

Table 4.7 shows the allowable type casts that do not potentially lose information and are automatically handled. Others such as assigning an int value to a byte variable require an explicit type cast expression prefaced with the target data type in parentheses.

Table 4.7. Safe type casts.

Value of type	Can be safely assigned to
byte	short, char, int, long, float, double
short	char, int, long, float, double
char	int, long, float, double
int	long, float, double
long	float, double
float	double
double	double

When casting floating point values to integer variables, the results are truncated—they are not rounded. For example, the program fragment

```
int result;
double v = 4.999999;
result = (int)v;   // Use type cast to assign v to result
```

sets the integer result equal to 4.

Flow Control Statements

You now have enough information about Java data types, variables, and expressions to begin writing simple programs that perform useful actions. To do this, you need to use *flow control statements,* which alter the program's default action of executing statements one at a time, in the order they are declared.

Flow control statements can select actions based on the values of variables, they can perform loops, and they can do other useful work. In most cases, one or more *relational expressions* fuel a flow control statement, so let's start there.

Relational Expressions

Relational operators create boolean expressions that have true or false values. Don't confuse them with integer operators, a common mistake. For example, the statement

```
a = b;
```

assigns the value of b to a, but the statement

```
a == b;
```

is a boolean expression that is true if a equals b. You might use such an expression in an if statement, which selects among two actions, depending on whether its relational expression is true:

```
if (a == b)
  System.out.println("a equals b");
```

If the value of a equals b, the program displays a message; otherwise, it skips the println() statement. A common mistake I've probably made as many times as I've gotten up in the morning is to write = in place of ==. If you mistakenly type

```
if (a = b)  // ???
  System.out.println("a equals b");
```

Java reports the error Cannot convert int to boolean because the result of the expression a = b is type int (if the operands are int). Boolean expressions are not interchangeable with integers, as they are in C and C++.

In addition to their use in flow-control statements, relational expressions can be assigned to boolean variables. For example, the following fragment sets a boolean variable, result, to true:

```
boolean result;
int a = 1, b = 1;
result = (a == b);
if (result == true)
  System.out.println("result is true!");
```

The third line evaluates the expression (a == b), producing a true or false result, which is assigned to the result variable. You could write this without parentheses, but it's less clear:

```
result = a == b;
```

Notice how the if statement compares the value of result with true. Because result is already of type boolean, this isn't necessary, and you can more simply write

```
if (result)
  System.out.println("result is true!");
```

Table 4.8 lists Java's relational operators, which give boolean results when used in expressions. You'll see examples of these operations in the next several sections.

Table 4.8. Relational operators.

Operator	Description	Example
<	Less than	(a < b)
>	Greater than	(a > b)
<=	Less than or equal	(a <= b)
>=	Greater than or equal	(a >= b)

Operator	Description	Example
==	Equal	`(a == b)`
!=	Not equal	`(a != b)`
&&	And	`(a <= b) && (b <= c)`
¦¦	Or	`(a <= b) ¦¦ (b >= c)`

if-else Statements

Use `if`, optionally followed by `else` statements, to conditionally execute code. For example, the following fragment tests whether an integer is less than another and displays an appropriate message:

```
int a = 10, b = 20;
if (a < b)
 System.out.println("a < b");
else
 System.out.println("a >= b");
```

I'll use equally simple examples to introduce other flow-control statements, so we can move quickly through this material and get to more interesting subjects.

An `else` statement is optional, and can be followed by another `if` statement to create multipath conditionals:

```
if (a < b)
 System.out.println("a < b");
else if (a == b)
 System.out.println("a = b");
else
 System.out.println("a > b");
```

Only one of the `println()` statements will execute, depending on the values of the compared integers.

To execute more than one statement, create a *statement block* delimited by braces:

```
if (a < b) {
 System.out.println("a < b");
 System.out.println("That's all folks!");
}
```

switch Statements

A `switch` statement (I call it the ol' switcheroo) selects statements to execute based on the value of a condition. It is a kind of shorthand for a complex `if-else` statement, also known as a multiway decision tree, something like this:

```
if (a == 1)
  // statement for a == 1
```

```
else if (a == 2)
  // statement for a == 2
else if (a == 3)
  // statement for a == 3
else
  // statement for all other values
```

There's nothing wrong with writing statements like that, but it makes the program work harder than necessary. Use a switch statement in these cases for clearer and more efficient code. Listing 4.6, Switcher.java, demonstrates how to create a switch statement as a multiway decision tree.

Listing 4.6. Switcher.java (Demonstrates switch statements).

```
class Switcher {
 public static void main(String args[]) {
  int a = 2;
  switch (a) {
   case 1:
    System.out.println("Case 1");
    break;
   case 2:
    System.out.println("Case 2");
    System.out.println("Final statement in case 2");
    break;
   case 3:
    System.out.println("Case 3");
    break;
   default:
    System.out.println("All other cases");
  }
 }
}
```

The control expression in parentheses after the keyword switch may be any expression or variable that can be compared to a literal integer or character. Follow the switch keyword and control expression with the word case, a value to compare to the control, and a colon. If the control expression matches the case value, the statements following that case are executed.

Use break statements in each case to exit the switch statement. If you forget to insert break, execution continues with the next case (in other words, the program "falls through" the current case to the next one). This is often a mistake, but it might be useful in rare circumstances. Try taking out the break from case 2 in the sample listing and run the program modified like this:

```
case 2:
 System.out.println("Case 2");
 System.out.println("Final statement in case 2");
 // falls through to next case
case 3:
 System.out.println("Case 3");
 break;
```

If the control expression equals 2, the program prints the two statements for that case, but also falls through to print the statement for case 3.

You may follow a `switch` statement with an optional `default` statement, which is executed if no case matches the control expression. You do not have to supply a `default` case, but if you do, it must be last. You don't need to insert a `break` in the `default` statements, but doing so is not an error:

```
switch (c) {
  case 'A':
    // statement(s) for c == 'A'
  case 'B':
    // statement(s) for c == 'B'
...
  default:
    // statement(s) for c == other characters
    break;  // okay but not required
}
```

while Statements

A `while` statement performs an operation as long as its control expression is true. Presumably, something in the `while` statement causes the expression to become false eventually; otherwise, the `while` loops endlessly. (Actually, this can be a useful technique—but I'll avoid the subject of endless loops until we examine multithreaded programming.)

Listing 4.7, `WhileCount.java`, uses a `while` loop to count from 1 to 10.

Listing 4.7. WhileCount.java (Demonstrates while).

```
class WhileCount {
 public static void main(String args[]) {
  int count = 0;
  while (count < 10) {
   count++;
   System.out.println("Count = " + count);
  }
 }
}
```

When the control expression (`count < 10`) becomes `false` as a result of the program incrementing count, the loop ends. In this case, so does the program because no other statement follows the `while` loop.

do-while Statements

You might never use a `do-while` statement, but they are handy on rare occasions. It's similar to a plain `while`, but the control expression comes at the end instead of at the beginning. For comparison, Listing 4.8, `DoWhileCount.java`, counts from 1 to 10 using a `do-while` loop.

Listing 4.8. `DoWhileCount.java` (Demonstrates do-while).

```
class DoWhileCount {
 public static void main(String args[]) {
  int count = 0;
  do {
   count++;
   System.out.println("Count = " + count);
  } while (count < 10);
 }
}
```

> **TIP**
>
> The key to selecting between `while` and `do-while` is to remember that a `while` loop does not execute its statements at all if the controlling expression is initially false. A `do-while` loop, however, always executes its statements at least once because its controlling expression is evaluated at the end of the loop.

for Statements

A `for` statement is a versatile beast, and you'll use it in many circumstances. It is usually preferred over `while` or `do-while` when you or the program can determine in advance how many loops to execute. All `for` statements have these elements:

> The keyword `for`
>
> A three-part expression in parentheses
>
> A statement or block to execute

The design of a `for` loop is easiest to learn in schematic form. It uses this layout:

```
for (statement; expression1; expression2) {
 // statement or block to execute
}
```

The braces are required only if the block to execute contains two or more statements, but you can use braces anyway for clarity as do many programmers. Listing 4.9 uses a `for` loop to count from 1 to 10.

Listing 4.9. `ForCount.java` (Demonstrates for).

```
class ForCount {
 public static void main(String args[]) {
  int count;
  for (count = 1; count <= 10; count++) {
   System.out.println("Count = " + count);
  }
 }
}
```

Rather than declare the integer count variable separately, you may insert the declaration directly in the for statement:

```
for (int count = 1; count <= 10; count++) {
 System.out.println("Count = " + count);
}
```

This example loop initially sets count to 1. It executes the loop's statement or statement block *while* the controlling expression, count <= 10, is true. After executing the loop's statement or block, it executes the final expression, which in this case increments count by one. As with other loops, it is usually important that this expression perform some action that will eventually cause the control expression to become false; otherwise, the loop will never end.

label, break, and continue Statements

These three types of statements are easily misused, and are best put into play only when absolutely necessary. A label marks any statement in a program. A break or continue statement halts a while, do-while, or for loop, and starts execution at the labeled position.

An example will help make these concepts clear and also show the subtle difference between break and continue. Listing 4.10 shows the correct way to use these statements, which as this listing also demonstrates, can lead to messy code. To make the sample program easier to follow, I commented the closing braces, showing the statement to which each belongs.

Listing 4.10. LabelDemo.java (Demonstrates label, break, and continue).

```
class LabelDemo  {
 public static void main(String args[]) {
  int i, j;
OuterLoop:
  for (i = 1; i < 100; i++) {
   System.out.println("\nOuter loop # " + i);
InnerLoop:
   for (j = 1; j < 10; j++) {
    if (j % 2 == 0)
     continue InnerLoop;  // Skip even j values
    if (i > 4)
     break OuterLoop;      // Abort if i > 4
    System.out.println("j = " + j);
   } // end of inner for statement
  }  // end of outer for statement
  System.out.println("Program exiting at OuterLoop:");
 }   // end of main() method
}     // end of class declaration
```

The sample program executes two for loops, one inside the other. Two labels—OuterLoop: and InnerLoop:—mark the position above each loop. A label is any unused identifier followed by a colon.

Inside a while, do-while, or for statement, a continue statement causes an immediate jump to the designated position. Use continue to continue executing the loop from a specific point when you do not want to execute any other statements from that point on. This might be easier to fathom in schematic form:

```
L1:
for (...) {
  // statements to always execute
  if (condition)
    continue L1; // keep executing loop, but skip following
  // statements to conditionally execute
}
```

If the condition is true, the if statement executes continue, skipping the rest of the loop but otherwise executing it normally.

A break statement is similar to continue, but completely exits the loop. Again, this might be easier to understand in schematic form:

```
L2:
for (...) {
  // statements to always execute
  if (condition)
    break L2; // exit loop completely
  // statements to conditionally execute
}
```

The difference is that, if the condition is true, the break statement halts execution of the loop, and the program continues after the for statement's closing brace. A good use for break is to get out of a nested flow-control statement because of an error or other condition.

Summary

- A Java program consists of one or more source code files, which are merely text files that end with the filename extension, .java.

- The example programs in this part's chapters are best compiled and run from a DOS command-line prompt. While primitive, this technique will help you to get through the tutorial information quickly and learn the Java programming language so you can move on to more sophisticated concepts such as graphics and Internet programming.

- The individual elements of a Java source code file are known as tokens. These include literals, operands, operators, separators, identifiers, and keywords.

- Java has three comment styles. Text bracketed with /* and */ is ignored. Text beginning with // is ignored to the end of the line. You may optionally use Java's documentation comment, /** ... */, which Visual J++ does not directly support.

- You declare variables using Java's many data types. There are several kinds of integer, floating point, character, and string types from which to choose.

- Operators perform actions on data values. Java supports numerous mathematical, logical, and bitwise operators that you can use to create expressions for manipulating data. Operators with higher precedence are evaluated before operators with lower precedence; otherwise, expressions are evaluated from left to right. Use parentheses to force a different expression evaluation order.

- Flow control statements conditionally select among a program's statements and perform other jobs such as creating loops. Java has `if`, `switch`, `while`, `do-while`, and `for` statements. Java also supports labeled statements for use with `break` and `continue`, which are occasionally useful for ending deeply nested `while` and `for` loops.

Exercises

1. Write a Java program that displays your name or another string of text 10 times. Number each line of output. Use comments to document the code.

2. Use the ++ operator to simplify the `while` loop in Listing 4.7, `WhileCount.java`.

3. Using only the elements introduced in this chapter, write a program that clears the screen.

4. Advanced: Write a program that displays the binary value of an integer variable. (The answer uses some elements not introduced in this chapter, but the purpose of this exercise is to get you to think about how you can use Java operators to extract the bits in an integer variable.)

5. Write a test program that shows the results of floating point underflow, underflow, and divide-by-zero errors. (This program makes a good addition to your benchmark library for testing how various Java interpreters perform.)

What's Next?

As I mentioned, everything in a Java program operates in the context of at least one class. The next chapter explains how to use classes and introduces the fundamentals of object-oriented programming.

5

CHAPTER

Classes and Objects

Java is completely object oriented. This means that every piece of data and every action in a Java program exists or takes place in the context of a class. As you will learn in this chapter, the class is Java's basic building block. You can use classes to perform all sorts of operations such as input and output, and you can also create your own classes.

Because classes have extensive features, it is impractical to cover everything about classes and objects in one chapter. This chapter introduces classes and the concepts of object-oriented programming with Java. We'll return to these topics in Chapter 8, when we examine "More About Classes and Objects."

> **NOTE**
>
> If you know C++, don't skip this chapter. Although Java and C++ classes resemble each other, their likeness is only skin deep. There are many differences, some subtle, between Java and C++ classes.

In This Chapter

This chapter introduces the following fundamentals about classes, objects, and object-oriented programming:

- Introduction to classes and objects
- Class methods
- Input and output methods
- Initializing class objects
- Cleaning up class objects

Introduction to Classes and Objects

The primary purpose of a class is to encapsulate data and the methods that operate on that data. Keeping data and methods together helps you create well-organized programs, and also prevents pitfalls that are common in conventional programming languages such as passing the wrong data to subroutines.

Declaring Classes

A class begins with the `class` keyword followed by braces that delimit the class's contents:

```
class AnyClass {
  ...
}
```

Most classes have one or more methods, such as `main()`, which is found in all stand-alone Java applications:

```
class AnyClass {
 public static void main(String args[]) {
  // statements inside main()
 }
}
```

As you have seen, statements inside `main()` perform the program's actions. You can also create other methods and call them from `main()` and from other places:

```
class AnyClass {
 public static void HiThere() {
  System.out.println("Hi there!");
 }
 public static void main(String args[]) {
  HiThere();  // Call HiThere() method
 }
}
```

This class has two methods, `HiThere()` and `main()`. The statement in `main()` calls the `HiThere()` method, which displays a string. (If you enter this program, save it in a `.java` file named the same as the class.)

As you know, you can declare variables inside functions. You also can declare variables in a class:

```
class AnyClass {
 static int i;  // Declare class variable
 public static void HiThere() {
  for (i = 0; i < 4; i++)
   System.out.println("Hi there!");
 }
...
}
```

The `static int i` declaration creates an integer variable that any method in the class can use.

You might wonder (rightly) at this point why I am using the word `static` in every variable and method declaration. This is because the sample programs have so far used classes in only a rudimentary way—as shell-like constructions that specify data and code. But classes are more than simply shells; they are templates for creating *objects*. In fact, a Java application is itself an object that can be loaded into a Java interpreter or a Web browser.

Declaring Objects

An object is also called an instance of a class. An object or instance is a variable, just like integers, characters, and those of other data types. An object occupies space in memory, and it must be initialized. You may create objects of any class, and you may create as many objects of a specific class as you need.

Listing 5.1, `DateObject.java`, demonstrates how to construct objects of a declared class that stores a date.

Listing 5.1. `DateObject.java` (Demonstrates class objects).

```java
// Declare DateClass
class DateClass {
 int month;
 int day;
 int year;
 public DateClass(int m, int d, int y) {
  month = m;
  day = d;
  year = y;
 }
 public void Display() {
  System.out.println(month + "/" + day + "/" + year);
 }
}

// Declare main program class
class DateObject {
 public static void main(String args[]) {
  // Create and display a DateClass object
  DateClass birthday = new DateClass(7, 18, 64);
  birthday.Display();
  // Create and display another DateClass object
  DateClass future = new DateClass(1, 1, 01);
  future.Display();
 }
}
```

The sample application declares two classes. `DateClass` stores a date as three integer *instance variables*—`month`, `day`, and `year`. A *constructor* method, named the same as the class, initializes these variables by assigning its parameters (`m`, `d`, and `y`) to the instance variables. The class also declares a method, `Display()`, that shows the date in `m/d/y` format. Some Java texts call constructors *creation methods*.

To use the class, the main program creates an object by using Java's `new` operator. This tells the interpreter to *instantiate* the class—in other words, to create an instance or object of the class:

```java
DateClass birthday = new DateClass(7, 18, 64);
```

The object is named `birthday`, and it is initialized by a new instance of the `DateClass` class. The integer arguments in parentheses are passed to the class constructor's parameters, which as mentioned, are saved in the object's instance variables. Given an initialized object, you may call methods in reference to it—to display the date, for example:

```java
birthday.Display();
```

It's useful to think of this statement as giving the `birthday` object a command to display itself. In object-oriented programming, it's common to perform actions this way by calling class methods. For example, you might tell a graphics object to display itself or to change its colors.

The sample program also shows that you may create multiple objects of the same class. The statement

```
DateClass future = new DateClass(1, 1, 01);
```

constructs another object, named `future`, of `DateClass`. The class is a template for a certain kind of data, just like other data types such as integers. Compare that statement to one that creates a simpler variable:

```
int count = 10;
```

The only difference is that, to create class objects, you use the `new` operator and you typically (but not always) pass values to the class constructor to initialize instance variables. As you can with simple variables, you can declare class objects and initialize them at another place. The fragment

```
DateClass d1;  // Declare d1 object
...
d1 = new DateClass(5, 6, 70);  // Initialize d1
```

declares a `DateClass` object, performs some other tasks (indicated by the ellipsis), and initializes `d1` using the statement shown on the last line. You may also reinitialize an object to give it other values. For example, the preceding fragment could be followed by

```
d1 = new DateClass(8, 9, 10);  // Reinitialize d1
d1.Display();  // Display object
```

which reinitializes the object and displays its value.

> **NOTE**
>
> You do not have to delete or dispose of the objects you create. When the program is finished using an object, Java automatically deletes it from memory, a process called *garbage collection*. Java's automatic garbage collector ensures that memory isn't wasted by unused objects.

Modifying Classes

One of the key benefits of object-oriented programming is that classes can control access to their data and methods. You'll learn more about this subject throughout this book, but for a simple demonstration, consider how you might improve the `DateClass` in the `DateObject.java` sample program.

A problem with that program is that it displays dates such as January 15, 2001, as

1/15/1

It would be better if the year were displayed in full, and to make that change, we can arbitrarily specify that the DateClass store years minus 1900. The year value 50 equals 1950; the year value 105 equals 2005, and so on. To make this change, modify the statement year = y; to

```
year = y + 1900;
```

Also modify the following statement in the main program class (change the year 01 to 101):

```
DateClass future = new DateClass(1, 1, 101);
```

When compiled and run, the program now displays dates such as

```
7/18/1964
1/1/2001
```

Another improvement might be to change the integer instance variables to smaller data types. There's hardly any good reason to waste space by storing month and day values as 32-bit integers! You can reduce the size of DateClass by declaring month and day as type byte:

```
class DateClass {
 byte month;
 byte day;
 int year;
 public DateClass(int m, int d, int y) {
  month = (byte)m;
  day = (byte)d;
  year = y;
 }
...
}
```

This change also requires using type cast expressions in the assignments to month and day in the DateClass() constructor.

Significantly, none of these changes affects the use of the class. The main program remains unchanged even though the storage format of the DateClass has been altered. This is another benefit of object-oriented programming. In general, you may make changes to well-designed classes without affecting their use in other parts of the program.

Importing Classes

Java comes with a rich class library of *packages* that provide ready-to-use classes for a variety of purposes. Try to use these classes whenever possible. They save you time, and they reduce the size of your programs. Also, because Java's classes are debugged, they help you create robust code.

For example, searching Visual J++'s online help reveals that Java already has a date class named java.util.Date. The class name is Date; it is declared as part of the java.util package, which provides other classes. (More about packages in Part III.)

To use a Java class library package, you *import* it into your program. Do this with an `import` statement such as

```
import java.util.Date;
```

Generally, this and other import statements should be at the top of your program's source file. You may also use a wild-card asterisk to import multiple classes. The statement

```
import java.util.*;
```

imports all classes declared in `java.util`. The statement

```
import java.*;
```

imports all `java` package classes.

> ### NOTE
>
> `System` classes are automatically imported into all applications. You do not have to import the `System` package in order to write statements such as `System.out.println();`.

Listing 5.2, `DateDemo.java`, shows how to import a class and use it in a program.

Listing 5.2. `DateDemo.java` (Demonstrates importing classes).

```
import java.util.Date;  // Import the Date class

// Use the imported Date class
class DateDemo {
 public static void main(String args[]) {
  Date today = new Date();
  System.out.println(today.toString());
  Date future = new Date("5/3/2006");
  System.out.println(future.toString());
 }
}
```

Use Java's classes the same way you do your own. Import the class with an `import` declaration as shown in the sample program, and then use the `new` operator to create one or more objects of the imported classes. For example, the sample application constructs a `Date` object with the statement

```
Date today = new Date();
```

which creates an initialized object, `today`, with the current date and time. Java's `Date` class doesn't have an output method, but it provides other ways to extract `Date` information. Call the `toString()` method for a string representation of the date and time.

```
System.out.println(today.toString());
```

When I ran the program, that statement printed the following line on my screen:

```
Sat Sep 14 15:54:34 Eastern Daylight Time 1996
```

Another way to construct a `Date` object is to pass it a string. The fragment

```
Date future = new Date("5/3/2006");
System.out.println(future.toString());
```

parses (translates) the date string passed to the `Date` class, and displays this text on screen:

```
Sat Jun 03 00:00:00 Eastern Daylight Time 2006
```

There are other ways to construct `Date` objects. You can pass integer values representing the year, month, and day:

```
Date anyDate = new Date(101, 1, 2);   // 1/2/2001
```

Year values are minus 1900, so the above sets the date to January 2, 2001. Call methods such as `setYear` to change a `Date` object's year value:

```
anyDate.setYear(56);   // Set year to 1956
```

You can also extract the date and time using various methods. For example, for the GMT (Greenwich Mean Time, but now more properly called Zulu time), call the `toGMTString()` method like this:

```
System.out.println(future.toGMTString());
```

There are numerous other `Date` methods you might want to try. Look them up in the `Date` class declaration using the Developer Studio's InfoViewer online help or the InfoView help in Visual Studio 97.

Inheriting Classes

When a class doesn't do exactly what you want, you can build a new class based on it. Your class *inherits* the original class's methods and instance variables, to which you can add your own code and data. Inheriting classes is a great way to reuse existing code.

> **NOTE**
>
> Contrary to what some programmers might tell you, the term *code reuse* does not refer to a text editor's cut and paste commands. Developing reusable code means writing and debugging classes, and then building new classes from them. You can get a lot of work done in a relatively short time by using as many existing classes as possible—either those of your own design, or those from Java's rich class library.

To demonstrate how to inherit and build on an existing class, Listing 5.3, `DateShow.java`, adds a `Display()` method to Java's `Date` class.

Listing 5.3. `DateShow.java` (Demonstrates inheriting classes).

```
import java.util.Date;  // Import the Date class

// Extend the imported Date class
class NewDate extends Date {
 public void Display() {
  System.out.println(toString());
 }
}

// Use the NewDate class
class DateShow {
 public static void main(String args[]) {
  NewDate today = new NewDate();  // Construct NewDate object
  today.Display();  // Call the new Display() method
 }
}
```

The sample program imports the `Date` class as before. It then extends `Date` by declaring a new class like this:

```
class NewDate extends Date {
  ...
}
```

The `NewDate` class inherits all members (instance variables and methods) from `Date`. To its inheritance, `NewDate` adds a `Display()` method, which uses the `println()` method to display the object's date in string form. Take a close look at the statement that makes this happen:

```
System.out.println(toString());
```

In past examples, you called methods such as `toString()` in reference to an object such as `today`. Because this statement is in the `NewDate` class, and because that class inherits `Date`'s members, the statement can call `toString()` directly. Whatever object the program uses to call our new `Display()` method is the same object used to call `toString()`.

For example, the sample program's `main()` method constructs a `NewDate` object and then calls the `Display()` method in reference to that object using the statements

```
NewDate today = new NewDate();  // Construct NewDate object
today.Display();  // Call the new Display() method
```

This calls our new `Display()` method, which calls the inherited `toString()` method for the `today` object, thus printing today's date and time.

Subclass and Superclass

An extended class such as `NewDate` in the preceding sample program is called a *subclass.* The class from which it is extended is called the *superclass.* Other object-oriented languages such as C++ and Object Pascal use the terms *ancestor* and *descendent* to describe class relationships—and you might also come across the term *base class,* which is analogous to a *superclass* in Java.

Any subclass can be used as a superclass, and there is no practical limit to the number of subclasses you can create for any class. You can import a class, extend it, import the resulting subclass, extend it again, and so on. In fact, most classes you import into a program are already extended from several other classes. All Java classes, even those that you create, are extended from a superclass, called `Object`. All classes, and all objects, are related through the `Object` class.

Among other members, the `Object` class declares a method, `toString()`, which you may call for any object. By default, this method returns a string equal to the object's class name, the character @, and the object's *hash code.* To try this method, insert the following statement at the end of the `main()` method in the `DateObject.java` sample program:

```
System.out.println(birthday.toString());
```

When I did this, my system displayed

```
DateClass@4283c0
```

This tells me that birthday is an object of the `DateClass`, and it has the hash code `4283C0` (in hexadecimal). Hash codes are used by the `java.util.Hashtable` class, which provides a convenient mechanism for storing objects. (More on this and other classes in Part III.)

There are several other aspects of inheritance that I'll cover later in this chapter and also in Chapter 8.

Class Methods

Class methods, as you have seen in all sample programs presented so far, execute statements. They can also declare variables and call other methods. As you know, every stand-alone Java application must have a `main()` method in a class named the same as the program's source code file.

Programming with Methods

A method can be a *function* that returns a value. Declare the return-value's data type ahead of the method's name, and list any parameters and their types in parentheses. In the sample

```
int sum(int a, int b, int c) {
 return a + b + c;
} // <-- no semicolon here!
```

a *return statement* passes back the `sum()` function's integer result—the sum of the three `int` parameters, a, b, and c, which are separated by commas. Notice that there is no semicolon after the method's closing brace. Another statement might call `sum()` like this:

```
int k = sum(x, y, 25);  // k = x + y + 25;
```

If a method returns no value, declare it as type `void`. This is typically done for methods that perform some action rather than calculate a value. For example, the function

```
void doSomething();
```

returns no value and requires no parameter arguments. Call the method simply by writing its name in statements such as

```
doSomething();     // Call method
o.doSomething();   // Call method for an object
```

> **NOTE**
>
> Reminder: In this text, empty parentheses indicate a function name. You know that `count()` is a function, but `count` is probably a variable.

Listing 5.4, `Methods.java`, demonstrates how to declare and use methods in a program.

Listing 5.4. `Methods.java` (Demonstrates methods).

```
// Method demonstration class
class MethodClass {
 int sum(int a, int b, int c) {
  return a + b + c;
 }
 double product(double x, double y) {
  return x * y;
 }
 void showErrorMessage(int code) {
  switch (code) {
  case 1:
   System.out.println("Error 1: Deep trouble!");
   break;
  case 2:
   System.out.println("Error 2: Deeper trouble!");
   break;
```

continues

Listing 5.4. continued

```
  default:
    System.out.println("Unknown code: Situation hopeless");
  }
 }
}

// Main program class
class Methods {
 public static void main(String args[]) {
  // Create demo object of the MethodClass class
  MethodClass demo = new MethodClass();

  // Call demo object's sum() method
  int k = demo.sum(10, 25, 16);
  System.out.println("sum = " + k);

  // Call demo object's product() method
  double f = demo.product(3.14159, 4.5);
  System.out.println("product = " + f);

  // Call demo object's showErrorMessage() method
  demo.showErrorMessage(1);
  demo.showErrorMessage(2);
 }
}
```

The sample program declares three methods: sum(), product(), and showErrorMessage(). The first two return int and double values respectively. The third returns void—that is, no value. As required in Java, each method is declared and implemented in a class, MethodClass. To call the methods, the program constructs an object, demo, of the class

```
MethodClass demo = new MethodClass();
```

and then calls each method in reference to the object. Dot notation shows the association with the object and the class method identifiers:

```
int k = demo.sum(10, 25, 16);
double f = demo.product(3.14159, 4.5);
demo.showErrorMessage(1);
```

Static Methods

Methods may be called in reference to a class, in which case they must be prefaced with the key word static. For example, the main() method is static so it can be called without having to construct an object of its class:

```
public static void main(String args[]) { ...
```

The main() method is also declared public, which makes it available to other classes. I'll cover this and other *access specifiers* in Chapter 8. Static methods are of limited use. Because they are not called in reference to an object, they may not access instance variables in the class. For example, the following statements illustrate a common mistake:

```
class DontDoThis {
 int i;  // instance variable
 public static void main(String args[]) {
  i = 10;  // ???
...
}
```

These statements do not compile because static methods may not use instance variables—there is no instance of the DontDoThis class, and therefore, the instance variable i is not available to the static method.

Overloaded Methods

A class may declare more than one method using the same name as long as each declaration differs by at least one parameter. This technique is called *overloading*, and it is useful for creating sensible code that can accept a variety of arguments.

You already used overloaded methods with the Date class, which as explained, can be initialized with various arguments as in these statements:

```
Date today = new Date();
Date future = new Date("5/3/2006");
```

The same method, Date(), differs only in the type and number of arguments it requires. The methods are actually separate, just as though they had different names, but it's more convenient to name them the same.

Listing 5.5, Overload.java, demonstrates how to declare, implement, and use overloaded methods.

Listing 5.5. Overload.java (Demonstrates overloaded methods).

```
class DemoClass {
 // Method #1
 void Show(int x) {
  System.out.println("int x = " + x);
 }
 // Method #2
 void Show(double x) {
  System.out.println("double x = " + x);
 }
 // Method #3
 void Show(char x) {
  System.out.println("char x = " + x);
 }
}

class Overload {
 public static void main(String args[]) {
```

continues

Listing 5.5. continued

```
DemoClass myObj = new DemoClass();  // Create object
myObj.Show(123);       // Call Show #1
myObj.Show(3.14159);   // Call Show #2
myObj.Show('Q');       // Call Show #3
}
}
```

DemoClass declares three methods, all named Show(). The methods differ in the types of parameters. As the sample program's main() method demonstrates, Java decides which method to call based on the type of argument passed to the method's int, double, or char parameters.

Understanding Scope

Variables declared in a method are available only to that method. This concept is called *scope*. Variables declared in a class are available to all methods in the class. Any *local variables* declared in methods, however, take precedence over any variables of the same names in the class. For example, the class

```
class AnyClass {
 int k = 20;
 void AnyMethod() {
  int k = 10;  // Local variable k hides instance variable k
  System.out.println(k);  // Displays 10
 }
}
```

declares an instance variable, k. Because AnyMethod also declares k, the output statement prints 10. If you delete the declaration of the local variable, the program displays 20 because AnyMethod() refers to the variable in the outer (class) scope.

It's useful to think of scope as a series of nested rooms with one way mirrors. Inside any room, you can see out to other rooms, but outside you can't peer in through the windows. Consequently, one method's local variables do not conflict with another method's. For example, two methods may declare integer variables named i without conflict:

```
class AnyClass {
 public static void f1() {
  int i = 10;  // Belongs to scope of f1()
 }
 public static void f2() {
  int i = 20;  // Belongs to scope of f2()
 }
...
}
```

Input and Output Methods

Although the purpose of this chapter is to introduce classes and object-oriented programming, it's useful to discuss the topics of input and output here. In order to begin presenting more useful sample programs, we need techniques to get data into and out of applications. Actually, output is simpler, so I'll cover that first.

Output Statements

You've already seen how to display text and other values using the `println()` method in statements such as

```
System.out.println("\nValue of k = " + k);
```

This displays a string and the value of k. The special character \n precedes the string with a new line. In general, a variable such as k may be of any data type because Java can convert most kinds of values to strings, which you can join using plus signs as shown here.

Calling `println()` this way, however, isn't always convenient, especially for displaying multiple values. It's often better, and probably faster, to construct a string and then display it using one output statement. Chapter 6 discusses strings in more detail, but Listing 5.6, `OutputDemo.java`, demonstrates the basic technique of using a string for displaying relatively complex output.

Listing 5.6. `OutputDemo.java` (Demonstrates string output).

```
class OutputDemo {
 public static void main(String args[]) {
  StringBuffer s = new StringBuffer();
  for (char c = 'A'; c <= 'Z'; c++) {
   s.append(c);
  }
  System.out.println(s);
 }
}
```

The sample program constructs a `StringBuffer` object, using the statement

```
StringBuffer s = new StringBuffer();
```

This creates an object, s, to which the program can append characters. In this program, a for loop appends the letters A through Z to s by calling the `StringBuffer` class's `append()` method. After constructing the string, the program displays it with a single `println()` statement.

> **NOTE**
>
> The output technique described here is suitable only for simple text output. Graphical output requires entirely different techniques, which you will meet in Part III.

Input Statements

To input characters and strings from the keyboard, call the `System.in.read()` method, as Listing 5.7, `InputDemo.java`, demonstrates.

Listing 5.7. `InputDemo.java` (Demonstrates string input).

```java
import java.io.IOException;

class InputDemo {
 public static void main(String args[]) {
  try {
   // Input a single character
   System.out.println("Type a character:");
   char ch = (char)System.in.read();
   System.out.println("You entered: " + ch);
   ch = (char)System.in.read();  // Throw out new line
   // Input a string
   System.out.println("Type a string:");
   StringBuffer s = new StringBuffer();
   while ((ch = (char)System.in.read()) != '\n')
    s.append(ch);
   System.out.println("You entered: " + s);
  } catch (IOException e) {
   System.out.println("Input error detected");
  }
 }
}
```

> **NOTE**
>
> The sample program inputs a class named IOException, and uses *exception handling* to trap any input errors that might occur. I'll cover exceptions in Chapter 9, but they are necessary here because Visual J++ requires input statements to handle their own errors.

Use the following statement to read a single character from the keyboard:

```java
char ch = (char)System.in.read();
```

Because the user must press Enter after typing the character, follow this statement with a similar one to throw out the `'\n'` new line character:

```java
ch = (char)System.in.read();  // Throw out new line
```

To read a string, use a loop such as the following, which builds a string from characters typed at the keyboard:

```java
StringBuffer s = new StringBuffer();
while ((ch = (char)System.in.read()) != '\n')
 s.append(ch);
```

The while loop calls System.in.read() as long as it does not equal a new line character, and appends all other characters to the StringBuffer object, s.

Cleaning Up Class Objects

Java automatically deletes objects from memory when those objects become out of scope. For example, any objects that a method creates are automatically deleted from memory when the method ends. This keeps memory free of unused objects, and helps make available as much free memory as possible for creating other objects.

Sometimes, it is necessary to perform one or more actions just before an object is deleted. A graphical program, for example, might erase some drawing on screen. To perform such cleanup activities, create a finalize() method in a class declared as

```
protected void finalize() {
...
}
```

A finalize() method, sometimes called a *destructor*, is never required, and most important, Java does not guarantee that it will ever be called. It will be called *only* if an object of its class is deleted, and this will occur only if Java needs to delete objects to free up some memory. As Listing 5.8, FinalDemo.java, demonstrates, you can therefore never rely on your finalize() methods being called.

Listing 5.8. FinalDemo.java. (Demonstrates finalize() method).

```
class AnyClass {
 AnyClass() {
  System.out.println("Inside AnyClass() constructor");
 }
 protected void finalize() {
  System.out.println("Inside AnyClass() destructor");
 }
}

class FinalDemo {
 public static void f() {
  System.out.println("Start method f()");
  AnyClass obj1 = new AnyClass();
  System.out.println("End method f()");
 }
 public static void main(String args[]) {
  System.out.println("Start method main()");
  f();
  AnyClass obj2 = new AnyClass();
  System.out.println("End method main()");
 }
}
```

The sample program also shows the difference between a class initializer method, or constructor, and `finalize()`, the destructor. The constructor is named the same as the class and has no return type, not even `void`. It is called when an object of the class is created with a statement such as

```
AnyClass obj1 = new AnyClass();
```

The `finalize()` destructor returns the data type `void` and is typically made `protected` (see Chapter 8), because it is never called by a program statement:

```
protected void finalize() {
  System.out.println("Inside AnyClass() destructor");
 }
```

Despite this declaration, when you compile and run the sample program, the preceding string is probably not displayed. This indicates that `AnyClass`'s `finalize()` method is not called. Because there's plenty of memory available for this small program's use, Java probably does not have to delete any objects.

Summary

- Java is completely object oriented. Every piece of data and every action takes place in the context of one or more classes.

- A class encapsulates data (instance variables) and code (methods). Programming with classes encourages the reuse of debugged code, which potentially simplifies software development.

- A class initializer, or constructor, is a method named the same as the class but with no return type. A class may declare a cleanup, or *destructor*, method named `finalize()`, which Java calls if it deletes an object of the class. This, however, is not guaranteed to happen.

- To use a class, it is usually instantiated. This creates an object of the class. You may create as many objects of a specific class as you need. Each such object receives separate copies of any instance variables. All objects of a class, however, share the class's methods.

- A source code module imports classes from Java's class library using an `import` statement. There are numerous classes such as `Date` from which to choose. You can create your own classes, but always check whether an existing class is available before reinventing the wheel.

- Classes may extend other classes. The original class is called a superclass. Its extension is called a subclass. Any subclass may be used as a superclass that may be further extended. All classes have the `Object` class as their most distantly related superclass.

- Methods are declared and implemented in a class. They may return a value or `void` (no value). Methods must be called in reference to an object of a class. Static methods, however, may be called in reference to the class itself, but static methods may not use any of the class's instance variables because there is no instance, or object, of the class in this case.

Exercises

1. Using Java's Date class, write a program that shows the day of the week for any date entered at the keyboard.
2. Create a utility class with a method, GetString(), that returns a string entered at the keyboard. Hint: Use Java's String class for your method's return data type.
3. To your utility class from the preceding exercise, add a boolean method named yes() that prompts users to enter Y or N in response to a displayed prompt. Use your method in a loop that repeats an action until the user requests the program to end.
4. Create a MenuClass that displays a menu and lets users choose from one or more selections.

What's Next?

As you will learn in the next chapter, Java's String and StringBuffer classes simplify character and string handling and provide numerous methods for manipulating string objects.

6

CHAPTER

Strings and Characters

You might think that the subjects of strings and characters could be done away with in a few brief paragraphs. But, while it is true that using strings and characters in Java is as easy as can be, there are many operations you might want to perform on text data that might not be obvious. As you will learn in this chapter, there's more than one way to skin string objects and character values.

In This Chapter

This chapter introduces the following techniques for programming with strings and characters:

- Declaring and using strings
- Declaring and using characters
- Java's `String` and `StringBuffer` classes
- `String` and `StringBuffer` constructors
- `String` and `StringBuffer` methods
- The `Character` wrapper class

Declaring and Using Strings

As already mentioned, literal strings are written as zero or more characters delimited with double quotes. For example, the statement

```
System.out.println("A string is a wonderful thing!");
```

displays a literal string on a text screen.

You may use the + and += operators to concatenate, or join, strings. You may also create strings from other types of data by attaching them to another string. The fragment

```
double distance = 45.5;
System.out.println("Distance = " + distance + " miles");
```

displays a string composed of three parts—two literal strings and the value of `distance`, which is converted to a string. If you run this fragment, you will see on screen this line:

```
Distance = 45.5 miles
```

Internally, all strings are represented as objects of the `String` or `StringBuffer` classes. I'll cover more about these classes in this chapter. It's important to understand, however, that when you use a string in a program, it is represented as an object, not as an array of characters as in some other languages.

You can create `String` objects for creating and storing string data, which is often more convenient than simply displaying strings. The fragment

```
double distance = 45.5;
String s = "Distance = " + distance + " miles";
System.out.println(s);
```

constructs a String object, s, and then displays it using a println() statement. Having strings as objects opens all sorts of possibilities for programs. You can, for example, find the length of a string by calling the String class's length() method as in this example:

```
System.out.println("Length = " + s.length() + " character(s)");
```

Attached to the preceding fragment, the statement displays

```
Length = 21 character(s)
```

One significant characteristic of a String object is that it may have a length of zero. If you create and assign a string as

```
String empty = "";
System.out.println("Length = " + empty.length());
```

the program displays empty's length as zero.

Later in this chapter, you explore more about String methods as well as those in another class you will find useful, StringBuffer.

> **NOTE**
>
> Java strings are not arrays of characters, as they are in C and C++. All strings are class objects.

Declaring and Using Characters

Java programs may also declare and use char variables, which are 16 bits in length and can store one character. The char data type is native to Java and is analogous to short, but is unsigned. Literal characters are represented as any character you can type delimited by single quotes. For example, the statement

```
char dollarSign = '$';
```

creates a char variable, dollarSign, and assigns it the dollar sign character. One significant difference between strings and characters is that a char variable can never have a length of zero.

Character Values

Character values in Java are represented in the Unicode worldwide standard. This standard defines a character code for every possible character. Strings are composed of Unicode characters, and thus your string objects are usable internationally. This is not true of 8-bit characters in other languages such as C and C++, and it is one of the significant advantages Java offers programmers.

You may mix strings and characters in several ways. For example, use the + operator to concatenate a character and a string:

```
char ch = 'Q';
System.out.println("Char = " + ch);
```

You can also use the += operator to construct String objects out of characters. For example, the fragment

```
String s = "";
for (char ch = 'a'; ch <= 'z'; ch++)
 s += ch;
System.out.println(s);
```

creates a String object, s, containing the lowercase alphabet characters a through z.

In addition to its native char data type, Java also provides a Character *wrapper class*. Later in this chapter, I'll explain more about how to use this class.

> **TIP**
>
> Wrapper classes provide an object-oriented interface to another type of data, often a simple type such as char or double. Chapter 7, "Numerical Classes," covers more about wrapper classes.

Character Arrays

Although strings are represented as String or StringBuffer objects, you may construct arrays of char values for a variety of purposes. For example, you might store arrays of characters for simplicity when you don't need a full string object.

You haven't learned about arrays yet (more about them in Chapter 10, "Arrays and Other Containers"), but they differ from arrays in other languages. In Java, arrays are constructed at runtime using the new operator. For example, this statement defines an array of 26 char values:

```
char letters[] = new char[26];
```

The empty square brackets state that letters is an array. The new operator constructs an array of 26 chars, which is assigned to the letters identifier. Each character in the array is initialized to the value zero.

You may also declare and define a char array using separate statements such as

```
char letters[];
...
letters = new char[26];
```

The first line declares that `letters` is an array of `char` values. Elsewhere in the program, the last line constructs the actual array and assigns its space to `letters`. Because the array is constructed at runtime, you may use a variable to specify its size. Here's yet another way to create the `letters` array:

```
char letters[];
int k = 26;
letters = new char[k];
```

At runtime, this creates the `letters` array with a size in `char` values equal to `k`.

String Classes

Now, let's get back to Java's string classes. There are two kinds:

- `String`: Use this one for fixed-length strings that will not change at runtime.
- `StringBuffer`: Use this class for variable-length strings that might change at runtime.

You may be surprised to learn that these two classes are each extended from the `Object` superclass, but are not otherwise related to each other. The next sections explain how to use each of Java's two string classes.

The `String` Class

Listing 6.1 shows the declaration for Java's `String` class. Refer to this listing for the following discussions of the class's constructors and methods.

Listing 6.1. Java's `String` class.

```
public  final  class  java.lang.String
extends  java.lang.Object
{
// Constructors
public String();
public String(byte  ascii[], int  hibyte);
public String(byte  ascii[], int  hibyte,
 int  offset, int  count);
public String(char  value[]);
public String(char  value[], int  offset, int  count);
public String(String  value);
public String(StringBuffer  buffer);
// Methods
public char charAt(int  index);
public int compareTo(String  anotherString);
public String concat(String  str);
public static String copyValueOf(char  data[]);
public static String copyValueOf(char  data[], int  offset, int count);
public boolean endsWith(String  suffix);
public boolean equals(Object  anObject);
public boolean equalsIgnoreCase(String  anotherString);
```

continues

Listing 6.1. continued

```
public void getBytes(int  srcBegin, int  srcEnd,
 byte  dst[], int  dstBegin);
public void getChars(int  srcBegin, int  srcEnd,
 char  dst[], int  dstBegin);
public int hashCode();
public int indexOf(int  ch);
public int indexOf(int  ch, int  fromIndex);
public int indexOf(String  str);
public int indexOf(String  str, int  fromIndex);
public String intern();
public int lastIndexOf(int  ch);
public int lastIndexOf(int  ch, int  fromIndex);
public int lastIndexOf(String  str);
public int lastIndexOf(String  str, int  fromIndex);
public int length();
public boolean regionMatches(boolean  ignoreCase,
int  toffset, String  other, int  ooffset, int  len);
public boolean regionMatches(int  toffset, String  other,
 int  ooffset, int  len);
public String replace(char  oldChar, char  newChar);
public boolean startsWith(String  prefix);
public boolean startsWith(String  prefix, int toffset);
public String substring(int  beginIndex);
public String substring(int  beginIndex, int endIndex);
public char[] toCharArray();
public String toLowerCase();
public String toString();
public String toUpperCase();
public String trim();
public static String valueOf(boolean  b);
public static String valueOf(char  c);
public static String valueOf(char  data[]);
public static String valueOf(char  data[], int  offset, int  count);
public static String valueOf(double  d);
public static String valueOf(float  f);
public static String valueOf(int  i);
public static String valueOf(long  l);
public static String valueOf(Object  obj);
}
```

String Constructors

The String class overloads seven constructors that give you a variety of ways to create String objects. The default, no-parameter, constructor is used when you construct a string like this:

```
String s;  // Default constructor
```

The object, s, has zero length, and because a String object cannot change, you won't usually declare strings this way. It's more useful to initialize a String object with a literal string:

```
String s1 = "Literal construction";
String s2 = new String("Alternate method");
```

Either technique is correct and produces the same compiled code, but the first line is more common.

There are also several constructors for creating `String` objects from `char` arrays. For demonstration, first create the array, and then assign it some characters:

```
char letters[] = new char[26];
for (int i = 0; i < 26; i++)
 letters[i] = (char)(i + 'a');
```

The sample code creates the array `letters`, and then assigns it the lowercase letters of the alphabet a through z. You may construct a `String` object using this array with the statement

```
String s1 = new String(letters);
```

Specify integer offset and count values to initialize a string using only a portion of a character array. For example, the statement

```
String s2 = new String(letters, 3, 7);
```

sets s2 to the string `"defghij"`.

To convert an ASCII character array to Unicode characters, specify a high-byte value, usually zero. All resulting 16-bit Unicode characters will have that high-byte value and the associated ASCII character in the lower byte. To try this, first construct an array of `byte` values, each representing one 8-bit ASCII character. This is similar to how you created the `char` array `letters`:

```
byte byteArray[] = new byte[26];
for (int i = 0; i < 26; i++)
 byteArray[i] = (byte)(i + 'a');
```

Convert this ASCII `byte` array to a Unicode `String` object using the statement

```
String s3 = new String(byteArray, 0);  // Set Unicode high byte to zero
```

This technique can be useful for converting between C and C++ character arrays and Java `String` objects. A similar constructor takes three integers representing the Unicode high-byte value, an integer offset into the byte array, and an integer count. The statement

```
String s4 = new String(byteArray, 0, 12, 4);
```

sets s4 to `"mnop"` by extracting four characters at index 12 from `byteArray`. Each character's high byte is set to zero.

Finally, you may construct a `String` object using another `String` or `StringBuffer` object. The statements

```
String original = "Copy me!";
String copy = original;
```

construct a String object, original, and then construct a second String, copy, initialized to the original string. The original object may also be of the StringBuffer class, but the programming is a little different because you must use the new operator to construct String objects at runtime, as this fragment demonstrates:

```
StringBuffer original = new StringBuffer("Copy me!");
String copy = new String(original);  // Must use new here
System.out.println(original);
```

The reason for the difference is that the compiler cannot determine the size of the StringBuffer object, because this is by definition able to change at runtime.

String Methods

The String class offers numerous methods for manipulating and interrogating String objects. Refer to the String class declaration in Listing 6.1 while you read the examples in this section. Try any of the following fragments by replacing the contents of the method main() in one of this part's sample programs.

To determine which character is at a certain index position in a string, call the charAt() method. It's a good idea to verify that the target string length is greater than any specified index, as this fragment demonstrates:

```
String s = "abcdefg";
if (s.length() >= 5) {
 char ch = s.charAt(4);
 System.out.println("Char at 4 = " + ch);
}
```

The code sets ch equal to 'e', the character at index four position in the test string. The first index is zero, so an index of four refers to the fifth character.

> **NOTE**
>
> If you call charAt() with an argument that is greater than or equal to the string length, Java generates a StringIndexOutOfBoundsException error. See Chapter 9, "Exceptions," for information about how to catch this and other exceptions.

To perform the reverse operation—finding the index of a specific character—call one of several indexOf() methods, possibly followed by a call to substring() to extract a portion of a string. The fragment

```
String s = "abcdefghijklmnop";
int index = s.indexOf('k');
if (index >= 0) {
 String sub = s.substring(index);
 System.out.println(sub);
}
```

searches a string for the letter k. If index is zero or greater, the program creates another string, sub, to which it assigns the string "klmnop"—the value from the reported index to the end of the original string. If indexOf() returns -1, the requested character was not found. Another form of substring() takes a second integer argument, representing the final index of the string to extract. Given the preceding code, the statement

```
String sub = s.substring(index, index + 3);
 System.out.println(sub);
```

sets sub to "klm".

Other forms of indexOf accept additional parameters. For example, you can specify an index to begin searching a string from a position other than the beginning. Listing 6.2, MonthNames.java, shows how to use indexOf() to parse a string composed of variable-length substrings and separator characters ('#').

> **TIP**
>
> Listing 6.2 also shows how to write a long literal string on multiple lines, which I did here so the listing would fit on the page. The backslash characters at the end of lines 3 and 4 *continue* the literal string on the next line. The continuation characters are not part of the final string.

Listing 6.2. MonthNames.java (Demonstrates substring() method).

```
class MonthNames {
 public static void main(String args[]) {
  String s = "#January#February#March#April\
#May#June#July#August#September#October\
#November#December#";
  int i = 0, j;
  while (i++ >= 0) {
   j = s.indexOf('#', i);
   if (j >= 0) {
    String month = s.substring(i, j);
    System.out.println(month);
   }
   i = j;
  }
 }
}
```

The sample program extracts the month names from the original string, using two integer index values and the indexOf() method to hop from separator to separator. Other forms of indexOf() accept a string argument, which is useful for finding substrings, as in the fragment

```
String s = "Passwords.txt";
int index = s.indexOf(".txt");
if (index >= 0)
 System.out.println(s + " is a text file");
```

which searches a filename string for the extension .txt. A potentially easier technique uses the endsWith() method, which returns a boolean true or false value:

```
String s = "LoveLetters.txt";
if (s.endsWith(".txt"))
 System.out.println(s + " is a text file");
```

Conversely, use startsWith() to find out if a string begins with a certain substring:

```
String s = "Accounts1.txt";
if (s.startsWith("Accounts"))
 System.out.println(s + " is an Accounts file");
```

To compare two strings, call compareTo(), which returns an integer value. Listing 6.3, Compare.java, shows how to use the method.

Listing 6.3. Compare.java (Demonstrates compareTo() method).

```
class Compare {
 public static void main(String args[]) {
 String s1 = "abcdefg";
 String s2 = "ABCDEFG";
 int result = s1.compareTo(s2);
 if (result == 0)
  System.out.println("s1 = s2");
 else if (result < 0)
  System.out.println("s1 < s2");
 else // if (result > 0)
  System.out.println("s1 > s2");
 }
}
```

The compareTo() method returns -1 if its string object is alphabetically less than the argument passed to the method. It returns 0 if the two strings are exactly equal. It returns +1 if the object is alphabetically greater than its argument.

You can also compare one string with another using the equals() method, as in

```
if (s1.equals(s2))
 System.out.println("s1 = s2");
```

> **TIP**
>
> Because equals() is inherited from Object, it can be used to compare *any* two objects, not only strings.

To compare strings ignoring case, call equalsIgnoreCase() like this:

```
if (s1.equalsIgnoreCase(s2))
 System.out.println("s1 = s2");
```

Compare substrings by calling one of two `regionMatches()` methods. The two methods differ only in having an initial `boolean` parameter, which you can set to `true` to ignore case; otherwise, or if this parameter is `false`, the comparison is case sensitive. The full method is defined as

```
public boolean regionMatches(boolean ignoreCase, int toffset,
 String other, int ooffset, int len);
```

The overloaded method is the same, but it lacks the `ignoreCase` parameter. The parameters are

- `boolean ignoreCase`: Set to `true` to ignore case for the comparison. Omit this argument, or set it to `false`, for a case-sensitive comparison.
- `int toffset`: The offset index to begin the comparison of the string object for which you call `regionMatches()`.
- `String other`: The second string to compare with the string object for which the method was called.
- `int ooffset`: The offset index to begin the comparison of the other string object parameter, `other`.
- `int len`: The number of characters to compare in both strings.

The following code shows how to use `regionMatches()` to determine whether a substring is part of another string.

```
String s = "Haste makes waste";
String sub = "waste";
if (s.regionMatches(true, 12, sub, 0, sub.length()))
 System.out.println("sub string found in s");
```

There are many other operations available in the `String` class. Call `toLowerCase()` and `toUpperCase()` to return a string with all lower- or uppercase characters. The methods do not alter the original string; to do that, reassign the results back to the object. The fragment

```
String s = "Haste makes waste";
System.out.println(s.toUpperCase());
System.out.println("s = " + s);
s = s.toUpperCase();
System.out.println("s = " + s);
```

first displays a string in uppercase, then converts it to uppercase and displays the result. Statements such as the last two `println()` calls use the plus sign to concatenate, or join, two strings. To concatenate *and* save string objects, use the `concat()` method. Because this method does not alter the original string, to actually append strings, you must reassign the results of the method back to the original object. For example, Listing 6.4, `Concat.java`, builds the string, `Testing One Two Three`, in the test `String` object.

Listing 6.4. `Concat.java` (Demonstrates `concat()` method).

```java
class Concat {
 public static void main(String args[]) {
  String s1 = " One";
  String s2 = " Two";
  String s3 = " Three";
  String test = "Testing";
  test = test.concat(s1);
  test = test.concat(s2);
  test = test.concat(s3);
  System.out.println(test);
 }
}
```

Call `replace()` to replace all occurrences of a specific character with another character. The fragment

```java
String s = "#January#February#March#April#May#";
System.out.println(s.replace('#', '@'));
```

changes the `'#'` separators to `'@'` characters in `String s`. The method does not alter the original string. Again, to do that, you must assign the results back to the object:

```java
s = s.replace('#', '@');
```

A series of highly useful overloaded methods are all named `valueOf()`. Use them to convert values of various types to string representations. For example, the statements

```java
double d = 3.14159;
String s = String.valueOf(d);
```

set `String s` to the string `"3.14159"`. All `valueOf()` methods are declared `static`, which means they may be called in reference to the `String` class as shown here. You may call them in reference to a `String` object, but there's no good reason to do so because you will more likely want to assign a string *representation* of a value. The methods accept the following types of parameters:

- `boolean b`: Converts `boolean` value to string `"true"` or `"false"`.
- `char c`: Converts a character to a string.
- `char data[]`: Converts an array of characters to a string.
- `char data[]`, `int offset`, `int count`: Converts an array of characters to a string using count characters starting with the offset index in the `data` array.
- `double d`: Converts a `double` value to a string.
- `float f`: Converts a `float` value to a string.
- `int i`: Converts an `int` value to a string.
- `long l`: Converts a `long` value to a string.
- `Object obj`: Converts any other object to a string.

There are several String methods available for converting between char and byte arrays and String objects. These methods give you the ability to store character data in various ways, and to prepare 8-bit ASCII arrays for passing to other languages such as C++.

Call toCharArray() to assign any String object to an array of characters. You do not have to initialize the array—the method creates it at runtime, as this fragment demonstrates:

```
char alpha[];
String s = "abcdefghijklmnopqrstuvwxyz";
alpha = s.toCharArray();
```

The result is the alphabetic characters in a newly allocated array of char, which is assigned to the array variable, alpha.

Another way to get character data out of a String object is to call one of two methods—getBytes() or getChars(). Each has similar parameters, but the former extracts 8-bit bytes (ASCII characters) and the latter extracts Unicode char values. To use either method, specify beginning and ending index values from which to extract bytes or characters from the original string. Also specify a byte or char array to hold the results, and finally, give the index in the destination array at which you want to begin depositing characters. The fragment

```
String s = "abcdefghijklmnopqrstuvwxyz";
char alpha16[] = new char[6];   // Char array
byte alpha8[] = new byte[6];    // Byte array
s.getChars(12, 18, alpha16, 0);
s.getBytes(12, 18, alpha8, 0);
```

copies six characters as Unicode 16-bit values and 8-bit bytes from a String object to arrays of char and byte. To go in the other direction, converting a char array to a String object, call copyValueOf() like this:

```
char alpha[] = new char[26];
for (char c = 'a'; c <= 'z'; c++)
  alpha[c - 'a'] = c;
String s = String.copyValueOf(alpha);
```

First, the program creates an array of char values equal to the alphabet. The final line calls copyValueOf() to convert the array to a String object. Because this method is static, you normally call it in reference to the String class as shown here. Alternatively, you may specify integer offset and count values to create a String object from a portion of a char array. Given the preceding code, the following statement creates String s equal to "jklmno":

```
String s = String.copyValueOf(alpha, 9, 6);
```

Finally in the String class is a miscellaneous method that might be useful from time to time. Call trim() to remove any leading and trailing blanks from a string. As with several other String methods, calling trim() does not alter the original string. If you want to do that, assign the result back to the object as the following fragment demonstrates:

```
String s = "    blankety blank    ";
System.out.println("Length before = " + s.length());
s = s.trim();  // trim blanks from string
System.out.println("Length after  = " + s.length());
```

The StringBuffer Class

Listing 6.5 shows the declaration for Java's StringBuffer class, which you can use to create string objects that can change at runtime. For example, you may append strings to a StringBuffer object without constructing a new object, as you must do with the String class. Refer to this listing for the following discussions of the class's constructors and methods.

Listing 6.5. Java's StringBuffer class.

```
public  class  java.lang.StringBuffer
 extends  java.lang.Object
{
// Constructors
public StringBuffer();
public StringBuffer(int  length);
public StringBuffer(String  str);
// Methods
public StringBuffer append(boolean  b);
public StringBuffer append(char  c);
public StringBuffer append(char  str[]);
public StringBuffer append(char  str[], int  offset, int  len);
public StringBuffer append(double  d);
public StringBuffer append(float  f);
public StringBuffer append(int  i);
public StringBuffer append(long  l);
public StringBuffer append(Object  obj);
public StringBuffer append(String  str);
public int capacity();
public char charAt(int  index);
public void ensureCapacity(int  minimumCapacity);
public void getChars(int  srcBegin, int  srcEnd,
 char  dst[], int  dstBegin);
public StringBuffer insert(int  offset, boolean  b);
public StringBuffer insert(int  offset, char  c);
public StringBuffer insert(int  offset, char  str[]);
public StringBuffer insert(int  offset, double  d);
public StringBuffer insert(int  offset, float  f);
public StringBuffer insert(int  offset, int  i);
public StringBuffer insert(int  offset, long  l);
public StringBuffer insert(int  offset, Object  obj);
public StringBuffer insert(int  offset, String  str);
public int length();
public StringBuffer reverse();
```

```
public void setCharAt(int  index, char  ch);
public void setLength(int  newLength);
public String toString();
}
```

StringBuffer Constructors

There are three ways to construct a StringBuffer object. To create one for later use, but not initialize it to any specific value or maximum size, declare the object like this:

```
StringBuffer buffer = new StringBuffer();
```

You must use the new operator to initialize all StringBuffer objects, as you must do for all Java class objects that are not fixed in size. Alternatively, however, you may delay construction of the object using two separate steps. The code

```
StringBuffer filler;
...
filler = new StringBuffer();
```

declares a StringBuffer object, filler, and elsewhere in the program initializes the object with new.

> ### WARNING
>
> You *must* initialize StringBuffer objects by using new before you may use the objects.

Specify a maximum length for storing string data by passing an integer value to the StringBuffer constructor. For example, the statement

```
StringBuffer buffer = new StringBuffer(80);
```

constructs a StringBuffer object that can hold up to 80 characters. Again, you may delay construction by declaring the object and initializing it separately, as in

```
StringBuffer buffer;  // Declare object
...
buffer = new StringBuffer(80);
```

Because construction takes place at runtime, you may also use a variable as the StringBuffer object's size:

```
int len = 45;
StringBuffer buffer = new StringBuffer(len);
```

The third and final way to create a `StringBuffer` object is to initialize it using a `String` object. Java calls the constructor

```
StringBuffer(String str);
```

for statements such as

```
StringBuffer buffer = new StringBuffer("Initial string");
```

This technique is useful also for converting a `String` object to a `StringBuffer`, as the following demonstrates:

```
String s = "Make me variable!";
StringBuffer canChange = new StringBuffer(s);
```

In that code fragment, `String` object s is fixed in size and cannot be directly changed. The second line converts the `String` object to a `StringBuffer` object, which can be changed by other statements. For example, you can append a new string to `canChange`.

StringBuffer Methods

Strings that will not change are best declared using the `String` class. Strings that might change during a program should be `StringBuffer` objects. Although it's true that the `String` class provides methods such as `concat()`, a close inspection of the method's declaration

```
public String concat(String str);
```

reveals that it returns a `String` object, indicating that calling `concat()` creates an entirely new instance of the `String` class. This is highly inefficient, especially when creating string variables out of multiple parts such as filenames. For example, the code

```
String name = "Account";
String extension = ".dat";
String fileName = name;
fileName = fileName.concat(extension);
```

creates the `String` object `fileName` equal to the string `"Account.dat"`. Compare this to the equivalent `StringBuffer` technique, which calls the `Append()` method using the same `name` and `extension` objects:

```
String name = "Account";
String extension = ".dat";
StringBuffer fileName = new StringBuffer(80);
fileName.append(name);
fileName.append(extension);
```

This might appear to be more work because (ignoring the first two declarations) it uses three statements instead of two. Actually, however, this is more efficient because the system needs to construct only one `fileName` `StringBuffer` object to which the `name` and `extension` are appended. Even better, the same `fileName` object is available for use elsewhere in the program without reinitializing.

There are numerous variations of `append()` that you may use to attach data in string form to `StringBuffer` objects. You may append `boolean`, `char`, `char[]` array, `double`, `float`, `int`, `long`, and `String` class values. You may also append any other object. This is possible because all classes are extensions of the superclass `Object`, which provides a `toString()` method. Thus, *any* object of *any* class has a string form that can be appended to a `StringBuffer` object.

To try the various `append()` methods, first declare and initialize a `StringBuffer` object that can hold 80 characters (it could also be smaller):

```
StringBuffer buffer = new StringBuffer(80);
```

Next, declare some variables:

```
boolean truth = false;
long value = 1000000;
char ch = '$';
```

Call `append()` to attach them in string form to the `StringBuffer` object:

```
buffer.append("You won ");
buffer.append(ch);
buffer.append(value);
buffer.append(" is a ");
buffer.append(truth);
buffer.append(" statement!");
```

Those statements create the string

```
You won $1000000 is a false statement!
```

which you can display using the statement

```
System.out.println(buffer);
```

For every `append()` method, there is a corresponding `insert()` method that you can use to insert data into any position in a `StringBuffer` object. This is often convenient for poking values into the middle of a string, as in this code:

```
double value = 65.7;
StringBuffer buffer =
 new StringBuffer("Value =  light years");
buffer.insert(8, value);  // Insert value at index 8
```

This fragment creates the string

```
Value = 65.7 light years
```

in the `StringBuffer` object. Because the first index in a `StringBuffer` is zero, the statement

```
buffer.insert(0, "Preface: ");
```

inserts a literal string at the front of `buffer`.

All `StringBuffer` objects have `length()` and `capacity()` methods. A `StringBuffer` object's *length* equals the number of characters it currently holds. The object's *capacity* is the total maximum number of characters it can hold. The following statements display each value for the `buffer` object:

```
System.out.println("Length = " + buffer.length());
System.out.println("Capacity = " + buffer.capacity());
```

If you append more data than a `StringBuffer` can hold, Java allocates additional space to the object. If that can't be done, an exception is generated (see Chapter 9). Too many of these reallocations are potentially inefficient, and you can prevent them generally by allocating enough space to your `StringBuffer` objects. The statement

```
StringBuffer buffer = new StringBuffer(128);
```

creates an object, `buffer`, that can hold up to 128 characters.

> **NOTE**
>
> All characters in a `StringBuffer` object are significant; there is no length byte or termination null character as in C, C++, and other languages. A `StringBuffer` object with a length of 80 can hold up to exactly 80 characters.

Call `setLength()` to alter the length of a `StringBuffer`'s string data. This, in effect, appends blanks to the end of any existing string, and might be useful for creating a series of strings all of the same length for display purposes, as this code demonstrates:

```
StringBuffer buffer = new StringBuffer(40);
buffer.append("Short");
buffer.setLength(40);
```

The last statement pads `buffer` with blank characters to ensure its length is equal to its capacity. The `setLength()` method is also useful for erasing a `StringBuffer` object's contents. The statement

```
buffer.setLength(0);
```

clears all character data from `buffer`. The object's capacity, however, is not changed. To do that—and ensure that a `StringBuffer` object can hold a string of a certain maximum length, for example—call `ensureCapacity()` like this:

```
buffer.ensureCapacity(128);
```

As long as enough memory is available, calling ensureCapacity() guarantees that buffer can hold at least 128 characters.

NOTE

Regardless of its length, if a string's capacity is already greater or equal to the argument passed to ensureCapacity(), Java makes no change to the StringBuffer object's capacity value.

Calling ensureCapacity() never reduces a StringBuffer object's size. To do that, you can reallocate the object by calling one of its constructors. For example, when you are finished using a StringBuffer object, you can reduce its memory size by reallocating the object with a statement such as

```
buffer = new StringBuffer();  // Reallocate buffer
```

This creates a buffer object with a length of zero and a capacity of 16 characters. Because Java defines this default value, it is probably consistent across all implementations.

Sometimes, it might be necessary to extract the string data from a StringBuffer object. There are two basic methods. Call toString() to convert a StringBuffer object to a String object, as in

```
StringBuffer buffer =
 new StringBuffer("A penny saved is a penny earned");
String s = buffer.toString();
```

which converts buffer to a String object.

To extract the individual characters from a StringBuffer object, call getChars with four arguments:

- int srcBegin: The index in the source StringBuffer of the first character to copy.
- int srcEnd: The index in the source StringBuffer where copying stops. The character at index srcEnd - 1 is the last to be copied. The character at srcEnd is *not* copied to the destination.
- char dst[]: The destination char array, with a length greater or equal to srcEnd - srcBegin;.
- int dstBegin: The starting index in the dst array to which characters should be copied.

These statements demonstrate how to use getChars() to extract a substring from a StringBuffer object:

```
StringBuffer buffer =
 new StringBuffer("A stitch in time saves nine");
char chArray[] = new char[6];
buffer.getChars(2, 8, chArray, 0);
```

This fragment first constructs a `buffer` and a six-char array, `chArray`. The final statement calls `getChars()` to extract the string `"Stitch"` from `buffer` into `chArray`.

Another way to extract character data from a `StringBuffer` object is to call `charAt()` with an integer index argument. For example, the code

```
char chArray[] = new char[buffer.length()];
for (int i = 0; i < buffer.length(); i++)
 chArray[i] = buffer.charAt(i);
```

uses a `for` loop to extract the characters from `buffer`, one at a time, and deposit each character in `chArray`. Notice how the array is constructed to be the same size as the `buffer`'s length. (Of course, it would be easier to call `getChars()`—this code merely demonstrates how to use the `charAt()` method.)

Conversely, you can change any character in a `StringBuffer` object by calling the `setCharAt()` method. For example, the following code fragment creates a 40-character `StringBuffer` object, sets its length to 40 (which pads it with blanks), and then calls `setCharAt()` to change every character in the object to an asterisk:

```
StringBuffer buffer = new StringBuffer(40);
buffer.setLength(40);
for (int i = 0; i < buffer.length(); i++)
 buffer.setCharAt(i, '*');
```

Finally, in `StringBuffer`, is a traditional string-processing method named `reverse()` that reverses an object's string, end for end. The following code demonstrates the method by reversing the alphabetic characters a through z:

```
StringBuffer buffer = new StringBuffer(26);
buffer.append("abcdefghijklmnopqrstuvwxyz");
buffer.reverse();  // Reverse alphabet in buffer
```

The Character Class

As you have learned, a variable of Java's native `char` data type is 16 bits long and can hold one Unicode character. Java strings, however, are represented as objects of the `String` or `StringBuffer` classes—they are not native data types. Among other benefits, these classes provide numerous methods you can use to manipulate string data, but these same benefits are not directly available for native data types such as `char`.

To rectify this situation, Java provides a *wrapper class,* `Character`, for its native `char` type. The `Character` wrapper class makes available various methods that you'll find invaluable in writing text-processing code. For example, you can determine the nature of a character, such as whether it is a lower- or uppercase alphabetic letter.

As you will discover, wrapper classes such as `Character` put an object-oriented face on Java's native data types, without the drawbacks associated with a completely pure object-oriented language. For instance, `char` values are stored efficiently as 16-bit integer values, but using the

Character class, you can choose to access character data as objects. Wrapper classes are a Java specialty, and I'll discuss other similar classes in the coming chapters.

Listing 6.6 shows Java's Character wrapper class declaration.

Listing 6.6. The Character wrapper class.

```
public final class java.lang.Character
 extends java.lang.Object
{
// Fields
public final static int MAX_RADIX;
public final static char MAX_VALUE;
public final static int MIN_RADIX;
public final static char MIN_VALUE;
// Constructors
public Character(char value);
// Methods
public char charValue();
public static int digit(char ch, int radix);
public boolean equals(Object obj);
public static char forDigit(int digit, int radix);
public int hashCode();
public static boolean isDefined(char ch);
public static boolean isDigit(char ch);
public static boolean isJavaLetter(char ch);
public static boolean isJavaLetterOrDigit(char ch);
public static boolean isLetter(char ch);
public static boolean isLetterOrDigit(char ch);
public static boolean isLowerCase(char ch);
public static boolean isSpace(char ch);
public static boolean isTitleCase(char ch);
public static boolean isUpperCase(char ch);
public static char toLowerCase(char ch);
public String toString();
public static char toTitleCase(char ch);
public static char toUpperCase(char ch);
}
```

The Character wrapper class provides only one constructor. You can use it to create a class object, which can hold one character value:

```
Character chObj = new Character('Q');
```

However, this isn't a practical technique for storing character data. Instead, you'll normally use the Character class to call one of several static methods, which do not require constructing a class object. For example, use one of the static "is..." methods to determine what kind of character the object holds. The statement

```
if (Character.isLowerCase(ch))
 System.out.println("is lowercase");
```

tests whether a `char` variable, `ch`, is a lowercase alphabetic character. Use other `"is..."` methods to test for digits, spaces, uppercase characters, and so on. Call `isJavaLetter()` to determine whether a character is a legal first character for a Java identifier:

```
if (Character.isJavaLetter(ch))
 // okay to use for first letter of identifier
```

Call `isJavaLetterOrDigit()` to determine whether `ch` is legal for a non-initial identifier character:

```
if (Character.isJavaLetterOrDigit(ch))
 // okay to use for identifier
```

You can obtain the `char` value of a `Character` class object by calling `charValue()`. For example, use the following technique to convert a `Character` object back to a `char` value:

```
char ch = chObj.charValue();  // Convert chObj back to char
```

Use the `digit()` method to convert a character to an integer value in a specific radix. This method might be useful in code that parses values in hexadecimal or another radix. For example, the code fragment

```
char ch = 'F';
int digit = Character.digit(ch, 16);
System.out.println(ch + " = " + digit);
```

converts the hexadecimal (radix 16) character `'F'` to a corresponding digit. Running the fragment displays

```
F = 15
```

To go the other way—determining what character represents a certain value in a specified radix—call `forDigit()`. For example, the code

```
int digit = 12;
char ch = Character.forDigit(digit, 16);
System.out.println(digit + " = " + ch);
```

sets `ch` to the character that represents the value 12 in radix 16 (hexadecimal). The output statement displays

```
12 = c
```

If you want an uppercase letter instead, call `toUpperCase()` like this:

```
int digit = 12;
char ch = Character.forDigit(digit, 16);
ch = Character.toUpperCase(ch);
System.out.println(digit + " = " + ch);
```

To ensure that radix and character values are within allowable ranges, the `Character` class provides the four constants `MIN_RADIX`, `MAX_RADIX`, `MIN_VALUE`, and `MAX_VALUE`. The `...RADIX` constants are type `int`. The `...VALUE` constants are `char`. Use them as in the following fragment, which displays an error if `radix` is outside of the allowable range of base values allowed by the `Character` class:

```
int radix = 16, result;
char ch = 'A';
if (Character.MIN_RADIX <= radix &&
    radix <= Character.MAX_RADIX) {
 result = Character.digit(ch, radix);
 System.out.println(
  ch + " in base " + radix + " = " + result);
} else
 System.out.println("Radix out of range");
```

The preceding code converts ch to its equivalent integer value in base 16 (hexadecimal) and displays this on screen:

```
A in base 16 = 10
```

If you change radix to an illegal value such as 255, the program displays

```
Radix out of range
```

> **NOTE**
>
> Methods in the Character class depend on a *Unicode attribute table,* which gives a name to every Unicode character, and specifies equivalents such as uppercase, lowercase, and so-called title-case (dual character) characters. Obtain this table on the World Wide Web in this file:
>
> `ftp://unicode.org/pub/MappingTables/UnicodeData1.1.5.txt`

Getting Input

Now that you know how to use strings and characters, it's time to clarify an important subject that will lead to more interesting sample programs—how to get input from users. The following sections explain two basic techniques—how to prompt users to enter data at the keyboard (usually in response to a prompt), and how to extract command-line arguments entered after the program's name.

Prompting for Input

There are two basic ways to read data at the keyboard, usually in response to a prompt displayed on screen. The first technique, demonstrated in Listing 6.7, InputBytes.java, shows how to enter input into an array of bytes and then convert that input into a String object.

Listing 6.7. InputBytes.java (Demonstrates prompting for input).

```
import java.io.IOException;  // or java.io.*

class InputBytes {
 public static void main(String args[]) {
```

continues

Listing 6.7. continued

```
try {
  // Get input from user
  byte buffer[] = new byte[128];        // Input buffer
  System.out.println("Enter text:");    // Prompt user
  System.in.read(buffer);               // Get input
  // Display string entered
  String str = new String(buffer, 0);   // Convert to String
  System.out.println("You entered: " + str);
} catch (IOException e) {               // Trap exception
  System.out.println(e.toString());     // Display error
 }
 }
}
```

The sample program declares an array of type `byte`, named `buffer`. The array is arbitrarily set to 128 characters, which is usually enough for most input (except for the wordiest users!). Input greater than that is ignored. To read bytes into the buffer, the program calls the `read()` method in the `System.in` object, using the statement

```
System.in.read(buffer);
```

That buffer's contents are then converted into a `String` object by the statement

```
String str = new String(buffer, 0);
```

As explained in the "String Constructors" section in this chapter, the `0` argument sets to zero the high byte of each Unicode character in the string.

The call to `read()` is surrounded in a `try` block, ending with a `catch` statement, which traps any `IOException` errors that occur during input. Chapter 9 covers exceptions, so I won't go into this subject in detail here. Notice, however, that it is necessary to import the exception class. You may, however, input all `io` classes with the directive

```
import java.io.*;  // Import all io classes
```

Listing 6.8, `InputString.java`, demonstrates the second way to get keyboard data into a program. This sample program builds a string by repeatedly calling `read()`, thus eliminating the need for a buffer array.

Listing 6.8. `InputString.java` (Demonstrates how to input strings).

```
import java.io.IOException;  // or java.io.*

class InputString {
 public static void main(String args[]) {
  try {
   StringBuffer str = new StringBuffer();
   char ch;
   // Get input from user
   System.out.println("Enter text:");  // Prompt user
   while ((ch = (char)System.in.read()) != '\n')
```

```
      str.append(ch);  // Build string using ch
     // Display string entered
     System.out.println("You entered: " + str);
    } catch (IOException e) {           // Trap exception
     System.out.println(e.toString());   // Display error
    }
  }
}
```

The new program declares a `StringBuffer` object, `str`, and a `char` variable, `ch`, which holds each character entered at the keyboard. A `while` loop builds the `StringBuffer` object by reading individual characters and appending each to `str`, using the statement

```
while ((ch = (char)System.in.read()) != '\n')
 str.append(ch);
```

The `while` loop repeats until the user presses the new-line key (Enter on PCs, but labeled Return on many other keyboards). This is the preferred string-input technique for text-only Java applications.

A significant difference between this method and the buffered input technique in `InputBytes.java` is the (`char`) type cast expression that prefaces `System.in.read()`. This method returns type `byte`, and it is therefore necessary to recast the return value to a `char` for assigning to `ch`.

Using Command-Line Arguments

Users may also pass data to Java applications by entering one or more arguments after the program name. Listing 6.9, `CommandLine.java`, shows the basic techniques. After compiling the program, run it with a command such as

```
jview commandline argument moreArguments lastArgument
```

This displays the number of arguments (3) and echoes their text. Each argument is separated by a space. Notice that, as with all examples in this part, you still must run the program using `jview`.

Listing 6.9. `CommandLine.java` (Demonstrates command-line arguments).

```
class CommandLine {
 public static void main(String args[]) {
  System.out.println("Number of arguments = " + args.length);
  for (int i = 0; i < args.length; i++) {
   System.out.println(args[i]);
  }
 }
}
```

All command-line arguments, if any, are stored in the `args[]` String array passed to the `main()` method. The number of arguments equals the array's length value. The sample code displays this value using the expression `args.length`. The program also uses it in a `for` loop to echo each argument's text using a `println()` statement. Running the program with the command

```
jview commandline arg1 arg2 arg3
```

displays the following on screen:

```
Number of arguments = 3
arg1
arg2
arg3
```

Summary

- Java represents all strings as class objects. This differs significantly from other languages such as C++ in which strings are arrays of characters.
- Use the `String` class for string objects that will not change during the course of a program.
- Use the `StringBuffer` class for string objects that are likely to change in size or content.
- The `String` and `StringBuffer` classes are not directly related to each other, although both are derived from the superclass `Object`. Both classes provide numerous methods you can call to perform many operations on string data.
- The `Character` wrapper class puts an object-oriented face on Java's native `char` data type. You will most often use the `Character` class's static methods such as `isLowerCase()` to determine the nature of character variables.
- There are two basic methods for getting keyboard input into a program—read keypresses into a byte array, or build a `StringBuffer` object from individual keyboard characters. The second method is generally preferred.
- Use the `args[]` String array passed to the `main()` method to extract command-line arguments passed to a program run by `jview.exe`. The expression `args.length` equals the number of arguments that the user entered.

Exercises

1. Write a filename parser that extracts a possible extension from a filename string.
2. Write a method that returns the index of a specified substring in a `StringBuffer` object.

3. Create a `boolean` function that tests whether a string is a *palindrome,* one that is spelled the same forward or back, ignoring punctuation. Some examples of palindromes are *party booby trap, tuna nut,* and that old standard *A man, a plan, a canal—Panama.*

4. Write a program that displays the minimum and maximum radix and character integer values allowed by the `Character` class.

What's Next?

Although I've introduced Java's integer and floating-point data types, I haven't scratched the surface of the numerical techniques you can use in applications. The next chapter shows how to perform these kinds of operations with the `Math` class. I'll also explain how to use numerical wrapper classes, which provide object-oriented interfaces to native integer and floating-point values.

7

CHAPTER

Numerical Classes

One of the myths about computers is their presumed mathematical nature, a fantasy perpetuated by computer news reports, usually headlined in tabloid style: "*Computer Calculates Possibility of Extraterrestrial Life!*" Consequently, much of the public still considers a computer as nothing more than a robotic math genius, though mathematics represents only a small percentage of the tasks computers perform.

I can confirm the public's misimpression firsthand. When I meet someone who knows little or nothing about computers, I'm invariably proclaimed a math whiz and, in the next breath, asked to help fill out the person's tax forms. Believe me, I'm no math whiz, and I hire an accountant to do my taxes. I can balance my checkbook, but until recently, I thought that algebra was the name of the green plant material that grows on the bottom of my boat.

Okay, that's an exaggeration, but arithmetic isn't one of my stronger skills. Fortunately for me, however, and for other numerically challenged programmers, Java's Math and numerical classes make even tough math chores as easy as counting on your fingers and toes.

In This Chapter

This chapter introduces the following techniques for using numerical information in Java applications:

- Math class methods
- Random-number generators
- Numerical wrapper classes

The Math Class

Java's Math class, shown in Listing 7.1, provides numerous methods that you can call to perform a variety of mathematical operations. All methods are static, and as sample programs in this chapter demonstrate, you call them without constructing an object of the Math class.

The Math class is automatically imported into every Java application. You do not have to write an import statement to use this class.

Listing 7.1. Java's Math class.

```
public final class java.lang.Math
 extends java.lang.Object
{
 // Fields
 public final static double E;
 public final static double PI;
 // Methods
 public static double abs(double a);
 public static float abs(float a);
 public static int abs(int a);
 public static long abs(long a);
```

```
public static double acos(double a);
public static double asin(double a);
public static double atan(double a);
public static double atan2(double a, double b);
public static double ceil(double a);
public static double cos(double a);
public static double exp(double a);
public static double floor(double a);
public static double IEEEremainder(double f1, double f2);
public static double log(double a);
public static double max(double a, double b);
public static float max(float a, float b);
public static int max(int a, int b);
public static long max(long a, long b);
public static double min(double a, double b);
public static float min(float a, float b);
public static int min(int a, int b);
public static long min(long a, long b);
public static double pow(double a, double b);
public static double random();
public static double rint(double a);
public static long round(double a);
public static int round(float a);
public static double sin(double a);
public static double sqrt(double a);
public static double tan(double a);
}
```

NOTE

Any attempt to create a Math class object as in the faulty statement

```
Math m = new Math();   // ??? Don't do this!
```

results in the obscure compilation error, `"cannot access member Math.Math()"`, a consequence of the Math class's constructor being intentionally inaccessible. This is entirely by design—it's not a bug—and you would gain no advantage in creating Math objects because the class declares no instance variables (it is purely code). See Chapter 8, "More About Classes and Objects," for more information on making constructors inaccessible and why you might want to do that.

Math Fields

The Math class declares two fields, so called because they are static. (In other words, they are not instance variables.) The double field E represents the base of the natural logarithms. The double field PI represents the value of π. The following statements (which you can insert in a test main() method)

```
System.out.println("E = " + Math.E);
System.out.println("Pi = " + Math.PI);
```

119

display these values:

```
E = 2.71828
Pi = 3.14159
```

Internally, however, the values are more accurately represented as E = 2.7182818284590452354 and PI = 3.14159265358979323846 respectively.

Math Utility Methods

The Math class provides a slew of what I call utility methods that perform miscellaneous mathematical operations. Some of these are overloaded, so you can pass them different types of arguments. For example, there are four versions of method abs(), which is not a reference to abdominal muscle tone but to *absolute value.*

Use the abs() methods in formulas requiring positive values when the argument might be negative. For example, suppose that it is possible that an integer value might be positive or negative as a result of some other operation. To ensure a positive value, perhaps for using the integer as a character, call Math.abs() like this:

```
int v = -100;
char ch = (char)Math.abs(v);
```

The second statement casts the absolute value of integer v into a char and assigns it to ch.

Other forms of abs() permit double, float, and long arguments. Similarly overloaded are the min() and max() methods, which compare double, float, int, and long values, and return the minimum or maximum of two arguments. Here's a sample you can try in a main() method:

```
long v1 = 99;
long v2 = v1 * 2;
System.out.println("v1=" + v1 + " v2=" + v2);
System.out.println("Maximum value = " + Math.max(v1, v2));
System.out.println("Minimum value = " + Math.min(v1, v2));
```

It's often necessary (for mathematicians, that is) to find the smallest or largest integer value close to a floating-point variable's value. The following official Visual J++ online descriptions of the methods that perform these tasks—ceil() and floor()—are virtual models of obscurity:

- ceil(): "Returns the smallest (closest to negative infinity) double value that is not less than the argument and is equal to a mathematical integer."

- floor(): "Returns the largest (closest to positive infinity) double value that is not greater than the argument and is equal to a mathematical integer."

In plain language, ceil() returns the closest integer value greater or equal to (at the ceiling of) a given floating-point value. The floor() method returns the closest integer less than or equal to (at the floor of) a floating-point value. Try the following statements to test the methods:

```
double d = 10.0;
while (d < 11.0) {
```

```
System.out.println("d=" + d + " ceil(d)=" + Math.ceil(d) +
  " floor(d)=" + Math.floor(d));
  d += 0.1;
}
```

Some other methods—which if you are mathematically inclined you will no doubt find valuable—are exp(), which returns E to the power of its double argument, and log(), which returns the natural logarithm of its double argument. Use pow() to raise any value to any exponent, as in the sample

```
int j = 2, k = 8;
System.out.println(
  "2 to the 8th power = " + Math.pow(j, k));
```

which displays the value of 2^8, or 256. You may pass integer or floating-point values to pow().

Two other methods fall into the miscellaneous category. Use IEEEremainder() to compute the IEEE remainder of the division of two floating-point arguments:

```
double arg1 = 3.14159;
double arg2 = 2;
double result = Math.IEEEremainder(arg1, arg2);
System.out.println(arg1 + " / " + arg2 + " = " + result);
```

This displays the following:

```
3.14159 / 2 = -0.85841
```

Note that this does not equal the modulo value of arg1 divided by arg2. If that's what you need, use the modulo operator instead of the method:

```
double result = arg1 % arg2;
```

That displays

```
3.14159 / 2 = 1.14159
```

Finally in the miscellaneous utility category is a method that computes the square root of a double argument. The statement

```
System.out.println("Square root of 2 = " + Math.sqrt(2));
```

displays the square root of 2.

Rounding Methods

There are three methods in the Math class for rounding double and float values. The first, rint(), returns a double value for a double argument. The fragment

```
double arg = 3.14159;
System.out.println("rint(arg) = " + Math.rint(arg));
```

displays 3 as the rounded value of 3.14159. Change arg's value to 3.54159, and the program displays 4.

The two overloaded round() methods each take a floating-point argument and return the equivalent rounded integer. The only difference between round() and rint() is that the former returns an integer value (either long or int, depending on context), and the latter returns a floating-point double value. Use round() similarly to rint(), as in this quick demonstration:

```
double arg = 3.54159;
long longResult = Math.round(arg);
```

Math Standard Methods

The Math class provides standard methods for computing the sine, cosine, tangent, and other trigonometry functions. Each of these takes a double argument and returns type double. The methods are simple to use, but a demonstration program shows an interesting factor in using these and all floating-point methods. Listing 7.2, CosDemo.java, displays the cosine values for -1.0 through 1.0.

Listing 7.2. CosDemo.java.

```
class CosDemo {
 public static void main(String args[]) {
  double fp, result;
  for (fp = -1.0; fp <= 1.0; fp += 0.1) {
   result = Math.cos(fp);
   System.out.println("fp = " + fp + ", cosine = " + result);
  }
 }
}
```

When you run the program, you'll see the following lines on screen (I deleted some lines to save space):

```
fp = -1, cosine = 0.540302
fp = -0.9, cosine = 0.62161
fp = -0.8, cosine = 0.696707
...
fp = -1.38778e-016, cosine = 1
...
fp = 0.9, cosine = 0.62161
fp = 1, cosine = 0.540302
```

As this shows, the value for zero (computed in the sample program as -1.9 + 0.1) is not necessarily 0.0 (see the line marked in bold). It is a very small value that is *close* to zero and will probably equal 0.0 in a comparison expression, but it is not physically zero (all bits set to zero) as you might assume. Remember always that floating-point values might be only approximately accurate.

Math Random Method

It always interests me that, in such an orderly and methodical business as computer programming, randomness intrigues programmers like no other subject. With all the effort spent writing code to put items in order, an equal amount of time (if not more) is expended to invent the ultimate algorithm for creating a true random sequence.

Call the `Math` class's `random()` method for the next `double` value between `0` and `1` in a presumed arbitrary sequence. Listing 7.3, `RandomDemo.java`, demonstrates how to use the method.

Listing 7.3. `RandomDemo.java` (Demonstrates `Math.random()` method).

```
class RandomDemo {
 public static void main(String args[]) {
  double fp;
  int rows, cols;
  StringBuffer buffer;
  for (rows = 1; rows <= 8; rows++) {
   buffer = new StringBuffer(128);
   for (cols = 1; cols <= 5; cols++)
     buffer.append(Math.random() + " \t");
   System.out.println(buffer);
  }
 }
}
```

The sample program displays a table of random floating-point values. Here's a portion of what my display showed, with spacing altered to fit on this page:

```
0.825197   0.718661   0.773833   0.216086     0.376129
0.617642   0.96141    0.381529   0.00279287   0.149163
0.993278   0.275149   0.900144   0.590038     0.846229
0.439925   0.912582   0.246319   0.291711     0.0227796
```

`Math.random()` returns a value r such that

```
0.0 <= r < 1.0
```

The method produces a different sequence each time a program using it is started.

To produce random integer values, multiply by a factor and round the results or simply cast to type `int` or `long` (or another integer type). For example, to create a table of random integers, replace the output statement in `RandomDemo.java` with

```
buffer.append((int)(Math.random() * 100) + " \t");
```

Although `Math.random()` is certainly a handy method, more exacting needs require a more sophisticated generator. See the next section's discussion of the `Random` class if you need additional random capabilities.

Random-Number Generators

Use the Random class when you need random-number capabilities beyond the simple floating-point sequences that the Math.random() method produces. Each instance of the Random class creates a unique pseudo-random-number generator, a technique that can be useful in simulation and game software. You can also create repeatable random sequences by *seeding* a Random generator object. Listing 7.4 shows the declaration of the Random class, minus private items, which are not accessible to application statements.

> **NOTE**
>
> A "pseudo" random sequence is so called because it is only statistically random. Random-number algorithms are capable of repeating the same sequence, which are therefore not *actually* random.

Listing 7.4. Java's Random class.

```
public class Random {
 public Random();
 public Random(long seed);
 synchronized public void setSeed(long seed);
 public int nextInt();
 public long nextLong();
 public float nextFloat();
 public double nextDouble();
 synchronized public double nextGaussian();
}
```

The Random class provides two constructors. Use them to create random-number generators. They are initialized by calling one or more methods or constructors. For example, to create a Random object, first import the class from java.util using this statement near the beginning of the source code file:

```
import java.util.Random;
```

Then, inside a method such as main(), call Random's default constructor to create the generator object:

```
Random generator = new Random();
```

This seeds the generator using the current time, thus guaranteeing a different sequence for each new object. After constructing the object, you can call various Random methods. For example, Listing 7.5, RandGen.java, displays a table similar to the one in RandomDemo.java, but using a Random object instead of the Math.random() method.

Listing 7.5. RandGen.java (Demonstrates the Random class).

```
import java.util.Random;

class RandGen {
 public static void main(String args[]) {
  Random generator = new Random();
  int rows, cols;
  StringBuffer buffer;
  for (rows = 1; rows <= 8; rows++) {
   buffer = new StringBuffer(128);
   for (cols = 1; cols <= 5; cols++)
     buffer.append(generator.nextDouble() + " \t");
   System.out.println(buffer);
  }
 }
}
```

Instead of calling nextDouble() as the sample program's output statement shows, you can call nextFloat() for a float value. To produce random integers, call the nextInt() or nextLong() methods. For example, replace the program's output statement with

```
buffer.append(generator.nextInt() + " \t");
```

TIP

For generating random integers, the preceding technique is superior to multiplying Math.random() by a constant and casting or rounding.

To seed a Random object using a specific value, construct the object by passing to the alternate constructor an integer long value:

```
Random generator = new Random(100);
```

Or, if the program has already constructed the generator, call the setSeed() method with a long integer value:

```
generator.setSeed(100);
```

Either way, the resulting generator object is guaranteed to produce the identical random sequence providing the program calls Random methods in the same way. These are useful techniques for creating repeatable test data, which you might do to debug simulations and other programming that uses random values.

> **NOTE**
>
> Java specifies the algorithms that all implementations are expected to use for the Random class. Because of this, random sequences should be identical across all Java sites, although this might not be true for locations using early Java versions.

Finally, in the Random class, you'll find the method NextGaussian(), which generates a random distributed value with a mean of 0.0 and standard deviation of 1.0. The algorithm used to produce this value is defined in Donald Knuth's *Art of Computer Science* series, section 3.4.1, Algorithm C.

Depending on which documentation you consult, you might find some protected methods in the Random class, which have recently been redeclared private. Such designations are discussed further in Chapter 8. The methods and declarations discussed here are current as of this writing.

Numerical Wrapper Classes

As you learned from the preceding chapter's discussion of the Character class, a *wrapper class* puts an object-oriented face on a native data type. In addition to Character, Java provides the wrapper classes Boolean, Integer, Long, Float, and Double for, respectively, the boolean, int, long, float, and double native data types. This section explains how to use Java's numerical wrapper classes.

> **TIP**
>
> Wrapper class names are capitalized; native types are not. For example, Boolean refers to the wrapper class for the boolean data type. The Integer class, however, represents native int values; there is no Int wrapper class.

The Boolean Wrapper Class

Listing 7.6 shows Java's Boolean wrapper class declaration. In this and other wrapper classes listed in this chapter, I deleted private declarations, which are not accessible to application statements. I'll discuss only applicable methods in full here. Others such as the hashcode() method are covered elsewhere (for example, see Chapter 10's discussions on container classes).

NOTE

All wrapper class declarations listed here were verified against Java's class library source code but are slightly rearranged for readability.

Listing 7.6. Java's `Boolean` wrapper class.

```
class Boolean {
 // Fields
 public static final Boolean TRUE;
 public static final Boolean FALSE;
 // Constructors
 public Boolean(boolean value);
 public Boolean(String s);
 // Methods
 public boolean booleanValue();
 public static Boolean valueOf(String s);
 public String toString();
 public int hashCode();
 public boolean equals(Object obj);
 public static boolean getBoolean(String name);
}
```

Two static fields provide the object-oriented equivalents of Java's native `true` and `false` values. The constants, `TRUE` and `FALSE`, which are spelled in all uppercase, are *objects* of the `Boolean` wrapper class.

When using the `Boolean` wrapper class, it's important to keep straight on whether you are using objects or native values. For example, Listing 7.7, `BooleanDemo.java`, demonstrates the differences between using a wrapper object and a native `boolean` variable.

Listing 7.7. `BooleanDemo.java` (Demonstrates `Boolean` class).

```
class BooleanDemo {
 public static void main(String args[]) {
  // Shows that TRUE and FALSE are objects
  Boolean boolObject = new Boolean(true);
  if (boolObject.equals(Boolean.TRUE))
   System.out.println("boolObject is true");
  // But that true and false are native values
  boolean boolValue = true;
  if (boolValue = Boolean.TRUE.booleanValue())
   System.out.println("boolValue is true");
 }
}
```

The sample listing constructs a `Boolean` class object using the statement

```
Boolean boolObject = new Boolean(true);
```

The class has no default constructor—you must specify an initial value, which is `true` here. Following this, an `if` statement tests whether the object is true:

```
if (boolObject.equals(Boolean.TRUE))...
```

You cannot simply use an equate expression. You must instead call a method such as `equals()`, and compare the *objects* with `TRUE` or `FALSE`, which are themselves objects. Contrast this with the second half of the sample program, which uses a convoluted technique to test whether a native `boolean` value is `true` or `false`:

```
if (boolValue = Boolean.TRUE.booleanValue())...
```

I'm not suggesting you actually do that, but the statement proves that `TRUE` is an object, and as such, it may be used to call a `Boolean` class method such as `booleanValue()`. This method returns the object's native `true` or `false` value.

Another way to construct a `Boolean` object is to pass it a string, as in this example:

```
Boolean boolObject = new Boolean("True");
```

Use this form to convert strings, either entered at the keyboard or taken from a command-line argument. For example, the fragment

```
Boolean boolObject = new Boolean(args[0]);
```

constructs a `Boolean` object using a command-line argument, which you might pass to a program by typing

```
jview YourProgram True
```

You must spell the word `True` in full, but case is ignored. The word `False` or any other string value is considered to be false.

One common use for the `Boolean` wrapper class is to convert a string to a `Boolean` object value. Call the static `valueOf()` method to translate a string into a `Boolean` object. The statement

```
Boolean boolObject = Boolean.valueOf(args[0]);
```

constructs `boolObject` by parsing a command-line string and calling the static `valueOf()`. To further convert a string to a native `boolean` value, call the object's `booleanValue()` method like this:

```
boolean boolValue = Boolean.valueOf(args[0]).booleanValue();
```

This might seem complex, but it simply translates a command-line argument (or any other `String` or `StringBuffer` object) to a `Boolean` object, using the `valueOf()` method. That result is then translated to a native `boolean` value by calling `booleanValue()`, which is assigned to the `boolValue` variable.

To go the other direction—converting a Boolean object to a string—call the toString() method. For example, the output statement

```
System.out.println(boolObject.toString());
```

displays true or false depending on the value of the Boolean class object, boolObject. The resulting string is all lowercase.

Call the getBoolean() method to determine if a *property* value is available. Java registers various properties, and so can applications. For example, the following fragment displays Java's home directory:

```
String home = System.getProperty("java.home");
System.out.println("Home = " + home);
```

The Integer Wrapper Class

Listing 7.8 shows Java's Integer wrapper class, which represents in class form values of type int. This and the rest of the wrapper classes discussed in this chapter are extended from the Number class, which provides these four methods:

```
public double doubleValue();
public float floatValue();
public int intValue();
public long longValue();
```

Call any of these methods to convert an object of a specific type to the indicated native type. You may call the methods for any object of the Integer, Long, Double, and Float classes.

Listing 7.8. Java's Integer wrapper class.

```
class Integer extends Number {
 // Fields
 public static final int MIN_VALUE;
 public static final int MAX_VALUE;
 // Constructors
 public Integer(int value);
 public Integer(String s);
 // Methods
 public static String toString(int i, int radix);
 public static String toHexString(int i);
 public static String toOctalString(int i);
 public static String toBinaryString(int i);
 public static String toString(int i);
 public static int parseInt(String s, int radix);
 public static int parseInt(String s);
 public static Integer valueOf(String s, int radix);
 public static Integer valueOf(String s);
 public int intValue();
 public long longValue();
 public float floatValue();
 public double doubleValue();
 public String toString();
```

continues

Listing 7.8. continued

```
public int hashCode();
public boolean equals(Object obj);
public static Integer getInteger(String nm);
public static Integer getInteger(String nm, int val);
public static Integer getInteger(String nm, Integer val);
}
```

The `Integer`, `Long`, `Double`, and `Float` wrapper classes provide two constants—`MIN_VALUE` and `MAX_VALUE`—that indicate the range of allowable values for objects of each type. They are static and, as such, may be called in reference to their respective classes; you don't have to declare an object to get to the values. For example, the statement

```
System.out.println("Max integer = " + Integer.MAX_VALUE);
```

displays the maximum allowed integer value:

```
Max integer = 2147483647
```

Replace `Integer` with `Long`, `Double`, or `Float` to find those maximums. Print `MIN_VALUE` to find the minimum allowed values for specific types.

Some of the most useful methods in the `Integer` class (also available in the `Long` class) convert values to `String` objects, and also parse strings into values. Listing 7.9, `ConvertInt.java`, demonstrates how to use these methods.

Listing 7.9. `ConvertInt.java` (Demonstrates `Integer` and string conversion methods).

```
class ConvertInt {
 public static void main(String args[]) {
  if (args.length < 1)
   System.out.println("ex. jview convertint 1234");
  else {
   int intValue = Integer.parseInt(args[0]);
   System.out.println("Default = "
    + Integer.toString(intValue));
   System.out.println("Hex = "
    + Integer.toHexString(intValue));
   System.out.println("Octal = "
    + Integer.toOctalString(intValue));
   System.out.println("Binary = "
    + Integer.toBinaryString(intValue));
   System.out.println("base 32 = "
    + Integer.toString(intValue, 32));
  }
 }
}
```

The sample program calls `Integer` methods such as `toString()` and `toHexString()` to convert a command-line argument to various string formats. For example, running the program with the command

```
jview convertint 1234
```

displays the integer value 1234 in the following ways:

```
Default = 1234
Hex = 4d2
Octal = 2322
Binary = 10011010010
base 32 = 16i
```

The Long Wrapper Class

Listing 7.10 shows Java's `Long` wrapper class, which represents `long` native values in class form. The `Long` class is similar to `Integer`, and most methods are the same, except that `parseInt()` is named `parseLong()`, and method return values are of type `long`.

Listing 7.10. Java's Long wrapper class.

```
class Long extends Number {
// Fields
public static final long MIN_VALUE;
public static final long MAX_VALUE;
// Constructors
public Long(long value);
public Long(String s);
// Methods
public static String toString(long i, int radix);
public static String toHexString(long i);
public static String toOctalString(long i);
public static String toBinaryString(long i);
private static String toUnsignedString(long i, int shift);
public static String toString(long i);
public static long parseLong(String s, int radix);
public static long parseLong(String s);
public static Long valueOf(String s, int radix);
public static Long valueOf(String s);
public int intValue();
public long longValue();
public float floatValue();
public double doubleValue();
public String toString();
public int hashCode();
public boolean equals(Object obj);
public static Long getLong(String nm);
public static Long getLong(String nm, long val);
public static Long getLong(String nm, Long val);
}
```

The `Float` Wrapper Class

For working with `float` and `double` floating-point values, Java provides the `Float` and `Double` object-oriented classes. Listing 7.11 shows Java's `Float` wrapper class. The next section lists the `Double` wrapper.

Listing 7.11. Java's `Float` wrapper class.

```
class Float extends Number {
 // Fields
 public static final float POSITIVE_INFINITY;
 public static final float NEGATIVE_INFINITY;
 public static final float NaN;
 public static final float MAX_VALUE;
 public static final float MIN_VALUE;
 // Constructors
 public Float(float value);
 public Float(double value);
 public Float(String s);
 // Methods
 public static native String toString(float f);
 public static native Float valueOf(String s);
 static public boolean isInfinite(float v);
 public boolean isNaN();
 public boolean isInfinite();
 public String toString();
 public int intValue();
 public long longValue();
 public float floatValue();
 public double doubleValue();
 public int hashCode();
 public boolean equals(Object obj);
 public static native int floatToIntBits(float value);
 public static native float intBitsToFloat(int bits);
}
```

As with the `Integer` and `Long` classes, `Float` provides `MAX_VALUE` and `MIN_VALUE` constants that show the range of values allowed by the `float` type. In addition, three more constants give the negative and positive values for infinity and a special value, `NaN`, or "not a number." These three constants are `POSITIVE_INFINITY`, `NEGATIVE_INFINITY`, and `NaN`. You may use them directly, but you will more often call a method that employs the constants. For example, the fragment

```
float value = Float.POSITIVE_INFINITY;
System.out.println("value = " + value);
if (Float.isInfinite(value))
 System.out.println("Value is infinite");
```

assigns the value for positive infinity to a `float` variable, and calls the `Float` class method `isInfinite()` to determine whether the value is infinite. Such a value is beyond the range of allowable values for the specified native type. A floating-point value may also have the special value "not a number," or `NaN`:

```
float value = Float.NaN;
...
if (Float.isNaN(value))
 System.out.println("Value is not a number");
```

As with the `Integer` and `Long` wrappers, some of the more useful `Float` methods convert values between floating-point and string formats. The statements

```
float value = (float)3.14159;
String s = Float.toString(value);
System.out.println(s);
```

convert a `float` variable to a `String` object for display. The type cast expression is necessary because Java normally represents floating-point values as type `double`.

The Double Wrapper Class

Listing 7.12 shows Java's `Double` wrapper class, which is similar to `Float` but is probably more useful because `double` is Java's default floating-point data type. Most floating-point values are best represented using the native `double` data type or the `Double` wrapper class.

Listing 7.12. Java's Double wrapper class.

```
class Double extends Number {
 // Fields
 public static final double POSITIVE_INFINITY;
 public static final double NEGATIVE_INFINITY;
 public static final double NaN;
 public static final double MAX_VALUE;
 public static final double MIN_VALUE;
 // Constructors
 public Double(double value);
 public Double(String s);
 // Methods
 public static native String toString(double d);
 public static native Double valueOf(String s);
 static public boolean isNaN(double v);
 static public boolean isInfinite(double v);
 public boolean isNaN();
 public boolean isInfinite();
 public String toString();
 public int intValue();
 public long longValue();
 public float floatValue();
 public double doubleValue();
 public int hashCode();
 public boolean equals(Object obj);
 public static native long doubleToLongBits(double value);
 public static native double longBitsToDouble(long bits);
}
```

In addition to various `String` and `double` conversion methods such as `toString()` and `longValue()`, the `Double` class provides two methods that you can use to convert IEEE floating-point bit patterns, in `long` storage format, to floating-point values. This provides exacting capabilities for data input and output—from binary files, for example, that store IEEE floating-point values. To try these methods, declare three variables:

```
double value;
long bits;
String s;
```

Then assign a `double` value such as `PI` for test purposes:

```
value = Math.PI;
System.out.println("PI as double    = " + value);
```

To convert `value` to IEEE `long` format, call `doubleToLongBits()` as follows:

```
bits = Double.doubleToLongBits(value);
s = Long.toString(bits);
System.out.println("PI as IEEE long = " + s);
```

To convert a bit pattern back to a floating-point `double` value, call `longBitsToDouble()` as follows:

```
value = Double.longBitsToDouble(bits);
s = Double.toString(value);
System.out.println("Back to double  = " + s);
```

If you run the foregoing examples, on screen you see this report:

```
PI as double    = 3.14159
PI as IEEE long = 4614256656552045848
Back to double  = 3.14159
```

Summary

- Java's numerical classes give you object-oriented interfaces for programming various mathematical operations.

- The `Math` class provides miscellaneous methods and is automatically imported into every application. You cannot instantiate the `Math` class. Instead, you call its methods and use its constants in reference to the class itself.

- Objects of Java's `Random` class are random-number generators. Call the `Random` class's methods to seed the generator, of which you may create as many instances as needed. Because Java carefully defines the algorithms used by the `Random` class, the resulting pseudo-random sequences are potentially repeatable across all conforming Java installations.

- Java's numerical and Boolean wrapper classes provide object-oriented interfaces for numeric and boolean data types. The wrapper class names are the same as the represented native types but are capitalized, except for Integer, which represents int values. Java's wrapper classes are Boolean, Integer, Long, Float, and Double. (The preceding chapter describes the Character wrapper class.)

Exercises

1. Write a program that sums one or more floating-point values entered as command-line arguments. For example, it should be possible to run your program using a command such as the following:

   jview fpsum 3.14159 7.88 123.5

2. Write a PowerOf program that raises any value to any power using command-line arguments.

3. Create a method that returns a String object containing a specified number of characters selected at random. (This method might be useful for testing string processing software.)

4. Write a program that converts any integer value to its hexadecimal and binary equivalents.

What's Next?

So far, I've only scratched the surface of what you can do with Java classes. In the next chapter, I'll dig deeper into Java's class and object capabilities and their roles in object-oriented programming.

CHAPTER

8

More About
Classes and Objects

As you have learned so far, everything in a Java program occurs in the context of a class, which can be instantiated as an object. With what you know about Java so far, however, you might not appreciate the value of classes and objects in writing robust software. In this chapter, I explain more about classes and objects, and their value to object-oriented programming.

In This Chapter

This chapter introduces the following advanced class and object-oriented programming techniques:

- Advanced class concepts
- Abstract classes
- Interface classes
- Public, protected, and private class access rules
- Friendly declarations

Advanced Class Concepts

Until now, I've purposely avoided some class techniques that would only have gotten in the way of Java's fundamentals. Now that you have a better grasp of Java programming—and now that you have used some of Java's prepackaged classes such as Math and StringBuffer—you're ready to move beyond simple class designs into the exciting world of object-oriented programming.

First in this section, I'll briefly review what you already know about classes. Then, I'll cover the subjects of access specifiers, inheritance techniques, polymorphism, static class members, and the concept of data hiding—all crucial ammunition in the battle to write code that's as indestructible as a Sherman tank but runs like a Porsche.

Class Review

Classes, as you know, encapsulate code and data. As a running example for this section, you examine different versions of a class named Rectangle that specifies the size of a rectangular area. This isn't a graphical object, but rather a conceptual model for a rectangular shape. You might use Rectangle objects in a variety of ways—to specify display regions, for example, or as the relative dimensions of a graphical window.

In its most basic form, the class needs some data declarations (called instance variables) and one or more methods. As with most classes, it also has a constructor method, which initializes a class object's data. Listing 8.1, RectDemo1.java, shows this basic design—not the finished goods, but a reasonable starting place for discussing class design considerations. You can compile the program, but it produces no output. Its purpose is purely to demonstrate concepts of object-oriented programming. Other listings in this chapter similarly produce no on-screen results.

Listing 8.1. `RectDemo1.java` (Demonstrates basic class design).

```
class Rectangle {
 // Instance variables
 int left, top, right, bottom;
 // Constructor
 Rectangle(int l, int t, int r, int b) {
  left = l;
  top = t;
  right = r;
  bottom = b;
 }
}

class RectDemo1 {
 public static void main(String args[]) {
  Rectangle rect = new Rectangle(4, 6, 24, 26);
 }
}
```

The sample program declares the `Rectangle` class with four integer instance variables representing the `left`, `top`, `right`, and `bottom` coordinate values of an arbitrary rectangular area. A single constructor method, named the same as the class and returning no value (not even `void`) initializes instance variables by assigning them parameter values.

> **NOTE**
>
> A constructor's parameters are usually named differently from the class instance variables those parameters are used to initialize. This can lead to awkward and confusing identifiers, and programmers use various naming conventions as a result. For example, in the sample program, I named the parameters using the first letters of their associated instance variables (`l` for `left`, `r` for `right`, and so on). If this isn't feasible, another solution is to double single-letter variables. In a class with a variable named `x`, for example, the constructor parameter to be assigned to that variable might be `xx`. Another popular convention is to use capitalization to distinguish among the identifiers. If I had adopted this technique, I would have named the `Rectangle` constructor parameters `Left`, `Top`, `Right`, and `Bottom`, and used them to initialize the non-capitalized `left`, `top`, `right`, and `bottom` instance variables.

The sample program's `main()` method demonstrates how to construct an object of the `Rectangle` class. This object contains its own copies of the class's instance variables. In other words, if you construct another object using the same `Rectangle` class, as in the statement

```
Rectangle rect2 = new Rectangle(10, 10, 50, 50);
```

the second object's instance variables are independent from the first's. The two objects, however, share the same class methods and constructors.

> **TIP**
>
> Objects do not *contain* code, a common misconception. Objects contain only data, which is associated with the class's methods.

Using this design for the `Rectangle` class, a statement can access the object's instance variables using dot notation. For example, the following statement displays the value of `rect`'s `left` instance variable:

```
System.out.println("rect.left = " + rect.left);   // ???
```

In general, this is *not* good object-oriented design because it allows too much freedom in the use of instance variables. Any statement anywhere in the program could modify a `Rectangle` object's data. In this simple example, no harm would probably result, but in more complex settings this kind of freedom typically produces chaos. One of the key goals in object-oriented programming is to restrict access to data, and in that way, ensure its proper use. You'll learn in this chapter numerous ways for achieving this goal, but for now, we'll leave `Rectangle` as is.

Before moving on, it is important to understand that a class is merely a schematic of an object's design. A class is like a drawing of a desk that you want to build. The drawing describes the desk's dimensions and shows its individual parts such as drawers, which might be shaped to hold specific objects—pencils, for example, or envelopes. A carpenter might use your drawing to construct an actual desk, into which you can place real pencils and paper. You might say the carpenter *instantiates* the drawing, making it real. In the same way, you declare classes and instantiate them into real objects that exist at runtime. The objects hold the program's data and perform its operations as specified by the class's constructors and methods.

Constructors

Many classes have multiple constructors, which provide different ways to initialize class objects. For example, using the `Rectangle` class from `RectDemo1.java`, there is only one way to construct an object—by specifying four integer values as arguments to the `Rectangle()` constructor:

```
Rectangle rect = new Rectangle(0, 0, 31, 26);
```

As designed, `Rectangle` is inconvenient to use because a program might need to construct one or more objects of the class and initialize them at runtime. To provide for this, the class needs a *default constructor,* one that requires no arguments. It could also use a method to assign values to the object's instance variables. Listing 8.2, `RectDemo2.java`, redesigns the `Rectangle` class to achieve these goals.

Listing 8.2. `RectDemo2.java` (Demonstrates overloaded constructors).

```java
class Rectangle {
 // Instance variables
 int left, top, right, bottom;
 // Default constructor
 Rectangle() {
  setDimensions(0, 0, 0, 0);
 }
 // Overloaded constructor
 Rectangle(int l, int t, int r, int b) {
  setDimensions(l, t, r, b);
 }
 // Assign values to instance variables
 void setDimensions(int l, int t, int r, int b) {
  left = l;
  top = t;
  right = r;
  bottom = b;
 }
}

class RectDemo2 {
 public static void main(String args[]) {
  Rectangle rect1 = new Rectangle();
  Rectangle rect2 = new Rectangle(0, 0, 10, 20);
  rect1.setDimensions(8, 9, 25, 25);
 }
}
```

The new `Rectangle` sports two overloaded constructors. They are *overloaded,* not because they stayed out too late last night, but because they have the same names but differ in one or more parameters. The default constructor declares no parameters:

```java
Rectangle();
```

Use it to create an object that you intend to initialize elsewhere. For example, the code

```java
Rectangle rect1 = new Rectangle();
...
rect1.setDimensions(8, 9, 25, 25);
```

constructs a default `Rectangle` object and, elsewhere in the program, calls the `setDimensions()` method to initialize the object's instance variables. Notice that in the listing, the overloaded constructors also call `setDimensions()` to assign values to the `left`, `top`, `right`, and `bottom` integer variables. This method provides a controlled access path to an object's data—but it is still possible for a program to directly access and modify that data simply by assigning values to `left`, `top`, `right`, or `bottom`. While we have provided an access method in `setDimensions()`, we have not prevented the indiscriminate use of the class's instance variables—a laudable goal in good object-oriented design. To do this, we need to *guarantee* that only `setDimensions()` or another designated method can change an object's data, which brings me to the next subject: *access specifiers.*

Access Specifiers

Access specifiers control the availability of instance variables and methods to a program's statements. They create varying levels of protection for controlling access to class data and code.

There are three types of access specifiers: public, protected, and private. The default access is *friendly,* which means that all classes within the same source file or package have access to the variables and methods. It is, however, generally best to designate an access specifier for all instance variables and methods. Do that by prefacing the declaration with the appropriate keyword. For example, to make two instance variables private, use a declaration like this:

```
class AnyClass {
 private int x, y;
...
}
```

As private members of a class, x and y are accessible *only* to methods in that same class. No other classes, not even a subclass of AnyClass, may access x and y, not to read or to write their values. Presumably, a method in AnyClass provides the means to modify and read the private instance variables. This hides the data inside the class and provides a controlled access path to the data values. Among other benefits, this class-design technique does the following:

- Makes it possible to modify the instance variables' data types without affecting the use of that data.
- Helps you find bugs related to the class data because you can trace all calls to methods in the class that modify the data values.
- Prevents bugs caused by accidental redeclaration of instance variables because the compiler will display an error if a subclass attempts to redefine the instance variables.

You may also make methods private, although this is not as common. A private method is callable only by other methods in that same class. Not even a method in a subclass may call an inherited private method. More commonly, therefore, methods are made protected, which makes them available only to other methods in their declaring class and also to any methods in a subclass of this class. Making instance variables and methods public makes them available to all statements anywhere in the program.

> **NOTE**
>
> Constructors are almost always public so that statements anywhere in the program may call them to construct objects of the class.

Classes themselves may be declared public, which makes them available to other classes for the purposes of constructing objects. This is the most common design. If unspecified, a class's access method is *friendly,* and the class is available only to other classes in the same module or package. Classes may not be declared protected or private.

Unless you have some experience with object-oriented design, it may be unclear at this stage why you would select one access specifier over another. The following general rules will guide your selection until you gain experience with objects and appreciate the reasons for data hiding and restricting access to data and code:

- Most instance variables should be `private`. There are few good reasons to declare variables `public`, because this effectively sidesteps the goals of object-oriented design by making it resemble conventional programming in which data is generally available to any part of the program.

- Most methods should be `public`. The exception is a method that you want to call only from other class methods or from methods in a subclass—in this case, designate the method `protected`. It is rarely useful to make a method `private`, but you can do so to prevent methods in a subclass from calling it.

- Constructors are almost always `public`. The one exception is a `private` constructor that is used in constructing an abstract class that cannot be instantiated (more on this later in the chapter).

From now on in this book, sample classes will more carefully use the `public`, `private`, and `protected` access specifiers. In the interests of brevity, however, I'll often make data `public` when demonstrating some aspect of Java programming. As a general rule, though, data is almost always best made `private` to its defining class.

> **TIP**
>
> You can mix `public`, `private`, and `protected` declarations in any order anywhere in a class. Many programmers, however, prefer to place all declarations of one type together.

Listing 8.3, `RectDemo3.java`, uses access specifiers in a third revision of the `Rectangle` class. The new class better controls access to its instance variables and, as such, is a superior example of robust object-oriented design.

Listing 8.3. `RectDemo3.java` (Demonstrates access specifiers).

```java
class Rectangle {
 // Private instance variables
 private int left, top, right, bottom;
 // Constructors:
 // Default constructor
 public Rectangle() {
  setDimensions(0, 0, 0, 0);
 }
 // Overloaded constructor
 public Rectangle(int l, int t, int r, int b) {
  setDimensions(l, t, r, b);
 }
```

continues

Listing 8.3. continued

```
// Public methods:
// Get values of instance variables
public int getLeft()   { return left; }
public int getTop()    { return top; }
public int getRight()  { return right; }
public int getBottom() { return bottom; }
// Set values of instance variables
public void setLeft(int n)   { left = n; }
public void setTop(int n)    { top = n; }
public void setRight(int n)  { right = n; }
public void setBottom(int n) { bottom = n; }
// Display values of instance variable:
public void displayDimensions(String label) {
 System.out.println(label +
   ": left=" + left + " top=" + top +
   " right=" + right + " bottom=" + bottom);
}
// Protected method:
// Assign values to instance variables
protected void
setDimensions(int l, int t, int r, int b) {
 setLeft(l);
 setTop(t);
 setRight(r);
 setBottom(b);
}
}

class RectDemo3 {
 public static void main(String args[]) {
  Rectangle rect1 = new Rectangle();
  Rectangle rect2 = new Rectangle(0, 0, 10, 20);
  rect1.setTop(5);
  rect1.displayDimensions("rect1");
  rect2.displayDimensions("rect2");
 }
}
```

Our demonstration `Rectangle` class is really growing. Its four instance variables are now private members of the class, and it is no longer possible for statements outside of class methods to access that data directly. For example, a statement such as

```
rect1.left = 10;  // ???
```

inserted into `main()` causes the compiler to issue the error message

```
RectDemo3.java(53,9) : error J0147: Cannot access private member
'left' in class 'Rectangle' from 'void main(String[] args)'
```

Instead of directly accessing the private instance variables, the program is now forced to use one of the public access methods—`getLeft()`, `getTop()`, `getRight()`, or `getBottom()`—to obtain the object's data values. Similarly, the public methods `setLeft()`, `setTop()`, `setRight()`, and `setBottom()` assign values to the object's instance variables. These methods control access to the data, and help make the program more reliable and more easily maintained.

In addition to these changes, for demonstration purposes, I also declared the `setDimensions()` method `protected`. This means that statements in `main()` can no longer call this method; however, statements in the class still can. For example, the constructors call `setDimensions()` to initialize the four instance variables. Methods in a class extended from `Rectangle` could also call the `protected` `setDimensions()`.

Even this expanded version of `Rectangle` is not necessarily the only or the ideal way to create this particular class, but it demonstrates some typical design considerations for classes. Some of these considerations are

- Make instance variables `private` unless you have excellent reasons for doing otherwise.

- For each instance variable, provide methods to read (get) and write (set) their values.

- Provide default (no parameter) and parameterized constructors that initialize instance variables. Instance variables should always be set to a known or computed value for all class objects no matter how they are constructed.

- Use the `protected` specifier sparingly, usually only when it is necessary to restrict calling a method to statements in a class's own methods or in methods of a subclass extended from this one.

When classes such as `Rectangle` reach a certain stage of complexity, it is a good idea to create a documentation listing of them for reference. For example, Listing 8.4, `Rectangle.txt`, shows the declarations for the `Rectangle` class minus its implementation details. The documentation might leave out `private` and `protected` declarations, especially if it is intended for end users only. This file is in the `RectDemo3` directory on the CD-ROM.

Listing 8.4. `Rectangle.txt` (Final `Rectangle` documentation).

```
class Rectangle {
 // Default constructor
 public Rectangle();
 // Overloaded constructor
 public Rectangle(int l, int t, int r, int b);
 // Get values of instance variables
 public int getLeft();
 public int getTop();
 public int getRight();
 public int getBottom();
 // Set values of instance variables
 public void setLeft(int n);
 public void setTop(int n);
 public void setRight(int n);
 public void setBottom(int n);
 // Display values of instance variable:
 public void displayDimensions(String label);
}
```

Inheritance Revisited

As you have learned, a new class (called the *subclass*) may extend an existing class (called the *superclass*). The subclass inherits the superclass's instance variables and methods, to which you may add new data and code. You may also override methods by redeclaring them. You cannot override instance variables—only methods. Using these techniques, you build programs by extending debugged classes from Java's library, or from your own.

For example, a typical technique is to import an existing class and extend it with new capabilities. To demonstrate, Listing 8.5 imports Java's own `Rectangle` class, from the `java.awt` (Another Window Toolkit) package. The program extends `Rectangle` to a new subclass, `MyRectangle`, to which I added a `String` label, a constructor, and a method for returning the label.

Listing 8.5. `InheritDemo.java` (Demonstrates inheritance).

```
import java.awt.Rectangle;

class MyRectangle extends Rectangle {
 private String rectName;
 // Constructor
 MyRectangle(String name, int x, int y, int h, int w) {
  super(x, y, h, w);
  rectName = new String(name);
 }
 public String getName() {
  return rectName;
 }
}

class InheritDemo {
 public static void main(String args[]) {
  MyRectangle r = new MyRectangle("My Rectangle", 0, 0, 10, 20);
  System.out.println("Name = " + r.getName());
 }
}
```

The imported `java.awt.Rectangle` class is already extended from `Object`, which as I have explained, is the base class of all Java classes, even if not specified with the `extends` keyword. Nevertheless, Java's `Rectangle` class is declared as

```
public class java.awt.Rectangle
 extends java.lang.Object
```

to show that it directly descends from `Object`. Our new `MyRectangle` subclass in the sample program is declared as

```
class MyRectangle extends Rectangle { ...
```

Thus `MyRectangle` inherits all members of the `Object` and `Rectangle` classes. It is not necessary to use the fully qualified name, `java.awt.Rectangle`, but you may do so in order to avoid possible conflicts with any other `Rectangle` classes in other packages. The fully qualified name also tells the compiler where to find the compiled `Rectangle` class byte codes.

Our new subclass inherits all members of the existing Rectangle superclass along with all members of Object. In a sense, this means MyRectangle is a specific kind of Rectangle—similar to the way an oak tree is a specific type of tree—but with additional characteristics. One of those attributes is the storage of a name, which the constructor assigns to the new private String field:

```
MyRectangle(String name, int x, int y, int h, int w) {
 super(x, y, h, w);  // Call inherited constructor
 rectName = new String(name);
}
```

The constructor first calls a special method, super(), which refers to the inherited method in the superclass. Thus, the statement shown here calls the Rectangle() constructor that takes four integer arguments. (There are other constructors, but we will override only this one for demonstration.) After this step, which initializes the instance variables inherited from Rectangle, the new constructor assigns the String name to its private field. This is a typical situation:

- You import an existing class, to which you add data and code.
- You also add a new constructor, which calls an existing one and then initializes any new data added to the class.

Finally, our new class provides a method, getName(), which returns the value of the new private field.

Our new class, MyRectangle, has all the capabilities of its ancestor classes. For example, a program can call the Rectangle class's grow() method, which expands the rectangle by specified height and width values. Because our class is a subclass of Rectangle, the program can do this in reference to a MyRectangle object:

```
MyRectangle r = new MyRectangle("Name", 0, 0, 10, 20);
r.grow(8, 12);
```

This code is possible because MyRectangle inherits the public grow() method. The second statement would not be possible, however, if grow() were declared private or protected. A private method is callable *only* from within its declaring class. A protected method is callable from within its class and any extended subclass. A public method is always callable.

Built-In Names

Java provides some built-in names to handle special situations. You saw one instance of this when a subclass constructor calls its superclass constructor with a statement such as

```
super(x, y, w, h);  // Call super class constructor
```

Another built-in name is null, which represents a nonexisting object. You may pass null to any method that requires an object of a class:

```
anyObject.DoSomething(null);  // Pass null object to method
```

You may also pass another name, `this`, that represents the object for which a method was called:

```
DoSomething(this);  // Pass current object to DoSomething
```

The word `this` inside a class method always refers to the object for which the method was called. It is implied in all references to a class object, as in the `MyRectangle` method:

```
public String getName() {
 return rectName;
}
```

The method's statement could also be written as

```
return this.rectName;
```

but it isn't necessary because `this` is implied when a statement in a class method refers to a class instance variable.

The concept of `this` confuses many beginners to object-oriented programming, but is easier to understand from a few more examples. When the program executes the statement

```
r.getName();
```

Java calls `getName()` in reference to the object `r`. That object is referenced inside the method as `this`. In other words, any statement in the class that uses `this`, in this case, refers to the object `r`.

As I mentioned, in most cases, it isn't necessary to use `this` explicitly; it is implied when statements refer to the object's methods and instance variables. Suppose, however, the `MyRectangle` class had a method that required a `Rectangle` object argument:

```
public void SomeMethod(Rectangle rr);
```

To call `SomeMethod()`, we need to provide a `Rectangle` argument. Inside another class method, use `this` to make that argument refer to the same object for which the method was called. For example, the statement

```
SomeMethod(this);  // Pass current object
```

passes the current object to `SomeMethod()`.

Polymorphism

The word *polymorphism* is one of the most misused and maligned words in object-oriented programming. In brief, polymorphism is the ability objects have to perform operations that conform to their class types. Using again the analogy of an oak tree, imagine all trees have a "method" named `grow()`. When nature "calls" the method, trees grow in ways that conform to their types: an oak tree produces leaves and branches that are distinct from a locust tree's. The object (tree) itself determines the effect of nature's command for it to "grow."

A common example of polymorphism in object-oriented programming is a graphical object in a class hierarchy of shapes. We'll examine real-life examples of polymorphism throughout this book, but the concept is easier to fathom with some hypothetical code fragments. Start with a superclass, named Shape:

```
class Shape {
...
 void Draw();
};
```

Among its other talents, the Shape class provides a Draw() method. Other classes extend Shape to create actual graphical classes:

```
class Circle extends Shape {
...
void Draw() {
 // method statements
 }
}
```

The redeclared Draw() overrides the inherited method from Shape. (The superclass Draw() can be called using super() as explained before.) Here's another class that overrides Draw():

```
class Square extends Shape {
...
 void Draw() {
 // method statements
 }
}
```

We now have two subclasses, Circle and Square, each of which overrides the inherited Draw() method. The Circle class implements Draw() to draw a circle. The Square class implements Draw() to draw a square. Because each class is extended from Shape, a statement in the program can draw *any* shape. We might, for example, create a method such as the following that receives a Shape object argument:

```
void DrawShape(Shape s) {
 s.Draw();
}
```

Elsewhere, the program can pass a Circle or a Square object to DrawShape's Shape parameter. This is a good example of *class typecasting*. It is permissible to pass Circle and Square objects to the DrawShape() parameter because these classes are subclasses of Shape. A good way to think of this is to consider that a Circle object is also a Shape, just as an oak is also a tree. When the program executes the statement

```
s.Draw();
```

the effect is to call the Draw() method that is defined by the object s's class. Because of polymorphism, even if that statement were buried in a precompiled class somewhere on the Internet, you could program a new class extended from Shape, and the statement would call your class's Draw() method. Simply extending a class, in other words, teaches the DrawShape() method how to draw a completely new shape that was unknown to the method's original programmers. Through polymorphism, you can plug in new code that modifies how programs work, and that allows them to use new objects, and you don't even have to recompile those programs.

> **TIP**
>
> Java does not allow class type casting between sibling objects. For example, using the hypothetical `Shape` classes from the preceding discussion, if a method declares a `Circle` parameter, you cannot pass it a `Square` object. `Circle` and `Square` objects are `Shape`s, but a `Circle` is not a `Square`, and neither is a `Square` a `Circle`.

Static Class Members

When you need only a method, and you don't intend to create objects of the method's class, you can make the method `static`. You can also declare variables `static`, but it is more common to use the technique with methods. Any `static` declaration is the same for all objects of a class, and it may be used in reference to the class itself without having to instantiate the class.

Listing 8.6, `StaticDemo.java`, demonstrates how to declare and use static class members.

Listing 8.6. `StaticDemo.java` (Demonstrates `static` class members).

```java
class AnyClass {
 static int x;
 static void ShowValue() {
  System.out.println("x = " + x);
 }
}

class StaticDemo {
 public static void main(String args[]) {
  // Use static items in reference to class
  AnyClass.x = 123;
  AnyClass.ShowValue();
  // Use static items in reference to object
  AnyClass v = new AnyClass();
  v.x = 456;
  v.ShowValue();
  // Try class reference again
  AnyClass.ShowValue();
 }
}
```

The sample program declares a class, `AnyClass`, with a static variable x and a static method `ShowValue()`. The main program demonstrates that it can access each of these items in reference to `AnyClass` without constructing an object of the class. The two statements

```java
AnyClass.x = 123;
AnyClass.ShowValue();
```

assign 123 to the static x variable, and call the static `ShowValue()` method to display that variable's value.

You may instantiate a class that has static members, and you may refer to them in reference to an object as you can with nonstatic items. For example, the main program in the sample listing executes the statements

```
AnyClass v = new AnyClass();
v.x = 456;
v.ShowValue();
```

which construct an object of the AnyClass class. The program assigns 456 to the static variable x and calls ShowValue(), this time in reference to the object v. However, when the program again calls ShowValue() in reference to AnyClass with the statement

```
AnyClass.ShowValue();
```

the code displays 456—the value assigned to v.x. This is because x is static, and it is therefore the same variable for *all* objects of the class. Unlike normal instance variables, objects do not have distinct copies of static data members. Also, as a consequence of this rule, static methods may not refer to nonstatic data members. If you add an integer declaration to AnyClass, such as

```
class AnyClass {
 int q;
...
}
```

it would not be possible for the static ShowValue() method to use q. This is because instance variables by definition must be used in reference to an instance of the class. Because a static method can be called without reference to an object, the method cannot use any instance variables that exist only in such an object. Likewise, a static data member is not an instance variable; only one copy of it exists for the class itself and for all objects of that class.

As Listing 8.7, Version.java, demonstrates, a version number is an excellent use for a static data member, because the version refers to the class revision and is therefore the same for all objects of that class.

Listing 8.7. Version.java. (Demonstrates a practical use for a static data member).

```
class AnyClass {
 static String version;
 AnyClass () {
  version = new String("1.2b");
 }
 static void ShowVersion() {
  System.out.println("AnyClass version " + version);
 }
}

class Version {
 public static void main(String args[]) {
  AnyClass v1 = new AnyClass();
  AnyClass v2 = new AnyClass();
```

continues

Listing 8.7. continued

```
  v1.ShowVersion();
  v2.ShowVersion();
 }
}
```

The sample program's `AnyClass` class declares a `static` `String` variable, named `version`. The class constructor assigns a literal string to the variable, which, because it is static, is the same for all objects of the class. The main program demonstrates this fact by constructing two objects of the class and calling `ShowVersion()` for each. Because the `static` `version` string is the same for all objects, the final two statements of the listing display the same version number:

```
AnyClass version 1.2b
AnyClass version 1.2b
```

Private Constructors

Classes in which all members are static are typically not instantiated as objects. Instead, programs access static data members and call static methods to perform various operations without constructing objects of the class. A good example of this type of class design is the `Math` class that you examined in Chapter 7. Rather than construct a `Math` object, to use one of the class's methods, you simply call it in reference to the class itself, as in this example:

```
System.out.println(Math.sqrt(2.0));
```

This statement computes and displays the square root of 2. There's no reason to create a `Math` object merely to call its static `sqrt()` method. In fact, due to `Math`'s design, constructing an object of this class is impossible. If you attempt to do so with a declaration such as

```
Math m = new Math();
```

the compiler issues this obscure error message:

```
error J0073: ... cannot access member 'Math.Math()'
```

This might seem odd at first glance, but it indicates that the reason you cannot construct a `Math` object is because the class's default constructor is `private`. This fact is evident from examining the `Math.java` source code file, which contains the constructor's declaration:

```
private Math() {}
```

The constructor performs no statements (its braces are bare), but because it is `private`, it is not possible for any statement to call it. In this way, construction of `Math` objects is neatly prevented! You might use this trick to prevent programs from constructing objects of any class, but it is a useful technique only when all class methods and variables are `static`.

In addition to its `private` constructor, the `Math` class is also declared `final`:

```
public final class Math { ...
```

This indicates that Math is complete, and that no subclasses are to be allowed that extend the class. Because Math is a final class, any attempt to extend it using a declaration such as

```
class NewMath extends Math {  // ???
}
```

produces this compilation error:

```
error J0048: Cannot extend final class 'Math'
```

Abstract Classes

An abstract class provides a model for creating other classes. Inside an abstract class are one or more *abstract methods,* which show the form of code subroutines, but don't actually provide their contents. To use an abstract class, you extend it with a subclass of your own design, and you complete the abstract methods. Other methods in an abstract class might be implemented in full, but you can override them as needed with your own methods, depending on what you are trying to do. You must, however, implement all inherited abstract methods before you may use an abstract class to instantiate an object.

An example of an abstract class might be one that provides a framework for a graphics system. The abstract class could specify various methods for drawing, printing, and animating shapes that other software requires. However, the techniques for actually drawing images on screen are left to you. In this way, you can plug in your own code (perhaps to accommodate specific hardware at your location) and take advantage of the software that recognizes the abstract class's design.

Declaring an Abstract Method

To declare an abstract method, precede it with the abstract keyword. Any class that has one or more such declarations must also be declared abstract, and it cannot be instantiated. The only way to use an abstract class is to extend it and implement its abstract methods. You do not repeat the abstract keyword in the subclass.

Using an Abstract Class

Listing 8.8, AbstractDemo.java, shows how to create an abstract class and extend it for use as an object.

Listing 8.8. AbstractDemo.java (Demonstrates abstract method and class).

```
// Declare abstract class
abstract class Model {
 protected String s;
 public Model(String ss) {
  s = ss;
```

continues

Listing 8.8. continued

```
 }
 // Abstract method
 public abstract void ShowString();
}

class Actual extends Model {
 public Actual(String ss) {
  super(ss);
 }
 // Implement abstract method
 public void ShowString() {
  System.out.println(s);
 }
}

class AbstractDemo {
 public static void main(String args[]) {
  // Use Actual class extended from Abstract class
  Actual object = new Actual("Actual object");
  object.ShowString();
 }
}
```

The sample program's abstract class, Model, declares a protected String variable, a public constructor, and an abstract method, ShowString(). Because its data is protected, only a subclass of Model may access it by name. Because the class and ShowString() method are abstract, the program cannot instantiate the class. For example, statements such as

```
Model object = new Model("Abstract object"); // ???
object.ShowString(); // ???
```

produce the compilation error

```
error J0109: Cannot 'new' an instance of abstract class 'Model'
```

(Apparently, according to Java, "new" is a verb, a fact that has escaped my learning until just now.) To use the abstract Model class, the sample program extends it with a subclass named Actual. The new class overrides the public ShowString() method, but does not repeat the abstract keyword. In its new implementation, the method displays the protected String data inherited from the Model abstract class. The subclass also provides a constructor, which is required so that the program can create an object of the Actual class. This new constructor merely calls the Model constructor using the built-in super() method to initialize the String variable.

The program's main() method uses the extended abstract class to create an object and call ShowString() in reference to that object. Although all of this might seem arbitrary, the program shows the practical use of abstract classes. Because the sample program's Model class does not implement ShowString(), a subclass is free to display the string data using any means—perhaps graphically, or by drawing it on a plotter. Other software may use the Model class, assuming that somewhere along the line, a programmer will provide an actual implementation of the ShowString() abstract method. For example, another method elsewhere could be written as

```
void AnyMethod(Model modelObject) {
 modelObject.ShowString();
}
```

This code could appear in the Model class, in the Actual class, or in another class that has access to Model. It can be compiled *in advance* of ShowString()'s implementation. Subsequently, you might instantiate a subclass of Model, and call the method using code like this:

```
Actual actualObject = new Actual("Your string");
```

And you can pass the object to AnyMethod():

```
AnyMethod(actualObject);
```

This code will call your implementation of the ShowString() method. In this way, you plug in your own methods to existing code—a tremendous advantage over conventional programming, which typically provides no counterpart to this object-oriented technique.

> **NOTE**
>
> Constructors, static methods, and private methods cannot be declared abstract. These items must be fully implemented in their declaring class.

Interface Classes

An *interface class* is a purely abstract class. All methods in an interface class are by definition abstract, and do not require prefacing with the abstract keyword. An interface class may also provide constant data. To use an interface class, you must implement it, similar to how you extend a class as a subclass, and write code for all or some abstract methods. An application can subsequently instantiate the class as an object and call its methods. A key advantage is that a class may implement multiple class interfaces, whereas a given subclass can extend from only one superclass.

Java's class library is filled with class interfaces that provide templates and protocols for a variety of purposes. You can also create your own interfaces, but for most application programming, you'll probably import and implement existing interface declarations. You will also use class interfaces that are implemented by various classes in Java's class library.

This section introduces class interfaces. First, I'll explain how to use interfaces with an example of random-access file input and output. Then, I'll explain how to create your own interface classes.

Using Interface Classes

In many cases, you will unknowingly take advantage of interface classes, which are frequently used to provide low-level protocols and services that you don't need to understand in full detail. Even so, it's useful to be aware of the mechanisms of an interface class. To demonstrate these mechanisms, this section presents a sample program that creates a file of double values on disk, writes 10 values at random to the file, and then reads the values back into memory. This also demonstrates a good way to read and write other kinds of file data, and you can use the sample program in this section as a template for many other file I/O tasks.

Two of the interface classes you will use frequently, if not explicitly, are DataOutput and DataInput, which provide input and output services. For example, Java's RandomAccessFile's declaration reveals how a class implements an interface class:

```
public class java.io.RandomAccessFile
 extends java.lang.Object
 implements java.io.DataOutput,
 java.io.DataInput
{
...
}
```

This declaration states that RandomAccessFile extends the Object superclass. In addition, it implements two purely abstract interface classes: DataOutput and DataInput. Notice there is one use of the implements keyword, and the two interface class names are separated by commas. The resulting class is an amalgam of all three classes: Object, DataOutput, and DataInput. Because the latter two classes are interfaces, RandomAccessFile implements their abstract methods. This provides file-access and other classes with standards for data I/O while greatly encouraging code reuse and portability.

Listing 8.9, FileDemo.java, demonstrates how to use the RandomAccessFile class. After explaining how the sample code operates, I'll show some of the ways this class implements its two interfaces.

Listing 8.9. FileDemo.java (Demonstrates interface classes and file I/O).

```
import java.io.*;

class FileDemo {
 public static void main(String args[]) {
  double value;
  try {
   // Open file for writing
   RandomAccessFile file = new RandomAccessFile("Test.dat", "rw");
   // Write 10 randomly selected doubles to file
   for (int i = 0; i < 10; i++) {
    value = Math.random();
    file.writeDouble(value);
   }
   // Rewind file for reading
   file.seek(0);
   try {
    while (true) {
```

```
      value = file.readDouble();
      System.out.println("Value = " + value);
    }
  } catch (EOFException e) {
    file.close();
    System.out.println("End of file reached");
  }
  } catch (IOException e) {
    System.out.println("Error: " + e.getMessage());
  }
 }
}
```

The sample program shows the correct way to create a file, write data to it, and read data back into memory. The first step is to create or open the file for I/O by constructing an object of the RandomAccessFile class:

```
RandomAccessFile file = new RandomAccessFile("Test.dat", "rw");
```

Pass two strings to the class constructor—a filename, and the string "rw" for reading and writing file data. If you want only to read data, use "r". There is no provision for write-only access; the specification "w" produces a runtime error.

> **NOTE**
>
> For security reasons, it might not be possible to create and write files remotely over the Internet. It should be possible, however, to read file data in most cases. The "rw" specification might work locally on your system, but it might produce a runtime error if executed remotely over the Internet.

After constructing the RandomAccessFile object, the sample program writes double values selected at random via the Math class's random() method. Doing this is simple. Just call the RandomAccessFile class's writeDouble() method as shown here:

```
file.writeDouble(value);
```

To read the data from the file, first rewind its internal byte pointer to the beginning, which positions the file for reading or writing at that location. Do this by seeking to byte zero:

```
file.seek(0);  // Be kind; rewind
```

After that, another call to a RandomAccessFile method reads double values into memory using the statement

```
value = file.readDouble();
```

There are other read and write methods in the RandomAccessFile class, so look them up in your online documentation. In all uses of this class, you will want to catch exceptions that are thrown—not only for errors, but also to indicate conditions such as the end of file. Carefully examine the following code fragment, which shows the correct way to read data from a file until reaching the file's end. This is extracted and simplified from the sample listing:

```
try {
 while (true) {
  value = file.readDouble();
 }
} catch (EOFException e) {
 file.close();
}
```

A try statement executes an apparently endless while loop, which calls the RandomAccessFile class's readDouble() method. Although the loop appears endless, it actually does end because readDouble() moves the internal file pointer ahead by the number of bytes occupied by its target data type—double in this case. Eventually, this action must reach the end of the file, at which time readDouble() throws an exception object of the EOFException class. This doesn't mean an error occurred, but rather, that the method has detected an exceptional condition—namely that there is no more data in the file to read. In response to this condition, a catch statement calls the RandomAccessFile class's close() method. This closes the file for future I/O. (To reopen it, you must reconstruct the class object.)

This sample read loop is further nested inside another try-catch block, which handles any IOExceptions that might be thrown. Generally, these represent error conditions—not finding a named file, for example, or attempting to create a file on a write-protected disk or a secure location. To see an example of this kind of error handling, change the "rw" designation to "r" in the statement that constructs the RandomAccessFile object, and then recompile and run the program. Because this opens the file for reading, if the file exists, the attempt to write a value to it generates this error:

```
Error: write error
```

If the file doesn't exist, attempting to construct the RandomAccessFile object in read-only mode generates the following error, which indicates a problem with the designated filename:

```
Error: Test.dat
```

Test this by deleting Test.dat and rerunning the modified program. In each instance, the program's outer catch statement displays the appropriate message by calling the exception object's getMessage() method:

```
System.out.println("Error: " + e.getMessage());
```

I'll go into the concept of exception handling in more detail in the next chapter. Here, I want only to show how using interface classes greatly increases the portability of file I/O and other code that is, by definition, system dependent. The sample program listed in this section might have to run on a wide variety of personal computers, mini-systems, and even mainframes, all running radically different operating systems. However, through the benefits of class interfaces, which implement low-level file I/O services, the *compiled* code remains completely portable.

It is interesting to trace how the RandomAccessFile class implements the two DataOutput and DataInput interfaces that provide low-level file I/O services. First, take a look at how the DataOuput interface is declared in Java's class library:

```
public interface java.io.DataOutput
{
 public abstract void write(byte b[]);
 public abstract void write(byte b[], int off, int len);
...
}
```

The interface keyword indicates that DataOutput is a purely abstract class, one that provides only the form of methods, but not their actual implementations. Any class that implements DataOutput must provide programming for its write() methods, and in that way, make it possible for completely general programs to write data on widely different computer systems.

In the source code to the RandomAccessFile class, which implements the DataOutput interface, the second method write() listed previously is implemented as a native function:

```
public native void write(int b) throws IOException;
```

The keyword native in RandomAccessFile's implementation of write() indicates that the actual code for this method is provided by the Java interpreter. This completes the linkage between the application (our sample program), a Java class (RandomAccessFile), and a class interface abstract method (DataOutput.write()). What's more, because the interface method's implementation is in the interpreter, *compiled* code can use that implementation. This means the program does not have to be recompiled to link with the machine-specific data-write subroutine.

> **NOTE**
>
> For most application programming, it is rare that you'll need to implement interface classes. It is important, however, to understand the mechanisms involved. For example, in order to fully understand how to use a class that implements one or more interfaces, you might need to study the documentation for the class *and* its various interfaces. Most interface methods, though, are low level and of more interest to system designers than application programmers.

Creating Interface Classes

Despite the common use of interface classes on the system level, they have value to application development. When a group of related classes requires the same methods, it might be wise to place those methods in an interface class. For example, if a set of animation classes needs a `drawFrame()` method, to maintain portability, an interface class can provide that method's declaration while leaving its implementation up to the software designer. This provides the program and class library with several organizational benefits:

- It specifies a low-level protocol that higher-level classes are expected to follow.
- It provides programmers with a common interface, encouraging code reuse and helping prevent reinventing of the wheel.
- It simplifies debugging because, if an application works correctly on one system but fails on another, the logical place to start looking for the bug is in the interface class implementations.
- It helps focus your thinking on the general nature of your class hierarchies, which can lead to discoveries of pure abstractions that you can build upon in future projects.

> **TIP**
>
> The default access specifier in an interface class is `private`. In most interfaces, however, methods are explicitly declared `public` or `protected`.

Listings 8.10 through 8.13 demonstrate how to create and use an interface class. All of these files are in the `Part2\InterfaceDemo` directory on the CD-ROM. The first listing, `Protocols.java`, is the simplest.

Listing 8.10. `Protocols.java`.

```
public interface Protocols {
 public abstract void ProtocolMethod(String s);
}
```

The interface class, named `Protocols`, provides one abstract method, `ProtocolMethod()`. This method requires a `String` argument, but it is not implemented in the interface. Any class using `Protocols` must implement `ProtocolMethod()`. For example, Listing 8.11, `LowClass.java`, implements the interface class.

Listing 8.11. `LowClass.java`.

```
import Protocols;

public class LowClass
implements Protocols {
 public void ProtocolMethod(String s) {
  System.out.println(s.toLowerCase());
 }
 public void ShowString(String s) {
  ProtocolMethod(s);
 }
}
```

In the public class `LowClass`, one version of `ProtocolMethod()` is implemented. Just for demonstration, the sample code calls the `String` class's `toLowerCase()` method to print the argument passed to the implemented method. In addition, a new method, `ShowString()`, is declared and implemented. Similarly, Listing 8.12, `HighClass.java`, also implements the `Protocols` class.

Listing 8.12. HighClass.java.

```
import Protocols;

public class HighClass
implements Protocols {
 public void ProtocolMethod(String s) {
  System.out.println(s.toUpperCase());
 }
 public void ShowString(String s) {
  ProtocolMethod(s);
 }
}
```

In this listing, however, the `ProtocolMethod()` implementation calls the `String` class's `toUpperCase()` method. We now have two implementations of the abstract method—one in `LowClass` and one in `HighClass`. The final source file, Listing 8.13, `InterfaceDemo.java`, brings all classes together.

Listing 8.13. InterfaceDemo.java.

```
import Protocols;
import LowClass;
import HighClass;

class InterfaceDemo {
 public static void main(String args[]) {
  LowClass object1 = new LowClass();
  HighClass object2 = new HighClass();
  String s = "AbCdEfGhIjKlMnOpQrStUvWxYz";
  System.out.println("LowClass string:");
  object1.ShowString(s);
  System.out.println("HighClass string:");
  object2.ShowString(s);
 }
}
```

The final demonstration creates two objects—`object1` of the `LowClass` class, and `object2` of the `HighClass` class. Calling the same `ShowString()` method for each object produces different results, which depend on the class interface implementations. Running the program displays this text on screen:

```
LowClass string:
abcdefghijklmnopqrstuvwxyz
HighClass string:
ABCDEFGHIJKLMNOPQRSTUVWXYZ
```

Class Interface Data

Any variables declared in a class interface are `final` by default and cannot be changed at runtime. This provides a handy way to create constant data. For example, to the `Protocols` class in `Protocols.java`, you can add this declaration:

```
public int d = 123;
```

You must initialize any such declarations as shown here—it is not possible for code to assign values to `final` declarations. Because d is a `public` data member, the value of d can be read by any user of the class, but as a `final` value, it cannot be changed, so `public` is usually the preferred access specifier.

Variables that are `final` are also `static`, and as such, they exist for all users of the class. If you insert the preceding declaration, the same integer variable is shared by the `LowClass` and `HighClass` implementations of the `Protocols` interface.

> **TIP**
>
> I've noticed that on several occasions, especially with multifile programs, the Visual J++ compiler reports "class format" problems and other strange errors. When this happened, on a hunch, I deleted all `.class` files from the directory and recompiled. This often worked, but may be due to the early versions of VJ that I used while writing this book. In any case, if you are certain the source files are correct, or if you receive unexplained compilation errors when compiling this book's CD-ROM examples, try deleting all `.class` files and compile again.

Class Access Rules

Class access rules are the kingpins of object-oriented programming, and before continuing with this book, it's essential that you understand them. So, I end this chapter with a review of `public`, `protected`, and `private` access rules, plus a clarification of the somewhat obscure subject of *friendly* access, which I briefly mentioned but did not explain in full.

Access Specifiers Revisited

As you know from this chapter, Java provides three access specifiers—`public`, `protected`, and `private`—which you may use in variable and method declarations. Classes may be `public`, but not `protected` or `private`. Each specifier affects access to its declared item in the following ways:

- A `public` declaration is available to all users of the class.
- A `protected` declaration is available only to the same class's methods, or to methods in subclasses extended from this one.
- A `private` declaration is available only to members of the same class.

Aside from memorizing these definitions, it's important you understand *why* you might choose one access specifier over another. In general, these rules will help you decide:

- Constructors are almost always `public` so that statements anywhere in the program can create objects of the class.

- Methods are usually `public` so that statements anywhere in the program can call them.

- Some methods might be `protected` to restrict their use to the class or a subclass of this class.

- It is rarely useful for a method to be `private`, but if you want only the declaring class to be able to call the method, this is the correct designation.

- Variables are often best declared `private` (accessible only in their declaring class) or `protected` (accessible in their class and any subclasses).

- Variables may be `public` to permit statements to access their values directly. However, a well-written class provides access methods to read and write `private` class instance variables.

Although it may seem inefficient to make data `private` and provide access methods for changing that data, this is an important technique in object-oriented programming. By privatizing data and providing methods that access it, you maintain a class's encapsulation, and you simplify future maintenance. For example, because statements outside of the class's methods cannot refer directly to a private instance variable, it is always safe to change that variable's data type without fear that you will affect other parts of the program. Good object-oriented programming *hides* data and *controls access* to it. Follow these rules now, and you will simplify your life later—even if the purpose of the rules might seem vague at this stage in your programming experience.

Classes may be declared `public`, but never `protected` or `private`. As with all `public` declarations, `public` classes are available to all users, but there is one complication with this designation that I haven't mentioned. If you declare a class like

```
public class AnyClass {
...
}
```

then that class *must* be written in a separate compilation unit (the fancy term for a source code text file) named the same as the class. The preceding declaration, for example, is not allowed in a program module with another class having a `main()` method. For casual use (in test programs, for instance), you may omit the `public` access specifier and declare the class as

```
class AnyClass {
...
}
```

This is an example of a friendly class, which brings me to the next subject.

Friendly Class Access

If you do not specify a `public`, `protected`, or `private` access specifier, a declaration is said to be *friendly*. All such declarations are available publicly throughout their compilation unit (source code file). For all other uses, the declarations are `private`. Listing 8.14, `AccessRules.java`, demonstrates friendly class access rules.

Listing 8.14. `AccessRules.java` (Demonstrates friendly class access rules).

```
class ImFriendly {
 int x, y;
 ImFriendly(int xx, int yy) {
  x = xx;
  y = yy;
 }
 void ShowValues() {
  System.out.println("x = " + x + ", y = " + y );
 }
}

class AccessRules {
 public static void main(String args[]) {
  ImFriendly object = new ImFriendly(10, 20);
  object.ShowValues();
  object.x = 30;
  object.y = 40;
  object.ShowValues();
 }
}
```

The sample program declares class `ImFriendly` with no access specifier. This makes the class friendly—accessible in the same compilation unit. If the class were in a separate file, it would require a `public` access specifier like this:

public class ImFriendly {...

This then requires other modules to import the class in order to make it available for use:

import ImFriendly;

As written, however, the sample `ImFriendly` class is available only in the demonstration module. Outside of this module, `ImFriendly` is private and cannot be made available with an `import` statement.

The data and code members of `ImFriendly` are also friendly because these do not use explicit access specifiers. As the main program demonstrates, statements may directly alter the values of the class's friendly instance variables with statements such as

object.x = 30;
object.y = 40;

Normally, to allow such direct access to class data, it would be declared `public`. However, because they exist in the same compilation unit as the use of that data, the instance variables are friendly. Outside of the module, the variables are strictly private.

In a module of multiple classes—a technique that becomes more important when you learn about packages in Part III—friendly declarations provide easy access to code and data within the same module, while restricting access outside of that compilation unit. This is an important technique that maintains encapsulation of data, but relaxes access within a module for simpler programming.

Throughout this book, you'll see numerous examples of friendly declarations, which are simply convenient for short examples that are self-contained in one module. In general, however, most declarations are best made explicitly `public`, `protected`, or `private` for one of the reasons already mentioned.

Summary

- Classes encapsulate data and code. Each object of a class contains distinct copies of the class's instance variables, but all objects of a class share the same methods.

- Access specifiers—`public`, `protected`, and `private`—control the availability of instance variables and methods.

- `private` members of a class are available only to that class's methods. `protected` members are available to that class's methods and methods in an extended class. `public` members are available to all class users.

- An abstract class provides a model for creating other classes. Any class with one or more abstract methods is an abstract class. To use an abstract class, you extend it as a subclass and implement its abstract methods.

- An interface class is a purely abstract class in which all methods are abstract by default. Interfaces are typically used to provide low-level protocols and services (such as system-dependent file I/O code), but are also useful in application programming for collecting methods that numerous other classes might use and implement. A class may implement one or more interface classes.

- If an access specifier is not designated, a declaration is friendly, meaning that it is accessible to all statements in the same compilation unit. Outside of the unit, friendly declarations are private.

Exercises

1. Create a class that automatically maintains a count of the number of objects that a program creates of the class.
2. Write a program that reads its own source code text and displays it on screen.

3. Create a class, Point, that can store an X,Y coordinate value. Use access specifiers to control access to the class's instance variables.

4. Extend the Integer wrapper class with a subclass of your own that adds a String label instance variable. (Hint: Don't spend too much time on this one—it's a "trick" question—but see if you can determine why.)

5. *Advanced.* Write a method that prints the name of the class of any object. (Hint: The answer requires you to do some additional research on your own into Java's class libraries.)

What's Next?

On several occasions, I've introduced and promised to expand upon the subject of exceptions. As you will learn in the next chapter, exception handling is the key to writing robust Java applications that can respond to any error or other exceptional condition.

9

CHAPTER

Exceptions

Exceptions are the key to writing robust Java code that elegantly handles all possible errors and other boundary conditions. As you will learn in this chapter, an *exception* is an object that is *thrown* to indicate an extreme event such as a file not found or an out-of-memory error. Programs *catch* exception objects so they can respond gracefully to unplanned events rather than crash and burn, possibly taking the user's system software—and a customer's good will—along for the ride.

In This Chapter

This chapter introduces the following fundamental topics about exception handling:

- Terminology
- Programming with `try`, `catch`, and `throw` blocks
- Using a `finally` statement
- Creating your own exception objects
- Class library exceptions

A Few Good Terms

Exceptions come with their own terminology and concepts. Following are some overviews that will help you to read and understand this chapter:

- An *exception* is just that—an *exceptional condition* that requires special handling. Exceptions are best used for a program's error handling, but they are not limited to that use. For example, some `RandomAccessFile` class methods throw an object of the `EOFException` class to indicate reaching the end of a file during a read operation.

- To create an exception, a statement *throws* an object that describes the nature of the exceptional condition. The object must be a subclass of the `Throwable` class or, preferably, of a descendent subclass such as `Exception` or `RuntimeException`.

- To handle an exception, a statement *catches* an exception object that another process *throws*. Any process may throw one or more exceptions to indicate various extreme conditions.

- Programs prepare to catch exceptions by *trying* one or more statements (including, but not limited to, calls to methods) that might throw exceptions. In general, to use exceptions, you simply *try* one or more methods and you *catch* any exceptions those methods *throw*.

Introducing Exceptions

The basic mechanism for handling exceptions is the *try block*. This is a brace-delimited block of one or more statements preceded with the keyword `try`. The following template shows the format of a try block:

```
try {
  // statements that might throw an exception
} catch(exceptionClass exObject) {
  // handle the exception
}
```

A try block is always followed by at least one catch block, which dictates the program's response to an exceptional condition. Inside the try block, the program calls methods or executes other statements that might throw one or more exception objects. The catch block lists these exception objects, and the code in that block is expected to take whatever evasive or other action is necessary to handle the reported problem.

> **TIP**
>
> An exception is a mechanism for reporting an extreme condition; it does not dictate a response to that condition. The actions taken in response to a specific exception are your job to program.

A single try block may catch multiple types of exceptions. For example, the following incomplete code fragment catches three types of exception objects:

```
try {
  // statements that might throw an exception
} catch (EOFException e) {
  // handle end-of-file exception
} catch (FileNotFoundException e) {
  // handle file-not-found exception
} catch (IOException e) {
  // handle all other I/O exceptions
}
```

The EOFException and FileNotFoundException classes are each subclasses of IOException. The preceding code tries one or more statements such as method calls that might throw these types of exceptions. After the try block, three catch blocks handle the first two specific types of I/O exceptions. The last catch block handles all other IOException class errors.

Handling All Exceptions

It's possible, but usually not wise, to write a catch block that handles all possible types of exception objects. For example, the following incomplete code fragment catches all exception objects of the Throwable class:

```
try {
  // Call method(s) which might throw an exception
} catch (Throwable e) {  // ???
  System.out.println(e.getMessage());
}
```

Because all exception objects must be of classes extended from Throwable, the program catches every possible exceptional condition. This includes, however, any exceptions that are better handled by the Java virtual machine—those that enable multithreaded processes to run

169

correctly, for example (more on this in Chapter 11, "Threads"). For this reason, the preceding technique, while technically acceptable, is not recommended for application programming.

Rather than catch `Throwable` objects, to handle most exceptions, you can catch `Exception` class objects, which are direct descendants of `Throwable` and are intended for application use. For example, the code

```
try {
 // Call method(s) which might throw an exception
} catch (Exception e) {
 System.out.println(e.getMessage());
}
```

catches most types of exceptions, but permits other more sensitive types of the `Throwable` and `Error` classes (another `Throwable` subclass) to pass on to the Java virtual machine for proper handling.

In most cases, however, rather than attempt to catch all exceptions (except, perhaps, in small test programs), it is almost always best to catch objects of specific classes. Each method in the Java class library specifies exactly what kinds of exceptions it might throw. Your code needs to respond to those and only those types of specific exceptions. Likewise, your own code should specify the exceptions it might throw so that users of that code can catch all possible boundary conditions and errors. Adding this kind of specific exception handling to your programs *as you write the code* is the best way to create robust programs that respond sensibly to every conceivable problem.

> **NOTE**
>
> The Java compiler is able to detect that your code, or the virtual machine interpreter, handles exceptions that might be thrown. You will receive errors from the compiler if it determines that a possible exception is not handled. For example, if you call a method that might throw a specific kind of exception, the compiler will complain, "Exception X not caught or declared by Y," where X is the exception class name and Y is your method that calls the exception-throwing method. When you see this error, you can insert the method call in a `try` block and provide a `catch` block that handles the reported exception. Alternatively, you can declare your own method as one that throws an exception of this type. This pushes, but does not eliminate, responsibility for handling the exception onto the caller of your method.

Using Exceptions

When a statement in a `try` block causes an exception to be thrown, the rest of the statements in that `try` block do not execute. Instead, the program jumps immediately to a `catch` block statement that either matches the declared exception class exactly or matches a superclass of the thrown exception object. If, in the following code, `method1()` throws an exception

```
try {
 method1();  // always executes
 method2();  // does not execute if m1 throws exception
 method3();  // does not execute if m1 or m2 throw an exception
} catch (Exception e) {
 System.out.println(e.getMessage());
}
```

then `method2()` and `method3()` are not called, and the program immediately jumps to the `catch` block statement, which in this example, calls the `Exception` class `getMessage()` method and (we hope) prints an intelligent message about what happened. Similarly, `method3()` does not execute if `method1()` or `method2()` throws an exception. If no exceptions are thrown, the `catch` block statement does not execute.

In addition to these rules, if the `try` block ends abnormally—that is, if an associated `catch` block does not handle the exception object—then the method in which this `try` block appears immediately returns to its caller. Any return value is uninitialized. In that event, the exception stays alive, and it must eventually be handled. If the `try` block ends normally—that is, if no exceptions occur or if any are handled by a `catch` statement—then the program continues running after the last `catch` block associated with this `try`. For example, if the preceding code is in method `main()`, and if `method2()` in the preceding example throws an object of the `Error` class, `main()` returns immediately to its caller—the Java virtual machine—which is expected to handle the problem.

It is also possible for a `catch` block to handle an exception, and then *rethrow* the object to pass the problem upward in the chain of method calls that led to a problem. Rethrowing an exception is an important technique that allows a program to indicate a problem but pass responsibility for handling that problem to a higher authority. For example, the hypothetical fragment

```
try {
 // call method(s) which might throw an exception
} catch (Exception e) {
 System.out.println("Trouble in paradise!");
 throw e;  // Rethrow the exception
}
```

catches an `Exception` object that might be thrown in the preceding `try` block. After displaying a message, the `catch` block rethrows the same exception to pass it upward in the chain of method calls that led to this code's execution.

Eventually, an exception object must be handled, either by your code, by code in Java's class library, or by the virtual runtime machine. There is actually no such thing as an unhandled exception, but if your code does not handle a thrown exception object, the end result might be the surprise ending of your application.

Programming with Exceptions

In addition to catching exceptions thrown by methods in Java's class library, you can also create your own exception classes and objects. It's a good idea to do this as you develop your programs—don't put off error-handling until the last moment! It's also good to use exception handling for *all* errors and exceptional conditions rather than attempt to create your own error protocols such as returning special values from functions to indicate error conditions. Exception handling has been widely accepted in the C++, Pascal, and Java communities as the best all-around system for writing robust code that responds to all possible boundary conditions. Don't hesitate to weave exception handling code into the fabric of your applications from the very start—you will be glad you did!

To demonstrate how to create your own exception classes and objects, Listing 9.1, ExceptDemo.java, implements a power() method that can raise any double value to any double exponent value. Although the Math class already provides a similar method, pow(), it does not generate exceptions for illegal values such as a zero base and negative exponent, or a negative base and fractional exponent (trying to raise -4, for example, by a power of 1.5). The sample program adds exception handling to a power() function that calls Math.pow() to do most of the hard work of the calculation.

Listing 9.1. ExceptDemo.java (Demonstrates user exceptions).

```java
class NewMathException extends Exception {
 // Constructor
 public NewMathException(double b, double e) {
  super("Domain error: base = " + b + " exp = " + e);
 }
}

final class NewMath {
 // Prevent instantiation of class
 private NewMath() { }
 // Return b raised to the power of e
 public static double power(double b, double e)
 throws NewMathException {
  NewMathException error = new NewMathException(b, e);
  if (b > 0.0) return Math.pow(b, e);
  if (b < 0.0) {
   Double d = new Double(e);
   double ipart = d.intValue();
   double fpart = e - ipart;
   if (fpart == 0) {
    if ((ipart % 2) != 0)  // i.e. ipart is odd
     return -Math.pow(-b, e);
    else
     return Math.pow(-b, e);
   } else
    throw error;
  } else {
   if (e == 0.0) return 1.0;
   if (e < 1.0) throw error;
   return 0.0;
  }
 }
}

class ExceptDemo {
 public static void main(String args[]) {
  if (args.length < 2) {
   System.out.println("Specify value and exponent");
```

```
       System.out.println("ex. jview exceptdemo -4 1.5");
     } else try {
       double base = new Double(args[0]).doubleValue();
       double exponent = new Double(args[1]).doubleValue();
       double result = NewMath.power(base, exponent);
       System.out.println("Result = " + result);
     } catch (NewMathException e) {
       System.out.println(e.getMessage());
     }
   }
}
```

The sample listing begins with a class declaration that creates a new exception type, extended from Java's Exception class. When creating your own exceptions, you'll often want to declare a similar class to report special conditions and their associated values. For instance, in this case, we want to report not only that an error occurred, but also what values caused a problem—specific actions that the Exception class doesn't do on its own. To do that, I extend that class with the declaration

```
class NewMathException extends Exception {
```

and then declare in the NewMathException class a constructor that takes as arguments two double values:

```
public NewMathException(double b, double e) {
```

To use the new exception class, the program's NewMath class declares the power() method and informs the world that this method might throw an object of the NewMathException type:

```
public static double power(double b, double e)
  throws NewMathException {
```

Because power() states that it might throw a NewMathException object, any statements that call power() must be in a try block, or they must themselves exist in a method that also throws NewMathException. Because the method explicitly declares an exception class, attempts to execute statements such as

```
double x = NewMath.power(1.2, 1.3);  // ???
```

cause the compiler to complain that the NewMathException is neither declared nor caught in the method that executed the preceding statement. The method could also declare this same exception, and in this way, pass any thrown object back up the method-call chain that led to the exception. For example, the method declaration

```
public void f() throws NewMathException {
  double x = NewMath.power(1.2, 1.3);
  ...
}
```

makes it okay to call NewMath.power() without using a try block because f() explicitly states that it might throw a NewMathException object. If power() throws an exception, f() immediately returns to its caller, which now has the responsibility for handling the exception. That code might be written like this:

```
try {
 f();
} catch (NewMathException e) {
 // handle exception
}
```

A method may state that it throws more than one type of exception class object. Separate multiple class names with commas after the `throws` keyword. For example, this declaration of a method named `test()` states that it might throw one of the three listed types of exceptions:

```
public void test()
 throws ArrayIndexOutOfBoundsException,
        NullPointerException,
        IllegalArgumentException {
...
}
```

Try always to declare methods this way, because it helps the compiler ensure that exceptions are properly handled.

Two important points to remember about `try` blocks are

- If any statement in the `try` block throws an exception, no other statements in that block are executed.

- If any statement in the `try` block throws an exception and that exception is not caught, the method that executed the `try` block immediately returns to its caller.

The second point might cause a method to skip critical code that must execute regardless of whether an exception is detected. The next section explains how to write this code using a `finally` block.

finally Block

As I just mentioned, if a `try` block detects an exception and that exception is not handled, the method that executed the `try` block immediately returns. Technically speaking, this happens because the `try` block ends abnormally, which causes the block that executes the `try` also to end. To deal with situations that require code to execute regardless of whether an exception is thrown or caught, insert a *finally block* after the try and any `catch` statements.

> **NOTE**
>
> The example code in Visual J++'s online help, section 14.18.2 (Execution of `try-catch-finally`), incorrectly suggests that a `finally` block's purpose is to catch unhandled exceptions. As explained in this chapter, only a `catch` block can perform this service by specifying an argument of type `Exception` or `Throwable`. A `finally` block's purpose is not to catch exceptions, but to guarantee that critical code is executed regardless of whether an exception is thrown and detected in a preceding try block.

Listing 9.2, FinallyDemo.java, demonstrates the purpose and effect of a finally block following a try block. The sample program tests three situations: throwing no exceptions, throwing an exception of a predefined Java class, and throwing an object of a class defined in the program itself. Running the program shows what you can expect from a finally block, and also shows what happens to any unhandled exceptions.

Listing 9.2. FinallyDemo.java (Demonstrates try-catch-finally statements).

```
// Exception class
class ThrowMe extends Exception {
 ThrowMe() { }
 ThrowMe(String s) {
  super(s);
 }
}

class FinallyDemo {
 // Test method -- pass 0, 1, or 2 for different exceptions
 static void testMethod(int n) throws ThrowMe {
  switch (n) {
  case 1:
   throw new NullPointerException();
  case 2:
   throw new ThrowMe("To the wolves");
  default:
   return;
  }
 }
 // Main program
 public static void main(String args[]) {
  int argument = 0;
  if (args.length > 0)
   argument = Integer.parseInt(args[0]);
  try {
   testMethod(argument);
  } catch (ThrowMe e) {
   System.out.println("ThrowMe: " + e.getMessage());
  } catch (Exception e) {
   System.out.println("Exception: " + e.getMessage());
  } finally {
   System.out.println("Finally statement");
  }
  System.out.println("Statement after try block");
 }
}
```

After compiling the program, run it three times by typing the following commands:

```
jview finallydemo
jview finallydemo 1
jview finallydemo 2
```

175

The first command shows what happens when no exceptions are thrown. On screen, the text

```
Finally statement
Statement after try block
```

shows that, in the absence of any exceptions, the main() method's finally block executes as does the statement following the try block. This last statement is significant because its execution proves that the preceding try block ended normally. Because of this, the try block did *not* cause main() to return prematurely.

The second test, which causes testMethod() to throw a NullPointerException object (a system error that is normally reported when a program attempts to use a null object, but is used here merely for demonstration), displays these results:

```
Exception: null
Finally statement
Statement after try block
```

The first line indicates that the sample program's catch statement handles the exception, but even so, the finally block still executes as does the statement after the try block. Again, this last statement executes because the try block handled the exception. Because the try ended normally, it did not cause an early return from main().

Similar results occur from the third and final experiment, which displays the text

```
ThrowMe: To the wolves
Finally statement
Statement after try block
```

The first line shows that the program's own ThrowMe class object is caught and handled. Again, because the exception was handled, the try block ended normally and did not cause main() to end prematurely. Thus, the Statement after try block executed normally.

As you can see, in each case, whether or not an exception was thrown, the finally block was executed. This is the purpose of finally—to execute critical code that the program must run regardless of any exceptions.

A modified test shows what happens if the application allows a so-called unhandled exception to remain uncaught. Locate these statements in the listing:

```
} catch (Exception e) {
 System.out.println("Exception: " + e.getMessage());
```

Type // in front of the two lines to turn them into comments. Compile the program and run it using the same three test commands from before. The first and third tests produce the same results. The second test, however, now fails to handle the NullPointerException. Consequently, the program displays this on screen:

```
Finally statement
ERROR: java.lang.NullPointerException
```

Because main() no longer handles Exception, the *unhandled exception* causes three important events to occur:

1. The exception causes the try block to end abnormally.

2. Because try ends abnormally, it exits the current method immediately. In this example, this causes main() to return prematurely without executing the Statement after try block.

3. Because main() is at the outermost level of method calls in the program, the exception is passed to the Java virtual machine, which reports the error and terminates the program.

In any event, despite the program not catching all exceptions, and despite the try block ending abnormally, the finally block still executes. This hammers home the point I made earlier—that catching Exception in main() is the correct way to trap most types of exceptions that would otherwise prematurely end the program. Use a finally block to execute critical code regardless of any exceptions, whether handled or not.

> **TIP**
>
> A finally block's statements also run even if the associated try block executes a return, break, continue, or throw statement. You can really trust a finally block to run regardless of what occurs in its try block.

Nested try Blocks

You may nest try blocks inside each other, which might simplify some kinds of error handling. This technique might be necessary to respond to an exception on more than one level; an inner try block, for example, may handle a specific kind of error that is additionally handled in a more general way in an outer try block. Listing 9.3, NestedTry.java, demonstrates how to program nested try blocks that each respond to the same exception object in different ways.

Listing 9.3. NestedTry.java. (Demonstrates nested try blocks).

```
class NestedTry {
 public static void test() {
  throw new NullPointerException();
 }
 public static void main(String args[]) {
  try {
   try {
    test();
   } catch (NullPointerException e) {
```

continues

Listing 9.3. continued

```
    System.out.println("Inner: " + e.getMessage());
    throw e;
    }
  } catch (Exception e) {
   System.out.println("Outer: " + e.getMessage());
   }
  }
}
```

The sample program's `main()` method calls a `test()` method from within a nested `try` block. That method throws a `NullPointerException` object (again, I'm using this class merely for demonstration purposes), which the inner `try` block catches with an argument of that class type.

So that the outer `try` block can also respond to this exception, the inner block's `catch` statement rethrows the same exception using the statement

```
throw e;
```

This keeps the exception alive, and gives the outer `try` block the opportunity to catch the same exception, using the standard technique:

```
} catch (Exception e) { ...
```

One practical use for nested `try` blocks is to abort a program in an extreme situation—a critical file that's missing, for example—but still give the user as much information about the problem as possible. Rather than relying on the Java interpreter to report the error, an inner `try` block in your code might display the name of the missing file, and the outer block might inform the user that the program is ending due to this error and give suggestions about how to repair the damage—reinstalling the software, for example, or downloading the correct file.

Tracing the Stack

Properly understanding why an exception occurred often requires knowing the order in which methods were called that led to the exception being thrown. A useful method in the `Exception` class can print this information for you. It's particularly effective as a debugging device, but is valuable also for application error-reporting.

Listing 9.4, `StackTrace.java`, shows how to display the method calls that led to an exception. This technique is especially good for debugging unhandled exceptions that remain alive in method `main()`.

Listing 9.4. `StackTrace.java` (Demonstrates `Exception` class stack tracing).

```
class StackTrace {
 // Cause an exception to be thrown
 public static void test() {
  int intArray[] = new int[3];  // Create array
  intArray[4] = 0;  // Use out-of-bounds array index
```

```
  }
  // Main program--catch the thrown exception
  public static void main(String args[]) {
   try {
    test();
   } catch (Exception e) {
    System.out.println("Exception: " + e.getMessage());
    e.printStackTrace();
   }
  }
}
```

The sample program calls a test() method in a try block. The method creates an integer array large enough to hold three values, then purposely attempts to assign a value using an index of 4. This causes the method to end with an ArrayIndexOutOfBoundsException exception (a mouthful of a class name to be sure) when the program executes this faulty statement:

```
intArray[4] = 0;  // ???
```

The main() method handles the exception in a catch statement that uses an Exception argument (it could instead specify the specific type of exception). After displaying this exception object's message by calling its getMessage() method, the program calls another method to print a trace of the method-call stack:

```
e.printStackTrace();
```

Running the program displays

```
Exception: null
java.lang.ArrayIndexOutOfBoundsException
        at StackTrace.test
        at StackTrace.main
```

The first line is printed by the call to println() in the catch statement. The next line tells you the name of the exception subclass. (Notice that this subclass information is obtainable even though the statement catches an Exception superclass object.) The final two lines of output trace the method calls in reverse order that led to the exception. From this information, you know that main() called test(), which threw the exception. These facts are of great value in finding where in the source code an exception occurred, and by using stack traces, you might be able to weed out numerous logical errors in your code.

Class Library Exceptions

Methods in Java's class library use exceptions extensively, and any program that uses the class library must also respond to the conditions that these exceptions indicate. As you read through the class library documentation (and also the information on specific classes in Part III of this book), you will discover notes that method so-and-so throws an exception of class such-and-such. To provide error handling, in most cases, you can simply call the method from within a try block, followed by one or more catch statements that handle the listed exception classes.

This plan gives you a good start to writing robust applications, but merely catching exceptions is not enough to respond sensibly to all possible error conditions. To use exceptions wisely, you also need to understand the purpose and meaning of Java's many different kinds of exception classes.

In this section, I examine the hierarchy of Java's exception classes, and I describe their categories and purposes. Use this section as a guide to writing your own exception handling code, and also to become familiar with the types of exceptions to which your programs might respond.

Exception Class Hierarchy

All exception classes extend from `Throwable`, a class in the `java.lang` package. Objects of this class and all its extensions contain two items:

- A string that describes the exceptional condition
- A snapshot of the execution stack, which as I've explained, you can use to print a trace of method calls that led to a problem

In this and subsequent sections of this chapter I'll discuss some of `Throwable`'s subclasses used throughout Java's class library. Rather than make this a complete reference to exception classes, however, I'll describe only the more significant classes used in the library. From this information, you can easily deduce how to use other exception subclasses. Also see the complete hierarchy chart in the Visual J++ online help.

Throwable Subclasses

Extensions of `Throwable` might add additional members or define an exception object's contents more specifically. The message in a `FileNotFoundException` object, for example, specifies the name of a file that could not be located. Sometimes, a subclass adds nothing new to its inherited members, but its class name makes a problem clear—the purpose of the `OutOfMemoryError` class needs no further explaining, for example. You may also extend the `Exception` class (a direct descendent of `Throwable`) and add any fields you want.

> **TIP**
>
> When declaring your own exception classes, its best to base them on `Exception` rather than `Throwable`, which is generally reserved for serious system problems and other critical events.

Figure 9.1 shows `Throwable`'s subclasses, which divide Java exception classes into two main categories.

Figure 9.1.
Throwable subclasses.

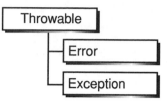

Error

An `Error` class exception and its subclasses signal a highly abnormal event that is unlikely to occur during a program's normal execution. Applications usually do not catch errors that descend from the `Error` class (but see `ThreadDeath` in the next section for an "exception" to this rule). If you have excellent reasons for trapping an `Error` class exception, you may certainly do so, but in general, these types of errors are best left to the Java virtual machine for resolution.

Exception

An `Exception` class exception and its subclasses signal a more common type of problem such as an array index out of bounds or an illegal argument. Applications are more likely to catch and deal with these types of exception objects, and the Java class library is programmed to throw them for various purposes. Your own exception subclasses are usually best extended from the `Exception` class or from one of its subclasses. For example, from Listing 9.1 in this chapter, the declaration

```
class NewMathException extends Exception {
 // Constructor
 public NewMathException(double b, double e) {
  super("Domain error: base = " + b + " exp = " + e);
 }
}
```

creates a new class, `NewMathException`, as a subclass of `Exception`. To throw an exception object of this class, a program might execute the statement

```
throw new NewMathException(d, e);
```

For informal uses, you can create `Exception` objects directly, perhaps to specify an error message as in this statement:

```
throw new Exception("Trouble in Paradise!");
```

Error Subclasses

As I mentioned, `Error` class exceptions tend to indicate highly abnormal conditions to which an application program normally does not respond. The Java virtual machine handles all exceptions of the `Error` subclass. Figure 9.2 shows some of `Error`'s main subclasses.

Figure 9.2.

Error subclasses (partial).

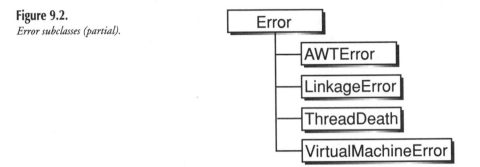

AWTError

An error of this class indicates a problem with the AWT (Another Window Toolkit) package. Applications will probably never receive a serious error of this type, which probably indicates an internal problem with the package's programming. Applications instead more commonly respond to `AWTException` class errors or other extensions of the `Exception` class as dictated in AWT's documentation.

LinkageError

Subclasses of the `LinkageError` class indicate a problem with a class dependency, usually caused when compiling a class that depends on another and that other class has since changed in declaration. Because this kind of error is caught at compile time, there is never any need for applications to catch objects of this type. Subclasses of `LinkageError` that you might want to read about in the Visual J++ online help include `ClassCircularityError`, `NoSuchFieldError`, `NoSuchMethodError`, and others (see the full hierarchy chart online).

ThreadDeath

The `ThreadDeath` exception class is thrown when a thread in a multithreaded application is about to die. An application may catch an exception of this type to clean up some other objects, for example, before the thread breathes its last. If you do this, however, be sure to rethrow the exception so that the virtual machine receives it and, consequently, the thread is humanely put out of its misery. Always `catch` this exception object using code such as

```
try {
 // statements that might throw exception
} catch (ThreadDeath e) {
 // clean up as needed
```

```
 throw e;   // rethrow the exception
}
```

The reason that `ThreadDeath` is a subclass of `Error` and not of `Exception` is because, as demonstrated in many of this chapter's sample programs, applications typically catch all instances of `Exception` in `main()`. If `ThreadDeath` were an `Exception` subclass—which would technically make more sense because this is really an application-oriented exception class—catching all `Exception` objects would complicate multithreaded programming and make it more difficult for individual threads to end.

VirtualMachineError

An error of type `VirtualMachineError` should never occur. It is thrown if the Java virtual machine detects an internal problem, or if the interpreter runs out of critical resources. Three subclasses of `VirtualMachineError` indicate self-descriptive problems—`InternalError`, `OutOfMemoryError`, and `StackOverflowError`. A fourth subclass—`UnknownError`—indicates an extremely serious problem with the virtual machine and, if ever received, would be cause for alarm about the integrity of the interpreter and installation.

Exception Subclasses

Applications are much more likely to catch and respond to subclasses of `Exception`, which is a direct descendent of the `Throwable` class. Figure 9.3 shows the main subclasses of `Exception` to which applications are likely to respond. See the Visual J++ online help and hierarchy diagram for a complete list of `Exception` subclasses.

Figure 9.3.
Exception subclasses (partial).

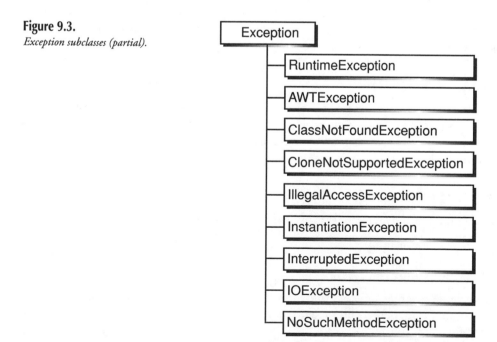

Exception
- RuntimeException
- AWTException
- ClassNotFoundException
- CloneNotSupportedException
- IllegalAccessException
- InstantiationException
- InterruptedException
- IOException
- NoSuchMethodException

RuntimeException

A RuntimeException object is probably the most common of all Exception subclasses. This class has numerous subclasses of its own, which are discussed in the next section. An application might respond to all such conditions by catching a RuntimeException object, but is more likely to respond to a specific subclass—such as ArrayIndexOutOfBoundsException, for example.

AWTException

An AWTException object indicates a problem with a use of the AWT package, but is less serious than AWTError. Applications can respond to an exception of this type, and your code might throw AWTException objects, but a search of the AWT source files strangely indicates that it is never thrown by methods in the AWT package itself.

ClassNotFoundException

Because Java stores classes in .ZIP archive format and also as individual .class files, it's possible that an application might discover at runtime that it doesn't have all of its needed classes. Usually, this indicates a faulty software installation—or perhaps, an incomplete download or compilation. The application might tell the user to reinstall the software and end the program if one of these errors is detected.

CloneNotSupportedException

An object of the CloneNotSupportedException class is thrown if a user attempts to clone an object of a class, and that class does not support cloning. If your class does not support cloned objects, you might indicate to users that receipt of this exception is not an error, but is rather a warning that they are attempting to use your class inappropriately.

IllegalAccessException

Receipt of an IllegalAccessException object indicates that a particular method could not be found. This might indicate a version problem in a dependent class, which compiled correctly but fails to run when it attempts to call a certain method. The similar IllegalAccessError class is more likely to be detected at compile time, and does not need to be caught by applications.

InstantiationException

An object of the InstantiationException class is thrown if an application attempts to instantiate an abstract class or interface.

InterruptedException

An InterruptedException object is thrown when one thread in a multithreaded application attempts to interrupt another thread. See Chapter 11 for more information about programming with threads.

IOException

The IOException class has numerous subclasses that indicate various I/O conditions, not all of which are errors. These subclasses are

- EOFException: Thrown when a file-read operation reaches the end of the file. This does not usually indicate a problem, but rather that a read-loop should end after reading the final data in the file.

- FileNotFoundException: Thrown when an attempt to open a file fails because the file cannot be found. This usually takes place on the creation of a file object—when a program creates a RandomAccessFile object, for example.

- InterruptedIOException: Thrown when an input or output operation is interrupted, which might occur due to a multithreaded process. The public instance variable, bytesTransferred, of type int indicates how many bytes were input or output before the interruption occurred. It might be possible to use this information to continue an interrupted I/O operation.

- MalformedURLException: Thrown if a URL (Uniform Resource Locator) is badly formed, either because of a parsing error (a typo, for example), or because a legal protocol could not be found. See also the java.net.URL class.

- ProtocolException: Thrown if an error in a protocol is detected (usually a TCP/IP error of some sort).

- SocketException: When using sockets, this error is thrown to indicate a problem of a general nature. See also the SocketInputStream and SocketOutputStream classes for more specific types of socket exceptions.

- UnknownHostException: Thrown if the IP address of a host cannot be determined.

- UnknownServiceException: Thrown in response to one of two unknown service conditions: a problem with the return of a URL connection, or an attempt to write to a read-only connection.

- UTFDataFormatException: Thrown to indicate that a malformed UTF-8 string appears in an input data stream or a class that implements the java.io.DataInput or java.io.DataOutput interfaces. See, for example, the writeUTF() method in the DataOutput interface, which might throw an exception of this type.

NoSuchMethodException

This class is included for backward compatibility only, and it is obsolete. Instead, Java throws an object of the NoSuchMethodError class for methods called but not found.

RuntimeException Subclasses

The RuntimeException class, a subclass of the Exception class, sports numerous subclasses that indicate a variety of conditions. Most applications will commonly catch one or more of these types of exceptions, and your code can also throw them to indicate problems such as an array index out of bounds or an illegal argument value passed to a method. Figure 9.4 lists the most significant subclasses of the RuntimeException class.

Figure 9.4.
RuntimeException subclasses (partial).

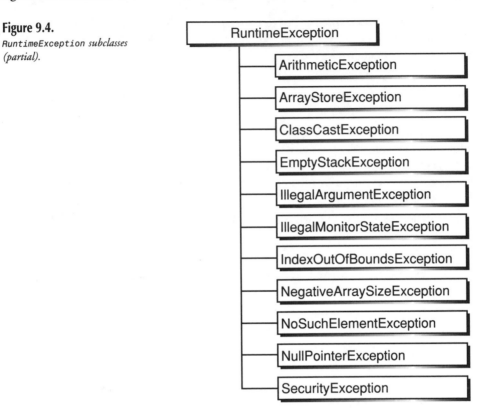

ArithmeticException

ArrayStoreException

ClassCastException

EmptyStackException

IllegalArgumentException

IllegalMonitorStateException

IndexOutOfBoundsException

NegativeArraySizeException

NoSuchElementException

NullPointerException

SecurityException

ArithmeticException

Catch ArithmeticException objects to trap errors in mathematical expressions such as an attempt to divide by zero.

ArrayStoreException

An object of type ArrayStoreException is thrown if a statement attempts to store the wrong type of object in an array. (See the next chapter for more information on using arrays.)

ClassCastException

Java throws an object of ClassCastException if a statement attempts to subclass an object to an inappropriate class. For example, an attempt to subclass an Integer object n with an expression such as (String)n throws an exception of this type.

EmptyStackException

The Stack class throws this exception to indicate that the stack is empty—on attempting to pop a value from an empty stack, for example. See the next chapter for more information on the Stack class.

IllegalArgumentException

Thrown by various methods to indicate that an argument value is illegal. Your methods can also throw exceptions of this type. Two further subclasses of this class are IllegalThreadStateException and NumberFormatException.

IllegalMonitorStateException

The IllegalMonitorStateException class does *not* indicate a problem with your CRT, but rather that a thread has attempted to wait on an unowned object's *monitor*—a term and technique that applies to multithreaded applications.

IndexOutOfBoundsException

You will probably catch and throw one of two subclasses of IndexOutOfBoundsException rather than use objects of this class directly. The two subclasses are ArrayIndexOutOfBoundsException and StringIndexOutOfBoundsException, and they are self descriptive.

NegativeArraySizeException

If a statement attempts to construct an array using a negative size argument (which might happen when using a variable as the array's size), Java throws an object of the NegativeArraySizeException class. Although this might seem a very strange error to trap, because arrays are sized at runtime, this is an important type of object to catch in programs that construct arrays. See the next chapter for more information about creating and using arrays.

NoSuchElementException

An object of the NoSuchElementException class is thrown when using the Enumeration class to indicate that there are no more elements in the enumeration. This class is an example of an exception that is not necessarily an error, but rather a condition that requires a special response or can be used to end a loop that accesses an unknown number of Enumeration elements.

NullPointerException

Java throws an object of the NullPointerException class to indicate that a statement has attempted to use an uninitialized object. Such an object, for example, might be declared but not constructed using the new operator.

SecurityException

The `java.lang.SecurityManager` class throws an exception of type `SecurityException` to indicate a security violation or a potential security-related problem. An application's security policy, for instance, might require verification before attempting a critical operation. For example, the `checkPackageAccess()` method in the `SecurityManager` class throws a `SecurityAccess` exception if the user does not have access to the package. By implementing a security policy, it's possible to safely restrict the use of a package or class—after a trial period has expired, for example, in a shareware collection of programming tools.

Summary

- An *exception* is an exceptional condition that requires special handling. Exceptions are normally used for reporting errors, but they are not restricted to that use. For example, the `EOFException` class is thrown when a program reads past the end of a file.

- To add exception handling to your code, call methods and execute statements in a `try` block. Any exceptions thrown by those methods or statements are handled in one or more `catch` blocks.

- If an exception is not handled by a `catch` block, the `try` block ends abnormally causing the method in which it exists to immediately return to its caller.

- To ensure that critical code is executed, insert it in a `finally` block. A `finally` block's statements are always executed, regardless of whether an exception is thrown in a `try` block.

- All exception classes are subclasses of `Throwable`. Application exceptions are normally subclasses of the `Exception` subclass (and further subclasses). System errors are typically of the `Error` subclass (and further subclasses). When declaring your own exception classes, it is usually best to base them on `Exception` or one of its subclasses.

- To catch most types of exceptions, and thus prevent the program from ending prematurely, use a `catch` statement in `main()` that declares an `Exception e` argument. Do not catch all `Throwable` exceptions unless you have excellent reasons for doing so and are prepared to handle system tasks such as ending threads in multithreaded applications. This is not generally recommended for most applications.

- This chapter provides overviews of most exception classes declared and thrown in the Java class library. When writing your applications, add exception handlers (`catch` statements) for all exception classes documented by specific methods—don't wait until you finish your program to program its error handling! The best way to ensure robust applications is to become familiar with Java's exception classes as listed near the end of this chapter.

Exercises

1. Write a program that uses exceptions to detect whether a user-supplied file exists.
2. Write a test program that safely catches all possible exceptions and prints a stack trace if a problem develops.
3. Write a program with a method that uses the `NullPointerException` class to indicate that a class object parameter is uninitialized.
4. Write a program that, if any exception is detected, displays an error message and prompts the user whether to continue execution.

What's Next?

Many, if not most, applications need versatile data storage mechanisms, of which Java offers several intriguing choices, including arrays and other container classes examined in the next chapter.

10

Arrays and Other Containers

Arrays are probably the most common multiple-item data storage containers—nearly all computer languages have them. Technically speaking, an array is merely a sequence of data elements stored one after the other in memory. What makes arrays interesting is not their structure, but the way that a language accesses the array's elements.

Java arrays are versatile and easier to use than in many languages. In this chapter, I explain how to declare and construct arrays, and also how to use other container classes such as `Hashtable`, `Properties`, `Vector`, and `Stack` for special data storage and retrieval needs.

In This Chapter

This chapter introduces the following techniques for programming with arrays and other containers:

- How to declare and construct arrays
- Using multidimensional arrays
- Initializing array elements
- Copying arrays and moving array elements
- Programming with array exceptions
- How to use the `Cloneable` and `Enumeration` interfaces
- Programming with Java's container classes

Arrays

The safety and versatility of arrays differ among various computer languages. Some languages such as C and Pascal require you to define an array's size when you write the program—a major inconvenience when an array's capacity needs to be determined at runtime. Consequently, C and Pascal programmers tend to rely on tricks that fool the compiler into allocating a variable amount of memory to arrays at runtime, but this often leads to hard to find bugs.

Various programming languages differ also in the level of safety for array-handling techniques. In C, for example, accessing an array element beyond the memory allocated to the array does not necessarily produce an error, but the program might not work correctly. In the worst case, an out-of-range array index—or *boundary error*—might cause a general protection fault and halt the program, especially when running under a multitasking operating system that places arrays in protected memory.

In Java, arrays are both safe and versatile. Array indexes are checked, and exceptions are thrown for out-of-range boundary errors. Arrays are declared in the program code, but are created at runtime; their sizes are therefore variable and can be determined by a program calculation. In addition, unlike in other object-oriented languages such as C++, the initialization rules for array elements are strictly defined and easy to use.

Furthermore, an array is a Java type that behaves as a class object and, as such, provides elements such as an instance variable `length` that equals the number of elements the array holds. Unlike true classes, however, arrays cannot be extended—there is no `Array` class per se.

Introduction to Java Arrays

An array is literally a *composite type,* which can be made of zero or more elements of another type. If that type is another array, the array is *multidimensional.* In a Java program, an *array variable* is a reference to an element of the array's type. Use empty brackets to inform the compiler that you intend to use an identifier as a typed array. For example, to declare an array of integers, you can use a statement such as

```
int intArray[];  // Declare integer array reference
```

This declaration states only that `intArray` is capable of referring to an array of multiple integer values. It does not create an array, nor does it reserve any memory for array elements. Before using the array, a program statement must allocate memory for the array. This is always done at runtime. For example, given the preceding declaration, at runtime, the statement

```
intArray = new int[10];
```

creates an array of 10 integer values in memory and sets the array variable `intArray` to refer to that array's first value. Each element of the array is initialized according to the specific type's default value—in this case, all elements are set to zero. (An array of class objects initially holds all `null` references.) To refer to a specific array element, follow the array variable with square brackets containing an index value. For example, this statement prints the contents of the preceding array:

```
for (int i = 0; i < 10; i++)
 System.out.println(intArray[i]);
```

Assign a value to a specific array element using a statement such as

```
intArray[4] = 123;
```

That assigns the value `123` to the fifth array element. Because the first index value is zero, the index `4` references the fifth element in the array.

You may also declare and construct an array in one easy motion using a single statement such as

```
int intArray[] = new int[10];
```

This actually performs two actions—declaring `intArray` to the compiler and, at runtime, constructing an array of 10 integer values referred to by `intArray`.

The array size may be variable. For example, the fragment

```
int n;
// ... code that sets n to some positive value
int intArray[] = new int[n];
```

declares and constructs intArray using the value of integer n, presumably set to a positive value by other code not shown here. The value of n could be calculated or even entered by the user. Java arrays are completely dynamic, and their sizes are determined at runtime.

In any case, after constructing the array, the program cannot change its size. A statement can, however, create another array and assign it to the array reference using a statement such as

```
intArray = new int[250];  // Create another array
```

Java's memory garbage collector automatically dumps the old array's elements in the trash can, making its memory available, if necessary, for other variables.

Because arrays are constructed at runtime, it's usually best to use the length field—available with all arrays—in loops and other statements that use array index values. For example, this statement sets intArray's values equal to their associated indexes:

```
for (int i = 0; i < intArray.length; i++)
 intArray[i] = i;
```

The expression intArray.length equals the number of array elements, and therefore the loop works correctly for all arrays regardless of size. The maximum index value allowed is always one less than the value of length.

Using an array index value outside of the range 0 ... length - 1 throws an ArrayIndexOutOfBoundsException object. To catch this error—and prevent the program from ending prematurely—enclose array statements in a try block as follows:

```
int intArray[] = new int[10];
try {
 intArray[12] = 123;  // ???
} catch (ArrayIndexOutOfBoundsException e) {
   System.out.println("Bad array index");
}
```

Because intArray was defined to hold 10 elements, the questionable statement attempts to assign 123 to a nonexistent array element. This throws the exception, which the catch block nabs before it can halt the program. There is no way to cheat: Java does not use pointers, and unlike with other languages, you cannot fool the compiler into accessing elements beyond the defined size of the array. (I'll cover this and other exceptions in more detail a bit later.)

When declaring arrays, you may place the empty brackets either after the array element data type or after the array variable identifier. For example, the declaration

```
int intArray[];
```

is syntactically identical to

```
int[] intArray;
```

Both statements declare intArray as a reference to an array of integer values; neither allocates any memory or actually constructs the array, which as I've explained, you must do using the new operator. The alternate declaration style is convenient for declaring multiple arrays of the same element type. For example, the statement

```
int[] array1, array2, array3;
```

declares three integer arrays, which might be constructed at runtime using the statements

```
array1 = new int[10];
array2 = new int[20];
array3 = new int[30];
```

The expression `int[]` is also useful when you need to refer to an array *type,* as when declaring method parameters.

> **NOTE**
>
> Keep in mind that any Java array may be empty, in which case its `length` field equals zero. Accessing a zero-length array using any index value will throw an exception.

Java permits any array to be assigned to a variable of type `Object`. For example, if `array1` is an array of integers, the statement

```
Object obj = array1;
```

causes `obj` to refer to the array. You cannot, however, use `obj` as an array because it is not legal to arbitrarily apply brackets, `[ ]`, to a variable of type `Object`. This technique, though, might be useful for passing arrays to method `Object` parameters.

> **NOTE**
>
> If enough space is not available to define an array at runtime, Java throws an `OutOfMemoryError` exception.

Multidimensional Arrays

A multidimensional array is merely an array of arrays. For instance, a two-dimensional array is similar to a chessboard with rows and columns. In Java, however, the rows do not have to be all the same length as they do in most programming languages that provide for multidimensional arrays. This is a consequence and an advantage of the fact that arrays are constructed at runtime.

Declare a multidimensional array by using multiple pairs of empty brackets. The statement

```
double trouble[][]
```

declares that `trouble` is a reference to a two-dimensional array of floating-point `double` values. Define the array's memory at runtime using a statement such as the following, which creates a 10 by 10 array of `double` values:

```
trouble = new double[10][10];
```

The two sizes can be different:

```
trouble = new double[10][20];
```

This creates an array having 10 rows of 20 `double` values each. Only the first size must be specified at runtime (but it can be variable rather than literal as shown here). The preceding statement, for instance, is equivalent to the code

```
trouble = new double[10][];
for (int i = 0; i < trouble.length; i++)
 trouble[i] = new double[20];
```

The fragment first defines space for 10-element arrays of `double` values, and it causes `trouble` to refer to that space. A `for` loop then creates 20-element arrays, assigned to each of `trouble`'s elements. It's important to understand that those elements are arrays—specifically, the data type of the expression `trouble[n]` is `double[]`, a reference to an array of `double` values.

Constructing arrays using the foregoing technique makes it possible to define variable-size, multidimensional arrays. For example, the fragment

```
trouble = new double[10][];
for (int i = 0; i < trouble.length; i++)
 trouble[i] = new double[i + 1];
```

creates an interesting structure known as a *triangular array.* This array has 10 columns, each of which refers to an array of `double` values with a length equal to the column index plus one. Thus, `trouble[0]` refers to an "array" of one `double` value, `trouble[1]` is an array of two values, `trouble[2]` is an array of three values, and so on. This is very difficult, if not downright impossible, to do in C++ or Pascal!

Because of the potential for array sizes to be variable, when programming with multidimensional arrays, it is especially important to respect the `length` field. The following shows how to use `length` to assign values to all positions in the `trouble` array:

```
for (int i = 0; i < trouble.length; i++)
 for (int j = 0; j < trouble[i].length; j++)
  trouble[i][j] = Math.random();
```

In this code, the outer loop limits the column index `i` to `trouble.length`. The inner loop limits the row index `j` to the `length` value for each column (`trouble[i].length`). This code works correctly even if each row is a different length, as it is in the preceding triangular definition.

Multidimensional arrays may have more than two dimensions. For example, the statement

```
double fifthDimension[][][][][];
```

declares `fifthDimension` as a five-level array of `double` values. This is of little practical value, because it is rarely useful to declare more than three dimensions. Though Java places no limit on the number of dimensions, you might want to use a `try` block to define the array as in this example:

```
try {
 fifthDimension = new double[10][4][8][6][9];
} catch (OutOfMemoryError e) {
 System.out.println("Out of memory!");
}
```

Arrays of numerous dimensions can consume huge amounts of memory. In one test of the preceding code, I multiplied the first two sizes by 10 (making them 100 and 40, respectively). Running the result put an enormous strain on the Windows 95 virtual memory manager, which until I interrupted the program, seemed bent on consuming every scrap of memory and disk space in my computer. After a minute or so of exercising my hard drive's seek arm, I halted the program, but I assume that an `OutOfMemoryError` exception would be thrown eventually.

Array Initializations

As I mentioned, you may assign values to array elements using expressions such as

```
myArray[i] = 3.14159;
```

which assigns a floating-point value to one of `myArray`'s elements (assuming the array is a floating-point type). Another way to initialize array elements is to assign them literal values in the declaration. For example, the statement

```
int[] fibonacci = {1, 2, 3, 5, 8, 13, 21, 34};
```

declares an array of `int` values (`fibonacci`), constructs an eight-element array at runtime, and initializes each element to the literal values shown in braces. The technique is often useful for creating arrays of strings as in this declaration:

```
String[] text =
 {"Humpty", "Dumpty", "sat", "on", "a", "wall"};
```

To print out the individual strings, use a loop such as

```
for (int i = 0; i < text.length; i++)
 System.out.println(text[i]);
```

Arrays may contain objects—either of any Java classes, or those of your own making. For example, a program can declare a class such as the following (which is incomplete and just for demonstration purposes, but it compiles):

```
class MyClass {
 String s;
 MyClass(String ss) { s = ss; }
}
```

Then it can define and initialize an array of `MyClass` elements using a statement such as

```
MyClass[] myArray = {
 new MyClass("Testing"),
 new MyClass("One, "),
 new MyClass("Two, "),
 new MyClass("Three")
};
```

This is a *single* statement (note the commas). In all cases, after defining the array at runtime, no matter how you construct it, the array's size can never change. You can, however, assign a new array to any array variable. For example, the statements

```
int[] array1 = {1, 2, 3};
System.out.println(array1.length);
```

define and initialize a three-integer array—the output statement displays 3. To redefine the array, use code such as

```
array1 = new int[100];
System.out.println(array1.length);
```

The first line replaces the original three-element array with one capable of holding 100 integers. The output statement now displays 100. Any data in the old array, however, is lost. (See the `Vector` class in this chapter if you need an array container that can be resized without losing data.)

You may redefine arrays this way as often as you like. You do not have to take any special action to dispose of the array's elements: Java's memory manager takes care of that chore automatically. This is yet one more advantage of Java arrays not found in other programming languages, which typically require you to follow torturous memory allocation and disposal rules.

Copying Arrays

When you need to copy an array, you may use one of three techniques, demonstrated in Listing 10.1, `ArrayCopy.java`. Each of the techniques is included in the listing, but only the first is active. The other two techniques are written as comments. Remove the unindented comment slashes to enable and test each method in turn.

Listing 10.1. `ArrayCopy.java` (Demonstrates array copying techniques).

```
class ArrayCopy {
 public static void main(String args[]) {
  // Declare the arrays
  double[] apples, oranges;
  // Construct and initialize the first array
  apples = new double[10];
  for (int i = 0; i < apples.length; i++)
   apples[i] = Math.random();
  // Copy technique #1
```

```
  oranges = apples;
  // Copy technique #2
// oranges = new double[apples.length];
// System.arraycopy(apples, 0, oranges, 0, apples.length);
  // Copy technique #3
// try {
//   oranges = (double[])apples.clone();
// } catch (CloneNotSupportedException e) {
//   System.out.println(e.getMessage());
// }
  // Display the copied array's values
  for (int i = 0; i < oranges.length; i++)
   System.out.println(oranges[i]);
  // Test whether the arrays are the same
  if (apples == oranges)
   System.out.println("Arrays are the same");
  else
   System.out.println("Arrays are NOT the same");
 }
}
```

The first way to copy an array is the simplest—just assign one array to another of the same type. For example, this statement in the sample listing assigns the apples array to oranges:

```
oranges = apples;
```

When you run the program with this statement enabled, you also see the message "Arrays are the same." This demonstrates an important aspect of array copying: Assigning one array to another as shown here does *not* create two separate arrays. It merely causes two array variables to refer to the *same* array. Thus, if you change a value in apples, that value also changes in oranges.

To copy and create an entirely new array, use one of the two other techniques demonstrated in the sample program. Delete or comment out the first technique, and enable the second, which uses these statements:

```
oranges = new double[apples.length];
System.arraycopy(apples, 0, oranges, 0, apples.length);
```

This code first constructs a new array of the same size as apples and causes oranges to refer to that new array. The second line calls the arraycopy() method in Java's System class to copy the values of apples to oranges. The two zero arguments refer to the source and destination array starting indexes. The final argument is the number of elements to copy (more on the arraycopy() method in a moment).

Because the two arrays are now distinct, the program tells you that the "Arrays are NOT the same." This is because two arrays are considered to be equal only if they refer to the same arrayed elements regardless of those elements' values. Even if all values in both arrays are equal, the arrays are not the same.

The sample program demonstrates a third technique for copying an array. Use try-catch blocks to call the array's clone() method, inherited from Object but overridden by all arrays:

```
try {
  oranges = (double[])apples.clone();
} catch (CloneNotSupportedException e) {
  System.out.println(e.getMessage());
}
```

The statement inside the try block calls clone() to create a duplicate of the apples array. Because clone() returns type Object, a type-cast expression is necessary to inform the compiler what type of array the program is cloning. The compiler also requires you to catch a possible object of type CloneNotSupportedException. Because all arrays are capable of being cloned—they override the clone() method inherited from Object—this exception can never actually be thrown. (If it is, something *really* weird is happening!)

As I mentioned, the System.arraycopy() method is useful for copying values between two arrays. It is also valuable for moving values around within the same array—especially in buffers of characters or bytes, for example. The System class declares the method and its parameters as

```
public static void
  arraycopy(Object src, int src_position,
            Object dst, int dst_position,
            int length);
```

The method's parameters are as follows:

- Object src: Pass the name of the source array from which you want to copy array elements.

- int src_position: Pass the starting index value of the first source-array element to copy.

- Object dst: Pass the name of the destination array to which you want to copy array elements.

- int dst_position: Pass the starting index value of the first destination-array element to which you want to assign copied values.

- int length: Pass the number of array elements to copy.

Using arraycopy() on the same array—in other words, passing the same array as the source and destination—moves the elements in the array up or down. This is a useful technique for shuffling data in buffers. For example, these statements define and initialize a 10-element array of integers, named buffer:

```
int buffer[] = new int[10];
for (int i = 0; i < buffer.length; i++)
  buffer[i] = i;
```

The code sets the element values in buffer to

```
0 1 2 3 4 5 6 7 8 9
```

To shuffle the values in `buffer`, specify the same array as the source and destination arguments using a statement such as

```
System.arraycopy(buffer, 3, buffer, 0, 7);
```

This moves seven values starting with the fourth element to the beginning (zero-index) of the array. After the preceding statement executes, the resulting buffer holds these values:

```
3 4 5 6 7 8 9 7 8 9
```

Notice that values beyond those moved are unchanged.

Array Members

Although there is no `Array` class per se in Java, an array behaves as though it is an object of a class extended from `Object`. Among other payoffs, this means every array inherits `Object`'s members, and every array variable may be assigned to another variable of type `Object`. (However, arrays override rather than inherit `Object`'s `clone()` method.)

For the purposes of programming with arrays, it is useful to imagine them to be declared of a class shown in Listing 10.2. This listing is not on disk, and you should *not* use it in a real program; it merely shows the structure of array objects as though they were declared this way. There is no `ArrayType` class in Java.

Listing 10.2. The `ArrayType` pseudo-class.

```
class ArrayType
implements Cloneable {
 public final int length = N;
 public Object clone() {
  try {
   return super.clone();
  } catch (CloneNotSupportedException e) {
   throw new InternalError(e.getMessage());
  }
 }
}
```

Because all arrays implement the `Cloneable` interface, as the listing shows, the `CloneNotSupportedException` object cannot be thrown. Nevertheless, Visual J++ exhibits the behavior of some Java compilers that fail to recognize this fact, and you must therefore catch this exception or the program will not compile. Perhaps this problem will be repaired by an updated Java compiler by the time you read this; if not, you can catch the object like this:

```
try {
 int ia1[] = { 1, 2 };
 int ia2[] = (int[])ia1.clone();
 // ...
```

```
} catch (CloneNotSupportedException e) {
 System.out.println("This shouldn't be necessary!");
}
```

This is similar to an example in the Visual J++ online help, which contrary to the documentation, does not compile without adding the try-catch blocks shown here.

Array Exceptions

When programming with arrays, you should prepare to catch the following exceptions:

- NegativeArraySizeException: Thrown if a statement attempts to construct an array with a negative size value, which could easily happen when using an integer variable to specify the array's size.

- ArrayIndexOutOfBoundsException: Thrown if a statement attempts to access an array element using an index value that is less than zero or greater than the array's length field.

- ArrayStoreException: Thrown if a statement attempts to store the wrong type of object in an array element.

- CloneNotSupportedException: Never thrown, but due to an error in Visual J++ (which might be cured by the time you read this) it must be caught by a program that calls the overridden clone() method as explained in this chapter.

Container Classes

When your data storage needs exceed what you can do with arrays, you can probably accomplish your goals using one of Java's container classes. For example, the Vector and Stack classes extend Java arrays and, most significantly, can change size at runtime—something arrays cannot do. The Vector class is similar to an array, but in addition to its ability to change size, it also provides numerous methods for inserting and removing data elements and searching for data. The Stack class extends Vector and adds traditional stack-handling methods such as pop() and push().

This section examines the Vector and Stack container classes. I'll also explain how to use the BitSet, Dictionary, and Hashtable classes, which are useful for highly specialized data storage needs. In addition, I'll show how to implement the Cloneable and Enumeration interfaces, which you'll often need to do when using Java's container classes.

Class Hierarchy

Figure 10.1 shows the hierarchy of Java's container classes. All are derived from Object (as are all classes). As the diagram shows, there are actually three containers: BitSet, Dictionary, and Vector. The Hashtable and Property classes are derived from Dictionary. The Stack class is derived from Vector.

Figure 10.1.
Container classes.

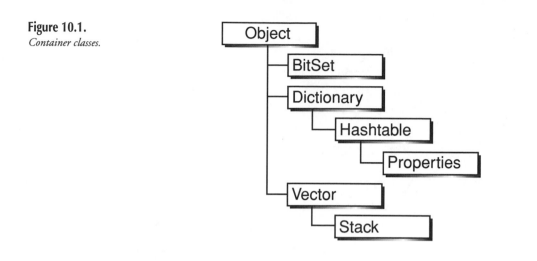

The `Cloneable` Interface

The `Object` class provides automatic cloning capabilities that you can implement for any class. But to provide you with the option of specifying whether a class object may be cloned, Java requires a class to implement the `Cloneable` interface. Objects of any class that implement `Cloneable` may be cloned by calling the `clone()` method inherited from `Object`. Objects that do not implement `Cloneable` may not be cloned. The `Cloneable` interface is declared as

```
public interface java.lang.Cloneable
{
}
```

As you can see, the `Cloneable` interface has no methods or data members; it is an empty class interface whose mere presence or absence determines the cloning capabilities of other class objects. Listing 10.3 demonstrates the effects of implementing and not implementing the `Cloneable` interface.

Listing 10.3. `CloneDemo.java` (Demonstrates `Cloneable` interface).

```
// Declare a class
class MyClass extends Object
implements Cloneable  // Comment out to test exception
{
 private int x, y;
 MyClass() { x = 0; y = 0; }
 MyClass(int xx, int yy) { x = xx; y = yy; }
 public int getx() { return x; }
 public int gety() { return y; }
}

// Main program class
class CloneDemo {
 // Display MyClass object data values
```

continues

Listing 10.3. continued

```java
public static void show(MyClass obj) {
  System.out.println(obj.toString() + " = (" +
   obj.getx() + ", " + obj.gety() + ")");
}
// Test cloning MyClass objects
public static void main(String args[]) {
  try {
   MyClass obj1 = new MyClass(10, 20);
   MyClass obj2 = (MyClass)obj1.clone();
   show(obj1);
   show(obj2);
  } catch (CloneNotSupportedException e) {
   System.out.println(
     "Cloning not supported for " + e.getMessage());
  }
 }
}
```

For demonstration purposes, the sample program declares a class, MyClass, with two data members—x and y. The class has a default constructor, MyClass(), and an alternate constructor that accepts two integer arguments. The class also provides methods getx() and gety(), which return the class object's instance variables. The class declaration

```java
class MyClass extends Object
implements Cloneable
...
```

indicates that it extends from Object. (It would anyway, but I included this to explicitly show MyClass's inheritance.) The second line of the declaration states that MyClass implements the Cloneable interface. This is all you need to do to enable object cloning. You do not have to supply any methods, and particularly, you should *not* override the inherited clone() method. This method is already programmed to work with any class declared as shown here. When you first compile and run the program, it displays the lines

```
MyClass@430590 = (10, 20)
MyClass@437f0c = (10, 20)
```

The address values might be different. The values in parentheses are from the main program's two MyClass objects, the second of which is created by calling the inherited clone() method:

```java
MyClass obj1 = new MyClass(10, 20);
MyClass obj2 = (MyClass)obj1.clone();
```

The first object is created normally, by calling MyClass's alternate constructor. The second object is created by calling clone() in reference to the first object. The type-cast expression indicates to the compiler the type of object that clone() returns. Because this method is inherited from Object, it returns type Object by default, so you'll nearly always need to supply a type-cast expression.

If a program attempts to call `clone()` for an object of a class that does not implement the `Cloneable` interface, `clone()` throws an exception of the `CloneNotSupportedException` class. To demonstrate the effect of this, comment out the following declaration by prefacing it with double slashes:

```
// implements Cloneable
```

Compile and run the modified program, which now displays

```
Cloning not supported for MyClass
```

This line is printed by the `catch` block in the sample program. Because a program might receive this exception for any class, when calling `clone()`, always use `try-catch` blocks as shown here:

```
try {
// ... call clone() here
} catch (CloneNotSupportedException e) {
 System.out.println(
   "Cloning not supported for " + e.getMessage());
}
```

When the `clone()` method clones an object, it creates an exact duplicate of that object in memory. Any data members in the destination object receive the same values as the members in the source object. However, the `clone()` method does not call a class constructor to initialize the new object.

> **NOTE**
>
> A class that implements `Cloneable` may optionally override the inherited `clone()` method. For example, the `BitSet` class described in this chapter uses this technique to provide its own cloning code. When doing this, your `clone()` method's statements should be in a `try` block that catches `CloneNotSupportedException`. Because the class implements `Cloneable`, this exception should never be thrown, and the proper response is to convert it to an internal error using code such as
>
> ```
> try {
> // ... statements in overriden clone() method
> } catch (CloneNotSupportedException e) {
>  throw new InternalError();
> }
> ```
>
> If you receive the internal error, which will probably halt the application, there might be a problem in the source code (check whether the class implements `Cloneable`). If not, the problem is more than likely in the compiler or interpreter.

The Enumeration Interface

The Enumeration interface provides the capability of traversing another container, usually of the Vector or Hashtable classes. You can implement the Enumeration interface in your own classes, but you'll most likely use it in conjunction with containers, as explained later in this chapter. Java declares the Enumeration interface as

```
public interface java.util.Enumeration {
 public abstract boolean hasMoreElements();
 public abstract Object nextElement();
}
```

A container class that implements Enumeration must supply the contents for the interface's two abstract methods. Such a container is expected to store a sequence or series of elements of some kind. The hasMoreElements() method returns true if the container object has more values in its sequence; it returns false if all values have been returned. The nextElement() method returns the next value, which must be an Object, in the container's sequence.

See the section on the Vector class in this chapter for more information on using the Enumeration interface.

The BitSet Class

The java.util package provides the BitSet class for storing and manipulating bit values. You might find the class handy for keeping true-false data compressed into single bits, or you might use it for Boolean logic code. Listing 10.4 shows the declaration of the BitSet class.

Listing 10.4. Java's BitSet class.

```
public final class BitSet
implements Cloneable {
// Constructors
 public BitSet();
 public BitSet(int nbits);
// Public methods
 public void set(int bit);
 public void clear(int bit);
 public boolean get(int bit);
 public void and(BitSet set);
 public void or(BitSet set);
 public void xor(BitSet set);
 public int hashCode();
 public int size();
 public boolean equals(Object obj);
 public Object clone();
 public String toString();
}
```

Technically, the BitSet class implements a vector of single bits—but it is not based on the Vector class. A module that uses the BitSet class must import it from Java's util package using the statement

```
import java.util.BitSet;
```

A `BitSet` container can grow as needed to accommodate additional bits, but in most cases, you'll construct the object of the size you need. Here are two ways to create a `BitSet` object:

```
BitSet setOfBits = new BitSet(16);
BitSet secondSet = new BitSet();
```

The first and most common form specifies the number of bits to store. The second form constructs a default empty `BitSet` object. All bits are initially set to `false`.

> **NOTE**
>
> Internally, `BitSet` containers store data in the individual bits of an array of `long` integer variables. Consequently, there is no practical limit on the number of bits that a `BitSet` container can store.

Bits in a `BitSet` container are indexed starting with zero. Set a particular bit to `true` by calling `set()` like this:

```
setOfBits.set(5);  // Set bit 6 true
```

Clear a bit, setting it to `false`, by calling `clear()`:

```
setOfBits.clear(3);  // Set bit 4 false
```

Calling `set()` or `clear()` with an index value greater than or equal to the `BitSet`'s current length automatically allocates more memory to the container. Index exceptions are not thrown, but if enough memory isn't available, an `OutOfMemory` exception is generated. To expand a `BitSet` object, you might use a statement such as

```
secondSet.clear(63);
```

There is no way to reduce the size of a `BitSet` except by re-creating it.

To obtain the value of a particular bit, call the `get()` method this way:

```
if (setOfBits.get(5))
 System.out.println("Bit 5 is true");
```

You may combine `BitSet` containers using AND, OR, and XOR (exclusive OR) Boolean logic. These methods are declared as follows, and they are used similarly:

```
public void and(BitSet set);
public void or(BitSet set);
public void xor(BitSet set);
```

Pass a `BitSet` container to one of these methods, called in reference to the destination `BitSet` that you want to alter according to the specific Boolean operation. Listing 10.5 demonstrates how to do this using the `xor()` method.

Listing 10.5. `BitSetDemo.java` (Demonstrates `BitSet` class).

```java
import java.util.BitSet;

class BitSetDemo {
 // Display string and value of BitSet object
 public static void show(String s, BitSet obj) {
  System.out.println(s + obj.toString());
 }
 // Main program--test BitSet Boolean logic
 public static void main(String args[]) {
  // Construct two BitSets
  BitSet set1 = new BitSet(16);
  BitSet set2 = new BitSet(16);
  // Set bits 2, 4, and 8 in set 1
  set1.set(2); set1.set(4); set1.set(8);
  // Set all bits in set 2
  for (int i = 0; i < set2.size(); i++)
   set2.set(i);
  // Test Boolean logic and show results
  show("before XOR set1 = ", set1);
  set1.xor(set2);
  show("after XOR set1  = ", set1);
  set1.xor(set2);
  show("after XOR set1  = ", set1);
 }
}
```

The sample program constructs two 16-bit `BitSet` containers. It sets the first container's bits 2, 4, and 8 to `true` and also sets all bits in the second container using a `for` loop along with the `BitSet` `size()` method to determine how many bits the set contains. Two calls to the `xor()` method then demonstrate one of the principles of Boolean XOR logic: Exclusive ORing any bit value with 1 twice in succession returns the original value. In other words, XOR can work as a bit toggle. The sample program's `show()` method proves this by displaying

```
before XOR set1 = {2, 4, 8}
after XOR set1  = {0, 1, 3, 5, 6, 7, 9, 10, 11, 12, 13, 14,
15, 16, 17, 18, 19, 20, 21, 22, 23, 24, 25, 26, 27, 28, 29,
30, 31, 32, 33, 34, 35, 36, 37, 38, 39, 40, 41, 42, 43, 44,
45, 46, 47, 48, 49, 50, 51, 52, 53, 54, 55, 56, 57, 58, 59,
60, 61, 62, 63}
after XOR set1  = {2, 4, 8}
```

The first line shows that the first set's bits 2, 4, and 8 are `true`. The next several lines show the results of exclusive ORing this set with another set with all bits equal to `true`. The final line shows that repeating that exclusive OR operation restores the first set's original values.

To display the `BitSet` contents, the sample program calls the `BitSet` class's `toString()` method using this statement:

```
System.out.println(s + obj.toString());
```

This provides a handy way to display the values of any `BitSet`. The resulting string shows the index values of all `true` bits, delimited with braces.

Other BitSet methods include hashCode() (covered in the section "The Hashtable Class," later in this chapter), equals(), and clone(). Use the clone() method as described earlier in this chapter for arrays.

Call equals() to compare an Object class object with a BitSet and determine whether they contain the same values. As with other classes that implement equals(), this is *not* equivalent to comparing two BitSet objects using the == operator, which is an important distinction. The statement

```
if (b1 == b2)
 System.out.println("Objects are the same");
else
 System.out.println("Objects are NOT the same");
```

tests whether b1 and b2 refer to the same object in memory. Even if the contained bits in each object are identical in value, the expression (b1 == b2) is false if the containers are distinct objects in memory. To compare the values *contained* by two BitSet containers, use a statement such as

```
if (b1.equals(b2))
...
```

The expression b1.equals(b2) is true if all bits in b2 have the same values as the bits in b1.

NOTE

The BitSet class appears to needlessly override the Object.clone() method. (See the BitSet.java file included with Visual J++ and installed in your Windows/Java directory under Classes/java/util.) Overriding clone() isn't necessary because the method can already copy any class object. Apparently, BitSet.clone() overrides the method merely to catch the CloneNotSupportedException error, which can't be generated anyway because BitSet implements the Cloneable interface. Even so, the overridden method seems to work harder than necessary. Here are the statements that perform the cloning:

```
BitSet set = (BitSet)super.clone();
set.bits = new long[bits.length];  // ???
System.arraycopy(bits, 0, set.bits, 0, bits.length);  // ???
```

The second and third statements are not needed because calling super.clone() has already re-created the object. Tests indicate that removing these two statements causes no ill effects. In fact, removing the entire method does no harm, but it requires BitSet users to catch CloneNotSupportedException errors.

I offer these observations for your information only, and I do not recommend modifying your source code libraries. If you choose to do that, you should thoroughly test the effects of this proposed change on your application.

The `Dictionary` Class

The `Dictionary` class shown in Listing 10.6 is abstract and cannot be used to create container objects. Instead, `Dictionary` serves as the parent to other containers, of which there currently is only one, `Hashtable`. Before learning how to use the `Hashtable` class, it's important to understand `Dictionary`'s members. In this section, I'll discuss those members, and then in the following section, I'll explain how to use them to create hash table containers.

Listing 10.6. The `Dictionary` class.

```
public abstract
class Dictionary {
 abstract public int size();
 abstract public boolean isEmpty();
 abstract public Enumeration keys();
 abstract public Enumeration elements();
 abstract public Object get(Object key);
 abstract public Object put(Object key, Object value);
 abstract public Object remove(Object key);
}
```

`Dictionary`'s seven methods provide the basic elements required for random-access containers. The `size()` method returns the number of elements that the `Dictionary` contains. As you might expect, method `isEmpty()` returns `true` if `size()` is zero.

The two `Enumeration` interface methods, `keys()` and `elements()`, provide for sequential access to key values and associated data elements. I'll explain how to use these in the next section. In brief, an `Enumeration` provides an object with two methods—`hasMoreElements()` and `nextElement()`—that you can use to walk through a container's contents. When using a `Dictionary`, for example, you can call `keys()` or `elements()` and use the resulting `Enumeration` to access the container's data.

For finding, inserting, and removing data elements from a container, the `Dictionary` class provides three methods. Use `get()` to search for an element based on its associated key. Use `put()` to insert a new element and key into the container. Use `remove()` to delete an element and its key, based on its associated key value.

Each of these methods returns type `Object`, which might be `null`. Method `get()` returns `null` if the specified key is not found. Method `put()` returns a previous value to which the specified key was associated, or `null` if that key was not already in the container. Method `remove()` returns the deleted key value, or `null` if that key was not found.

None of `Dictionary`'s methods is implemented in the abstract class. To use `Dictionary`, you must extend it to a new class and implement each of its abstract methods to perform as just described. Rather than doing this yourself, however, it is far easier to use an existing `Dictionary` subclass such as `Hashtable`, described in the next section.

The `Hashtable` Class

The `Hashtable` class extends `Dictionary` and implements the inherited methods as described in the preceding section. `Hashtable` also provides additional methods for creating hash table containers.

A hash table is a random-access data structure that stores elements with associated key values. Hash tables are designed for extremely fast searches: They are typically used, for example, by a compiler to look up keywords and identifiers. Hash tables achieve their speed by computing a data element's location from its associated key and a *hash code* algorithm. All keys stored in a `Hashtable` container must therefore implement the `hashcode()` method inherited from `Object`. Because `Hashtables` are designed to use the `hashcode()` method, which returns type `int`, the hashing algorithm is totally up to you. Many Java classes provide `hashcode()` methods, and in many cases, you won't need to program a hashing algorithm, but it's good to know you can do this if you want. A useful performance-profiling technique, for example, is to modify a process's algorithm and compare runtime speeds.

NOTE

Hash codes are converted to hash table index values using the algorithm

```
int index = (hash & 0x7FFFFFFF) % tab.length;
```

where `hash` is the hash code, and `tab` is the array of `HashtableEntry` objects that stores the actual hash table.

Many existing classes provide ready-to-use `hashcode()` methods. For example, the `Float` class implements `hashcode()` as follows:

```
public int hashCode() {
 return floatToIntBits(value);
}
```

This simply converts a floating-point value to an integer bit pattern, which is used as the hash key value by the container.

> **NOTE**
>
> All keys and data stored in a Hashtable container must be objects of a class—either one that already exists, or one of your own making. Internally, Hashtable containers store keys and values as objects of the HashtableEntry class. You probably won't have any cause to use the HashtableEntry class—it is not necessary to construct your data elements using this class—so I won't describe it here. If you are interested, however, you can find HashtableEntry's declaration in file Hashtable.java, supplied with Visual J++.

One of the disadvantages of using a hash table is the potential for two different keys to return the same hash code. Because this maps data values to the same table location, the effect is called a *collision*. The Hashtable class handles collisions by storing keys and associated elements on a *collision list* composed of HashtableEntry objects. Because the collision list is searched sequentially, if there are too many collisions, the hash table's performance rapidly degrades.

Another disadvantage is that hash tables work best when they are allocated large amounts of memory. This provides more space for data values and lessens collisions, but it causes hash tables to be sparsely populated and can waste memory. Choosing the correct amount of memory to allocate to a Hashtable container requires much trial and error—and no small amounts of luck and intuition.

Despite their disadvantages, hash tables are unmatched in speed for inserting, searching, and removing data. If you have data to store, and if retrieval speed is critical, a Hashtable container is a good choice. Listing 10.7 shows Java's Hashtable class declaration.

Listing 10.7. The Hashtable class.

```
public class Hashtable
extends Dictionary implements Cloneable {
// Constructors
 public Hashtable(int initialCapacity, float loadFactor);
 public Hashtable(int initialCapacity);
 public Hashtable();
// Public methods
 public int size();
 public boolean isEmpty();
 public synchronized Enumeration keys();
 public synchronized Enumeration elements();
 public synchronized boolean contains(Object value);
 public synchronized boolean containsKey(Object key);
 public synchronized Object get(Object key);
 public synchronized Object put(Object key, Object value);
 public synchronized Object remove(Object key);
 public synchronized void clear();
 public synchronized Object clone();
 public synchronized String toString();
}
```

Probably the best way to learn how to use the Hashtable class is to experiment with a Hashtable container object in a program. Listing 10.8, HashtableDemo.java, demonstrates some of the ways you can use the Hashtable class.

Listing 10.8. HashtableDemo.java (Demonstrates the Hashtable class).

```java
import java.util.Hashtable;
import java.util.HashtableEnumerator;

class HashtableDemo {
 public static void main(String args[]) throws Exception {

  // Construct a table of Float objects
  Hashtable floatTable = new Hashtable();

  // Insert some objects
  floatTable.put("1.5", new Float(1.5));
  floatTable.put("3.14159", new Float(3.14159));
  floatTable.put("9.9", new Float(9.9));

  // Search for an object key
  Float floatObject = (Float)floatTable.get("3.14159");
  if (floatObject != null)
   System.out.println("Found value: " + floatObject.toString());

  // Construct database of account numbers and names
  Hashtable nameTable = new Hashtable(100);

  // Insert some account numbers and names
  nameTable.put("10003", "John Lennon");
  nameTable.put("10005", "Paul McCartney");
  nameTable.put("10006", "George Harrison");
  nameTable.put("10009", "Ringo Starr");

  // Output database keys
  System.out.println("\nDatabase keys:");
  HashtableEnumerator keyEnum =
   (HashtableEnumerator)nameTable.keys();
  while (keyEnum.hasMoreElements()) {
   String key = (String)keyEnum.nextElement();
   System.out.println(key);
  }

  // Output database names
  System.out.println("\nDatabase names");
  HashtableEnumerator nameEnum =
   (HashtableEnumerator)nameTable.elements();
  while (nameEnum.hasMoreElements()) {
   String name = (String)nameEnum.nextElement();
   System.out.println(name);
  }

  // Output database keys and names by searching
  System.out.println("\nDatabase keys and names:");
  keyEnum = (HashtableEnumerator)nameTable.keys();
  while (keyEnum.hasMoreElements()) {
```

continues

Listing 10.8. continued

```
  String key = (String)keyEnum.nextElement();
  String name = (String)nameTable.get(key);
  if (name == null)
   throw new Exception("Error in hash table");
  System.out.println(key + " : " + name);
 }
 }
}
```

Most applications that use hash tables need two import statements, shown in the sample listing:

```
import java.util.Hashtable;
import java.util.HashtableEnumerator;
```

The Hashtable class is the main honcho—it creates the actual table. The HashtableEnumerator class is optional and is needed only for sequentially accessing hash table keys and elements. You can also import HashtableEntry, but as I mentioned, you probably won't ever use this class.

The sample program demonstrates two ways to construct a hash table. The first is simplest: Let the Hashtable class choose a default table size and something called the *load factor*, which the Hashtable class uses to determine when to rehash a full or nearly full table. Rehashing expands the hash table so it can accommodate more data elements.

For example, the statement

```
Hashtable floatTable = new Hashtable();
```

constructs floatTable with default parameters. Notice that you don't tell the table what kind of objects the container contains—it can hold all types of objects. To store items in the container, call put() like this:

```
floatTable.put("3.14159", new Float(3.14159));
```

The first object is the element's associated key value, usually a string. The second is the element value. Both items must be objects (literal strings are objects of the String class). Because of this rule, it isn't possible to store values such as 3.14159 directly; instead, you must construct a class using a wrapper such as Float and pass the resulting object to put().

Call get() to search for a hash table entry by its key value. For example, the statement

```
Float floatObject = (Float)floatTable.get("3.14159");
```

searches for the object with the string key value "3.14159". Because get() returns type Object, a type-cast expression is necessary to indicate that this is really a Float object. If the resulting object is null, the search failed.

Use a similar statement (not in the sample listing) to remove an element. The fragment

```
Float floatObject = (Float)floatTable.get("9.9");
if (floatObject != null)
 System.out.println("Item removed");
```

searches for and removes the element with the string key value "9.9". If that element is not found, remove() returns null.

The sample program shows another way to construct a hash table using the statement

```
Hashtable nameTable = new Hashtable(100);
```

This specifies an initial table size of 100 elements. The default load factor is 0.75. To specify a different load factor, pass two arguments to the third and final Hashtable constructor as in the statement

```
Hashtable nameTable = new Hashtable(250, 0.5);
```

This creates a hash table with room for 250 elements and a load factor of 0.5. Given that value, the table will be expanded (rehashed) when the table's number of elements exceeds a threshold value computed using the algorithm

```
threshold = (int)(initialCapacity * loadFactor);
```

In other words, with an initial capacity of 250 and a load factor of 0.5, the table will be rehashed and expanded when it contains 125 elements and the program attempts to insert another element. Load factors must be greater than 0 and less than 1.0. Greater load factors use memory more efficiently at the expense of speed. Smaller load factors waste memory but tend to produce faster search times.

> **NOTE**
>
> The default hash table capacity is 101 elements. The default load factor is 0.75. These defaults may differ among Java implementations.

Strings are commonly stored in hash tables to create an *association database*. For example, the sample program enters an account number and name using the statement

```
nameTable.put("10003", "John Lennon");
```

Literal strings and String variables are objects, so you can use strings directly as keys and data elements in a hash table. The arguments can also be String variables.

Use the Enumeration methods keys() and elements() to access all objects in a hash table. For example, to find all keys in a table, first construct a HashtableEnumerator object like this:

```
HashtableEnumerator keyEnum =
 (HashtableEnumerator)nameTable.keys();
```

After obtaining the enumeration object, named `keyEnum` here, call its methods to peruse the database. The code

```
while (keyEnum.hasMoreElements()) {
 String key = (String)keyEnum.nextElement();
 System.out.println(key);
}
```

prints all keys in the hash table. You can similarly find all data elements. Again, first construct the enumeration object, but this time, construct it by calling the `elements()` method:

```
HashtableEnumerator nameEnum =
 (HashtableEnumerator)nameTable.elements();
```

Next, call the enumeration's methods to sequentially access data elements in the table:

```
while (nameEnum.hasMoreElements()) {
 String name = (String)nameEnum.nextElement();
 System.out.println(name);
}
```

To find key values and their associated data elements, combine the preceding techniques. First, construct an enumeration object. I'll simply reinitialize the same `keyEnum` object from earlier:

```
keyEnum = (HashtableEnumerator)nameTable.keys();
```

Next, in a loop (see the last `while` statement in the sample listing), locate each object by obtaining the key values from the enumerator and passing them to `get()`:

```
String key = (String)keyEnum.nextElement();
String name = (String)nameTable.get(key);
```

This gives you the key and its associated name, which you can print or use however you wish.

> **TIP**
>
> A hash table exhibits worst-case performance when all keys hash to the same location. This can make a useful torture test for applications using `Hashtable` containers, and it can also help you find the minimum memory to allocate to the container. To perform the test, program your data-key class's `hashcode()` method to return zero or another literal integer. This will cause all keys to hash to the same location and be stored on the hash table's collision list. After testing your application, restore the `hashcode()` method to normal. Keep increasing the size of the allocated hash table until the application's performance shows a significant improvement.

The `Properties` Class

A `Properties` class object is essentially a formatted hash table that can be saved and loaded from a file stream. Use `Properties` to create initialization files. For example, a word processor might store tab settings and other configuration details in a `Properties` table and save it to a setup file that is read back into memory the next time the program is run. Listing 10.9 shows the declaration of the `Properties` class in the `java.util` package.

Listing 10.9. The Properties class.

```
class Properties extends Hashtable {
// Constructors:
 public Properties();
 public Properties(Properties defaults);
// Public methods:
 public synchronized void load(InputStream in);
 public synchronized void save(OutputStream out, String header);
 public String getProperty(String key);
 public String getProperty(String key, String defaultValue);
 public Enumeration propertyNames();
 public void list(PrintStream out);
}
```

Because Properties extends Hashtable, all of the operations for hash tables described in the preceding section apply equally to Properties containers. In addition to these capabilities, the Properties class adds methods for loading and saving property lists using input and output streams. Methods are also provided for listing property values, discovering property names, and searching for specific property values. A Properties container may hold another Properties list of default values, a feature that might be useful for creating hierarchies of nested properties.

A Properties list written to an output stream is formatted in text as a key value followed by an equals sign and an associated value. For example, a list of font names might look like this:

```
font1=Courier New
font2=Arial
font3=Braggadocio
```

In addition, a Properties list has a date and time stamp, and it may have an optional header. This information, along with property keys and values, is stored as strings separated by line-feed control codes (hexadecimal 0A). The characters in this text are 8-bit ASCII codes, not Unicode values.

Listing 10.10, PropertiesDemo.java, demonstrates how to use the Properties class to create a property list, save it to disk, load it back into memory, and search for specific keys and values.

Listing 10.10. PropertiesDemo.java (Demonstrates Properties class).

```
import java.io.FileOutputStream;
import java.io.FileInputStream;
import java.io.IOException;
import java.util.Properties;

class PropertiesDemo {
 public static void main(String args[]) {
  // Construct and initialize a property list
  Properties props = new Properties();
  props.put("1", "One");
  props.put("2", "Two");
  props.put("3", "Three");
  try {
```

continues

Listing 10.10. continued

```
   // Save the property list to disk
   FileOutputStream fout = new FileOutputStream("props.inf");
   props.save(fout, "Test properties");
   // Load the property list from disk and list all values
   Properties inprops = new Properties();
   FileInputStream fin = new FileInputStream("props.inf");
   inprops.load(fin);
   inprops.list(System.out);
   // Search for a specific property
   String val = inprops.getProperty("2");
   if (val != null)
     System.out.println("Property 2 = " + val);
   } catch (IOException e) {
     System.out.println("I/O exception: " + e.getMessage());
   }
 }
}
```

Running the sample program creates the file props.inf in the current directory. (The filename and extension are up to you—it doesn't have to end with .inf.) To create the initial Proper-ties container in memory, the program executes the statement

```
Properties props = new Properties();
```

Alternatively, but not shown here, you may pass another Properties object as an argument to construct the container with a set of default property values. These properties will be used for keys not found in the main list. After constructing the container, use it as you would a hash table—for example, insert keys and properties using statements such as

```
props.put("1", "One");
props.put("2", "Two");
props.put("3", "Three");
```

The first argument passed to put() is the lookup key. The second is the value to be associated with that key. To save the Properties container to a file, create an output stream object of a class such as FileOutputStream, and pass it along with an optional header string to the Proper-ties class save() method. This should be in a try block that catches the IOException error. The statements

```
FileOutputStream fout = new FileOutputStream("props.inf");
props.save(fout, "Test properties");
```

first create the file object (which also creates or overwrites the disk file) and then save the Prop-erties container with the header string "Test properties". If you examine the bytes written to disk, you'll find they resemble those in Figure 10.2. Notice that all values are 8-bit ASCII character codes and that each header and property association is separated by a line-feed con-trol code, hexadecimal 0A. Comments are preceded by the pound sign #, which is automati-cally added to header text.

Figure 10.2.

Byte values in the prop.inf file.

```
0100   23 54 65 73 74 20 70 72-6F 70 65 72 74 69 65 73    #Test properties
0110   0A 23 46 72 69 20 4F 63-74 20 32 35 20 30 39 3A    .#Fri Oct 25 09:
0120   35 30 3A 35 31 20 45 61-73 74 65 72 6E 20 44 61    50:51 Eastern Da
0130   79 6C 69 67 68 74 20 54-69 6D 65 20 31 39 39 36    ylight Time 1996
0140   0A 33 3D 54 68 72 65 65-0A 32 3D 54 77 6F 0A 31    .3=Three.2=Two.1
0150   3D 4F 6E 65 0A                                     =One.
```

To load a property list from disk, first construct an empty `Properties` container:

```
Properties inprops = new Properties();
```

Next, create an input stream object of a class such as `FileInputStream`, and specify the filename as a string argument. After that, call `Properties`'s `load()` method, passing the input stream object as an argument:

```
FileInputStream fin = new FileInputStream("props.inf");
inprops.load(fin);
```

This loads the properties into memory as a hash table. To access and modify the property information, you may use all of the `Hashtable` class methods described in this chapter, or you may use methods provided by the `Properties` class. For example, list all properties using the statement

```
inprops.list(System.out);
```

Pass the argument shown here to display properties on screen—a useful debugging tool. Alternatively, pass any other output stream object to write properties elsewhere. In the sample program, the preceding statement displays

```
-- listing properties --
3=Three
2=Two
1=One
```

To search for a specific property and get its value, use a statement such as

```
String val = inprops.getProperty("2");
```

The `getProperty()` method returns a `String` object for a specified key, or `null` if that key doesn't exist. Alternatively, you may specify a default value for `getProperty()` to return. For example, a word processor might load a tab setting using this statement:

```
String val = inprops.getProperty("Tabs", "4");
```

If the `"Tabs"` key isn't in the property list, this `getProperty()` statement returns the default value `"4"`.

219

TIP

> If a specified key is not found, getProperty() searches the containers' default Properties list if one was specified when constructing the main container. If that search comes up empty, the two-argument form of getProperty() returns the specified default value.

To obtain a list of the property keys in a Properties container, but not the associated values, call the propertyNames() method, which returns an Enumeration object. Because this is actually a HashtableEnumerator, import that class in your module:

```
import java.util.HashtableEnumerator;
```

You can then construct the enumerator by calling propertyNames() for a Properties object such as inprops from the sample listing:

```
HashtableEnumerator enum =
 (HashtableEnumerator)inprops.propertyNames();
```

Use the resulting Enumeration to access key values in sequence. For example, this while loop prints all keys in the inprops property list:

```
while (enum.hasMoreElements()) {
 String key = (String)enum.nextElement();
 System.out.println(key);
}
```

The Vector Class

The Vector class is similar to an array, but it can grow and shrink as necessary to accommodate different amounts of data. Internally, Vector elements are stored in a Java array. Unlike an array, however, which after being constructed cannot change size, a Vector container may increase its capacity by a specified chunk size if the program attempts to store data into a full container. Likewise, a Vector can shrink down to the minimum size required to hold its items. With careful programming, these facts make Vectors highly efficient containers. The Vector class also provides numerous methods you can call to add, remove, search, and perform other operations on array elements. Listing 10.11 shows the declaration for the Vector class.

Listing 10.11. The Vector class.

```
class Vector implements Cloneable {
// Constructors:
 public Vector(int initialCapacity, int capacityIncrement);
 public Vector(int initialCapacity);
 public Vector();
// Methods:
 public final synchronized void copyInto(Object anArray[]);
 public final synchronized void trimToSize();
 public final synchronized void ensureCapacity(int minCapacity);
 public final synchronized void setSize(int newSize);
 public final int capacity();
```

```
  public final int size();
  public final boolean isEmpty();
  public final synchronized Enumeration elements();
  public final boolean contains(Object elem);
  public final int indexOf(Object elem);
  public final synchronized int indexOf(Object elem, int index);
  public final int lastIndexOf(Object elem);
  public final synchronized int lastIndexOf(Object elem, int index);
  public final synchronized Object elementAt(int index);
  public final synchronized Object firstElement();
  public final synchronized Object lastElement();
  public final synchronized void setElementAt(Object obj, int index);
  public final synchronized void removeElementAt(int index);
  public final synchronized void insertElementAt(Object obj, int index);
  public final synchronized void addElement(Object obj);
  public final synchronized boolean removeElement(Object obj);
  public final synchronized void removeAllElements();
  public synchronized Object clone();
  public final synchronized String toString();
}
```

> **NOTE**
>
> When speed is not absolutely critical, and especially when memory consumption is the more important factor, a `Vector` container is a better choice than a `Hashtable`. Searching large `Vector` containers, however, will be much slower on the average than searching the same information inserted into a `Hashtable`.

As you can see from the listing, the `Vector` class provides numerous methods. I'll explain how to use some of these, but you can probably figure out the others. For example, the purpose of `removeElementAt()` is obvious. To demonstrate how to use `Vector` containers, Listing 10.12 sorts an array of integer values, stored in the container as strings.

Listing 10.12. `VectorDemo.java` (Demonstrates `Vector` class).

```
import java.util.Vector;
import java.util.VectorEnumerator;
import java.util.Random;

class VectorDemo {
 // Declare Vector object
 static Vector array;
 // Display contents of Vector object
 public static void showVector(String msg, Vector v) {
  System.out.println("\n" + msg);
  VectorEnumerator enum = (VectorEnumerator)v.elements();
  while (enum.hasMoreElements()) {
   String s = (String)enum.nextElement();
   System.out.print(s + "   ");
```

continues

Listing 10.12. continued

```java
  }
  System.out.println();
}
// Return 3-digit integer as string padded with 0s at left
public static String getNextInt(Random gen) {
  int n = Math.abs(gen.nextInt()) % 1000;
  StringBuffer s = new StringBuffer(new Integer(n).toString());
  while (s.length() < 3)
    s.insert(0, '0');
  return s.toString();
}
// Sort contents of Vector object
// Quicksort algorithm by C. A. R. Hoare
public static void quickSort(int left, int right) {
  int i = left;
  int j = right;
  String test = (String)array.elementAt((left + right) / 2);
  String swap;
  do {
    while (((String)array.elementAt(i)).compareTo(test) < 0) i++;
    while (test.compareTo((String)array.elementAt(j)) < 0) j--;
    if (i <= j) {
      swap = (String)array.elementAt(i);
      array.setElementAt(array.elementAt(j), i);
      array.setElementAt(swap, j);
      i++;
      j--;
    }
  } while (i <= j);
  if (left < j) quickSort(left, j);
  if (i < right) quickSort(i, right);
}
// Main program -- demonstrates using Vector container
public static void main(String args[]) {
  int n, i;   // Miscellaneous variables
  String s;
  // Construct Vector container and random-number generator
  array = new Vector(100);
  Random gen = new Random();
  // Fill container with unique values selected at random
  // Values are converted to strings for demonstration
  for (i = 0; i < 100; i++) {
    do {
      s = getNextInt(gen);
    } while (array.contains(s));
    array.insertElementAt(s, i);
  }
  // Show container values before and after sorting
  showVector("Before sorting:", array);
  if (array.size() > 1 )
    quickSort(0, array.size() - 1);
  showVector("After sorting:", array);
}
}
```

The sample program is a little more complex than most of the tutorial examples in this part. To understand the code, start with the main program near the bottom of the listing. The program constructs a Vector container, initially capable of holding 100 elements, with the statement

```
array = new Vector(100);
```

If you don't specify a container size, a default size of 10 is used. You may also specify a *capacity increment* value using a statement such as

```
array = new Vector(100, 25);
```

This causes the Vector to expand by chunks of 25 elements. If you don't specify a capacity increment value, a default of zero is used, which causes the Vector to double in size during an expansion.

After creating the Vector container, call a method such as insertElementAt() to insert data. The sample program uses a for loop, and calls a local method getNextInt(), to obtain an integer value at random converted to a string. I used strings here for two reasons: One, this is the most common type of data you will probably want to store in Vectors, and two, a Vector's elements must be objects. This means you cannot store int, double, and other native data types in Vectors—but you could wrap those types of values into objects using Integer, Double, and similar wrapper classes. For arrays of integer and other native-type values, then, it's probably best to use plain Java arrays rather than Vector containers.

Local method showVector() in the sample program demonstrates how to use an enumerator object to access a Vector container's elements sequentially. This code is similar to that used in this chapter to access Hashtable elements. The module must import the Vector and VectorEnumerator classes:

```
import java.util.Vector;
import java.util.VectorEnumerator;
```

In your method, construct the enumerator object by calling the Vector container's elements() method:

```
VectorEnumerator enum = (VectorEnumerator)v.elements();
```

Call the enumerator object's hasMoreElements() and nextElement() methods as shown in the listing to browse the Vector's data items, and in this case, to print them using the System.out.print() method.

The sample program shows some other ways to access Vector elements. For example, the statement

```
String test = (String)array.elementAt((left + right) / 2);
```

in the quickSort() method copies to the String variable test the Vector element located at the computed index—a prerequisite for the Quick Sort algorithm I used to sort the container's strings. This method is used at other places in quickSort() to access elements at various index locations. Another method copies a value into an array at a specified index. The statement

```
array.setElementAt(swap, j);
```

sets the Vector element at index j equal to the value of swap, a temporary variable used here to transpose two items in the container during sorting. Notice that the integer index is the second argument to setElementAt(). Use this method to replace an element in a Vector with another value. Use the insertElementAt() method to insert new elements into a Vector. If the container already holds some elements, calling insertElementAt() moves those existing values upward in the array to make room for the insertion. Thus, insertElementAt() is the correct method to use when initially filling an array, and setElementAt() is probably what you will use to assign new values to those elements.

To search a Vector, call the contains() method as shown in the main program's initialization loop. The section of code

```
do {
  s = getNextInt(gen);
} while (array.contains(s));
```

continuously calls getNextInt() to obtain a string not already in the container. To find the index location of a value, call indexOf() like this:

```
int k = array.indexOf("Find this string");
```

This searches the entire array. To start searching from a specific index and proceed upward in the Vector, use the alternate two-argument indexOf() method. For example, the statement

```
int k = array.indexOf("Keep searching", 10);
```

searches for the specified string starting at index 10 (the eleventh item in the array). If the container might have duplicate values, call lastIndexOf() to find the last duplicate:

```
int k = array.lastIndexOf("sdrawkcab hcraes", 50);
```

This finds the last element in the container by searching backwards from the specified index down to index zero. If you don't specify a starting index, the search begins at the end of the Vector and proceeds backwards from there to index zero.

TIP

If methods indexOf() and lastIndexOf() do not find a specified element value, they return -1.

When using Vectors, you will often need to adjust and inspect their sizes. There are various methods for these purposes. Call capacity() for the potential number of elements a Vector can hold. Call size() for the actual number of elements the Vector currently holds. It's important to understand the difference between these two methods: Because Vector elements must be objects, Vectors initially hold null object references until you insert data into the container. Thus, it is possible for a Vector to have a capacity() of 100 or another positive integer value, but a size() of zero.

> **NOTE**
>
> Internally, the Vector class stores individual elements in an Object[] array.

To vary the size of an array (but not its capacity), call setSize() like this:

```
array.setSize(50);
```

This might expand or shrink the array, depending on its current size (number of elements). If you set the new size to less than the current value, elements above the new maximum are permanently lost. If you set the size greater, new element positions are set to null.

Another way to downsize a Vector is to call trimToSize() like this:

```
array.trimToSize();
```

This trims the new maximum capacity of the Vector to equal its size. Use this technique to trim the fat from a container to the number of elements currently contained.

Call ensureCapacity() to verify that a Vector container can hold at least a specified number of elements. This never shrinks the container, but it might expand it, in which case any newly added element positions are initialized to null.

The Stack Class

Java's Stack class is short but sweet. It extends the Vector class, adding classic stack-handling methods such as push() and pop(). Besides being a useful container, the Stack class is a good example of how to build code using object-oriented inheritance. Listing 10.13 shows the Stack class declaration.

Listing 10.13. The Stack class.

```
class Stack extends Vector {
// Public methods
 public Object push(Object item);
 public Object pop();
 public Object peek();
 public boolean empty();
 public int search(Object o);
}
```

Because the `Stack` class has no declared constructors, the only way to construct a `Stack` container is to call its default constructor, which Java automatically provides. For example, the statement

```
Stack fruit = new Stack();
```

constructs a new `Stack` container, using the default capacity and increment values for the `Vector` class. Because a `Stack` grows and shrinks as needed to hold data, its initial size is never specified.

Listing 10.14, `StackDemo.java`, demonstrates some `Stack` class-handling techniques.

Listing 10.14. `StackDemo.java` (Demonstrates `Stack` class).

```java
import java.util.Stack;

class StackDemo {
 public static void main(String args[]) {
  String s;
  Stack fruit = new Stack();
  fruit.push("Apples");
  fruit.push("Peaches");
  fruit.push("Pumpkin");
  s = (String)fruit.peek();
  System.out.println("\nTop of stack = " + s);
  s = "Peaches";
  System.out.println("\nSearching stack for " + s);
  int n = fruit.search(s);
  if (n >= 0)
   System.out.println("distance from top = " + n);
  else
   System.out.println("search argument not found");
  System.out.println("\nStack contents");
  while (!fruit.empty()) {
   s = (String)fruit.pop();
   System.out.println(s);
  }
 }
}
```

The sample program creates a new `Stack` named `fruit`, and calls `push()` to insert some string values into the container. Each new item is inserted on top of any others; thus, the most recently pushed element is said to be at the top of the stack. Popping an item removes the topmost item from the stack. These rules make a stack a LIFO (last in, first out) data structure.

The demonstration program shows how to use all `Stack` class methods. To peek at, but not remove, the topmost element from the stack, call the `peek()` method. The statement

```
s = (String)fruit.peek();
```

sets `String s` equal to the item at the top of the stack, or to `null` if the stack is empty. You can also search a stack for a specific element using statements such as

```
s = "Peaches";
int n = fruit.search(s);
```

This sets n to –1 if the specified element is not in the stack. If the element is found, `search()` returns the element's distance from the top of the stack. This does not equal the element's index in the `Vector` container, but rather the number of `pop()` instructions required to get to that element. For example, if `search()` returns 4, calling `pop()` four times will return the specified element.

The `Stack` class is strictly programmed to follow the rules of good stack handling—you cannot pull out items at any position. The only way to get elements out of a stack is to pop them off the top. The program demonstrates this by calling `pop()` and `empty()` in concert to remove and display all elements from the stack. The code

```
while (!fruit.empty()) {
 s = (String)fruit.pop();
 System.out.println(s);
}
```

is commonly used to empty a stack in the reverse order in which the elements were pushed.

Summary

- An array is a composite data structure. As in most programming languages, Java's arrays consist of data elements one after the other in memory.

- Declaring an array merely creates a variable that can refer to an array of elements. Java arrays are allocated memory at runtime using the new operator. As a consequence, and a decided advantage, array sizes can be computed by program statements. Once an array is defined (allocated memory), however, its size cannot be changed.

- A multidimensional array is simply an array of arrays. There is no limit on the number of dimensions you may declare; however, it is rarely useful to declare more than three levels. Unlike in most computer languages, nested arrays in Java multidimensional arrays do not have to all be of the same size.

- Java also provides container classes for specialized data storage needs. This chapter explains how to use the `BitSet`, `Dictionary`, `Hashtable`, `Properties`, `Vector`, and `Stack` container classes. The chapter also explains how to use the related `Cloneable` and `Enumeration` interfaces.

Exercises

1. Write a program that sorts an array of 100 unique integer values selected at random.
2. Write a program that copies the array of command-line arguments passed to an application's main() method. Convert the arguments to uppercase strings, and display them from the copied array.

3. Write a program that creates a hash table of Java's keywords. Print the table to the display, and also permit users to enter a command-line argument to search for a specific word. (Hint: Consider using the identifier as both key and data value. What are the consequences of doing this?)

4. Starting with the VectorDemo.java program in this chapter, write a method that returns true if the elements in the container are in sorted order. Use your method to prove that the sorting algorithm works.

5. Write a method that can extract any element from a Stack container without disturbing other values.

What's Next?

The next chapter, and the last in Part II, introduces the exciting subject of multithreaded programming. As you will discover, a Java application is capable of running multiple processes simultaneously—sort of like patting your head while rubbing your tummy and scrambling eggs all at the same time. You might not want to do that, but you'll certainly want to take advantage of Java's multitasking features to create processes that run in the background of other jobs.

11

CHAPTER

Threads

Java can execute multiple threads, which you might think of as chunks of code that appear to run simultaneously and independently of one another. Some possible uses for multithreaded applications include printing in the background, performing lengthy calculations while carrying out other tasks, programming multiple-player games, implementing parallel processing algorithms, and backing up files automatically. With threads, all of these tasks can take place while the application performs other operations in the foreground.

In This Chapter

This chapter covers the following fundamentals of multithreaded application development:

- Understanding multithreaded-programming concepts
- Extending the Thread class
- Implementing the Runnable interface
- Synchronizing code for safe data access

Concepts of Multithreaded Programming

If you sewed a line through the instructions of a program, the thread would follow the code's sequence of execution. A *multithreaded* application has two or more such lines, each identifying separately executing code sequences that weave in and out of each other like threads on a loom.

Every Java application is already multithreaded. The Java virtual machine executes an application as a thread, and the internal garbage collector, which frees memory occupied by unused objects, runs in the background as a separate thread. A program can also spawn its own threads to perform operations in the background, foreground, and anywhere in between. To control relative activity among threads, you may specify a priority level. Threads having highest priority get first crack at system resources; those with lower priorities operate in the shadows of more critical tasks.

> **NOTE**
>
> Because Java code is interpreted, it can execute multiple threads by time-slicing on a single-tasking processor or by spawning tasks that are handled on the operating system and processor levels. For application development, however, the implementation details are unimportant. If the Java interpreter is programmed correctly, multithreaded applications will run on simple single-tasking systems as well as under the control of sophisticated multitasking operating environments. Of course, multithreaded applications work as expected on Visual J++, but it's nice to know that your code will perform equally well on other platforms.

A Few Good Terms

Multithreaded programming comes with its own terminology that you need to understand before you can make good use of the involved techniques. Following are some multithreaded-programming terms and related concepts you'll meet throughout this chapter:

- *Daemon:* A daemon thread is one that does not have to die in order for the application to end. Specifically, the Java virtual machine exits when all non-daemon threads have terminated. An executing thread cannot be changed to a daemon, and only a daemon thread can spawn another daemon. (Although I can find no explicit guarantees on the subject, I'll go out on a limb and assume that the Java garbage collector is most likely a daemon thread, because there would be no logical reason for the interpreter to free unused objects immediately before the virtual machine exits.)

- *Monitor:* Although threads appear to run concurrently, they are still deterministic, and their independence is mere illusion. Because of the potential for interactions among threads, it is frequently necessary to synchronize thread activity through the use of monitors. This uses a system of locks, which control thread execution within defined regions of code. A thread comes to own an object's monitor by executing synchronized code for the object and, in that way, protecting data from disaster—preventing one thread from changing data, for example, while another thread prints the data's value. Some operations such as waiting for thread notification require the thread to own the object's monitor; or, to say that another way, the thread must be synchronized with other processes that modify the object's data.

- *Multitasking operating system:* This is generally defined as an operating system that can run more than one program simultaneously. A multitasking operating system also typically provides protected memory so that errant code in one application cannot destroy the code and data in another. Java's threads do not require, but can take advantage of, an operating system's multitasking capabilities. Because Java does not have pointers, and because all memory allocations are internally controlled, even in a single-tasking environment, it is highly unlikely for a Java program to overstep its assigned memory boundaries.

- *Multithreaded application:* This refers to a program that runs two or more concurrent tasks, each given a priority level that defines relative access to system resources. In Java, a thread is an object—usually an instance of the Thread class—but it is also possible to create threads by implementing the Runnable interface. Multithreaded Java applications do not require a multitasking operating system.

- *Sleep:* This term refers to the state of a thread that is temporarily inactive. The thread awakens after a specified amount of time passes or when another thread notifies the sleeper. A thread may go to sleep only if it owns the object's monitor, but sleeping does not relinquish ownership of that monitor.

- *Thread:* A thread is the sequence of execution in a program's instructions. In a multithreaded application, each thread's individual instructions execute as though interspersed with one another. Once started, a thread can pause in its execution by sleeping or waiting. Once stopped, however, a thread cannot be restarted. When all threads that are not daemons end, the Java virtual machine exits.

- *Wait:* This term refers to the state of a thread that is waiting for notification from another thread. Such notification comes typically when the state of the object or its data has changed due to some other thread's activities. A thread may wait only if it owns the object's monitor. Unlike sleeping, however, waiting for notification relinquishes ownership of the object's monitor.

And a Few Good Classes

As with all Java techniques, programming with threads makes use of one or more classes, all of which I'll explore in this chapter. The key classes are as follows:

- `Thread`: Used to construct an individual thread. Constructing an object of this class and calling its `start()` method creates a separately executing thread. However, if your class does not override any `Thread` methods, you can more simply achieve the same results by implementing the `Runnable` interface.

- `ThreadGroup`: Used to create thread sets, arranged in a tree-like hierarchy. The system thread group is at the root of this tree, which provides a measure of security to applications. For example, threads may spawn new threads only within their own group; to spawn a thread in another group requires approval from a security manager object.

- `Runnable`: Used to construct an individual thread, with the same results as instantiating the `Thread` class, but without requiring your class to extend `Thread`. Using the `Runnable` interface is appropriate when you don't need to override any `Thread` class methods; otherwise, building your class on `Thread` is the recommended technique.

- `ThreadDeath`: An object of this exception class is thrown to indicate that a thread is terminating. The Java virtual machine must receive this exception object in order to properly shut down the thread that originally threw the exception. An application may, however, catch this exception to perform cleanup chores for specific threads. When doing so, the `catch` block statement *must* rethrow the same `ThreadDeath` object so that the thread is properly extinguished.

- `InterruptedException`: An object of this class is thrown for a `Thread` object that is waiting or sleeping and interrupted by another thread that calls the `Thread.interrupt()` method.

- `IllegalMonitorStateException`: An object of this class is thrown if a thread attempts a monitor operation such as waiting or sleeping when the thread does not own its object's monitor.

- IllegalThreadStateException: An object of this class is thrown if a Thread object attempts an illegal operation—for example, attempting to start a thread that is already running.

Programming Multithreaded Applications

There are two ways to create a multithreaded application. The first and most common is to extend the Thread class, provided by the java.lang package. The second is to implement the Runnable interface, which is advantageous only if you have no need to override any of the methods inherited from Thread. The end results are operationally identical; only the programming techniques differ.

> **NOTE**
>
> To identify threads, you may assign them names, which is usually a good idea. Threads may have the same names, but if you don't specify one when you create the thread object, Java assigns one for you.

Extending the Thread Class

Before learning how to extend the Thread class, it's helpful to become generally familiar with its fields, constructors, and public methods. Listing 11.1 lists Java's Thread class declaration.

Listing 11.1. The Thread class.

```
class Thread implements Runnable {
// Fields:
 public final static int MIN_PRIORITY = 1;
 public final static int NORM_PRIORITY = 5;
 public final static int MAX_PRIORITY = 10;
// Constructors:
 public Thread();
 public Thread(Runnable target);
 public Thread(ThreadGroup group, Runnable target);
 public Thread(String name);
 public Thread(ThreadGroup group, String name);
 public Thread(Runnable target, String name);
 public Thread(ThreadGroup group, Runnable target, String name);
// Public methods:
 public static native Thread currentThread();
 public static native void yield();
 public static native void sleep(long millis);
 public static void sleep(long millis, int nanos);
 public synchronized native void start();
 public void run();
 public final void stop();
```

continues

Listing 11.1. continued

```
public final synchronized void stop(Throwable o);
public void interrupt();
public static boolean interrupted();
public boolean isInterrupted();
public void destroy();
public final native boolean isAlive();
public final void suspend();
public final void resume();
public final void setPriority(int newPriority);
public final int getPriority();
public final void setName(String name);
public final String getName();
public final ThreadGroup getThreadGroup();
public static int activeCount();
public static int enumerate(Thread tarray[]);
public native int countStackFrames();
public final synchronized void join(long millis);
public final synchronized void join(long millis, int nanos);
public final void join();
public static void dumpStack();
public final void setDaemon(boolean on);
public final boolean isDaemon();
public void checkAccess();
public String toString();
}
```

As you can see, the Thread class has numerous members. Rather than tediously describe them all, I'll briefly touch on some of the more important items, and cover others in due course.

Three static fields specify the minimum, default, and maximum priority levels that a thread object can have. Priorities range from 1 to 10, and are normally set in the middle at 5. You can inspect a thread's priority by calling getPriority(). Change the level by calling setPriority(). As I mentioned, threads with higher priorities get preferential treatment when it comes to accessing system resources, but regardless of priority, there is no guarantee that a thread will get any specific amount of operating time. (The maximum priority of 10 might prevent other threads from barely executing and should be used with care.)

To inspect the name of a thread, call getName(). To set its name, call setName(). Usually, however, you'll specify a thread's name when you create the object.

Start a thread by calling the start() method, which calls run(). (Don't call run() directly.) Put a thread to sleep for a specified amount of time by calling one of two sleep() methods. Tell a thread to wait for another thread's notification by calling suspend().Continue execution by calling resume(). Tell a thread to yield to other threads by calling yield().

To stop a thread, a program typically calls its stop() method. This causes the thread to throw a ThreadDeath exception object. You may also specify a different object to be thrown, but this is highly unusual and may skip important shutdown procedures. Normally, you should call stop() to halt a thread's execution. It is also possible to kill a thread by calling destroy(), but this does not throw ThreadDeath and should be considered strictly as a last-ditch technique for killing a thread.

When the Java virtual machine receives the ThreadDeath exception, it halts the thread's operation. As I mentioned, if the program catches this exception, it is important to rethrow it so the thread will actually die. The only way to restart a thread after it dies is to construct a new Thread object.

To wait for a thread to die, call one of the three join() methods. The one with no parameters waits forever. The others wait only for the specified amount of time. You have the option of specifying the number of milliseconds to wait or, for more precision, the number of milliseconds and nanoseconds. (Similar parameters are available for the two sleep() methods.)

Specify that you want a thread to be a daemon by passing true to the setDaemon() method. If you don't call this method, or if you pass it a false argument, the thread will be a normal non-daemon. After a thread starts running, its daemon status may not be changed, and calling setDaemon() will throw an IllegalThreadStateException object.

Now, let's examine a program that creates and runs multiple thread objects. Listing 11.2, ThreadDemo.java, shows how to use the Thread class to create a process that runs in the background, one of the most common uses you'll have for multithreaded programming.

Listing 11.2. ThreadDemo.java (Demonstrates multithreaded programming).

```java
// Extend Thread class and override the run() method
class Background extends Thread {
// Fields:
long count;         // Number of loops in run()
long trigger;       // Controls printing speed
boolean finished;   // True when thread should die
// Constructor:
Background(String name) {
 super(name);
 finished = false;    // Allows run() to continue
 trigger = 1000000;   // Increase to slow printing
 count = trigger / 2; // Makes first message appear sooner
}
// Override run() method (BUT DON'T CALL IT!)
public void run() {
 try {
  while (!finished) {   // Note: loops "forever!"
   count++;
   if (count == trigger)
    System.out.println("\nHurry up!");
   else if (count == trigger * 2)
    System.out.println("\nWhat's taking you so long?");
   else if (count == trigger * 3) {
    System.out.println("\nC'mon, press that key!");
    count = 0;  // Reset count to repeat messages
   }
  }
```

continues

Listing 11.2. continued

```
  } catch (InterruptedException e) {
   halt();
  }
 }
 // Causes run() method to halt
 public void halt() {
  finished = true;
  System.out.println("Stopping thread " + getName() + "\n");
  stop();  // Throws ThreadDeath exception
 }
}

// Main program demonstrates background processing
class ThreadDemo {
 public static void main(String args[]) throws Exception {
  Background background =
   new Background("Background process");
  System.out.println(
    "Starting thread. Press Enter to stop.");
  background.start();  // Start background thread
  while ((char)System.in.read() != '\n');  // Wait for key
  background.halt();   // Stop background thread
 }
}
```

Compile and run the sample program, which asks you to press Enter—but don't do that. Instead, wait for a few moments and you will soon see some messages that tell you to hurry up and press that key! These messages are printed by a background thread object, executing simultaneously with this statement, which waits for you to press Enter:

```
while ((char)System.in.read() != '\n');
```

Despite the fact that this statement appears to wait "forever" for read() to return a new-line control code, in fact other processes such as Java's garbage collector and the sample's thread object continue to execute normally in the background. Let's see how this works.

The first step in creating a thread is to extend the Thread class. In this case, the program declares a new class, Background, like this:

```
class Background extends Thread {
...
}
```

There are three critical tasks for the extended class to perform. These are

1. Provide a constructor to initialize instance variables. Although this step is technically not required, it is almost always included.

2. Override the run() method to perform the thread's activity. This method must catch or throw an InterruptedException object. Typically, the method executes until some external condition tells it to stop. This might be a notification from another thread, or as in the sample, it can be a simple boolean flag that causes a so-called "do-forever" loop to exit.

3. Provide some method for the program to halt the thread. This too is not required, but it is usually included as in the sample to set the `run()` method's flag and thus end the thread's execution.

These three steps are not set in concrete, and there are many possible ways to create thread objects. However, it's helpful to understand the straightforward technique before branching out to more sophisticated multithreaded tasks. Things can get confusing quickly! Take the sample's `Background` class a line at a time. Its constructor executes the statements

```
super(name);
finished = false;
trigger = 1000000;
count = trigger / 2;
```

Calling `super(name)` executes the `Thread` constructor, and this must be the first statement. It is optional to pass a `String` name, but usually you'll want to do this to distinguish multiple threads. The key statement here is the one that sets flag `finished` to `false`. This causes the thread's `while` loop in method `run()` to execute until the thread is halted. The other two variables, `trigger` and `count`, are merely used for the demonstration to control the output speed of the messages that impatiently hurry you along.

Of prime importance is the overridden `run()` method. Every extended `Thread` class *must* override this method to provide the code that the thread object is to execute. Remember that classes such as the demo's `Background` are merely declarations—the actual thread isn't created until the program instantiates the class by creating a `Background` object and calling `start()`. But more on that in a moment. First, examine closely how `run()` is programmed. The basic template is a `try` block that executes code while an external condition remains true:

```
try {
 while (!finished) {
  // put the thread's code here
 }
} catch (InterruptedException e) {
   halt();
}
```

The "do-forever" `while` loop in the sample executes some code while the `!finished` (not-finished) flag is true. The `try` block catches the `InterruptedException` object, which another thread could throw to interrupt this one's execution. In this sample, the exception calls local `halt()` method, which sets the `finished` flag true and calls `stop()`.

Inside `run()`, your code can perform whatever actions you want the thread to take. Here, the sample program increments a `count` variable and uses it to display some messages at intervals that are probably not too fast to read nor too slow to appear. Increase the value assigned to `trigger` for slower output; decrease it to speed up the program.

The important observation is that `run()` never exits normally! Other forces must therefore come to bear on the thread to cause it to end.

> **TIP**
>
> Never call `run()` in a statement. When started, the thread itself automatically calls `run()`.

To create the thread object, the sample program's `main()` method executes the statement

```
Background background =
 new Background("Background process");
```

This does not create the actual thread—it merely creates the `Thread` class *object*, which serves as an interface to the thread. To create the real thread and start it running, call the `start()` method as in this demonstration:

```
background.start();
```

This creates the thread, which calls the object's `run()` method. You may construct as many other threads of the same class as you want, and they may have the same or different names.

The program continues almost immediately after calling `start()`. Simply continue your code on its merry way, knowing that the background process is or soon will be started. As I mentioned, the sample program executes a `while` loop that waits for you to press Enter. However, because a thread is executing in the background, instead of pausing, the program prints messages telling you to hurry up.

After you finally press Enter, the main `while` loop ends. To stop the thread, the program executes the statement

```
background.halt();
```

It could also call `stop()` to do the same, but this might end the thread at any place inside `run()`. If you want `run()` to end normally, provide another method that changes a flag as in this sample. This is not required, but gives better control over how and when `run()` ends. Calling `stop()` directly is perfectly acceptable.

> **NOTE**
>
> The sample program has a potential quirk that might cause it to display a hurry-up message between the time you press Enter and the time that `halt()` calls `stop()`. Such is the difficult nature of multithreaded programming: Conflicts among simultaneous processes are likely to occur in places and at times when you least expect them!

Implementing a `Runnable` Interface

The second way to create a thread is to implement the `Runnable` interface. The only reason to do this is to avoid having to extend the `Thread` class, and you only want to do that to override one or more inherited methods. If you don't need to override any `Thread` methods, then implementing the `Runnable` interface is the recommended technique for creating a thread. Another advantage is that, by using this technique, any class can be made to execute in a separate thread. In fact, the `Thread` class itself implements `Runnable`, which provides a common protocol for threaded code. Listing 11.3 shows the declaration for the `Runnable` interface.

Listing 11.3. The `Runnable` interface.

```
interface Runnable {
 public abstract void run();
}
```

As you can see, `Runnable` is simplistic. It declares a single abstract method named `run()`, which the Java source code calls the "soul of a thread." As you do when extending the `Thread` class, insert statements in `run()` to execute concurrently with other threads. All classes that implement `Runnable` must provide a `run()` method.

Listing 11.4, `Primes.java`, demonstrates how to implement the `Runnable` interface. The program is becoming an old standard for Java thread demonstrations, but I'll do it a little differently than the usual labeled-loop and `break` statements that appear in several other sources.

Listing 11.4. `Primes.java` (Demonstrates the `Runnable` interface).

```
class Background implements Runnable {
 // Fields:
 boolean finished = false;  // True to end run()
 int num = 3;               // Prime number candidates
 // Return true if num is a prime number
 public synchronized boolean isPrime(int n) {
  for (int i = 2; i < n; i++)
   if ((n % i) == 0)
    return false;
  return true;
 }
 // Search for prime numbers in the background
 public void run() {
  while (!finished) {
   if (isPrime(num))
    System.out.println(num);
   num++;
  }
 }
 // Set flag to stop run()
 public synchronized void halt() {
  finished = true;
 }
}

// Compute prime numbers in the background
class Primes {
 public static void main(String args[]) throws Exception {
```

continues

Listing 11.4. continued

```
Background background = new Background();
System.out.println(
  "Starting thread. Press Enter to stop.");
new Thread(background).start();  // Start background thread
char ch = (char)System.in.read();  // Wait for key
background.halt();    // Stop background thread
 }
}
```

> **NOTE**
>
> If you are using an early release of Visual J++, the Prime.java program in this chapter might halt after a minute or so when executed under the DOS-prompt jview.exe interpreter. Other prime-number and multithreaded code exhibits this same behavior, indicating a bug in that interpreter. I include this note just in case you are having this trouble; chances are, this problem will be fixed in your release of Visual J++.

To create a class that can execute its code in a separate thread, declare it as the sample program does its Background class:

```
class Background implements Runnable {
...
}
```

The only requirement is that your class provides a run() method, which is called when the thread starts. (As mentioned several times, never call run() directly in a program statement!) In addition, however, you'll probably need a flag or some other variable to indicate when the thread should exit. The sample uses a boolean flag declared in the class as

```
boolean finished = false;
```

Implement the run() method to execute your code while the finished flag remains false (or until some other external condition changes). For example, the sample program calculates and displays prime numbers with this code:

```
public void run() {
 while (!finished) {
  if (isPrime(num))
   System.out.println(num);
  num++;
 }
}
```

The isPrime() method in the Background class returns true if the integer argument is a prime number. (I'm not trying to win any awards for prime-number algorithms here; there are better ways to calculate them than simply dividing test values by integers from 2 to n - 1!)

In addition to `run()`, you'll probably also want to program a method that changes the `finished` flag, and thus ends the thread. The sample program does this with a simple `halt()` method encoded as

```
public void halt() {
 finished = true;
}
```

That's all that is needed to implement the `Runnable` interface, which as I mentioned, you can do for any class. Because classes can implement multiple interfaces, but can extend only a single other class, this is especially convenient when you have other interfaces to import. It is also object-oriented "friendly," because it adheres to the general rule that extending a class merely to inherit its members, but not revise them in some way, is a poor programming practice.

To use the class, construct an object as you would for most other classes. Our sample class declares no constructors, so the main program uses the default no-parameter constructor form to create the object:

```
Background background = new Background();
```

It's important to realize that the `background` object is special only in that it *can* be executed in a thread due to the implementation of the `Runnable` interface protocol. It is otherwise a normal object no different than any other. To start the `run()` method rolling, construct an object of the `Thread` class using the `background` object, and call the thread's `start()` method:

```
new Thread(background).start();
```

Alternatively, you may save the `Thread` object so that you can call its members such as `setPriority()`:

```
Thread bgThread = new Thread(background).start();
```

Either way, as you can see, you still need to use the `Thread` class, but your class doesn't have to inherit `Thread`'s members. Passing the `background` object (the one of the `Background` class that implements `Runnable`) to the `Thread` constructor tells `Thread` to create an actual thread for your object's `run()` method. Calling `start()` calls `run()` automatically. I know I've said this before, but again, *do not call run() directly!* Let `start()` call `run()`—that's what it's for.

The thread is now running, and the program can proceed to other tasks—waiting for a keystroke, for example, as in the sample listing:

```
char ch = (char)System.in.read();
```

Because the prime-number thread is running independently of the main thread, prime numbers race by until you press Enter. When you do that, the preceding statement releases its grip on the main program thread, after which the statement

```
background.halt();
```

halts the prime-number thread by setting the `Background` class `finished` variable to `true`. You might see a couple of additional numbers printed after you press Enter because of the time it takes for `run()` to recognize that its flag has become `true`. Remember this quirk in your own code. It is virtually impossible to predict the exact moment that a thread will begin or end. All you can say with certainty is that a thread will begin soon after you start it, and it will end soon after you kill it. The meaning of "soon," however, depends on too many variables to be precisely defined.

Synchronizing Threads

When two or more concurrent processes access the same data, conflicts can arise that might lead to serious bugs. For example, suppose thread A calculates some test results that are saved in a series of variables in an object. Thread B displays the data values. Obviously, the program must ensure that thread A finishes updating all variables before thread B displays them. Although this means that the two threads essentially operate linearly—and there would seem to be no reason to program them as separate threads—other processes could continue while Thread A performs its calculations. On the other hand, if all code and data are synchronized, the program reverts to non-concurrent execution, and multithreaded techniques may not be appropriate. It takes a lot of careful thought to determine which methods need to be synchronized with what data.

To synchronize a method, declare it with the `synchronized Thread` class modifier like this:

```
public synchronized void anyMethod() {
...
}
```

This states that `anyMethod()` will not be permitted to run concurrently with other synchronized methods. Specifically, the method must obtain a *lock* on the object for the class in which the method is declared. There is only one such lock available per object, and therefore, only one synchronized method at a time may obtain the lock, also called a monitor. When `anyMethod()` returns, the lock is released, and another synchronized method is permitted to execute.

Presumably, each synchronized method accesses the same data, which could be instance variables in the class, or variables in another object. The location and type of data are unimportant. What matters is that the conflicting methods are permitted exclusive access to data by obtaining a lock on their class object.

It is also possible, however, to pass an object to the `synchronized` keyword, which indicates to the compiler that subsequent statements are not to be executed concurrently. For example, given an object `myData`, you can synchronize access to it by using code such as

```
synchronized(myData) {
 myData.f1();
}
synchronized(myData) {
 myData.f2();
}
```

This assumes that f1() and f2() are called by a separately executing thread. Synchronizing the methods this way for a specific object ensures that f1() and f2() will not run concurrently, and thus, any potential conflicts with data accessed by those methods is effectively prevented.

The preceding technique is usually a poor choice, because it puts the burden of synchronization on the user rather than on the supplier (that is, the class). It is far better to design a class with properly synchronized code than it is to expect your users to call methods correctly. If they make an error, chaos will result—and if you are in the business of selling Java class libraries, your phone will undoubtedly ring off the hook with complaints.

There's one other way to synchronize portions of code by using the synchronized modifier inside a method. For example, to synchronize one or more statements, pass the this keyword to synchronized as in this sample:

```
public void f1() {
 // unsynchronized code
 synchronized(this) {
  // synchronized code
 }
 // more unsynchronized code
}
```

The beauty of this method is that it narrows the synchronization down to just the statements that need a lock on the object in order to prevent conflicting access to data. Only the code inside the synchronized block is required to obtain the lock before it runs. Other statements in the method can run concurrently with other threads.

Summary

- Java can execute multiple threads, or processes, that appear to run concurrently.

- Every Java program is already multithreaded. The main program executes in one thread, while the Java garbage collector executes in another.

- There are two ways to create a separate thread. The first, and most common, is to extend the Thread class. The second is to implement the Runnable interface. The end results are the same, but implementing Runnable does not require you to inherit the Thread class, which you need to do only to override one or more inherited methods.

- In both cases, program the thread's code by providing a method named run() in your class. Never call this method directly. Instead, call the Thread class start() method, which creates the actual thread and calls run().

- To prevent conflicting access to data used by two or more threads, use the synchronized modifier. You may synchronize entire methods, blocks of code, or any statements that access data objects.

Exercises

1. Change the priority level of the Background object in ThreadDemo.java to the minimum possible value. Change it to the maximum. Test the differences these values have on the program's speed and user-friendliness.

2. Convert the ThreadDemo.java demonstration to one that implements the Runnable interface instead of extending the Thread class.

3. Show the declarations you would use for two methods, one named inputString() and the other outputString(), that access the same String object in a thread object.

What's Next?

This is the last chapter in Part II, and it concludes this book's fundamental Java tutorials. Congratulations—if you've understood the material so far and can do most of the exercises, you are well on your way to becoming a Java wizard! Next up are some in-depth examinations of Java's class library *packages*. As you will discover, there is literally a *ton* of prepackaged code you can import into your applications for all sorts of purposes.

PART

III

Packages

12

CHAPTER

Introducing Packages

No programming language can possibly provide all the tools that a software developer needs. In addition to a language's fundamental elements, programmers need toolkits that provide ready-to-use classes for creating user interfaces, accessing networks, performing input and output, displaying graphics, and performing other tasks. A language provides a program's basic structure. Toolkits add walls, windows, doors, and other extensions that help you turn the program's frame into a finished dwelling.

In Java, a toolkit is called a *package*. Collectively, all of Java's toolkits comprise its *class library*. This chapter explains how to use the packages and classes provided with your Visual J++ development system (and with most other Java installations), and also how to write your own packages. The rest of the chapters in Part III provide in-depth coverage for many of the classes in Java's standard packages.

In This Chapter

This chapter covers the following fundamentals of programming with packages:

- Using packages
- Importing Java's standard packages
- Writing your own packages

Introducing Java Packages

A package is simply a group of related classes. For example, a set of graphics classes might be grouped into a package named *graphics*. To use the classes, one or more modules in a program can import the entire package, or any of its individual classes with a declaration such as this hypothetical statement:

```
import graphics.*;
```

It's important to note that this statement imports the *classes* in the package. It is not correct to import the package by name itself. For example, the declaration

```
import graphics;  // ???
```

produces a compilation error. You'll better understand the reason for this rule when you discover that the package's name corresponds to its directory location on disk or its hierarchy in a compressed ZIP file such as classes.zip. Thus the java.awt package is located in a directory named java\awt, which is typically a subdirectory in another path. For example, under Windows 95 using Visual J++, the source code for the java.awt package is located in C:\Windows\Java\Classes\java\awt. In the classes.zip file, it is located in the hierarchical path java\awt.

Java provides a number of preprogrammed packages, some of which you have already seen in Part II's tutorial. A package such as java.io provides input and output services. The java.lang package provides general-purpose classes such as String, System, and Math. There are several other packages introduced in this chapter and covered in detail in the rest of the chapters in Part III.

Packages are also great for organizing a complex application into reusable modules. In this chapter, you also learn how to develop your own packages, which you might reuse in numerous applications. Remember that old saw of programming, which is as true today as yesteryear: "divide and conquer." Rather than attempt to construct a major application from top to bottom, it's far better—and usually a lot easier—to divide its complexity into manageable chunks. Try to identify the generalities among these pieces, and program them as packages of classes that you can reuse in other projects.

Another key advantage of packages is the encapsulation of code and data on a module level. Even though classes are commonly written and stored in separate compilation units (source-code files), multiple classes within the same package can access friendly declarations in the package's other classes. Those same declarations, however, are inaccessible to the package's users, an arrangement that solves one of object-oriented programming's stickier messes—the need for classes to have ready-access to data, but still deny users that same level of access. We'll examine a working example of this technique later in the chapter.

import Statements

As you have seen in many of this book's sample programs, to use a class or an interface declared in a package often requires an import statement. Actually, however, this isn't the whole story: import statements are an optional convenience, and are technically not required. For example, to use the Stack class in the java.util package, a module can import the class using the statement

```
import java.util.Stack;
```

This tells the compiler to load the declaration for the class and make it available to statements such as the following, which constructs a Stack object:

```
Stack storage = new Stack();
```

Alternatively, however, you may specify the full package and class name *without* using an import statement. For example, the statement

```
java.util.Stack storage = new java.util.Stack();
```

fully qualifies the Stack class, telling the compiler in which package it is located—importing the class is not necessary. Using fully qualified expressions is more work, of course, but eliminates the need for an import statement. The long form is possibly useful for debugging—to temporarily use a test version of a class, for example. An import statement, though, is better in most cases.

`import` statements may also use an asterisk wildcard character to load all class declarations within a package. For instance, the statement

```
import java.util.*;
```

imports all classes in the `java.util` package. Because you'll often use numerous classes in a single package, this form of `import` statement is probably the most common. It might, however, cause the compiler to work a little harder loading all class declarations, and when you need only one or two, you can save a little time importing them individually by name. In either case, all of a package's code winds up in the finished application even if you import only one class. This is because a package's classes automatically import one another—but importing only specific classes relieves the compiler from opening unused `.class` files.

You can import the class library's whole ball of wax with the statement

```
import java.*;
```

In most cases, however, it's better to bring in just the classes you intend to use.

> **NOTE**
>
> `import` statements require the compiler to be able to locate class declarations, which are stored in a compressed ZIP file, known as a *database*, or in individual bytecode `.class` files. The command-line compiler uses an environment variable named `CLASSPATH` to locate these files. Visual J++ uses the Developer Studio's, or the newer Visual Studio 97's, *Tools/Options* dialog's *Directories* settings for *Class files*.

Java's Standard Packages

Java provides eight standard packages, some of which you have already met such as `java.lang` and `java.util`. Others are the subjects of the remaining chapters in Part III. In alphabetical order, these packages are

- `java.applet`: Provides the means to create Java applets, which are typically executed using a Web browser such as Microsoft's Internet Explorer or HotJava. Applets are usually referenced by statements in HTML (Hypertext Markup Language) documents, which when viewed in a suitable browser, load and execute the necessary applets. The `java.applet` package, though small, contains the classes you'll need to construct your own Java applets. This package also provides the `AudioClip` class for playing audio files. See Chapter 13, "Applets."

- `java.awt`: Provides classes for *Another Window Toolkit* (AWT), which as its name suggests, provides a class-based graphical user interface with the usual windows, buttons, dialog boxes, and other controls that are undoubtedly second nature to all readers. See Chapter 14, "Another Window Toolkit," for descriptions of the classes in this extensive package.

- `java.awt.image`: Provides graphics classes for use with the `java.awt` package. Notice that this is an example of a nested package. See Chapter 15, "Events and Layouts."

- `java.awt.peer`: Provides AWT with interfaces to the operating system's graphical elements. For example, these classes are how AWT interfaces with Windows 95 buttons and other controls. Most Java installations, and all those using Visual J++, provide ready-to-use `awt.peer` classes, and therefore, I do not discuss them in this book. (You don't need to use these classes in applications.)

- `java.io`: Provides various input and output service classes for the keyboard, display, printer, and disk files. You'll find numerous classes in this package for file streams, buffers, filters, pipes, printer stream objects, and more. See Chapter 16, "Windows, Menus, and Dialogs."

- `java.lang`: Provides wrapper classes such as `Character`, `Integer`, and `Double`, and also `String` and `StringBuffer` classes. In addition, the essential `System`, `Thread`, and `Object` classes are declared in this package. Java automatically imports all of these classes into every module; you do not need to import them explicitly, although doing so is harmless. You have already met most of these classes in Part II.

- `java.net`: Provides network and socket handler classes, for communications with input and output protocols.

- `java.util`: Provides various low-level and miscellaneous utility classes such as the containers `Vector`, `Hashtable`, and `Stack`, covered in Chapter 10, "Arrays and Other Containers," and also the generally useful `Date` class, introduced in Chapter 5, "Classes and Objects."

> **NOTE**
>
> Java installations are required to implement only three packages: `java.lang`, `java.util`, and `java.io`. Most installations, however—and, of course, all Visual J++ sites—fully implement all eight standard packages.

Programming with Packages

Creating your own packages is a great way to preserve useful classes that you construct during the course of writing an application. By organizing your program's classes into packages, you make them more readily available to future applications, and a little thought now in collecting generally useful classes into packages will go a long way in the future. This section explains how to create your own packages.

Package Names

If you are creating packages for your own use, you can name them whatever you like. (Don't use Java's standard package names, though.) Many developers, however, will share packages or distribute them via the Internet. In that case, it's a good idea to use your Web page or e-mail address in your package names. This way, you ensure that your package names are unique. For example, if Ugly Duckling Software's URL is ugly.com, the company developers might name their packages `com.ugly.util`, `com.ugly.io`, and `com.ugly.graphics`. By convention, a URL is reversed so that `name.edu` becomes `edu.name`. Microsoft's Java classes, for example, are prefaced with the pathname `com\ms`. You don't have to use this convention, but it's an easy way to prevent conflicts with the names of packages from other sources.

In Visual J++, as in most Java installations, package names correspond with the operating system's directory structure. This provides a convenient method for storing and accessing packages, and simplifies the development system's configuration. Under Visual J++, package names are case sensitive, and the corresponding directories must match exactly. This might not be true, however, under all Java installations, and it is unwise to rely only on upper- and lowercase to distinguish among package names.

How to Create a Package

Creating a package is easy—simply preface the module with a statement such as

```
package Stuff;
```

This line must come before any other declarations or statements except comments. A `package` declaration states that subsequent classes are to be collected within the named package—`Stuff` in this case—and as such, the `.class` files are to be found in a subdirectory of that same name. Typically, `.class` and `.java` source code files are stored together in the same directories, but this isn't required, and to use the package, only the `.class` files need be provided.

The classes in a package may declare any classes, and they may import other classes, either of your own design or from Java's standard library. Most developers prefer to implement one class per `.java` source code file, but there is no restriction on the number of classes you may declare within a compilation unit. Classes within the same package automatically import the other classes in that package, so there's no advantage to bunching them together within the same file. As a rule, only classes that are intimately related should be implemented in the same file. Use separate `.java` source files for all other classes.

Use your own packages as you do Java's. For example, to use the classes in the `Stuff` package, a program would declare

```
import Stuff.*;
```

Or, you can import the package's classes individually by name, using declarations such as

```
import Stuff.TClass1;
import Stuff.TClass2;
```

An example will clarify how this works and also show how classes in a package can access friendly declarations. The next three listings go together. (See the following Note box for compilation instructions.) Listing 12.1, PackageTest.java, shows the program's main application class. Listing 12.2, Stuff\TClass1.java, implements one of the package's two test classes. Listing 12.3, Stuff\TClass2.java, implements the other test class and also shows how one class in a package can access friendly declarations in another.

> **NOTE**
>
> To compile the classes in the Stuff package, and to compile and run the demonstration program, first change to the PackageTest\Stuff subdirectory at a DOS prompt. Compile the two classes by entering the command jvc tclass1 tclass2. This compiles both classes in their separate source code modules. Next, change to the PackageTest directory, and compile the test program by entering jvc packagetest. Finally, run the test by issuing the command jview packagetest. This displays two lines of text by virtue of methods in the two test classes.

Listing 12.1. PackageTest.java (Demonstrates packages).

```java
import Stuff.*;
class PackageTest {
 public static void main(String args[]) {
  TClass1 x = new TClass1("Test");
  System.out.println("via TClass1: " + x.getName());
  TClass2 y = new TClass2();
  System.out.println("via TClass2: " + y.returnName(x));
 }
}
```

Listing 12.2. Stuff\TClass1.java (Stuff test class #1).

```java
package Stuff;
public class TClass1 {
 String name;  // Friendly declaration
 public TClass1(String name) {
  this.name = name;
 }
 public String getName() {
  return name;
 }
}
```

Listing 12.3. Stuff\TClass2.java (Stuff test class #2).

```
package Stuff;
public class TClass2 {
 public String returnName(TClass1 obj) {
  return obj.name;
 }
}
```

To understand how the Stuff package works, first take a look at its directory structure. The two test classes, TClass1 and TClass2, have their .class and .java files stored in the directory PackageTest\Stuff. When directory PackageTest is current, the compiler automatically looks in the Stuff subdirectory to find classes imported from the Stuff package. If another directory were current, you would have to set the CLASSPATH environment variable—or use the equivalent *Directory* setting in Developer Studio or Visual Studio 97—to tell the compiler where to look for package subdirectory names. For example, you might execute this DOS command:

```
set CLASSPATH=c:\packages\source
```

This assumes that the Stuff directory is inside c:\packages\source. To check the current setting, type SET at a DOS prompt and press Enter. (Pardon me if this is old hat, but many programmers today know only a smidgen of DOS commands, so I thought I'd better be explicit.)

Each of the two test classes in the sample Stuff package is written in a separate compilation unit, named the same as the class. TClass1.java, for example, implements the TClass1 class. This class declares a friendly String instance variable, and it provides a constructor and method. Because these two methods are declared public, they are available to users of the package. (Though not shown here, protected declarations, of course, are available only to classes that extend the class.) Notice also that the class declaration itself *must* be public for it to be available outside of the package. Because no public, private, or protected access specifier is used for the String instance variable, it defaults to friendly status. Other classes in this compilation unit, and also all other classes in the same package, have direct access to this friendly variable as though it were declared public. Outside of the package, however, the variable is private. This means the test program must call a method to access TClass1's data; the program cannot access the name variable directly. In this way, the package provides a measure of safety in the use of its classes by hiding sensitive data, but without restricting access to that data within the package. This is a tremendous advantage over C++ and other object-oriented languages, which offer no similar organizational mechanisms for class libraries.

Classes within the same package automatically import one another, and references may be circular. (For example, class A may use class B, which may reference class A.) Compilation units may import other classes, but should not import classes in the same package, or the compiler will probably issue a warning that a package has already been imported.

Each compilation unit within the package must begin with the identical `package` declaration, which in this example is

```
package Stuff;
```

As I mentioned, this declaration and its associated directory are case sensitive under Windows 95 and Visual J++, but they might not be so under another Java installation.

NOTE

When you construct an application or applet, its classes are considered to be members of an *unnamed package*. All Java installations are required to support at least one such unnamed package, the use of which is automatic and requires no `package` or `import` declarations. However, if you receive an error message that tells you a class is in the package <none> rather than one of an expected name, the likely cause is a spelling error (you might have typed `stuff` rather than `Stuff`, for instance) or an incorrect `CLASSPATH` setting.

Summary

- Java's packages provide libraries of related classes that perform all sorts of useful operations. The Java programming language provides fundamental capabilities for writing code. Packages provide I/O, network, graphics, window, and other toolkits of classes that you can use to build applications.

- As you have seen in many of this book's sample programs, to use a package's classes, a program declares it in an `import` statement. An `import` statement may import all classes in a package, or individual classes by name. An `import` statement, however, can import only types (classes), not packages themselves.

- Java provides eight standard packages, most of which are described in the next several chapters of Part III. Java installations are not required to support all of these packages, but most do.

- You can create your own packages, which is a good way to collect generally useful classes and make them available for future projects. Package names correspond with their storage locations on disk and, in Visual J++, are case sensitive.

- Classes within a package automatically import and may refer to one another. Only `public` declarations are available outside of the package. Protected declarations are, of course, available to classes that extend those in the package. If a declaration does not use a `public`, `private`, or `protected` access specifier, it is friendly and is freely available to all classes in the package. Friendly declarations, however, are private to classes outside of the package.

What's Next?

Now that you have a working knowledge of how to use and create packages, you are ready to dig into Java's rich class library. The next chapter presents one of the most generally useful and extensive packages in the set—`java.applet`. As you will see, this package is the essential ingredient for constructing applets embedded in Web page HTML documents.

13

Applets

Applets and Java go together like peanut butter and jelly. Of course you can write stand-alone applications using Java, but the real excitement in Java programming is the development of applets distributed over the World Wide Web. With a few simple strokes of your pen—make that keyboard—you can insert applets into your Web page's HTML documents. When loaded into a suitable browser, the documents reach out over the Web and pull in needed applet classes to be executed on the user's system. Simple, right? Yes, but through this singular concept of adding interactive code to HTML documents, applets are literally transforming the way people are using the Internet, and its an idea whose impact will be felt long into the future of network programming.

In This Chapter

This chapter covers the following fundamentals of creating and using applets for Web-page documents and other HTML documents:

- Ways to create an applet
- The HTML `<applet>` tag
- Applet class methods
- Applet programming techniques

How to Create an Applet

An applet is simply a Java class that is executed within another application. That other application is usually a Web page browser such as Netscape, Hot Java, or Internet Explorer, which you received with your Visual J++ CD-ROM. You can also run an applet for test purposes using the `jview.exe` application, also supplied with Visual J++. This requires some additional code, as I'll explain in this chapter, but it's a little faster and doesn't require opening an HTML document. You normally run `jview.exe` from a DOS prompt, but an applet's output appears in a graphical window just as it does in a graphical Web browser.

The following sections explain several methods for creating and viewing applets. Try each technique so you'll know which one to use for your own code.

> **NOTE**
>
> Not all Web browsers support Java applets, although the situation is far better today than in the recent past. There are also text-only browsers still in use that don't support graphics. Probably, this won't be a concern to most readers. Just make sure you are using the latest version of your favorite browser; it will probably support Java applets as described in this chapter. Of course, if you installed Microsoft's Internet Explorer shipped with Visual J++, you are ready to run any and all applets in this book and from other sources.

Simple Method

You probably won't use the simple method described in this section to create your own applets, but even so, it's useful to go through the motions. This will introduce the basic layouts of applet source code and related files, and it's also a handy technique for testing various ideas. Use this applet-creation method if you just want to try an algorithm without recompiling your entire 10,000-line, whiz bang, 3D spreadsheet applet.

Although the resulting files of the following instructions are on the CD-ROM in the Part3\AppletADay directory, it's beneficial to go through the steps from scratch. Create an empty directory named AppletADay anywhere on you hard drive, and then follow these numbered steps to create the applet:

1. Start Developer Studio or Visual Studio 97, or if Studio is running, close the current workspace. Answer Yes if asked to close all document windows.

2. Choose *File\New* and select *Text File.*

3. Enter the text from Listing 13.1, AppletADay.java, into the blank text-file window created in step 2. (Hint: To turn on syntax coloring, do step 4 before typing. This names the file and tells Developer or Visual Studio 97 which algorithms to use for coloring statements.)

4. Choose *File\Save.* The first time you do this, browse to your AppletADay directory and enter AppletADay.java for the file name. Press Enter or select OK to save the applet's source code file.

5. Choose *Build\Build AppletADay* to compile the applet. The first time you do this, you are asked whether to create a default project workspace—answer Yes. This also creates some related files in the directory, which I'll explain in a moment.

6. Make sure the Output window shows no compilation errors, and then choose *Build\Execute.* Enter AppletADay for the *Class file name* (this is case sensitive and must be typed exactly as printed here). Make sure *Run project under* is set to *Browser,* and then press Enter or click OK.

You should soon see Internet Explorer or your favorite browser start up and display the applet's message: "An Applet a Day Keeps the Debugger Away!" Or, anyway, you'll see most of the message. Because we are using the default window size, the message is probably chopped off somewhere in the middle. No problem—we'll take care of things like that in due course.

Listing 13.1. AppletADay.java (Demonstrates a simple applet).

```
import java.awt.Graphics;
class AppletADay
extends java.applet.Applet {
 // Paint method draws a string on screen
 public void paint(Graphics g) {
  g.drawString(
   "An Applet a Day Keeps the Debugger Away!", 10, 25);
 }
}
```

Up to now, I've recommended using the command-line compiler `jvc.exe` and viewer `jview.exe` from a DOS prompt to learn Java fundamentals. For constructing applets, however, you will need the more sophisticated programming environment offered by Developer Studio or Visual Studio 97. I developed most of the applets and code in this and the next chapters in Part III using these tools along with the Visual J++ Applet Wizard. To view the CD-ROM's project files, open the `.mdp` workspace file in the subdirectories under `Part3` on the CD-ROM.

A couple of interesting events take place when you run the simple `AppletADay` class in a browser. First, notice that the URL address of the HTML file is something like this:

```
C:\Mvj\Part3\AppletADay\VJC003.HTML
```

This is *not* your typical URL—it's obviously a directory pathname. You might also notice the same path displayed elsewhere along with the notation (`local`), which indicates that the file is being opened on your system rather than over the Web. Browsers of only recent vintage were not capable of this magic—but most current ones are, and of course, Internet Explorer can load HTML documents both locally and over the network.

Before moving to the next technique for creating applets, examine `AppletADay`'s source code. This is just about the simplest possible applet. It imports the `Graphics` class to give the applet a method to call for displaying text, and it extends the `Applet` class. All applets must extend this class, which provides the interface that Java-capable browsers require. Inside the class, the overridden `paint()` method provides the code that runs when the browser executes the applet. Don't be concerned at this point about what's going on in the program. I want to introduce general applet programming techniques before discussing what you can do with them. We'll get to these items later in this chapter and then go into them more fully in the next several chapters, which discuss interfacing, graphics, and other visual-programming techniques.

Look also in the directory for other files created when you compiled the applet. One of those files is the HTML document that embeds the applet (actually, it just references the file, but it's common to say that the applet is "embedded" in the document even though it's not). Listing 13.2, `Vjc003.html`, shows the document's contents. (It might be named something else because Developer Studio or Visual Studio 97 created it.)

Developer Studio and Visual Studio 97 add several comment lines to the HTML listing shown here. To save space, I deleted those lines, which you will see if you re-create the file.

Listing 13.2. `Vjc003.html` (Created by Developer Studio).

```
<html>
<head>
<title>AppletADay</title>
</head>
<body>
<hr>
<applet
code=AppletADay
width=200
height=200>
```

Later in this chapter, you'll examine the format for `<applet>` tags, which as shown here, must have a minimum of three parts: a `code` name, a `width`, and a `height`. You'll probably also see a dire warning in this file, which I deleted here, admonishing you never to edit the text because it will be re-created when you compile the applet. That's true, so you'll probably want to load the file into Notepad or another text editor, and save it as `AppletADay.html`. Change the width to 300, and then load that document into your browser. You should now see the full message that was previously chopped in half.

Use these steps to create a permanent HTML file that will not be regenerated when you compile:

1. Create a new text file and save it.
2. Insert the file into your project.
3. Select *Settings* from the *Build* menu, and then perform the following steps:
   a. Choose the *Debug* tab.
   b. Set *Category* to Browser.
   c. In the *Parameters* section, select *Use parameters from HTML page*.
   d. Specify the new HTML filename in the edit box for *HTML page*.

Using the Applet Wizard

The preceding section illustrates some important aspects of applet programming and their association to HTML documents. However, you won't use the foregoing technique in practice. Real live applets need to be multithreaded (usually), they might display animated graphics, and they require critical initialization and termination programming. It's certainly possible to construct all of these details from scratch, but why work harder than necessary? In almost all cases, you are best advised to use the Applet Wizard to create an applet shell that you can fill in with your applet's code. This section explains how to do that, and also examines the resulting shell's parts. I used this method to develop most of the sample applets included on this book's CD-ROM.

To experiment with the technique, it's useful to create a raw, do-nothing shell. You can use the supplied files on the CD-ROM if you want, but I urge you to roll your own applet for experience. Follow these steps to create an applet shell using the Visual J++ Applet Wizard:

1. Start Developer or Visual Studio 97, or if Studio is already running, close the current workspace. Answer Yes if asked to close all document windows.

2. Choose *File|New* and select *Project Workspace* to bring up the New Project Workspace dialog box, or if using Visual Studio 97, select the Projects tab. Select *Java Applet Wizard* under *Type,* and then enter WorldView in the Name field. Click the Browse button (shown as an ellipsis button in Visual Studio 97) and change to any working directory; the Applet Wizard will create a WorldView subdirectory in that location into which it will store all of the project's files.

3. Click the Create button (named OK in Visual Studio 97), which displays the first of five dialog box pages in this wizard. Examine each page, but don't make any changes. Click the Next button until it dims, and then click Finish on the final page. This displays a summary of the applet's attributes. Click OK to generate the source files.

4. Compile and run the applet as you did AppletADay in the preceding section. First, choose *Build\Build WorldView,* and then select *Build\Execute WorldView.* Because you used the Applet Wizard to create the project workspace, the applet's class name is already entered in the *Execute* command.

You should soon see a spinning world displayed in your default browser. Figure 13.1 shows Internet Explorer running the WorldView shell on my system. This is a dramatic example of what an applet can do! Although not evident, the entire animation is running in a thread, and therefore, if this were taking place through a Web connection, the user might see other parts of the downloaded document while the graphic is being initialized and while the Java code is executing. Of course, everything is currently running locally on your system—but you are seeing *exactly* what the end user will see on his or her computer, and that's the way it should be. (The browser might be different, of course, but the applet should appear just as it does for you, or at least as closely as is possible given the end user's system parameters.)

Figure 13.1.
The WorldView applet running in the Internet Explorer Web browser.

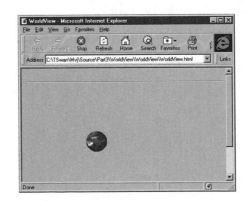

Listing 13.3 shows the code shell generated by the Visual J++ Applet Wizard. There are many pieces to this file, some of which we'll examine in future chapters. However, I'll give an overview of its contents following the listing for those who are itching to get started writing their own applets. (To accomplish that, you'll need to read at least the next two chapters—so hold off for a while longer if you can.)

Listing 13.3. WorldView.java (Applet Wizard shell).

```
//******************************************************************************
// WorldView.java: Applet (Applet Wizard shell)
//******************************************************************************
import java.applet.*;
import java.awt.*;

//==============================================================================
// Main Class for applet WorldView
//==============================================================================
public class WorldView extends Applet implements Runnable
{
 // THREAD SUPPORT:
 //   m_WorldView is the Thread object for the applet
 //--------------------------------------------------------------------------
 Thread  m_WorldView = null;

 // ANIMATION SUPPORT:
 //   m_Graphics  used for storing the applet's Graphics context
 //   m_Images[]  the array of Image objects for the animation
 //   m_nCurrImage the index of the next image to be displayed
 //   m_ImgWidth  width of each image
 //   m_ImgHeight  height of each image
 //   m_fAllLoaded indicates whether all images have been loaded
 //   NUM_IMAGES  number of images used in the animation
 //--------------------------------------------------------------------------
 private Graphics m_Graphics;
 private Image    m_Images[];
 private int      m_nCurrImage;
 private int      m_nImgWidth  = 0;
 private int      m_nImgHeight = 0;
 private boolean  m_fAllLoaded = false;
 private final int NUM_IMAGES = 18;

 // WorldView Class Constructor
 //--------------------------------------------------------------------------
 public WorldView()
 {
  // TODO: Add constructor code here
 }

 // APPLET INFO SUPPORT:
 //   The getAppletInfo() method returns a string describing the applet's
 //   author, copyright date, or miscellaneous information.
 //--------------------------------------------------------------------------
 public String getAppletInfo()
 {
```

continues

Listing 13.3. continued

```java
  return "Name: WorldView\r\n" +
         "Author: Tom Swan\r\n" +
         "Created with Microsoft Visual J++ Version 1.0";
}

// The init() method is called by the AWT when an applet is first loaded or
// reloaded.  Override this method to perform whatever initialization your
// applet needs, such as initializing data structures, loading images or
// fonts, creating frame windows, setting the layout manager, or adding UI
// components.
//-----------------------------------------------------------------------
public void init()
{
// If you use a ResourceWizard-generated "control creator" class to
// arrange controls in your applet, you may want to call its
// CreateControls() method from within this method. Remove the following
// call to resize() before adding the call to CreateControls();
// CreateControls() does its own resizing.
//----------------------------------------------------------------
  resize(320, 240);

  // TODO: Place additional initialization code here
}

// Place additional applet clean up code here.  destroy() is called when
// when your applet is terminating and being unloaded.
//-----------------------------------------------------------------------
public void destroy()
{
  // TODO: Place applet cleanup code here
}

// ANIMATION SUPPORT:
//   Draws the next image, if all images are currently loaded
//-----------------------------------------------------------------------
private void displayImage(Graphics g)
{
 if (!m_fAllLoaded)
  return;
 // Draw Image in center of applet
 //-------------------------------------------------------------
 g.drawImage(m_Images[m_nCurrImage],
  (size().width - m_nImgWidth)  / 2,
  (size().height - m_nImgHeight) / 2, null);
}
// WorldView Paint Handler
//-----------------------------------------------------------------------
public void paint(Graphics g)
{
 // ANIMATION SUPPORT:
 //   The following code displays a status message until all the
 //   images are loaded. Then it calls displayImage to display the current
 //   image.
 //-------------------------------------------------------------
 if (m_fAllLoaded)
 {
  Rectangle r = g.getClipRect();
```

```
  g.clearRect(r.x, r.y, r.width, r.height);
  displayImage(g);
 }
 else
  g.drawString("Loading images...", 10, 20);

 // TODO: Place additional applet Paint code here
}


//   The start() method is called when the page containing the applet
// first appears on the screen. The AppletWizard's initial implementation
// of this method starts execution of the applet's thread.
//-------------------------------------------------------------------------
public void start()
{
 if (m_WorldView == null)
 {
  m_WorldView = new Thread(this);
  m_WorldView.start();
 }
 // TODO: Place additional applet start code here
}



//   The stop() method is called when the page containing the applet is
// no longer on the screen. The AppletWizard's initial implementation of
// this method stops execution of the applet's thread.
//-------------------------------------------------------------------------
public void stop()
{
 if (m_WorldView != null)
 {
  m_WorldView.stop();
  m_WorldView = null;
 }

// TODO: Place additional applet stop code here
 }


// THREAD SUPPORT
// The run() method is called when the applet's thread is started. If
// your applet performs any ongoing activities without waiting for user
// input, the code for implementing that behavior typically goes here. For
// example, for an applet that performs animation, the run() method controls
// the display of images.
//-------------------------------------------------------------------------
public void run()
{
 m_nCurrImage = 0;

 // If re-entering the page, then the images have already been loaded.
 // m_fAllLoaded == TRUE.
 //-------------------------------------------------------------------
       if (!m_fAllLoaded)
 {
     repaint();
     m_Graphics = getGraphics();
     m_Images   = new Image[NUM_IMAGES];
```

continues

Listing 13.3. continued

```java
    // Load in all the images
    //------------------------------------------------------------------
    MediaTracker tracker = new MediaTracker(this);
    String strImage;

    // For each image in the animation, this method first constructs a
    // string containing the path to the image file; then it begins
    // loading the image into the m_Images array.  Note that the call to
    // getImage will return before the image is completely loaded.
    //------------------------------------------------------------------
    for (int i = 1; i <= NUM_IMAGES; i++)
    {
     // Build path to next image
     //------------------------------------------------------------
     strImage = "images/img00" + ((i < 10) ? "0" : "") + i + ".gif";
     m_Images[i-1] = getImage(getDocumentBase(), strImage);

            tracker.addImage(m_Images[i-1], 0);
    }

    // Wait until all images are fully loaded
    //------------------------------------------------------------------
try
{
 tracker.waitForAll();
 m_fAllLoaded = !tracker.isErrorAny();
}
catch (InterruptedException e)
{
 // TODO: Place exception-handling code here in case an
 //       InterruptedException is thrown by Thread.sleep(),
 //    meaning that another thread has interrupted this one
}

if (!m_fAllLoaded)
{
 stop();
 m_Graphics.drawString("Error loading images!", 10, 40);
 return;
}


    // Assuming all images are same width and height.
    //------------------------------------------------------------
    m_nImgWidth  = m_Images[0].getWidth(this);
    m_nImgHeight = m_Images[0].getHeight(this);
        }
repaint();

while (true)
{
 try
 {
  // Draw next image in animation
  //------------------------------------------------------------
  displayImage(m_Graphics);
  m_nCurrImage++;
```

```
      if (m_nCurrImage == NUM_IMAGES)
       m_nCurrImage = 0;

      // TODO:  Add additional thread-specific code here
      Thread.sleep(50);
     }
    catch (InterruptedException e)
    {
     // TODO: Place exception-handling code here in case an
     //       InterruptedException is thrown by Thread.sleep(),
     //    meaning that another thread has interrupted this one
     stop();
    }
   }
  }
 }
 // TODO: Place additional applet code here
}
```

TIP

The Visual J++ Applet Wizard creates class and file browser information that makes it easy to view an applet's parts and pieces. (If you closed the WorldView workspace, reopen `WorldView.mdp` now, or open that file from the CD-ROM.) Notice that the InfoViewer panel, usually on the left side of the Developer Studio screen (named InvoView under Visual Studio 97), has some new tabs below it. Click the one that looks like a hierarchical chart to display the project's classes. Open any class by clicking its plus sign; you'll see all of its methods and instance variable declarations. To hop to that place in the source files, double-click the method or other identifier you want to see. Use this method while following the discussions of the applet shell in this chapter—its a lot easier than hunting through a long listing or searching for text. Another way to find items is to select the tab that looks like a page of paper. This displays the project's files, in this case including the animation's `.gif` graphics files and the `WorldView.java` and `WorldView.html` source files. Double-click any of these to open the files or, if they are already open, to display them in the text editor window. You can also open a `.gif` file to edit the graphics image using Developer Studio's or Visual Studio 97's image editor.

The applet's `WorldView` class is typical of most applets. It's declared as

```
public class WorldView extends Applet implements Runnable {
...
}
```

This performs two essential functions. It causes `WorldView` to inherit `Applet`'s members and, thus, become qualified for running as an applet. The class also implements `Runnable`, which enables the applet to run in a separate thread. Declare most applets this way so other processes such as the display of text and other applet graphics can continue while the user downloads this portion of your document.

A WorldView object saves its own Thread-class object as an instance variable declared as the friendly variable

```
Thread  m_WorldView = null;
```

This is a neat trick, and avoids having to extend the class from Thread. To call Thread methods such as sleep(), you can use code such as

```
m_WorldView.sleep(10);
```

The next seven variables—m_Graphics through m_fAllLoaded and one constant NUM_IMAGES—are explained with comments in the source code listing. The Applet Wizard adds the variables only if you specify that your applet is to perform an animation. (This also requires the applet to be multithreaded.) In lieu of using your own image files, the wizard installs a set of whirling-world snapshots.

> **TIP**
>
> For a quick heads up on writing a fresh applet, hunt for comments that begin with // TODO:. Applet Wizard inserts these comments to suggest where you can add your own code.

The default constructor does nothing—insert your own initialization statements here. However, it's important to understand the difference between the constructor and the overridden init() method, which also performs applet initializations. Use the constructor to assign values to instance variables, and to prepare other values when the applet object is created. Use init() to initialize the applet just before the thread's start() method is called. When the system calls init(), the applet has been loaded and is ready to begin running. This is an appropriate time, for example, to spawn any separate threads that the applet is to run as separate processes. Kill those threads in method destroy(). You can also put other shutdown code in destroy(), which is guaranteed to be called when the applet is terminated and in the process of being unloaded.

Method getAppletInfo() has the obvious purpose of identifying the applet, its author, and source. You can modify the default-generated string as you wish.

Local method displayImage() does nothing unless all images are loaded—a good example of how to construct multithreaded code, by the way. It wouldn't do to start displaying images until the system ensures they are in memory, which because the various pieces of code are running concurrently, could very well happen. This method otherwise displays the current image indicated by variable m_nCurrImage, which is set elsewhere. This method along with paint() draws the animation that you see when you load the WorldView.html document. (The next two chapters go into graphical output more fully.)

When the applet is loaded, and when its page first appears on screen, the browser calls the applet object's start() method. The code in this method reveals how an applet configures itself to run in a separate thread:

```
if (m_WorldView == null) {
 m_WorldView = new Thread(this);
 m_WorldView.start();
}
```

This statement does nothing if the Thread object m_WorldView is already initialized, indicating that start() has already been called. If this is the first such call, m_WorldView is assigned a reference to a new Thread object, created using this object (that is, the WorldView object for which start() was called). Calling that Thread object's start() method creates the actual process thread, which because this class implements Runnable, calls the object's run() method. This may seem somewhat convoluted on a first reading, but after some study you'll soon appreciate the beauty of this piece of code. It's a shining example of solid object-oriented programming. The object literally installs itself in a separate thread, and then gives itself a kick in the pants to start itself running! (This also basically describes how I get up in the morning.)

The stop() method performs as expected. It stops the thread's process by calling Thread.stop() in reference to the m_WorldView Thread-class object. It then sets WorldView to null so that start() could potentially re-create the thread. You may insert other code here to perform activities when the thread ends.

The sample listing's run() method performs some graphical duties. Except for the thread-specific code and exception handling, the programming is straightforward and simply displays each snapshot from the m_Images[] array to make the world spin like a top.

You may insert other methods and declarations, and you can also reference and create other classes, as you wish. There's a comment at the end of the default listing where Microsoft suggests you add additional code. You can place your code elsewhere if you wish, but it's best to separate it as suggested so that you can more easily regenerate the shell (perhaps using a future upgraded Wizard). You'll have to keep track of any changes you make, and make them again in a newly generated shell, but with careful commenting this shouldn't be too difficult. Any major code should probably go in its own class anyway, which won't be affected by a regeneration.

That's it—one tasty applet shell, ready for filling with your favorite fruits and pudding. Just bake in Visual J++ at 350 degrees for a few seconds, pour into a warm HTML document, and serve to your Web page paths (along with the associated .class files, of course). Users with Java-aware browsers can then load your document and run the applet's bytecodes on their own systems. It's literally as easy as pie.

As an Application

What's the difference between an applet and an application? Answer: five letters and two syllables. Actually, there aren't any real differences, except that, as I've mentioned, an applet runs under control of a browser or other viewer while an application runs as a stand-alone program (but also via an interpreter such as jview.exe).

On a technical level, the only differences in source code between an applet and an application are the presence of a `main()` method and the fact that an applet class extends `Applet`. A stand-alone application class, however, may also be derived from `Applet`—an observation that provides the key to the secret of creating a Java program that runs *both* as an applet and as an application. All that's needed is a suitable `main()` method. When you load the class under `jview.exe`, `main()` runs the program. When you load it under control of a browser or other viewer, `main()` is not called and the applet runs normally. Actually, as I'll explain in a moment, `jview.exe` can perform on both ends of this stick, even though applications normally run in text-only mode. Before seeing how that works, however, let's create a version of WorldView that runs both ways.

Follow the steps in the preceding section to create another WorldView application (I named it WorldView2 on the book's CD-ROM). This time, however, when you get to the first page in the Applet Wizard dialog, (Step 1 of 5), select the radio button labeled *As an applet and as an application.* Rather than view the remaining Wizard pages, you can simply click Finish and then select OK to generate the applet's files. Build the application by selecting the *Build* menu's *Build WorldView2* command. To run the program as an applet, execute it using the *Build* menu's *Execute WorldView2* command. To run the program as a stand-alone application, open a DOS prompt window, change to the WorldView2 directory, and issue the command `jview WorldView2`. (The `jview.exe` program must be on the current path.) This runs the applet inside a graphical frame window as shown in Figure 13.2.

Figure 13.2.
*WorldView2 running as a
stand-alone application inside
a graphical frame window.*

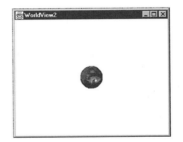

Listing 13.4, `WorldView2.java`, shows the portion of the generated shell that enables running an applet as a stand-alone application. The full listing is on disk, or if you created it using Applet Wizard, it is loaded into Developer Studio or Visual Studio 97. If you created the application, use the InfoView panel's `WorldView2` class's outline to locate method `main()` while you read the discussion about the listing.

Listing 13.4. `WorldView2.java` (partial listing).

```
// STANDALONE APPLICATION SUPPORT:
//   m_fStandAlone will be set to true if applet is run standalone
//-----------------------------------------------------------------------
boolean m_fStandAlone = false;
// STANDALONE APPLICATION SUPPORT
//   The main() method acts as the applet's entry point when it is run
// as a standalone application. It is ignored if the applet is run from
// within an HTML page.
//-----------------------------------------------------------------------
```

```
public static void main(String args[])
{
 // Create Toplevel Window to contain applet WorldView2
 //-------------------------------------------------------------------
 WorldView2Frame frame = new WorldView2Frame("WorldView2");
 // Must show Frame before we size it so insets() will return valid values
 //-------------------------------------------------------------------
 frame.show();
 frame.hide();
 frame.resize(frame.insets().left + frame.insets().right  + 320,
 frame.insets().top  + frame.insets().bottom + 240);
 // The following code starts the applet running within the frame window.
 // It also calls GetParameters() to retrieve parameter values from the
 // command line, and sets m_fStandAlone to true to prevent init() from
 // trying to get them from the HTML page.
 //-------------------------------------------------------------------
 WorldView2 applet_WorldView2 = new WorldView2();
 frame.add("Center", applet_WorldView2);
 applet_WorldView2.m_fStandAlone = true;
 applet_WorldView2.init();
 applet_WorldView2.start();
 frame.show();
}
```

In the modified listing, WorldView2.java, a boolean variable m_fStandAlone indicates, if true, that the program is being run as a stand-alone application. Except for this flag's initialization in main(), it is referenced at only one other place in the shell. This is in method run(), which loads the graphical images. Because the stand-alone application can't rely on code in the browser to perform interface and graphical functions, the program calls the Toolkit class's getDefaultToolkit() to obtain access to AWT methods such as getImage(), called here. (This will make better sense when you examine AWT in the next chapter. The significance here is that the stand-alone application needs alternate ways to call graphical output methods because applications normally support text-only I/O. Applets are graphical by default, and simply use the I/O capabilities of their browser.)

Getting back to main() in WorldView2.java, running an applet as an application amounts to executing the following sequence:

```
WorldView2Frame frame = new WorldView2Frame("WorldView2");
// ... frame initialization
WorldView2 applet_WorldView2 = new WorldView2();
frame.add("Center", applet_WorldView2);
applet_WorldView2.m_fStandAlone = true;
applet_WorldView2.init();
applet_WorldView2.start();
frame.show();
```

To emphasize the application-specific code, I cut out some statements that merely adjust the frame's window size. The first statement constructs a WorldView2Frame object, using the Frame-derived class in the file WorldView2Frame.java. I did not list this class here—we'll get into frames in the next chapter—but you might want to examine it. Applet Wizard creates this source code file when you specify that you want to run an applet also as a stand-alone application.

After constructing the frame window in which the applet will run, `main()` constructs a `WorldView2` class object, assigning its reference to variable `applet_WorldView2`. Consider what's happening here. The `WorldView2` object for which `main()` is called creates a *second* `WorldView2` object, which becomes the applet encased within the stand-alone graphical frame! This implies a certain amount of inefficiency in the problem's solution, and if your applet has any large variables, you'll want to think about the consequences of constructing two class objects just so that one of them can represent the applet and the other can provide a `main()` method. (For example, you might make large variables static, but remember that arrays are merely references and, until they are allocated memory, occupy no space. The duplication of the `m_Images[]` array in the sample shell is therefore of no consequence because it occupies only a few bytes.) In any case, to indicate that the applet is running in stand-alone mode, its `boolean` flag is set to `true` before `main()` calls `init()` and `start()`, in that order. This simulates the way a browser executes an applet and, thus, runs the code inside the stand-alone frame. The only remaining job is to call the frame's `show()` method to make it visible and start the animation.

HOW TO ADD FILES TO AN APPLET WORKSPACE

After you create an applet shell using Applet Wizard and the techniques described in the preceding sections, you'll probably need to add additional files to the applet's workspace as \you develop your code. For example, you'll want to add any packages and separate class source code files so they will be compiled as needed to bring the entire project up to date. To do that, follow these steps:

1. Using the *Insert* menu, select *Files into Project*.

2. In the resulting Insert Files into Project dialog, select a file type or enter `*.java;*.html` into the File Name field. This will display files of these two types.

3. Browse to any subdirectories as necessary, and select the files you want to add.

4. Click OK to add the selected files to your project.

HTML <applet> Tag

There isn't room in this book to cover the extensive subjects of HTML document files and the construction of World Wide Web pages. Plenty of books have been published on these subjects, so in this section, I'll cover HTML commands that relate only to the embedding of applets using the `<applet>` tag.

TIP

I found the following note in a Visual J++ help file, which might help you to locate more information about HTML document creation: "A complete description of HTML is available from the web site http://www.w3.org and also through the Internet documentation database at http://www.internic.net, where the document 'Hypertext Markup Language -Version 2.0' by T. Berners-Lee and D. Connolly may be found as RFC1866."

Minimum Requirements

Use the <applet> tag, formerly named <app>, to insert an applet into your HTML document. Follow this with any parameters, ending with the end-tag, </applet>. In the recent past, there was reason for concern about the support for this tag, but it's pretty much universally accepted today.

Listing 13.5 shows the minimum required attributes that you must specify when using the <applet> tag. The command begins with <applet and is followed by code, id, width, and height attributes, the values of which are, of course, up to you. End the attribute list with a closing bracket, >, followed by the end tag, </applet>.

Listing 13.5. Minimum <applet> syntax for HTML documents.

```
<applet
  code=YourApplet.class
  id=YourApplet
  width=320
  height=240 >
</applet>
```

Full Syntax

Listing 13.6 shows the full syntax for an <applet> tag. Optional attributes are in square brackets, which are not typed in the actual command.

Listing 13.6. Full <applet> tag syntax for HTML documents.

```
<applet
 [codebase=URL]
 code=YourApplet.class
 id=YourApplet
 [alt=text]
 [name=instance name]
 width=100
 height=100
 [align=alignment]
 [vspace=pixels]
 [hspace=pixels] >
</applet>
```

An applet's codebase can indicate a URL where a class is to be found. Use this attribute to store your classes in a separate server directory, which is usually a good idea. For example, you can use the command

```
codebase="http://www.server.com/mvj/myclass.class"
```

to reference a class in directory MVJ on the indicated server. You can also use partial URLs such as "/mvj/myclass.class" as the codebase.

The alt attribute is rarely needed but provides a message to users who don't have a Java-capable browser. Some early browsers that are Java aware will still display this message, although this bug has pretty much been stamped out. Java applets, however, are still new enough to warrant an alternative message such as

```
alt="Applets require a Java-aware browser"
```

The name attribute provides a defined instance name for the Applet object as constructed on the user's system. You can use this name to locate the object from within another method—in a separate applet, a button object for example, also executing on this HTML page. Assign the name as a quoted string:

```
name="AppletInstance"
```

Then refer to it by calling getAppletContext(), a method provided by the Applet class. For example, suppose you want to call a method of your own design named m() in your Applet-derived class for the AppletInstance object. To do that, use code such as the following in your Applet-derived class. First, obtain the Applet object by calling getAppletContext(), and then calling the interface method getApplet() for the resulting object:

```
Applet appletObject = getAppletContext().getApplet("AppletInstance");
```

Following this, use the Applet object to call your method:

```
(YourClassName)appletObject.m();
```

Because appletObject is of type Applet, you need to cast it to your class name before calling m(). If you need to make a lot of such calls, create another reference to the object, which you can use without casting:

```
YourClassName yourObject = (YourClassName)appletObject;
yourObject.m();  // Call a method
yourObject.n();  // Call another method
yourObject.q();  // Call yet another method, ... .
```

Use the align attribute to align the applet according to a variety of schemes, and also to affect how text wraps around the applet's graphic. (Consult an HTML reference for more information on this, possibly listed under the <img> tag.) To align, you may assign any of the following attributes: left, right, top, texttop, middle, absmiddle, baseline, bottom, and absbottom. It's highly instructive to test the effects of each of these settings using a test applet.

Finally in the <applet> tag are the vspace and hspace attributes, which specify the number of pixels to reserve around the applet's border. The value of vspace represents vertical pixels reserved above and below the applet. The value of hspace represents horizontal pixels reserved to the left and right of the applet outline.

TIP

Developer Studio and Visual Studio 97 support syntax coloring for HTML document statements. To use this feature, open the document file using *File|Open* or by selecting it from the InfoView window pane. Because double-clicking an .html document using the Windows Explorer loads it into the default browser, you must use Developer or Visual Studio to open a document file for editing. (You can, of course, drag a document file into Studio's text editor window.)

Parameters

The HTML document may pass one or more parameters to an applet, which are easily retrieved using the getParameter() method in the Applet class. To create a parameter, attach one or more param tags after your <applet> attributes. Each param tag has two settings: a name and a value, the second of which must be a quoted string. For example, Listing 13.7 shows the <applet> attributes for a sample applet named Temp.class, which defines two parameters.

Listing 13.7. Applet parameters in the HTML file.

```
<applet
 code=Temp.class
 id=Temp
 width=320
 height=240 >
 <param name=Title value="Temp Applet">
 <param name=Speed value="100">
</applet>
```

The first parameter is named Title, and it has the value "Temp Applet". The second parameter is named Speed, and it has the value "100". To retrieve these string parameters, call getParameter() with a string argument equal to the name of the parameter you want. The method returns the parameter's value as a string, which you can assign to a String object using code such as

```
String nameParam = getParameter("Title");
if (nameParam == null)
 nameParam = "Default Title";
```

It's important to always check whether getParameter() returns null, in which case a good response is to assign a default string as shown here. If your applet requires a critical parameter, however, it might shut down or throw an exception—the exact response depends on your needs.

Because all parameter values are strings, to obtain numerical parameters requires converting the returned strings to the data type you want. Again, it's important to guard against exceptions thrown by badly formatted values—but the techniques are easy and are covered in Part II. For example, to read the Speed parameter from Listing 13.7, the applet could use code such as

```
int speed = 500;  // Default speed
String ts = getParameter("Speed");
try {
 speed = Integer.parseInt(ts);
} catch (NumberFormatException nfe)
}
```

This catches, but ignores, a possible exception thrown by the parseInt() method in the Integer wrapper class. If the exception is thrown, speed is left holding its default value of 500.

To create parameters, you can edit your HTML file's <applet> commands, or you can use the Applet Wizard to enter parameters if you know what they are when you create the shell source files. Enter your parameters in step 4 of 5 while using the wizard. Figure 13.3 shows the screen you'll see along with the two parameters listed earlier (see Listing 13.7). The columns in this dialog require some extra explanation. (The dialog's use also requires some patience—it's not exactly user-friendly. Hint: Try clicking on each field to enter, and *don't* press Tab unless you want to jump to the next line.)

Figure 13.3.

The Applet Wizard's parameter entry screen.

Although each <applet> parameter has only two parts—a name and a value—the Applet Wizard parameter entry screen provides five columns for each parameter. The extra columns are used to generate source code that loads the parameters into typed variables. Though it's a bit confusing at first, after you play with the dialog, you'll appreciate how slick all this is. You can specify parameters of any Java type and automatically generate their <applet> HTML attributes and the source code to initialize and load their values.

Refer again to Figure 13.3. First enter the name that you want the parameter to be called in the HTML file. This is the value assigned to the <param>'s name field. Next, click on the *Type* field, and you'll see that Applet Wizard creates a Member name such as m_Title or m_Speed automatically. The Member name represents the identifier used for the parameter variable in the applet source code. You can enter a different Member identifier if you want, but the default is usually good enough.

The *Type* field is normally set to String. Click the small down arrow next to this field (it must first be highlighted, which is not shown in the figure), and select the Member's data type. For example, to create an integer parameter, select int from the drop-down list.

Click the *Def-Value* field and enter a default value. You must do this after selecting the Member's type; otherwise, the default value will be zeroed. Finally, enter a *Description* that you want Applet Wizard to enter as a comment in the source code. This is optional, but a good idea to include.

> **TIP**
>
> When creating a new applet with Applet Wizard, enter a few dummy parameters of various types. Although you can insert additional parameters into the HTML document at any time, this is the only chance you get to automatically generate the associated variables and source code statements that load the parameter values. By creating some dummy parameters, you might save the effort of writing those statements manually. You can always delete the extra parameters you don't need. (Or just leave them in for future revisions.)

After you are finished specifying your parameters, review their settings and finish creating the applet shell. When you open the generated .java source code file, you'll find several additions to the code that declare and load the parameter values. Using the parameters illustrated in Figure 13.3, Applet Wizard declares the following two instance variables in the Applet-derived class:

```
private String m_Title = "Temp Applet";
private int m_Speed = 500;
```

Notice that these are declared private to the class—not essential, but usually a good practice. You can make them public or protected, or delete the private specifier to make the declarations friendly. The default assignments are those that you specified in the Applet Wizard dialog. To identify each parameter by its name in the HTML document, Applet Wizard also declares two other constants:

```
private final String PARAM_Title = "Title";
private final String PARAM_Speed = "Speed";
```

These are made final to indicate that they are constant and cannot be changed.

Because the applet has parameters, the Applet-derived class is expected to override and implement a method named getParameterInfo(). Listing 13.8 shows the method generated for the parameters illustrated in Figure 13.3.

Listing 13.8. The `getParameterInfo()` method for the parameters illustrated in Figure 13.3.

```
public String[][] getParameterInfo()
{
 String[][] info =
 {
  { PARAM_Title, "String", "Applet title string" },
  { PARAM_Speed, "int", "Animation speed (int)" },
 };
 return info;
}
```

The return type of the `getParameterInfo()` method is an array of `String` arrays, each of which has three elements: the parameter name, its data type, and its description. Thus, `info[0]` refers to the first `String` array having the literal values shown for `PARAM_Title`, and `info[1]` has the second `String` array values for `PARAM_Speed`. To access this information, use statements such as the following. I've included the resulting strings as comments to make it clear how each element is stored in the multidimensional array:

```
String[][] info = getParameterInfo();
String s;
s = info[0][0];  // "Title"
s = info[0][1];  // "String"
s = info[0][2];  // "Applet title string"
s = info[1][0];  // "Speed"
s = info[1][1];  // "int"
s = info[1][2];  // "Animation speed (int)"
```

> **TIP**
>
> The `getParameterInfo()` method is not called by the Applet Wizard shell. If you make any additions or modifications to your HTML parameters, be sure to make the same changes to the `getParameterInfo()` method. To add new parameters, you can create a dummy shell with the wizard, cut and paste the generated code into your application, and then delete the dummy shell.

In any applet with one or more parameters, Applet Wizard adds code to the `init()` method in your `Applet`-derived class. This code loads the parameter values from the HTML document when the `Applet` object is instantiated and initialized, but just before it begins running. You can be sure, then, that the variables (`m_Title` and `m_Speed`) are properly initialized in your applet's `run()` method and in any other methods called from `run()` or started as separate processes (because those threads would also usually be created in `init()`). For example, to load the `m_Title` parameter, Applet Wizard inserts this code into `init()`:

```
String param;
param = getParameter(PARAM_Title);
if (param != null)
 m_Title = param;
```

First, getParameter() is called for the parameter, using the constant PARAM_Title, and assigning the result to a local String variable, param. If this is not null, m_Title is assigned the loaded value. Because m_Title is given an initial value, any problems will not cause severe trouble; if the parameter is not available for some reason, m_Title will simply have the default value you assigned in the wizard.

Unfortunately, the same is not true for parameters of other types. For example, take a look at the relatively poor code that the wizard generates to load our sample m_Speed int parameter:

```
param = getParameter(PARAM_Speed);
if (param != null)
 m_Speed = Integer.parseInt(param);
```

Here again, getParameter() loads the value of PARAM_Speed, which is actually a string (as are all HTML value parameter attributes). As I mentioned earlier, to obtain the int value, you can use the Integer wrapper class, but the wizard fails to insert the necessary exception handling to guard against a NumberFormatException object thrown from parseInt(). As generated, an exception could halt the applet, so you will want to add this by modifying the preceding code to the following (changes are shown in bold):

```
param = getParameter(PARAM_Speed);
try {
 if (param != null)
  m_Speed = Integer.parseInt(param);
} catch (NumberFormatException nfe) {
}
```

You must do this for each generated code fragment that the wizard creates to load parameter values. This is a bit tedious, but all of the source lines are together in the init() method, so at least it's easy to find the lines you must change.

Remember that generated HTML files are subject to regeneration. You will probably want to specify a different file for your finished applet than the one generated by the wizard. Use the technique explained in the following tip to change your workspace to another HTML document.

> **TIP**
>
> Normally, a project's HTML file is named the same as the project workspace file, but using the filename extension .html. Follow these steps to specify another HTML document file for a project:
>
> 1. Choose *Build|Settings*.
> 2. From the Project Settings dialog, select the Debug tab. Under Category, select Browser.
> 3. Select the button labeled *Use parameters from HTML page* and enter your HTML document name.

4. Alternatively, select the other button, labeled *Enter parameters below*, and enter the parameters you want Visual J++ to add automatically to the HTML document it will create if you don't specify an existing document. This is a kind of tedious way to create an HTML document, however, so you'll probably want to use another method and specify its filename as explained in step 3. (This book doesn't explain how to create HTML documents except as related to Java applets, nor does it cover the extensive subject of Web page construction and design. As you are no doubt aware, there are numerous books on these subjects.)

Applet Class Methods

From the preceding discussions, you now have a fairly good working knowledge of how to create and run an applet. To understand more about what you can do in your applet's class, look more closely at the `Applet` declaration, shown in Listing 13.9.

NOTE

The `Applet` class hierarchy reads like a biblical family tree. `Applet` is derived from `Panel`, which is derived from `Container`, which is derived from `Component`, which is derived from `Object`. For now, concentrate on `Applet`. We'll cover some of the methods in the other superclasses in the coming chapters.

Listing 13.9. Java's `Applet` class.

```
public class Applet extends Panel {
// Public methods:
 public final void setStub(AppletStub stub);
 public boolean isActive();
 public URL getDocumentBase();
 public URL getCodeBase();
 public String getParameter(String name);
 public AppletContext getAppletContext();
 public void resize(int width, int height);
 public void resize(Dimension d);
 public void showStatus(String msg);
 public Image getImage(URL url);
 public Image getImage(URL url, String name);
 public AudioClip getAudioClip(URL url);
 public AudioClip getAudioClip(URL url, String name);
 public String getAppletInfo();
 public String[][] getParameterInfo();
 public void play(URL url);
 public void play(URL url, String name);
 public void init();
```

```
public void start();
public void stop();
public void destroy();
}
```

I'll explain only some of the more significant methods in Applet that you are likely to use at this stage in your understanding of applet construction. I'll skip methods such as setStub() that you'll never need to call. The first method to examine is init(). Use it for initializing your applet's instance variables and for other tasks to perform, especially any that call methods in the parent class or that use code in the browser. You may also insert initialization code in your class constructor, but realize that this is called only to construct the Applet object, and other window and graphics services may not be available at that time. For example, the init() method, as you have seen, is the proper place to load parameters from the HTML document and also to construct any separate threads to run concurrently.

It's also vital to understand the purposes of the start(), stop(), and destroy() methods. The browser calls start() when the applet is first loaded, and then calls it again if the user revisits the applet's page. Be aware that the Applet object is not necessarily destroyed between times— all that start() needs to do, usually, is to start the applet's thread unless it has already been started. It would also start any other threads as necessary.

The browser calls stop() when the user shifts away from the applet's page. You should stop any running threads at this point, but don't kill them. Instead, keep them alive in case the user decides to revisit the applet's page. This will enable the applet to come alive more quickly than the first time it's viewed.

When the browser removes the applet's page from its cache memory, or when the user closes the browser, it calls the applet's destroy() method. You may kill threads and release any other resources in this method. If the user decides to revisit the same page, the Applet object will be re-created from scratch.

Use the resize() methods (there are two variations) to specify a size for the applet's window, which is not outlined. You may pass two literal integer values representing the horizontal and vertical sizes respectively. You may alternatively pass a Dimension-class object to resize() to specify these values. Applets that have control objects, a subject for the next chapter on AWT programming, size themselves according to their component layout. In that case, you may remove the resize() statement generated by Applet Wizard from method init().

The isActive() method is also valuable, especially in multithreaded applet code. This method is set to return true immediately before the applet's start() method is called. It is set to return false immediately after the applet's stop() method is called. Thus, if isActive() returns false, you can be fairly certain that the applet is not visible, although the Applet object is probably still alive and kicking. You might call this method to avoid tying up the system with graphical gymnastics that nobody will see anyway.

Applet Programming Techniques

With the information so far in this chapter, you should now be able to construct simple applets. You'll need more information, however, on techniques for interfacing and graphics before you can write applets that do useful chores. These are the subjects of the next two chapters, starting with interfacing techniques. However, I need to jump the gun a little and introduce a few graphics topics that you must know to construct applet user interfaces with buttons and other controls. I'll end this chapter, then, with an example program that shows some basic graphics operations that you'll use in most of your applets.

Listing 13.10, `Sketch.java`, is a simple but fully developed applet for drawing sketches with the mouse. Figure 13.4 shows the applet's display in the Internet Explorer. You can use Developer Studio or Visual Studio 97 to compile and execute the program; open the `Sketch.mdp` workspace file on the CD-ROM, or open `Sketch.html` to run the sample applet directly. The listing shows the program's source code, which I created with Applet Wizard and then modified. I also added fresh comments to explain the purpose of each method and many statements. Just to be different, and for simplicity's sake, I made this applet single-threaded.

Figure 13.4.

The Sketch applet running in Internet Browser.

Listing 13.10. `Sketch.java` (Mouse sketching applet).

```java
import java.applet.*;
import java.awt.*;
import java.util.*;
// Objects of the Line class are stored in a Vector
// container to keep track of lines drawn. This class
// and any others in this compilation unit may not be
// public therefore it is declared with no access
// specifier.
class Line {
 // Fields that define a line's end points
 int startx, starty;
 int endx, endy;
 // Constructor
 public Line(int x1, int y1, int x2, int y2) {
  startx = x1;
  starty = y1;
  endx = x2;
```

```
    endy = y2;
  }
}
// The Applet-derived class (this one is single-threaded)
public class Sketch extends Applet
{
 boolean dragging;      // True while clicking and dragging
 int startx, starty;    // Current line's start point
 int endx, endy;        // Current line's end point
 Vector points;         // Vector of lines drawn
 // Constructor
 public Sketch()
 {
  points = new Vector();   // Create empty Vector
 }
 // Return name and author information
 // Insert a copyright notice here if you want
 public String getAppletInfo()
 {
  return "Name: Sketch\r\n" +
         "Author: Tom Swan\r\n" +
         "Created with Microsoft Visual J++ Version 1.0";
 }
 // Initialize the applet's instance variables and
 // also size its window.
 public void init()
 {
  resize(320, 240);
  dragging = false;
  points.removeAllElements();
 }
 // Complements constructor, but does nothing here
 public void destroy()
 {
 }
 // Paint applet window
 public void paint(Graphics g)
 {
  // Draw a message string
  g.drawString("Click and drag mouse to sketch", 10, 20);
  // Draw or erase the current line
  if (dragging) {
   g.drawLine(startx, starty, endx, endy);
  }
  // Draw all lines saved in the points Vector
  VectorEnumerator enum =
   (VectorEnumerator)points.elements();
  while (enum.hasMoreElements()) {
   Line k = (Line)enum.nextElement();
   g.drawLine(k.startx, k.starty, k.endx, k.endy);
  }
 }
// Reinitialize when applet becomes active
 public void start()
 {
  dragging = false;
 }
```

continues

283

Listing 13.10. continued

```
// Deinitialize when applet becomes inactive
public void stop()
{
 dragging = false;
}
// Respond to mouse click inside applet window
public boolean mouseDown(Event evt, int x, int y)
{
 dragging = true;  // Start a dragging operation
 startx = x;        // Initialize line start point
 starty = y;
 endx = x;          // Set start=end point initially
 endy = y;
 return true;  // Tell system event was handled
}
public boolean mouseUp(Event evt, int x, int y)
{
 dragging = false;  // End the dragging operation
 endx = x;          // Save new line's end point
 endy = y;
 Line k = new Line(startx, starty, endx, endy);
 points.addElement(k);  // Add Line object to Vector
 repaint();             // Repaint to show new line
 return true;  // Tell system event was handled
}
public boolean mouseDrag(Event evt, int x, int y)
{
 if (dragging) {  // Ignore if not dragging
  endx = x;         // Reset new end point to mouse
  endy = y;
  repaint();        // Paint current line being drawn
 }
 return true;  // Tell system event was handled
}
}
```

Sketch.java demonstrates three essential areas of interactive applet programming:

- Handling mouse events
- Performing startup and shutdown chores
- Painting graphics

Understanding each of these techniques is essential to constructing useable applets. To handle mouse events—generated when the user clicks, moves, and drags the mouse pointer inside the applet's defined window—the Sketch class overrides three methods inherited from Applet by way of its distant ancestor, the Component class. The full set of mouse-event handlers are

```
public boolean mouseDown(Event  evt, int  x, int  y);
public boolean mouseDrag(Event  evt, int  x, int  y);
public boolean mouseEnter(Event  evt, int  x, int  y);
public boolean mouseExit(Event  evt, int  x, int  y);
public boolean mouseMove(Event  evt, int  x, int  y);
public boolean mouseUp(Event  evt, int  x, int  y);
```

Each method receives an `Event` object that describes exactly when, where, and how the event was generated. You often can ignore this parameter except in special circumstances—checking whether a certain key was held down while the mouse button was clicked, for example. Each method also receives two integer values representing the x and y coordinate position of the mouse pointer. This position is relative to the component's upper-left corner; in this case, the applet window is the component, so the coordinate is the mouse's relative position inside the applet's window. Each method returns `true` to indicate that it has successfully handled the event. It may return `false` to indicate that it has ignored the event, in which case the browser executes any default code it has for the event. (This probably means that nothing at all happens, but it is a tenet of graphical user interface programming that all events be handled.)

The `MouseDown()` and `MouseUp()` methods are called when the user clicks and releases the mouse button. `MouseEnter()` is called when the mouse pointer moves inside the applet or other component's window. `MouseExit()` is called when the pointer leaves the component's screen space. `MouseDrag()` is called when the user moves the mouse while holding down the mouse button. `MouseMove()` is called when the user moves the mouse and does not hold down the button. (Chapter 15, "Events and Layouts," explains how to distinguish among left, middle, and right mouse button clicks. For now, we'll use only the left button.)

To respond to a mouse event, simply override the appropriate method as shown in `Sketch.java`. For our purposes, we need only three events: `MouseDown()`, `MouseUp()`, and `MouseDrag()`. A boolean `dragging` variable indicates to other methods whether a click-and-drag operation is taking place. `MouseDown()` sets the flag true; `MouseUp()` sets it false.

In addition, we need to keep track of the end points of the lines that the user draws. For this, the program maintains four integer variables: `startx`, `starty`, `endx`, and `endy`. These are assigned the mouse coordinate values in the mouse events. When `MouseUp()` is called, the program assumes that the four variables represent the current line, which is fixed in place by constructing a `Line` object using the coordinate values with the statement

```
Line k = new Line(startx, starty, endx, endy);
```

The `Line` class is declared in `Sketch.java`, and it simply holds four public integer variables. We need an object to do this so we can store line coordinates in a `Vector` container, using the next statement:

```
points.addElement(k);
```

This brings up an important concept in interactive graphics programming: An applet must be able to redraw all of its graphical elements on demand. This is true because the applet might be covered by another window, or the user might scroll it away temporarily. In these and other instances, the applet needs to re-create its contents, which might happen at any time. To draw the applet's contents, the browser calls a method named `paint()`, which we'll examine soon. This might happen at any time, but to force it to happen as soon as possible, the program can call `repaint()` using the statement

```
repaint();
```

You'll see two instances of this in `Sketch.java`—once in `MouseUp()` and once in `MouseDrag()`. The first instance draws the current line when you release the mouse button. The second instance draws and erases the current line as you click and drag the mouse. There's no need to `repaint()` the screen in `MouseDown()` because nothing has changed on screen until you move the mouse.

Notice how the program's `start()` and `stop()` methods set the dragging flag to `false`. This might not be necessary, but it's a good idea to carefully consider the state of the applet when the browser calls these methods. Keep in mind that your applet's user will probably enter and leave the page many times, and might switch willy-nilly from applet to applet using the browser. Just in case the user manages to leave the applet while drawing a line, I decided to set the `dragging` flag false in `stop()`, and also to reinitialize it in `start()`. A little caution might go a long way toward keeping the applet running smoothly.

Notice that the applet also has a constructor, `Sketch()`, which constructs the program's `Vector` container for saving `Line` objects using the statement

```
points = new Vector();
```

This demonstrates an appropriate use for a constructor—creating and initializing a locally declared object. Remember, however, that it is generally not proper to call inherited methods or to effect browser actions such as drawing graphics in the applet's constructor. Such chores are best done, as I have mentioned, in the `init()` method, which `Sketch` uses to execute these statements:

```
resize(320, 240);
dragging = false;
points.removeAllElements();
```

The first statement sizes the applet's window, calling the inherited `resize()` method with the indicated arguments. I also took this opportunity to initialize `dragging` to false, but this statement could have gone in the constructor. Finally, `init()` calls the `Vector` method `removeAllElements()` to ensure that the container is empty when the applet is initialized. This last step also might be unnecessary, but I included it as food for thought. You'll want to carefully consider the interactions, and the effects on your applet's data, that starting, stopping, destroying, and initializing have on your applet's operation. In some cases, you'll want to erase an applet's display and zero any graphical containers; in others, you'll want to preserve the applet's graphics throughout its life cycle. The choices are yours, but the programming might require some experimentation with your applet class's constructor and other methods.

The third and final aspect of applet construction to cover in this introduction is the painting of graphics. We'll use the `paint()` method extensively in upcoming examples. In almost all cases, this is the method to use to display your applet's contents. The method is declared as

```
public void paint(Graphics g);
```

This method, inherited from the `Component` class, is called whenever the system needs your applet to draw itself. Clipping is automatic, so that if only the lower right corner of the applet needs drawing (perhaps because the user moved another window aside), `paint()` can simply go ahead and draw everything. Only the required graphics are actually transferred to the display.

It's important to understand that `paint()` redraws *everything* in the applet's window. Beginners to GUI programming sometimes attempt to draw only one or another item, using confusing systems of flags to indicate what has already been drawn. To their surprise, they quickly discover that objects drawn don't stick as expected. Instead, when uncovered by another window, the objects disappear. Actually, they weren't there in the first place—and `paint()` is expected to redraw the objects in such cases.

The `paint()` method receives one all-important parameter, a `Graphics` object simply labeled `g`. This object is called a *context variable.* It defines the output context to which graphics are drawn—usually the applets window in the browser. The `Graphics` class provides many methods for performing graphical sorcery—but here, we use only two of its methods, `drawString()` and `drawLine()`.

> **NOTE**
>
> Until this chapter, many Java sample programs have used the `System.out.println()` method to display text. This works, however, only on a text-output display such as a DOS window. Applets are graphics based, and they require different techniques for displaying text. Among other differences, this means you can't use the `print()` and `println()` methods to display text in applet windows.

Carefully examine the `paint()` method in `Sketch.java`. It illustrates the fundamental techniques you will use to produce output in most if not all of the applets you write. The method begins by displaying a message using the statement

```
g.drawString("Click and drag mouse to sketch", 10, 20);
```

The first argument is the text to display. The second and third are the x and y coordinates, relative to the component (in this case, the applet window) where the line should appear.

To draw the current line, `paint()` executes the following statement but only if `dragging` is true:

```
if (dragging) {
 g.drawLine(startx, starty, endx, endy);
}
```

This is how the program displays the line that appears to move along with the mouse while you click and drag. This line must be drawn separately because it hasn't yet been entered into the `Vector points` database. To draw all of those lines—the `Line` objects previously stored in the container—the `paint()` method executes the statements

```
VectorEnumerator enum =
 (VectorEnumerator)points.elements();
while (enum.hasMoreElements()) {
 Line k = (Line)enum.nextElement();
 g.drawLine(k.startx, k.starty, k.endx, k.endy);
}
```

This is a standard `Vector` enumeration loop, which I explained in Part II. Here, each `Line` object is pulled out of the container inside a `while` loop. The `g.drawLine()` statement draws each line by referencing the objects' integer instance variables.

The important concept here is that `paint()` not only draws the current line, but it *redraws* all lines saved in the `Vector` database. In this way, every time `paint()` is called, it re-creates the program's entire display. If it drew only the current line (a common beginner mistake), scrolling away from the applet's window or covering it with another window would erase the existing drawing. If this is your first introduction to windowed graphics programming, you might find that it takes some time to fully grasp this concept. But take heart—we'll explore more about this and other aspects of applet window design and construction in the next two chapters.

Summary

- An applet is a Java program that runs under the control of another application, usually a Web browser such as Internet Explorer.

- Using the Applet Wizard in Developer Studio or Visual Studio 97 is the best way to construct an applet shell along with an associated `.html` file, ready for programming. Most of the applets in this book were created using this method.

- An applet can be multithreaded, and it usually supports graphics animations and other sophisticated techniques. This chapter introduces the fundamentals of applet design. The next two chapters cover user interfacing and graphics programming.

- The HTML `<applet>` tag embeds an applet in an HTML document. This tag supports numerous optional attributes and can also pass parameters to applets.

- All applets are classes that extend the `Applet` class. A multithreaded applet also implements the `Runnable` interface. An applet may be executed as a stand-alone application by programming a `main()` method in the class that extends `Applet`. The `Applet` class is derived from several other classes, which are described more fully in the next chapters.

- Applet programming requires you to master three fundamental techniques demonstrated by this chapter's `Sketch.java` sample applet. The techniques are handling mouse events, performing startup and shutdown chores, and painting graphics.

What's Next?

Applets incorporate the AWT—Another Window Toolkit—which provides a full complement of interface objects. Using AWT, you can add buttons, input boxes, and other interface elements for interacting with your applet's users. You can also use AWT in stand-alone applications. The next chapter explains the ins and outs of AWT programming techniques.

14

Another Window Toolkit

Get your thinking cap ready. This and the next several chapters could be the most important in this book. With the classes in the AWT package—commonly called the *("oh no, not") Another Window Toolkit*—you add interactive graphical components to your applet's user interface. The AWT provides classes for text objects, buttons, scrollbars, lists, and other interactive visual controls. In fact, there are so many classes in this package, it will take four chapters to cover them all. In this chapter, I'll discuss the basics for creating user interfaces and inserting components such as buttons, lists, and editable text areas. In the next three chapters, I'll cover events and layouts; menus, windows, and dialogs; and graphics, animation, and multimedia programming.

In This Chapter

This chapter covers the following fundamentals of the AWT package classes and user-interface programming:

- Designing graphical applet interfaces
- Understanding AWT classes
- Programming with components
- Handling events
- Component and container classes
- Miscellaneous classes

Graphical Applet Interfaces

It's a safe bet that most readers of this book are thoroughly familiar with Windows and the basic concepts of a graphical user interface, or GUI. These concepts, known to only a few pioneers just a few years ago, are now pretty much standard worldwide, though the exact elements still differ widely. Not everyone uses Windows, however, and it's important to realize that your applets might run under a variety of operating systems. Some will be Macintosh systems; others will run X-Windows and Sun Solaris. Their users will want to see the buttons and other graphical components that are familiar to them. This is the primary goal of AWT's classes—to provide *platform-independent* tools for creating graphical user interfaces.

This chapter, then, is not about how to program Windows 95 buttons, scrollbars, and other components. It's about how to use Java's tools for constructing user interfaces that run correctly under all Java-aware Web browsers. When they run your applets, Windows users see Microsoft's familiar buttons and controls. Solaris users see X-Windows widgets. Macintosh owners see Apple's tried-and-true visual components. Your program, however, creates its user interface in exactly the same way, completely independent of the target operating system.

So, being a properly skeptical programmer, you might ask, what's the catch? What must you give up in return for this enticing platform independence? The answer is, you give up some versatility and a little bit of control, but not as much as you might fear. For example, rather than position components exactly where you want them, you'll most likely use a relative layout technique that ensures good-looking, if not perfectly equivalent, results on all displays. You also have fewer selections among specific elements—only a few fonts to choose from, for instance, rather than the hundreds of TrueType font sets you probably have in your CD-ROM collection. But at least you can be sure that Java's limited set of fonts is available on all systems—and that's saying a lot.

Because you can't know what system your users have, it's vital to play by the rules of AWT's design constraints. At first, these rules may seem restrictive, but in time you'll appreciate their simplicity. Rather than place a component at a specific coordinate, you might insert it in a panel's northwest corner and let the browser figure out where this should be. As you will discover in the coming chapters, this plan is surprisingly effective for creating graphical user interfaces that look good and work reliably well under a variety of display environments.

WARNING

Before you rush out and purchase third-party Java-component toolkits to enhance your applets with the latest flashy graphical craze, consider carefully the consequences this might have on your applet's general usefulness. Many third-party tools require users to install or download special code files—those users who don't have the necessary files, won't be able to use your applets. Worse, multiple toolkits floating around on zillions of user systems is a versioning nightmare waiting to trap you and your code in the doom and gloom of continual customer support. (Take a look, however, at Microsoft's Java SDK described in Chapter 20. Sun Microsystems is reportedly considering general support for these tools.)

For best results, toe the line and stick to the techniques outlined in this and the next three chapters. If you do this, your applets will run correctly on all Java-compatible browsers. Furthermore, because the AWT is built into those browsers, your code files will be ridiculously small. There's no need for users to download code to create components such as buttons and text fields because that code is *already* built into their browsers.

Creating a User Interface

Before hiking deeply into AWT's classes, it's useful to look at an example program as a model of how to program applet user interfaces. This will illustrate some of the principles to be covered in more detail later in this chapter. It will also lead you gently into the morass of the AWT's class hierarchy, which can be confusing when you first blaze its trails.

Listing 14.1, `ButtonTest.java`, demonstrates how to program a simple interactive component— a button, as shown in Figure 14.1. To run the program, open the HTML file on the CD-ROM in the `Part3\ButtonTest` directory to run the applet in your default browser. This file was named by Visual Studio 97, and might be something like `VJ60E3.html`. Alternatively, for practice writing applets, enter the listing into a new text file. Save it as ButtonTest.java in a fresh directory, and then select the *Build* menu's *Build\ButtonTest* command. Answer Yes when asked whether to create a default workspace. After compiling, select *Build\Execute* and specify ButtonTest for the requested class name. This will load and run the applet in the default browser. When you see the button, click it to change the applet's background color at random. This demonstrates how an applet can reprogram the browser using interactive controls. An applet is literally an interactive piece of code embedded in a Web page document that executes on the user's system.

Figure 14.1.

Clicking ButtonTest's sample button changes the applet's background color at random.

Listing 14.1. ButtonTest.java (Demonstrates component programming).

```java
import java.applet.*;
import java.awt.*;
import java.util.*;

class ButtonTest extends Applet {
 Random gen;  // Random number generator for color selection
 // Initialize applet
 // Constructs random number generator and button object,
 // and then adds button to applet's window.
 public void init() {
  gen = new Random();
  Button colorButton = new Button("Click Me");
  add(colorButton);
 }
 // Responds to button click. Creates new color not
 // equal to current background, and then paints applet
 // background using that color.
 public boolean action(Event evt, Object what) {
  Color c;
  if ("Click Me".equals(what)) {
   do {
    c = new Color(gen.nextInt());
   } while (c == getBackground());
   setBackground(c);
   repaint();
  }
```

```
  return true;
 }
}
```

ButtonTest.java shows the general organization used by most applet user interfaces. The program imports three packages using the statements

```
import java.applet.*;
import java.awt.*;
import java.util.*;
```

The first two statements are required by all applets that use the AWT package. The third imports the Random class used for this demonstration only. As mentioned in the preceding chapter, use the init() method to initialize the applet. In this case, the method creates a random number generator, and then adds a button component to the display with these statements:

```
gen = new Random();
Button colorButton = new Button("Click Me");
add(colorButton);
```

The string passed to the Button class constructor is displayed inside the button. Notice that you do not specify the object's size or location—details that are handled automatically. As I will explain in Chapter 15, "Events and Layouts," however, it's possible to designate a relative layout for multiple components, but in this sample program, it doesn't matter where the button appears and the browser displays it where it will.

Having initialized the button, the only remaining job is to respond to its selection. This is handled by an inherited method named action(), declared as

```
public boolean action(Event evt, Object what);
```

The method receives two arguments. The Event is an object that describes the type of action that is taking place—whether it's a control's selection, a keypress, a mouse button click, and so on. The Object argument represents a parameter passed along with this event, and its nature depends on the type of event. For some events, you won't use this parameter at all. In this case, we need it to identify which button was clicked. (I know, there's only one, but in most cases there will be several components, so in most cases, you will need to determine which one caused this event to occur.) The sample code uses the following if statement to determine whether the "Click Me" button was selected:

```
if ("Click Me".equals(what)) {
...
}
```

The expression inside parentheses might seem a little odd until you consider that even literal strings are objects, and therefore, you can call methods of their classes. Here, the program calls the String class equals() method to compare the action() Object parameter to the quoted string. If they are equal, then the user clicked the named button. (Obviously, you need to use different labels for all of your applet's buttons, but you'll probably do that anyway.)

What you do in response to a component's selection is your business. I programmed the button's response to select a new background color at random, set the applet's background to that color, and then repainted the window, using the statements

```
do {
 c = new Color(gen.nextInt());
} while (c == getBackground());
setBackground(c);
repaint();
```

Call getBackground() to obtain the current background color as an object of the Color class, to be covered in Chapter 17, "Graphics, Animation, and Multimedia." Call setBackground() to change the applet's background to this color. Nothing happens, however, until the applet is repainted, so you also have to call the repaint() method to force a display update event, which calls the applet's paint() method. (In this case, it's the inherited paint() because our applet doesn't provide an implementation of this method.)

The final step in action() is to return a boolean true value to indicate that the event was handled. If your code does not handle the event, return false so that the AWT's default event handlers receive the event. In this small example, we don't care about those events, so action() simply returns true. (I'll explain more about handling events in Chapter 15.)

> **NOTE**
>
> Components such as buttons are displayed using the operating system's native capabilities by calling methods in the java.awt.peer package. You will have little reason to call these methods. In fact, doing so might cause your code to become system dependent—anathema for the well-constructed Java applet. For this reason, this book does not cover the peer package classes.

Introducing AWT Classes

Now that you have seen the basics of applet user interfaces, you are ready to take your first step into the AWT class hierarchy, diagrammed in Figure 14.2. As you can see, there are numerous classes to study. The indicated classes are all extended directly from Object.

The following sections briefly describe each class and interface shown in Figure 14.2. Read through these sections to become generally familiar with the available classes. After this text, I'll explain how to use Component and some other classes to construct interface controls. Subsequent chapters explain how to respond to events, how to lay out multiple components for a pleasing display, how to create pull-down menus, and how to construct separate windows and dialogs. There's a lot of ground to cover, so the following descriptions will be exceedingly sparse. The idea here is to get you up to speed on the AWT package's many classes, variables, and methods. I'll discuss each class in more detail at the appropriate times within this and the next three chapters.

Figure 14.2.
*AWT classes extended
from* Object.

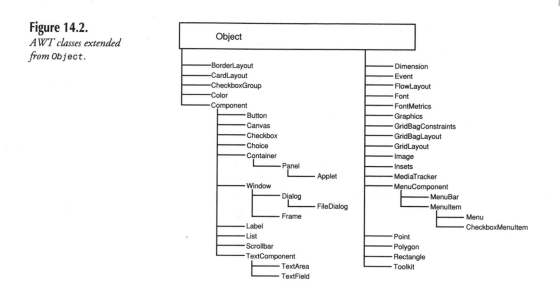

Component Classes

Component class objects provide visual elements through which the applet's user communicates with your program. The applet itself is a Component object—one that, through the services of the Container class can hold other components. The classes derived from Component, along with one related class (CheckboxGroup), are

- Button: A selectable, labeled button that users can click with the mouse or select by pressing the spacebar.

- Canvas: An onscreen area into which the applet can draw graphics. The inherited paint() method comes from this class.

- Checkbox: A button, which can be square or round, that displays a check or other mark to indicate its selection.

- CheckboxGroup: Extended from Object, this class is used to group multiple Checkbox buttons, also sometimes called radio buttons. However, the class itself does not create a visual element.

- Choice: Presents a pull-down menu or list of selectable text items.

- Container: An abstract superclass that enables other classes to contain components. You will use this class's services to lay out multiple components in the applet's display space. Notice that the Applet class is derived from Panel, which extends Container.

- Label: Displays a text item that the applet can change, but users cannot edit.

- List: Presents users with a scrollable list of text items, from which an item may be selected.

- Scrollbar: Displays a horizontal or vertical scrollbar, typically used to select a range of values or to scroll another object's contents.

- `TextArea`: Extended from `TextComponent`, this class displays a multiline text box that users can edit. You can use this class also to create multiline static text messages that users cannot change.

- `TextField`: Extended from `TextComponent`, this class displays a single-line text box that users can edit.

- `Window`: Provides a fundamental window (see the "Window Classes" section, later in this chapter).

Except for the `Window` class, which is covered in Chapter 16, "Menus, Windows, and Dialogs," and `Canvas`, which is covered in Chapter 17, this chapter explains all of the preceding component classes. The `Component` class itself, from which most of these classes extend, is discussed near the end of this chapter (see the "Components" section).

Container Classes

There are two classes derived from the abstract `Container` superclass (see Figure 14.2), which is extended from `Component`. The two classes are

- `Applet`: Provides the basis for applet classes. As explained in the preceding chapter, all Java applets are classes extended from the `Applet` class. Because `Applet` is derived from `Panel`, which is derived from `Container`, an `Applet` object is capable of holding other `Component` objects such as `Buttons`, `TextFields`, and `Scrollbars`.

- `Panel`: Extends and implements the abstract `Container` class to provide objects with the capability of containing, displaying, and arranging other `Components`. This class is discussed briefly near the end of this chapter, under the heading "Components." Chapter 15 explains how to use `Panel` to create surfaces for holding other `Component` objects.

> **NOTE**
>
> Web browsers such as HotJava that are written in Java are themselves objects of the `Container` class, which is derived from `Component`. Such a browser is potentially extendible using the same techniques presented in this book, but unfortunately, the same isn't true of all browsers. You cannot, for instance, attach a new menu item to Internet Explorer by adding it to the applet's parent container. This sounds like an exciting capability—and some references suggest that you can do exactly that—but in reality, extending the browser itself through AWT's services is unlikely to produce reliable results. Besides, would *you* want an applet to modify *your* browser's interface?

Window Classes

The Window class, which is derived from Component, provides a top level window that has no border or menu. Objects of the Window class are used to create various types of windows such as pull-down menus and dialog boxes. They are described in Chapter 16. The Window class's default layout is an object of the BorderLayout class. There are two main classes, and one nested subclass, extended from Window. These are

- Dialog: Used to construct a separate window for prompting users to input information such as configuration settings.

- FileDialog: Extended from Dialog, this class prompts users to select or enter a filename.

- Frame: Adds title, border, and menu capabilities to the basic Window class.

Layout Classes

Layout classes are all derived from Object (there is no class named "Layout"). Each is used to arrange the components in a Container's window according to various schemes that I'll explain in Chapter 15. The layout classes are

- BorderLayout: Lays out components in a container using relative North, South, East, West, and Center directions.

- CardLayout: Lays out components using a series of cards, like those in a Rolodex file, that the user can flip through.

- FlowLayout: Lays out components so that they "flow" in left to right order, spaced according to their native shapes and sizes.

- GridBagConstraints: Specifies parameters, or *constraints*, for layouts that use the GridBagLayout class.

- GridBagLayout: Lays out components in a row and column format. Each intersecting cell in the grid may be variable in size, making this the most versatile of layout classes.

- GridLayout: Lays out components in a row and column format. Each intersecting cell in the grid is of equal size, and each component is placed in the middle of a cell. Useful for creating neatly organized sets of objects such as the buttons in a calculator or a monthly calendar.

- LayoutManager: This is an interface class that specifies the fundamental protocols all other layout classes must follow. All of the preceding layout classes implement this interface.

Font Classes

Two classes, each extended directly from Object, provide fonts for displaying text as described in Chapter 17. The two classes are

- Font: Represents a font object, of which Java provides several selections. A font can be styled using attributes such as bold and italic.

- FontMetrics: Provides information about the rendering of specific fonts. Typically used to control the spacing of text characters and lines, and to calculate the space required to display text using a specific font.

Graphics Classes

The following classes, all of which are derived directly from Object, are used mostly by graphical applications. They are discussed in detail in Chapter 17. The classes are

- Color: Represents a color, the exact nature of which depends on the user's system.

- Graphics: An extensive, abstract base class that provides numerous system-independent methods for drawing lines, polygons, rectangles, text, and other visual elements. The paint() method receives an object of a class derived from Graphics that is tailored to the user's system.

- Image: An abstract class that represents bitmapped image objects.

- MediaTracker: A relatively new class that simplifies loading and displaying multiple image objects in a multithreaded environment. A future edition of this class is expected to handle other media such as sound clips, but it currently supports only bitmapped images. You will typically use this class to create animations in applets.

Menu Classes

The following classes are derived from MenuComponent, which extends Object. These classes are used to create pull-down (some call them pop-up) menus in applet windows, and are described in Chapter 16. The classes are

- CheckboxMenuItem: Extended from MenuItem, this class represents a menu item that shows its selection by displaying a check or other mark, usually to its left.

- Menu: Extended from MenuItem, this class represents an individual pull-down menu of a MenuBar object. It can also be used to create a *tear-off* menu that can stay open after the mouse button is released. (This is also sometimes referred to as a floating pop-up menu.)

- MenuBar: Extended from MenuComponent, this class provides a menu bar that can be attached to a window's frame. A MenuBar is a kind of container that can hold one or more pull-down Menu objects.

- MenuContainer: An interface class that is implemented by the MenuBar class to provide the capability of containing Menu objects.

- MenuItem: Extended from MenuComponent, this class represents an individual item in a pull-down menu.

Dimensional Classes

Dimensional classes—this is my term—are used to define areas, locations, and dimensions for other objects. Except for Polygon, the classes are discussed throughout this chapter at their first use. They are not visual components and have no onscreen appearance, a fact that beginners often find confusing. For example, the Rectangle class does *not* create a visible rectangle; it merely defines a rectangular area that might be used to position another object. To create visual rectangles and other shapes, see the Graphics class described in Chapter 17, which also covers the Polygon class. The dimensional classes are

- Dimension: Determines the width and height of another component.
- Insets: Determines the reserved space around a component's border.
- Point: Represents x and y coordinate values.
- Polygon: Represents a list of x and y coordinate values.
- Rectangle: Defines a rectangular area.

Miscellaneous Classes

Finally in this section are two classes that don't fit into any other categories. Both are derived directly from Object. The two classes, described in Chapter 15, are

- Event: Describes the nature of an event passed to the action() method.
- Toolkit: Provides an abstract class for implementations of the AWT package, which calls methods in Toolkit to bind platform-independent code with the target system's native tools. There are few good reasons, if any, to call any of this class's methods from an applet. (However, doing that is one way to create a program that can run both as an applet and as an application. For example, see the WorldView2.java program in the preceding chapter.)

NOTE

As you can see from the preceding introductions, the AWT package provides a wealth of classes. It will take some time for you to learn how to use them all, but in the course of writing your applet, you probably will use most of them. The rest of this chapter will help you get started using many of AWT's classes, and as I mentioned, the next three chapters explore specific programming techniques for a variety of topics. Also remember to consult the Visual J++ online help files and Java's source code files, which reveal many secrets for developing successful user interfaces.

Components

Now let's take a look at how to use interactive components in applets. Listing 14.2, Components.java, shows examples of each common component control object. Figure 14.3 illustrates the program's display, showing each control of the classes Button, Checkbox, Choice, Label, List, Scrollbar, TextArea, and TextField. Refer to the listing and figure as you read about each class in the following sections. I'll also explain in the following sections how to use the related CheckboxGroup class, which is not itself extended from the Component class, and is not therefore a control object.

> **NOTE**
>
> Although you might be interested in particular classes, it's best to read the following information straight through the first time. At various places, I introduce some general topics such as methods shared by all Component classes, and if you skip around, you might miss this important information.

Figure 14.3.

Common component controls in the Components applet.

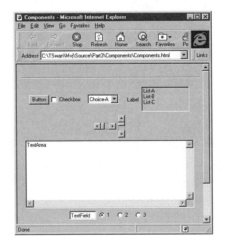

Listing 14.2. Components.java (Demonstrates component controls).

```java
import java.applet.*;
import java.awt.*;

public class Components extends Applet {

    // Component control objects.
    Button          buttonControl;
    Checkbox        checkboxControl;
    CheckboxGroup   group;
    Choice          choiceControl;
    Label           labelControl;
```

```
List           listControl;
Scrollbar      scrollbarHControl, scrollbarVControl;
TextArea       textAreaControl;
TextField      textFieldControl;

public void init()
{
 // Set the applet's display size
 resize(400, 350);

 // Construct the control objects
 buttonControl = new Button("Button");
 checkboxControl= new Checkbox("Checkbox");
 choiceControl = new Choice();
 labelControl = new Label("Label");
 listControl = new List();
 scrollbarHControl =
  new Scrollbar(Scrollbar.HORIZONTAL, 0, 5, 0, 99);
 scrollbarVControl =
  new Scrollbar(Scrollbar.VERTICAL, 0, 5, 0, 99);
 textAreaControl = new TextArea("TextArea");
 textFieldControl = new TextField("TextField");

 // Specify a layout strategy
 setLayout(new FlowLayout(FlowLayout.CENTER));

 // Add control objects to applet display
 add(buttonControl);
 add(checkboxControl);
 add(choiceControl);
 add(labelControl);
 add(listControl);
 add(scrollbarHControl);
 add(scrollbarVControl);
 add(textAreaControl);
 add(textFieldControl);

 // Construct a "radio-button" group
 group = new CheckboxGroup();
 Checkbox c1 = new Checkbox("1", group, true);
 Checkbox c2 = new Checkbox("2", group, false);
 Checkbox c3 = new Checkbox("3", group, false);
 add(c1);
 add(c2);
 add(c3);

 // Insert selections into the Choice control
 choiceControl.addItem("Choice-A");
 choiceControl.addItem("Choice-B");
 choiceControl.addItem("Choice-C");

 // Insert selections into the List control
 listControl.addItem("List-A");
 listControl.addItem("List-B");
 listControl.addItem("List-C");

}
}
```

The Button Class

The first sample program in this chapter demonstrated how to add a Button object to an applet display. The Components.java applet does the same, passing a label for the button's interior to its constructor with the statement

```
buttonControl = new Button("Button");
```

Alternatively, you can create a button without a label by using the default constructor like this:

```
buttonControl = new Button();
```

But unnamed buttons are confusing and should probably be avoided. Perhaps, however, a grid of them might be useful for a specialized purpose. After constructing the object, add it to the applet container using the statement

```
add(buttonControl);
```

Listing 14.3 shows the Button class's declaration.

Listing 14.3. The Button class.

```
public class Button extends Component {
// Constructors:
 public Button();
 public Button(String label);
// Public methods:
 public synchronized void addNotify();
 public String getLabel();
 public void setLabel(String label);
}
```

In addition to its two constructors, the Button class provides three methods, but only two that applets normally call. The first, addNotify(), is called by the AWT to bind a Button object with its peer class, which connects the object to the operating system's native control. Applets have little if any reason ever to call addNotify(), which is provided by most of the classes discussed in this chapter. (The fact that this method is public points out a minor weakness in Java. Methods that shouldn't be called are best not made available in the first place.)

Call getLabel() to retrieve the label string displayed by a Button object. You might use the method to distinguish between one button or another. Call setLabel() to change the button's text. You may do this as often as necessary. For example, an action() method could call setLabel() to change between two labels, thus making a Button function as a toggle.

The Checkbox Class

You normally construct a Checkbox control the same way as a button. Pass it a string label as in the sample program's statement:

```
checkboxControl= new Checkbox("Checkbox");
```

There are two other ways to construct Checkbox controls. You can create a nameless one (which, as with buttons, is probably unwise in most cases):

```
checkboxControl = new Checkbox();
```

And you can create one assigned to a CheckboxGroup object. (See the next section.) After constructing the Checkbox object, add it to the applet container using the statement

```
add(checkboxControl);
```

Listing 14.4 shows the Checkbox class declaration.

Listing 14.4. The Checkbox class.

```
public class Checkbox extends Component {
// Constructors:
 public Checkbox();
 public Checkbox(String label);
// Public methods:
 public Checkbox(String label, CheckboxGroup group, boolean state);
 public synchronized void addNotify();
 public String getLabel();
 public void setLabel(String label);
 public boolean getState();
 public void setState(boolean state);
 public CheckboxGroup getCheckboxGroup();
 public void setCheckboxGroup(CheckboxGroup g);
}
```

Call the Checkbox methods getLabel() and setLabel() to get and set the control's label text, respectively. Call getState() to determine whether the control is selected (true) or not (false). Call setState() to change the control's selected state under program control—initially, the control is unselected (its state is false). The getCheckBoxGroup() and setCheckBoxGroup() methods are used in conjunction with the CheckboxGroup class, explained in the next section.

The CheckboxGroup Class

A CheckboxGroup object is not itself a control, but a means for organizing multiple Checkbox objects. Some systems such as Windows call these groups *radio buttons* because they resemble the station-selector buttons on an automobile radio—at least those in the pre-electronic age. Only one button within the group may be selected. Selecting another button turns off the currently selected one. This makes CheckboxGroup objects suitable for presenting multiple choices such as a set of colors or difficulty levels in a game.

Under Windows, each button is a round shape with a black bullet inside to indicate the selected control. Under other systems, the buttons might be triangular or another shape, but they are usually not square as are individual Checkbox components. Listing 14.5 shows the CheckboxGroup class.

Listing 14.5. The CheckboxGroup class.

```
public class CheckboxGroup {
// Constructor:
 public CheckboxGroup();
// Public methods:
 public Checkbox getCurrent();
 public synchronized void setCurrent(Checkbox box);
 public String toString();
}
```

The sample applet uses a `CheckboxGroup` object to create a three-way radio button group, displayed at the bottom of the applet's window. Create the group object by calling the `CheckboxGroup` class's default and only constructor:

```
group = new CheckboxGroup();
```

This is usually done before constructing the individual buttons to insert in the group. Construct those objects using the `Checkbox` class, but specify two additional parameters in addition to each button's label:

```
Checkbox c1 = new Checkbox("1", group, true);
Checkbox c2 = new Checkbox("2", group, false);
Checkbox c3 = new Checkbox("3", group, false);
```

The parameters label each button, specify its group, and set its initial value. Only one button may be selected (`true`). The others should be `false`. To display the buttons in their group, add them to the applet using statements such as

```
add(c1);
add(c2);
add(c3);
```

Notice that you add the `Checkbox` controls to the *applet*. You do *not* add the group object. A `CheckboxGroup` is not a container, nor is it a component, but it is merely an organizer for multiple `Checkbox` buttons. Each button knows the group to which it belongs, and therefore, adding the buttons to the applet container organizes them within the desired group.

If it is more convenient to construct the buttons first, you can call the `Checkbox` method `setCheckboxGroup()` to insert a button into any group object, or even to change its group at runtime (though this might produce a strange effect). For example, use statements such as the following to add a fourth button to the sample program:

```
Checkbox c4 = new Checkbox("4");
c4.setCheckboxGroup(group);
add(c4);
```

That code first constructs the `Checkbox` object, and gives it a label. It next calls that object's `setCheckboxGroup()` method to assign the button to a group. Finally, it adds the `Checkbox` (again not the group) to the applet container. When using this method, you might also need to specify the initially selected button. Do this by calling the group object's `setCurrent()` method as in this statement:

```
group.setCurrent(c4);
```

Call the group's `getCurrent()` method to determine which button is selected. This returns a `Checkbox` object reference, which can be compared to the button objects using code such as

```
Checkbox cb = group.getCurrent();
if (cb == c3) { ... }
```

Or, if you don't want to save references to each button in a group, you can call the `Checkbox` object's `getLabel()` method and compare it to determine which button is selected. Use code like this:

```
Checkbox cb = group.getCurrent();
if (cb.getLabel().equals("3")) { ... }
```

You might also call the group's `toString()` method, which returns a string in the form

```
[current=4]
```

where the 4 is the button object's name. This technique makes me uneasy, however, because it relies too much on the implementation. If the programmer decides to add a space on each side of the equal sign, for example, a comparison on this string might fail.

The `Choice` Class

A `Choice` object presents the applet's user with a pull-down menu of selectable items. It is particularly handy in a busy display where you need to conserve room; otherwise, a `List` object might be a better choice because it doesn't require users to open the window. Figure 14.3 shows a sample `Choice` control labeled *Choice-A*. Click the arrow next to the label (usually it's to the right, but there's no guarantee of this) to open the control's window and see its other choices.

There's only one way to construct a `Choice` object—call its default constructor as in the sample listing:

```
choiceControl = new Choice();
```

Add the object to the applet's container using the statement

```
add(choiceControl);
```

Before or after you do that, you can also insert the `Choice` control's selections using statements such as

```
choiceControl.addItem("Choice-A");
choiceControl.addItem("Choice-B");
choiceControl.addItem("Choice-C");
```

Listing 14.6 shows the `Choice` class. Internally, by the way, the list of selection strings is stored in an object of the `Vector` class.

Listing 14.6. The Choice class.

```
public class Choice extends Component {
// Constructor:
 public Choice();
// Public methods:
 public synchronized void addNotify();
 public int countItems();
 public String getItem(int index);
 public synchronized void addItem(String item);
 public String getSelectedItem();
 public int getSelectedIndex();
 public synchronized void select(int pos);
 public void select(String str);
}
```

The Choice class provides several useful methods. Call countItems() for the number of selections stored in the object. This is useful in applets that interactively add new selections such as filenames.

Call getItem() to retrieve any specific entry by index number, with zero representing the first one. This is *not* necessarily the selected item. For that, call either getSelectedItem() for its string value, or getSelectedIndex() for its integer index, which you might pass to getItem().

To insert a selection into the list, call addItem() at any time, either before or after adding the Choice object to the applet. The item is added to the bottom of the current list—no provision is made for inserting items elsewhere. (This is one of the restrictions of using generic controls, but it's nothing to fuss about.)

Call one of the two overloaded select() methods to select any item under program control. You may pass a string argument (perhaps obtained from another control such as a TextField object), or an integer index of the item to be selected. The methods are potentially useful for giving applet users alternate ways to select choices.

The Label Class

The preceding chapter showed how to draw text by calling Graphics.drawString() in a paint() method. I'll also explain more about this technique in the next chapter. When constructing interactive applets or dialogs, however, it's often more convenient to use a Label object, which displays a single line of static text. Users cannot tab to, nor can they edit, this text; it is purely for labeling purposes.

A Label object is advantageous also because its layout class ensures its position relative to another control. For example, by adding a Label next to another object such as a CheckboxGroup, you can be fairly certain that the two objects will go together. Note I said, *fairly*. In the next chapter's discussion of layout objects, I'll explain more about how to position controls where you want them 99.9 percent of the time.

There are three ways to construct a Label object. The sample program uses the most common, passing a string object for the Label's text:

```
labelControl = new Label("Label");
```

You can also construct the Label object, and then fill in its text later using code such as

```
labelControl = new Label();
...
labelControl.setText("Label text");
```

A third method specifies an alignment, which can be LEFT, CENTER, or RIGHT. When using this technique, you must reference the Label class for each specification. For example, the statement

```
labelControl = new Label("Text", Label.CENTER);
```

centers the label's text within its layout space. You might use the technique with a grid layout to center a label within a column under which other controls appear.

After constructing the Label object, add it to the applet container with the statement

```
add(labelControl);
```

Listing 14.7 shows the Label class declaration.

Listing 14.7. The Label class.

```
public class Label extends Component {
// Fields:
 public static final int LEFT;
 public static final int CENTER;
 public static final int RIGHT;
// Constructors:
 public Label();
 public Label(String label);
 public Label(String label, int alignment);
// Public methods:
 public synchronized void addNotify();
 public int getAlignment();
 public void setAlignment(int alignment);
 public String getText();
 public void setText(String label);
}
```

Although you'll usually construct Label objects that merely annotate other controls or provide users with messages, the class offers some methods that you might find useful in special circumstances. Call getAlignment() to find out how a label is aligned—it returns the integer value of the LEFT, CENTER, or RIGHT field. Call setAlignment() to change the label's justification. (Call repaint() afterwards to update the display.)

The getText() and setText() methods do the expected jobs of returning and changing the label's text, respectively. It's usually a good idea to call repaint() after calling setText() if you've already added the label to the applet container.

The List Class

The List class presents the applet's user with a window of one or more selections, each a string of text on its own line. If more selections are available than fit inside the window, the List object displays a vertical scrollbar that users can click and drag to view selections out of view. The class also generates various events to indicate whether users have selected an item or double-clicked one. It's also possible to choose between Lists from which only one or more than one item can be selected. The next chapter, "Events and Layouts," explains how to respond to events. In this section, I explain how to construct and initialize List objects.

There are two ways to create a List component. The easiest, and the one illustrated in this chapter's sample program, calls the class's default constructor with the statement

```
listControl = new List();
```

Alternatively, you can specify two arguments using a statement such as

```
listControl = new List(10, true);
```

The first argument represents the number of rows to be visible in the object's window, and the second if true indicates that you want users to be able to select multiple items. Listing 14.8 shows the List class's declaration.

Listing 14.8. The List class.

```
public class List extends Component {
// Constructors:
 public List();
 public List(int rows, boolean multipleSelections);
// Public methods:
 public synchronized void addNotify();
 public synchronized void removeNotify();
 public int countItems();
 public String getItem(int index);
 public synchronized void addItem(String item);
 public synchronized void addItem(String item, int index);
 public synchronized void replaceItem(String newValue, int index);
 public synchronized void clear();
 public synchronized void delItem(int position);
 public synchronized void delItems(int start, int end);
 public synchronized int getSelectedIndex();
 public synchronized int[] getSelectedIndexes();
 public synchronized String getSelectedItem();
 public synchronized String[] getSelectedItems();
 public synchronized void select(int index);
 public synchronized void deselect(int index);
 public synchronized boolean isSelected(int index);
```

```
    public int getRows();
    public boolean allowsMultipleSelections();
    public void setMultipleSelections(boolean v);
    public int getVisibleIndex();
    public void makeVisible(int index);
    public Dimension preferredSize(int rows);
    public Dimension preferredSize();
    public Dimension minimumSize(int rows);
    public Dimension minimumSize();
}
```

There are more than a few List methods you can call, but you'll probably need only a small subset of them. Some methods such as countItems() have obvious purposes. Others that you can no doubt figure out are addItem(), delItem(), getRows(), and so on.

It is sometimes useful to preselect an item by calling the select() method. Or, you can also pass a selected item's index (zero is the first item) to indicate the item you want selected—perhaps due to the editing of another control. In methods such as this that accept or return integer indexes, the range of allowable values is zero to one less than the number of listed selections. A value less than zero indicates that an operation failed for some reason—no item was selected, for example, when calling getSelectedIndex().

You can also request the string text of a selected item, which is often the easiest method for using a List control. Call getSelectedItem() for the currently selected string. The method returns null if no item is selected. Call getSelectedItems() for an array of all selected strings in Lists that allow multiple selections. Use the array's count to determine how many items are returned. (Review Chapter 10, "Arrays and Other Containers," if you need help with this.)

Several methods in the List class have the word *visible* in them. This indicates items that are currently visible in the List's window. For example, call makeVisible() to force the List to scroll a specific selection into view. You might use this capability in a word lookup program, perhaps a dictionary or thesaurus that automatically scrolls to various words as users enter text into another field.

In programs that need precise control over the size and placement of List objects, you can request information about the control's size by calling four methods. These methods are

```
    public Dimension preferredSize(int rows);
```
Returns the preferred size of a List object having the specified number of rows.

```
    public Dimension preferredSize();
```
Returns the preferred size of a List object created with a specified number of rows, or one with zero rows (the default).

```
    public Dimension minimumSize(int rows);
```
Returns the minimum size of a List object having the specified number of rows.

```
    public Dimension minimumSize();
```

Returns the minimum size of a List object created with a specified number of rows, or one with zero rows (the default).

Each of the preceding four methods returns a Dimension class object that indicates the size of the control. Listing 14.9 shows the Dimension class declaration. You might find your own uses for this class in cases where you need to store or describe the size of an object.

Listing 14.9. The Dimension class.

```
public class Dimension {
// Public variables:
 public int width;
 public int height;
// Constructors:
 public Dimension();
 public Dimension(Dimension d);
 public Dimension(int width, int height);
// Public method:
 public String toString();
}
```

There are three ways to construct a Dimension object—by calling its default constructor, by passing another Dimension object, or by specifying a width and height. In normal use, these values, which are obtainable directly from the class's public width and height instance variables, are in pixels, but when using this class for your own purposes, the values could represent whatever you want. The toString() method is mostly useful for debugging—printing the values of a Dimension object, for example. You might also call toString() after obtaining a List control's size by calling one of the aforementioned methods.

> **NOTE**
>
> The TextArea class, described in this chapter, provides similar methods that return Dimension objects.

The Scrollbar Class

Scrollbars are probably the most generally useful objects ever invented for the graphical control of computer software. Just about every program seems to have several scrollbars for viewing lists and for scrolling text and graphics that won't fit entirely on screen.

Java applets create scrollbars as instances of the Scrollbar class. Create a default Scrollbar object using the class's default constructor like this:

```
scroller = new Scrollbar();
```

Scrollbars created that way are vertical by default, but it is more common to specify the object's orientation. For example, the sample listing in this chapter creates horizontal and vertical scrollbars with the statements

```
scrollbarHControl =
 new Scrollbar(Scrollbar.HORIZONTAL, 0, 5, 0, 99);
scrollbarVControl =
 new Scrollbar(Scrollbar.VERTICAL, 0, 5, 0, 99);
```

The first statement (on two lines) creates a horizontal scrollbar, passing as an argument the HORIZONTAL field in the Scrollbar class. The second statement passes the VERTICAL field to create an upright, and no doubt upstanding, scrollbar control.

The integer arguments shown here are optional—you can specify just the orientation if you want—but you'll normally include the values as well. The four arguments, each of type int, are

- value: The initial value of the scrollbar, usually zero, which places the slider (also sometimes called the thumb) at the top or leftmost range of the control.

- visible: The size that the slider represents, used to determine how much travel paging should produce.

- minimum: The scrollbar's minimum possible value, usually zero.

- maximum: The scrollbar's maximum value, which must be greater than the minimum.

Listing 14.10 shows the Scrollbar class declaration.

Listing 14.10. The Scrollbar class.

```
public class Scrollbar extends Component {
// Fields:
 public static final int HORIZONTAL;
 public static final int VERTICAL;
// Constructors:
 public Scrollbar();
 public Scrollbar(int orientation);
 public Scrollbar(int orientation, int value,
  int visible, int minimum, int maximum);
// Public methods:
 public synchronized void addNotify();
 public int getOrientation();
 public int getValue();
 public void setValue(int value);
 public int getMinimum();
 public int getMaximum();
 public int getVisible();
 public void setLineIncrement(int l);
 public int getLineIncrement();
 public void setPageIncrement(int l);
 public int getPageIncrement();
 public void setValues(int value, int visible,
  int minimum, int maximum);
}
```

The class's methods get and set various attributes of a `Scrollbar` object. For example, call `getMaximum()` for the control's maximum value. Call `setValues()` to alter all of the scrollbar's parameters.

More than likely, however, you won't call these methods—you'll simply construct the scrollbar and call `getValue()` to obtain the relative position of the slider. This will be a value between the control's minimum and maximum value. A scrollbar control's operation is otherwise automatic, and requires little program intervention. Again, see the next chapter for information about how to respond to events generated by the use of a scrollbar control.

The `TextArea` Class

The AWT provides two classes, `TextField` and `TextArea`, each of which extends the `TextComponent` class in Listing 14.11. You won't construct objects of this class, but you'll call some of its methods inherited by `TextField` and `TextArea` components. For example, refer back to Figure 14.3. The large field labeled `TextArea` shows this object's multiline display—similar in functionality to the Windows Notepad utility. The `TextField` control near the bottom of the display provides a single-line entry space where users can type text such as a filename or a password.

Listing 14.11. The `TextComponent` class.

```
public class TextComponent extends Component {
// Constructor:
 TextComponent(String text);
// Public methods:
 public synchronized void removeNotify();
 public void setText(String t);
 public String getText();
 public String getSelectedText();
 public boolean isEditable();
 public void setEditable(boolean t);
 public int getSelectionStart();
 public int getSelectionEnd();
 public void select(int selStart, int selEnd);
 public void selectAll();
}
```

The `TextComponent` class provides several useful methods. Call `setText()` to change the object's text under program control—perhaps to transfer an item from a `List` object to be edited, for example. Call `getSelectedText()` to obtain the portion of the string that the user has highlighted, perhaps by double-clicking or by clicking and dragging the mouse. If you don't want users to be able to edit a field, pass `false` to `setEditable()`. This is unusual, however, and if you just want to display some text, you might want to use a `Label` object instead.

It is often useful to preselect the entire text display in a `TextComponent` control—especially of the `TextField` class. Do this by calling `selectAll()`, usually in response to the control's selection.

For multiline text windows into which users can type notes, poems, even an entire novel, construct a TextArea control as the sample program does with the statement

```
textAreaControl = new TextArea("TextArea");
```

The string is the one you want displayed initially inside the control's window (see Figure 14.3). You may also construct an empty window by using the class's default constructor like this:

```
textAreaControl = new TextArea();
```

And you may optionally specify the number of rows and columns, in that order. The statement

```
textAreaControl = new TextArea(4, 40);
```

creates a TextArea control with four rows and 40 columns. This is a good way to manage the size of the control object. Finally, you may specify an initial string and size arguments using a statement such as

```
textAreaControl = new TextArea("Type here!", 4, 40);
```

Listing 14.12 shows the TextArea class declaration.

Listing 14.12. The TextArea class.

```
public class TextArea extends TextComponent {
// Constructors:
 public TextArea();
 public TextArea(int rows, int cols);
 public TextArea(String text);
 public TextArea(String text, int rows, int cols);
// Public methods:
 public synchronized void addNotify();
 public void insertText(String str, int pos);
 public void appendText(String str);
 public void replaceText(String str, int start, int end);
 public int getRows();
 public int getColumns();
 public Dimension preferredSize(int rows, int cols);
 public Dimension preferredSize();
 public Dimension minimumSize(int rows, int cols);
 public Dimension minimumSize();
}
```

Call the insertText(), appendText(), and replaceText() methods to alter the object's text under program control. A spelling checker, for example, might call replaceText() to change a word selected from a list. The start and end index values indicate the position of the text, which is treated as one long string. You can call the inherited getSelectedText() method to obtain the highlighted word. Call the inherited getSelectionStart() and getSelectionEnd() for the selected text's positions. See the TextComponent class in this chapter for these methods' declarations.

The TextField Class

The TextField class is similar to TextArea but creates a single-line, editable control. There are four methods for constructing TextField objects. Call the default constructor for a default size field:

```
textFieldControl = new TextField();
```

Or, specify the size of the control as the number of columns it should have:

```
textFieldControl = new TextField(80);
```

This does not limit the amount of text, but only the control's size. Users may type beyond the control's boundaries; it scrolls left and right automatically to the usual keyboard commands on the user's system, such as pressing the left and right arrow keys.

You will often construct a TextField object as in the sample program by passing it an initial string for editing. Use this statement:

```
textFieldControl = new TextField("TextField");
```

Or, you may also specify the initial text and a number of columns—a good way to limit the control's size. The statement

```
textFieldControl = new TextField("c:\", 45);
```

constructs an edit field of 45 columns initialized to the pathname string, "c:\". Listing 14.13 shows the TextField class declaration.

Listing 14.13. The TextField class.

```
public class TextField extends TextComponent {
// Constructors:
 public TextField();
 public TextField(int cols);
 public TextField(String text);
 public TextField(String text, int cols);
// Public methods:
 public synchronized void addNotify();
 public char getEchoChar();
 public boolean echoCharIsSet();
 public int getColumns();
 public void setEchoCharacter(char c);
 public Dimension preferredSize(int cols);
 public Dimension preferredSize();
 public Dimension minimumSize(int cols);
 public Dimension minimumSize();
}
```

To use a TextField object for entering passwords, call setEchoCharacter() using code such as

```
TextField password = new TextField(20);
password.setEchoCharacter('#');
```

The *echo character* is displayed in place of the user's typing, so that the actual password entry is never made visible but is still entered in memory for the program to retrieve. You might call getEchoChar() to obtain the current character, and echoCharIsSet() to determine whether the control is set properly—a possibly useful security measure. If by some chance the echo character is not set, the applet could exit and prevent the user from accidentally revealing a password. Another possible use for these methods is to disable the echo character temporarily for debugging.

Other Classes

I'll end this chapter with brief descriptions of some related classes that provide methods you will find useful at times. Many of the methods have obvious purposes, so I won't dwell on these. I'll point out some highlights, however, that might prove useful.

The Component Class

Listing 14.14 shows the Component class declaration, from which all component classes such as Button and List extend. All of these component classes inherit the methods of the Component class, a fact that is helpful to keep in mind when puzzling through a problem. You might find the answer in the ancestor class rather than in the one you are using.

> **TIP**
>
> This brings up a general principle of object-oriented programming that is always useful to keep in mind. When investigating a class such as Button, also take a look at its ancestor classes— Component and Object, in this case. Remember that the derived subclass inherits the public and protected instance variables, fields, and methods from its superclass ancestor. A subclass declaration often shows only the tip of the iceberg of what the class can do.

Listing 14.14. The Component class.

```
public abstract class Component implements ImageObserver {
// Constructor:
 Component();
// Public methods:
 public ComponentPeer getPeer();
 public Toolkit getToolkit();
 public boolean isValid();
 public boolean isVisible();
 public boolean isShowing();
 public boolean isEnabled();
 public Point location();
 public Dimension size();
 public Rectangle bounds();
```

continues

Listing 14.14. continued

```
public synchronized void enable();
public void enable(boolean cond);
public synchronized void disable();
public synchronized void show();
public void show(boolean cond);
public synchronized void hide();
public Color getForeground();
public synchronized void setForeground(Color c);
public Color getBackground();
public synchronized void setBackground(Color c);
public Font getFont();
public synchronized void setFont(Font f);
public synchronized ColorModel getColorModel();
public void move(int x, int y);
public void resize(int width, int height);
public void resize(Dimension d);
public synchronized void reshape(int x, int y, int width, int height);
public Dimension preferredSize();
public Dimension minimumSize();
public void layout();
public void validate();
public void invalidate();
public Graphics getGraphics();
public FontMetrics getFontMetrics(Font font);
public void paint(Graphics g);
public void update(Graphics g);
public void paintAll(Graphics g);
public void repaint();
public void repaint(long tm);
public void repaint(int x, int y, int width, int height);
public void repaint(long tm, int x, int y, int width, int height);
public void print(Graphics g);
public void printAll(Graphics g);
public boolean imageUpdate(Image img, int flags,
        int x, int y, int w, int h);
public Image createImage(ImageProducer producer);
public Image createImage(int width, int height);
public boolean prepareImage(Image image, ImageObserver observer);
public boolean prepareImage(Image image, int width, int height,
    ImageObserver observer);
public int checkImage(Image image, ImageObserver observer);
public int checkImage(Image image, int width, int height,
    ImageObserver observer);
public synchronized boolean inside(int x, int y);
public Component locate(int x, int y);
public void deliverEvent(Event e);
public boolean postEvent(Event e);
public boolean handleEvent(Event evt);
public boolean mouseDown(Event evt, int x, int y);
public boolean mouseDrag(Event evt, int x, int y);
public boolean mouseUp(Event evt, int x, int y);
public boolean mouseMove(Event evt, int x, int y);
public boolean mouseEnter(Event evt, int x, int y);
public boolean mouseExit(Event evt, int x, int y);
public boolean keyDown(Event evt, int key);
public boolean keyUp(Event evt, int key);
```

```
    public boolean action(Event evt, Object what);
    public void addNotify();
    public synchronized void removeNotify();
    public boolean gotFocus(Event evt, Object what);
    public boolean lostFocus(Event evt, Object what);
    public void requestFocus();
    public void nextFocus();
    public String toString();
    public void list();
    public void list(PrintStream out);
    public void list(PrintStream out, int indent);
}
```

Of all the methods in the Component class—and as you can see, there are more than plenty—the most useful are show() and hide(), which you can use to make a control visible and invisible in an applet window. Some methods you'll have little use for unless you are creating your own control and need to override one of the paint() methods. The gotFocus(), lostFocus(), requestFocus(), and nextFocus() methods are useful for directing users to specific controls, often in response to various events such as keypresses and mouse clicks. Notice that the Component class also provides default methods for various events. You generally don't call methods such as MouseEnter(), which is called from the default action() method to provide a control's operation.

The three overloaded list() methods are frequently useful for debugging applet displays. You may call list() for any Component—even the Applet itself, which is a distant relative—to output information about one or more components.

The Point Class

The Component.location() method returns the x,y coordinate of a control's position. This method returns an object of the Point class, as shown in Listing 14.15. You will find numerous uses for this class, which is used in other places in the AWT.

Listing 14.15. The Point class.

```
public class Point {
// Public variables:
 public int x;
 public int y;
// Constructor:
 public Point(int x, int y);
// Public methods:
 public void move(int x, int y);
 public void translate(int dx, int dy);
 public int hashCode();
 public boolean equals(Object obj);
 public String toString();
}
```

The Point class holds two integer values, x and y, which are public instance variables. A hashCode() method is provided so multiple points can be stored in a hash table container.

There are two ways to manipulate a Point object. Call the move() method to change the object's coordinate to the specified new x and y values. Call translate() to add values (which can be negative) to the Point. This method's two parameters are called *delta* values because they are added to the Point's current x and y variables.

The Rectangle Class

Another utility class used by the Component.bounds() method is Rectangle, shown in Listing 14.16. Call bounds() for a control's upper-left-corner location and its width and height in pixels.

Listing 14.16. The Rectangle class.

```
public class Rectangle {
// Public variables:
 public int x;
 public int y;
 public int width;
 public int height;
// Constructors:
 public Rectangle();
 public Rectangle(int x, int y, int width, int height);
 public Rectangle(int width, int height);
 public Rectangle(Point p, Dimension d);
 public Rectangle(Point p);
 public Rectangle(Dimension d);
// Public methods:
 public void reshape(int x, int y, int width, int height);
 public void move(int x, int y);
 public void translate(int x, int y);
 public void resize(int width, int height);
 public boolean inside(int x, int y);
 public Rectangle intersection(Rectangle r);
 public Rectangle union(Rectangle r);
 public void add(int newx, int newy);
 public void add(Point pt);
 public void add(Rectangle r);
 public void grow(int h, int v);
 public boolean isEmpty();
 public int hashCode();
 public boolean equals(Object obj);
 public String toString();
}
```

The Rectangle class provides numerous methods for adjusting rectangular regions. As I mentioned, the class does not produce a visible shape on screen. It merely represents the values of a rectangular area, obtainable from the class's public instance variables x, y, width, and height. (I was glad to see that Java's designers did not try to define Rectangle in terms of Dimension and Point objects, as in so many object-oriented libraries, with the result being a mass of confusing methods and nested dot-notation expressions just to obtain simple values.)

Most of Rectangle's methods have obvious purposes. You can resize an object, move it, and translate its values—all useful for relative positioning of various shapes and controls onscreen. You can also call intersection() and union() to determine the relative positioning or overlap of two rectangular regions.

A Rectangle can be empty, indicated by its empty() method returning true. This is important to keep in mind, especially in code that might perform some pixel-by-pixel operation within the rectangle's borders.

The Container Class

The next class, Container in Listing 14.17, is also an integral element in the AWT. Refer back to Figure 14.2, in which Container extends Component and, therefore, inherits all of Component's methods. Container, however, is an abstract class and, as such, cannot be instantiated as an object. Its purpose, also evident from the figure, is to provide a base for the Panel and Applet classes.

The Container class's methods will be more meaningful when you investigate layouts in the next chapter. It's important to understand at this stage that Container objects (of derived classes such as Panel and Applet) are capable of holding other Components. It is through the Container class's services that Applets are able to display and organize multiple controls such as buttons and lists. The figure also reveals an important relationship among these classes. For example, an Applet is related to a Button in the same way that a Button is related to a Scrollbar. However, only an Applet or other class derived from Panel can hold other Component objects.

Listing 14.17. The Container class.

```
public abstract class Container extends Component {
// Constructor:
 Container();
// Public methods:
 public int countComponents();
 public synchronized Component getComponent(int n);
 public synchronized Component[] getComponents();
 public Insets insets();
 public Component add(Component comp);
 public synchronized Component add(Component comp, int pos);
 public synchronized Component add(String name, Component comp);
 public synchronized void remove(Component comp);
 public synchronized void removeAll();
 public LayoutManager getLayout();
 public void setLayout(LayoutManager mgr);
 public synchronized void layout();
 public synchronized void validate();
 public synchronized Dimension preferredSize();
 public synchronized Dimension minimumSize();
 public void paintComponents(Graphics g);
```

Listing 14.17. continued

```
public void printComponents(Graphics g);
public void deliverEvent(Event e);
public Component locate(int x, int y);
public synchronized void addNotify();
public synchronized void removeNotify();
public void list(PrintStream out, int indent);
}
```

You will probably use only two methods from the Component class. These are getLayout() and setLayout(), which are described in the next chapter.

One very useful Container method is getComponents(), which returns an array of references to all contained components. In applets where you want to perform some action on all components, you can call this method and then use a simple loop—to change all background colors for all onscreen controls, for example, or to erase the contents of an array of TextField entry areas.

The Insets Class

Another Container method, insets(), returns an object of the Insets class, shown in Listing 14.18. This class provides reserved space around controls in a container. These values are controlled with the layout classes to be discussed in the next chapter, but you might call insets() to determine the current values.

Listing 14.18. The Insets class.

```
public class Insets implements Cloneable {
// Public variables:
 public int top;
 public int left;
 public int bottom;
 public int right;
// Constructor:
 public Insets(int top, int left, int bottom, int right);
// Public methods:
 public String toString();
 public Object clone();
}
```

The Panel Class

Finally in this chapter, just for the sake of completeness, is the Panel class, which extends Container. I show this class (found in Listing 14.19) only to emphasize its position in the hierarchy stemming from Object and Component, and leading through Container, Panel, and Applet. Though Panel's main purpose in life is to provide an implementation of Container for the Applet class, you can use `Panel` to create platforms on which you can install other `Component` objects. We'll see this use in the next chapter in the discussion of layouts.

Listing 14.19. The `Panel` class.

```
public class Panel extends Container {
// Constructor:
 public Panel();
// Public method:
 public synchronized void addNotify();
}
```

Summary

- The AWT (Another Window Toolkit) provides an extensive selection of classes for developing graphical user interfaces.

- The purpose of the AWT is to provide generalized user-interface tools that produce reliable, and repeatable, results regardless of target operating system.

- This chapter introduces the classes in the AWT, and covers components and related classes. There are lots of classes in the toolkit, and to master them all will take some time and effort. The next three chapters cover other aspects of AWT programming.

What's Next?

Events and layouts are two subjects that will occupy a lot of your programming time while developing applets. As you will learn in the next chapter, you respond to a control's activities—such as the selection of items in a list or the click of a button—by programming event handlers. You also designate the relative locations of controls, and thus the appearance of your applet's display, not by specifying rigid coordinates, but by the use of a set of *layout* classes. Understanding these two topics is the key to creating good looking applet displays that respond intelligently to user input.

15

Events and Layouts

After selecting the types of controls to display in your applet's window, the next step is to write the code that makes those controls perform the actions you want. You'll also need to lay out the controls for a pleasing and well-organized display. This chapter explores these "controlling" subjects. First, I'll explain how to write code to respond to control events such as selecting an item from a list and clicking a scrollbar button. After that, I'll demonstrate several methods for laying out control objects in an applet's window using AWT techniques that are completely independent of the target operating system.

In This Chapter

This chapter covers the following fundamentals of events and layouts:

- Understanding the Event and Toolkit classes.
- Programming event handlers.
- Using AWT's layout classes.
- Layout strategies.

Events

Java programs are *event driven*, which means that the order in which a program's statements execute is controlled by external actions. Those actions, or events, might be keypresses or mouse button clicks. The events are intercepted by low-level code and distributed to the appropriate objects for processing. The objects, which might be buttons, lists, or even the applet itself, receive the events intended for them, and execute code commonly called an *event handler*. In this way, when the user clicks a button control, the object itself dictates its own response.

The Event Class

All events arrive in the form of Event-class objects, which provide a number of details about the event. Listing 15.1 shows Java's Event class declaration from the java.awt package.

Listing 15.1. The Event class.

```
public class Event {
// Public variables:
 public Object target;
 public long when;
 public int id;
 public int x;
 public int y;
 public int key;
 public int modifiers;
 public int clickCount;
 public Object arg;
 public Event evt;
```

```
// Constructors:
 public Event(Object target, long when,
  int id, int x, int y, int key,
  int modifiers, Object arg);
 public Event(Object target, long when,
  int id, int x, int y, int key, int modifiers);
 public Event(Object target, int id, Object arg);
// Special key masks:
 public static final int SHIFT_MASK;
 public static final int CTRL_MASK;
 public static final int META_MASK;
 public static final int ALT_MASK;
// Named function keys:
 public static final int HOME;
 public static final int END;
 public static final int PGUP;
 public static final int PGDN;
 public static final int UP;
 public static final int DOWN;
 public static final int LEFT;
 public static final int RIGHT;
// Numbered function keys:
 public static final int F1;
 public static final int F2;
 public static final int F3;
 public static final int F4;
 public static final int F5;
 public static final int F6;
 public static final int F7;
 public static final int F8;
 public static final int F9;
 public static final int F10;
 public static final int F11;
 public static final int F12;
// Window events:
 public static final int WINDOW_DESTROY;
 public static final int WINDOW_EXPOSE;
 public static final int WINDOW_ICONIFY;
 public static final int WINDOW_DEICONIFY;
 public static final int WINDOW_MOVED;
// Keyboard events:
 public static final int KEY_PRESS;
 public static final int KEY_RELEASE;
 public static final int KEY_ACTION;
 public static final int KEY_ACTION_RELEASE;
// Mouse events:
 public static final int MOUSE_DOWN;
 public static final int MOUSE_UP;
 public static final int MOUSE_MOVE;
 public static final int MOUSE_ENTER;
 public static final int MOUSE_EXIT;
 public static final int MOUSE_DRAG;
// Scrollbar events:
 public static final int SCROLL_LINE_DOWN;
 public static final int SCROLL_PAGE_UP;
 public static final int SCROLL_PAGE_DOWN;
 public static final int SCROLL_ABSOLUTE;
```

continues

Listing 15.1. continued

```
// List selection events:
 public static final int LIST_SELECT;
 public static final int LIST_DESELECT;
// Miscellaneous events:
 public static final int ACTION_EVENT;
 public static final int LOAD_FILE;
 public static final int SAVE_FILE;
 public static final int GOT_FOCUS;
 public static final int LOST_FOCUS;
// Miscellaneous public methods:
 public void translate(int dx, int dy);
 public boolean shiftDown();
 public boolean controlDown();
 public boolean metaDown();
 public String toString();
}
```

As you can see, the Event class is mostly composed of variables and static fields, but it also has a few public methods you can call. It will be more instructive to examine instances of this class in use, so for the moment, I'll describe its sections briefly. Ten public variables describe the nature of an event and provide other parameters for specific types of events. The variables are

- Object target: This is the object for which the event occurred. Because its type is Object, you'll normally have to use a type-cast expression such as (Button)evt.target to indicate the type of object, where evt is an object of the Event class.

- long when: This represents the date and time of the event. You can use the java.util.Date class to convert this value to a useable date and time.

- int id: This tells you the type of event that occurred. It is one of the values in the Event class under the categories labeled Window, Keyboard, Mouse, Scrollbar, List, and Miscellaneous events.

- int x: This is the x coordinate value of the pointer for mouse events relative to the target component.

- int y: This is the y coordinate value of the pointer for mouse events relative to the target component.

- int key: This is the value of the key for keyboard events. It can be the value of a character for a KEY_PRESS or KEY_RELEASE event, or a named or numbered function key for a KEY_ACTION or KEY_ACTION_RELEASE event.

- int modifiers: This is a bit mask that equals the logical OR of one or more mask field values: SHIFT_MASK, CTRL_MASK, ALT_MASK, or META_MASK.

- int clickCount: This is the count of mouse clicks for a mouse event—two for a double-click, for example.

- Object arg: This is an optional argument supplied with some events—the name of a button control as a string, for example. Not all events supply an argument.

- `Event evt`: This field, if not `null`, is the next event in a linked list of `Event` objects. Applets and applications do not normally use this field.

The `Event` class provides three constructors that you can use to create your own events. You might, however, never need to do this: Events are normally created internally for interception by your code's event handlers. At times, though, you might find it useful to send an event to an object—for example, to alter a button label or set a text field based on some other happening. Construct the event by selecting an appropriate constructor, and then call the `Component` class's `deliverEvent()` or `postEvent()` method. For example, to simulate a keypress, you can use code such as

```
Event evt = new Event(edit, 0, Event.KEY_PRESS,
 0, 0, Event.F1, 0, null);
deliverEvent(evt);
```

Alternatively, you can call `postEvent()`, which returns `true` or `false`, to determine whether the event was handled:

```
if (postEvent(evt)) {
 // ... event was handled
}
```

In addition to its variables, constructors, and fields, the `Event` class provides five public methods you might find useful. You may call these methods for any `Event` object. They are:

- `void translate(int dx, int dy)`: Call this method to add `dx` and `dy` to the event's coordinate values. You might use this method to add a component's window position to create new coordinate values relative to the applet window instead of to the component object.

- `boolean shiftDown()`: This method returns `true` if the shift key was held down during an event such as a mouse click or keypress.

- `boolean controlDown()`: This method returns `true` if the Ctrl key was held down during an event such as a mouse click or keypress.

- `boolean metaDown()`: This method returns `true` if an unspecified *meta* key is held down during an event such as a mouse click or keypress.

- `String toString()`: This method returns a string representation of the event, and is useful mostly for debugging.

The `shiftDown()` and `controlDown()` methods are valuable in providing multiple function keys—distinguishing between function key F1 and Shift+F1 or Ctrl+F1, for example. The `metaDown()` function, however, is less useful because no specific key is defined for this value. (My PC laptop, for example, has no such key.) The function, however, is used in conjunction with mouse button clicks to indicate the right button. There is no method named `altDown()` because the Alt key is generally reserved for system use and should not be used by Java programs. Users press Alt and another key, for instance, to open a browser menu, and interfering with this usage is a bad idea.

Now let's take a look at an actual applet that uses the Event class. Listing 15.2, DynaButton.java, demonstrates two different event-handling techniques. Figure 15.1 shows the program's display. To run the program, copy the files to your hard drive from the CD-ROM, and use *File|Open Workspace* to load the DynaButton.mdp project file. Use the *Build* menu to build and execute the applet. Alternatively, you can load the DynaButton.html file into your browser if you aren't currently running Visual J++. Use similar techniques to load and run the other applets in this chapter.

Figure 15.1.

DynaButton's display demonstrating event handling.

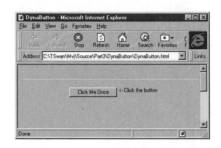

Listing 15.2. DynaButton.java (Demonstrates event handling).

```
import java.applet.*;
import java.awt.*;

public class DynaButton extends Applet
{
 Button theButton;   // Button control
 String message;     // Text message
 int count = 0;      // Switch control variable

 // Initialize applet
 public void init()
 {
  // Size the window
  resize(320, 240);
  // Create and insert a button
  theButton = new Button("    Click Me Once    ");
  add(theButton);
 }

 // Respond to component events
 public boolean action(Event evt, Object what)
 {
  if (evt.target instanceof Button) {
   if (evt.target.equals(theButton)) {
    count++;
    switch (count) {
    case 0:
     theButton.setLabel("    Click Me Once    ");
     break;
    case 1:
     theButton.setLabel("    Click Me Twice    ");
     break;
    case 2:
     theButton.setLabel(" Click Me Once Again ");
```

```
      count = -1;
    }
    theButton.repaint();
  }
 }
 return true;
}

// Paint the applet's window
public void paint(Graphics g) {
 if (message.length() !=0) {
  Point p = theButton.location();
  Dimension d = theButton.size();
  g.drawString(message,
   p.x + d.width + 4, p.y + d.height / 2);
 }
}

// Respond to the mouse clicks in the applet's
// window, but NOT in the button (see action()).
public boolean mouseDown(Event evt, int x, int y) {
 if (message == null) {
  message = new String("<- Click the button");
  repaint();
 }
 return true;
}
}
```

When DynaButton's display appears, click the button to change its text. This demonstrates how a component can respond to specific events intended for the control. Next, click in the applet window near the button (you can't see this window because it is the same color as the browser's background). This displays a message indicating you should click the button—which is an example of another way to handle events, this time those events intended for the applet rather than a contained component.

The program defines three variables:

```
Button theButton;
String message;
int count = 0;
```

The Button object is, of course, the button you see on screen. The message is the string displayed when you click outside of the button. The count variable alters which message the button displays when you click the control. To create the Button, the applet's init() method executes the following statements:

```
theButton = new Button("   Click Me Once    ");
add(theButton);
```

The first statement constructs the Button. The second adds it to the applet's display using the default layout strategy. (As I mentioned, I'll cover layouts in the second half of this chapter.) Notice that I left space around the button's text. This generally makes labels more readable, and I usually surround button and other text with at least one space on each end.

The applet's `action()` method demonstrates one way to handle events. The method is declared as

```
public boolean action(Event evt, Object what);
```

The `Event`-class object represents the event that occurred. The `what` parameter, of type `Object`, depends on the specific event but seems to usually be `null`, and is rarely (if ever) used. Generally, you can use an `action()` method to handle events that filter up to a component's parent. For example, in this case, clicking the button sends an event to that object, which passes the event on to its parent (the applet) for possible handling. By overriding the `action()` method in your applet's class, you can trap this and other events and program what they should do.

The first step in `action()` is usually to determine what type of event occurred. There are several techniques for doing this, and I'll try to use many of them throughout this chapter so you can investigate the best ways for your program. In this case, I use an `if` statement to check whether the event object is a button:

```
if (evt.target instanceof Button) {...
```

This expression is true if the target field of the `Event` parameter object is an instance of the `Button` class—a most useful way to determine what type of object is associated with an event. This also helps speed the program along by eliminating lengthy checks for event values that simply could not occur—checking for keypress values, for example, in response to mouse events.

After determining that a button event has occurred, the program checks which button was selected. Of course, there's only one button in this example, but I've included the code because, in practice, you'll normally have to distinguish between multiple controls using code such as

```
if (evt.target.equals(theButton)) {...
```

This calls the inherited `equals()` method for the target object to determine if the target instance is a *particular* button. If both `if` statements succeed, then the user has clicked our button, and the `action()` method uses a `switch` statement to select an appropriate message. This is passed to the button component using the statement

```
theButton.setLabel("   Click Me Twice   ");
```

which changes the button's text. So that users see that change, the program also calls `repaint()`. This causes an immediate update to the display, and calls the applet's `paint()` method, which executes the following code:

```
if (message.length() !=0) {
 Point p = theButton.location();
 Dimension d = theButton.size();
 g.drawString(message,
  p.x + d.width + 4, p.y + d.height / 2);
}
```

If the message has been initialized, two variables of the `Point` and `Dimension` classes are used to find the button object's position and size. These values are used to draw the message so that it appears next to the button. You'll want to use similar techniques to position text and other items on screen. Remember, you can't be certain of your users' display characteristics, and it is always necessary to use relative positioning techniques for all visible objects.

The `action()` method returns `true` to indicate that it has handled the event. It returns `false` to indicate that its parent object, or its native-system peer class, should handle the event. If your `action()` method does not handle an event, it is appropriate to return the value of its super class method using the following statement:

```
return super.action(evt, what);
```

We'll see examples of this type of response in other examples in this chapter. In DynaButton, `action()` simply returns `true`, because it effectively handles all events we care about.

DynaButton also demonstrates another way to respond to events by overriding one of several methods provided by the `Component` class. (You can generate shells for mouse-event methods using the Applet Wizard.) In this case, the program uses a `mouseDown()` event to display a message when you click outside of the button. The method is declared as

```
public boolean mouseDown(Event evt, int x, int y) {...
```

The `Event` object represents the event; the coordinate values locate the mouse pointer. In this program, I used the event to initialize the message string and call `repaint()` to display it using the `paint()` method already described. Overriding a `Component`-class mouse method this way is usually the best technique for responding to mouse events.

> **TIP**
>
> You cannot use an `action()` method to respond to mouse events because these are normally handled in a method called `handleEvent()`, which calls `action()`. Other sample applets in this chapter demonstrate how to override `handleEvent()`.

The `Toolkit` Class

In the course of discussing events and event handlers, you'll often come across the terms "peer" and "peer class." These are references to the `java.awt.peer` package, which provides classes that link system-independent components to their native counterparts. For example, an object of the `Button` class is linked to the native button element in the operating system so that users see the button shape familiar to them.

To perform this linkage, Java provides the abstract `Toolkit` class shown in Listing 15.3. `Toolkit` is subclassed (extended) in the browser to link your program to the operating system—an activity that is of no concern to application developers. There are several methods, however, in the `Toolkit` class that you'll find useful. Although all of these are abstract, you may call them to interrogate the system's subclass object, the exact type of which depends on the operating system that is running your code.

Listing 15.3. The `Toolkit` class.

```
public abstract class Toolkit {
 public abstract Dimension getScreenSize();
 public abstract int getScreenResolution();
 public abstract ColorModel getColorModel();
 public abstract String[] getFontList();
 public abstract FontMetrics getFontMetrics(Font font);
 public abstract void sync();
 public static synchronized Toolkit getDefaultToolkit();
 public abstract Image getImage(String filename);
 public abstract Image getImage(URL url);
 public abstract boolean prepareImage(Image image,
  int width, int height, ImageObserver observer);
 public abstract int checkImage(Image image,
  int width, int height, ImageObserver observer);
 public abstract Image createImage(ImageProducer producer);
}
```

Call the `Toolkit` class's `getScreenSize()` and `getScreenResolution()` methods to find out these characteristics of the user's display. The `getColorModel()` method returns a `ColorModel` class object, which you can look up online. It provides low-level information about how a specific system translates red, green, and blue color values, plus the size of pixels—information that is obviously useful only for critical graphical applications. Other methods such as `getImage()` work with bitmapped images, a subject to which I return in Chapter 17, "Graphics, Animation, and Multimedia."

A very useful `Toolkit` method is `getFontList()`, which you can call to prepare a list of available font names. Listing 15.4, `FontList.java`, demonstrates how to prepare this list. Figure 15.2 shows the program's display.

Figure 15.2.
Use `FontList` to list
available fonts.

Listing 15.4. `FontList.java` (Lists available fonts).

```
import java.applet.*;
import java.awt.*;
```

```
public class FontList extends Applet
{

 List fonts;

 public void init()
 {
  try {
   fonts = new List();
   Toolkit tools = Toolkit.getDefaultToolkit();
   String[] fontNames = tools.getFontList();
   for (int i = 0; i < fontNames.length; i++)
    fonts.addItem(fontNames[i]);
  } catch (AWTError e) {
   throw e;
  }
  resize(320, 240);
  add(fonts);
 }
}
```

This short program simply uses an init() method to create a List object named fonts. A Toolkit object is obtained by using the following statement:

```
Toolkit tools = Toolkit.getDefaultToolkit();
```

You must call getDefaultToolkit() this way to obtain an object of the *subclass* that the system creates to implement the abstract Toolkit methods. You never can be certain exactly what class this is, but it's okay to define it using Toolkit as shown here for the purpose of calling getFontList(). The method returns an array of String objects that you can reference with a variable using the following statement:

```
String[] fontNames = tools.getFontList();
```

It's up to you to use this information. Here, I transfer the strings to the fonts List control using the for loop:

```
for (int i = 0; i < fontNames.length; i++)
 fonts.addItem(fontNames[i]);
```

The program also shows how to call methods such as getFontList() that might throw an exception. This is good programming, but in this short example, any exceptions are merely rethrown to halt the applet if an error occurs.

Programming Events

To demonstrate several different types of event-handling problems—representing those you are likely to encounter in your own applets—I developed several sample programs described in this section. Use this information and sample code to explore more about event handling techniques, and also as guides for programming specific event handlers for keypresses, mouse actions, button, scrollbar, list, and choice controls.

Event Handlers

So far, I've shown two ways to respond to events: override the `action()` method, or use an event-specific method such as `mouseDown()`, inherited from the `Component` class. A third technique overrides an event called `handleEvent()`. It's important to program `handleEvent()` correctly or you might find your applets fail to respond to critical events. For example, `handleEvent()` calls `action()`, and you must not interfere with this linkage.

Listing 15.5, `MouseXY.java`, demonstrates the full range of event-specific mouse methods inherited from `Component`, and shows how to program a `handleEvent()` method as an alternative technique for responding to mouse activities. The program also demonstrates how to paint an applet's window in a color, which I did in this case to make its boundaries visible. Figure 15.3 shows the program's display. Notice that in this example the applet window is a different color from the browser's background.

Figure 15.3.

The MouseXY program display showing the applet window in a different color from the browser background.

Listing 15.5. `MouseXY.java` (Demonstrates mouse and `handleEvent()` methods).

```java
import java.applet.*;
import java.awt.*;

public class MouseXY extends Applet {
 String location;  // String for X=0 Y=0 display

 // Initialize applet variables and window
 public void init() {
  setBackground(Color.yellow);
  resize(200, 200);
  location = new String("Move mouse inside window");
 }

 // Paint the location string inside window
 public void paint(Graphics g) {
  g.drawString(location, 10, 10);
 }

 // Create the location string from x and y
 public void makeString(int x, int y) {
  location = new String(
   " X=" + String.valueOf(x) +
   " Y=" + String.valueOf(y) );
 }
```

```
// Respond to mouse-drag event
public boolean mouseDrag(Event evt, int x, int y) {
 makeString(x, y);
 repaint();
 return true;
}

// Respond to mouse-move event
public boolean mouseMove(Event evt, int x, int y) {
 makeString(x, y);
 repaint();
 return true;
}

// Respond to mouse-enter (applet window) event
public boolean mouseEnter(Event evt, int x, int y) {
 makeString(x, y);
 repaint();
 return true;
}

// Respond to mouse-exit (applet window) event
public boolean mouseExit(Event evt, int x, int y) {
 location = new String("Move mouse inside window");
 repaint();
 return true;
}

/* Alternate technique. To use:
 * 1) enable this method
 * 2) delete the preceding mouse...() methods.
public boolean handleEvent(Event  evt) {
 boolean eventHandled = false;
 switch (evt.id) {
  case Event.MOUSE_DOWN:
  case Event.MOUSE_UP:
  case Event.MOUSE_DRAG:
  case Event.MOUSE_ENTER:
  case Event.MOUSE_MOVE: {
   makeString(evt.x, evt.y);
   repaint();
   eventHandled = true;
   break;
  }
  case Event.MOUSE_EXIT: {
   location = new String("Move mouse inside window");
   repaint();
   eventHandled = true;
  }
 }
 if (eventHandled)
  return true;
 else
  return super.handleEvent(evt);
}
*/
}
```

To paint the applet background, call the `setBackground()` method inherited by your applet class. You can pass a `Color` class value such as `yellow`, as in the following sample listing statement:

```
setBackground(Color.yellow);
```

You can use a similar technique to color a component. For example, to paint a `Button` object, call `setBackground()` in reference to that object:

```
dangerButton.setBackground(Color.red);
```

Run the MouseXY program now and move the mouse pointer inside the applet's yellow window. As you can see, this displays the mouse pointer's location. To do this, the program overrides several mouse event methods such as `mouseDrag()`, which executes the following code:

```
makeString(x, y);
repaint();
return true;
```

Local method `makeString()` creates a string out of the mouse pointer's coordinate values. Calling `repaint()` causes the program's `paint()` method to update this string on screen. The mouse method returns `true` to indicate that it has handled the event.

Except for `mouseExit()`, which resets the string that tells you to move the mouse inside the window, the other mouse-event methods in the sample program perform these exact same steps, which is obviously wasteful programming. Because of the similarity of responses to all mouse activity, it is more efficient in this case to handle the events in one method. To do this, delete or comment-out the four mouse-event methods, and then enable the `handleEvent()` method listed as a comment. Compile and run the modified program, and you'll see it operates as before—but this time, one method instead of four handle the mouse events. This method is declared as

```
public boolean handleEvent(Event  evt):
```

A single `Event` parameter describes the event. It's important to program `handleEvent()` correctly so as not to interfere with events that your code doesn't handle. A good first step is to define a flag that indicates if the overridden method has handled an event:

```
boolean eventHandled = false;
```

You can then inspect variables and fields in the `Event` parameter passed to the method. In this case, I use a `switch` statement to compare the `evt.id` variable with `MOUSE` values defined in the `Event` class. Each `case` in this statement is run together so that the same code executes for all mouse events. However, I programmed `MOUSE_EXIT` differently to display the message `Move mouse inside window` when the mouse pointer leaves the applet's window.

The sample program ends `handleEvent()` by inspecting the `boolean` flag and returning a value using the following code:

```
if (eventHandled)
 return true;
else
 return super.handleEvent(evt);
```

If the event was handled, `handleEvent()` returns true. Otherwise, it returns the value of the ancestor method, using the expression `super.handleEvent(evt)`. It is important to call the ancestor method this way for all events your code does not handle. However, even if your method handles an event, you may call the ancestor method. You might do this, for example, to add new behavior to a certain event rather than reprogram it entirely.

Button Events

You've already seen several examples of `Button` events, but in all of those cases, the actions were not necessarily representative of what applets normally do. Usually, for example, you'll want to perform an activity such as obtaining the values of other components when the user clicks a button, perhaps labeled *OK*. Listing 15.6, `EditText.java`, demonstrates how to write this type of event handler for a `Button` object. The program also illustrates the important concept of *focus*, which directs keyboard events to a particular component. Figure 15.4 shows the program's display after I entered some text into the edit field and clicked the *OK* button.

Figure 15.4.
The EditText applet display.

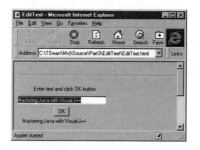

Listing 15.6. `EditText.java` (Demonstrates `Button` events and keyboard focus).

```java
import java.applet.*;
import java.awt.*;

public class EditText extends Applet {
 // Components and variables
 Button okButton;
 TextField entryField;
 String entryString;
 Label label;

 // Initialize components and applet window
 public void init()  {
  okButton = new Button(" OK ");
  entryField = new TextField(" ", 32);
  label = new Label("Enter text and click OK button");
  entryString = new String();
  resize(200, 200);
  add(label);
```

continues

Listing 15.6. continued

```
   add(entryField);
   add(okButton);
 }

 // Give TextField control the focus
 // when the applet starts or restarts
 public void start() {
  entryField.selectAll();
  entryField.requestFocus();
 }

 // Display the current entry string
 public void paint(Graphics g)  {
  Point p = okButton.location();
  Dimension d = okButton.size();
  g.drawString(entryString, 10, p.y + d.height + 15);
 }

 // Extract the entry string from the TextField control
 public boolean action(Event evt, Object what) {
  if (" OK ".equals(what)) {
   entryString = entryField.getText();
   repaint();
   entryField.selectAll();
   entryField.requestFocus();
  } else {
   return super.action(evt, what);
  }
  return true;
 }
}
```

The program's class declares three component controls of the Button, TextField, and Label classes. These variables are initialized in the usual way in the init() method, and added to the applet window. In addition, a String object is initialized. During the program, this string holds a copy of the text from the TextField control when you click the program's button.

These actions demonstrate typical responses to button events, but more importantly, they also show how to shift the keyboard focus to a particular control. When you click the *OK* button, for example, you'll notice that the text in the TextField control is highlighted, and you can again type another entry. This does not happen automatically. Normally, clicking a button would transfer the focus to that control, and if no further action were taken, the user would have to click inside the edit window before typing another entry. Having the button shift the focus *back* to the edit control simplifies the user interface.

Most of the significant programming in this example takes place in the action() method. First, the program determines that the *OK* button has been clicked, using the following statement:

```
if (" OK ".equals(what)) {...
```

If this succeeds, the code picks up the current entry from the `TextField` control and directs the program to update the display with these two statements:

```
entryString = entryField.getText();
repaint();
```

This displays the entered string below the button (see method `paint()` for details). At this point, the button has the keyboard focus. To direct the focus back to the edit control, and to select all text in that window, the program executes two statements:

```
entryField.selectAll();
entryField.requestFocus();
```

The `selectAll()` method is inherited by `TextField` and `TextArea` components from `TextComponent`. The `requestFocus()` method is inherited from the `Component` class, and may be called for any component. The applet itself may also call `requestFocus()` to direct keyboard events to the applet window.

As all `action()` methods should, the applet's `action()` method returns `true` if it handled an event; otherwise, it returns the value of its ancestor class using the following statement:

```
return super.action(evt, what);
```

> **NOTE**
>
> I'm not sure whether this is a Visual J++ bug or a general problem with Java, but I needed to add extra programming to the `EditText.java` applet to cause the edit field to have a blinking cursor when the program begins. First, I called `selectAll()` and `requestFocus()` in the `start()` method to give the field the keyboard focus when the applet becomes active. However, in order to make the flashing text cursor visible, I also had to initialize the `TextField` control with a single space; otherwise, the cursor was there (I could type into the field), but wasn't to be seen. To check whether you have the same trouble, initialize the `TextField` control in `init()` using the following statement:
>
> ```
> entryField = new TextField(32);
> ```

Keyboard Events

Java greatly simplifies programming responses to keypresses by providing standard function keys in the `Event` class. Finally, there's a reliable method to intercept function keypresses in a system-independent manner that actually works.

A useful utility program displays the values of keys as you press them. You can use the program to investigate key values, and as the next applet illustrates, to inspect other aspects of the user's system. Listing 15.7, `KeyEvent.java`, displays a lengthy string that describes various keys. Run the program and press any key to see its values. Figure 15.5 shows my display after I pressed my laptop's PgUp key.

339

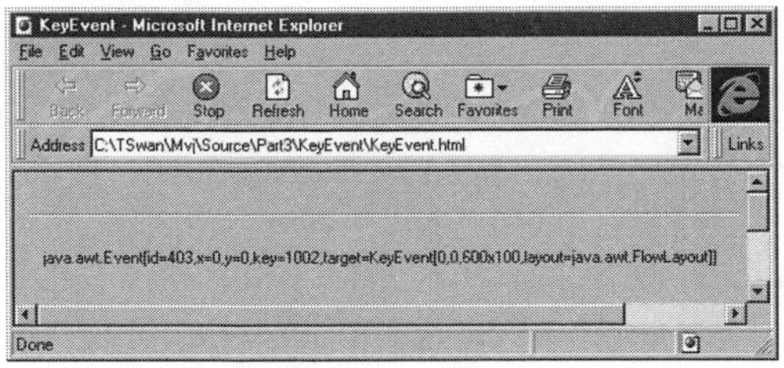

Figure 15.5.

The KeyEvent applet makes a useful utility for investigating key event values.

Listing 15.7. KeyEvent.java (Demonstrates keyboard focus and events).

```java
import java.applet.*;
import java.awt.*;

public class KeyEvent extends Applet {
 String keyString;  // String displayed in applet

 // Initialize the applet
 public void init() {
  resize(600, 100);
  keyString = new String("Press various keys");
 }

 // Give applet the keyboard focus so pressing
 // a key calls the applet's keyDown() method.
 public void start() {
  requestFocus();  // Gives applet the focus!
 }

 // Draw string inside applet window
 public void paint(Graphics g) {
  g.drawString(keyString, 10, 20);
 }

 // Respond to applet keypress events
 public boolean keyDown(Event evt, int key) {
  keyString = evt.toString();  // Get description
  repaint();  // Force repainting of window
  return true;
 }
}
```

So that the applet window receives the keyboard focus, the program's start() method calls the inherited requestFocus() method. This puzzled me at first, but apparently, no control has the focus until one requests it, including the applet container itself.

To display its debugging string, the applet class's keyDown() method executes these statements:

```java
keyString = evt.toString();
repaint();
```

The first line obtains a string representation of the event courtesy of the Event class's toString() method. This is a highly useful method to use for debugging not only keyboard events, but all types of Event objects. To update the display, the program calls repaint() as you have seen in numerous other samples.

In addition to the keyDown() method demonstrated here, your applet class also inherits method keyUp() from Component. You can override this method to respond to the release of a key, which might be useful in special circumstances. It is declared the same as keyDown(). In fact, you can replace keyDown() with keyUp() in the sample program to investigate keyboard release events.

Mouse and Keyboard Modifiers

Samples in this and the preceding chapter demonstrate how to program mouse and keyboard event handlers. In this code, you might often need to check whether the user has also held down the Shift or Ctrl keys, or both keys, while pressing another key or moving the mouse. For example, you might want to perform a different action when users Shift-click a button than when they simply click it. To do this, you need to inspect the bit settings in the Event class's modifiers variable.

You can experiment and debug this value by converting it to a string. For instance, a statement such as

```
String message = Integer.toString(evt.modifiers);
```

creates a string equal to the modifiers integer value. You can then display this string. The modifiers variable is the logical OR combination of four masks declared in the Event class: ALT_MASK, CTRL_MASK, META_MASK, and SHIFT_MASK. These masks also indicate whether the user has clicked the left, middle, or right mouse buttons. If the META_MASK bit is set, the user clicked the right button. If the ALT_MASK bit is set, the user clicked the middle button (my mouse doesn't have one, so I couldn't test this). If neither mask bit is set, the user clicked the left button.

> **TIP**
>
> I recommend not programming critical tasks for middle mouse buttons. Three blind mice might be common, but three button ones aren't.

You can use Boolean-logic expressions to detect whether specific mask values are contained in the modifiers field (see Part II if you need help with this), but rather than program this contortionist code, it's easier to prepare a simple table of values for each possible combination. For example, Table 15.1 shows all values for the modifiers variable for left and right mouse button clicks in combination with the Shift, Ctrl, and Ctrl+Shift keys. You can use the values in this table compared with the Event object's modifiers variable passed to an event handler method such as mouseDown() to determine which combination of keys where held down during the mouse event.

Table 15.1. Modifier values for mouse click events.

	Left button	Right button
No key	0	4
Shift	1	5
Ctrl	2	6
Ctrl+Shift	3	7

Scrollbar Events

One of the most versatile components in the AWT package is the `Scrollbar` class. Scrollbars appear like magic in controls such as `Lists` and `TextAreas`, but you can also use scrollbars to give users a graphical, interactive way to select values within a range. Listing 15.8, `ColorScroll.java`, demonstrates this technique. The program also demonstrates the critical technique of extending an existing component class to add new code and data, and thus, re-program the control's actions. The color resulting from manipulating the program's controls is shown in the box at left, as illustrated in Figure 15.6.

Figure 15.6.

ColorScroll demonstrates how to program scrollbar event handlers.

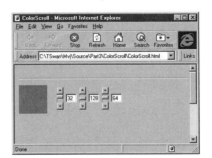

Listing 15.8. `ColorScroll.java` (Demonstrates `Scrollbar` event handling).

```java
import java.applet.*;
import java.awt.*;

// Extended TextField class
class ColorTextField extends TextField {
 // Scrollbar associated with this text field
 private Scrollbar colorScroller;

 // Constructor
 ColorTextField(Scrollbar colorScroller) {
  super("0");  // Call ancestor constructor
  this.colorScroller = colorScroller;  // Save Scrollbar
 }

 // Update scroller in response to key presses
 public boolean keyUp(Event evt, int key) {
```

```
  int value;
  try {
   value = Integer.parseInt(getText());
  } catch (NumberFormatException e) {
   value = 0;
  }
  value = Math.abs(value);
  if (value > 255)
   value = 255;
  colorScroller.setValue(value);
  colorScroller.invalidate();
  getParent().repaint();
  return super.keyUp(evt, key);
 }
}

// Extended Scrollbar class
class ColorScrollbar extends Scrollbar {
 // TextField associated with Scrollbar
 private ColorTextField colorText;

 // Constructor
 ColorScrollbar(Applet theApplet) {
  super(Scrollbar.VERTICAL, 0, 10, 0, 255);
  colorText = new ColorTextField(this);
  theApplet.add(this);
  theApplet.add(colorText);
 }

 // Update text field with scrollbar value
 public void updateText() {
  colorText.setText(String.valueOf(getValue()));
 }
}

// The Applet class
public class ColorScroll extends Applet {
 // Components
 ColorScrollbar redScroll, grnScroll, bluScroll;

 // Initialize components and applet window
 public void init() {
  // Size the applet window
  resize(320, 240);
  // Construct the Scrollbar controls
  redScroll = new ColorScrollbar(this);
  grnScroll = new ColorScrollbar(this);
  bluScroll = new ColorScrollbar(this);
 }

 // Paint a rectangle using the color values
 public void paint(Graphics g) {
  g.setColor(new Color(
   redScroll.getValue(),
   grnScroll.getValue(),
   bluScroll.getValue()));
  g.fillRect(0, 0, 64, 64);
```

continues

Listing 15.8. continued

```
}

// Respond to Scrollbar control events
public boolean handleEvent(Event evt) {
 switch (evt.id) {
  case Event.SCROLL_ABSOLUTE:
  case Event.SCROLL_LINE_DOWN:
  case Event.SCROLL_LINE_UP:
  case Event.SCROLL_PAGE_DOWN:
  case Event.SCROLL_PAGE_UP:
   ((ColorScrollbar)evt.target).updateText();
   repaint();
   return true;
  default:
   return super.handleEvent(evt);
  }
 }
}
```

Run the program and click the buttons on the three scrollbars, or click and drag their sliders, to adjust the red, green, and blue color values shown to the right of each control. You can also enter color values in the edit controls, which automatically update the associated Scrollbars and the color display box. This illustrates how, by extending Component classes, a control can be made to perform new operations, and is also a good example of solid object-oriented programming.

The main problem to solve in the ColorScroll applet is to program bidirectionally interactive controls. That is to say, altering a Scrollbar component must update the numeric value in the associated TextField control, and changing the text control must likewise update the associated scrollbar. At the same time, any such changes need to be reflected in the sample color box. Such interactions are common in graphical user interfaces.

To state the problem in an object-oriented manner, we need a TextField control that keeps track of its associated Scrollbar object. That Scrollbar object must in turn keep track of its associated TextField. The natural, object-oriented solution is to extend both classes as shown in the listing. The first new class, ColorTextField, along with its instance variables, is declared as

```
class ColorTextField extends TextField {
 private Scrollbar colorScroller;
...
}
```

The private variable is this TextField's associated Scrollbar control. The other class is declared similarly:

```
class ColorScrollbar extends Scrollbar {
 private ColorTextField colorText;
...
}
```

The colorText variable is this Scrollbar's associated ColorTextField component. To initialize the ColorTextField object, its constructor executes the following two statements:

```
super("0");
this.colorScroller = colorScroller;
```

The first statement calls the ancestor class constructor, passing the initial text to show in the edit window. After this, the program saves a reference to the associated ColorScrollbar object in the ColorTextField's private instance variable.

The extended TextField class also overrides method keyUp() inherited from TextComponent. This is done so that, when you press and release a key, the component itself can update its associated scrollbar. Try this: Run the program and type into any text field. As you type, you'll see the associated scrollbar move to the appropriate position. To make this happen, keyUp() sets an integer value to the text control's current value, allowing for errors and exceptions. After getting this value, three statements update the associated Scrollbar object:

```
colorScroller.setValue(value);
colorScroller.invalidate();
getParent().repaint();
```

Memorize this sequence—you'll find it invaluable in countless programs. The statements first pass the newly obtained value to the ColorScrollbar control, but this isn't enough to update the visual component. To do that, you must also tell the object that it has changed (you might think it would know this, but it doesn't). Calling invalidate() tells the control that it needs to update its visual display, which is completed in the usual way by calling repaint(). However—and this is important—calling repaint() directly would call that method *for the TextField object*. Thus, to update the entire display—and therefore repaint the sample color box as well as updating the changed scrollbar—we need to call the repaint() method in the Container object that owns this TextField control. This is done by calling getParent(), and then calling repaint() for the resulting object. You can use getParent() this way for any component to find the Applet container that owns a control.

The final step in the overridden keyUp() method is to call the ancestor subroutine so that keypresses work as they normally do. This is done by executing the following statement:

```
return super.keyUp(evt, key);
```

If you wanted to completely override keyUp(), you could simply return true. However, I merely wanted to add new programming to this method—not to interfere with existing behavior—and in this case, returning the value of the ancestor method is the proper way to end the extended subroutine.

> **NOTE**
>
> I probably could have overridden keyDown() in the sample program, but I used keyUp() just to be different. Either method would probably work equally well in this case.

The extended ScrollBar class is a little simpler, because it needs only to construct the object and update the text field. The resulting ColorScrollbar class constructor executes these statements:

```
super(Scrollbar.VERTICAL, 0, 10, 0, 255);
colorText = new ColorTextField(this);
theApplet.add(this);
theApplet.add(colorText);
```

This fragment demonstrates several interesting techniques. First, the ancestor constructor is called to construct the actual Scrollbar control, using the arguments shown here (and discussed in the preceding chapter). Next, the associated ColorTextField object is constructed. Passing this as the argument gives the ColorTextField control a reference to this ColorScrollbar object. The final two statements add the scrollbar and text field components to the applet window. The variable theApplet is passed to the ColorTextField constructor.

In addition to its constructor, the ColorTextField class provides a method, updateText(), which executes the following single statement:

```
colorText.setText(String.valueOf(getValue()));
```

This may seem a bit confusing, but take it one piece at a time and it will soon be clear. The statement obtains the current scrollbar value by calling getValue(). This is passed to the String class valueOf() method to convert the value to a string. Finally, this string is passed to the associated ColorTextField's setText() method. In this way, a simple call to updateText() sets the text field window equal to the numeric value of its associated scrollbar. Change the scrollbar, and the edit window automatically reflects the current setting.

Having written the two extended classes, it is a simple matter to use them to create the sample program. The applet class declares three variables, one for each scrollbar:

```
ColorScrollbar redScroll, grnScroll, bluScroll;
```

It's not necessary to declare the text fields because these are created and referenced in the ColorScrollbar objects. The scrollbar objects are constructed in method init() with the following statements:

```
redScroll = new ColorScrollbar(this);
grnScroll = new ColorScrollbar(this);
bluScroll = new ColorScrollbar(this);
```

Passing this to the constructor provides the reference to the applet class, which ColorScrollbar needs in order to add the scrollbar and text field objects to the applet's window.

The program paints the sample color window by executing two simple statements in method paint():

```
g.setColor(new Color(
 redScroll.getValue(),
 grnScroll.getValue(),
 bluScroll.getValue()));
g.fillRect(0, 0, 64, 64);
```

The first statement (on four lines) creates a Color class object using the red, green, and blue values of the three ColorScrollbar components. The second statement calls the Graphics class method fillRect() to paint a rectangle filled with the color passed to Graphics.setColor().

The final task in the sample program is to respond to scrollbar events. This is done in the overridden method handleEvent(). All five possible scrollbar events are intercepted to update the associated text field, and to repaint the display. These actions are performed with just two statements:

```
((ColorScrollbar)evt.target).updateText();
repaint();
```

The evt.target field represents the scrollbar object associated with the event. The type-cast expression (ColorScrollbar) is necessary so that we can call the extended class's updateText() method, which as I explained, sets the associated text field to the value of the scrollbar. As usual, calling repaint() forces a call to paint() to update the sample color box.

> **NOTE**
>
> The preceding discussion of the ColorScroll applet is a bit longer than most in this book. However, the program demonstrates several important object-oriented techniques that you will find invaluable in Java applications, and you might want to reread this section until you thoroughly understand how the code works. Remember that when searching for a solution to a tricky problem, you might find an easy answer by extending an existing class and adding new data and code. It's amazing how many programmers forget this ground rule of object-oriented programming. When stuck, *think objects*.

List and Choice Events

Finally in this half of the chapter is a demonstration of the two list-classes, List and Choice. As you may recall from the preceding chapter, a List object displays a window of selections, with scrollbars automatically added if the list is longer than can be comfortably shown. A Choice object displays a single line window with a button that, when clicked, drops down a menu of selections. The two controls are similar in operation, but are programmed differently as the next example shows. Listing 15.9, ListSelect.java, uses both controls to display a list of color strings. Selecting any string from either control alters the sample color box and also adjusts the corresponding control's setting. Figure 15.7 shows the program's display.

Figure 15.7.
The ListSelect applet's display.

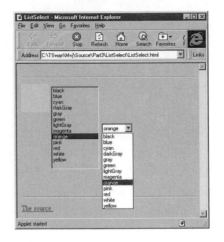

Listing 15.9. `ListSelect.java` (Demonstrates `List` and `Choice` events).

```java
import java.applet.*;
import java.awt.*;

public class ListSelect extends Applet {
 // Components and variables
 List colorList;
 Choice colorChoice;
 Color selectedColor;
 String[] colorStrings = {
   "black", "blue", "cyan", "darkGray", "gray",
   "green", "lightGray", "magenta", "orange",
   "pink", "red", "white", "yellow"};

 // Initialize components and applet window
 public void init() {
  // Create list of color strings
  colorList = new List(colorStrings.length, false);
  colorChoice = new Choice();
  for (int i = 0; i < colorStrings.length; i++) {
   colorList.addItem(colorStrings[i]);
   colorChoice.addItem(colorStrings[i]);
  }
  // Size the applet window
  resize(320, 240);
  // Add list and choice controls to applet
  add(colorList);
  add(colorChoice);
  // Preselect first item and set focus
  // to the control so user can press keys
  // to select colors.
  colorList.select(0);
  colorList.requestFocus();
 }

 // Draw a filled rectangle using current color
 public void paint(Graphics g) {
  g.setColor(selectedColor);
```

```
     g.fillRect(0, 0, 64, 64);
   }

   // Return a Color object from string parameter
   public Color getColor(String s) {
     if ("black".equals(s))
       return Color.black;
     else if ("blue".equals(s))
       return Color.blue;
     else if ("cyan".equals(s))
       return Color.cyan;
     else if ("darkGray".equals(s))
       return Color.darkGray;
     else if ("gray".equals(s))
       return Color.gray;
     else if ("green".equals(s))
       return Color.green;
     else if ("lightGray".equals(s))
       return Color.lightGray;
     else if ("magenta".equals(s))
       return Color.magenta;
     else if ("orange".equals(s))
       return Color.orange;
     else if ("pink".equals(s))
       return Color.pink;
     else if ("red".equals(s))
       return Color.red;
     else if ("white".equals(s))
       return Color.white;
     else if ("yellow".equals(s))
       return Color.yellow;
     else
       return Color.black;  // Default
   }

   // Handle list-selection event
   public boolean handleEvent(Event evt) {
    if (evt.id == Event.LIST_SELECT) {
     String s = colorList.getSelectedItem();
     selectedColor = getColor(s);
     colorChoice.select(s);
     repaint();
     return true;  // Event handled
    }
    return super.handleEvent(evt);  // Other events
   }

   // Handle choice-selection event
   public boolean action(Event evt, Object what) {
    if (evt.target.equals(colorChoice)) {
     selectedColor = getColor((String)what);
     colorList.select(((Choice)evt.target).getSelectedIndex());
     repaint();
     return true;  // Event handled
    }
    return super.action(evt, what);  // Other events
   }
}
```

The sample program's applet class declares several variables using these statements:

```
List colorList;
Choice colorChoice;
Color selectedColor;
String[] colorStrings = {
 "black", "blue", "cyan", "darkGray", "gray",
 "green", "lightGray", "magenta", "orange",
 "pink", "red", "white", "yellow"};
```

In addition to `List`, `Choice`, and `Color` objects, the program defines and initializes an array of strings equal to the color selections to be shown in each control. Creating a string array like this isn't strictly necessary, but it is easier in this case because both controls will be set to the same list. You might not need to do this, but using a string array has other advantages. For example, method `init()` constructs the `List` and `Choice` controls, and then initializes their selections with the `for` statement:

```
for (int i = 0; i < colorStrings.length; i++) {
 colorList.addItem(colorStrings[i]);
 colorChoice.addItem(colorStrings[i]);
}
```

After adding the two initialized controls to the applet window, `init()` ends with two key statements:

```
colorList.select(0);
colorList.requestFocus();
```

The first statement selects the first entry in the `List` control. The second gives the control the keyboard focus. With this bit of code, users can press the arrow keys to select items from the list as soon as the applet starts. It's often best to give *some* control the focus this way, so that users don't have to select a component with the mouse.

Method `paint()` simply updates the sample color using the value of the applet class's `Color` object:

```
g.setColor(selectedColor);
g.fillRect(0, 0, 64, 64);
```

To update `selectedColor`, the applet class implements a method, `getColor()`, which receives a string argument from a `List` or `Choice` control's selection. (I could have used an associative array or other data structure to simplify this method, but I was pressed for time so I used a long `if-then-else` construction, which is less than ideal.)

Two event handlers demonstrate how to respond to `List` and `Choice` selections. Method `handleEvent()` is called with `evt.id` equal to `Event.LIST_SELECT` when users select an item from a `List`. The program intercepts this event and executes the following statements:

```
String s = colorList.getSelectedItem();
selectedColor = getColor(s);
colorChoice.select(s);
repaint();
```

First, the List object's getSelectedItem() method is called for the string value of the selection. This value is passed to our getColor() method to convert it into a Color object, and is also passed to the Choice control's select() method to update that control. This way, the List and Choice components are kept in synch. Calling repaint() updates the sample color box using the current value of selectedColor.

The second event handler, action(), responds to selections in a Choice control. If the control is identified by comparing it to evt.target, the program executes the following statements:

```
selectedColor = getColor((String)what);
colorList.select(((Choice)evt.target).getSelectedIndex());
repaint();
```

First, our getColor() method is called to convert the string selection, passed in parameter what, to a Color object. In addition, the List control's select() method is called to update the list to the Choice component's selection. This keeps the two controls in synch when you select an item using the Choice's pull-down menu. Finally, calling repaint() causes paint() to update the sample color box using the current value of selectedColor.

Layouts

Foremost in the goals of writing Java software is the challenge of creating system-independent applications. Most important in this venture is the need to avoid placing interface components at specific coordinates. This important concern in all graphical user interfaces becomes even more critical with Java. There's just no telling what type of system an applet's users will have.

Java's solution to creating system independent interfaces is the use of layout objects. One of these creatures is simply attached to the interface container—the applet, for example—and it takes care of organizing controls according to one of several ingenious schemes. This section explores Java's layout classes, and shows how to use them to arrange components in ways that are guaranteed to be equivalent, if not exactly the same, regardless of the target operating system.

> **NOTE**
>
> One advantage of using layout classes that I've not seen mentioned elsewhere is the lack of need for visual component construction software. Layout classes simplify the design of dialog boxes and windows so much that there is little to be gained by using a component editor that lets you drag controls around. It's far easier, as I'll show in this section, to design interfaces directly in the program's source code.

Introducing Layouts

All layout classes implement the `LayoutManager` interface class shown in Listing 15.10. It's useful to know that this class forms the basis of layout objects, but you probably won't call its methods. You might, however, call `preferredLayoutSize()` and `minimumLayoutSize()` to obtain the dimensions of a proposed layout scheme. See the preceding chapter for more information about `Dimension` objects returned by these functions.

Listing 15.10. The `LayoutManager` interface class.

```
public interface LayoutManager {
 void addLayoutComponent(String name, Component comp);
 void removeLayoutComponent(Component comp);
 Dimension preferredLayoutSize(Container parent);
 Dimension minimumLayoutSize(Container parent);
 void layoutContainer(Container parent);
}
```

To use a layout class such as `FlowLayout`, which implements the `LayoutManager` interface, call `Container.setLayout()`. The method is declared as

```
public void setLayout(LayoutManager mgr);
```

Because the method's lone parameter is an object of the `LayoutManager` interface class, you may pass any object of a class extended from the interface. For example, to specify a `FlowLayout` object for an applet's window, the applet class's `init()` method can call `setLayout()` like this:

```
setLayout(new FlowLayout());
```

It's usually not necessary to keep a reference to the layout object—you can simply construct it using `new` as shown here and pass the resulting object directly to `setLayout()`. Often, you'll also pass an argument to the layout class constructor, as in the statement

```
setLayout(new FlowLayout(FlowLayout.CENTER));
```

which selects an optional arrangement provided by a constant in the `FlowLayout` class.

After specifying a layout object, subsequent controls added to the container by the `add()` method are laid out according to the layout's strategy. The visual effect, as you will see in the next several sections, depends on the class you elect to use.

> **TIP**
>
> The `Applet` class supposedly uses `BorderLayout` as its default layout object, but at least one source implies that this might not be rigidly the case in all Java implementations. For that reason, just to be on the safe side, all commercial quality applets should specify an explicit layout object using the techniques introduced here.

The `FlowLayout` Class

The `FlowLayout` class lays out components from left to right, in rows starting from top to bottom. This is a good strategy to use in cases where you don't care too much about component arrangements, but you want to ensure a reasonably good looking result.

Listing 15.11 shows the `FlowLayout` class declaration. In this and other layout class listings in this chapter, the important elements are any constants and variables and the constructors. You probably won't call layout methods, but I list them here for reference purposes.

Listing 15.11. The `FlowLayout` class.

```
public class FlowLayout implements LayoutManager {
// Fields:
 public static final int LEFT;
 public static final int CENTER;
 public static final int RIGHT;
// Constructors:
 public FlowLayout();
 public FlowLayout(int align);
 public FlowLayout(int align, int hgap, int vgap);
// Public methods:
 public void addLayoutComponent(String name, Component comp);
 public void removeLayoutComponent(Component comp);
 public Dimension preferredLayoutSize(Container target);
 public Dimension minimumLayoutSize(Container target);
 public void layoutContainer(Container target);
 public String toString();
}
```

There are three ways to construct a `FlowLayout` object. You can call its default constructor, or more likely, you can pass one of the three constants—`LEFT`, `CENTER`, and `RIGHT`—as an argument. For example, the statement

```
setLayout(new FlowLayout(FlowLayout.CENTER));
```

specifies that components are to be centered within their respective cells, using a scheme that lays them out from left to right and top to bottom. You may optionally specify the amount of space in pixels to reserve between component cells. The statement

```
setLayout(new FlowLayout(FlowLayout.RIGHT, 5, 10));
```

aligns components from left to right, flush with the right border, and also reserves five pixels horizontally and 10 vertically between each cell.

The next program shows examples of each `FlowLayout` strategy using five button components. The buttons don't perform any actions; they simply represent the positions of controls, which can be any extended from the `Component` class. Figure 15.8 illustrates `LEFT` alignment. Figure 15.9 shows the same program using `CENTER` alignment. Figure 15.10 shows `RIGHT` alignment. The number of objects per row depends on the size of the window relative to the sizes of each component. Listing 15.12, `FlowDemo.java`, shows the sample program's source code.

Figure 15.8.
FlowLayout using LEFT alignment.

Figure 15.9.
FlowLayout using CENTER alignment.

Figure 15.10.
FlowLayout using RIGHT alignment.

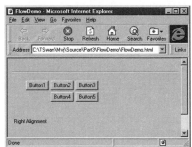

Listing 15.12. FlowDemo.java (Demonstrates FlowLayout class).

```
import java.applet.*;
import java.awt.*;

public class FlowDemo extends Applet
{
 int alignment;  // Current FlowLayout alignment

 // Initialize applet and add some dummy controls
 public void init() {
  resize(200, 120);
  alignment = FlowLayout.LEFT;
//  alignment = FlowLayout.CENTER;
//  alignment = FlowLayout.RIGHT;
  setLayout(new FlowLayout(alignment));
  add(new Button("Button1"));
  add(new Button("Button2"));
```

```
 add(new Button("Button3"));
 add(new Button("Button4"));
 add(new Button("Button5"));
 }

 // Display which alignment is used
 public void paint(Graphics g) {
  String s = null;
  if (alignment == FlowLayout.LEFT)
   s = "Left Alignment";
  else if (alignment == FlowLayout.CENTER)
   s = "Center Alignment";
  else if (alignment == FlowLayout.RIGHT)
   s = "Right Alignment";
  g.drawString(s, 4, 100);
 }
}
```

The sample program assigns a FlowLayout constant to an integer variable, and then passes that value to the FlowLayout constructor. Remove the comment slashes from one of the following statements in method init() to try out the other layout strategies:

```
alignment = FlowLayout.LEFT;
//   alignment = FlowLayout.CENTER;
//   alignment = FlowLayout.RIGHT;
setLayout(new FlowLayout(alignment));
```

The BorderLayout Class

The BorderLayout class provides more capabilities than its simple declaration reveals. Listing 15.13 shows the BorderLayout class.

Listing 15.13. The BorderLayout class.

```
public class BorderLayout implements LayoutManager {
// Constructors:
 public BorderLayout();
 public BorderLayout(int hgap, int vgap);
// Public methods:
 public void addLayoutComponent(String name, Component comp);
 public void removeLayoutComponent(Component comp);
 public Dimension minimumLayoutSize(Container target);
 public Dimension preferredLayoutSize(Container target);
 public void layoutContainer(Container target);
 public String toString();
}
```

There are two ways to construct a BorderLayout object. You can call its default constructor as follows (and presumably as used by default in applets):

```
setLayout(new BorderLayout());
```

Or you can specify the number of pixels to reserve horizontally and vertically between component cells with a statement such as

```
setLayout(new BorderLayout(5, 10));
```

The `BorderLayout` class's real power, however, comes from its ability to use compass coordinates to specify control locations. With this method, the resulting controls fill their assigned space, creating a pleasing display for some types of components, especially buttons. For example, Figure 15.11 shows five buttons laid out using the `BorderLayout` class's North, East, South, West, and Center compass directions. Listing 15.14, `BorderDemo.java`, shows the source code of the sample program that creates the display in the figure.

Figure 15.11.

Layout using the
`BorderLayout` class.

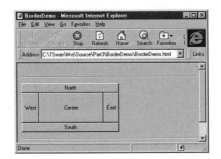

Listing 15.14. `BorderDemo.java` (Demonstrates `BorderLayout` class).

```
import java.applet.*;
import java.awt.*;

public class BorderDemo extends Applet
{
 // Initialize applet and add some dummy buttons
 public void init() {
  resize(220, 110);
  setLayout(new BorderLayout());
  add("North",  new Button("North"));
  add("South",  new Button("South"));
  add("East",   new Button("East"));
  add("West",   new Button("West"));
  add("Center", new Button("Center"));
 }
}
```

This simple applet brings up a subject that I've postponed until now. There are actually three forms of the add() method you can use to insert components into a `Container` such as an applet. You can pass a component object to add() like this:

```
add(new Button("Label"));
```

You may also specify a component's relative position as an integer value. The statement

```
add(new Button("Label"), 4);
```

places the button in the fourth position—whatever that happens to mean for the current layout strategy. (Frankly, I haven't had much luck with this method, though it is supposed to permit placing components in arbitrary positions. The value -1 supposedly adds a component at the end of others. Perhaps you will have better success with the technique than I.)

A third form of add() specifies a string tag that comes first in the argument list. For instance, the statement

```
add("North", new Button("Label"));
```

passes the tag string "North" to add() along with the component object to insert at that position. Only the BorderLayout class understands these compass-heading tags. The CardLayout class uses this third form of add(), but the string tags in that case represent the card names, not their positions.

The GridLayout Class

GridLayout is one of the most versatile of the layout classes. It provides a layout grid—like the rows and columns in a spreadsheet—into which you can plunk down component objects. Listing 15.15 shows the GridLayout class declaration.

Listing 15.15. The GridLayout class.

```
public class GridLayout implements LayoutManager {
// Constructors:
 public GridLayout(int rows, int cols);
 public GridLayout(int rows, int cols, int hgap, int vgap);
// Public methods:
 public void addLayoutComponent(String name, Component comp);
 public void removeLayoutComponent(Component comp);
 public Dimension preferredLayoutSize(Container parent);
 public Dimension minimumLayoutSize(Container parent);
 public void layoutContainer(Container parent);
 public String toString();
}
```

There are two ways to construct a GridLayout object. The statement

```
setLayout(new GridLayout(4, 8));
```

specifies a layout grid having four rows and eight columns. The grid cells are juxtaposed. To insert some space between cells, specify the number of pixels to reserve horizontally and vertically. For example, the statement

```
setLayout(new GridLayout(3, 4, 6, 12));
```

creates a grid of three rows and four columns, with six pixels between cells horizontally and 12 pixels between columns vertically.

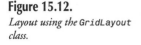

Figure 15.12 shows a typical use for a GridLayout object—arranging buttons as in a telephone touch-tone pad. Listing 15.16, GridDemo.java, shows the source code of the sample program used to create the figure.

Figure 15.12.

Layout using the GridLayout class.

Listing 15.16. GridDemo.java (Demonstrates GridLayout class).

```java
import java.applet.*;
import java.awt.*;

public class GridDemo extends Applet
{

// Initialize applet and add telephone pad buttons
public void init() {
  resize(150, 220);
  setLayout(new GridLayout(4, 3, 8, 16));
  add(new Button("   1"));
  add(new Button("ABC 2"));
  add(new Button("DEF 3"));
  add(new Button("GHI 4"));
  add(new Button("JKL 5"));
  add(new Button("MNO 6"));
  add(new Button("PRS 7"));
  add(new Button("TUV 8"));
  add(new Button("WXY 9"));
  add(new Button("  *  "));
  add(new Button("Opr 0"));
  add(new Button("  #  "));
 }
}
```

The GridBagLayout Class

The GridBagLayout class, relatively new to the AWT package and not discussed in many Java books, is similar to the GridLayout class but provides many more options. Like GridLayout, GridBagLayout provides a row-and-column grid of cells, each of which can hold a component object. However, the cells do not all have to be the same size. You may also specify whether a component should fill its cell completely. Listing 15.17 shows the `GridBagLayout` class declaration.

Listing 15.17. The `GridBagLayout` class.

```
public class GridBagLayout implements LayoutManager {
// Public variables:
 public int columnWidths[];
 public int rowHeights[];
 public double columnWeights[];
 public double rowWeights[];
// Constructor:
 public GridBagLayout ();
// Public methods:
 public void setConstraints(Component comp, GridBagConstraints constraints);
 public GridBagConstraints getConstraints(Component comp);
 public Point getLayoutOrigin();
 public int [][] getLayoutDimensions();
 public double [][] getLayoutWeights();
 public Point location(int x, int y);
 public void addLayoutComponent(String name, Component comp);
 public void removeLayoutComponent(Component comp);
 public Dimension preferredLayoutSize(Container parent);
 public Dimension minimumLayoutSize(Container parent);
 public void layoutContainer(Container parent);
 public String toString();
}
```

Of all the layout classes, `GridBagLayout` will probably require the most experimentation to master. An example program, similar to one in the Visual J++ online help file but with some additional parameters and comments, will help you to understand how to use the class. Figure 15.13 shows the resulting display of the program in Listing 15.18, `GridBagDemo.java`.

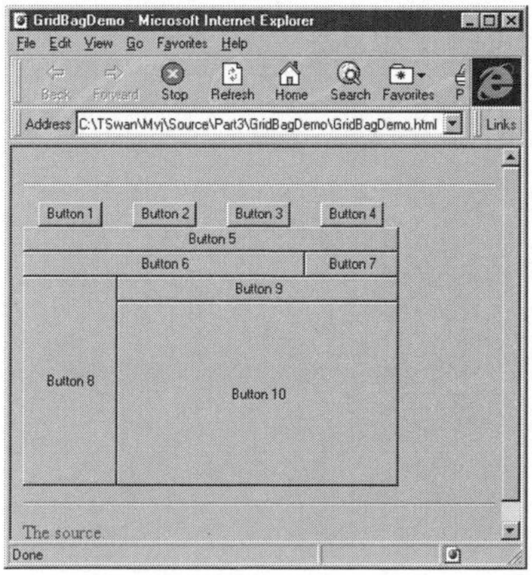

Figure 15.13.

Layout using the GridBagLayout class.

Listing 15.18. `GridBagDemo.java` (Demonstrates `GridBagLayout` class).

```java
import java.applet.*;
import java.awt.*;

public class GridBagDemo extends Applet
{

 void makebutton(String name, GridBagLayout gridbag,
  GridBagConstraints c)
 {
  Button button = new Button(name);
  gridbag.setConstraints(button, c);
  add(button);
 }

 // Initialize applet and dummy buttons
 public void init() {
  // Create GridBagLayout and Constraints objects
  GridBagLayout gridbag = new GridBagLayout();
  GridBagConstraints c = new GridBagConstraints();
  setLayout(gridbag);   // Tell container to use layout

  // Create four "normal" buttons on the top row
  c.fill = GridBagConstraints.NONE;
  c.weightx = 1.0;
  makebutton("Button 1", gridbag, c);
  makebutton("Button 2", gridbag, c);
  makebutton("Button 3", gridbag, c);
  c.gridwidth = GridBagConstraints.REMAINDER;
  makebutton("Button 4", gridbag, c);

  // Create a long button filling entire row
  c.fill = GridBagConstraints.BOTH;
  c.weightx = 0.0;
  makebutton("Button 5", gridbag, c);

  // Create two buttons that fill the row
  c.gridwidth = GridBagConstraints.RELATIVE;
  makebutton("Button 6", gridbag, c);
  c.gridwidth = GridBagConstraints.REMAINDER;
  makebutton("Button 7", gridbag, c);

  // Create a vertical button
  c.gridwidth = 1;
  c.gridheight = 2;
  c.weighty = 1.0;
  makebutton("Button 8", gridbag, c);
  c.weighty = 0.0;

  // Create buttons to right of vertical Button 8
  c.gridwidth = GridBagConstraints.REMAINDER;
  c.gridheight = 1;
  makebutton("Button 9", gridbag, c);
  makebutton("Button 10", gridbag, c);
  resize(300, 100);
 }
}
```

The `GridBagLayout` class uses objects of the `GridBagConstraints` class to specify various options for arranging components. Listing 15.19 shows the `GridBagConstraints` class declaration.

Listing 15.19. The `GridBagConstraints` class.

```
public class GridBagConstraints implements Cloneable {
// Fields:
 public static final int RELATIVE;
 public static final int REMAINDER;
 public static final int NONE;
 public static final int BOTH;
 public static final int HORIZONTAL;
 public static final int VERTICAL;
 public static final int CENTER;
 public static final int NORTH;
 public static final int NORTHEAST;
 public static final int EAST;
 public static final int SOUTHEAST;
 public static final int SOUTH;
 public static final int SOUTHWEST;
 public static final int WEST;
 public static final int NORTHWEST;
// Public variables:
 public int gridx, gridy, gridwidth, gridheight;
 public double weightx, weighty;
 public int anchor, fill;
 public Insets insets;
 public int ipadx, ipady;
// Constructor:
 public GridBagConstraints ();
// Public method:
 public Object clone ();
}
```

As the sample program shows, to use the `GridBagLayout` class, begin the applet's `init()` method with three statements such as these:

```
GridBagLayout gridbag = new GridBagLayout();
GridBagConstraints c = new GridBagConstraints();
setLayout(gridbag);
```

The first statement constructs a `GridBagLayout` object. The second constructs an object of the `GridBagConstraints` class. The third specifies that the container use the `GridBagLayout` object for its component layout strategy.

After these initial steps, assign various values to the `GridBagConstraints` object. This process will probably take some trial and error to achieve the effects you want. For example, to specify that components exactly fill their cells, use a statement such as

```
c.fill = GridBagConstraints.BOTH;
```

To grapple a component to a specific location, assign a constant to the `anchor` field:

```
c.anchor = GridBagConstraints.NORTHEAST;
```

361

You can also specify a variety of other attributes such as gridHeight and gridWidth, which determine the number of cells used by the object. The values of gridx and gridy control where a component is placed. Normally set to GridBagConstraints.RELATIVE, which places the component next to last in its row or column, you can change these values to insert a component relative to another's cell position. Other variables such as weightx and weighty alter the distribution of extra space left over in rows and columns. Again, experimenting with these parameters will show you their purposes better than long-winded explanations here.

Use the sample program to test different settings. For example, to cause the top buttons to fill their cells, as do the others, change NONE in the following statement to BOTH:

```
c.fill = GridBagConstraints.NONE;
```

NOTE

A useful trick is to construct a Panel object, and add it to the applet using a GridBagLayout class object. Add your components to the Panel to place them in various spots in the display. For example, rather than use Button objects in the sample listing in this section, these might be Panel objects that contain other controls.

The CardLayout Class

Last but not least among the layout classes is CardLayout, which offers the most intriguing possibilities for organizing complex applet displays. Use this class to create a series of panels, each of which can hold any number of components arranged according to one of the aforementioned strategies. By adding some additional buttons to the display, users can navigate from card to card. The result is similar to the tabbed windows in a multipage Windows dialog, or the cards in a Macintosh's Hypercard application. Listing 15.20 shows the CardLayout class declaration.

Listing 15.20. The CardLayout class.

```
public class CardLayout implements LayoutManager {
// Constructors:
 public CardLayout();
 public CardLayout(int hgap, int vgap);
// Public methods:
 public void addLayoutComponent(String name, Component comp);
 public void removeLayoutComponent(Component comp);
 public Dimension preferredLayoutSize(Container parent);
 public Dimension minimumLayoutSize(Container parent);
 public void layoutContainer(Container parent);
```

```
    public void first(Container parent);
    public void next(Container parent);
    public void previous(Container parent);
    public void last(Container parent);
    public void show(Container parent, String name);
    public String toString();
}
```

As the next program demonstrates, it takes some extra care to use the CardLayout class properly. The class also provides some methods you will need to call so users can navigate among cards. Figure 15.14, Figure 15.15, and Figure 15.16 show the three cards created by the sample applet. To navigate among the cards, run the program and click one of the four buttons along the bottom edge of the display. Listing 15.21, CardDemo.java, shows the source code of the program that creates the three figures.

Figure 15.14.

Card A of the CardDemo applet using the CardLayout *class.*

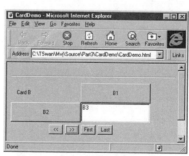

Figure 15.15.

Card B of the CardDemo applet using the CardLayout *class.*

Figure 15.16.

Card C of the CardDemo applet using the CardLayout *class.*

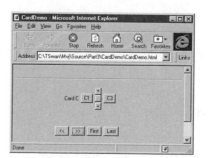

Listing 15.21. **CardDemo.java** (Demonstrates **CardLayout** class).

```java
import java.applet.*;
import java.awt.*;

public class CardDemo extends Applet {
 // Variables
 Panel cardPanel;
 CardLayout cards;

 // Initialize applets and cards
 public void init() {
  // Size the applet window
  resize(320, 120);

  // Construct Panel and CardLayout objects
  cardPanel = new Panel();
  cards = new CardLayout();

  // Set the applet layout object
  setLayout(new BorderLayout());

  // Set the cardPanel's layout to CardLayout
  // and add the panel to the applet
  cardPanel.setLayout(cards);
  add("Center", cardPanel);

  // Construct the first card
  Panel cardA = new Panel();
  cardA.setLayout(new FlowLayout());
  cardA.add(new Label("Card A"));
  cardA.add(new Button("A1"));
  cardA.add(new Button("A2"));
  cardA.add(new Button("A3"));
  cardPanel.add("Card A", cardA); // Add to panel

  // Construct the second card
  Panel cardB = new Panel();
  cardB.setLayout(new GridLayout(2, 2));
  cardB.add(new Label("Card B"));
  cardB.add(new Button("B1"));
  cardB.add(new Button("B2"));
  cardB.add(new TextField("B3"));
  cardPanel.add("Card B", cardB); // Add to panel

  // Construct the third card
  Panel cardC = new Panel();
  cardC.setLayout(new FlowLayout());
  cardC.add(new Label("Card C"));
  cardC.add(new Button("C1"));
  cardC.add(new Scrollbar());
  cardC.add(new Button("C3"));
  cardPanel.add("Card C", cardC); // Add to panel

  // Create a panel of controller buttons
  // for navigating through the cards
  Panel controller = new Panel();
  controller.setLayout(new FlowLayout());
  controller.add(new Button(" << "));
```

```
  controller.add(new Button(" >> "));
  controller.add(new Button("First"));
  controller.add(new Button("Last"));
  add("South", controller);
 }

 // Respond to card-controller button selections
 public boolean action(Event evt, Object arg) {
  if (" << ".equals(arg)) {
   cards.previous(cardPanel);  // Previous card
   return true;
  } else if (" >> ".equals(arg)) {
   cards.next(cardPanel);     // Next card
   return true;
  } else if ("First".equals(arg)) {
   cards.first(cardPanel);    // First card
   return true;
  } else if ("Last".equals(arg)) {
   cards.last(cardPanel);     // Last card
   return true;
  }
  return super.action(evt, arg);
 }

}
```

To use the CardLayout class, your applet class needs at least two variables declared as follows:

```
Panel cardPanel;
CardLayout cards;
```

The first is a Panel object, upon which the individual cards are placed. Think of this as a surface that can hold separate card objects. The second variable represents the layout strategy for the Panel to use. Remember that this is the *panel's* strategy, not the applet's. The panel itself is laid out in the applet window according to the applet's strategy—BorderLayout by default.

In the applet's init() method, construct the two objects using code such as

```
cardPanel = new Panel();
cards = new CardLayout();
```

This gives you two objects for specifying the surface to hold individual cards (cardPanel) and the layout strategy for that surface (cards). As I mentioned, the panel uses the applet's layout strategy, which you may set using any of the methods in this chapter. For example, the sample program executes the following statement:

```
setLayout(new BorderLayout());
```

This could also be FlowLayout or another object (but probably not CardLayout, which might result in a confusing display). To tell the panel to use the CardLayout object as its layout strategy, call setLayout() a second time, and then add the panel to the applet's container:

```
cardPanel.setLayout(cards);
add("Center", cardPanel);
```

365

The first statement specifies that the panel should use the CardLayout strategy, and thus can display individual cards. The second statement adds the panel to the applet window. Any left over space is static—that is, any components outside of the panel are displayed regardless of which card is currently showing. You might use this space, as illustrated in the demonstration program, to display a toolbar of buttons for navigating through individual cards.

To construct those cards, create a new Panel object for each card, and then add your component controls to that surface. The panels may use any layout strategy, except as I mentioned, another level of CardLayouts might be more confusing than helpful. For example, the statements

```
Panel cardA = new Panel();
cardA.setLayout(new FlowLayout());
```

construct a Panel object, cardA, and call its setLayout() method to specify a layout strategy managed by the FlowLayout class. You can then add any component you want to the panel using statements like these:

```
cardA.add(new Label("Card A"));
cardA.add(new Button("A1"));
```

Finally, add the card to the original panel with the following statement:

```
cardPanel.add("Card A", cardA);
```

This statement adds the individual card panel, cardA, to the Panel object, cardPanel, for which you earlier specified the CardLayout strategy. Remember, the cardPanel object is added to the applet. Individual components are added to separate Panel objects, which are added to cardPanel. If this seems confusing, review the preceding text before continuing.

To construct a navigation toolbar—or to display any other controls outside of the cards—construct another Panel object, just as you do for the individual cards. For example, the sample program creates a controller toolbar Panel with the following statement:

```
Panel controller = new Panel();
```

Specify a layout strategy to use, and then add buttons or other objects to this panel using statements like these:

```
controller.setLayout(new FlowLayout());
controller.add(new Button(" << "));
```

Finally, add the Panel object to the applet container in the usual way:

```
add("South", controller);
```

It's important to add this object to the applet, not to the card panel! The goal is to create a toolbar that remains visible in the applet's window regardless of which card is currently displayed.

TIP

The preceding technique is useful in other situations for positioning controls within a panel that is added to the applet container.

After you have created the cards and navigational controls, you need to program an `action()` method similar to the one in the sample listing. The method intercepts events generated by the user clicking navigational buttons, and calls methods in the `CardLayout` class to display one or another card. For example, the statement

```
cards.previous(cardPanel);
```

displays the previous card. If the first card is showing, it displays the last one. The statement

```
cards.next(cardPanel);
```

displays the next card—or the first if the last one is showing. The next two statements display the first and last cards respectively:

```
cards.first(cardPanel);
cards.last(cardPanel);
```

Summary

- Objects of the `Event` class represent the nature of events such as keypresses and mouse button clicks.
- The `Toolkit` class binds components to their native counterparts in the operating system. Some `Toolkit` methods, however, are useful for obtaining system information such as display resolution and lists of available fonts.
- Java programs are event driven, and a lot of code involves responding to events. This chapter describes several different ways to write event handlers.
- One of the goals of Java applets is to create system-independent user interfaces. For this purpose, the AWT package provides a collection of layout classes that arrange controls according to various strategies.

What's Next?

With the information presented so far, you should now be able to write credible applets. Some tasks, however, might require additional interface elements such as menus, windows, and dialog boxes—subjects coming up next.

16

Windows, Menus, and Dialogs

16

In this chapter we embark on a dangerous journey into the wild and untamed land of windows, menus, and dialogs. It's a perilous trip because, although most of the techniques I'm about to show you will probably work just fine, these three subjects are in relatively uncharted territory. Creating separate windows and dialogs (a menu is a kind of window, too) comes as close as one dares to communicating directly with the operating system. Any problem with the interface to those services is practically guaranteed to bring bugs crawling out of the undergrowth in your code.

If you decide to blaze the trails described in this chapter, be prepared to carefully test your applets, preferably on more than one system. To give you the best chance at success, I'll concentrate on techniques that are fairly well proven. If, however, you discover other workable solutions—and especially if you encounter difficulties with any of this chapter's information—I'd like to hear about your solutions.

In This Chapter

This chapter covers the following fundamentals of windows, menus, and dialogs:

- Creating separate windows
- Creating separate frames
- The differences between windows and frames
- Creating a menu bar
- Responding to menu selections
- Creating dialogs containing control objects
- Transferring data to and from dialog controls
- Using a file dialog to prompt for filenames

Windows

The Window class is too low-level to be of any practical use for constructing objects, but it's necessary to understand how to use the class before proceeding to more advanced subjects. Java windows are merely on-screen areas that can be fashioned into the windows with which you are more familiar. Most importantly, a Window object has a parent (usually the applet) that is responsible for creating and maintaining the Window object.

Introducing Windows

It's useful to take a look at a demonstration program before examining the Window class. Figure 16.1 shows the result of the program running in Internet Explorer. Clicking the sample applet's button creates the window shown as a gray rectangle to the left (it's red on your monitor). This demonstrates that a Java window has no border or title, and it also cannot have a menu bar.

For these reasons, windows are not useable on their own—but, as I mentioned, the techniques for creating them are fundamental to creating practical windows, menus, and dialogs. Listing 16.1, WindowDemo.java, shows the source code of the sample applet that produced the figure.

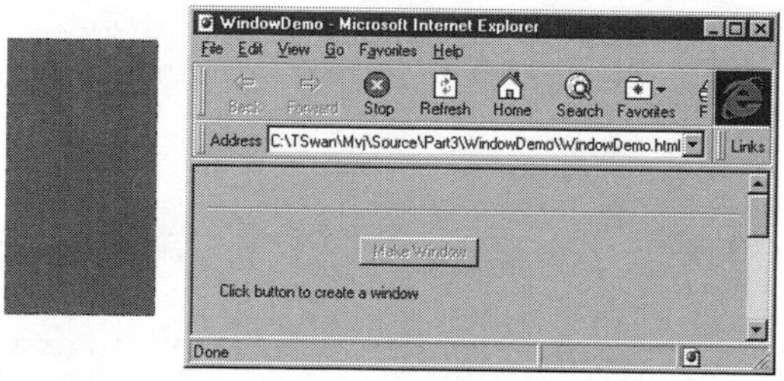

Figure 16.1.

The rectangle next to the WindowDemo applet shows that a fundamental Window object has no border, title, or menu bar.

Listing 16.1. WindowDemo.java (Demonstrates fundamental Window objects).

```
import java.applet.*;
import java.awt.*;

public class WindowDemo extends Applet {
// Button and Window components
 Button makeWindowButton;
 Window theWindow;

 // Initialize applet and button object
 public void init() {
  resize(320, 240);
  makeWindowButton = new Button(" Make Window ");
  add(makeWindowButton);
 }

 // Paint instructions in applet window
 public void paint(Graphics g) {
  g.drawString("Click button to create a window", 10, 50);
 }

 // Respond to button click
 public boolean action(Event evt, Object what) {
  if (theWindow == null) {
   if (evt.target.equals(makeWindowButton)) {
    // Locate parent Frame
    Component c = this;
    Frame f = null;
    while (f == null) {
     c = c.getParent();
     if (c instanceof Frame)
      f = (Frame)c;
    }
    // Construct Window attached to parent Frame
    theWindow = new Window(f);
    theWindow.resize(100, 200);
    theWindow.setBackground(Color.red);
    theWindow.show();
```

continues

371

Listing 16.1. continued

```
    // Disable button so it can't be reselected
    makeWindowButton.disable();
    // Signal that we've handled this event
    return true;
  }
 }
 // Other events
 return super.action(evt, what);
 }
}
```

The WindowDemo applet declares two variables in its applet class. These are

```
Button makeWindowButton;
Window theWindow;
```

The `Button` object is shown in the applet. The `Window` object is shown separately. When you run this demonstration and click the button to display a window, you'll notice that you can select the window, but because it has no border or system buttons, you can't move it or do anything with it.

Method `init()` creates the `Button` object and adds it to the applet. Method `paint()` draws instructions in the applet. You've seen these techniques before.

Method `action()` is literally where the action is in this demonstration. Creating a `Window` requires the object to have a parent, which must be an object of the `Frame` class or one extended from `Frame`. Though essential for creating separate windows, techniques for finding this parent object are not well documented. My solution (there might be others) is straightforward. First, declare two variables:

```
Component c = this;
Frame f = null;
```

The `Component` object is initialized to `this`, representing the current applet object; thus, this code must be in an `Applet`-extended class method. The `Frame` object is initialized to `null`. After these preliminaries, a `while` loop finds the `Frame` that is the applet's parent:

```
while (f == null) {
 c = c.getParent();
 if (c instanceof Frame)
  f = (Frame)c;
}
```

Because an applet *must* have a `Frame` parent object, this loop will always find the parent as long as it is executed inside an `Applet`-class method. Calling the current object's `getParent()` method finds its immediate parent. Checking whether that parent is an instance of the `Frame` class confirms whether we have located the frame.

Having found the parent, we can now create a separate window using the following code:

```
theWindow = new Window(f);
```

Pass the parent `Frame` object to the `Window` class constructor. After this, but before making the window visible, you can perform various initializations. For example, you can size the window and color its background with statements such as

```
theWindow.resize(100, 200);
theWindow.setBackground(Color.red);
```

When the window is configured, show it by calling `show()`:

```
theWindow.show();
```

To hide the window, you can call `hide()`, or you can call the `destroy()` method, which essentially does the same.

> **TIP**
>
> To prevent you from creating more than one window, the sample program calls the `disable()` method for the `Button` control. This dims the button (or another type of component) and prevents its selection. To restore a `Button` or other component, call `enable()`.

The Window Class

The `Window` class, a descendent of `Container`, is a fundamental structure without the capabilities of having a border, title, or menu bar. This class, however, forms the basis of the more practical `Frame` class, which you will use to create practical windows. It is also the base class for the `Dialog` and `FileDialog` classes discussed near the end of the chapter. Listing 16.2 shows the `Window` class declaration.

Listing 16.2. The `Window` class.

```
public class Window extends Container {
// Constructor:
 public Window(Frame parent);
// Public methods:
 public synchronized void addNotify();
 public synchronized void pack();
 public void show();
 public synchronized void dispose();
 public void toFront();
 public void toBack();
 public Toolkit getToolkit();
 public final String getWarningString();
}
```

There is only one way to create a `Window` object: You must find an existing `Frame` object, and pass it to the `Window` class constructor as the `WindowDemo.java` applet shows. The class provides several public methods, some of which you will find useful when creating separate windows.

These methods are

- `void addNotify()`: Never call this method; the AWT package calls it to connect a `Window` object with its peer class, which forms the interface between objects and the operating system's native windows.

- `void pack()`: Usually called automatically, this method arranges components inside a window according to the current layout strategy and their preferred sizes.

- `void show()`: You must call this method to make a window visible. Call `hide()`, inherited from `Component` but not redefined in the `Window` class, to make a window invisible.

- `void dispose()`: This is supposed to destroy the window and any components that it contains, but it actually only hides the window and detaches it from its peer class. It doesn't "dispose" anything, but it might help conserve system resources.

- `void toFront()`: Makes a window visible and, if necessary, brings it to the front of other windows. Note: I have had little success using this method; it may or may not work as documented.

- `void toBack()`: Moves a window behind all others. Note: I have had just as little success using this method; like `toFront()`, it may or may not work as documented.

- `Toolkit getToolkit()`: Returns the default toolkit in use for this object. Although this method's return value is an object of the `Toolkit` class, it is actually an object of a system-dependent class extended from `Toolkit`. This makes the returned object valuable for obtaining information about the system such as its resolution and color values. See Chapter 15, "Events and Layouts," for more information on the `Toolkit` class.

- `String getWarningString()`: This rather unusual method returns a string that, if `null`, indicates the window is secure. If the window is insecure—meaning that a security manager object is in effect, and a method such as `checkTopLevelWindow()` method has returned `false` for the window object—then the warning string will be set to something like `Warning: Applet Window`. This string will also be displayed inside the window. You may, however, call `getWarningString()` to determine whether the window is insecure, in which case you might prevent the window from being shown in the first place.

> **NOTE**
>
> In the event that a security manager object is in effect on a user's system, your applet might be prevented from creating separate windows. In the absence of security measures, such windows could possibly provide an avenue for a virus to infiltrate the system—just one of the reasons that separate windows, menus, and dialogs are fraught with potential danger.

Introducing Frames

The Frame class builds on Window to add a border and title bar, complete with system menu and buttons as appropriate for the target operating system. A Frame object may also have a menu bar. These features make Java Frames more like the windows with which you are familiar. (In a perfect world, the Frame class would be named Window, and Window would be named Frame, which would more closely resemble the counterpart objects in most graphical user interfaces.)

You can use Frame objects to create separate, modeless windows that users can drag, size, hide, and show, at will. They behave very much like separate applications, although they are owned by a parent object, which is usually the applet container.

The next sample applet shows how to use the Frame class to create a separate window. Figure 16.2 shows the result of running the applet—as you can see, the separate window is shown to the left of Internet Explorer. The program in Listing 16.3, FrameDemo.java, is similar to the preceding demonstration, but shows how much easier (and more practical) it is to create a Frame object than a Window.

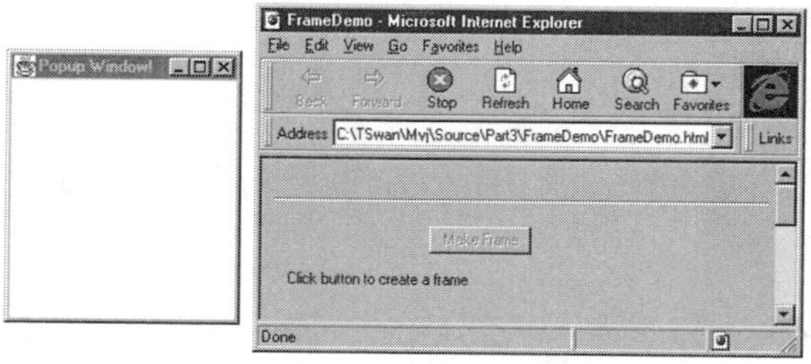

Figure 16.2.

The FrameDemo applet shows that a Frame window has a title and a border. Though not shown here, a frame may also have a menu bar.

Listing 16.3. FrameDemo.java (Demonstrates fundamental Frame objects).

```java
import java.applet.*;
import java.awt.*;

public class FrameDemo extends Applet {
// Button and Frame components
Button makeFrameButton;
Frame theFrame;

// Initialize applet and insert Button
public void init() {
 resize(320, 240);
 makeFrameButton = new Button(" Make Frame ");
 add(makeFrameButton);
}

// Draw instructions in applet window
public void paint(Graphics g) {
 g.drawString("Click button to create a frame", 10, 50);
}

// Respond to button selection
```

continues

Listing 16.3. continued

```
public boolean action(Event evt, Object what) {
 if (theFrame == null) {
  if (evt.target.equals(makeFrameButton)) {
   // Construct new Frame window
   theFrame = new Frame("Popup Window!");
   theFrame.resize(200, 200);
   theFrame.show();
   // Disable button so it can't be reselected
   makeFrameButton.disable();
   // Signal that we've handled this event
   return true;
  }
 }
 // Other events
 return super.action(evt, what);
 }
}
```

The sample applet declares two variables, one for the button shown in the applet and the other for the separate Frame object. These variables are

```
Button makeFrameButton;
Frame theFrame;
```

The action() method constructs and displays the Frame object when you click the applet's button. To construct a Frame object, execute a statement such as

```
theFrame = new Frame("Popup Window!");
```

The string passed to the Frame constructor is displayed in the window's title bar. Before showing the frame, you can size it and perform any other initializations needed; then call show() as follows:

```
theFrame.resize(200, 200);
theFrame.show();
```

A Frame object may contain components such as Buttons and Lists, and it may display graphics and text. For complex windows, however, it is usually more appropriate to create a dialog as this chapter explains—but Frames are still potentially useful for displaying messages and for relatively simple chores that require separate windows. Doing this requires a good understanding of how to handle Frame events, which I'll explain in a moment. First, however, let's take a look at the Frame class.

The Frame Class

The Frame class extends Window, and it provides for a title bar and border. In addition, a Frame object may have a menu bar—but more on that later. Listing 16.4 shows the Frame class declaration.

The Frame class implements the MenuContainer interface class, discussed later in this chapter. This enables Frame objects to have menu bars.

Listing 16.4. The Frame class.

```
public class Frame extends Window implements MenuContainer {
// Fields:
 public static final int DEFAULT_CURSOR;
 public static final int CROSSHAIR_CURSOR;
 public static final int TEXT_CURSOR;
 public static final int WAIT_CURSOR3;
 public static final int SW_RESIZE_CURSOR;
 public static final int SE_RESIZE_CURSOR;
 public static final int NW_RESIZE_CURSOR;
 public static final int NE_RESIZE_CURSOR;
 public static final int N_RESIZE_CURSOR;
 public static final int S_RESIZE_CURSOR;
 public static final int W_RESIZE_CURSOR;
 public static final int E_RESIZE_CURSOR;
 public static final int HAND_CURSOR;
 public static final int MOVE_CURSOR;
// Constructors:
 public Frame();
 public Frame(String title);
// Public methods:
 public synchronized void addNotify();
 public String getTitle();
 public void setTitle(String title);
 public Image getIconImage();
 public void setIconImage(Image image);
 public MenuBar getMenuBar();
 public synchronized void setMenuBar(MenuBar mb);
 public synchronized void remove(MenuComponent m);
 public synchronized void dispose();
 public boolean isResizable();
 public void setCursor(int cursorType);
 public int getCursorType();
}
```

The Frame class declares several integer fields that select and indicate various cursor shapes. You can pass these values to the setCursor() method; they are returned by getCursorType(). One of these shapes is displayed when the user moves the mouse pointer over the frame's interior window (called the *client area* in Windows, but not necessarily so named in all operating systems). The exact shape depends entirely on the operating system itself, and is not drawn by the AWT package—so beware of telling your customers to expect to see a specific image such as a hand or hourglass. These images could be similar, or completely different, and you have no control over their actual shapes.

There are two ways to construct a `Frame` object. You may call the default constructor like this:

```
Frame untitled = new Frame();
```

But you are more likely to pass a window title as a string argument using a statement such as

```
Frame titled = new Frame("Window Title");
```

If you use the former technique, call `setTitle()` to display a title string in the window. The `Frame` class declares several public methods that you'll find useful for manipulating separate frame windows. These methods are

- `void addNotify()`: Never call this method, which connects a `Frame` object with the peer class that interfaces the `Frame` with its native counterpart in the operating system.

- `String getTitle()`: Returns the current title displayed in the frame window's title bar.

- `void setTitle(String title)`: Changes the title displayed in the frame window's title bar.

- `Image getIconImage()`: Returns the `Image` object that represents a minimized window's icon. The `Image` class is discussed in Chapter 17, "Graphics, Animation, and Multimedia."

- `void setIconImage(Image image)`: Changes the `Image` object that represents this window when minimized as an icon.

- `MenuBar getMenuBar()`: Returns a reference to the `Frame`'s menu bar. If there is no menu bar, this method returns `null`.

- `void setMenuBar(MenuBar mb)`: Sets or changes the `Frame` object's menu bar. You may change a `Frame`'s menu bar at any time and as many times as you want.

- `void remove(MenuComponent m)`: Removes a menu component from the `Frame`'s menu bar.

- `void dispose()`: This is supposed to destroy the `Frame` window and remove any associated menu and other components, but it merely hides the window and detaches it from its peer class. After disposing a window, you may call `show()` to display it again.

- `boolean isResizable()`: This method presumably returns `true` if the frame window size can be changed. However, because there is no defined way to create a window that *can't* be resized, this method is of dubious value. Only true dialogs can be fixed in size (see the `Dialog` class discussion in this chapter). Perhaps some Java installation somewhere allows applets to create `Frame` objects only of a fixed size. That seems highly unlikely, but if you suspect a problem with this, you might call `isResizable()` to check what's going on.

- `void setCursor(int cursorType)`: Changes the cursor image displayed when the user moves the mouse pointer over the frame's interior. This image is probably not displayed when the user moves the mouse over the title bar and menu. As I mentioned, it's best not to assume that users will see a specific shape. Pass this method an integer field such as CROSSHAIR_CURSOR defined in the Frame class. Attempting to use any other values will throw an exception of the IllegalArgumentException class.

- int getCursorType(): Returns the current cursor image as one of the ..._CURSOR fields defined in the Frame class.

Frame Events

Now that you know how to create a separate Frame-class window, you will probably want to add component objects, handle events, and draw graphics. You can certainly do all that and more—but I need to voice a caution before you start writing the code. The techniques described in this section work well enough, but for more control over the resulting windows, you will want to study this chapter's discussion of dialogs. This will give you a deeper knowledge of how to arrange, insert, and use control objects in frames—information that you will find invaluable in constructing separate windows.

The sample applet in this section describes the following essential Frame-object techniques:

- How to add a component to a frame window.
- How to respond to a component's selection.
- How to close a frame window under program control.

Figure 16.3 shows the result of running the sample applet. The window displays a string, which illustrates how to paint graphics inside a frame window. The frame also displays a Button object that you can click to close the window. The button demonstrates how to add and use components in separate windows. Selecting the window's system close button, its close menu item, or pressing the close-window keys (Alt+F4 under Microsoft Windows) also closes the separate frame window. Listing 16.5, FrameEvents.java, shows the sample applet's source code.

Figure 16.3.

This window's Exit button demonstrates how to respond to component events in separate Frame windows.

Listing 16.5. FrameEvents.java (Demonstrates Frame event handling).

```java
import java.applet.*;
import java.awt.*;

// Extend the Frame class
class CustomFrame extends Frame {
 // Button object used to create Frame window
 Button creationButton;
 // Constructor
 CustomFrame(Button aButton, String title) {
```

continues

Listing 16.5. continued

```
  super(title);
  creationButton = aButton;  // Save reference to button
}
// Handle events intended for this frame window
public boolean handleEvent(Event evt) {
 if (evt.id == Event.WINDOW_DESTROY) {
  creationButton.enable();
  hide();  // "Close" window by hiding it
  return true;
 }
 return super.handleEvent(evt);
 }
}

public class FrameEvents extends Applet {
 // Button and Frame components
 Button makeFrameButton;
 CustomFrame theFrame;

 // Initialize applet and create button
 public void init() {
  resize(320, 240);
  makeFrameButton = new Button(" Make Frame ");
  add(makeFrameButton);
 }

 // Display instructions in applet window
 public void paint(Graphics g) {
  g.drawString("Click button to create a frame", 10, 50);
 }

 // Respond to applet button selection
 public boolean action(Event evt, Object what) {
  if (evt.target.equals(makeFrameButton)) {
   // Construct new Frame window if necessary
   if (theFrame == null) {
    theFrame = new CustomFrame(makeFrameButton,
      "Popup Window!");
   }
   theFrame.resize(200, 200);
   theFrame.show();
   // Disable button so it can't be reselected
   // until window is closed (hidden)
   makeFrameButton.disable();
   // Signal that we've handled this event
   return true;
  }
  // Other events
  return super.action(evt, what);
 }
}
```

Posing it as a question, the problem to solve in this applet is, "What is the best way to extend the capabilities of a Frame object?" The answer lies in the question itself: Extend the Frame class and write new data and code to enhance the class as you wish.

This is the technique I used to create the sample applet's frame and to display a `Button` object and string. The rest of the listing is similar to the preceding sample applet, `FrameDemo.java`, so I'll discuss only the new code in `FrameEvents`. The extended class responds to events intended for the frame such as those generated when the user clicks the Exit button. The extended class and its two instance variables are declared as

```
class CustomFrame extends Frame {
 Button creationButton;
 Button exitButton = null;
 ...
}
```

The first `Button` in `CustomFrame` is a reference to the applet button that, when clicked, creates the `Frame` object. This button isn't required in the extended class, but I included it to demonstrate one way for a `Frame` class to communicate with applet components. As you will see, the extended class uses this button reference to enable the applet's button so that, when you close the frame, you can again click that button to redisplay the frame.

The second `Button` in `CustomFrame` is a reference to the frame's own button component, labeled *Exit*. This shows that a `Frame` can have its own components—which is expected, because the `Frame` class is descended from `Container`. However, unlike the `Applet` class—a further `Container` descendent—`Frame` does not provide an `init()` method for initializing components. For that reason, you can't use the same techniques for adding components to separate frames that you have seen in this book's other examples. (This also shows a decided weakness in the AWT class hierarchy—`init()` probably should have been added to the `Component` or `Container` classes so that the method would be available in classes such as `Frame`.)

I have found that I can install component objects into `Frames` by initializing those objects in the class constructor. However, despite the fact that the `Window` class is supposed to have a default layout strategy (in the form of a `BorderLayout` object), this does not seem to be effective for frames. Attaching a new layout object to the `Frame` is the answer to making components visible, as the sample applet demonstrates. First, though, the extended class's constructor begins by executing these statements:

```
super(title);
creationButton = aButton;
resize(200, 200);
```

The first statement is required; it calls the ancestor constructor to initialize the `Frame` class portion of the object. The second statement is optional, and is used in this demonstration to save a reference to the applet button that, when clicked, creates the frame window. If you don't need to do this, you can eliminate this statement and the associated `creationButton` variable in your own class. The last statement sizes the `Frame` window, which you should probably do before attaching the layout. That step is carried out with the following statement:

```
setLayout(new FlowLayout());
```

You may use any of the layout classes described in the preceding chapter, "Events and Layouts." After this step, create your component objects and add them to the frame. For example, the next statements create a Button and insert it into the frame:

```
exitButton = new Button("Exit");
add(exitButton);
```

A Frame object's paint() method is called whenever the window requires updating. It is called also when the window first appears. You may insert graphics statements into paint() to draw in a frame window, as this statement demonstrates:

```
g.drawString("Click button to exit", 10, 50);
```

In the next chapter, I'll explain more about calling Graphics class methods such as drawString().

The final essential technique to master for frames is how to handle events. The programming is the same as you have seen for other examples, but it is added to the class extended from Frame rather than Applet. For instance, examine the sample listing's handleEvent() method. The method intercepts the WINDOW_DESTROY event, which is sent to the window when the user requests that the window be closed.

The handleEvent() method also checks for selection of the Frame's Exit button. Although the sample window has only one such button, I added programming to distinguish among other possible components, which most frames will probably have. The two if statements

```
if (evt.target instanceof Button) {
 if ("Exit".equals(evt.arg))
  exitWindow = true;
}
```

set a flag, exitWindow, to true if the event's target is a Button and if that object's label is "Exit". Finally in handleEvent(), if the flag is true, the program performs the window's exit maneuvers, repeated here:

```
creationButton.enable();
hide();
return true;
```

The applet's creationButton object is enabled so you can select it again. Calling hide(), as mentioned, makes the frame window temporarily invisible. The handleEvent() method returns true to indicate that it has handled this event.

Rather than call hide(), the program can call dispose() instead. Despite the documentation for dispose(), however, this does not destroy the window object. All it does is call hide() and detach the object and any components from their peer classes. Subsequent calls to show() reattach the peers, so even though you have called dispose(), it is still proper to call show() to redisplay the window. You do not have to re-create the Frame object. This implies that dispose() is of limited value and doesn't really dispose anything, although by detaching the peers, it might conserve system resources (but this is in no way guaranteed).

To completely destroy a window, *after* calling dispose(), you would have to set the Frame class variable to null, or create another frame window and assign it to the variable. Because these actions are messy, I recommend not calling dispose(). Instead, call hide() to make a separate window temporarily invisible, and then call show() to redisplay it. When users close your applet (assuming this is the frame's parent), it will destroy any separate windows regardless of whether they are visible.

Menus

Where would programmers be without menu bars in graphical user interfaces? I don't know about you, but I'd probably be out of a job, since I have written thousands of words about creating and using pulldown menus. Following are a few hundred more words on the subject, but this time, of course, for Java applets.

Introducing Menus

Because the Frame class implements the MenuContainer interface, a Frame object can have a menu bar similar to those in your operating system. Most of the time, however, you will extend the Frame class so you can write code to respond to menu selections. I'll discuss all of these techniques in this and the following sections, but first there are some preliminary items to consider. In addition to the programming techniques, you also need to design your menu as a resource. This information is necessarily Windows based, but the end results are system independent.

The MenuDemo project on the CD-ROM demonstrates fundamental menu creation and event handling. Copy the files to your hard drive, and open the MenuDemo.mdp project file; or, to create the project from scratch using Studio 97 or Developer Studio, close any current workspace, and then follow these steps:

1. Create a new applet using Applet Wizard. Select *File|New,* choose *Project Workspace,* and highlight *Java Applet Wizard.* Enter the applet name, click the Create button, and then follow the steps in the Applet Wizard's multipage dialog. If you are following along, name the file MenuDemo.

2. You can do this step and the next one before or after creating the applet. If you already have menu templates from other projects—they can even be from another development system such as Visual C++—you can skip to step 4. To create a new menu template, again select *File|New,* but this time choose *Resource Template.* This displays a resource icon, which looks similar to a directory in the Windows Explorer. Click on this icon using the right mouse button, and select *Insert* from the popup menu.

3. Select the type of resource to insert into the template. For this demonstration, choose Menu and click OK. Design your menu by typing menu bar entries and items below them. To do this, double-click the item to change, or click the right mouse button on any item and select *Properties*. When you are done designing the template, go to the template window by pressing Alt+W and select it from the Studio's Window menu. Use *File\Save* to save the template as `Templ1.rct` (resource template file) in any directory. You might want to save all your templates in a directory such as `C:\MsDev\templates`.

4. Next, convert the menu template into a form that Java can use. Do this by selecting *Tools\Java Resource Wizard*. Click the Browse button and choose the template you created in steps 2 and 3, or you may select a template from another project. Click the Wizard's Next button and choose the `IDR_MENU1` class name, or another class, to create. Click the Finish button to create the source code file, `IDR_MENU1.java`. (You may have to move this file to your working directory.) You may rename the file, but I'll use the default name in this demonstration.

5. To make the new source code file a part of your applet project, select *Insert\Files into Project,* and choose the `IDR_MENU1.java` file created in step 4. Click the Add button to add this file to the applet project.

You have now completed most of the steps required to create a menu in a frame window. However, you'll also need to add programming to the applet source file to construct the necessary objects and display the menu in its separate frame. I'll explain these steps after the applet and menu listings.

Figure 16.4 shows the result of that code. Notice that the separate frame window has a menu bar under the window title. The menu bar has two entries, *File* and *Edit.* These are dummy menus. Selecting *File\Exit* closes the frame window, but the other menu items merely update the message in the frame window that tells you which menu item you selected. However, this demonstrates how to respond to menu events, which you will, of course, need to do in your own programs.

Listing 16.6, `MenuDemo.java`, and Listing 16.7, `IDR_MENU1.java`, show the source code for the MenuDemo applet on the CD-ROM. The main source is in `MenuDemo.java`. Resource Wizard created the second listing, `IDR_MENU1.java`. You need to study both listings to fully understand how menus are created and used in frame windows. You can use the code listed here also to construct menus from scratch if you do not want to use Studio 97 and the resource wizard, which might not be available on another Java development system. I'll fully explain both listings so that if you must move to another system, you'll have the necessary tools for creating menus.

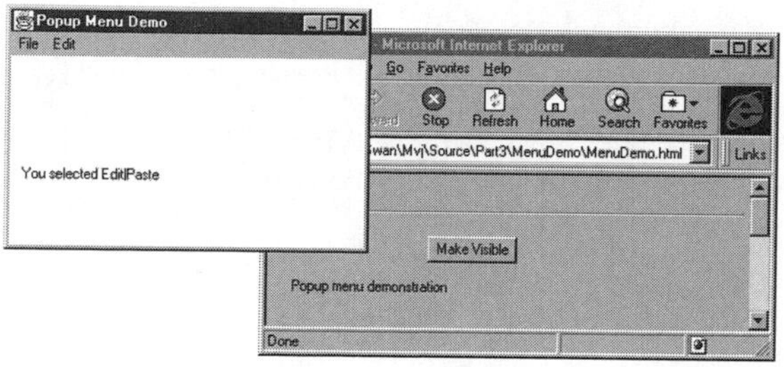

Figure 16.4.

The MenuDemo applet displays a separate Frame window with a title, border, and menu bar.

Listing 16.6. MenuDemo.java (Demonstrates menu creation and use for the MenuDemo project).

```java
import java.applet.*;
import java.awt.*;


//================================================================
// Separate Frame class with popup menu
//================================================================

// Extend the Frame class
class MenuFrame extends Frame {
 // Instance variable
 String message = null;

 // Constructor
 MenuFrame(String title) {
  super(title);
 }

 // Paint string message in frame window
 // This shows which menu item was last selected
 public void paint(Graphics g) {
  g.drawString(message, 10, 100);
 }

 // Handle events intended for this frame window
 public boolean handleEvent(Event evt) {
  if (evt.id == Event.WINDOW_DESTROY) {
   hide();  // "Close" window by hiding it
   return true;
  }
  return super.handleEvent(evt);
 }

 // Respond to menu selections
 public boolean action(Event evt, Object what) {
  if ("Open".equals(what)) {
   message = new String("You selected File¦Open");
  } else if ("Close".equals(what)) {
   message = new String("You selected File¦Close");
  } else if ("Exit".equals(what)) {
   message = new String("You selected File¦Exit");
   Event e = new Event(this, Event.WINDOW_DESTROY, null);
   deliverEvent(e);
  } else if ("Copy".equals(what)) {
```

continues

Listing 16.6. continued

```
  message = new String("You selected Edit¦Copy");
 } else if ("Cut".equals(what)) {
  message = new String("You selected Edit¦Cut");
 } else if ("Delete".equals(what)) {
  message = new String("You selected Edit¦Delete");
 } else if ("Paste".equals(what)) {
  message = new String("You selected Edit¦Paste");
 }
 repaint();
 return super.action(evt, what);
 }

}

//==============================================================
// MenuDemo applet class
//==============================================================

public class MenuDemo extends Applet {
 // Button for making hidden window visible
 Button makeVisibleButton;
 // Frame object of our extended class
 MenuFrame frame;

 // Information method
 public String getAppletInfo() {
  return "Name: MenuDemo\r\n" +
         "Author: Tom Swan\r\n" +
         "Created with Microsoft Visual J++ Version 1.0";
 }

 // Initialize applet and create frame window
 // with popup menu
 public void init() {
  // Size applet window
  resize(320, 240);
  // Construct Button and add to applet window
  makeVisibleButton = new Button("Make Visible");
  add(makeVisibleButton);
  // Construct separate frame window
  frame = new MenuFrame("Popup Menu Demo");
  frame.resize(300, 200);
  // Construct menu object and call CreateMenu()
  IDR_MENU1 menu = new IDR_MENU1(frame);
  menu.CreateMenu();
  // Show the frame window with its menu bar
  frame.show();
 }

 // Display information in applet window
 public void paint(Graphics g) {
  g.drawString("Popup menu demonstration", 10, 50);
 }

 // Handle applet's button selection
 public boolean handleEvent(Event evt) {
  if (evt.target.equals(makeVisibleButton)) {
   frame.show();      // Display frame if hidden
```

```
    frame.toFront();  // Bring to front if obscured (???)
    return true;
  }
  return super.handleEvent(evt);
}
}
```

As in the FrameEvents project, MenuDemo extends the `Frame` class. This class and its single instance variable are declared as

```
class MenuFrame extends Frame {
  String message = null;
...
}
```

The `String` variable holds the text that the frame window displays as a confirmation of the menu item you most recently selected. You don't have to declare this string in your own code. The `MenuFrame` constructor doesn't perform any new duties. I included it, however, because this is where you will insert any components such as `Buttons` and `Lists` in the frame window, using the techniques outlined for the FrameEvents project.

The critical code to study in the extended class is in the two methods, `handleEvent()` and `action()`. The first method responds to events such as `WINDOW_DESTROY`, which is intercepted here to close the frame window. Actually, as I explained in the preceding section, the code simply calls `hide()` so the window can be easily redisplayed—the window object is not actually destroyed.

To respond to menu selections, write an `action()` method using the techniques illustrated in the sample listing. When the user selects a menu item, the method receives an `Event` object and an argument equal to the menu item's string. It is a simple matter of comparing this string to determine which menu item was selected. For example, the statement

```
if ("Open".equals(what)) {
  message = new String("You selected File¦Open");
}
```

sets the `message` variable to the string shown if the user selects *File|Open*. Notice that the string argument equals only the menu item (`Open`, not `File|Open`), and therefore, all commands in all menus must be named uniquely.

As the extended `Frame` class shows, responding to menu selections is as simple as can be. The rest of the listing shows how to construct the frame window with its menu bar. Declare the `Frame` object as you normally do using a statement such as the following in your `Applet` class:

```
MenuFrame frame;
```

This uses the extended class just described. Construct the frame object in the applet's `init()` method using code such as

```
frame = new MenuFrame("Popup Menu Demo");
frame.resize(300, 200);
```

To attach a menu bar to the menu frame, construct the menu by passing the frame object as an argument, and then call the menu's CreateMenu() method. Finally, call the frame's show() method to display the window along with its menu. These statements show the required steps:

```
IDR_MENU1 menu = new IDR_MENU1(frame);
menu.CreateMenu();
frame.show();
```

The first statement creates an object of the IDR_MENU1 class, which is created by Resource Wizard to correspond to the chosen menu resource template. The second statement calls that class's CreateMenu() method, which is also programmed by the wizard. This method, as described in the next listing, constructs the individual menu items and adds them to the frame window.

Listing 16.7, IDR_MENU1.java, shows the source code that Resource Wizard created for the MenuDemo project. You do not have to modify this code, but you may do so to add additional menu items. However, it may be best to re-create the menu resource template, and then follow the numbered steps in this chapter to re-create the source.

Listing 16.7. IDR_MENU1.java (Menu source code created by Java Resource Wizard for the MenuDemo project).

```java
import java.awt.*;

public class IDR_MENU1 {
 Frame   m_Frame        = null;
 boolean m_fInitialized = false;

 // MenuBar definitions
 MenuBar mb;

 // Menu and Menu item definitions
 Menu m1;                  // File
 MenuItem ID_FILE_OPEN;    // Open
 MenuItem ID_FILE_CLOSE;   // Close
 MenuItem m4;              // Separator
 MenuItem ID_FILE_EXIT;    // Exit

 Menu m6;                  // Edit
 MenuItem ID_EDIT_CUT;     // Cut
 MenuItem ID_EDIT_COPY;    // Copy
 MenuItem ID_EDIT_PASTE;   // Paste

 // Constructor
 public IDR_MENU1 (Frame frame) {
  m_Frame = frame;
 }

 // Initialization.
 public boolean CreateMenu() {
  // Can only init controls once
  if (m_fInitialized || m_Frame == null)
   return false;

  // Create menubar and attach to the frame
```

```
mb = new MenuBar();
m_Frame.setMenuBar(mb);

// Create menus and menu items and assign to menubar

// Create File menu
m1 = new Menu("File");
mb.add(m1);
 ID_FILE_OPEN = new MenuItem("Open");
 m1.add(ID_FILE_OPEN);
 ID_FILE_CLOSE = new MenuItem("Close");
 m1.add(ID_FILE_CLOSE);
 m4 = new MenuItem("-");
 m1.add(m4);
 ID_FILE_EXIT = new MenuItem("Exit");
 m1.add(ID_FILE_EXIT);

// Create Edit menu
m6 = new Menu("Edit");
mb.add(m6);
 ID_EDIT_CUT = new MenuItem("Cut");
 m6.add(ID_EDIT_CUT);
 ID_EDIT_COPY = new MenuItem("Copy");
 m6.add(ID_EDIT_COPY);
 ID_EDIT_PASTE = new MenuItem("Paste");
 m6.add(ID_EDIT_PASTE);

 m_fInitialized = true;
 return true;
 }
}
```

Understanding the source created by Resource Wizard for menus is not essential to using them, but you will at least benefit from a cursory glance at the code. To create menus from scratch, though, you need to fully understand this listing's contents. A menu consists of several objects. In the sample listing, these are as follows:

- MenuBar mb: The menu bar itself is an object of the MenuBar class. The class is a menu component. The class implements the MenuContainer interface so that it can hold individual menu items. I'll discuss these elements in more detail when we examine the class declarations.

- Menu mn: Each pulldown menu in a menu bar is an object of the Menu class, and is named by the wizard *mn* where *n* is a integer number (m1 and m6, for example, in the sample listing). The Menu class is a menu item.

- MenuItem ID_FILE_OPEN: Each element in a pulldown menu is an object of the MenuItem class, which extends MenuComponent.

Examine the declarations in the sample IDR_MENU1 class from Menubar mb down to MenuItem ID_EDIT_PASTE. These declarations neatly form the entire menu bar and all of its components to match the design specified by the menu resource template.

389

The menu needs to keep track of its owning object, and to do this, the IDR_MENU1 class constructor saves the Frame object passed as an argument. The constructor performs no other duties. Because IDR_MENU1 is extended from Object, there's no need to call the super() class constructor here.

Most of the guts of the IDR_MENU1 class are in the CreateMenu() method, which as I explained, you must call after constructing the frame and menu objects. This method performs several essential tasks. It begins by checking whether the menu has already been initialized, returning false in that case with the code

```
if (m_fInitialized || m_Frame == null)
 return false;
```

This is not essential, but it is good programming. The next two statements construct the menu bar and attach it to the frame window:

```
mb = new MenuBar();
m_Frame.setMenuBar(mb);
```

Calling the Frame class's setMenuBar() method inserts the menu bar, which at this stage has no elements. To create the actual menus, you first need a Menu class object, constructed with a statement such as

```
m1 = new Menu("File");
```

This object must be added to the menu bar, so follow that statement with

```
mb.add(m1);
```

Do this for each of the pulldown menus you need. To each menu, add individual commands as objects of the MenuItem class. For example, the statements

```
ID_FILE_OPEN = new MenuItem("Open");
m1.add(ID_FILE_OPEN);
```

create a MenuItem labeled "Open" and add it to the menu object m1. This object was already added to the menu bar, and therefore, these steps are all that are needed to create menus of any complexity.

To create a separator line between menu items, construct the MenuItem object using a single hyphen as the string argument:

```
m4 = new MenuItem("-");
m1.add(m4);
```

You may alternatively call the Menu class's addSeparator() method to create a separator line.

Because the Menu class extends MenuItem, you may use all of these same techniques to create multilevel menus—provided, however, that the target operating system supports this feature. Simply construct the Menu object, add commands in the usual way, and then add the *menu* to the outer menu. For example, the following code fragment creates a menu command named *More* that, when selected, opens a nested menu with two more commands:

```
mlevel2 = new Menu("More");
L2_C1 = new MenuItem("Level2 Command1");
mlevel2.add(L2_C1);
L2_C2 = new MenuItem("Level2 Command2");
mlevel2.add(L2_C2);
m1.add(mlevel2);
```

If you want to try this, insert the preceding statements into the IDR_MENU1 class in the sample MenuDemo applet. Also declare the following Menu and MenuItem objects in the IDR_MENU1 class:

```
Menu mlevel2;
MenuItem L2_C1, L2_C2;
```

This approach to creating hierarchical menus works, but you might find it easier to use the menu designer in Studio 97 to create the menu and convert it using Resource Wizard.

Another potential technique not illustrated in the sample applet is to create a tear-off menu—known as a floating popup menu in Windows. I've had no success with these, but maybe your luck will be better. Create the menu using statements such as these:

```
m2 = new Menu("TearOff", true);
mb.add(m2);
item1 = new MenuItem("Item1");
m2.add(item1);
item2 = new MenuItem("Item2");
m2.add(item2);
```

If you want to try this, add the following declarations also to the IDR_MNENU1 class:

```
Menu m2;
MenuItem item1, item2;
```

These changes create the tear-off menu, but for the life of me, I cannot coax it away from its mother menu bar. Anyway, such elements as floating menus are so dependent on the target operating system, that I can't recommend this technique even if you can get it to work under Windows.

TIP

Specifying Alt menu selection keys by preceding menu item characters with an ampersand (&) is at best a dicey technique. You can try this, but it's impossible to say whether it will work on every system. Also, inserting tabs and other control characters may or may not produce the expected results. For best results, keep your applet menus as simple as possible. However, if you are certain your code will run under Windows, see Chapter 19, "Microsoft's Java SDK," under "Using Windows Menus," for advice on programming Alt menu keys, tabs, and other control characters.

The `MenuContainer` Class

In this and the next several sections, I'll list and explain all of the menu classes that you can use in constructing menu bars in frame windows. Because the classes are interrelated, I'll necessarily mention several classes before listing them—so you might have to read through all of the following sections a couple of times to understand how the classes fit together. First is the `MenuContainer` class, shown in Listing 16.8. This is an interface class that the `Menu` and `Menubar` classes implement.

Listing 16.8. The `MenuContainer` interface class.

```
public interface MenuContainer {
// Methods:
 Font getFont();
 boolean postEvent(Event evt);
 void remove(MenuComponent comp);
}
```

A class that implements the `MenuContainer` interface can hold `MenuComponent` and `MenuItem` objects. This does not make a `Menu` or `Menubar` a fully fledged container like one created of the `Container` class, but provides only the protocols necessary for pulldown menus. As you can see, the interface provides only the following three methods:

- `Font getFont()`: Returns the menu's current font or, if none is set, that of the parent `MenuContainer` object's.

- `boolean postEvent(Event evt)`: Posts a menu event. Applications usually don't call this method.

- `void remove(MenuComponent comp)`: Removes a menu component from a menu container.

The `MenuComponent` Class

The `MenuComponent` class in Listing 16.9 is abstract and cannot be instantiated. The class provides the basic methods required by menu items added to a menu container.

Listing 16.9. The `MenuComponent` class.

```
public abstract class MenuComponent {
// Public methods:
 public MenuContainer getParent();
 public MenuComponentPeer getPeer();
 public Font getFont();
 public void setFont(Font f);
 public void removeNotify();
 public boolean postEvent(Event evt);
 public String toString();
}
```

The abstract `MenuComponent` class provides the following methods. You may call these methods in reference to any object of the extended classes: `MenuItem`, `Menu`, `Menubar`, and `CheckboxMenuItem`. The `MenuComponent` methods are as follows:

- `MenuContainer getParent()`: Returns the parent `MenuContainer` object that owns this menu component. Usually, this will be a `Menu` or a `Menubar` object. (Hint: Use the `instanceof` keyword to determine which type of object this method returns.)

- `MenuComponentPeer getPeer()`: Returns the native peer component associated with this system-independent menu item. Because peer objects are necessarily system-dependent, you'll rarely if ever call this method.

- `Font getFont()`: Returns the font used by the menu component or, if no font is set, by its parent container.

- `void setFont(Font f)`: Changes the font used by this menu component. Each component may have a different font setting, though in most cases, the parent container will specify the font.

- `void removeNotify()`: Removes the peer object associated with this menu component. Applications should probably never call this method.

- `boolean postEvent(Event evt)`: Posts a menu event such as the selection of a menu item. Applications don't need to call this method.

- `String toString()`: Returns a string representation of the menu component, which includes the class name, the component name, and any assigned parameter. The parameter string is returned by the protected `paramString()` method, which is overridden by extended classes. For example, the `MenuItem` class's `paramString()` method returns a string in the form `Label=label`, where `label` is the menu item's text. The `MenuComponent`'s `toString()` method is useful for debugging. For example, you might use it to construct a `List` object of menu items for inspection.

The `MenuItem` Class

Each element in a menu is an object of the `MenuItem` class, shown in Listing 16.10. For example, a menu command labeled `"Open"` would be represented in the program as a `MenuItem` object that is added to an instance of the `Menu` class.

Listing 16.10. The `MenuItem` class.

```
public class MenuItem extends MenuComponent {
// Constructor:
 public MenuItem(String label);
// Public methods:
 public synchronized void addNotify();
 public String getLabel();
 public void setLabel(String label);
 public boolean isEnabled();
```

continues

Listing 16.10. continued

```
public void enable();
public void enable(boolean cond);
public void disable();
public String paramString();
}
```

There is only one way to construct a MenuItem object. Declare the object and initialize it by passing a string to the class constructor using statements such as

```
MenuItem ID_FILE_OPEN;
ID_FILE_OPEN = new MenuItem("Open");
```

You'll normally follow this sequence with a statement that adds the MenuItem object to an instance of the Menu class. For example, the sample MenuDemo project adds the preceding MenuItem to the *File* menu (m1) by executing this statement:

```
m1.add(ID_FILE_OPEN);
```

The MenuItem class provides several useful public methods. Remember that the Menu and CheckboxMenuItem classes extend MenuItem, so you can call the following methods for objects of those two classes as well:

- void addNotify(): As with similarly named methods scattered throughout the AWT package, this method attaches a MenuItem object to the operating system's native peer. It is through this attachment that the menu takes on its local characteristics, but there is rarely any reason for an application to call this method.

- String getLabel(): Returns the MenuItem's current label, which is the text displayed in the item and used to construct the object.

- void setLabel(String label): Changes the MenuItem's current label. This method is highly useful for creating dynamic menus that change according to other activities. For example, an *Open* command might be changed to *Close*—a neat and simple way to restrict users to opening one file at a time.

- boolean isEnabled(): Returns true if this menu item is enabled. Users can select only enabled menu items. Rather than maintain separate boolean flag variables for individual menu items, you might enable and disable the menu items and call isEnabled() to check their current states. In this way, the menu items themselves serve as their own on-and-off flags.

- void enable(): Enables this menu item. This method is highly useful for creating dynamic menus that disable and enable selected menu items according to other activities. For example, a menu item named *Save* might be enabled only if a change is made to a document. Newly created MenuItem objects are enabled by default.

- void enable(boolean cond): Changes the current enable-state of a MenuItem object. This is useful in programs that keep boolean flags that indicate whether a specific MenuItem should be enabled. Rather than test that flag using an if statement, and then calling `enable()` or `disable()`, you can more simply pass the flag to this overloaded form of the `enable()` method.

- `void disable()`: Disables this menu item, preventing its selection. Calling this method causes the menu item to be displayed in dim or mottled text that indicates it cannot currently be selected. (The exact look depends on the operating system.)

- `String paramString()`: Returns the current text of the `MenuItem` object in the form `Label=label`. This method is used primarily for debugging, often by way of the `MenuComponent.toString()` method. To obtain only the text of the `MenuItem` object, call `getLabel()` instead of `paramString()`. (I suspect this method was declared `public` by mistake, since there is little reason for an application to call it.)

The Menu Class

A popup menu is a container of the `Menu` class that typically holds one or more `MenuItem` objects. Because the `Menu` class is itself extended from `MenuItem`, a contained item can be another `Menu` object. As I explained, you can use this technique to create a multilevel, nested menu, as long as the target operating system provides this capability. Listing 16.11 shows the `Menu` class declaration.

Listing 16.11. The `Menu` class.

```
public class Menu extends MenuItem implements MenuContainer {
// Constructors:
 public Menu(String label);
 public Menu(String label, boolean tearOff);
// Public methods:
 public synchronized void addNotify();
 public synchronized void removeNotify();
 public boolean isTearOff();
 public int countItems();
 public MenuItem getItem(int index);
 public synchronized MenuItem add(MenuItem mi);
 public void add(String label);
 public void addSeparator();
 public synchronized void remove(int index);
 public synchronized void remove(MenuComponent item);
}
```

There are two ways to construct a `Menu` object. Usually, you'll simply pass it a string to be displayed in a menu bar. For example, the statement

```
m1 = new Menu("File")
```

taken from the MenuDemo project, creates a `Menu` object named `m1`, labeled *File* in the program's menu bar. Alternatively, you may pass a second argument equal to true to create a tear-off menu, using a statement such as

```
mfloat = new Menu("TearMe", true);
```

It is senseless to pass a `false` argument, because this simply creates a normal `Menu` object; however, you might pass a `boolean` variable to allow users to select which kind of menu to create. As I mentioned, I've had no luck creating tear-off menus, which depend entirely on the operating system having this capability. Although Windows does, tear-off menus still don't seem to work properly in Java applets.

The `Menu` class provides several methods you can call. Keep in mind also that `Menu` extends the `MenuItem` class, which extends from `MenuComponent`—so you may also call methods in those classes. In addition, `Menu` implements the `MenuContainer` interface described in this chapter. The public methods in the `Menu` class are as follows:

- `void addNotify()`: As I've mentioned several times, this method attaches a native operating system peer object to the `Menu`, and applications should have little if any reason to call `addNotify()`.

- `void removeNotify()`: This method detaches the menu from its peer. As with the preceding method, you should have little if any reason to call this method.

- `boolean isTearOff()`: Returns `true` if this menu can be torn away from its mother menu bar. In theory, such a menu can remain on screen and possibly be moved as though it were a separate window.

- `int countItems()`: This returns the number of `MenuItem` objects held by the `Menu` container. (An item, remember, can also be an object of the `Menu` class, which extends from `MenuItem`.)

- `MenuItem getItem(int index)`: Returns the `MenuItem` object, which could also be an object of the `Menu` class, having the specified index. The first item in a menu has the index zero.

- `MenuItem add(MenuItem mi)`: Adds a new `MenuItem` object to the bottom of the menu. For reasons that are not entirely clear (but possibly for debugging purposes), this method returns the same object passed as an argument. `MenuItems` are stored internally in a `Menu` object in a `Vector` container. Calling `add()` uses `Vector.addElement()` to add the new item to the menu, a fact that might be useful for debugging or in custom menu creation software. It is interesting to note that calling `add()` first *removes* the specified item from the menu so that no item can accidentally be added twice (see the `remove()` method). This observation leads to a cute trick—calling `add()` for any existing menu item moves it to the end of its popup menu. I've yet to find a practical use for this side effect, but perhaps you will.

- `void add(String label)`: Adds a new `MenuItem` object that is created using the specified `String label`. Use this form of `add()` to create new `MenuItems` if you do not want to save references to those items. Use the former method, as in the `MenuDemo` project, if you construct `MenuItems` separately and maintain references to them. You cannot use this string-argument form of `add()` to create nested menus; to do that, construct the `Menu` object separately and pass it to the preceding `add()` method.

- **void addSeparator()**: Adds a separator line to the bottom of the menu. This is handy for segmenting lengthy menus, but don't overdo it—too many separators are perhaps more confusing than too few. Alternatively, you may pass the string "-" (a single hyphen in quotes) to the add() method to create a separator, which is all that addSeparator() does.

- **void remove(int index)**: Removes the MenuItem or Menu object at the specified index. This method would be highly useful in constructing dynamic menus that add new commands according to external circumstances except for a glaring omission in the Menu class—there is no corresponding insert() method! Although you can remove a menu item from the middle of a menu, you can add new ones only at the end. (Tip: An extended class might manipulate the internal Vector object to insert menu items at random locations.)

- **void remove(MenuComponent item)**: Removes the specified MenuComponent (which is probably an object of the Menu or MenuItem classes). No error occurs if the component doesn't exist. Adding new menu items internally calls remove() so that no item can accidentally be added twice to a menu.

The MenuBar Class

As you no doubt expect, the MenuBar class represents the menu bar displayed in a Frame window under its title. Individual labels in the menu bar are represented programmatically as objects of the Menu class, which contain individual MenuItem (or Menu) elements. The MenuBar class extends MenuComponent (see its description in this chapter), and also implements MenuContainer. Listing 16.12 shows the MenuBar class declaration.

Listing 16.12. The MenuBar class.

```
public class MenuBar extends MenuComponent implements MenuContainer {
// Constructor:
 public MenuBar();
// Public methods:
 public synchronized void addNotify();
 public void removeNotify();
 public Menu getHelpMenu();
 public synchronized void setHelpMenu(Menu m);
 public synchronized Menu add(Menu m);
 public synchronized void remove(int index);
 public synchronized void remove(MenuComponent m);
 public int countMenus();
 public Menu getMenu(int i);
}
```

There is only one way to construct a MenuBar object. Declare the object and call the MenuBar() constructor with no parameters, using statements such as

```
MenuBar mb;
mb = new MenuBar();
```

This sequence, however, is only part of the complete story for creating and using a menu bar. You will normally follow the preceding code with

```
m_Frame.setMenuBar(mb);
```

which attaches the MenuBar object to a Frame window. You may make this attachment at any time, but usually you'll perform the preceding three steps together. After creating the MenuBar object and adding it to a Frame window, you can insert popup menus into the bar with statements such as

```
m1 = new Menu("File");
mb.add(m1);
```

The MenuBar class provides the following public methods. Because the class extends MenuComponent and also implements the MenuContainer interface, you'll want to also examine those two classes for additional methods you can call. MenuBar's public methods are as follows:

- void addNotify(): As with similarly named methods scattered throughout the AWT package, this method attaches a MenuBar object to the operating system's native peer. There is rarely any good reason for an application to call this method.

- void removeNotify(): This detaches the MenuBar object from its native peer. Calling removeNotify() also detaches all menus from their peers (which detaches the individual menu items as well). If you are writing system software, or if you are doing your own menu classes, you can call this method to detach an entire menu bar and all its elements. Applications, however, should have no reason to call this method.

- Menu getHelpMenu(): Returns the Menu object that is currently designated as the help menu (see the next method). If there is no such menu, getHelpMenu() returns null.

- void setHelpMenu(Menu m): Sets the current help menu. This changes an internal helpMenu flag to true for the help Menu-class object, which is maintained as an instance variable in MenuBar. The flag is passed to the peer, which might use it to display the help menu differently, or perhaps in a different location on the menu bar, depending on the native operating system's characteristics. To take advantage of these features, call setHelpMenu() for your menu's Help Menu object. This might, however, do absolutely nothing if the operating system does not treat help menus differently from others.

- Menu add(Menu m): Adds a new Menu object to the menu bar. Notice that this method returns the same object passed as an argument, which might be useful for debugging but otherwise seems to have little practical value. Internally, Menu objects are stored in the MenuBar class in an object of the Vector class, and are added by calling that class's addElement() method. Unlike the Menu class's add() methods, however, Menubar.add() does *not* first remove the Menu argument object, an unfortunate inconsistency in Java's menu-class design. For this reason, you must take care not to add the same Menu object to a MenuBar twice by accident, an error the class does nothing to prevent.

- void remove(int index): Removes the specified Menu item from the menu bar. Menus are numbered from left to right starting with zero.

- **void remove(MenuComponent m):** Removes the specified `MenuComponent` object (usually a `Menu` object) from the menu bar. Use this overloaded form of `remove()` if your code maintains a reference to its popup menus; otherwise, use the preceding indexed method.

- **int countMenus():** Returns the number of `Menu` objects in this `MenuBar`. This equals the internal `Vector`'s `size()` return value.

- **Menu getMenu(int i):** Returns the `Menu` item at the specified index. Menus are numbered from left to right starting with zero.

The `CheckboxMenuItem` Class

The AWT package provides one additional menu class, which is extended from `MenuItem`. Use the `CheckboxMenuItem` class shown in Listing 16.13 to create a menu item that, when selected, displays a check or other mark. This is useful for creating menu items that operate as toggles—selecting a checked item removes the mark. The actual shape displayed depends entirely on the target operating system.

> **NOTE**
>
> This note comes under the heading of *personal gripe,* but I've never been overly fond of check mark menu items because they force me to open menus twice in succession just to see which items are checked. Rather than have numerous check mark menu items, I prefer my programs to offer radio buttons that remain visible, or that I can display by opening a dialog box.

Listing 16.13. The `CheckboxMenuItem` class.

```
public class CheckboxMenuItem extends MenuItem {
// Constructor:
 public CheckboxMenuItem(String label);
// Public methods:
 public synchronized void addNotify();
 public boolean getState();
 public void setState(boolean t);
 public String paramString();
}
```

Create a `CheckboxMenuItem` object as you do a `MenuItem`. (Note that the b in box is lowercase.) For example, to add a check mark menu item to the `MenuDemo` project in this chapter, declare a `CheckboxMenuItem` object in the `IDR_MENU1` class with the following statement:

```
CheckboxMenuItem check_item;
```

To create the menu item, add the following statements to method `CreateMenu()`:

```
check_item = new CheckboxMenuItem("Check me");
m6.add(check_item);
```

399

This adds a check mark menu item, labeled "Check me", to the sample program's *Edit* menu. Select that item; then reopen the menu, and you'll see a check mark to its left. Select it again to remove the check mark.

The CheckboxMenuItem class provides the following public methods. Because the class extends from MenuItem, which extends from MenuComponent, you may also call methods in those two classes. The CheckboxMenuItem methods are as follows:

- void addNotify(): Need I say again that you will have little if any reason to call this method? It attaches the menu item to its native peer object, the class of which depends entirely on the operating system.

- boolean getState(): This method returns true if the menu item is currently checked. It returns false if the item is not checked.

- void setState(boolean t): Changes the state of the CheckboxMenuItem object, which is unchecked by default. Pass true to this method to add a check mark to the menu item. Pass false to remove a check mark. You might use this method to initialize menu items that you want users to see as checked when they first open a menu.

- String paramString(): This method overrides the method of the same name inherited from the MenuItem class. Call paramString() to obtain a string in the form "Label=*label*,state=*state*" where *label* is the menu item's text, and *state* is true or false, depending on whether the menu item is checked. The method is mostly useful for debugging. Call the inherited getLabel() method instead to obtain only the CheckboxMenuItem object's menu text.

> **WARNING**
>
> You might be tempted to use the preceding information to write an applet that manipulates a Web browser's menus. This is theoretically possible in browsers such as HotJava, which are written in Java and, therefore, use the same menu objects described in this chapter. However, crawl with utmost care onto this highly dangerous branch of Java programming. Most other browsers probably won't allow you to access their menus, so the attempt is probably futile. If you try it, I wish you lots of luck. You'll need it.

Dialogs

Dialogs in Java applets are similar to those in most Windows programs, including of course, Visual J++. As you probably know, a dialog is a specialized window with various control objects typically used for selecting options and configuring program settings. Dialogs also make good data-entry screens, and they are perfect for prompting users to supply bits of information that might be needed in response to clicking a button, for example, or selecting a menu item.

Unfortunately, although Java provides the `Dialog` class specifically for creating dialogs, the class falls short of the requirements needed for using dialogs effectively. For example, there is no clearly defined way for a dialog to communicate with its parent applet, nor is there any method for transferring control data to and from the program's variables. Developer Studio makes up for some of these shortcomings in its Java Resource Wizard and dialog resource template editor, which make creating dialogs easier than writing the code from scratch. I'll add some additional techniques—along with a data-transfer class—that take up the rest of the slack and will help you create practical dialogs and controls for your Web page applets.

Introducing Dialogs

On a technical level, a Java dialog is simply a frame window with control objects. It can have a menu bar, although this is not traditional in dialog design. You can create dialogs the hard way—by typing the code from scratch. However, I highly recommend using Developer Studio's Resource Template editor to create all of your dialogs. This way, you can share your templates with other development systems. For example, by using the techniques described here, you can use the same dialog template in Visual C++ and Visual J++ projects.

> **NOTE**
>
> The dialog techniques described here do not use Java's `Dialog` class. Later in this chapter, I'll describe that class and show how to use it.

Follow these numbered steps to create a dialog template, and then convert it into Java source code:

1. Refer to the numbered steps under the "Introducing Menus" heading in this chapter for creating a menu, but choose *Dialog* as the type of resource to create in the original step 2. Also create a sample applet named DialogDemo using Applet Wizard. For reference, the finished code files are on the CD-ROM in the `Part3\DialogDemo` directory.

2. After laying out your dialog's controls, save it as a template file. Figure 16.5 shows a sample dialog in construction; if you want to follow along with these steps, make your dialog resemble the figure. After saving the resource template, select *Tools\Java Resource Wizard* to convert the template to Java source code files.

3. You now have two new files in the applet's directory. For the DialogDemo project, which I'll describe in a moment, the wizard created files `DialogLayout.java` and `IDD_DIALOG1.java`. (You can name them something else if you prefer when prompted by the wizard.) The first file provides a new layout class suitable for constructing separate dialog frame windows that contain one or more component objects. The second is the class to use for creating the frame window.

Figure 16.5.

Demonstration dialog in construction using Developer Studio's resource-template editor.

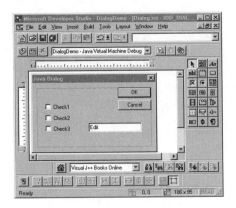

The preceding steps do not complete the process of creating a useable dialog. You still need to create the applet code, construct the dialog frame window, and figure out a way to transfer control data to and from your applet and the frame's components. The DialogDemo project that follows demonstrates how to do all of this, and you can use the code as a shell for creating your own dialogs.

Figure 16.6 shows the finished dialog in action, along with its parent applet running in Internet Explorer. The sample dialog has three check boxes, two buttons, and one text-entry field—enough components to demonstrate the basic techniques for handling dialog control data. When you run the sample program, click the dialog's OK button to display in the applet window the current control values. This shows how a dialog can communicate with its parent applet—an essential ingredient in using dialogs effectively, but one that as you will see requires some hocus-pocus to accomplish.

Figure 16.6.

The demonstration dialog displayed by an applet, which shows the current control values.

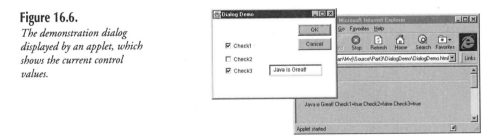

The next two listings show the sample applet's source code and the class that are used to create the dialog's controls. A third listing, which is not printed here, provides a layout class used by the dialog window. You can safely ignore the contents of this listing and its layout class, which do not provide any methods useful to your applet's code. (The file is on the CD-ROM, however, and is created using the preceding numbered steps.)

The first source code file—Listing 16.14, IDD_DIALOG1.java—declares and implements the IDD_DIALOG1 class created by Studio 97's Java Resource Wizard. This class is extended from

Object and not, as you might expect, from the Dialog class. The generated class is used as an organizer for the dialog's control components, which are named according to the identifiers in the resource template. I have retained all default identifiers to make it easier for you to re-create the source files for practice. You will probably want to use other names, however, and in particular, not use all uppercase text as in the generated code.

Listing 16.14. `IDD_DIALOG1.java` (Implements class `IDD_DIALOG1`).

```
import java.awt.*;
import DialogLayout;

public class IDD_DIALOG1 {
 Container    m_Parent       = null;
 boolean      m_fInitialized = false;
 DialogLayout m_Layout;

 // Control definitions
 Button       IDOK;
 Button       IDCANCEL;
 Checkbox     IDC_CHECK1;
 Checkbox     IDC_CHECK2;
 Checkbox     IDC_CHECK3;
 TextField    IDC_EDIT1;

 // Constructor
 public IDD_DIALOG1 (Container parent) {
 m_Parent = parent;
 }

 // Initialization.
 public boolean CreateControls()
 {
 // CreateControls should be called only once
 if (m_fInitialized || m_Parent == null)
  return false;

 // m_Parent must be extended from the Container class
 if (!(m_Parent instanceof Container))
  return false;

 // Since a given font may not be supported across all
 // platforms, it is safe to modify only the size of the
 // font, not the typeface.
 Font OldFnt = m_Parent.getFont();
 if (OldFnt != null) {
  // Note: I changed the following font size from 8 to 12!
  Font NewFnt = new Font(OldFnt.getName(),
   OldFnt.getStyle(), 12);
  m_Parent.setFont(NewFnt);
 }

 // All position and sizes are in dialog logical units,
 // so we use a DialogLayout as our layout manager.
 m_Layout = new DialogLayout(m_Parent, 186, 95);
```

continues

403

Listing 16.14. continued

```
  m_Parent.setLayout(m_Layout);
  m_Parent.addNotify();

  Dimension size   = m_Layout.getDialogSize();
  Insets    insets = m_Parent.insets();

  m_Parent.resize(insets.left +
   size.width  + insets.right,
   insets.top  + size.height + insets.bottom);

  // Control creation
  IDOK = new Button ("OK");
  m_Parent.add(IDOK);
  m_Layout.setShape(IDOK, 129, 7, 50, 14);

  IDCANCEL = new Button ("Cancel");
  m_Parent.add(IDCANCEL);
  m_Layout.setShape(IDCANCEL, 129, 24, 50, 14);

  IDC_CHECK1 = new Checkbox ("Check1");
  m_Parent.add(IDC_CHECK1);
  m_Layout.setShape(IDC_CHECK1, 19, 28, 41, 10);

  IDC_CHECK2 = new Checkbox ("Check2");
  m_Parent.add(IDC_CHECK2);
  m_Layout.setShape(IDC_CHECK2, 19, 44, 41, 10);

  IDC_CHECK3 = new Checkbox ("Check3");
  m_Parent.add(IDC_CHECK3);
  m_Layout.setShape(IDC_CHECK3, 19, 58, 41, 10);

  IDC_EDIT1 = new TextField ("");
  m_Parent.add(IDC_EDIT1);
  m_Layout.setShape(IDC_EDIT1, 84, 55, 81, 14);

  m_fInitialized = true;
  return true;
 }
}
```

The IDD_DIALOG1 class imports the java.awt package and the DialogLayout class, which the Resource Wizard also creates. The three variables

```
Container    m_Parent      = null;
boolean      m_fInitialized = false;
DialogLayout m_Layout;
```

define the dialog's parent container (usually a Frame window), a boolean flag that indicates whether the dialog object has been initialized, and an object of the DialogLayout class. Each control is also declared as an instance variable in the IDD_DIALOG1 class. The full set of controls are

```
Button      IDOK;
Button      IDCANCEL;
Checkbox    IDC_CHECK1;
Checkbox    IDC_CHECK2;
```

```
Checkbox        IDC_CHECK3;
TextField       IDC_EDIT1;
```

The IDD_DIALOG1 class constructor merely saves the parent Container object passed as an argument. This object is used to lay out the controls, and also to attach them to their native operating system peers—actions that take place in the all-important CreateControls() method. The applet calls this method to construct the dialog's components.

CreateControls() begins with some code that checks whether the object has already been initialized, and whether the parent that owns this object is a Container or an extended class. The method returns false if neither of these conditions is satisfied. If, however, you are the careful type, you don't have to check this return value.

After performing its initial tests, the method selects a font by interrogating the parent Container. For this reason, you will normally want to select a font for the parent before calling CreateControls(). For reasons not entirely clear, however, the generated code changes the font size to 8 points, which is too small for most systems. I therefore changed this setting to 12 points in the statement

```
Font NewFnt = new Font(OldFnt.getName(),
 OldFnt.getStyle(), 12);
```

If your selected font size seems to be ignored, try making a similar change in your dialog's generated file. (All of this could stand some improvement in the Wizard-generated code.)

The next several statements create and configure a DialogLayout object. The statements

```
m_Layout = new DialogLayout(m_Parent, 186, 95);
m_Parent.setLayout(m_Layout);
m_Parent.addNotify();
```

create the DialogLayout object and specify its window size. This places the control objects within a defined area according to their relative positions, in dialog units, from the resource template. The second and third statements set the parent Container's layout to the DialogLayout object, and call addNotify() to attach the parent's peers. This is one of the rare instances where an applet calls addNotify(). Because we are doing our own layout, however, this step is necessary.

The parent Container is also sized by the next statements:

```
Dimension size   = m_Layout.getDialogSize();
Insets     insets = m_Parent.insets();
m_Parent.resize(insets.left +
 size.width  + insets.right,
 insets.top  + size.height + insets.bottom);
```

This code is the reason that the Applet Wizard inserts a comment telling you not to call resize() when calling CreateControls(). The statements shown here interrogate both the layout and Container for size information, and then resize the parent window accordingly.

Finally in CreateControls() is the code that creates each component. This is done in the usual way with the addition of calling the layout object's setShape() method. For example, these three statements create the sample dialog's OK button:

```
IDOK = new Button ("OK");
m_Parent.add(IDOK);
m_Layout.setShape(IDOK, 129, 7, 50, 14);
```

The Button object is added to the parent Container. The layout's setShape() method sizes the component in dialog units according to the object's size in the resource template.

Listing 16.15, DialogDemo.java, demonstrates how to use the IDD_DIALOG1 class to create a dialog frame window. The listing also shows how to transfer control data to and from an applet and dialog, and also shows how a dialog can communicate with the applet—essential techniques that are not provided by the Wizards.

Listing 16.15. DialogDemo.java (Demonstrates how to create a dialog).

```
import java.applet.*;
import java.awt.*;
import IDD_DIALOG1;

//===========================================================
// DataClass class (holds copy of dialog control values)
//===========================================================

class DataClass {
 // Instance variables for each dialog control
 boolean check1Value;   // Value of Checkbox 1
 boolean check2Value;   // Value of Checkbox 2
 boolean check3Value;   // Value of Checkbox 3
 String edit1Value;     // Value of TextField 1

 // Constructor initializes instance variables
 DataClass(boolean check1, boolean check2, boolean check3,
  String edit1)
 {
  check1Value = check1;  // Initialize instance variables
  check2Value = check2;  // to the arguments passed to
  check3Value = check3;  // the constructor.
  edit1Value  = edit1;
 }

 // Return string representation of data for display
 // This isn't required, but is used by the demonstration
 // to display the dialog control values in the
 // applet's window.
 public String toString() {
  return new String(edit1Value + " " +
   "Check1=" + check1Value + " " +
   "Check2=" + check2Value + " " +
   "Check3=" + check3Value);
 }
}

//===========================================================
// DialogFrame class (forms a window for the dialog)
//===========================================================

class DialogFrame extends Frame {
```

```java
// Instance variables
private IDD_DIALOG1 dialogBox;  // The dialog object
private Component parent;       // Dialog's parent
private DataClass dialogData;   // Copy of dialog's data

// Constructor
DialogFrame(Component parent, String title) {
 super(title);  // Call ancestor method first
 this.parent = parent;  // Save container parent
 // Select font so that this parent's getFont() method
 // will return a known entity. However, you must also
 // set the font size in the CreateControls() method
 // in the dialog source file (IDD_DIALOG1.java here).
 setFont(new Font("Arial", Font.PLAIN, 12));
 dialogBox = new IDD_DIALOG1(this);  // Create dialog
 dialogBox.CreateControls();  // Also resizes window
 dialogData = getData();      // Initialize data object
 show();  // Display our frame and dialog's controls
}

// Respond to dialog events
public boolean action(Event evt, Object what) {
 if (evt.target instanceof Button) {
  if ("OK".equals(what)) {  // If it's the OK button...
   dialogData = getData();  // Get control values
   parent.repaint();        // Update applet display
   // hide();   // Enable this to hide dialog box
   return true; // We handled the event
  }
 }
 return super.action(evt, what);  // Other events
}

// Return dialog data in raw form
// You'll always want a method like this to get
// the dialog control values.
public DataClass getData() {
 boolean check1 = dialogBox.IDC_CHECK1.getState();
 boolean check2 = dialogBox.IDC_CHECK2.getState();
 boolean check3 = dialogBox.IDC_CHECK3.getState();
 String edit1   = dialogBox.IDC_EDIT1.getText();
 DataClass data =
  new DataClass(check1, check2, check3, edit1);
 return data;
}

// Return string representation of data
// This method is designed to never return null.
// It is not necessary to program this method, which
// is used by the demonstration to display the
// dialog control values in the applet window.
public String toString() {
 dialogData = getData();   // Make sure data is current
 if (dialogData == null)
  return "";
 else
  return dialogData.toString();
}
```

continues

Listing 16.15. continued

```
}

//================================================================
// Applet class (constructs dialog and shows values)
//================================================================

public class DialogDemo extends Applet {

 // Frame object for holding our dialog
 DialogFrame theFrame = null;

 public void init() {
  // When using the techniques demonstrated here, ignore
  // the message from the Applet Wizard about deleting
  // this statement. Our own DialogFrame class calls
  // the createControls() method mentioned in the
  // Wizard's note that normally appears here.
  resize(320, 240);
  // Construct the frame using our DialogFrame class
  // This initializes and displays the dialog box
  // along with all of its controls!
  theFrame = new DialogFrame(this, "Dialog Demo");
 }

 // Display the values of the dialog's controls
 public void paint(Graphics g) {
   g.drawString(theFrame.toString(), 10, 40);
 }
}
```

Understand the programming in DialogDemo.java, and you'll be well on your way to creating your own applet dialogs. The key feature is a class, named DataClass (you can call it something else), which provides the basis for transferring control data between the dialog and the applet. The class declares one instance variable for each of the dialog's controls for which you need to transfer data:

```
boolean check1Value;
boolean check2Value;
boolean check3Value;
String edit1Value;
```

There are no instance variables for objects such as Buttons, which have no stored values. The DataClass constructor, which is declared as

```
DataClass(boolean check1, boolean check2, boolean check3,
 String edit1)
```

initializes the instance variables. For your own dialogs, modify this class to declare instance variables for each control, and modify the constructor to initialize the variables.

The sample DataClass declaration also provides a toString() method, which is not required. The demonstration program uses this method to echo the control values in the applet window. You do not need to program a similar method for your own dialogs.

Next in the `DialogDemo.java` file is the program's `Frame` class, which is declared along with three instance variables as follows:

```
class DialogFrame extends Frame {
 private IDD_DIALOG1 dialogBox;
 private Component parent;
 private DataClass dialogData;
...
}
```

This class creates the frame window that will hold the dialog's component controls. The first variable, `dialogBox`, is an object of the `IDD_DIALOG1` class created by the Java Resource Wizard. The second variable, `parent`, refers to the applet that owns the frame window, and provides the means for the dialog to communicate with its parent. Because the `Applet` class is extended from `Component` (among other classes), I declared this variable as a `Component`, which is the more general case—but you could just as well declare it as an `Applet` object. The third instance variable in our `Frame` class, `dialogData`, is an object of the `DataClass` just described. This object holds a copy of each of the dialog's control values.

The `DialogFrame` class constructor must perform several critical maneuvers to initialize the frame window object. Two statements begin the constructor:

```
super(title);
this.parent = parent;
```

The first calls the `Frame` constructor, passing the dialog's specified window title. The second saves the parent object, which as I mentioned is probably the applet that created the frame. Next, you must specify a font to use for the control labels. Do this with a statement such as

```
setFont(new Font("Arial", Font.PLAIN, 12));
```

However, as I mentioned, because of the way Resource Wizard generates the `IDD_DIALOG1` class code, you might also have to modify that code to set the font size—an annoyance that you might consider eliminating. (We'll just have to live with this oddity until, and if, the Wizard is upgraded.) Next, create the `IDD_DIALOG1` class object and initialize its controls by calling `CreateControls()`, using these statements:

```
dialogBox = new IDD_DIALOG1(this);
dialogBox.CreateControls();
```

At this stage, the initialization process is nearly complete. However, to provide the means for transferring control data to and from the applet, it is necessary also to synchronize the `DataClass` object to match the control values. This is done with the following statement:

```
dialogData = getData();
```

Now, `dialogData` contains instance variables with values that match each of the dialog's controls. It is like a box that the program can use to transfer the control values *en masse* to and from the applet. Finally, the dialog frame window is ready for prime time, and is displayed by calling `show()`.

You will undoubtedly need to respond to various events in your dialog's frame window. For this, you may use the techniques in Chapter 15. To demonstrate, the sample class programs an `action()` method, which responds to selecting the dialog's OK button. This also shows how the dialog communicates with its parent applet. First, the method determines which button was selected, and it then copies the control values to the `DataClass` object with this statement:

```
dialogData = getData();
```

This is the same statement used to initialize the object. To tell the applet to echo the control values, the `action()` method executes the statement

```
parent.repaint();
```

which is made possible by saving a reference to the parent in the `DialogFrame` constructor. Calling the parent's `repaint()` method causes AWT to call its `paint()` method, thus updating the string in the sample applet's window. You can use similar code to call other methods in the applet in response to the user selecting dialog controls.

The next method in the `DialogFrame` class, `getData()`, shows how to obtain the dialog's individual control values. For example, the statement

```
boolean check1 = dialogBox.IDC_CHECK1.getState();
```

gets the current state of the dialog's first check box control, saving the value in a `boolean` variable. In your own code, do this for each of the control objects in the class created by Resource Wizard (`IDD_DIALOG1`, in this example). Use these values to construct a `DataClass` object with a statement such as

```
DataClass data =
 new DataClass(check1, check2, check3, edit1);
```

and then return that object as `getData()`'s return value. You now have a handy method for obtaining all of the dialog's current control values. This is also much cleaner than scattering statements all over an applet for accessing individual controls.

The sample project's `DialogFrame` class also provides a `toString()` method, which the applet calls to display the string that echoes the dialog's control values. You don't need to program a similar method in your own dialogs, but it might be useful for debugging purposes.

Finally, in the `DialogDemo.java` source file we come to the `Applet` class itself. Because the other classes perform much of the demonstration's work, this part of the program is the simplest. The `DialogDemo` class declares an object of the `DialogFrame` class to represent the frame window:

```
DialogFrame theFrame = null;
```

The applet constructor sizes its window in the usual way, and then constructs the `DialogFrame` object using these statements:

```
resize(320, 240);
theFrame = new DialogFrame(this, "Dialog Demo");
```

Ignore the comment that the Wizard inserts here telling you not to call `resize()` if you are calling `CreateControls()`. Whoever wrote this comment apparently did not understand that this use of `resize()` is for the *applet's* window, not for the separate frame that displays the dialog. It is correct not to call `resize()` for the frame because `CreateControls()` does this to make the dialog's size match the resource template. But this has nothing to do with the applet's window, and you may call `resize()` for the applet as you normally do, despite what the comment suggests.

The applet echoes the dialog's control values by executing this statement in method `paint()`:

```
g.drawString(theFrame.toString(), 10, 40);
```

Be sure to understand the process that leads up to this code; it is essential to your understanding of how a dialog can communicate with its applet. As you may recall, when you click the dialog's OK button, its `action()` menu calls the parent's `repaint()` method. Because that parent is the applet, this action causes `paint()` to execute the preceding statement, which calls the frame object's `toString()` method. At this point, it is essential that the `DataClass` object hold an updated copy of each of the dialog's control values.

> **NOTE**
>
> The preceding techniques and code represent only one way to create dialog frame windows. You are free to invent other ways to insert and use controls in frames, and you are equally at liberty to call the result a *dialog*. I tried to examine techniques and code that illustrate the basic steps for using the code generated by the Java Resource Wizard, but you will undoubtedly want to tailor the generated statements to better suit your exact needs. By no means does the preceding code represent the only way to create a Java dialog!

The `Dialog` Class

Strangely, dialogs created using Visual J++ resource editors and Wizards do not use Java's `Dialog` class. If you have been following along up to this point, you probably realize by now that the dialog windows created using the techniques in the preceding sections are actually separate windows with control components. They *look* like dialogs, but they are technically just windows. In particular, the pseudo-dialogs we've examined so far lack several characteristics of a true dialog window, including the following:

- The capability of being modal or modeless.
- The capability of preventing users from resizing and minimizing the window.
- The restriction against having a menu bar.
- The capability of automatically tracking along with the parent window.
- The capability of painting the dialog window background the same as its parent.

Dialogs differ from common frame windows mostly in their capability to be modal or modeless. A *modal dialog* retains the input focus until closed. A *modeless dialog* behaves like any other window, and users can switch between the dialog and the applet or other windows at will.

True dialog windows also typically prevent users from changing the windows' sizes. This results in a cleaner display with controls positioned just as you want them. Because all controls are displayed in the dialog window, there's no good reason for users to zoom a true dialog window to full screen, and it is usually best to prevent this.

True dialogs cannot have menu bars. They also tag along with their parent windows. This means users cannot minimize a true dialog window, and they can switch to other applications, but not between a modal dialog and its applet window. Minimizing the parent window also minimizes the dialog, which typically does not receive a separate icon on the desktop display.

Finally, a true dialog window's background is painted the same as its parent window. This is, of course, not a critical feature, but it might indicate to users that a dialog belongs to another parent window.

To create true dialogs for applets using Java requires some undocumented techniques that I have developed largely through experimentation. These are the basic steps:

1. Locate the applet's parent frame window.
2. Create an instance of the `Dialog` class using the frame from step 1.
3. Specify the dialog window's size.
4. Call the dialog's `show()` method to make it visible.

For example, create a new applet using the Applet Wizard (or copy any of the applet demonstration listings in Part III of this book), and add the programming in Listing 16.16 to method `init()`. This same programming can be used in other places—in response to users selecting a menu command, for instance, or clicking a button. The listing is purely illustrative and is not on the CD-ROM. I'll show more complete code later in this chapter in listing `TrueDialog.java`. Figure 16.7 shows the true dialog window, which has only a close button but no minimize or maximize buttons.

Figure 16.7.
A true dialog window displayed by the code in Listing 16.16.

Listing 16.16. Steps to create a true dialog (add to an applet's `init()` method).

```
// Locate parent Frame
Component c = this;
Frame f = null;
while (f == null) {
 c = c.getParent();
 if (c instanceof Frame)
  f = (Frame)c;
}
// Construct and show dialog window
Dialog diag = new Dialog(f, "Test Dialog", false);
diag.resize(200, 100);
diag.show();
```

The first task is to locate the parent's `Frame` object, which all applets possess. This is done by a `while` loop that repeatedly calls the applet's `getParent()` method. Eventually, the loop tracks down the parent `Frame` object that encases the applet and creates its visible window.

Using the parent `Frame` object, next create an instance of the `Dialog` class. The first argument passed to this class's constructor is the parent frame. The second argument is a string to display in the dialog title bar. The third argument is `false` to create a modeless dialog. You can change this argument to `true` to create a modal dialog, but first read the following warning.

> **WARNING**
>
> Because the `Dialog` class does not provide any means to close true dialog windows, if you create a modal window using the techniques described here, extraordinary measures will be needed to regain control of your browser. For example, when I changed `false` to `true` in Listing 16.16 to create a modal dialog in Windows 95, I could close my browser only by pressing Ctrl+Alt+Del and shutting down the Internet Explorer task. In the upcoming Listing 16.18, `TrueDialog.java`, I'll show you how to create a modal dialog that users can properly close—but for now, if you play around with the techniques in this section, be aware that you can easily lock up your browser.

After creating the `Dialog` object, two steps are required to display its window. First, call `resize()` as shown to specify the window's size. If you don't do this, the dialog window has no size, and like a black hole, it cannot be seen. Obviously, this will cause you some problems, so always remember to call `resize()`. Finally, call `show()` to make the dialog window visible. Because the `Dialog` class does not provide any means to close a true dialog window, you must close the browser to erase the dialog window from your display. (Later in this section, I'll explain how to fix this problem.)

The resulting dialog window shown in Figure 16.7 is resizable. To create a window that is fixed in size, which is best for most true dialogs, insert the following statement between the calls to `resize()` and `show()` in Listing 16.16:

```
diag.setResizable(false);
```

Listing 16.17 shows the `Dialog` class declaration. As the listing shows, `Dialog` extends from `Window`, not from `Frame`. Among other effects, this means a true dialog's cursor is determined by the operating system and cannot be changed to a different style. A true dialog also cannot have a menu bar—only `Frame` windows can have menus. After explaining the `Dialog` class's public members, I'll show a more practical example of how to use objects of the class to create true dialog windows.

Listing 16.17. The `Dialog` class.

```
public class Dialog extends Window {
// Constructors:
 public Dialog(Frame parent, boolean modal);
 public Dialog(Frame parent, String title, boolean modal);
// Public methods:
 public synchronized void addNotify();
 public boolean isModal();
 public String getTitle();
 public void setTitle(String title);
 public boolean isResizable();
 public void setResizable(boolean resizable);
}
```

There are two ways to construct a `Dialog` object. Each requires finding the applet's parent `Frame` object, which is the first argument to pass to the `Dialog` constructor. The second argument is optional, and can be eliminated if you want a dialog with no title. Set the final argument to `true` for a modal dialog or to `false` for a modeless one. For example, the statement

```
Dialog diag = new Dialog(f, "Dialog Title", false);
```

creates a modeless dialog window, assuming that `f` represents the applet's parent `Frame` object. To create a true dialog with no title, use a statement such as

```
Dialog diag = new Dialog(f, false);
```

This is generally useful only if your code changes the dialog title—to display an error message, for example. Most true dialog windows should have descriptive titles.

The `Dialog` class provides several public methods that applets can call. Because the class extends `Window`, it inherits that class's methods along with those inherited by `Window` from `Container`, `Component`, and `Object`. For the full set of available methods, examine all of these classes. The methods declared in the `Dialog` class are as follows:

- `void addNotify()`: As I've mentioned, this method attaches a component to its native operating system peer class. Applications and applets normally never call this method.

- `boolean isModal()`: Returns `true` if the dialog window is modal, and as such, captures the input focus until the dialog is closed. If this method returns `false`, the dialog window is modeless and does not capture the input focus.

- `String getTitle()`: Returns the current title string displayed in the dialog window. If no title is set during the `Dialog` object's construction, this method returns `null`—it does *not* return a zero-length string.

- `void setTitle(String title)`: Changes the dialog window's title to the specified `String`. Calling this method forces an immediate update of the dialog window.

- `boolean isResizable()`: Returns `true` if the dialog window can be resized. Returns `false` if the dialog window is fixed in size.

- `void setResizable(boolean resizable)`: Prevents the dialog window from being resized if the `boolean` argument is `false`, or allows the window to be resized if the argument is `true`. A dialog window is sizable by default. To create a fixed-size dialog window, you must call `setResizable()` with its argument set to `false`.

The next sample applet demonstrates how to use the `Dialog` class. The program shows the correct way to create a modal dialog window, and works around some apparent bugs—such as the browser losing the input focus when a modal dialog window closes. To keep things interesting, I also threw in some odds and ends that you'll find useful in creating your own true dialogs. Listing 16.18, `TrueDialog.java`, shows the program's source code. Figure 16.8 shows the window displayed when you click the applet's button.

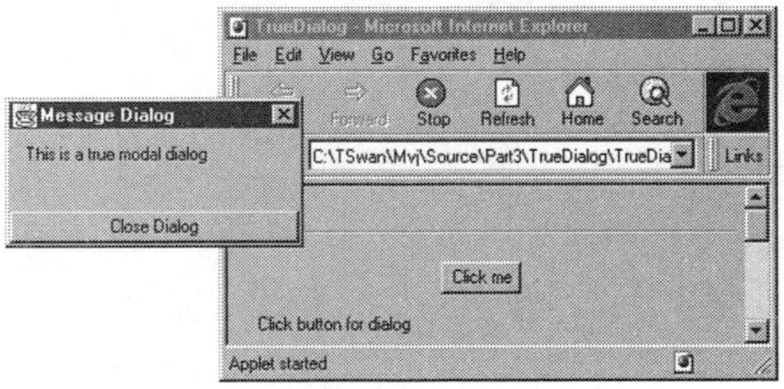

Figure 16.8.
The TrueDialog applet displays a modal dialog when you click the button.

Listing 16.18. `TrueDialog.java` (Demonstrates modal true dialogs).

```java
import java.applet.*;
import java.awt.*;


//=============================================================
// MessageDialog class
//=============================================================

class MessageDialog extends Dialog {
 // Instance variables
 private String message;
 private Button closeButton;
 private Frame parent;

 // Constructor
```

continues

Listing 16.18. continued

```
MessageDialog(Frame parent) {
 super(parent, "Message Dialog", true);
 this.parent = parent;
 resize(200, 100);
 setResizable(false);
 message = "";
 closeButton = new Button("Close Dialog");
 add("South", closeButton);
}

// Display message in dialog window
public void paint(Graphics g) {
 g.drawString(message, 10, 20);
}

// Handle events for dialog window
public boolean handleEvent(Event evt) {
 boolean exitWindow =
  (evt.id == Event.WINDOW_DESTROY ||
   evt.target.equals(closeButton));
 if (exitWindow) {
  hide();  // Hide dialog window
  parent.requestFocus();  // Make parent visible ???
  return true;
 }
 return super.handleEvent(evt);
}

// Change current message string
public void setMessage(String message) {
 if (message == null)
  this.message = "";
 else
  this.message = message;
 if (isVisible())
  repaint();
}
}

//================================================================
// Applet class
//================================================================

public class TrueDialog extends Applet {
// Instance variables
 MessageDialog md;
 Button makeDialogButton;

 // Find applet's parent Frame object
 public Frame parentOf(Component c) {
  Frame f = null;
  while (f == null) {
   c = c.getParent();
   if (c instanceof Frame)
    f = (Frame)c;
  }
  return f;
 }
```

```
// Initialize applet and its components
public void init() {
 resize(320, 240);
 // Construct dialog object, but don't show it
 md = new MessageDialog(parentOf(this));
 makeDialogButton = new Button("Click me");
 add(makeDialogButton);
}

// Display applet instructions
public void paint(Graphics g) {
 g.drawString("Click button for dialog", 10, 50);
}

// Handle selection of applet button
public boolean handleEvent(Event evt) {
 if (evt.target.equals(makeDialogButton)) {
  md.setMessage("This is a true modal dialog");
  md.show();  // Display dialog
  md.move(100, 100);  // Optional
  return true;
 }
 return super.handleEvent(evt);
}
}
```

To provide the means to close a modal dialog, the sample program extends the Dialog class. The new class is useful for displaying simple messages, but you can also use it as a starting place for your own dialogs. Because the sample dialog is modal, users must close the window to continue using the applet—a good way to direct users' attention to a critical message such as an error or warning. The extended MessageDialog class along with its instance variables is declared as

```
class MessageDialog extends Dialog {
 private String message;
 private Button closeButton;
 private Frame parent;
 ...
}
```

A String field holds the message displayed in the dialog window. The Button is labeled "Close", and in this example, takes up the bottom portion of the dialog window. The Frame variable holds a reference to the container object that owns the dialog. This is highly useful for communicating between the dialog and its applet.

MessageDialog's constructor initializes the modal dialog. It calls the ancestor class constructor using the super() method, and then initializes the extended class's instance variables. The dialog window is made fixed in size, so users cannot expand or shrink it. Notice also that the Close button is added to the dialog frame window using the statement

```
add("South", closeButton);
```

417

The first argument causes the button to occupy the bottom portion of the dialog window. This takes advantage of the default BorderLayout class used by Dialog (by virtue of its extending the Window class). To use a different layout class, call setLayout()as explained in Chapter 15.

Method paint() simply shows the dialog's message. You are free to add any other code to display items in dialog windows. In many cases, dialogs with control objects do not need a paint() method.

Method handleEvent() shows the correct way to permit closing a modal dialog, which as I mentioned, you must do to prevent locking up the browser. In the extended class, handleEvent() intercepts two events—WINDOW_DESTROY and the selection of a Close or other button that users can click to end the dialog. In response to these events, the program performs two actions:

```
hide();
parent.requestFocus();
```

Calling requestFocus() is apparently necessary so that the parent window is displayed when the dialog closes. This statement works around a bug that hides the browser window if it is not the only one on display. The fix causes a momentary and annoying screen flash, but until the bug is repaired, this is necessary to bring the browser back up when the dialog is closed.

Finally, method setMessage() changes the message displayed in the dialog window. This method also demonstrates an important aspect of dialogs. Because the parent program most likely creates the dialog object before displaying the window, a method such as setMessage() is best programmed to test whether the dialog is visible before forcing an update of its contents. This is easily done with a statement such as

```
if (isVisible())
 repaint();
```

Continuing in the sample listing, the TrueDialog class, extended from Applet, shows how to use MessageDialog. The applet declares the dialog object using this statement:

```
MessageDialog md;
```

In method init(), construct that object using the following statement:

```
md = new MessageDialog(parentOf(this));
```

The parentOf() function encompasses the code listed earlier that finds the applet's Frame parent. This object is passed to the MessageDialog constructor, which calls the Dialog constructor as previously explained.

At this stage, the dialog is not yet displayed, but it is ready for use at a moment's notice. This gives good response times. For example, in the sample applet, when you click the button labeled "Click me," the program displays the message dialog using these statements:

```
md.setMessage("This is a true modal dialog");
md.show();
md.move(100, 100);
```

Because the `Dialog` object has already been created, this quickly displays the dialog window on demand. The first statement changes the message to display inside the dialog window. The second statement makes the dialog visible. The third moves the dialog to a new position on screen. I included this statement because it is evidently not possible to position a dialog *before* making it visible—another probable bug, as there ought to be some way of presetting a window's position. In your own code, however, you might want to find a different way to obtain position coordinates rather than use literal coordinate values as I do here. (You might, for example, call `ToolKit` methods to interrogate the system's display resolution.)

WARNING

As I mentioned earlier in this chapter, separate windows such as the true dialogs displayed here might be prohibited by a security manager. At the very least, and as Figure 16.9 shows, Web page users are warned that the window has been created by the applet. You can see this effect by opening the `TrueDialog.html` file on the CD-ROM.

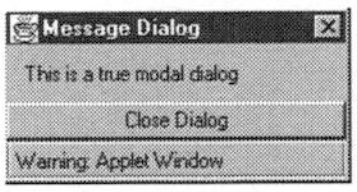

Figure 16.9.
Web page users receive a warning that the applet created a separate window.

The `FileDialog` Class

The `FileDialog` class is one of the most poorly documented in the AWT package. If you attempt to use it, you will probably receive an exception error that tells you something like this:

```
exception: com.ms.applet.AppletSecurityException: security.filedialog
```

That's about as informative as the instructions on an IRS tax form. The reason for this exception is that applets are prohibited from accessing a user's disk, and a file dialog definitely steps over that line. You should use the techniques explained here only in stand-alone applications, or in applets executed in debug mode. The applet will work also if the browser does not enforce a security manager.

NOTE

When executing applets using Visual J++, you won't see the security exception; it is displayed only if the applet is loaded by opening or downloading a document `.html` file.

The `FileDialog` class extends from `Dialog`, and is used similarly. For example, add the text from Listing 16.19 to a fresh applet's `init()` method (use the Applet Wizard to create the shell). This displays a standard Windows File-Open dialog, with which you are no doubt thoroughly familiar. The program works fine when executed from Visual J++ in debug mode, but the security error is displayed if you attempt to open the applet's `.html` file directly.

Listing 16.19. Steps to create a File-Open dialog (this works only in stand-alone applications or when run in debug mode from Visual J++).

```
Component c = this;
Frame f = null;
while (f == null) {
 c = c.getParent();
 if (c instanceof Frame)
  f = (Frame)c;
}
FileDialog fd = new FileDialog(f, "Open file");
fd.show();
```

Listing 16.20 shows the `FileDialog` class declaration. After explaining the class's constructors and public methods, I'll list an example program that demonstrates how to use the dialog to prompt users for filenames and allow them to browse their systems' directories.

Listing 16.20. The `FileDialog` class.

```
public class FileDialog extends Dialog {
// Fields:
 public static final int LOAD;
 public static final int SAVE;
// Constructors:
 public FileDialog(Frame parent, String title);
 public FileDialog(Frame parent, String title, int mode);
// Public methods:
 public synchronized void addNotify();
 public int getMode();
 public String getDirectory();
 public void setDirectory(String dir);
 public String getFile();
 public void setFile(String file);
 public FilenameFilter getFilenameFilter();
 public void setFilenameFilter(FilenameFilter filter);
}
```

There are two ways to construct a `FileDialog` object. Each approach requires two arguments—one for the applet's `Frame` object that is to own the `FileDialog`, and a string for the dialog window's title. For example, the statement

```
FileDialog fd = new FileDialog(f, "Open file");
```

constructs a standard File-Open dialog, assuming that `f` represents the applet's `Frame` parent. (See Listing 16.19 for one way to locate this parent.) To construct a File-Save dialog, pass an optional third argument as follows:

```
FileDialog fd = new FileDialog(f, "Save file", FileDialog.SAVE);
```

The third argument, if not specified, defaults to `FileDialog.LOAD`. If you wish to specify this explicitly, use a construction statement such as

```
FileDialog fd = new FileDialog(f, "Open file", FileDialog.LOAD);
```

After constructing the `FileDialog` object, you may use it simply by calling the inherited `show()` method. For example, follow any of the preceding three statements with

```
fd.show();
```

It is not necessary to size the window, nor can you call inherited methods to attempt to create a modeless window. File dialogs are always modal, and must be closed before continuing with the application. In general, it's best not to attempt anything too fancy with file dialogs; they are intended merely to prompt users for file and directory names, and they are best implemented to use the native services of the operating system for these purposes.

The `FileDialog` class provides several public methods that you can call. These methods are as follows:

- void `addNotify()`: As usual, this method connects the `FileDialog` object with its native operating system peer. Applications should have no reason ever to call this method.

- int `getMode()`: Returns the current mode setting, which is equal to `FileDialog.LOAD` or `FileDialog.SAVE`, as defined in the `FileDialog` class.

- String `getDirectory()`: Returns the current directory path string as set by the user. You will normally call this method after showing a file dialog.

- void `setDirectory(String dir)`: Changes the current directory path that the file dialog initially displays. You will normally call this method before showing the dialog.

- String `getFile()`: Returns the currently selected or entered filename. You will normally call this method after showing the dialog to obtain the user's file entry.

- void `setFile(String file)`: Changes the initial filename displayed in the file dialog. You will normally call this method before showing the dialog. It is particularly useful in a File-Save dialog that suggests a current filename as the one to use for saving an open document.

- FilenameFilter `getFilenameFilter()`: Returns an object of the `FilenameFilter` class, which specifies wild cards such as `*.*` and `*.TXT` for restricting directory lists to specific categories of files. This method is particularly useful for updating or modifying the filter list. By default, the only filter used by a file dialog is the "all files" wild card, `*.*`. (At least this is true for Windows 95.)

- void `setFilenameFilter(FilenameFilter filter)`: Sets the file dialog's list of filename filters. You will normally call this method before showing the dialog window.

The `FilenameFilter` class is a simple interface class that is implemented by other classes such as `File`. The interface declares a single method, `accept()`, that determines whether a specific file is acceptable for listing its name in the dialog window. See Chapter 18, "Input and Output," for more information about using files and filename filters.

Listing 16.21, `FileDialDemo.java`, demonstrates how to use the `FileDialog` class to create File-Open and File-Save dialogs. The listing also shows how to determine whether the user clicked the Open or Save button to close the dialog box—a very poorly documented feature of the class. Run the program and click the sample applet's button to open the dialog. Browse directories and select a file—nothing is read or written to disk, and no files are changed by the demonstration. As I mentioned, you might receive a security violation if you attempt to load the sample applet's `.html` file. To run the program successfully, execute it from Studio 97 in debug mode, or you can convert the listing to a stand-alone application.

Listing 16.21. `FileDialDemo.java` (Demonstrates `FileDialog` class).

```
import java.applet.*;
import java.awt.*;

public class FileDialDemo extends Applet {
// Instance variables
 String filename = null;
 String pathname = null;
 FileDialog fd;
 Button makeDialogButton;

  // Find applet's parent Frame object
 public Frame parentOf(Component c) {
  Frame f = null;
  while (f == null) {
   c = c.getParent();
   if (c instanceof Frame)
    f = (Frame)c;
  }
  return f;
 }

// Initialize applet, file dialog, and button
 public void init() {
  resize(320, 240);

  // Use this to create File-Open dialog
  fd = new FileDialog(
   parentOf(this), "File Dialog");

  // Enable this to create File-Save dialog
  // fd = new FileDialog(
  //  parentOf(this), "File Dialog", FileDialog.SAVE);

  // Create button in applet window
  makeDialogButton = new Button("Click me");
  add(makeDialogButton);
 }
```

```
// Display current file- and pathname settings
public void paint(Graphics g)  {
 String fn = filename, pn = pathname;
 if (filename == null) fn = " none";
 if (pathname == null) pn = " none";
 g.drawString("File name = " + fn, 10, 50);
 g.drawString("Path name = " + pn, 10, 70);
}

// Handle selection of applet button
public boolean handleEvent(Event evt) {
 if (evt.target.equals(makeDialogButton)) {

  // Set filename null to provide a way
  // to determine if user clicked OK button:
  filename = null;
  fd.setFile("");
  // Change to specified directory returned
  // by prior use of the file dialog:
  if (pathname != null)
   fd.setDirectory(pathname);

  // Display the dialog. The program
  // continues only after show() returns:
  fd.show();

  // Obtain current file- and pathname settings
  filename = fd.getFile();
  pathname = fd.getDirectory();
  repaint();  // Display the new settings
  return true;
 }
 return super.handleEvent(evt);
 }
}
```

There is apparently no defined way to determine if users closed a file dialog by clicking the Open, Save, or Cancel buttons—an indication that this AWT class could stand upgrading. However, by experimentation, I discovered that a null filename is always returned if the user clicks Cancel, and this is the work-around implemented in the sample listing. This may or may not work on all systems, and you are best advised to carefully test your applets before relying on the technique shown here.

The program creates the file dialog as explained before. Enable the commented-out statements duplicated here to create a File-Save dialog:

```
// Enable this to create File-Save dialog
fd = new FileDialog(
 parentOf(this), "File Dialog", FileDialog.SAVE);
```

A File-Save dialog differs from a File-Open dialog in only two ways. First, it displays a Save button rather than an Open button. Second, if the specified file already exists and the user clicks Save, another dialog asks whether to overwrite the file. Only if the user answers Yes to this prompt does getFile() return a non-null string.

Summary

- The Window class provides the basis for creating separate windows, but you will normally not use Window to construct objects. A window has no border, title, or menu.

- The Frame class extends Window to provide for a separate window with a border, a title bar, and optionally, a menu bar.

- You can construct pulldown menus from scratch, but it is far easier to use Studio 97 to create a menu template. You can then use the Java Resource Wizard to convert the template into Java code. This chapter explains how to use the generated code to attach and use a menu bar in a separate frame window.

- Likewise, it is best to create dialogs as resource templates, and then use Resource Wizard to convert the template to code. Dialogs created this way, however, do not use the Dialog class.

- This chapter fills in some of the gaps in generated dialogs, such as how to transfer control data to and from a dialog, and also how a dialog can communicate with its parent applet.

- The Dialog class creates a true dialog window that can be modal or modeless.

- The FileDialog class extends Dialog and can be used to create File-Open and File-Save dialogs. However, because disk access is prohibited in downloaded Web page documents, the FileDialog class is usable only in stand-alone applications or when running applets in debug mode from Studio 97.

What's Next?

The next chapter explains graphics, animation, and multimedia techniques that you can use in applets and also in stand-alone applications.

17

CHAPTER

Graphics, Animation, and Multimedia

Believe it or not, some Internet surfers still use text-only terminals to browse the Web. But most users have graphical browsers such as Internet Explorer and Netscape that take advantage of the native operating system's graphics capabilities. Using Java classes, you can tap into these features to spruce up your applets with color, graphics, animation, and multimedia.

> **NOTE**
>
> Java's multimedia features are currently limited to playing simple sounds, but the techniques described in this chapter will probably be valid for future multimedia developments.

In This Chapter

This chapter covers the following fundamentals of graphics, animation, and multimedia programming:

- Using the Graphics class to draw shapes in the applet's window.
- Using related classes such as Color, Polygon, and Font along with the Graphics class.
- Loading and displaying image files that use the popular GIF format.
- The proper use of multithreaded programming with image graphics.
- How to animate a sequence of images using threads to control file loading, image display, and animation speed.
- How to play a sound file in the standard .AU format.

Graphics Fundamentals

The extensive Graphics class brings a wide range of system-independent graphics capabilities to applets. You'll never create an object of this class; instead, you'll normally use it in a method such as paint(), which receives a Graphics object as a parameter. Actually, the object that paint() receives is of an unspecified subclass of Graphics that depends on the browser and operating system. As defined in Java, the Graphics class is abstract, and as such, it operates as an interface to the operating system's graphical capabilities. This is why you cannot create Graphics objects with the new operator.

Because of the interactive nature of a graphical user interface such as Windows 95, most of an applet's graphics are programmed in a paint() method. The operating system, via the browser and Java, calls paint() whenever the applet's window needs updating. As you will learn in this chapter, a properly written graphics program must be able to create *and re-create* its graphics on request—it is never enough for any method merely to draw shapes on screen. When the user switches away and then back to the applet, the program needs to redraw any shapes that were obscured by another window.

Another important aspect of graphics programming, especially when embedded in HTML documents, is to keep in mind that display speeds are likely to fluctuate widely from system to system. Web page visitors will see much different, and slower, graphics than you see on your development system. For example, it might take only a brief moment to load and display an image file locally, but this same operation might take several seconds or longer when performed over a busy network connection. For this reason, a good understanding of multithreaded concepts is vital to producing graphics that look good and run smoothly. So that a lengthy download of a large image file does not lock up the system, the applet must perform the loading using a separate thread that permits other activities to run concurrently.

This chapter introduces classes that you will use in graphics programming and also explores techniques for displaying images and animation using multithreaded programming. I'll also explain how to create multimedia applets, although Java currently limits this avenue to playing simple sounds. This will at least introduce key concepts for future multimedia features such as full-motion video and stereo sound.

The Graphics Class

Because the Graphics class has so many different capabilities, I'll discuss it here briefly. Throughout the rest of the chapter, I'll cover various aspects of the class as needed to explain specific programming techniques. Listing 17.1 shows the Graphics class declaration. Remember that this class is abstract and, as such, cannot be instantiated with the new operator.

Listing 17.1. The Graphics class.

```
public abstract class Graphics {
// Constructor:
 protected Graphics();
// Utility methods:
 public abstract Graphics create();
 public Graphics create(int x, int y, int width, int height);
 public abstract void translate(int x, int y);
 public abstract Color getColor();
 public abstract void setColor(Color c);
 public abstract void setPaintMode();
 public abstract void setXORMode(Color c1);
 public abstract Rectangle getClipRect();
 public abstract void clipRect(int x, int y,
  int width, int height);
 public abstract void copyArea(int x, int y,
  int width, int height, int dx, int dy);
 public abstract void clearRect(int x, int y,
  int width, int height);
// Drawing methods:
 public abstract void drawLine(int x1, int y1,
  int x2, int y2);
 public void drawRect(int x, int y,
  int width, int height);
 public abstract void drawRoundRect(int x, int y,
  int width, int height, int arcWidth, int arcHeight);
 public void draw3DRect(int x, int y,
```

Listing 17.1. continued

```
 int width, int height, boolean raised);
public abstract void drawOval(int x, int y,
 int width, int height);
public abstract void drawArc(int x, int y,
 int width, int height, int startAngle, int arcAngle);
public abstract void drawPolygon(int xPoints[],
 int yPoints[], int nPoints);
public void drawPolygon(Polygon p);
// Filling methods:
public abstract void fillRect(int x, int y,
 int width, int height);
public abstract void fillRoundRect(int x, int y,
 int width, int height, int arcWidth, int arcHeight);
public void fill3DRect(int x, int y,
 int width, int height, boolean raised);
public abstract void fillOval(int x, int y,
 int width, int height);
public abstract void fillArc(int x, int y,
 int width, int height, int startAngle, int arcAngle);
public abstract void fillPolygon(int xPoints[],
 int yPoints[], int nPoints);
public void fillPolygon(Polygon p);
// Image methods:
public abstract boolean drawImage(Image img, int x, int y,
 ImageObserver observer);
public abstract boolean drawImage(Image img, int x, int y,
 int width, int height, ImageObserver observer);
public abstract boolean drawImage(Image img, int x, int y,
 Color bgcolor, ImageObserver observer);
public abstract boolean drawImage(Image img, int x, int y,
 int width, int height,
 Color bgcolor, ImageObserver observer);
// Font methods:
public abstract Font getFont();
public abstract void setFont(Font font);
public FontMetrics getFontMetrics();
public abstract FontMetrics getFontMetrics(Font f);
// Text methods:
public abstract void drawString(String str, int x, int y);
public void drawChars(char data[], int offset,
 int length, int x, int y);
public void drawBytes(byte data[], int offset,
 int length, int x, int y);
// Miscellaneous methods:
public abstract void dispose();
public void finalize();
public String toString();
}
```

To understand how to use the Graphics class, it helps to study it in sections. I divide the class into the following categories:

- *Constructor:* As I mentioned, Graphics is abstract, and it cannot be instantiated as an object with the new operator. To use the class, you'll normally program a method such as paint(), which receives a Graphics object tailored to the operating system. For this reason, you'll never have any reason to use the class's constructor, which is declared protected and is therefore available only to a subclass of Graphics, not to an applet's programming.

- *Utility methods:* These are various methods that can clone a Graphics object, select colors and drawing modes, set clipping regions, and perform other utilitarian chores.

- *Drawing methods:* Methods in this relatively large category draw lines and other outline shapes in the current color.

- *Filling methods:* Methods in this large category mirror many of those under *Drawing methods,* but produce filled shapes in the current color.

- *Image methods:* These methods display image files, but as explained in this chapter, doing this requires additional multithreaded programming to create smoothly operating displays.

- *Font methods:* Use these four methods to select fonts for displaying text, and also to obtain font metrics that provide useful information for accurately positioning and spacing text characters.

- *Text methods:* These methods draw strings and character arrays using the current font settings.

- *Miscellaneous methods:* Rarely if ever called by applications, these methods are used mostly by Graphics subclasses, and you can ignore them for the purposes of application and applet development. The toString() method, however, which returns a string representation of a Graphics object, might be useful for debugging.

Programming with paint()

A sample application shows the most common way to use the Graphics class. Figure 17.1 shows the program's display, consisting of a grid on a yellow background, with a shaded blue rounded rectangle and the text "Mastering Java with Visual J++!" These elements demonstrate the basic graphics techniques of painting background colors, drawing lines, filling shapes, and showing text. Listing 17.2 shows the program's source code.

Figure 17.1.
GraphicsDemo shows how to draw various shapes, lines, and text in an applet's window.

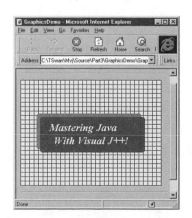

Listing 17.2. `GraphicsDemo.java` (Demonstrates the Graphics class).

```java
import java.applet.*;
import java.awt.*;
public class GraphicsDemo extends Applet
{
 // Initialize applet
 public void init()
 {
  resize(321, 241);
 }
 // Paint window contents
 public void paint(Graphics g)
 {
  // Get window size
  Rectangle r = bounds();
  // Paint background yellow
  g.setColor(Color.yellow);
  g.fillRect(0, 0, r.width, r.height);
  // Outline window in black
  g.setColor(Color.black);
  g.drawRect(0, 0, r.width, r.height);
  // Draw grid inside window
  for (int h = 0; h < r.height; h += 10)
   g.drawLine(0, h, r.width, h);
  for (int v = 0; v < r.width; v += 10)
   g.drawLine(v, 0, v, r.height);
  // Draw overlapping round rectangles
  int cx = r.width / 8;
  int cy = r.height / 3;
  int w = (r.width / 4) * 3;
  int h = cy;
  g.setColor(Color.gray);
  g.fillRoundRect(cx - 4, cy - 4, w, h, 10, 10);
  g.setColor(Color.blue);
  g.fillRoundRect(cx + 4, cy + 4, w, h, 10, 10);
  // Draw text inside outer rectangle
  Font f = new Font("TimesRoman",
   Font.BOLD + Font.ITALIC, 24);
  g.setFont(f);
  g.setColor(Color.orange);
  g.drawString("Mastering Java", cx + 25, cy + 36);
  g.drawString("With Visual J++!", cx + 35, cy + 66);
 }
}
```

Except for its `init()` method, which simply sets the applet's display size, GraphicsDemo consists of a large `paint()` method that draws the applet's shapes. The `paint()` method is declared as

```java
public void paint(Graphics g) {
...
}
```

The Graphics object g received by paint() is of a subclass provided by your browser. This subclass is tailored to the operating system so that, when you draw a shape such as a rectangle, it is the operating system's rectangle-draw function (if one exists) that performs the actual maneuver.

As I've mentioned, paint() is called whenever the applet's display needs updating. For example, if the user opens or moves another window that obscures the applet, when the user returns to the browser, paint() is called to re-create the display. For this reason, your code must always be prepared to draw its graphics as many times as necessary. This might mean storing coordinate values in variables that can be used to draw shapes at known locations.

GraphicsDemo's paint() method begins with a statement that you will find handy in your own graphical escapades. To find the boundaries of the current window, the method executes the statement

```
Rectangle r = bounds();
```

This creates and sets a Rectangle object, r, to the height and width of the applet window—information that is highly useful in drawing graphics within that region. The bounds() method is provided by the Applet class. The sample program uses the returned information in various ways. For example, to paint the window's background yellow, the applet executes these statements:

```
g.setColor(Color.yellow);
g.fillRect(0, 0, r.width, r.height);
```

Notice that each statement calls a Graphic's class method in reference to the g object received by paint(). The first statement sets the drawing color to yellow, specifying that constant in reference to the Color class, which I'll explain in the next section, "Using Color."

Calling fillRect() paints a rectangular area in that color. The coordinate values passed to fillRect() use the information returned by bounds() to paint the applet's entire background. To outline that same region in black, the program executes these statements:

```
g.setColor(Color.black);
g.drawRect(0, 0, r.width, r.height);
```

Methods with "draw" in their names draw outline shapes; those with "fill" in their names draw filled shapes. Using the current color, the program draws a grid on top of the yellow background with two for statements. These statements call the drawLine() method, which simply connects two points with a solid line in the current drawing color.

> **TIP**
>
> Because there is no line-width setting in the Graphics class, you might attempt to draw heavy lines by calling drawLine() multiple times. However, for lines heavier than two or three pixels, it might be faster to call fillRect().

After calculating some integer variables, GraphicsDemo draws two rounded rectangles by calling the fillRoundRect() method. The program then creates and selects a font with the following statements:

```
Font f = new Font("TimesRoman",
 Font.BOLD + Font.ITALIC, 24);
g.setFont(f);
```

This font is used to draw the text you see inside the outer blue rectangle. The statements

```
g.drawString("Mastering Java", cx + 25, cy + 36);
g.drawString("With Visual J++!", cx + 35, cy + 66);
```

display the text at the indicated coordinates, a technique that is adequate for many purposes, but not as exacting as I explain elsewhere in this chapter. (See the section "The Font Class.")

You might want to try experimenting with other Graphics methods using the GraphicsDemo applet as a testbed. In general, statements in paint() may call any Graphics class methods. However, as I mentioned, displaying image files requires additional multithreaded programming that I'll explain when we get to images and animation techniques.

Using Color

The Color class, shown in Listing 17.3, provides versatile methods for specifying color values.

Listing 17.3. The Color class.

```
public final class Color {
// Fields:
 public final static Color white;
 public final static Color lightGray;
 public final static Color gray;
 public final static Color darkGray;
 public final static Color black;
 public final static Color red;
 public final static Color pink;
 public final static Color orange;
 public final static Color yellow;
```

```
   public final static Color green;
   public final static Color magenta;
   public final static Color cyan;
   public final static Color blue;
// Constructors:
   public Color(int r, int g, int b);
   public Color(int rgb);
   public Color(float r, float g, float b);
// Public methods:
   public int getRed();
   public int getGreen();
   public int getBlue();
   public int getRGB();
   public Color brighter();
   public Color darker();
   public int hashCode();
   public boolean equals(Object obj);
   public String toString();
   public static Color getColor(String nm);
   public static Color getColor(String nm, Color v);
   public static Color getColor(String nm, int v);
   public static int HSBtoRGB(float hue, float saturation, float brightness);
   public static float[] RGBtoHSB(int r, int g, int b, float[] hsbvals);
   public static Color getHSBColor(float h, float s, float b);
}
```

In many cases, you will use this class simply by referring to one of several constant values such as Color.white and Color.red. These constants are objects of the Color class, and they can be used wherever a Color object is allowed. For example, in a paint() method, you can set the current drawing or fill color using a statement such as

```
g.setColor(Color.green);
```

Or, you can construct a Color object and pass it to setColor() using code like this:

```
Color c = new Color(255, 0, 128);
g.setColor(c);
```

If you don't want to keep the Color object, create a temporary one as the method argument, and pass it directly to setColor():

```
g.setColor(new Color(0, 0, 64));
```

Any drawing, filling, or text method will use the selected color until you choose another. In some cases, it is useful to preserve the current drawing color. Do that by calling getColor() with code such as

```
Color saveColor = g.getColor();
g.setColor(Color.red);
// ... insert drawing statements here
g.setColor(saveColor);   // Restore original color
```

Internally, Color class objects store color values in a single 32-bit private integer. This integer stores individual red, green, and blue color intensities as byte values ranging from 0 to 255. To construct the Color.pink constant, for example, the class uses the statement

```
public final static Color pink = new Color(255, 175, 175);
```

This indicates that the color pink is internally represented as a full blob of red, with approximately two-thirds of a portion each of green and blue. You can similarly construct your own Color objects, and then call various methods for them. For example, Listing 17.4, Gradient.java, displays graduated bands of color from lighter to darker shades. Figure 17.2 shows the applet's display.

Figure 17.2.

The Gradient applet displays bands of color from lighter to darker shades.

Listing 17.4. Gradient.java (Demonstrates the Color class).

```
import java.applet.*;
import java.awt.*;
public class Gradient extends Applet
{
 // Initialize applet
 public void init() {
  resize(400, 250);
 }
 // Paint window contents
 public void paint(Graphics g) {
  int increment = 40;
  Rectangle r = bounds();
  Color c = new Color(255, 175, 175);
  int x = 0;
  while (x < r.width) {
   g.setColor(c);
   g.fillRect(x, 0, x + increment, r.height);
   c = c.darker();
   x += increment;
  }
 }
}
```

The sample program constructs a `Color` object using this statement:

```
Color c = new Color(255, 175, 175);
```

Alternatively, you can create `Color` objects with a single integer value. This value is conveniently expressed in hexadecimal. For example, the statement

```
Color c = new Color(0x00112233);
```

creates a `Color` object with red, green, and blue component values of `0x11`, `0x22`, and `0x33`, respectively. The most significant byte, set to `0x00` here, is ignored.

You can also specify floating-point red, green, and blue color values. Each value must be greater or equal to zero and less than 1.0. For example, the statement

```
Color c = new Color(1.0f, 0.75f, 0.75f);
```

constructs a color value with floating-point arguments. Each argument value represents a desired fraction of `255`, the maximum color integer component value. For instance, the floating-point argument `0.75f` is equivalent to an integer component value of `191`.

> **TIP**
>
> Floating-point constants passed to the `Color` constructor must be followed by the letter `f` to indicate that they are of type `float`.

The sample Gradient program calls the `darker()` method to create a color slightly darker than the current one. Because this method returns a new `Color` object, you'll normally assign its result to the same object for which you call the method:

```
c = c.darker();
```

Similarly call `brighter()` for a color slightly brighter than the current one. Again, this method returns a `Color` object that you'll need to assign to a variable. If you don't do this, nothing seems to happen. For example, calling either method in the following way merely throws away the method results and produces no effects on the `Color` object `c`:

```
c.darker();    // ???
c.brighter();  // ???
```

To obtain a `Color` object's component red, green, or blue values, call methods `getRed()`, `getGreen()`, or `getBlue()`. You can also obtain a single integer representation of a `Color` object by calling `getRGB()` as follows:

```
int colorInt = Color.magenta.getRGB();
```

This assigns to `colorInt` the 32-bit integer representation of the `Color` constant, `magenta`.

There are other methods in Color that you might want to investigate on your own. The ones that accept string arguments prepare Color objects based on system property settings, which are not well defined for all Java installations and might have varying results. Methods such as HSBtoRGB() use hue, saturation, and brightness values to represent colors—but the end results are the same as specified by red, green, and blue component values. There's no real advantage to using these methods over the others, but they are available if the need arises—for example, to implement an algorithm that calls for hue, saturation, and brightness levels. In the "Filtered Images" section of this chapter, I show how to use these methods to convert a color image to a gray-scale black-and-white picture.

The Polygon Class

The Graphics class provides four ways to draw outlined and filled polygons, which are defined as a set of coordinate points. Polygons are useful for drawing wire-frame graphics and for other complex figures. Two of the polygon methods accept integer arrays of coordinate values. These methods are defined as

```
void drawPolygon(int xPoints[], int yPoints[], int nPoints);
void fillPolygon(int xPoints[], int yPoints[], int nPoints);
```

Call drawPolygon() for an outlined shape; call fillPolygon() for one that is filled with the current color. Pass two arrays of integer values, representing the x and y coordinates of each polygon point. The third argument equals the number of points in the array—a less-than-ideal design because the methods could more simply use the array's size value to determine the number of elements, and also because there is no way to begin drawing from an arbitrary starting index.

> **TIP**
>
> The online documentation states that Polygon objects are automatically completed—meaning that the last point is automatically joined to the first. My tests indicate that this is true *only* for filled shapes. An outlined polygon drawn by the drawPolygon() method must repeat its starting point in order to close the shape.

More convenient are the two overloaded Graphics methods—also named drawPolygon() and fillPolygon()—which take as arguments an object of the Polygon class, shown in Listing 17.5. These methods are defined as

```
void drawPolygon(Polygon p);
void fillPolygon(Polygon p);
```

Listing 17.5. The Polygon class.

```
public class Polygon {
// Public variables:
 public int npoints;
 public int xpoints[];
 public int ypoints[];
```

```
// Constructors:
 public Polygon();
 public Polygon(int xpoints[], int ypoints[], int npoints);
// Public methods:
 public void addPoint(int x, int y);
 public Rectangle getBoundingBox();
 public boolean inside(int x, int y);
}
```

> **NOTE**
>
> The `Polygon` class does not seem to be one of Java's best designed classes. There is no way to specify a starting array size, and worse, integer coordinates are stored in simple arrays, which are doubled in size *and temporarily duplicated* when a new point is added to a full array! A better class—perhaps you'll design one—might use the `Vector` class (or be subclassed from it) to take advantage of this container's more sophisticated array-storage features.

To use the class, construct a `Polygon` object using code such as

```
Polygon p = new Polygon();
```

Or, if you have arrays of integer coordinates, construct the object with this statement:

```
Polygon p = new Polygon(xints, yints, numElements);
```

Here again, I would prefer having a means to specify a starting index in the arrays. Nevertheless, the stock class has some useful methods. To add a new point to the object, call the `addPoint()` method. For example, the code fragment

```
Polygon p = new Polygon();
p.addPoint(50, 0);
p.addPoint(75, 50);
p.addPoint(25, 50);
p.addPoint(50, 0);
```

creates a triangular `Polygon` object, which you can display in a `paint()` method using the following code:

```
g.setColor(Color.blue);
g.drawPolygon(p);
g.setColor(Color.white);
g.fillPolygon(p);
```

Notice that the starting point is repeated in order to fully outline the shape. To outline *and* fill the polygon, I selected different colors and called `drawPolygon()` and `fillPolygon()` using the same `Polygon` object. If you were only filling the shape, you would not need to repeat the starting point's coordinate values.

Two additional methods are handy for working with `Polygon` objects. Call `getBoundingBox()` as follows for a `Rectangle` object in which all the polygon's points lie:

```
Rectangle r = p.getBoundingBox();
g.drawRect(r.x, r.y, r.width, r.height);
```

This sample code outlines the polygon with a rectangle; note the order of the `Rectangle` object's parameters passed to `drawRect()`. The width is specified before the height.

The final `Polygon` method determines whether a specified coordinate is inside the polygon's boundaries. Use the method like this:

```
if (p.inside(10, 20))
...
```

Listing 17.6, `PolyDemo.java`, draws polygon shapes at random in an applet window. Figure 17.3 shows the program's display.

Figure 17.3.

PolyDemo displays random-ized, filled polygons inside the applet's window.

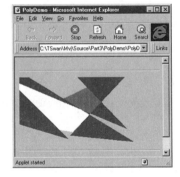

Listing 17.6. `PolyDemo.java` (Demonstrates polygons).

```java
import java.applet.*;
import java.awt.*;
import java.util.Random;
public class PolyDemo extends Applet
{
 // Initialize applet
 public void init()
 {
  resize(300, 150);
 }
 // Create randomized polygon with num points
 // constrained to width and height.
 public Polygon newPolygon(int num, int w, int h)
 {
  Polygon p = new Polygon();
  Random r = new Random();
  while (num > 0) {
   p.addPoint(r.nextInt() % w, r.nextInt() % h);
   num--;   // i.e. num = num - 1
  }
  return p;
 }
```

```
// Paint graphics in applet window
public void paint(Graphics g)
{
 Rectangle r = bounds();
 g.setColor(Color.red);
 g.fillPolygon(newPolygon(6, r.width, r.height));
 g.setColor(Color.white);
 g.fillPolygon(newPolygon(8, r.width, r.height));
 g.setColor(Color.blue);
 g.fillPolygon(newPolygon(10, r.width, r.height));
 }
}
```

Though PolyDemo demonstrates the `Polygon` class along with `Graphics` methods such as `fillPolygon()`, the code uses less-than-ideal drawing techniques. When you run the program, you'll notice that every time you resize the browser window or switch away from it and then back, new shapes are drawn. Perhaps I could have called this a "feature," but a better program would store each polygon and redraw it on demand—perhaps in response to clicking a button. I left the example as it is because, later in the "Creating a Graphics Object" section of this chapter, I'll discuss far better techniques for displaying, storing, and animating graphics.

The Font Class

In Part II of this book, you used the command-line `Jvc.exe` compiler at a DOS-prompt window to learn Java fundamentals. This approach makes it easy to display text simply by writing strings to the display with a method such as `System.out.println()`.

Unfortunately, graphical applets and applications cannot use this same method to display text. In addition to drawing rectangles, ovals, polygons, and other shapes, a graphics program must *draw* text by calling `Graphics` class methods. Although this requires more complex programming, it makes it possible to use fonts for your applets' text data. You can also display colored characters and use boldface and italic styles.

For programming graphical text, Java provides two classes—`Font` and `FontMetrics`. The classes are typically used together to create a font, and to obtain spacing information for that font's characters. By *font*, I mean not only its family—Helvetica or Times Roman, for example—but also its size and style. Listing 17.7 shows the `Font` class declaration. After explaining this class and showing a demonstration program, I'll discuss the `FontMetrics` class, which provides information about a font.

Listing 17.7. The Font class.

```
public class Font {
// Fields:
 public static final int PLAIN;
 public static final int BOLD;
 public static final int ITALIC;
```

continues

Listing 17.7. continued

```
// Constructor:
 public Font(String name, int style, int size);
// Public methods:
 public String getFamily();
 public String getName();
 public int getStyle();
 public int getSize();
 public boolean isPlain();
 public boolean isBold();
 public boolean isItalic();
 public static Font getFont(String nm);
 public static Font getFont(String nm, Font font);
 public int hashCode();
 public boolean equals(Object obj);
 public String toString();
}
```

Java's official documentation states that all installations are required to support the following set of fonts:

- Dialog
- Helvetica
- TimesRoman
- Courier
- Symbol

When specifying fonts by name, you may use these family titles as strings. Note that there is no space in TimesRoman. Installations may support other font family names, but the preceding ones are guaranteed to be available, although their exact appearances depend on the local installation. Visual J++, for example, adds `DialogInput` to the standard list.

Listing 17.8, `FontDemo.java`, shows how to use the `Font` and `FontMetrics` classes. Figure 17.4 shows the program's display, which paints each font name in its own style and uses `FontMetrics` to space the lines. The `Symbol` font displayed on the bottom line has no alphabetical characters, so its name is unreadable.

Figure 17.4.

FontDemo displays available font names using the `FontMetrics` *class to position each line.*

Listing 17.8. FontDemo.java (Demonstrates fonts and font metrics).

```
import java.applet.*;
import java.awt.*;
public class FontDemo extends Applet
{
 String[] fontNames;
 // Initialize applet
 public void init()
 {
  // Size window
  resize(400, 240);
  // Get available font names
  Toolkit tools = Toolkit.getDefaultToolkit();
  fontNames = tools.getFontList();
 }
 // Paint window contents
 public void paint(Graphics g)
 {
  Font f;
  int y = 0;
  for (int i = 0; i < fontNames.length; i++) {
   f = new Font(fontNames[i], Font.BOLD, 18);
   g.setFont(f);
   y += g.getFontMetrics().getHeight();
   g.drawString(fontNames[i], 10, y);
  }
 }
}
```

Although it is simple, FontDemo shows the basic techniques for displaying text in applet windows. The program first prepares a list of available font names, stored in an array of strings declared as

```
String[] fontNames;
```

In the applet's init() method, the two statements

```
Toolkit tools = Toolkit.getDefaultToolkit();
fontNames = tools.getFontList();
```

obtain the current Toolkit object (tailored to the system's characteristics), and call getFontList() for the available font family names.

To use these fonts, the program's paint() method executes a for loop once for each available font name. A Font class object is created with this code:

```
f = new Font(fontNames[i], Font.BOLD, 18);
```

This specifies three items: the font name as a String object; a style, which can be Font.BOLD, Font.ITALIC, or Font.PLAIN; and a size in points. If a specific size or style is not available, assume that at least some close representation will be created. Pass the resulting Font object to the Graphics class setFont() method:

```
g.setFont(f);
```

441

You can then call a method such as drawString() to display text using the specified font:

```
g.drawString(fontNames[i], 10, y);
```

As you can see, using the Font class is easy. However, the more difficult job is determining where to position text on screen for a pleasing display that will look good on a wide variety of output devices. For example, even in this simple demonstration, using a constant for the y coordinate value might fail to space lines properly for all systems and available fonts. So that the program works correctly on all installations, it calls the FontMetrics method getHeight() to determine the maximum headroom to allow for each line:

```
y += g.getFontMetrics().getHeight();
```

This works, but it is only the most rudimentary way to position text. More sophisticated text placement requires information provided by the FontMetrics class, explained next.

The FontMetrics Class

Listing 17.9 shows Java's FontMetrics class, which provides information that is vital for accurately positioning text in graphical applet and application windows.

Listing 17.9. The FontMetrics class.

```
public abstract class FontMetrics {
// Public methods:
 public Font getFont();
 public int getLeading();
 public int getAscent();
 public int getDescent();
 public int getHeight();
 public int getMaxAscent();
 public int getMaxDescent();
 public int getMaxDecent();
 public int getMaxAdvance();
 public int charWidth(int ch);
 public int charWidth(char ch);
 public int stringWidth(String str);
 public int charsWidth(char data[], int off, int len);
 public int bytesWidth(byte data[], int off, int len);
 public int[] getWidths();
 public String toString();
}
```

Using FontMetrics requires understanding a few terms from the world of professional typesetting. These terms—*Baseline, Leading, Ascent, Descent, Height,* and *Advance*—represent specific elements in the spacing of characters on lines of text. (By the way, *Leading* is pronounced "ledding," not "leeding." The term refers to the amount of spacing above the tallest character in the olden days of hot-lead typesetting.)

Figure 17.5 shows how the various typesetting terms apply to the spacing of text. The Reference point is the location of the coordinate values passed to a method such as `Graphics.drawString()`. This location is on the baseline at the beginning of the first character in the string. The other values are relative to this position.

Figure 17.5.

Typesetting terms exactly describe the spacing of text using a specific font.

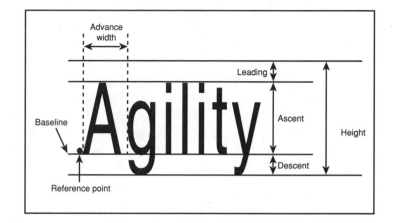

To use the `FontMetrics` class, first assign a `Font` object by calling the `Graphics` method `setFont()`. Usually, you'll do this in a `paint()` method, but if you want to prepare text-positioning variables elsewhere, you can obtain a `Graphics` context object by calling `getGraphics()`, which is inherited by your `Applet` subclass:

```
Graphics g = getGraphics();
```

Next, create a `Font` object, and assign it to the `Graphics` context:

```
Font f = new Font("Helvetica", Font.PLAIN, 14);
g.setFont(f);
```

You may skip those two steps if you want to use the default font, or if one has been set into the `Graphics` object by other means. Finally, obtain a `FontMetrics` object for the selected font by calling `getFontMetrics()` in reference to the `Graphics` context object:

```
FontMetrics fm = g.getFontMetrics();
```

This gives you extensive information in one handy package that you can use to position text with precision. Remember that this information is accurate for only the current font. If you set a different font into the `Graphics` context object, you must again call `getFontMetrics()`. To inspect the `Font` referenced by a `FontMetrics` object, call the `getFont()` method. For example, you can save the current `Font` object using this statement:

```
Font saveFont = fm.getFont();   // Save font referenced by fm
```

The `FontMetrics` class provides eight methods that return basic spacing information. (Refer back to Figure 17.5.) These methods are as follows:

- `int getLeading()`: Returns the standard leading, also called the *inter-line spacing*, to reserve below the descent of a preceding line. This is not necessarily the maximum leading for all characters in the font.

- `int getAscent()`: Returns the standard ascent of most characters in the font, equal to the space from the average tallest character to the baseline. This is not necessarily the maximum ascent for all characters in the font.

- `int getDescent()`: Returns the standard descent of most characters in the font, equal to the space below the baseline that characters such as *g* and *y* dangle their tails. Some characters may extend beyond the space indicated by this method.

- `int getHeight()`: Returns the standard height of most characters in the font, equal to the sum of the leading, ascent, and descent standard values. Some characters may be taller than indicated by this method.

- `int getMaxAscent()`: Returns the maximum ascent of any character in the font.

- `int getMaxDescent()`: Returns the maximum descent of any character in the font.

- `int getMaxDecent()`: Included for backwards compatibility with older Java versions in which this method name was accidentally misspelled. Do not call this method—it merely calls the correctly spelled `getMaxDescent()`.

- `int getMaxAdvance()`: Returns the maximum advance width of any character in the font, equal to the character's width plus space to the right, up to the beginning of the next character. If this value is not known, `getMaxAdvance()` returns -1. (From the AWT source code, it appears that this method *always* returns -1 and is therefore of no practical use. Specific Java installations may implement this method, but don't count on it.)

The first four of the preceding eight methods return standard information that is probably accurate for most purposes. If you use these standard values, some text might not be exactly spaced—a character's descent might extend a bit too low and touch another character on a line below. The other methods return maximum values that are guaranteed not to be violated, but might produce too widely spaced text for most characters. In most cases, it is safe to use the standard values and risk an occasional spacing problem.

Six methods in `FontMetrics` provide additional information about the width of specific characters and strings. (Refer again to Figure 17.5.) Here are the methods:

- `int charWidth(int ch)`: Returns the advance width of the specified character code value.

- `int charWidth(char ch)`: Returns the advance width of the specified character.

- `int stringWidth(String str)`: Returns the sum of the advance widths of all characters in the specified `String` object.

- int charsWidth(char data[], int off, int len): Returns the sum of the advance widths of len characters in the char array, starting with the character at data[off].

- int bytesWidth(byte data[], int off, int len): Returns the sum of the advance widths of len characters in the byte array (presumably holding ASCII character data), starting with the character at data[off].

- int[] getWidths(): Returns an array of integer values equal to the advance widths of the first 256 characters in the selected font.

Creating a Graphics Object

At times, it is necessary to draw an object immediately rather than wait for paint() to get around to updating the display. To do this, you may obtain a temporary Graphics context object and use it to draw a shape or display text in an applet's window. Although this is easy to do, when using this technique, it's important to follow two guidelines:

- Retain any necessary values so that paint() can re-create any object you draw in a different method.

- Limit your use of temporary Graphics objects as much as possible. Some operating systems may not support more than a few Graphics context objects at a time, and creating more than a limited number could overtax the system's resources.

Obtaining a temporary Graphics context is also a key technique in animated and busy graphics displays. For example, a program that draws numerous shapes might need several methods, each programmed to draw a specific object. Those methods might be called from paint(), or from other methods in the applet or application.

These kinds of programs, however, can quickly tow your code into troubled waters. As your paint() method becomes more and more complex, you will begin to notice a reduction in speed, and you might also notice a lack of responsiveness in the browser. This happens because a complex paint() method *blocks* other processes that contribute to smoothly running software, a situation that must not be allowed to occur.

The solution to this common problem is to use the multithreaded techniques introduced in Chapter 11, "Threads." This way, other processes continue to run concurrently with your program's graphics code, resulting in smoother operation and at least the appearance of improved speed. Users can, for example, click buttons, enter text, and perform other activities while complex graphics form in the background. Multithreaded programming is also an important ingredient in image animation, covered later in this chapter in the "Multimedia Sound and Animation" section.

Listing 17.10 demonstrates the correct way to program multithreaded graphics applets. The program also shows how to obtain and use a Graphics context object for drawing in a method other than paint(). Although the program is simple—it merely draws colored lines at random—the applet's methods make a useful shell for your own complex graphics programming. Simply remove my output statements and insert your own to create a smoothly operating, multithreaded graphical applet.

Listing 17.10. RandLine.java (Demonstrates multithreaded graphics).

```
import java.applet.*;
import java.awt.*;
import java.util.Vector;
import java.util.VectorEnumerator;
import java.util.Random;
//===============================================================
// Line class
//===============================================================
class Line {
 // Fields that define a line's end points
 public int x1, y1, x2, y2;
 public Color c;
 // Constructor
 public Line(int x1, int y1, int x2, int y2, Color c) {
  this.x1 = x1;
  this.y1 = y1;
  this.x2 = x2;
  this.y2 = y2;
  this.c  = c;
 }
}
//===============================================================
// Applet RandLine class
//===============================================================
public class RandLine extends Applet implements Runnable
{
 // Instance variables
 Thread gThread = null;  // Graphics thread
 Random gen = null;      // Random number generator
 Vector lines = null;    // Holds Line objects
 // Initialize applet window
 public void init() {
  resize(320, 240);
  gen = new Random();     // Construct random generator
 }
 // Draw line object using Graphics context
 public void drawLine(Line ln, Graphics g) {
  g.setColor(ln.c);
  g.drawLine(ln.x1, ln.y1, ln.x2, ln.y2);
 }
 // Redraw all saved lines
 public void paint(Graphics g) {
  if (lines == null)
   return;
  VectorEnumerator enum =
   (VectorEnumerator)lines.elements();
  while (enum.hasMoreElements()) {
   Line ln = (Line)enum.nextElement();
   drawLine(ln, g);
  }
```

```
}
// Start the graphics thread
public void start() {
 if (gThread == null) {
  gThread = new Thread(this);
  gThread.start();
 }
}
// Stop the graphics thread
public void stop() {
 if (gThread != null) {
  gThread.stop();
  gThread = null;
 }
}
// Construct and return a new Line object
public Line newLine(Line previousLine) {
 int x1, y1, x2, y2;
 Rectangle r = bounds();
 x1 = previousLine.x2;
 y1 = previousLine.y2;
 x2 = Math.abs(gen.nextInt()) % r.width;
 y2 = Math.abs(gen.nextInt()) % r.height;
 Color c = new Color(
  gen.nextInt() % 255,
  gen.nextInt() % 255,
  gen.nextInt() % 255 );
 Line ln = new Line(x1, y1, x2, y2, c);
 return ln;
}
// Runs the separate graphics thread
public void run() {
 // Create starting line
 Line ln = new Line(0, 0, 0, 0, Color.black);
 // Create vector to hold Lines objects
 lines = new Vector(100);
 // Create temporary graphics context
 Graphics context = getGraphics();
 // Perform threaded loop
 while (true) {  // Do "forever"
  try {
   ln = newLine(ln);       // Create a Line object
   lines.addElement(ln);   // Add Line to Vector
   drawLine(ln, context);  // Draw the new Line
   Thread.sleep(50);       // Sleep for a while
  } catch (InterruptedException e) {
   stop();
  }
 }
}
}
```

Multithreaded programs can be difficult to understand, so to make it easier for you to follow along with the code, I'll describe each declaration and method as it appears in the listing. After a set of import statements, the applet declares a new class, Line, for the purpose of storing the color and coordinate values of a single line.

The applet class, RandLine, extends in the usual way from Applet, but also implements the Runnable interface. This enables the applet to execute threaded code. If you did not select multithreaded programming with the Applet Wizard, you can manually add implements Runnable to your applet class's declaration.

The class next declares three variables so that they are available to all methods:

```
Thread gThread = null;
Random gen = null;
Vector lines = null;
```

The first variable represents the thread that will draw the program's graphics concurrently with other processes. The second variable is used to create line coordinate values at random. The third variable stores all lines generated so that paint() can easily re-create the program's display.

Method init() performs only two simple jobs: sizing the applet's window and constructing the random number generator from the Random class. The next method, declared as

```
public void drawLine(Line ln, Graphics g);
```

is a good example of code that, in a complex graphical program, draws an individual shape. As the method's name implies, drawLine() draws a Line object using the specified Graphics context. A statement in paint() could pass its Graphics object to drawLine(), or another method can obtain a Graphics context and use it to draw lines. For example, in this applet, paint() uses standard Vector techniques to pass all saved Line objects to drawLine(), thus updating the display as needed. To see how this works, run the program and obscure the browser with another window. Move that window aside and watch each line being redrawn.

Notice especially that paint() does not generate the program's graphics. This is vital to the program's smooth running appearance!

> **TIP**
>
> If you discover that you are programming lengthy for or other loops in paint(), this is a good sign that you need to consider using the multithreaded techniques described here. Try never to write a paint() method that blocks other processes.

The applet's start() and stop() methods begin and halt the thread responsible for the creation and display of each line. Method start() executes these statements:

```
if (gThread == null) {
 gThread = new Thread(this);
 gThread.start();
}
```

If the Thread object gThread is not null, and therefore has not yet been constructed, the statement creates a new Thread object and calls its start() method. Conversely, the stop() method stops the thread and sets gThread to null:

```
if (gThread != null) {
 gThread.stop();
 gThread = null;
}
```

The program's newLine() method returns a Line object with randomly selected coordinate values and color. The programming is straightforward, so I won't describe it further.

Finally, in the listing, we come to its heart—the run() method that creates the graphics display. The first three statements in run() create a starting Line object, a Vector for holding all generated lines, and a graphics context. The statement

```
Graphics context = getGraphics();
```

shows how to obtain a separate Graphics object for drawing in a method other than paint().

After these preliminary steps, a so-called do-forever while loop draws lines repeatedly until you halt the applet or close the browser. The statements in this part of the code are encased in a try block so the do-forever loop can exit upon the receipt of an InterruptedException object. Meanwhile, the program executes these statements:

```
ln = newLine(ln);
lines.addElement(ln);
drawLine(ln, context);
Thread.sleep(50);
```

First, newLine() is called to create a new Line object, which is added to the Vector for safekeeping, and so that paint() can faithfully update the applet's display. Next, drawLine() draws this single line—a simple-seeming action that is actually key to keeping the program running smoothly. By passing the Graphics context object to drawLine(), the program satisfies two basic design goals:

- It avoids blocking other processes during the creation of its graphics.
- It retains information (the Vector of Line objects) so that paint() can re-create the applet's display on demand.

The final step in the preceding code fragment shows how to use the Thread class to control the speed of an applet's display. Executing the statement

```
Thread.sleep(50);
```

causes the program to pause for the specified number of milliseconds, but does not block other processes from running.

> **NOTE**
>
> Some possible improvements to RandLine come to mind—perhaps you'll want to try making them. The program's paint() method could display the lines Vector using another thread so that the repainting of even hundreds of lines would not block other processes. Another possibility would be to draw lines to an offscreen image, and then display the resulting bitmap rather than repaint each individual line (see "Offscreen Images" in this chapter). In that case, the Vector would not be needed.

Image Processing

Although the Graphics class provides several overloaded drawImage() methods for displaying bitmap-image files (I'll call them image files from now on), and the Applet class provides overloaded getImage() methods for loading image data, using these methods correctly takes careful programming. Loading image data—especially over remote network connections—is a time-consuming process that must not be allowed to interfere with other processes. This is especially important when animating multiple images and when displaying large pictures. While an image is loading and forming onscreen, users expect to be able to read other text and to interact with an applet's components. This means that calling getImage() and drawImage() must be handled in a separate thread that runs concurrently with other processes.

The following sections explain how to program applets to display static images, and also how to create animations that display multiple image files. In both cases, multithreaded code handles the loading and displaying of image data to ensure a smoothly running result.

The Image Class

Numerous classes are associated with image data files, which in the current implementation are limited to files using the GIF format. Even if this limitation is lifted in the future, the techniques for loading and displaying images will most likely remain the same regardless of storage format. For the moment, I'll concentrate on those classes you will most likely use for displaying and animating images. Later in this chapter, in the sections "Offscreen Images" and "Filtered Images," I'll describe other classes in the awt.image package that are available for advanced work. See the "Animation" section near the end of this chapter for information on animating multiple images.

The AWT package organizes its image classes into four categories:

- *Images:* These objects represent the actual image data, which is rendered in memory according to the requirements of the local operating system.

- *Image observers:* These are objects that monitor image loading, and display images only when ready. Technically, an image observer is an object of any class that implements the `ImageObserver` interface, which requires a method, `imageUpdate()`, that is called when an image, or a portion of an image, is ready for display.

- *Image producers:* These are objects that provide a source for image data. Think of them as conduits through which image data flows.

- *Image consumers:* These are objects that provide for the use or display of image data. A component such as a button that displays an image is a good example of an image consumer. Because the `Applet` class lists `Component` among its ancestors, applets can also be image consumers.

Listing 17.11 shows the `Image` class declaration. An object of this class represents an image loaded into memory—as returned, for example, by the `Applet.getImage()` method.

Listing 17.11. The `Image` class.

```
public abstract class Image {
// Constant:
 public static final Object UndefinedProperty = new Object();
// Constructor:
 public Image();
// Public methods:
 public abstract int getWidth(ImageObserver observer);
 public abstract int getHeight(ImageObserver observer);
 public abstract ImageProducer getSource();
 public abstract Graphics getGraphics();
 public abstract Object getProperty(String name, ImageObserver observer);
 public abstract void flush();
}
```

You do not construct `Image` objects as you do others, even though the class has a default constructor. Instead, to construct an `Image` object, you will use one of two methods:

- Call `Applet.getImage()` to load an image file.

- Call `Component.createImage()` to prepare a new image, usually for preparing an offscreen drawing surface.

I'll focus in this section on the first technique—loading and displaying image files. Later in this chapter (in the "Offscreen Images" section), I'll discuss how to use the second technique to prepare and use offscreen `Image` objects.

It's important to realize that an object of the `Image` class is not simply a collection of graphics bits in memory. In fact, there is no defined way to access an image's actual bitmap data. An `Image` object is an abstraction of that data—a mere interface to the visual image, the nature of which is necessarily system-dependent. On disk, a GIF file is essentially a set of instructions for creating this data. In memory, the format of the image depends entirely on the operating system.

The Image class's public methods are as follows:

- int getWidth(ImageObserver observer): Returns the width of the image in pixels, or if the image is still loading and the width is therefore unknown as dictated by the ImageObserver parameter, it returns -1.

- int getHeight(ImageObserver observer): Returns the height of the image in pixels, or if the image is still loading and the height is therefore unknown as dictated by the ImageObserver parameter, it returns -1.

- ImageProducer getSource(): Returns the producer that is the source of the image. Used most often with filtered images—those that are cropped to a portion of a full image bitmap, for example. (See the "Filtered Images" section in this chapter.)

- Graphics getGraphics(): Returns a Graphics context object for drawing to offscreen images. (See the "Offscreen Images" section in this chapter).

- Object getProperty(String name, ImageObserver observer): Returns a property defined for the image and labeled according to the String name. A commonly available property is "comment", which identifies the image's author or other source. If the property is not available, or if the image is still loading as dictated by the ImageObserver parameter, this method returns UndefinedProperty, an object of the Object class, defined as a public member of the Image class.

- void flush(): Flushes any system resources associated with this image—an in-memory cache, for example. Calling this method resets the image to its just-loaded or just-created state. Subsequent uses of the image require reloading or reforming the image from its source.

Using the Image class properly requires the help of another class, MediaTracker, which I'll list and explain a bit later. As you will see in the next sample program, MediaTracker simplifies the multithreaded aspects of loading and displaying image files, which as I've said, must not interfere with the program's and browser's other processes. Listing 17.12, ShowGIF.java, shows the correct way to use Image and MediaTracker to load and display a single GIF image file. Figure 17.6 shows the program's display of a sample GIF file included on the CD-ROM.

Listing 17.12. ShowGIF.java (Loads and displays a GIF image).

```
import java.applet.*;
import java.awt.*;
public class ShowGIF
extends Applet
implements Runnable
{
 // Instance variables
 Image pic;                // GIF image producer
 int picID;                // Arbitrary image ID
 MediaTracker tracker;     // Tracks loading of image
 Thread loadingThread;     // Thread for loading image
 String filename = "Parasol.gif";  // File name
 // Initialize applet
 public void init() {
```

```
   // Size applet window
   resize(320, 320);
   // Create MediaTracker object
   tracker = new MediaTracker(this);
   // Start image loading
   pic = getImage(getDocumentBase(), filename);
   picID = 0;
   tracker.addImage(pic, picID);
   // Create thread to monitor image loading
   loadingThread = new Thread(this);
   loadingThread.start();
 }
 // Run loading thread
 // Allows other processes to run while loading
 // the image data
 public void run() {
  try {
   tracker.waitForID(picID);
  } catch (InterruptedException ie) {
   return;
  }
  repaint();  // Cause paint() to draw loaded image
 }
 // Paint window contents
 // Displays loading or error message until
 // image is ready, then shows image
 public void paint(Graphics g) {
  if (tracker.isErrorID(picID))
   g.drawString("Error loading " + filename, 10, 20);
  else if (tracker.checkID(picID))
   g.drawImage(pic, 0, 0, this);
  else
   g.drawString("Loading " + filename, 10, 20);
 }
}
```

Figure 17.6.

ShowGIF demonstrates the correct way to load a graphics image using a separate thread.

You might see far simpler image-display programs in various Java tutorials, but as I've said, doing this correctly in a multithreaded environment requires more care than might be obvious. The first step is to make the `Applet` subclass capable of executing a threaded `run()` method. Be sure to add `implements Runnable` to your class declaration as shown here.

The applet class needs several variables for loading and displaying the image. In the sample program, these variables are

```
Image pic;
int picID;
MediaTracker tracker;
Thread loadingThread;
String filename = "Parasol.gif";
```

The `Image` object represents the image data and serves as a conduit for its importation from a source into memory. The integer `picID` is optional, but it can be used to numerically identify multiple images. The ID numbers are up to the program to assign and do not come from the images themselves. A `MediaTracker` object operates as a kind of director that monitors image loading and causes an image to be displayed only when ready. A single `MediaTracker` object can monitor the loading of an unlimited number of images. Using `MediaTracker` helps keep the program running fast and also simplifies error detection. A `Thread` object cooperates with `MediaTracker` to load and display one or more images concurrently with other processes. Finally, a `String` object represents the image's filename, which might be in reference to a URL or, for locally executing code, a subdirectory on disk.

> **NOTE**
>
> In other publications and listings, you might find image loading and display techniques that do not use `MediaTracker`. Ignore them. The `MediaTracker` class was recently added to the AWT package specifically for simplifying image programming. Image applets that don't use `MediaTracker` are out of date.

The sample applet's `init()` method prepares the class's variables for use. After sizing the applet's window, the program creates a `MediaTracker` object with the statement

```
tracker = new MediaTracker(this);
```

Passing `this` to the constructor tells the `MediaTracker` object which component, or `Applet` subclass object, will display the images. This argument can be any object of a class extended from `Component`. For example, a custom component could use a `MediaTracker` object to load a bitmap.

The next step is to load the actual image. This uses a sequence of steps that might appear a little odd:

```
pic = getImage(getDocumentBase(), filename);
picID = 0;
tracker.addImage(pic, picID);
```

Despite the method's name, getImage() does not actually load the specified image file, optionally referenced by a document base URL. Calling getImage() merely starts the process by which the image will be loaded, and this method returns immediately. As shown here, save the returned Image object in a variable (named pic, in this case) and prepare an optional ID value if needed. The final step adds the Image object and its ID to the MediaTracker object, which monitors the image's loading in a separate thread. None of these steps actually loads any image data from disk. That will happen a bit later.

By interrogating the MediaTracker object, the applet can determine when an image is available for use. To allow other processes to continue concurrently, you will usually call MediaTracker methods in a separate thread, which the sample program's init() method creates and starts by using these statements:

```
loadingThread = new Thread(this);
loadingThread.start();
```

The final statement causes the applet's run() method to be called. Meanwhile, the MediaTracker object is loading the image from disk. To detect when the image is ready, run() calls MediaTracker.waitForID(), passing the image's ID value assigned by init(). This is done in a try block that catches an InterruptedException, which is thrown if another thread interrupts this one:

```
try {
 tracker.waitForID(picID);
} catch (InterruptedException ie) {
 return;
}
```

When the program calls waitForID(), the image begins to load into memory from disk or over the network. Because this code is executed in a separate thread, other processes can interrupt this one, in which case run() immediately returns. This might happen, for example, if the user leaves the applet. When waitForID() returns normally, run() forces a display update by executing

```
repaint();
```

which eventually calls paint(). However, even though waitForID() returned normally, the image might not be ready for display. For example, its file might be missing, or a glitch might have caused the download to fail. To detect such problems, paint() again interrogates the MediaTracker object using this if statement:

```
if (tracker.isErrorID(picID))
 g.drawString("Error loading " + filename, 10, 20);
```

If isErrorID() returns false, an error occurred and the image cannot be displayed. To see the effect of this code, make an intentional error in the image's filename string, and rerun the applet.

Even if no errors are detected, and despite all the preceding code, it's important to keep in mind that image-loading is taking place in a separate thread—thus, you still have to verify that the image is ready for display. Do this by calling a MediaTracker method such as checkID(), which returns true only if the specified image (or other data) is completely loaded and ready for use. The sample program does this by following the preceding code with

```
else if (tracker.checkID(picID))
 g.drawImage(pic, 0, 0, this);
```

Only if checkID() returns true does paint() call the drawImage() method in reference to the Graphics context object passed to paint(). The arguments passed to drawImage() identify the Image, its relative display coordinates, and this as the ImageObserver object responsible for the image's actual transfer to the display.

Finally, if no errors are detected, but the image is still not ready for display, paint() shows a message stating that the image is loading:

```
else
 g.drawString("Loading " + filename, 10, 20);
```

When running the sample applet locally, you will have only a brief moment to see this message. Another possibility is to paint an empty rectangle where the image will eventually appear; users will probably understand that the image inside the rectangle is either unavailable or is being downloaded.

> **NOTE**
>
> Calling Graphics.drawImage() might paint only a portion of a large image—or it might paint the interlaced lines of a GIF image as more data becomes available. Along with MediaTracker's help, the code in the sample applet in this section correctly handles these situations, but it's important to realize that calling drawImage() in itself is not enough to ensure that an entire image is actually drawn.

The MediaTracker Class

The sample ShowGIF applet in the preceding section uses the MediaTracker class to manage the loading of image data. Currently, this class is limited to use with graphics images, but it is expected to be used in the future for more sophisticated multimedia software. Though the class declaration, shown in Listing 17.13, appears complex, it is relatively easy to use, and most methods have obvious purposes. Following the listing, I'll describe how to use selected methods.

Listing 17.13. The MediaTracker class.

```
public class MediaTracker {
// Fields:
 public static final int LOADING;
 public static final int ABORTED;
 public static final int ERRORED;
```

```
 public static final int COMPLETE;
// Constructor:
 public MediaTracker(Component comp);
// Public methods:
 public void addImage(Image image, int id);
 public synchronized void addImage(Image image, int id, int w, int h);
 public boolean checkAll();
 public synchronized boolean checkAll(boolean load);
 public synchronized boolean isErrorAny();
 public synchronized Object[] getErrorsAny();
 public void waitForAll() throws InterruptedException;
 public synchronized boolean waitForAll(long ms);
 public int statusAll(boolean load);
 public boolean checkID(int id);
 public synchronized boolean checkID(int id, boolean load);
 public synchronized boolean isErrorID(int id);
 public synchronized Object[] getErrorsID(int id);
 public void waitForID(int id) throws InterruptedException ;
 public synchronized boolean waitForID(int id, long ms);
 public int statusID(int id, boolean load);
}
```

A MediaTracker object may be created for any Component but is often associated with the applet's object. For example, the ShowGIF applet in this chapter creates a MediaTracker object using this statement from method init():

```
tracker = new MediaTracker(this);
```

To add an Image object to this MediaTracker, call addImage():

```
tracker.addImage(pic, picID);
```

This assumes that the Image (pic here) has been constructed by some other means. The ID is useful when working with multiple images, all of which may be managed by the same MediaTracker. Alternatively, you may specify width and height values to scale an image using code such as

```
tracker.addImage(pic, picID, 100, 50);  // ???
```

I question the value of this technique. I haven't had any luck with it, and in Visual J++, this appears to have no effect on the final image size.

After adding an image to a MediaTracker, call the class's methods to determine the image's status. There are numerous ways to proceed. For example, you can receive a status integer by calling statusID():

```
int status = tracker.statusID(picID, true);
```

This assigns to status the bitwise OR of the appropriate MediaTracker flags: ABORTED, COMPLETE, ERRORED, and LOADING. The true argument passed to statusID() tells MediaTracker to begin loading the specified image if it hasn't already done so. You might try this code, perhaps in a small loop or, better, in a thread, to retry loading in the event of an error.

Some `MediaTracker` methods check that all images are available. This is especially useful in animation programming when you don't want to begin displaying a sequence of images until they are all ready. Code such as

```
if (tracker.checkAll(true))
 showPictures();
```

calls a method only if `MediaTracker` confirms that all images assigned by `addImage()` are ready for use. The `true` argument, which is optional, tells `MediaTracker` to begin loading the images if it hasn't already done so.

Inside your image thread, call a method such as `waitForAll()` to allow `MediaTracker` to continue loading image data without blocking other threads. This will usually be in a `run()` method, using a `try` statement to catch a thread interruption. For example, the code

```
try {
 tracker.waitForAll(50);
} catch (InterruptedException ie) {
 return;
}
repaint();   // Or other method
```

gives the `MediaTracker` 50 milliseconds to load or scale its monitored images. The `paint()` method, or its equivalent if using other display techniques, needs to check with the `MediaTracker` to determine whether the images are ready for use.

> **NOTE**
>
> I'll return again to `MediaTracker` in this chapter's animation example near the end of the chapter under the section titled "Animation."

Offscreen Images

Creating an image offscreen and then displaying the results all at once can help give an applet a snappier appearance by hiding the individual steps that go into forming complex graphics. The program might also run faster because, unlike a GIF file laboriously downloaded over the network, an offscreen image is formed by program statements that call subroutines in the user's browser and operating system. Because the compiled byte codes for those statements are probably much fewer than the bytes in an equivalent image file, complex images produced locally under program control are potentially faster to appear—in many cases, even when compared to compressed image data. The technique also figures prominently in animation—a technique called *double buffering*—when two or more images with minor changes are kept offscreen, ready for displaying in sequence.

There are four basic steps in creating and using an offscreen image:

1. Prepare an `Image` object in memory to serve as the drawing surface.
2. Obtain a `Graphics` context object for drawing to the offscreen image.
3. Draw to the offscreen image using `Graphics` class methods.
4. Display the `Image` object the same way you display one loaded from a GIF file.

Listing 17.14, `Offscreen.java`, demonstrates how to create and display an offscreen image. As with other sample applets in this chapter, the code is multithreaded so that, while the image is forming, other processes continue to run concurrently. Figure 17.7 shows the program's display of 100 colorful ovals, which are painted to an offscreen image and then displayed all at once with a single command.

Figure 17.7.

The Offscreen applet demonstrates how to paint and display graphics using an offscreen image.

Listing 17.14. `Offscreen.java` (Creates and displays an offscreen image).

```java
import java.applet.*;
import java.awt.*;
import java.util.Random;
public class Offscreen extends Applet
 implements Runnable {
 // Instance variables
 Thread drawingThread;
 Image offscreenImage;
 Graphics offscreenContext;
 Random gen;
 boolean imageReady = false;
 int imageW, imageH;
 int numOvals = 100;
 // Initialize applet
 public void init() {
 // Size applet window
 resize(320, 240);
 // Construct random number generator
 gen = new Random();
 // Create offscreen image and Graphics context
 imageW = size().width;
 imageH = size().height;
```

continues

Listing 17.14. continued

```java
    offscreenImage = createImage(imageW, imageH);
    offscreenContext = offscreenImage.getGraphics();
  }
  // Create and start drawing thread
  public void start() {
    drawingThread = new Thread(this);
    drawingThread.start();
  }
  // Stop the thread
  public void stop() {
    if (drawingThread != null) {
      drawingThread.stop();
      drawingThread = null;
      imageReady = false;
    }
  }
  // Return positive integer at random between
  // low and high. Assumes low < high and are positive
  public int nextInt(int low, int high) {
    return low + (Math.abs(gen.nextInt()) % (high - low));
  }
  // Create image using separate thread
  public void run() {
    // Paint image background white
    offscreenContext.setColor(getBackground());
    offscreenContext.fillRect(0, 0, imageW, imageH);
    // Create and paint ovals at random
    for (int i = 0; i < numOvals; i++) {
      // Select oval color at random
      Color c = new Color(nextInt(0, 0xffffff));
      offscreenContext.setColor(c);
      // Select oval position
      int x = nextInt(20, imageW - 20);
      int y = nextInt(20, imageH - 20);
      // Calculate oval width and height
      // so it remains inside image boundaries
      int w = nextInt(10, Math.min(imageW - x, x));
      int h = nextInt(10, Math.min(imageH - y, y));
      // Draw oval to offscreen image
      offscreenContext.fillOval(x, y, w, h);
      Thread.yield();
    }
    imageReady = true;
    repaint();
  }
  // Paint window contents
  public void paint(Graphics g) {
    if (imageReady) {
      showStatus("Showing image...");
      g.drawImage(offscreenImage, 0, 0, this);
    } else {
      g.setColor(getBackground());
      g.fillRect(0, 0, imageW, imageH);
      showStatus("Preparing image...");
    }
  }
}
```

```
// Override inherited update() method
// to prevent screen flicker
public void update(Graphics g) {
  paint(g);
 }
}
```

This sample applet might seem overly complex, but as with other image code in this chapter, the extra programming—which handles image creation and display using separate threads—is required for a smooth result. Because the applet is multithreaded, its class implements the Runnable interface. The class also declares several instance variables, the most important of which are

```
Thread drawingThread;
Image offscreenImage;
Graphics offscreenContext;
```

The Thread object forms the offscreen image using a separate thread, so that other processes can run concurrently. The Image object provides a surface for drawing offscreen. The Graphics context object is provided by the image for calling graphics methods such as fillOval() and directing the results to the offscreen surface.

Method init() constructs the essential objects to prepare for drawing offscreen. The statements

```
imageW = size().width;
imageH = size().height;
offscreenImage = createImage(imageW, imageH);
offscreenContext = offscreenImage.getGraphics();
```

specify the width and height of the image to be the same as the applet's window; you can use different values, but in most cases, you won't create images larger than the applet. Call Component.createImage(), inherited by your Applet class, to create an Image object that you can draw to offscreen. To obtain a Graphics context object for drawing to the image, call Image.getGraphics().

To draw to the offscreen image, call Graphics class methods in reference to the associated Graphics context object. For example, fill an offscreen image's background to a color using code such as

```
offscreenContext.setColor(Color.red);
offscreenContext.fillRect(0, 0, imageW, imageH);
```

The sample applet performs similar instructions in method run(), which runs concurrently with other processes. For example, after creating each oval's position and size, the statement

```
offscreenContext.fillOval(x, y, w, h);
```

adds a new oval to the forming image. To give other processes the opportunity to run, each loop executes this statement:

```
Thread.yield();
```

When the image is finished, the thread sets the `imageReady` flag to `true`, and calls `repaint()`. This initiates an eventual call to `paint()`, which displays the offscreen image using this statement:

```
g.drawImage(offscreenImage, 0, 0, this);
```

This is the same way this chapter's ShowGIF applet displays a GIF file—the entire image appears at once. Sometimes, you might want users to see the image forming, but still use offscreen drawing. To do this, simply call `repaint()` inside the loop that creates the graphics. For example, modify the sample program by inserting the following two statements into the `run()` method's `for` loop, immediately after the call to `Thread.yield()`:

```
imageReady = true;
repaint();
```

When you run the modified program, you will see each oval as it is created. Even so, the code is properly multithreaded, and the image is formed offscreen as before—but the entire image is redisplayed to show each new oval, which is not as efficient as drawing them directly to the screen. (Click the browser's Refresh button to create a new set of shapes.)

The Offscreen applet also demonstrates a useful trick that eliminates an annoying flicker you might see when displaying multiple images. Normally, the `update()` method inherited from `Component` by your `Applet` class executes the statements

```
g.setColor(getBackground());
g.fillRect(0, 0, width, height);
g.setColor(getForeground());
paint(g);
```

This paints the window with the background color, sets the foreground color, and calls `paint()`. To eliminate the background painting, which causes the flicker, override `update()` and replace it with this streamlined model:

```
public void update(Graphics g) {
 paint(g);
}
```

To see what a difference the modified method makes, delete it from the sample applet (or turn it into a comment), and make the aforementioned modification that displays each oval as it is formed. When you run the program, it flickers worse than an old movie, but it is useful to see the problem so that if it occurs to you, you'll know how to fix it.

Filtered Images

The AWT package includes a nested package of classes that you can use to filter images. As a demonstration of these classes, the next sample applet shows how to convert a colored image into a gray-scale picture. Each pixel of the original image is filtered to an equivalent pixel of the same intensity, but lacking any color information.

This technique also brings up the subject of image producers and consumers. In general terms, a producer is an object that is used as a source of image data—whether that data is downloaded over the network, or is loaded from a file on disk. A consumer is an object that serves as a destination for image data. The applet, for example, is a consumer that can display an image. Programmatically speaking, an image producer is an object of a class that implements the `ImageProducer` interface. A consumer is an object of a class that implements `ImageConsumer`. These protocols provide the necessary methods for obtaining and using image pixel data.

By creating your own image producer object, you can filter that pixel data as requested by an image consumer. The filtered image is formed offscreen as explained in the preceding section, and it is displayed in the usual way.

The AWT image package provides ready-to-use filters. For example, the `CropImageFilter` class is useful for loading portions of large graphics files—a more efficient method than loading the entire image and displaying only a chunk of the picture. First, import the AWT image package with the statement

```
import java.awt.image.*;
```

Load the image file as demonstrated by this chapter's showGIF applet:

```
Image gifPic = getImage(getDocumentBase(), "filename.gif");
```

To insert a filter into the works, obtain the image's producer by calling `getSource()`:

```
ImageProducer picSource = gifPic.getSource();
```

This provides the means to tap into the image's source of pixels. To modify those pixels, create a filter object, in this case, using the supplied `CropImageFilter` class:

```
CropImageFilter picFilter = new CropImageFilter(0, 0, 50, 50);
```

The arguments specify the coordinates of the portion of the image to use. Finally, create an offscreen image using a new object of the `FilteredImageSource` class, which takes two arguments—the image producer and filter objects:

```
pic = createImage(new FilteredImageSource(picSource, picFilter));
```

This assumes that `pic` is an object of the `Image` class, probably declared as an instance variable in your `Applet` class. When the image is loaded via the specified producer, its pixels are filtered by the specified filter object, which in this example restricts loading pixels to those that fall within the defined coordinates. Display the filtered offscreen image in the usual way. For example, `paint()` might execute the following statement:

```
g.drawImage(pic, 0, 0, this);
```

As a more sophisticated example, Listing 17.15 shows how to extend an existing filter class to create your own filters. The applet is similar to the ShowGIF sample—I used a copy of that program as a starting place—but it adds a new class and additional code to convert a color image to a gray-scale picture. This is done by filtering each pixel using the Color class's hue, saturation, and brightness capabilities. Figure 17.8 shows the program's display of a clown in black-and-white. Load this file (Clown.gif in the Filter subdirectory) into your browser or other GIF viewer to see the image in its original colors.

Figure 17.8.

The Filter applet displays a color GIF image converted to a gray-scale image.

Listing 17.15. Filter.java (Converts color GIF file to gray-scale image).

```java
import java.applet.*;
import java.awt.*;
import java.awt.image.*;
//================================================================
// BWFilter (black and white filter) class
//================================================================
class BWFilter extends RGBImageFilter {
 // Constructor
 public BWFilter() {
  canFilterIndexColorModel = true;
 }
 // Return rgb color converted to shade of gray
 public int filterRGB(int x, int y, int rgb) {
  // Reduce rgb to hue, saturation, brightness elements
  Color c = new Color(rgb);
  float[] hsbvals = Color.RGBtoHSB(c.getRed(), c.getGreen(),
   c.getBlue(), null);
  // Return new color value of same brightness but
  // with hue and saturation set to zero
  return Color.HSBtoRGB(0.0f, 0.0f, hsbvals[2]);
 }
}
//================================================================
// Applet class
//================================================================
public class Filter
 extends Applet
 implements Runnable {
  // Instance variables
  Image pic;                // GIF image producer
  int picID;                // Arbitrary image ID
  MediaTracker tracker;     // Tracks loading of image
```

```
Thread loadingThread;  // Thread for loading image
String filename = "Clown.gif";  // File name
boolean imageReady = false;  // Offscreen image flag
Image bwPic;                   // Offscreen image object
// Initialize applet
public void init() {
 // Size applet window
 resize(320, 320);
 // Create MediaTracker object
 tracker = new MediaTracker(this);
 // Start image loading
 pic = getImage(getDocumentBase(), filename);
 picID = 0;
 tracker.addImage(pic, picID);
 // Create thread to monitor image loading
 loadingThread = new Thread(this);
 loadingThread.start();
}
// Run loading thread
// Allows other processes to run while loading
// the image data
public void run() {
 try {
  tracker.waitForID(picID);
  if (tracker.checkID(picID, true)) {
   // Create offscreen image using loaded GIF
   // file filtered by our BWFilter class
   ImageProducer picSource = pic.getSource();
   BWFilter bwFilter = new BWFilter();
   bwPic = createImage(new
    FilteredImageSource(picSource, bwFilter));
   imageReady = true;
  }
 } catch (InterruptedException ie) {
  return;
 }
 repaint();  // Cause paint() to draw loaded image
}
// Paint window contents
// Displays loading or error message until
// image is ready, then shows image
public void paint(Graphics g) {
 if (tracker.isErrorID(picID))
  g.drawString("Error loading " + filename, 10, 20);
 else if (tracker.checkID(picID) && imageReady)
  g.drawImage(bwPic, 0, 0, this);  // Show offscreen image
 else
  g.drawString("Loading " + filename, 10, 20);
}
}
```

BWFilter extends an existing filter class, RGBImageFilter, in the AWT.image package. This provides a filter that can modify individual pixels of an Image object. For faster results, the extended class's constructor sets the following flag true:

```
canFilterIndexColorModel = true;
```

This obscurely named flag, when `true`, indicates that the `filterRGB()` method uses only its `rgb` color parameter, and ignores its `x` and `y` integer coordinate values. This way, pixels of the same color need to be filtered only once each. If you do not set the flag `true`, *every* pixel of the image will be sent to `filterRGB()` for filtering. Needless to say, this might be a lengthy process, so unless you must examine every pixel, it's best to set the `canFilterIndexColorModel` flag to `true` in your filter class's constructor.

Implement the `filterRGB()` method to return its `rgb` parameter modified however you wish. In this case, I use the `Color` class to construct gray-scale pixels. To do that, the program creates a `Color` object using the `rgb` parameter in the following statement:

```
Color c = new Color(rgb);
```

Next, the program obtains an array of hue, saturation, and brightness floating point values by calling `Color.RGBtoHSB()`:

```
float[] hsbvals = Color.RGBtoHSB(c.getRed(), c.getGreen(),
 c.getBlue(), null);
```

It is now a simple matter to create the equivalent gray-scale pixel for any color. The final statement in the `filterRGB()` method

```
return Color.HSBtoRGB(0.0f, 0.0f, hsbvals[2]);
```

returns an integer value with the hue and saturation levels set to zero and the brightness unchanged.

To display the filtered image, the rest of the program uses code similar to that in the ShowGIF demonstration. Two new variables, however, are required:

```
boolean imageReady = false;
Image bwPic;
```

The `boolean` flag indicates when the filtered image is ready for display. The `Image` object represents the offscreen surface used to form that image.

The GIF picture is loaded using a separate thread. (See the ShowGIF sample in this chapter for a discussion of this code.) However, the `run()` method adds new code to create a filtered image. The following statements obtain an `ImageProducer` object for the original color GIF image, and create an object of our `BWFilter` class:

```
ImageProducer picSource = pic.getSource();
BWFilter bwFilter = new BWFilter();
bwPic = createImage(new
 FilteredImageSource(picSource, bwFilter));
imageReady = true;
```

These two objects are passed to `createImage()` to construct an offscreen image whose pixels are filtered by running them through our new `filterRGB()` method. Finally, the `imageReady` flag is set to true so that `paint()` can display the modified image.

Multimedia Sound and Animation

The word "multimedia" in Java combines the practicalities of network programming with a large helping of wishful thinking. We are nowhere close to realizing an Internet surfer's dreams of full-motion video applets and virtual reality Web sites bathed in stereophonic sound. On the other hand, technology seems to be moving at warp speed in this direction.

For the present, however, multimedia Java presentations are restricted to animation and sound, with audio quality limited to an embarrassingly simple monophonic .AU file format. With these facts in mind, I offer the following sample sound and animation applets—which I shamelessly label "multimedia"—with the admonishment that all of this information could, and probably will, change overnight.

Playing Sound

The simplest way to add sound to an applet is to call the Applet class's play() methods, which are defined as

```
public void play(URL url);
public void play(URL url, String name);
```

Each method loads and plays the specified audio file, which must be in the .AU format. When the sound stops, it can be restarted only by another call to play(); you can use this method, for example, to create a sound loop (more on that later). Each method accepts a URL object that defines a network address. The first form of play() takes an absolute URL; the second takes a relative address plus a filename. Most often, you'll use the second form with a statement such as

```
play(getDocumentBase(), filename);
```

This passes the current base path to play(), and specifies the name of an audio file. Listing 17.16, SoundDemo.java, demonstrates how to use this method to play the sound file Gong.au. You can substitute any other .AU file for the one specified in the listing.

Listing 17.16. `SoundDemo.java` (Plays a sound file).

```java
import java.applet.*;
import java.awt.*;
public class SoundDemo extends Applet {
 // Audio path and filename
 String filename = "Gong.au";
 // Initialize applet
 public void init() {
  // Size applet window
  resize(320, 240);
  Button playButton = new Button("Click Me");
  add(playButton);
 }
 // Play sound file in response to button click
 public boolean action(Event evt, Object arg) {
  if ("Click Me".equals(arg)) {
   play(getDocumentBase(), filename);
   return true;
  } else {
   return super.action(evt, arg);
  }
 }
}
```

Compile and run the SoundDemo program, and then click the applet's button to play the sound file. You may repeat this as many times as you wish. Each time you click the button, the program's `action()` method calls `Applet.play()` to play the sound file specified by the filename `String` object.

The `AudioClip` Class

Another way to play a sound is to construct an object of the `AudioClip` class, and then call methods for that object. Because the class is used to implement `Applet.play()`, `AudioClip` is a member of the applet package. For example, to play a sound, the second form of `play()` executes these statements:

```java
AudioClip clip = getAudioClip(url, name);
if (clip != null) {
 clip.play();
```

Listing 17.17 shows the `AudioClip` class declaration.

Listing 17.17. The `AudioClip` class.

```java
public interface AudioClip {
// Public methods:
 void play();
 void loop();
 void stop();
}
```

The `AudioClip` interface class provides the following three public methods:

- `void play()`: Plays the sound associated with this `AudioClip` object. The method returns immediately, which might be before the sound finishes playing.

- `void loop()`: Continuously plays the sound associated with this `AudioClip` object. This is done using a separate background thread.

- `void stop()`: Stops the sound started by either the `play()` or `loop()` methods. The sound can be restarted by again calling either of the two preceding methods. Calling `stop()` for a sound that is not already playing causes no ill effects.

The `AudioClip` class is an interface, and as such, it lacks any constructors. Because of this, you cannot create `AudioClip` objects by using the `new` operator. Instead, to use the class, call `Applet.getAudioClip()`, which is overloaded in two ways:

```
public AudioClip getAudioClip(URL url);
public AudioClip getAudioClip(URL url, String name);
```

The parameters are the same as used by `Applet.play()`. The actual `AudioClip` object returned is conditioned for the local operating system—and it's entirely possible that some of those systems will have no sound capabilities. Listing 17.18, `SoundLoop.java`, demonstrates how to use the `AudioClip` class methods to continuously play the `Music.au` sound file. You may substitute another `.AU` file, but those that are written to be played in a loop might sound better with this technique than those such as `Gong.au` that are designed for one-time use.

Listing 17.18. SoundLoop.java (Demonstrates the AudioClip class).

```java
import java.applet.*;
import java.awt.*;
public class SoundLoop extends Applet {
 // Instance variables
 AudioClip soundObject;
 String filename = "music.au";
 Button startButton, stopButton;
 // Initialize applet
 public void init() {
  resize(320, 240);
  soundObject = getAudioClip(getDocumentBase(), filename);
  startButton = new Button("Start");
  stopButton = new Button("Stop");
  add(startButton);
  add(stopButton);
  // Disable start button because sound
  // plays automatically when applet starts
  startButton.disable();
 }
 // Start playing sound when applet starts
 public void start() {
  soundObject.loop();
 }
```

continues

469

Listing 17.18. continued

```
// Stop playing sound when applet stops
public void stop() {
 soundObject.stop();
}
// Start and stop playing sound in response
// to user clicking buttons
public boolean action(Event evt, Object arg) {
 if ("Start".equals(arg)) {
  soundObject.loop();     // Start playing sound
  startButton.disable();
  stopButton.enable();
  return true;
 } else if ("Stop".equals(arg)) {
  soundObject.stop();     // Stop playing sound
  startButton.enable();
  stopButton.disable();
  return true;
 }
 return super.action(evt, arg);
}
}
```

The sample SoundLoop applet demonstrates some important aspects of playing sound files. Because sounds are played in a background thread, the program needs to be sure it starts and stops playing .AU files at the appropriate times. SoundLoop satisfies these requirements by first constructing an AudioClip object in method init(). The statement

```
soundObject = getAudioClip(getDocumentBase(), filename);
```

loads the specified .AU file, and returns it as an AudioClip object tailored for use on the local system. The variable soundObject holds this object throughout the applet's life.

To start playing the sound as soon as the applet is loaded and started, the method start() calls the interface's loop() method:

```
soundObject.loop();
```

You don't have to do this—I added the code so that the sound begins immediately. To ensure that the sound stops when the user switches away from the applet, method stop() calls the interface's stop() method:

```
soundObject.stop();
```

When playing sounds continuously, this step is important so that an applet's sounds don't interfere with another applet's audio.

To play the sound in response to selecting the program's Start and Stop buttons, the method action() also calls the interface's loop() and stop() methods. In addition, the program enables and disables the buttons so that you can stop a sound only if it is playing, and you can start it only if the sound is stopped. However, these steps are not strictly required, and you may start and stop sounds at any time.

Animation

I end this chapter with a sample applet that can animate a series of bitmap images. Figure 17.9 shows the program's display, which, of course, is not animated on this page. (Wouldn't that be a neat trick?)

Figure 17.9.

The Animation demo displays a series of bitmap images in a separate thread.

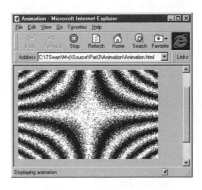

Listing 17.19, `Animation.java`, shows the sample applet's source code. I generated the program using the Visual J++ Applet wizard, and to make it easier to correlate this program's statements with your own, I kept all generated identifiers. However, I added my own comments to explain the listing, and I cleaned up the formatting to suit my tastes and for consistency with other listings in this book. I made a few other modifications here and there. Following the listing, I'll explain the purpose of each method and my changes. This will help you to modify your own Wizard-generated animation applets, but you can instead use my modified listing as a shell if you prefer.

Listing 17.19. `Animation.java` (Demonstrates image animation).

```
import java.applet.*;
import java.awt.*;
public class Animation extends Applet implements Runnable
{
 // Instance variables
 // Thread for loading and displaying images
 Thread m_Animation = null;
// private Graphics m_Graphics;    // Graphics context
 private Image m_Images[];        // Array of images
 private int m_nCurrImage;        // Index of current image
 private int m_nImgWidth  = 0;    // Width of all images
 private int m_nImgHeight = 0;    // Height of all images
 private boolean m_fAllLoaded = false;  // true = all loaded
 private final int NUM_IMAGES = 10;  // Number of image files
 private MediaTracker tracker;    // Tracks image loading
 // Initialize applet
 public void init() {
  resize(320, 240);
```

continues

Listing 17.19. continued

```
    // Create MediaTracker object. The string is
    // for creating the image filenames.
    tracker = new MediaTracker(this);
    String strImage;
    // Load all images. Method getImage() returns immediately
    // and all images are NOT actually loaded into memory
    // by this loop.
    m_Images = new Image[NUM_IMAGES];  // Create image array
    for (int i = 1; i <= NUM_IMAGES; i++) {
     strImage = "images/img00" + ((i < 10) ? "0" : "")
      + i + ".gif";
     m_Images[i-1] = getImage(getDocumentBase(),
      strImage);
     tracker.addImage(m_Images[i-1], 0);
    }
   }
   // Paint window contents
   public void paint(Graphics g)
   {
    // Draw current image
    if (m_fAllLoaded) {
     g.drawImage(m_Images[m_nCurrImage],
      (size().width - m_nImgWidth) / 2,
      (size().height - m_nImgHeight) / 2, null);
    }
   }
   // Create and start animation thread
   public void start() {
    if (m_Animation == null) {
     m_Animation = new Thread(this);
     m_Animation.start();
    }
   }
   // Stop animation thread
   public void stop() {
    if (m_Animation != null) {
     m_Animation.stop();
     m_Animation = null;
    }
   }
   // Run image load and display thread
   public void run() {
    // Load images if not already done
    if (!m_fAllLoaded) {
     showStatus("Loading images...");
     // Wait for images to be loaded
     // Other processes continue to run normally
     try  {
      tracker.waitForAll();
     }
     catch (InterruptedException e) {
      stop();  // Stop thread if interrupted
      return;  // Abort loading process
     }
     // If all images are not loaded by this point,
     // something is wrong and we display an error
     // message.
```

```
    if (tracker.isErrorAny()) {
     showStatus("Error loading images!");
     stop();
     return;
    }

    // All images are loaded. Set the loaded flag
    // and prepare image size variables
    m_fAllLoaded = true;
    m_nImgWidth  = m_Images[0].getWidth(this);
    m_nImgHeight = m_Images[0].getHeight(this);
   }

   // Loop endlessly so animation repeats
   // User ends loop by leaving the page or exiting
   // the browser.
   showStatus("Displaying animation");
   while (true) {
    try {
     repaint();
     m_nCurrImage++;
     if (m_nCurrImage == NUM_IMAGES)
      m_nCurrImage = 0;
     Thread.sleep(50);  // Controls animation speed
    }
    catch (InterruptedException e) {
     stop();
    }
   }  //· end of while statement
  }  // end of run() method
}
```

The applet declares several instance variables to control image loading and the display of individual bitmaps. The variables are

```
Thread m_Animation = null;
// private Graphics m_Graphics;
private Image m_Images[];
private int m_nCurrImage;
private int m_nImgWidth  = 0;
private int m_nImgHeight = 0;
private boolean m_fAllLoaded = false;
private final int NUM_IMAGES = 10;
private MediaTracker tracker;
```

The Applet Wizard declares all but one variable private to the class, but they can just as well be public. For reasons unknown, however, the m_Animation Thread object is made friendly even though no other class in the module needs access to this object—so, it too probably can be public.

I commented out the private Graphics context object and removed its use from the generated code. The stock programming uses this object to display a message during image loading, but I prefer to do this by calling showStatus().

The private `Image` array holds each bitmap image in the animation. Actually, however, it is more correct to say that the array holds references to the image producers, which are responsible for loading the actual bitmap data from disk. Integer variable `m_nCurrImage` specifies the array index of the current image to display during the animation. Variables `m_nImgWidth` and `m_nImgHeight` specify the images' width and height, which are expected to be the same for all images.

The `boolean` flag, `m_fAllLoaded`, indicates that, when `true`, the program may begin the animation. Constant `NUM_IMAGES` indicates the number of image files, which are stored in the images subdirectory in the form `img0001.gif`. You could, of course, use another file-naming scheme—I used this one because the Applet Wizard generates code to automatically create the filenames. You might want to eliminate the `NUM_IMAGES` constant and instead load this value as a parameter from the HTML file. (For suggestions on how to do this, see Chapter 13, under the section titled "Parameters.")

The final instance variable is an object of the `MediaTracker` class introduced in this chapter. This object, named `tracker`, greatly simplifies the process of loading multiple image files using a separate thread. It also makes error detection easier.

Method `init()` initializes the program's instance variables and constructs the `tracker` object. Each image is loaded using the `Applet.getImage()` method and is stored in the `m_Images` array. Remember, this array actually holds references to the image producers, not the actual bitmap data. Each image is added to the tracker object by calling `MediaTracker.addImage()`. After this `for` loop ends, the `tracker` is ready to begin loading the images from disk. It's important to realize, however, that this process continues to execute as a separate thread, and the images might not be ready for display until some time after `init()` ends.

> **TIP**
>
> If you need access to an animation's bitmap data, use the image filtering techniques described in this chapter, and then display the resulting offscreen images instead of the image files as shown here.

The program's `paint()` method is simply written—a desirable characteristic in all graphics programs. The method's `if` statement

```
if (m_fAllLoaded) {
 g.drawImage(m_Images[m_nCurrImage],
  (size().width - m_nImgWidth) / 2,
  (size().height - m_nImgHeight) / 2, null);
}
```

checks the `boolean` flag `m_fAllLoaded` to determine whether all images have been loaded and the animation is ready to begin. If so, `Graphics.drawImage()` is called to display the current image using some optional calculations to reduce the image sizes. It's important to realize that paint() merely draws one image; it would be a grievous error to use a loop in paint() to animate the display. This would block other processes and cause the applet to perform badly. Always keep paint() simple, and use multithreaded code to control potentially lengthy graphics operations.

Key elements toward that goal are the construction of a Thread object and the calling of its start() and stop() methods. This is done in the sample program's start() and stop() methods. The statement

```
m_Animation = new Thread(this);
```

constructs the Thread object and specifies our applet object using this. As a result, the Thread looks for a run() method in the specified argument—and it finds the code listed in the final portion of the sample program's listing.

Understanding Animation's run() method might take a couple of readings. The code demonstrates several techniques with broad application in multithreaded programming, and it also presents numerous opportunities for modifications. An initial if statement checks whether the images are already loaded, in which case the method can proceed directly to its display statements. This might happen, for example, if the user switches away and then back again to the applet.

If the images are not already loaded, a try statement calls the tracker's waitForAll() method, which returns only after all monitored images—as specified by MediaTracker.addImage()—are either loaded or an error is detected. However, if another thread interrupts the process, waitForAll() throws an InterruptedException object, which the code catches in this statement:

```
try {
 tracker.waitForAll();
}
catch (InterruptedException e) {
 stop();  // Stop thread if interrupted
 return;  // Abort loading process
}
```

The Wizard-generated code calls stop(), which might not be absolutely necessary because this causes the thread to be canceled. Revisiting the applet will then re-create the thread (by calling start()), but it might be just as well to simply return from run() and allow the same thread to continue.

After the try block ends normally, the images are either in memory, or an error has occurred. To detect any problems, run() executes this code:

```
if (tracker.isErrorAny()) {
 showStatus("Error loading images!");
 stop();
 return;
}
```

Method isErrorAny() returns true if any errors were detected for any of the images—even if only one file, for example, could not be found. In that case, showStatus() displays a message in the browser, and the program kills the image-loading thread.

Finally, if all is well, the global flag is set to true so that paint() can begin displaying images, and the width and height variables are initialized using the first image referenced at index 0 in the Image object array:

```
m_fAllLoaded = true;
m_nImgWidth  = m_Images[0].getWidth(this);
m_nImgHeight = m_Images[0].getHeight(this);
```

The purpose of this as an argument passed to getWidth() and getHeight() might seem obscure. These methods require an object known as an *image observer*, which can be an object of any class that implements the ImageObserver interface. This interface specifies that the implementing class should provide an imageUpdate() method, which is called when image data is ready for display. It is through this protocol that an image consumer (such as a component or the applet) receives its image data via the image producer.

Following these preliminary steps—all of which are concerned with preparing the animation's multiple images—the program is ready to begin displaying each image in sequence. This is done inside run() using a so-called "do-forever" while loop that continues until another thread interrupts this one, or until the applet ends. To display each image, a try block executes the statements

```
repaint();
m_nCurrImage++;
if (m_nCurrImage == NUM_IMAGES)
 m_nCurrImage = 0;
Thread.sleep(50);
```

This shows the proper way to perform potentially time-consuming graphics operations, which must not be allowed to inhibit other processes. (Heaven save us from inhibited processes.) Calling repaint() causes paint() to display a single image as specified by the m_nCurrentImage variable. So that the animation loops continuously, the index is rotated through the values 0 to NUM_IMAGES - 1. Finally, to give other processes time to run—and also to control the speed of the animation—a call to Thread.sleep() pauses in a thread-friendly way for 50 milliseconds between each image.

You might want to study the foregoing code carefully and use it, not only in creating animated applets, but also as a guide to other complex graphics programming. The results will undoubtedly benefit from the multithreaded techniques described here.

Summary

- Use `Graphics` class methods to draw outlined and filled shapes, to paint text, to display images, and to show other kinds of graphics.

- Most often, you will use the `Graphics` context object passed to method `paint()`. However, you may create your own `Graphics` context objects by calling `Component.getGraphics()`.

- Loading and displaying image files requires careful multithreaded programming. Simply loading and displaying a GIF image can potentially block other processes, which a well-written applet must not allow to happen.

- Use the `Color` class to create color values of red, green, and blue components. The class can also specify colors as hue, saturation, and brightness levels.

- Use the `Font` class to select a font family, size, and style for use with `Graphics` class methods that display text. Use the `FontMetrics` class to obtain spacing information for selected fonts.

- The `Image` class, which represents the source or producer of a bitmap image, is typically used in conjunction with the `MediaTracker` class to load image files. This chapter shows in detail the multithreaded code needed for using these classes to smoothly load and display bitmap images.

- You may prepare an offscreen image and draw to it by calling `Graphics` class methods. The image is displayed using the same techniques for displaying an image loaded from disk file.

- By obtaining an image's producer and creating an offscreen image, you can plug in an image filter that modifies the image's pixels. This chapter explains how to program a filter that converts a color GIF image to a gray-scale, black-and-white picture.

- Java's multimedia features are hardly state of the art, but they are likely to be improved in the future. Until then, you can use the information in this chapter to add limited multimedia capabilities to play sound files and animate multiple images.

What's Next?

For obvious security reasons, reading and writing files on a user's disk is generally prohibited. Even so, Java contains file I/O capabilities that are useful to know—in writing local applications, for example, or for code that will run over a restricted intranet that requires file input and output.

478

18

Input and Output

Although Java has no native input and output capabilities, the java.io package provides a full set of I/O tools. With the classes in this package, you can read and write file data, load text files into memory, randomly access database files, and perform other I/O operations.

> **NOTE**
>
> For security reasons, applets are strictly prohibited from using the I/O techniques described in this chapter. Only Java stand-alone programs running locally are permitted to read and write disk files.

In This Chapter

This chapter covers the following fundamentals of input and output programming:

- Review of standard input and output techniques.
- Using the File class to represent files and directories.
- Accessing files as binary data using streams and buffered streams.
- Reading and writing files containing typed data.
- Randomly accessing file records.

Standard Input and Output

Way back in Part II, I introduced standard input and output techniques that you can use to prompt users for input and to display strings. Before getting into this chapter's information on disk file programming, it will be useful to briefly review Java's standard I/O capabilities provided by the System class. In that class are three static declarations:

```
public static PrintStream err;
public static InputStream in;
public static PrintStream out;
```

Because the three objects are static, you may use them in reference to their class or to an object of their class. For example, the statement

```
System.out.println("Please enter your password:");
```

prompts users to enter a password. The message is displayed by the println() method in reference to the out object of the PrintStream class. That object is attached to the operating system's standard output file, which is not a disk file, but a file in the sense of a destination for a stream of data—in this case, bytes representing characters.

Another PrintStream object, System.err, represents the standard error output file. This file may not be redirected and is therefore guaranteed to send its output to the display. Use it to report error messages such as

```
System.err.println("Error: System has lost its marbles.");
```

Inputting data takes a little more work. For example, to read text entered at the keyboard, define a StringBuffer object and then call System.in.read() to build a string as the user types each character:

```
while ((ch = (char)System.in.read()) != '\n')
 str.append(ch);
```

The read() method is fundamental to all input techniques in this chapter. Here, a while loop calls read() to input bytes from the standard input device (usually the keyboard) until the user presses Enter, represented as the new-line escape character '\n'. Because read() inputs bytes, the (char) type-cast expression is needed to assign each byte to the character variable ch. The StringBuffer.append() method appends each of those characters to the str object.

Listing 18.1, StandardIO.java, shows the correct way to use the in, out, and err objects in the System class. The program also shows how to trap IOException errors, which are thrown by many I/O methods.

COMPILING THIS CHAPTER'S LISTINGS

Because applets cannot perform input and output tasks, all sample listings in this chapter are stand-alone programs. Compile and run them using one of the following techniques (although the first method works best for me):

1. From a DOS prompt, compile a .java source code file by typing a command such as jvc standardio, and then run the resulting .class byte-code file with a command such as jview standardio. The jvc.exe and jview.exe command-line programs are provided by your Visual J++ installation, but you might need to set the current Path to refer to them; or, if you don't want to fiddle with the Path, copy the two programs to C:\Windows.

2. To run the sample programs using Developer Studio or Studio 97, open a .java source code file such as StandardIO.java, and select the Build menu's Build StandardIO command. Answer yes when asked whether to create a default project workspace. After building, select the Build menu's Execute command, and when prompted, enter the program's class name (StandardIO in this example). Select the Stand-alone interpreter button and press Enter to run the program.

Listing 18.1. `StandardIO.java` (Demonstrates standard input and output).

```java
import java.io.*;
class StandardIO {
 public static void main(String args[]) {
  try {
   StringBuffer str = new StringBuffer();
   char ch;
   // Get input from user
   System.out.println("Enter text:");  // Prompt user
   while ((ch = (char)System.in.read()) != '\n')
    str.append(ch);  // Build string using ch
   // Display string entered
   System.out.println("You entered: " + str);
  } catch (IOException e) {             // Trap exception
   System.err.println(e.toString());   // Display error
  }
 }
}
```

To use the I/O classes in this chapter, insert this import statement at the top of your module:

```java
import java.io.*;
```

Because the Java compiler carefully monitors a program's exception handling, the `try-catch` blocks in the sample program are required. To ensure that any errors are displayed onscreen—even if, for example, output is redirected to the printer—the program's `catch` statement writes an error message to the `System.err` output object.

For any I/O method such as `read()` that can throw an exception, your code must either be executed in a `try` block followed by one or more `catch` statements, or the method must itself declare that it throws the exception. For example, you could write a method `f()` as

```java
public void f() throws IOException {
...
}
```

Any statements that call `f()` must themselves assume responsibility for handling any exceptions by either calling `f()` from a `try` block, or by similarly passing the exception upward in the call chain. Especially in file I/O programming, it's important to understand these exception-handling techniques. (See Chapter 9, "Exceptions," if you need to refresh your memory on the topic.) As you will see from this chapter's samples, exception handling is an integral part of I/O programming. Don't wait until the last moment to add this code; weave it into your methods as you write every statement.

TIP

For additional examples of standard I/O programming, examine these sample applications from Part II: `InputBytes`, `InputDemo`, and `InputString`.

Files and Directories

Despite attempts in the computer industry to create a standard disk operating system, files and directories in the real world remain highly system dependent. Filenames and the characters allowed in them, and also separator characters in directory paths, are just a few of the many details that make system-independent I/O programming difficult if not downright impossible.

In this section, I examine techniques you can use to access files and directories in system-independent fashion. The end results are not perfectly independent of the operating system's peculiarities, but they are as close to the ideal as currently possible.

The `File` Class

A lot of the pain that comes from writing system-independent I/O code is soothed by Java's `File` class. You can use the class to create objects that represent files and directories in system-independent ways. However, a path string in DOS or Windows might not be compatible with another operating system such as UNIX, which does not use drive letters such as `C:` and uses the forward slash rather than the backslash to separate directory names in a path. Nevertheless, the `File` class, shown here in Listing 18.2, does a fairly good job of providing a system-independent abstraction of a file or a directory.

Listing 18.2. The `File` class.

```
public class File {
// Fields:
 public static final String separator;
 public static final char separatorChar;
 public static final String pathSeparator;
 public static final char pathSeparatorChar;
// Constructors:
 public File(String path);
 public File(String path, String name);
 public File(File dir, String name);
// Public methods:
 public String getName();
 public String getPath();
 public String getAbsolutePath();
 public String getParent();
 public boolean exists();
 public boolean canWrite();
 public boolean canRead();
 public boolean isFile();
 public boolean isDirectory();
 public native boolean isAbsolute();  // not implemented
 public long lastModified();
 public long length();
 public boolean mkdir();
 public boolean renameTo(File dest);
 public boolean mkdirs();
 public String[] list();
 public String[] list(FilenameFilter filter);
```

continues

Listing 18.2. continued

```
public boolean delete();
public int hashCode();
public boolean equals(Object obj);
public String toString();
}
```

It is a little unusual, and perhaps questionable, that one class represents both a file and a directory. However, this design is possibly advantageous because, in some operating systems such as UNIX, a directory *is* a kind of file—one with the specific purpose of listing other files and their locations. Even so, you'll need to be on your toes to use the File class to create file *and* directory objects.

The class provides four constants that represent the separator and path separator characters in the operating system. By using these constants, you can construct pathnames and filenames in a completely system-independent way. The separator and separatorChar constants represent, as String and char objects, the character used to separate directories in a pathname—the backslash in DOS and Windows, for example. The pathSeparator and pathSeparatorChar constants represent, again as String and char objects, the character that separates multiple paths—a semicolon under DOS and Windows, for example.

Create a File object using one of the class's three constructors. For example, the statement

```
File fobj = new File("C:\Wizbang\Readme.txt");
```

creates a File object that refers to the Readme.txt file in the C:\Wizbang directory. You may also construct a File object that represents a directory name using a statement such as

```
File dobj = new File("C:\Wizbang");
```

It doesn't matter whether the file or the directory actually exist. A File object may refer to an existing or nonexistent file, directory, or path.

> **NOTE**
>
> Most readers probably know about files, directories, and paths, but it's critical to clearly understand the differences between these terms, so for the sake of accuracy, I'll define them briefly. A *filename* such as Readme.txt is, of course, the name of an individual file, and it may optionally have a name and extension separated by a period. A *directory* is the name of a storage location such as C:Wizbang. A *path* is a directory optionally combined with a filename—C:\Wizbang\Readme.txt, for example—that fully locates a file. Paths may be absolute or relative. The path Wizbang\Readme.txt refers to the Readme.txt file in the Wizbang subdirectory of the current directory. Some operating systems may impose strict limits on the lengths of file, directory, and pathnames, and may also restrict the characters they may contain. Even though Windows now allows long filenames with punctuation and spaces, it's always safest to use short names and alphanumeric characters.

A second way to construct a `File` object is to specify a path and filename separately. The following statement creates a `File` object that refers to the `C:\Wizbang\Readme.txt` file:

```
File fobj = new File("C:\Wizbang", "Readme.txt");
```

This `File` construction technique is useful when the program stores pathnames and filenames separately in `String` variables. Finally, you may specify a path using another `File` object plus a filename. For example, this fragment creates two `File` objects:

```
File dobj = new File("C:\Wizbang");
File fobj = new File(dobj, "Readme.txt");
```

The first object refers to the path `C:\Wizbang`. The second is created using the first object as the path and a string as the filename.

ABSOLUTELY *PATHETIC*

Some `File` class methods refer to *absolute paths,* the exact definition of which is system-dependent. For example, under UNIX, an absolute path is one that begins with that system's separator character. Under Windows, an absolute path begins with a backslash, with a slash, or with a drive letter and colon followed by a backslash or slash. Any path that is not absolute is relative to the current directory.

In addition to its constructors, the `File` class provides several useful methods that you can call to determine various facts about a file, directory, or path. Beware that some of these methods—`mkdir()`, for example—can make changes to your disk. The class's public methods are

- `String getName()`: Returns the name of the file or directory.
- `String getPath()`: Returns the full pathname.
- `String getAbsolutePath()`: Returns the current absolute path, or if the `File` object does not represent an absolute path, returns the concatenation of the current directory, a separator character, and the object's relative path or filename. The definition of an absolute path is system-dependent. (See the preceding sidebar.)
- `String getParent()`: Returns the directory of the file represented by this `File` object. This is the pathname up to the separator character before the filename. If the path has no such separator character, this method returns `null`.
- `boolean exists()`: Returns `true` if the file or directory exists.
- `boolean canWrite()`: Returns `true` if a program can write to the file—if it is not marked read-only, for example.
- `boolean canRead()`: Returns `true` if a program can read from the file—if it contains data and is not a directory, for example.
- `boolean isFile()`: Returns `true` if the `File` object represents a disk file.
- `boolean isDirectory()`: Returns `true` if the `File` object represents a directory name.

485

- native boolean isAbsolute(): Returns true if the represented path is absolute. (See the preceding sidebar.) Note: Java's source code indicates that this method is not implemented, and it always returns true. This might not be so, however, under all Java installations.

- long lastModified(): Returns the date and time of the file's most recent modification or creation. Use the Date class to convert the returned value to a useable form.

- long length(): Returns the length of the file in bytes.

- boolean mkdir(): Creates the directory represented by this File object. Any higher-nested directories in the path must already exist (see also mkdirs()). Returns true if the directory was successfully created.

- boolean renameTo(File dest): Renames the file represented by this File object to the name represented by the dest File object. Returns true if the filename was successfully changed.

- boolean mkdirs(): Works the same as mkdir(), but also creates any higher-nested directories in the path. Returns true if all directories were successfully created.

- String[] list(): Returns an array of String objects representing the filenames in the directory referenced by this File object.

- String[] list(FilenameFilter filter): Works the same as list(), but returns only filenames matching the specified filter (for an example, see the "File Filters" section in this chapter).

- boolean delete(): Deletes the file or directory referenced by this File object. Returns true if the deletion was completed successfully.

- int hashCode(): Returns a hash code that you can use to store filenames in hash tables for fast lookup. (See Chapter 10, "Arrays and Other Containers," under the section "Hashtable Class.")

- boolean equals(Object obj): Returns true if this File object equals another File object.

- String toString(): Returns a string representation of this File object. In the standard implementation, this method simply returns getPath().

File and Directory Programming

Listing 18.3, Directory.java, demonstrates how to use the File class to obtain the names of files in a specified directory. Compile and run the program at a DOS prompt, and when prompted, enter a pathname such as C:\Windows\Command.

Listing 18.3. Directory.java (Demonstrates the File class).

```
import java.io.*;
class Directory {
// Prompt user for pathname
 public static String getPathname()
  throws IOException {
```

```
   StringBuffer path = new StringBuffer();
   char ch;
   System.out.println("Path? ");
   while ((ch = (char)System.in.read()) != '\n')
    path.append(ch);
   return path.toString();
 }
// Construct File object for directory path
 public static File getFileForPath(String path)
  throws IOException {
  File dir = new File(path);
  if (!dir.isDirectory())
   throw new IOException("Not a directory");
  return dir;
 }
// Main program method
 public static void main(String args[]) {
  try {
   String path = getPathname();
   File dir = getFileForPath(path);
   String[] filenames = dir.list();
   for (int i = 0; i < filenames.length; i++)
    System.out.println(filenames[i]);
  } catch (IOException e) {                // Trap exception
   System.err.println(e.toString());   // Display error
  }
 }
}
```

After prompting you to enter a pathname (see method `getPathname()`), the program calls the local method `getFileForPath()`. This method converts the entered pathname string into a `File` object, created with the statement

```
File dir = new File(path);
```

The method then checks whether this object represents a directory. If the `File.isDirectory()` method returns `false`, the local method throws an object of the `IOException` class. This is a good example of how file I/O programming uses exceptions to report not merely errors, but also exceptional conditions—in this case, entering the name of a file when a directory is required.

To catch this problem, the main program calls the local method inside a `try` block. Run the program again and enter a nonexistent pathname or the name of an existing file to see how the code handles these conditions.

NOTE

For another example of directory handling, refer to the FileDialDemo sample program described in Chapter 16, "Windows, Menus, and Dialogs," under the section titled "The `FileDialog` Class."

File Information

Listing 18.4, `FileInfo.java`, shows another way to use the `File` class. Compile and run the program, but this time, when prompted, enter the name of a file. To test the program's exception handling, try entering nonexistent pathnames. Only if you enter the name of an existing file does the program report information such as the file's name, size, and modification date.

Listing 18.4. `FileInfo.java` (Gets information about any file).

```java
import java.io.*;
import java.util.Date;
class FileInfo {
// Prompt user for filename
 public static String getFilename()
  throws IOException {
  StringBuffer filename = new StringBuffer();
  char ch;
  System.out.println("Filename? ");
  while ((ch = (char)System.in.read()) != '\n')
   filename.append(ch);
  return filename.toString();
 }
// Construct File object for named file
 public static File getFileForFilename(String filename)
  throws IOException {
  File fi = new File(filename);
  // Do not move the following statements;
  // order is critical
  if (!fi.exists())
   throw new IOException("File not found");
  if (!fi.isFile())
   throw new IOException("Not a file");
  return fi;
 }
// Show a labeled string
 public static void showLabel(String label, String s) {
  System.out.print(label);
  System.out.println(s);
 }
// Display information about file fi
 public static void showInformation(File fi) {
  showLabel("Path     = ", fi.getPath());
  showLabel("Filename = ", fi.getName());
  showLabel("Length   = ",
   new Long(fi.length()).toString());
  showLabel("Readable = ",
   new Boolean(fi.canRead()).toString());
  showLabel("Writable = ",
   new Boolean(fi.canWrite()).toString());
  showLabel("Modified = ",
   new Date(fi.lastModified()).toString());
 }
// Main program method
 public static void main(String args[]) {
  try {
   String filename = getFilename();
   File fi = getFileForFilename(filename);
   showInformation(fi);
```

```
  } catch (IOException e) {        // Trap exception
   System.err.println(e.toString());   // Display error
  }
 }
}
```

File Filters

A filename filter uses *wildcards* to represent characters that match any pattern. For example, the filter *.* represents all files with a name, period, and extension. The filter *.txt represents all files ending with .txt. The filter *.00? represents all files with any name, a period, two zero characters, and any final character.

Java's official documentation contains little useful information on how to use filename filters with the File class, but with a little experimentation, I was able to figure out most of the particulars. The key is to create your own class that implements the FilenameFilter interface, which specifies the single method:

```
boolean accept(File dir, String name);
```

The method returns true if the designated file, directory, or path should be included in the File.list() method's return value. Return false to exclude a file, directory, or path. Listing 18.5, FilterDir.java, demonstrates how to implement the FilenameFilter interface to list only the subdirectories in a given path. The listing is a modified copy of the Directory.java program in this chapter. Only the new statements are listed here (but the full listing is, of course, on the CD-ROM).

Listing 18.5. FilterDir.java (Demonstrates filename filters: partial listing).

```
import java.io.*;
//==============================================================
// FilenameFilter interface implementation
//==============================================================
class FilterClass implements FilenameFilter {
 public boolean accept(File dir, String name) {
  File f = new File(dir, name);
  if (f.isDirectory())
   return true;
  else
   return false;
 }
}
```

The program's FilterClass implements the FilenameFilter interface. That interface's accept() method receives two parameters:

- File dir: The absolute or relative pathname or directory of the indicated file.
- String name: The candidate file or directory name to be returned by File.list().

It takes some care to correctly program an accept() method. For example, it might not be enough to examine the passed arguments; as shown here, to detect whether each candidate name is a directory, the method creates a new File object using both parameters. This forms a complete absolute path to the candidate, which can now be tested by calling isDirectory().

The modified main program (not listed here) uses these statements to create a filtered directory:

```
String[] filenames = dir.list(new FilterClass());
for (int i = 0; i < filenames.length; i++)
 System.out.println("<DIR> " + filenames[i]);
```

The first statement calls the overloaded File.list() method, passing an object of our FilterClass. Every candidate name is filtered through our accept() method, which returns true only if the name is a directory. The resulting String array, printed in a for loop, contains only directory names.

> **NOTE**
>
> The File.list() method does not return the current (.) or outer (..) directory names.

File Streams and Buffers

For some odd reason, many programmers think of *file streams* as magical objects with hidden data sources and unknown destinations to which information flows via secret processes that only a guru can fathom. But the concept of file streams has been around since the early days when engineers figured out how to store binary information on tape, and then, later, on magnetic disks. A file stream is simply a sequential source of data bytes that flow from one location to another. An object-oriented file stream is a class that represents this concept.

The word "sequential" is the clue to unraveling the mysteries of file streams. Think of a file stream as though it were a real stream, exactly one molecule wide. Each molecule is a byte in the stream. You are the troll under the bridge, and you can examine only one molecule at a time as it passes beneath your arch. You can collect molecules in a bucket, you can redirect them to a branching stream, and you can even cause your stream to move in either direction. (You are a very talented troll who can control the tides.)

My analogy might not be perfect, but it's important to keep in mind that file streams may or may not be associated with disk files. If they are, it is the sequential access of data in those files that makes them streams. The files themselves are merely storage locations on a device such as a disk drive.

The FileInputStream Class

The FileInputStream class in Listing 18.6 provides methods for accessing file stream data.

Listing 18.6. The `FileInputStream` class.

```
public class FileInputStream extends InputStream {
// Constructors:
 public FileInputStream(String name);
 public FileInputStream(File file);
 public FileInputStream(FileDescriptor fdObj);
// Public methods:
 public native int read();
 public int read(byte b[]);
 public int read(byte b[], int off, int len);
 public native long skip(long n);
 public native int available();
 public native void close();
 public final FileDescriptor getFD();
// Protected method:
 protected void finalize();
}
```

You can construct `FileInputStream` objects in three ways. Pass a string representing the filename or path:

```
FileInputStream fin =
 new FileInputStream("C:\Wizbang\Accounts.dat");
```

Another, and I think superior, method is to pass a `File` object to the constructor. This gives you the opportunity to check the status of the file before creating the stream. For example, the following code fragment throws an exception if the indicated file does not exist:

```
File fi = new File("C:\Wizbang\Accounts.dat");
if (!fi.exists())
 throw IOException("Not a file");
FileInputStream fin = new FileInputStream(fi);
```

The final statement creates the input stream object using the verified `File` object.

A third way to construct a `FileInputStream` object is to pass it a `FileDescriptor` object, which serves as an interface to a file handle—a term that typically refers to the object the operating system uses to keep track of opened files. Because `FileDescriptor` is necessarily system-dependent, you won't use it directly. You might, however, call the `FileInputStream` class's `getFD()` method to obtain the `FileDescriptor` object for an existing stream. You can then use this object to construct another stream—perhaps to clone a stream so that you can reference the same file data using two objects.

The `FileInputStream`'s public and protected methods are as follows:

- `int read()`: Reads a single byte from the stream.
- `int read(byte b[])`: Reads `b.length` bytes from the file into the byte array. Returns the number of bytes read, or -1 if the end of the file is reached. This method does not construct its array—you must do that before calling `read()`.

- `int read(byte b[], int off, int len)`: Similar to the preceding method, but ignores the array length. Deposits bytes from the stream starting at `b[off]` and reading up to `len` bytes or to the end of the file.

- `long skip(long n)`: Throws away the specified number of bytes from the stream, thus skipping from the current file position to a new position n bytes away. Returns the number of bytes skipped.

- `int available()`: Returns the number of bytes that can be read from the stream without a `read()` method blocking for another thread's process.

- `void close()`: Closes the input stream. It is always optional to close your file streams, but this is usually a good idea because it frees system resources.

- `FileDescriptor getFD()`: Returns the system-dependent file descriptor object for this input stream. You can use this object to clone a file input stream by passing the method's return value to the `FileInputStream` constructor.

- `void finalize()`: This method is protected, and you cannot call it from a program. However, I list it here as a rare example of a `finalize()` method with a useful purpose—in this case, closing a file if an unused `FileInputStream` object is deleted by Java's memory garbage collector.

The `FileOutputStream` Class

As counterpoint to the `FileInputStream` class, Java's `FileOutputStream` class represents a destination for a file stream of data bytes. Listing 18.7 lists the `FileOutputStream` class.

Listing 18.7. The `FileOutputStream` class.

```
public class FileOutputStream extends OutputStream {
// Constructors:
 public FileOutputStream(String name);
 public FileOutputStream(File file);
 public FileOutputStream(FileDescriptor fdObj);
// Public methods:
 public native void write(int b);
 public void write(byte b[]);
 public void write(byte b[], int off, int len);
 public native void close();
 public final FileDescriptor getFD();
// Protected method:
 protected void finalize();
}
```

You may construct `FileOutputStream` objects using the same three methods described for the `FileInputStream` class. Public methods that differ from those in `FileInputStream` are as follows:

- `void write(int b)`: Writes a single byte, b, to the output stream. The data is written to disk immediately.

- `void write(byte b[])`: Writes an entire array of bytes to the output stream.

- void write(byte b[], int off, int len): Writes len bytes starting with b[off] to the output stream.

File Programming

Listing 18.8, CopyFile.java, demonstrates how to use the FileInputStream and FileOutputStream classes to copy a disk file. Because the program uses low-level data streams, it can copy a file of any type.

Listing 18.8. CopyFile.java (Demonstrates file stream input and output).

```
import java.io.*;
class CopyFile {
// Prompt user for filename
 public static String getFilename(String prompt)
  throws IOException {
  StringBuffer filename = new StringBuffer();
  char ch;
  System.out.println(prompt);
  while ((ch = (char)System.in.read()) != '\n')
   filename.append(ch);
  return filename.toString();
 }
// Construct File object for named file
 public static File getFileForFilename(
  String filename, boolean checkExistence)
  throws IOException {
  File fi = new File(filename);
  if (checkExistence) {
   // Do not move the following statements;
   // order is critical
   if (!fi.exists())
    throw new IOException(fi.getName() + " not found");
   if (!fi.isFile())
    throw new IOException(fi.getName() + " is not a file");
  }
  return fi;
 }
// Returns true if user answers yes to prompt
 public static boolean yes(String prompt)
  throws IOException {
  System.out.println(prompt);
  char ch = (char)System.in.read();
  if (ch == 'y' || ch == 'Y') {
   return true;
  }
  return false;
 }
// Copy and old file to a new one
// Overwrites or creates the new file
 public static void copy(File fileOld, File fileNew)
  throws IOException {
  FileInputStream fin = new FileInputStream(fileOld);
  FileOutputStream fout = new FileOutputStream(fileNew);
  System.out.println("Copying...");
```

Listing 18.8. continued

```
  int b = fin.read();
  while (b != -1) {
   fout.write(b);
   b = fin.read();
  }
  System.out.println("Finished");
 }
// Main program method
 public static void main(String args[]) {
  try {
   String fileOldname = getFilename("Copy what file?");
   File fileOld = getFileForFilename(fileOldname, true);
   String fileNewname = getFilename("To what file?");
   File fileNew = getFileForFilename(fileNewname, false);
   if (fileNew.isDirectory())
    throw new IOException(fileNew.getName() + " is a directory");
   if (fileNew.exists()) {
    if (!yes("Overwrite file " + fileNew.getName() + "? "))
     throw new IOException("File not copied");
   } else {
    if (!yes("Create new " + fileNew.getPath() + "? "))
     throw new IOException("File not copied");
   }
   copy(fileOld, fileNew);
  } catch (IOException e) {              // Trap exception
   System.err.println(e.toString());    // Display error
  }
 }
}
```

Most of the sample program's code is concerned with prompting for filenames, checking that the source file exists, and asking for permission to overwrite an existing destination file. File copying takes place in method `copy()`, which creates `FileInputStream` and `FileOutputStream` objects. The two statements

```
FileInputStream fin = new FileInputStream(fileOld);
FileOutputStream fout = new FileOutputStream(fileNew);
```

create the stream objects using the `File` objects passed to `copy()`. At this point in the program, the files have been verified, and copying proceeds immediately using a `while` loop of a classic design:

```
int b = fin.read();
while (b != -1) {
 fout.write(b);
 b = fin.read();
}
```

The first statement reads the first source-file byte. While that byte is not -1, the loop writes it to its destination file and reads the next byte. As a side benefit, the `copy()` method, along with other statements in the program, also demonstrates how exception handling keeps the code simple while trapping all possible errors.

The `BufferedInputStream` Class

Plain file streams are adequate for small data files, but to maintain good performance, you'll want to use extensions of the basic file stream classes that add buffered I/O. A buffer is simply a block of memory that collects file stream data on its way to and from memory and disk. Because entire blocks of data are read and written at a time, disk accesses are kept to a minimum, which usually results in a great improvement in speed. The downside of using buffers is that, if the computer should be shut down prematurely, a greater amount of data is at risk. You can minimize this danger by flushing the file. (Output classes provide a flush() method for this purpose.)

Listing 18.9 lists the `BufferedInputStream` class, which you can use to construct buffered input file stream objects.

Listing 18.9. The `BufferedInputStream` class.

```
public class BufferedInputStream extends FilterInputStream {
// Constructors:
 public BufferedInputStream(InputStream in);
 public BufferedInputStream(InputStream in, int size);
// Public methods:
 public synchronized int read();
 public synchronized int read(byte b[], int off, int len);
 public synchronized long skip(long n);
 public synchronized int available();
 public synchronized void mark(int readlimit);
 public synchronized void reset();
 public boolean markSupported();
}
```

To construct a `BufferedInputStream` object, you must first construct an unbuffered `FileInputStream`. Actually, you may use any `InputStream` object, but in file I/O programming, this will usually be of the `FileInputStream` class. For example, the statements

```
FileInputStream fin = new FileInputStream(fi);
BufferedInputStream bin = new BufferedInputStream(fin);
```

construct a `FileInputStream` object using a `File` object, `fi`. The resulting unbuffered stream object (`fin`) is passed to the `BufferedInputStream` constructor to create the buffered stream.

You can optionally pass a size argument to the constructor to specify a buffer of a certain length. The statement

```
BufferedInputStream bin = new BufferedInputStream(fin, 1024);
```

constructs the buffered input stream object using the file stream, but increases the buffer size to 1024 bytes.

The following are public methods in the `BufferedInputStream` class that you can call:

- `int read()`: Reads a single byte from the input stream. Returns -1 if the end of file is reached.

- `int read(byte b[], int off, int len)`: Reads `len` bytes and deposits them in the `byte` array starting at `b[off]`. Returns the number of bytes actually read, or -1 if the end of the file has been reached.

- `long skip(long n)`: Throws away `n` bytes from the input stream starting at the current position. Returns the number of bytes actually skipped.

- `int available()`: Returns the number of bytes that can be read from the input stream without blocking another threaded process.

- `void mark(int readlimit)`: Sets a marker at the current position so that `reset()` can return to this position. The parameter `readLimit` equals the number of bytes that are permitted to be read before the mark becomes invalid.

- `void reset()`: Returns the file pointer to the position most recently recorded by `mark()`. The default mark is -1, which represents no valid position. Because of this, calling `reset()` without a preceding call to `mark()` throws an `IOException` error.

- `boolean markSupported()`: Returns true if `mark()` and `reset()` are supported by the operating system. Although the standard Java implementation always returns `true` for this method, a local installation may not support file marking, and it's a good idea to call `markSupported()` before using `mark()` and `reset()`.

> **NOTE**
>
> The `mark()` and `reset()` methods are typically used to remember the current position and then peek ahead to see what kind of data is coming up. Calling `reset()` repositions the file to its marked location. A parser might use these methods to look ahead for a specific character. It's important to realize, however, that reading more bytes than passed to `mark()` invalidates the mark, and throws an exception if `reset()` is subsequently called. An exception is also thrown if `reset()` is called without a prior call to `mark()`. The two methods are not intended for skipping around at will in a file; if you need that capability, see the `RandomAccessFile` class described in this chapter.

The BufferedOutputStream Class

The counterpart to the BufferedInputStream class is BufferedOutputStream, shown in Listing 18.10.

Listing 18.10. The BufferedOutputStream class.

```
public class BufferedOutputStream extends FilterOutputStream {
// Constructors:
 public BufferedOutputStream(OutputStream out);
 public BufferedOutputStream(OutputStream out, int size);
// Public methods:
 public synchronized void write(int b);
 public synchronized void write(byte b[], int off, int len);
 public synchronized void flush();
}
```

As with BufferedInputStream, there are two ways to construct a BufferedOutputStream object. Each requires an existing OutputStream object, which in file I/O programming, is typically an object of the FileOutputStream class. For example, the two statements

```
FileOutputStream fout = new FileOutputStream(fi);
BufferedOutputStream bout = new BufferedOutputStream(fout);
```

construct a FileOutputStream object using a File object, fi. The resulting unbuffered output stream fout is passed to the BufferedOutputStream constructor to create the buffered output object.

You may optionally specify a buffer size by passing an integer argument to the class constructor. The statement

```
BufferedOutputStream bout =
 new BufferedOutputStream(fout, 1024);
```

creates a buffered output stream object with a buffer size of 1024 bytes.

The BufferedOutputStream class provides only three public methods:

- void write(int b): Writes a single byte to the output stream. Because the stream is buffered, the data is not necessarily transferred to disk immediately.

- void write(byte b[], int off, int len): Writes len bytes to the output stream starting with b[off]. As with the other form of write(), the actual transfer of data to disk might not occur immediately.

- void flush(): Flushes the current buffer, causing any data held in memory to be written to disk immediately.

Buffered File Programming

Listing 18.11, CopyBuf.java, is a modified version of the CopyFile.java program in this chapter. Because most of the two programs are the same, I list only the new copy() method, which shows how to create and use buffered input and output file streams.

Listing 18.11. CopyBuf.java (Copies a file using buffered file streams: partial listing).

```
// Copy an old file to a new one
// Overwrites or creates the new file
public static void copy(File fileOld, File fileNew)
 throws IOException {
 FileInputStream fin = new FileInputStream(fileOld);
 BufferedInputStream bin = new BufferedInputStream(fin);
 FileOutputStream fout = new FileOutputStream(fileNew);
 BufferedOutputStream bout = new BufferedOutputStream(fout);
 System.out.println("Copying...");
 byte buffer[] = new byte[BUFSIZE];
 int n;
 while (bin.available() > 0) {
  n = bin.read(buffer);
  if (n > 0)
    bout.write(buffer, 0, n);
 }
 System.out.println("Finished");
}
```

The new program creates plain unbuffered file input and output streams as in the original code. Those stream objects are then used to create buffered streams. The statements

```
FileInputStream fin = new FileInputStream(fileOld);
BufferedInputStream bin = new BufferedInputStream(fin);
```

construct an unbuffered stream object, and then use that object to create the buffered stream. The buffered output stream is created similarly.

To read the buffered data, the program creates an array of byte values and then calls the available() method to determine whether more file data is available. The buffered input file's read() method reads data from disk (or from its internal buffers), and the output stream's write() method transfers those bytes to their new destination.

This is only one way to write a buffered I/O program, and the array of bytes shown here is not required. The original code from the unmodified sample, CopyFile.java, would work just as well. Whether you read and write multiple bytes using an array as shown here, or read and write them one byte at a time, the buffered file stream objects still collect blocks of bytes to and from disk.

It's typical for several layers of buffering to exist in programs such as the preceding example. The program itself can declare an array of bytes, which serves as a kind of top-level buffer. Meanwhile, the `BufferedInputStream` and `BufferedOutputStream` objects themselves maintain midrange buffers for collecting data on its way in and out of memory. Descending to a lower level, the operating system probably also buffers data, which it might conceivably do even for plain file streams. In general, it's best to use the largest buffer size possible, but because there might be multiple layers of buffers, a large buffer size does not necessarily guarantee better speed. It is the combination of the program's array sizes, the file object buffers, and the operating system's internal buffers that put a top limit on I/O performance, and finding the right combination of variables will take careful experimentation.

Typed Input and Output

The file I/O classes and methods presented so far blindly treat file data as no more than a pool of bytes. Although all files are at one level mere binary collections, their bits and bytes are more interestingly viewed as the values of various data types. File streams are highly useful for loading files wholly into memory, and for performing data operations that disregard the information's nature; but in many cases, you will want to access not files of bytes, but files of strings, floating point values, integers, and other typed input and output. For that, Java provides several useful classes such as `DataInputStream`.

The `DataInputStream` Class

The `DataInputStream` class can read data of any type from a file. Though it is not directly derived from the file stream classes examined in this chapter, it uses buffered and unbuffered streams as I will explain. Listing 18.12 shows the class's declaration.

Listing 18.12. The `DataInputStream` class.

```
public class DataInputStream extends FilterInputStream implements DataInput {
// Constructor:
 public DataInputStream(InputStream in);
// Public utility method:
 public final int skipBytes(int n);
// Public input methods:
 public final int read(byte b[]);
 public final int read(byte b[], int off, int len);
 public final void readFully(byte b[]);
 public final void readFully(byte b[], int off, int len);
```

continues

18

Listing 18.12. continued

```
// Public typed input methods:
 public final boolean readBoolean();
 public final byte readByte();
 public final int readUnsignedByte();
 public final short readShort();
 public final int readUnsignedShort();
 public final char readChar();
 public final int readInt();
 public final long readLong();
 public final float readFloat();
 public final double readDouble();
 public final String readLine();
 public final String readUTF();
 public final static String readUTF(DataInput in);
}
```

There is only one apparent way to construct a `DataInputStream` object. However, because the class constructor requires an `InputStream` object, you may connect a `DataInputStream` to any type of input stream. This can be a file stream, or it can be a buffered file stream—the two most common constructions in file I/O programming. In most cases, you'll probably want to use a buffered file stream. Doing this takes three steps:

1. Construct a file stream of the `FileInputStream` class.
2. Construct a buffered file stream of the `BufferedInputStream` class using the object from step 1.
3. Construct a `DataInputStream` object using the buffered stream from step 2.

These steps build the data input stream in stages, starting with a plain unbuffered stream, progressing to a buffered stream, and finishing with the typed data file stream object. Here are the three steps in code:

```
FileInputStream fin = new FileInputStream(fi);
BufferedInputStream bin = new BufferedInputStream(fin);
DataInputStream din = new DataInputStream(bin);
```

The first line constructs the plain, unbuffered file stream object, `fin`, using a `File` class object `fi` that represents the file's pathname. The resulting file stream object is passed to the `BufferedInputStream` constructor to create the buffered file object, `bin`. Finally, that object is passed to the solitary `DataInputStream` constructor, creating the finished typed data stream, `din`. That object is now ready for reading typed data from the file.

Listing 18.13, `ReadLines.java`, demonstrates one common use for typed file I/O—reading the lines of a text file. Compile and run the program, and then when prompted, enter the name of a text file to display.

Listing 18.13. `ReadLines.java` (Reads a text file using typed input).

```java
import java.io.*;
class ReadLines {
// Prompt user for filename
 public static String getFilename(String prompt)
  throws IOException {
  StringBuffer filename = new StringBuffer();
  char ch;
  System.out.println(prompt);
  while ((ch = (char)System.in.read()) != '\n')
   filename.append(ch);
  return filename.toString();
 }
// Construct File object for named file
 public static File getFileForFilename(String filename)
  throws IOException {
  File fi = new File(filename);
  // Do not move the following statements;
  // order is critical
  if (!fi.exists())
   throw new IOException(fi.getName() + " not found");
  if (!fi.isFile())
   throw new IOException(fi.getName() + " is not a file");
  return fi;
 }
// Main program method
 public static void main(String args[]) {
  try {
   String filename = getFilename("Read what file?");
   File fi = getFileForFilename(filename);
   FileInputStream fin = new FileInputStream(fi);
   BufferedInputStream bin = new BufferedInputStream(fin);
   DataInputStream din = new DataInputStream(bin);
   String line = din.readLine();  // Read first line
   while (line != null) {         // Loop until end of file
    System.out.println(line);     // Print current line
    line = din.readLine();        // Read next line
   }
  } catch (IOException e) {            // Trap exception
   System.err.println(e.toString());  // Display error
  }
 }
}
```

As with many of the listings in this chapter, a great deal of the programming in `ReadLines.java` is concerned with prompting for a filename and with exception handling. I'll describe here only the code directly responsible for reading typed data—in this case, the characters of a text file.

After prompting you to enter a filename (see the method `getFilename()`), the program constructs a `File` object by calling its `getFileForFilename()` method. This method verifies that the specified file exists and is not a directory.

After obtaining the `File` object for the specified text file, the main program executes the three steps for constructing the typed `DataInputStream` object. Armed with this object, a simple loop reads all lines of text into memory, each in the form of a `String`:

```
String line = din.readLine();
while (line != null) {
 System.out.println(line);
 line = din.readLine();
}
```

The `DataInputStream` class's `readLine()` method reads one line of text and returns it as a `String`. If the method returns `null`, the end of the file was reached by a preceding read operation. Each string is assigned to the program's `line` variable for display via `println()`. By virtue of the program's exception handling, the loop is clean and simple, but it rigorously traps all possible error conditions.

The `DataOutputStream` Class

As you might suppose, the counterpart to `DataInputStream` is `DataOutputStream`. Use this class to construct a typed output stream object to which you can write strings, integers, floating point values, and other typed data. Listing 18.14 shows the class's declaration.

Listing 18.14. The `DataOutputStream` class.

```
public class DataOutputStream extends FilterOutputStream implements DataOutput {
// Constructor:
 public DataOutputStream(OutputStream out);
// Public utility methods:
 public void flush();
 public final int size();
// Public output methods:
 public synchronized void write(int b);
 public synchronized void write(byte b[], int off, int len);
// Public typed output methods:
 public final void writeBoolean(boolean v);
 public final void writeByte(int v);
 public final void writeShort(int v);
 public final void writeChar(int v);
 public final void writeInt(int v);
 public final void writeLong(long v);
 public final void writeFloat(float v);
 public final void writeDouble(double v);
 public final void writeBytes(String s);
 public final void writeChars(String s);
 public final void writeUTF(String str);
}
```

Construct a `DataOutputStream` object using the same three steps described for `DataInputStream`. The only difference is that, if the file does not exist, it is created. An existing file is overwritten by the class's output methods, some of which are described in the next section.

Typed File Programming

As an example of how to use the DataOutputStream class, Listing 18.15, WriteData.java, writes typed data to a file. The program also demonstrates an effective, though not foolproof, way to check that the file contains the expected type of data.

Listing 18.15. WriteData.java (Writes typed data to a file).

```java
import java.io.*;
import java.util.Random;
class WriteData {
// Main program method
 public static void main(String args[]) {
  // Instance variables
  int dataSize = 10;
  Random gen = new Random();
  try {
   // Create file objects
   FileOutputStream fout = new FileOutputStream("Data.bin");
   BufferedOutputStream bout = new BufferedOutputStream(fout);
   DataOutputStream dout = new DataOutputStream(bout);
   // Write data to file in this order:
   // 1. number of data elements
   // 2. elements
   dout.writeInt(dataSize);
   for (int i = 0; i < dataSize; i++) {
    dout.writeDouble(gen.nextDouble());
   }
   dout.flush();
   fout.close();
   System.out.println(dout.size() + " bytes written");
  } catch (IOException e) {            // Trap exception
   System.err.println(e.toString());   // Display error
  }
 }
}
```

The sample program constructs the typed output stream using three statements:

```java
FileOutputStream fout = new FileOutputStream("Data.bin");
BufferedOutputStream bout = new BufferedOutputStream(fout);
DataOutputStream dout = new DataOutputStream(bout);
```

Rather than use a File object, as I normally do, this time I specified the name of a data file as a string—a perfectly acceptable technique for creating the underlying FileOutputStream object. I did this to keep the code simple (it does not prompt you for a filename), and so that the data file would be written to the current directory—the same one that holds the sample's source code files. The buffered output file object is created from the plain stream, and finally, the DataOutputStream object, dout, is constructed using the buffered stream from the second step.

It is now a simple matter to write typed data to the file. The file may contain any values, of any type, and in any order. To provide a simple verification, the program first writes the number of data elements to the file using this statement:

```
dout.writeInt(dataSize);
```

Next, a for loop writes that many double values, generated at random using an object of the Random class:

```
for (int i = 0; i < dataSize; i++) {
 dout.writeDouble(gen.nextDouble());
}
```

After this, to ensure that the buffered values are written immediately to disk, the program executes two more statements:

```
dout.flush();
fout.close();
```

These actions are optional, but they flush any buffered data to disk and close the file, releasing any held system resources. An output statement displays the number of bytes written by calling the DataOutputStream method, size():

```
System.out.println(dout.size() + " bytes written");
```

The generated file contains two types of data: an integer that represents the number of following items, each of which is an 8-byte double value. Listing 18.16, ReadData.java, shows the solution to the reverse problem: how to read the formatted file data back into memory.

Listing 18.16. ReadData.java (Reads typed data from a file).

```
import java.io.*;
class ReadData {
// Main program method
 public static void main(String args[]) {
  // Instance variables
  int dataSize;
  double data[];
  try {
   // Create file objects
   FileInputStream fin = new FileInputStream("Data.bin");
   BufferedInputStream bin = new BufferedInputStream(fin);
   DataInputStream din = new DataInputStream(bin);
   // Read data from file in this order:
   // 1. number of data elements
   // 2. elements
   dataSize = din.readInt();      // Get number of elements
   data = new double[dataSize];   // Create array for data
   // Read elements into array
   for (int i = 0; i < dataSize; i++) {
    data[i] = din.readDouble();   // Read each element
   }
   fin.close();
   // Display results:
```

```
    System.out.println("\n" + dataSize + " data elements:\n");
    for (int i = 0; i < dataSize; i++) {
     System.out.println("data[" + i + "] = " + data[i]);
    }
  } catch (EOFException eof) {          // Trap EOF exception
   System.err.println("File damaged or in wrong format");
  } catch (IOException e) {             // Trap exception
   System.err.println(e.toString());   // Display error
  }
 }
}
```

The sample program uses the same DataInputStream class that the ReadLines.java program used to read lines from a text file. This time, however, the class is put to work reading the integer and floating point values from the sample data file created by WriteData.java. (A copy of this data file is in the ReadData directory on the CD-ROM.)

To hold the data loaded from disk, the program declares an array of double values:

```
double data[];
```

Because Java arrays are created at runtime, the exact size of this array is determined after opening the file and determining how many values it contains. To do this, the program opens the data file as a buffered stream using three statements:

```
FileInputStream fin = new FileInputStream("Data.bin");
BufferedInputStream bin = new BufferedInputStream(fin);
DataInputStream din = new DataInputStream(bin);
```

These are the same three steps you have seen in other examples. After constructing the input data stream object, din, the program loads the integer stored at the head of the file that indicates how many double values follow:

```
dataSize = din.readInt();
```

The array is now constructed to hold the indicated number of elements:

```
data = new double[dataSize];
```

Being able to create arrays at runtime this way is one of the many advantages that Java offers over other programming languages, such as C++, that have no similar capability. After this step, a simple for loop loads the double values into the array:

```
for (int i = 0; i < dataSize; i++) {
 data[i] = din.readDouble();  // Read each element
}
```

The readDouble() method reads and returns one double value from the file. The rest of the code in the sample displays these values.

You could, of course, write a simpler program that reads and displays each value without first transferring it to an array, but in practice, you'll probably want to load data into memory in advance of some operation on that information. I also wanted to show the simple but effective technique of storing the number of file elements as an integer at the head of the file. This provides a useful, though not foolproof, method for checking that the file contains the expected type of data.

As an example of how effective this technique can be—and, more important, how exception handling is used to trap an error in the file's format—follow the steps in Listing 18.17, which I copied and numbered from my DOS prompt display. The steps modify the Data.bin file's leading integer, thus simulating the effects of a damaged or badly formatted file. To follow along, type the text shown in bold. (At step 5, press the spacebar three times to skip to the byte 0A, and then type **ff** to change that value.)

Listing 18.17. Data.bin (Steps for modifying the data file to force an EOFException error).

```
 1: C:\Mvj\Part3\ReadData>debug data.bin
 2: -d
 3: 0D9B:0100  00 00 00 0A 3F 93 EF 99-A9 6F A0 20 3F DB 80 EF
 ...
 4: -e 0100
 5: 0D9B:0100  00.    00.    00.    0A.ff
 6: -d 100
 7: 0D9B:0100  00 00 00 FF 3F 93 EF 99-A9 6F A0 20 3F DB 80 EF
 ...
 8: -w
 9: Writing 00054 bytes
10: -q
```

After modifying the file, run ReadData.java. You will receive an exception error that states File damaged or in wrong format. This happens when the program catches an object of the EOFException class, which is thrown if a read() method attempts to read past the end of the file. Obviously, if this happens, something is amiss.

I don't mean to suggest that storing the number of elements at the head of the file is a perfect solution to detecting badly formatted or damaged data. For example, if the number were too small, no exception would be thrown. However, you can use the sample code here as a starting place to invent a more sophisticated verification. For example, you might store a checksum of the file's data, or you might write an identifying string at the head of the file.

Random Access File I/O

The term *random access* is often associated with database file programming, but the term has general application in other types of file I/O programming. Using the RandomAccessFile class, you can access a file's data randomly at any position. For example, you can skip to a particular byte and read data of a known type at that location. That data can be of any type, and with careful programming, it can be of different types as long as the exact file structure is known.

> **NOTE**
>
> For other examples of random-access file programming, see Chapter 8, "More About Classes and Objects," under the section titled, "Using Interface Classes."

The RandomAccessFile Class

Listing 18.18 shows the RandomAccessFile class declaration.

Listing 18.18. The RandomAccessFile class.

```
public class RandomAccessFile implements DataOutput, DataInput {
// Constructors:
public RandomAccessFile(String name, String mode);
public RandomAccessFile(File file, String mode);
// Utility methods:
public int skipBytes(int n);
public native long getFilePointer();
public native void seek(long pos);
public native long length();
public native void close();
// Input methods:
public native int read();
public int read(byte b[], int off, int len);
public int read(byte b[]);
public final void readFully(byte b[]);
public final void readFully(byte b[], int off, int len);
// Output methods:
public native void write(int b);
public void write(byte b[]);
public void write(byte b[], int off, int len);
// Typed input methods:
public final boolean readBoolean();
public final byte readByte();
public final int readUnsignedByte();
public final short readShort();
public final int readUnsignedShort();
public final char readChar();
public final int readInt();
public final long readLong();
public final float readFloat();
public final double readDouble();
public final String readLine();
public final String readUTF();
// Typed output methods:
public final void writeBoolean(boolean v);
public final void writeByte(int v);
```

continues

507

Listing 18.18. continued

```
public final void writeShort(int v);
public final void writeChar(int v);
public final void writeInt(int v);
public final void writeLong(long v);
public final void writeFloat(float v);
public final void writeDouble(double v);
public final void writeBytes(String s);
public final void writeChars(String s);
public final void writeUTF(String str);
}
```

When using random access methods, it's typical for a program to read and write to the same file. For this reason, Java defines a single whopping class that handles input and output using random-access techniques. I don't want to bloat this chapter by listing methods such as `writeInt()` that have obvious purposes, but to help you wade through this enormous class, I organized its declaration into categories:

- *Constructors:* There are two ways to construct a `RandomAccessFile` object. Pass a string filename and a mode string. Or, to use the method I prefer, pass a `File` object and a mode string. The mode string may be `"r"` to create a read-only random access file object, or `"rw"` to create a file object to which you can read and write data. The mode `"w"` is not permitted: You cannot create a write-only file object, which would be of no practical value anyway.

- *Utility methods:* Use these methods to perform general operations on a random access file object. The most useful method in this group is `seek()`, which positions the internal file pointer for a subsequent read or write operation.

- *Input methods:* Call these methods to read data as a stream of bytes. For example, you might first call `seek()` to position the file pointer, and then call one of the `read()` methods in this group to load a number of bytes from that location into an array.

- *Output methods:* Call these methods to write data as a stream of bytes. Again, you might first call `seek()` to position the file pointer, and then call a `write()` method to write data to the file at this location. The new data overwrites existing bytes; new data is *not* inserted into the file. Writing data also might extend the file.

- *Typed input methods:* Call these methods to read typed data from the file, usually after calling `seek()` to position the file pointer. These methods are analogous to those in the `DataInputStream` class.

- *Typed output methods:* Call these methods to write typed data to a file, again usually after calling `seek()` to position the file pointer. These methods are analogous to those in the `DataOutputStream` class. As with other output methods, those in this group overwrite existing data in the file; they do *not* insert new values. The methods might also extend the file.

Random Access File Programming

As an example of random-access file programming, Listing 18.19, ReadRandom.java, uses the Data.bin file created by the WriteData.java sample application in this chapter. It was convenient to use this same file, but the demonstrated techniques are applicable to other files—a database of records, for example.

Listing 18.19. ReadRandom.java (Reads typed data using random access).

```
import java.io.*;
class ReadRandom {
 // Prompt user for record number
 public static int getRecordNumber()
  throws IOException {
  StringBuffer sb = new StringBuffer();
  char ch;
  System.out.println("Record number (-1 to quit)? ");
  while ((ch = (char)System.in.read()) != '\n')
   sb.append(ch);
  return new Integer(sb.toString()).intValue();
 }
 // Main program method
 public static void main(String args[]) {
  // Instance variables
  int dataSize;          // Number of elements in file
  int rn;                // Record number
  double value;          // Value of requested record
  int sizeOfInt = 4;     // Size of int variable
  int sizeOfDouble = 8;  // Size of double variable
  boolean wantsToQuit = false;
  try {
   // Create file objects
   File fi = new File("Data.bin");
   RandomAccessFile rin = new RandomAccessFile(fi, "r");
   dataSize = rin.readInt();     // Get number of elements
   // Prompt user for element to read
   System.out.println("\nFile has " +
    dataSize + " elements\n");
   while (!wantsToQuit) {
    rn = getRecordNumber();
    wantsToQuit = (rn == -1);
    if (!wantsToQuit) {
     // Seek to requested record
     rin.seek(sizeOfInt + (rn * sizeOfDouble));
     // Read and display value
     value = rin.readDouble();
     System.out.println("Record " + rn + " = " + value);
    }
   }
  } catch (IOException e) {          // Trap exception
   System.err.println(e.toString()); // Display error
  }
 }
}
```

Compile and run the sample program. (For convenience, a copy of `Data.bin` is in the CD-ROM `ReadRandom` directory.) To access the data in the file at random, the program constructs two objects using these statements:

```
File fi = new File("Data.bin");
RandomAccessFile rin = new RandomAccessFile(fi, "r");
```

The first line creates a `File` object that refers to `Data.bin`. That object and the mode string `"r"` are passed to the `RandomAccessFile` constructor. The resulting object, `rin`, is ready for use in randomly accessing the file's data.

As preparation for that operation, the program reads and reports the number of elements from the head of the file. After prompting you to enter a record number, which can be from zero to the number of reported elements minus one, the program positions the file pointer using `seek()`:

```
rin.seek(sizeOfInt + (rn * sizeOfDouble));
```

This statement multiplies the requested record number by the size of a record (a single `double` value). Added to the size of an integer—which accounts for the value written to the head of the file—the statement positions the file pointer to the first byte of the required record. The next statement

```
value = rin.readDouble();
```

reads that value into a `double` variable. You could use similar techniques to read data of any type—even objects of classes that might, for example, represent database records.

Summary

- The `java.io` package provides numerous classes for file I/O programming. However, for obvious security reasons, you may use these classes only in stand-alone programs. Applets are strictly prohibited from performing file I/O.

- Use the `File` class to represent filenames, directories, and paths.

- Use the `FileInputStream` and `FileOutputStream` classes to access file data using simple unbuffered streams.

- Use the `BufferedInputStream` and `BufferedOutputStream` to access file data using buffered streams, which can often improve the program's I/O performance.

- For reading and writing typed file data, Java provides the `DataInputStream` and `DataOutputStream` classes. Use these classes to read and write data of any type—strings in text files, for example, or floating point values.

- To read and write data at random locations in files, construct an object of the `RandomAccessFile` class. This class contains numerous methods for seeking to a file position and then reading and writing data at that location. The class has numerous methods you can use to read and write typed and untyped file data.

18

What's Next?

This chapter concludes Part III's look at many of the classes in Java's packages. In the next part, I'll examine some additional tools that extend standard Java. I'll also compare Java and C++.

PART

IV

Developer's Toolbox

19

Microsoft's Java SDK

19

Microsoft's Java Software Development Kit (SDK) extends the standard language's `lang` and `awt` packages, and also provides additional classes along with some highly useful Windows programming tools. This chapter, the first in Part IV, "Developer's Toolbox," explains what's in the Java SDK, how you can get it, and how to use many of its offerings for advanced Windows programming tasks.

> **NOTE**
>
> Programs written using the Java SDK run only under Windows 95 or Windows NT. Users must also install the modified Java Virtual Machine (VM) supplied with the SDK. Although these facts negate one of Java's key advantages—the capability of generating system-independent applications and applets—if you are targeting your code for Windows, you'll find the Java SDK packed with many powerful classes and utilities.

In This Chapter

This chapter covers the following fundamentals of Microsoft's Java SDK:

- Overview of the Java SDK: where to get it, what's in it, and how to install and use it
- How to generate stand-alone Windows `.Exe` code files from Java interpreted programs using the Jexegen utility
- How to use the SDK's WJiew, ClassVue, AppletViewer, and other utility programs
- Advantages and disadvantages of using the SDK's `FontX`, `MenuX`, and other extended classes
- Displaying text using Windows TrueType fonts
- Creating and using true Windows menu bars in application graphical windows

SDK Overview

The following sections describe Microsoft's Java SDK, and explain where to get it, how to install it, and what's in it. I'll also cover additional requirements needed for using some SDK tools such as native code access and programming DirectX video and sound.

Where to Get It

Microsoft's Java SDK is contained in two archive files. The two files are

- `SDK-Java.exe`: Compressed installation file for the Java SDK.
- `SDK-Docs.exe`: Compressed installation file for the Java SDK documentation and other help files.

For the latest update of the SDK, download the two archive files from http://www.microsoft.com/java. For online support, send your comments and questions to sdkjava@microsoft.com.

You can also obtain the latest SDK files from the Microsoft Developer Network CD-ROM, with a Level II or higher-level subscription. (This level has recently been renamed "Professional Subscription.") The installation files are located on CD-ROM #9, "Additional SDKs and Tools."

How to Install It

To install the complete SDK, run the first file, SDK-Java.exe. Follow onscreen instructions to create and install the SDK to the default directory, C:\SDK-Java. (The directory name has a hyphen in it, which is difficult to see onscreen.) Run SDK-Docs.exe to install the documentation. The default directory for these files, all of which are in .HTML format, is C:\SDK-Docs. I changed this to C:\SDK-Java\Docs on my system. Restart Windows after completing the installation.

> **WARNING**
>
> Under Windows NT, do not specify long filenames for the SDK installation directories.

What's in It

The Microsoft Java SDK contains the following tools, utilities, and other items:

- The newest release of the Java VM (Virtual Machine), including class extensions and support for Component Object Model (COM) services.
- New classes for a variety of special needs such as accessing Windows menus and fonts, and for programming with DirectX video and sound.
- The newest releases of the Java compiler, Jvc.exe, and application viewer, Jview.exe.
- A new AppletViewer.exe utility that you can use to run applets from a DOS prompt. This is faster than loading Internet Explorer or another browser from Visual J++, and it is especially handy for testing applets developed with the command-line Jvc.exe compiler.
- The Classvue.exe utility for viewing and debugging compiled Java code files. This program provides detailed information about a byte-code .class file; it can even disassemble a program's compiled instructions.
- The Javatlb.exe utility for converting type library files into Java classes. This program can also partially disassemble a .class file into a .java text-file, showing the file's class declarations in text form.
- The Jexegen.exe utility for converting compiled Java applications to stand-alone .Exe code files. Users can run the resulting file as they do any application.

517

- The `Msjavah.exe` utility, which generates a header file that can be used with a C or C++ program to access the methods and data in a compiled Java `.class` file.

- The `Guidgen.exe` utility for generating Globally Unique Identifiers (GUIDs), used to uniquely mark OLE and ActiveX components, objects, and interfaces. The Windows help file `Guidgen.hlp`, also provided with the Java SDK, explains how to use this utility.

- Various header files such as `Native.h` and `Nativecom.h`, for use with Visual C++ in writing native-code applications and accessing the Java VM's COM interfaces. In theory, you can use any C compiler with these files and their associated libraries; however, if you are not using Visual C++, you might have to modify the files' declarations.

- The CAB Developer's Kit for compacting `.class` and other files into archives, called *cabinets*, for faster download times.

- Documentation on APIs (application programming interfaces) for Java's Just-in-time (JIT) debugger, native code interfaces for raw and COM access, and the VM. To find more information on these topics, search the SDK's installed documentation files for sections titled "Java and COM," "Raw Native Interface," and "Working with Microsoft VM."

- Various sample applications. In this chapter, I refer to some of these applications to illustrate aspects of SDK programming.

The SDK also provides several new classes for accessing Windows 95 and NT services. Of course, if you use these classes, your application will require Windows 95 or NT. The classes are contained in these SDK packages:

- `com.ms.lang`: Win32 system-level features.

- `com.ms.awt`: Win32 window-management and graphics.

- `com.ms.awt.peer`: Low-level system interface classes.

- `com.ms.com`: Component Object Model (COM) services.

- `com.ms.util`: Access to version control services.

- `com.ms.com.directx`: Access to DirectX services.

> **NOTE**
>
> Users of applets and applications developed using the SDK must have the updated VM installed on their systems. To redistribute the VM in `IE32Java.exe`, you must register and agree to Microsoft's SDK license. Precise instructions about how to do this, and about which files are redistributable, are provided in `SDK-Docs.exe`.

Other Requirements

To install the SDK, in addition to the space occupied by the SDK-Java.exe archive file, you will need 45MB of free disk space during installation. After installation, the SDK files use 15MB of disk space.

To install the SDK documentation files, in addition to the space occupied by the SDK-Doc.exe archive file, you will need 20MB of free disk space during installation. After installation, the SDK documentation files use 7.8MB of disk space.

Total combined disk space required after installation of all files is 22.8MB. To remove the SDK from your hard drive, you may simply delete the installation directories SDK-Java and SDK-Doc. However, this does not delete the extended VM. Apparently, the only way to return to the standard VM is to reinstall Visual J++. Just to be on the safe side, if you decide to remove the VM, it might be a good idea to reinstall Internet Explorer 3.0. Installing the SDK does not in any way affect the capability of creating system-independent Java applets and applications—just don't use the SDK's classes and other tools, and the generated code will be the same as it is in the absence of an installed SDK.

To run DirectX video and sound programs, you must download and install the beta DirectX SDK, version 2 or 3, which is not provided in the Java SDK. For information about how to obtain the DirectX SDK, see http://www.microsoft.com. The complete SDK is also available on the Microsoft Developer Network CD-ROM. (By the way, this SDK has some cool examples of animated 3D video, games, and sound; it's worth looking at the sample programs even if you have no intentions of programming DirectX applications.)

The DirectX SDK installs updated Windows drivers for 3D video and stereo sound. To remove the SDK from your hard drive, first use the Control Panel's "Add/Remove Programs" utility to uninstall the drivers. You can then manually delete the SDK base directory (C:\Dxsdk by default) and its subdirectories.

The Java SDK's native-code examples require a C or C++ compiler capable of producing a Windows DLL (dynamic link library). Although the documentation states that any compiler will work, the header files appear to use declarations unique to Visual C++. If you use a different compiler, you will probably have to modify the stock header files.

To upgrade to the latest VM, remember to run IE30Java.exe, located in the installation directory SDK-Java\bin. The SDK has the same platform requirements as Internet Explorer 3.0, but the extended VM adds support for the SDK's enhanced and Windows-specific classes. If you haven't installed Internet Explorer from your Visual J++ CD-ROM, do that *before* updating the VM.

> **TIP**
>
> After installation, you may find multiple copies of the command-line utilities Jvc.exe and Jview.exe on your hard drive. Because installing the SDK does not update your system Path in Autoexec.bat, to ensure that your system uses the newest releases, either add C:\SDK-Java to your system Path or copy the utilities and other tools from that directory to C:\Windows.

Utilities

Read the following sections to get started using SDK tools such as the Exe code file generator, class viewer, and other utilities. Update your system path, or copy the utilities to C:\Windows or to C:\Windows\Command so that you can run them at a DOS prompt from any directory.

Jexegen Code File Generator

Jexegen.exe converts a Java application to a stand-alone Windows .exe code file. The utility cannot convert an applet because, by definition, applets run under control of a browser such as Internet Explorer.

> **NOTE**
>
> It *might* be possible to convert an applet to a stand-alone .exe code file by using the techniques for writing a Java program that can run as both an applet and an application. See Chapter 13, "Applets," under the section titled "As an Application." I haven't tried this, but there is no technical reason that would prevent it from working.

After conversion, the resulting .exe code file will run only on MS-DOS and Windows systems. The program's primary class to be converted must have a main() method declared in the standard way as

```
public static void main(String args[]) {
...
}
```

Jexegen is simple to use. For example, to convert Part II's CommandLine sample application, which demonstrates how to pass command-line arguments to a program, get to a DOS prompt and switch to the CommandLine directory. Compile the program in the usual way with this command:

```
jvc commandline
```

Normally, to run the resulting Commandline.class file, you must use the Jview interpreter. For example, the command

```
jview commandline arg1 arg2 arg3
```

runs `Commandline.class` and passes the three arguments to the program, which reports

```
Number of arguments = 3
arg1
arg2
arg3
```

To convert the interpreted program to a stand-alone executable code file, issue this Jexegen command all on one line:

```
jexegen /MAIN:CommandLine /OUT:commandline.exe
 /V commandline.class
```

This generates `Commandline.exe`, which you can run as you do any stand-alone application—just type the program's name. You no longer need to use `Jview.exe`. For example, type this command:

```
commandline arg1 arg2 arg3
```

Jexegen has several options. `/MAIN:classname`, which is required, specifies the name of the class that has a `main()` method. If you don't specify an output file with the `/OUT:exename` option, the resulting file is named `Jex.exe`, which you can rename after conversion. The `/V` option used in the preceding sample command selects verbose output, which reports progress notes such as

```
Adding file: CommandLine.class as CommandLine
```

Jexegen's syntax is as follows:

```
jexegen [options] [@command file] files
```

The `[options]` settings may be any combination of the program's options, which I'll detail in this section. The command file—more formally called a *command response file*—may be a text file containing option settings, one on each line. This is useful if you specify many options, so that you don't have to type them repeatedly. Preface the command filename with the @ character. Specify all `.class` files to be included in the conversion. This may be one or more filenames separated with a space, or a wildcard specification such as `*.class`.

OPTIONS SYMBOLOGY

For consistency, all options in this chapter are preceded with a forward slash, even when the program itself indicates a hyphen is the proper escape character. In general, you may type either a hyphen or a slash. For example, the options -v and /v are identical.

I believe that all SDK utility options are case-insensitive, and you may type them in upper- or lowercase as you prefer. However, I haven't tested this theory rigorously. Case is ignored for filenames, but when an argument designates a class name, you must type it exactly as declared in the program. Class names are always case-sensitive, as they are in the program's source code.

Some command-line options accept optional switches. A plus sign switches on a command; a dash turns it off. These characters are shown in square brackets to indicate they are optional. The option /R[-], for example, may be typed two ways: as /R and as /R-. Do not type the brackets.

A set of options is enclosed in curly braces. For example, the Jvc.exe warning-level option /w{0-4} indicates five possible settings: /w0, /w1, /w2, /w3, and /w4.

A few options have parameters that you must specify. These are listed in angle brackets as in /MAIN:<classname> to indicate that the argument is required. The option /MAIN:CommandLine, for example, passes the CommandLine class name to this option. Because the argument is a class name, this is one of the rare instances when case is significant. Do not type the angle brackets.

Most, but not all, utilities display a list of options when fed the command /?, and I therefore excluded this option from the following descriptions. For example, to see a list of Jvc options, enter the command

```
jvc /?
```

See the preceding sidebar for explanations of symbols used in the following descriptions and elsewhere in this chapter to describe command-line options for the SDK's utility programs. Jexegen's command-line options are as follows:

- /MAIN:<classname>: Specifies the class that has the application's public, static, main() method. The <classname> is case-sensitive, and it may be a class in a package: MyPackage.MyClass, for example.

- /NOMAIN: Use this command to prevent an error and allow the conversion even if the application doesn't have a main() method. This command is typically used with the /RAW method—to write resource data to the output file, for example.

- /BASE:<dir>: Specifies the base directory for any packages of class files involved in the conversion. Can be used with /NOMAIN and /RAW options simply to specify a starting directory rather than one containing packaged classes. The default base directory is the current one, and thus, in the absence of this option, all packages are expected to be in subdirectories of the current path.

- /OUT:<filename>: Specifies the output .exe code filename. If you don't use this option, Jexegen creates the file Jex.exe, which you can rename as you wish. Note that this file is created when using the /RAW command—but the resulting code is *not* executable.

- /R[-]: Causes Jexegen to recurse into subdirectories for other class files associated with this program. Append a dash after this option, as in /R-, to disable it—for example, if the command is already used in a command response file, and you want to turn it off. This may be useful in cases where some directories have packages in subdirectories, while others do not.

- /V: Produces verbose output that reports the class names Jexegen is converting.

- /W: Combines a stub with no console window capabilities to the resulting .exe code file. As a result, the finished program has no standard I/O capabilities, and it must be run in a window frame, which presumably, the program creates. Usually, this will be a graphical window, but this isn't required. Use /BINDTO: to specify the stub, which is your responsibility to provide.

- /BINDTO:<stub>: Binds the class resources to the specified stub .exe or .dll file.

- /RAW: Writes class resource data to the specified output file and does not create an executable code file. If you do not specify an output file, Jexegen still creates Jex.exe, but running this file causes a fatal exception that terminates the current DOS session. This command is intended for use along with the /NOMAIN and /BINDTO options to generate a data file suitable for use with the IJavaExecute2::SetClassSource() C++ method. Locate that method declared in the SDK's header file Javaexec.h. Its code is implemented in the SDK's MSJava.dll library, which provides Java invocation services for C++.

If your application uses its own packages—as do most significant applications—extra care is needed to preserve package names when converting the program with Jexegen. For best results, create your packages as subdirectories in your main application project path, and use the /R option to recurse into those directories for the package class files. To convert, use a command such as

```
jexegen /MAIN:MainClass *.class
```

This will not work, however, if the package names are not nested in the current path. In that case, there are two possible solutions. Specify the starting path containing the project and nested package directories:

```
jexegen /MAIN:MainClass /TheProject/*.class
```

If that's not convenient—as it probably isn't when sharing packages among multiple applications, for example—you can use the /BASE option to set the starting path.

A *stub*, as referenced here, is simply a short program that binds the application to the VM. This is done by calling SetClassSource() in the IJavaExecute2 C++ class, implemented in the MSJava.dll library. If the VM isn't in memory, it is instantiated and directed where to look for the specified program's code. Use the /BINDTO option to bind your code to another stub if the default one is not sufficient for your purposes, or use /RAW to generate data that you can pass to SetClassSource() by other means. An example of such a call appears in the Stub.cpp file:

```
hr = pJV->m_pJE->SetClassSource(
 CLASS_SOURCE_TYPE_MODULERESOURCES,
 &jcri, sizeof(JAVACLASSRESOURCEINFO) );
```

This, along with other code, runs the class thread. See the Jexegen directory in the SDK's Samples path for a complete example of a custom stub written in C++. The example demonstrates how, by writing a custom stub, a stand-alone executable code file can be created for an applet.

Jvc Command-Line Compiler

As you probably realize from this book's sample programs, especially those in Part II, Jvc.exe is Java's command-line compiler. It is highly useful for quick tests and demos, and it is fully capable of compiling any applet or application regardless of complexity and size. The program, which is executed from a DOS prompt, creates .class byte-code files from .java source code files. Jvc's syntax is

```
jvc [options] <filename>
```

You do not have to specify the .java extension in the filename. Jvc's command-line options are as follows:

- /cp <classpath>: Specifies the class path for this compilation by way of the CLASSPATH environment variable. This path is where the compiler looks for system and also user-defined classes. Semicolons may separate multiple paths.

- /cp:o[-]: Use this option to display the current class path setting. This is useful when you have trouble compiling, and you want to check whether Jvc can find Java's system classes, and also in preparation for using the /cp command to set a new class path. It's possible to append a dash to this command to disable it, but this switch is shown simply because it is the default setting.

- /cp:p <path>: Inserts the specified path in front of the current class path as specified by the CLASSPATH environment variable or by the /cp command. To specify multiple paths, separate them with semicolons; or you can use multiple /cp:p options.

- /d <directory>: Specifies the output directory where you want Jvc to write .class files. If the output directory does not exist, Jvc creates it—so use this option with care. After compilation, if you can't find your program's output, check whether you made a mistake entering the output directory name.

- /g[-]: Selects full debug information. It is equivalent to the combined options g:l and g:d. The default setting, /g-, selects no debug information in generated .class files. The following two subcommands select specific types of debug options:
  - /g:l[-]: Generates line number information only. The default is /g:l- (no line number information). Note that the option character is a lowercase letter "l" and not the digit 1.
  - /g:t[-]: Generates debug tables. The default option is /g:t- (no debug tables).

- /nowarn: Disables all warning messages. See also the /w command for selecting warning levels. The default is all warnings enabled (/warn, which is not an actual option, despite its being listed by the /? command).

- /nowrite: Compiles the specified source code files, but does not create or write to class files. When compiling large applications, use this option to view errors and warnings.

Strangely, there is no alternate option; to disable /nowrite, you have to exclude it from the command line or delete it from the command response file.

- /O[-]: Enables full optimization. This command is equivalent to issuing the separate commands O:I and O:J. The default option /O- disables all optimizations. Use one of these two subcommands to select specific types of optimizations:

  - /O:I[-]: Optimizes the generated class files by in-lining method calls. This "unrolls" the calls by replacing them with the method's statements, and it can create much larger output. The default is /O:I- (no in-lining).

  - /O:J[-]: Optimizes byte-code jumps to use the fastest possible instructions. The default is /O:J- (no jump optimization).

- /verbose: Produces verbose output messages. This option is especially useful for tracking down problems loading class files specified in an import statement. Unfortunately, you must type this option in full, because Jvc does not understand the usual /v shorthand option.

- /w{0-4}: Sets the level for warning messages. The default setting is /w2. See also /nowarn, which is the same as /w0 (no warnings).

- /x[-]: Use this option to disable all Microsoft extensions to standard Java. With the /x option in effect, any extension is treated as a common identifier, which will probably produce a compilation error. The default setting /x- switches off this option and *enables* all Microsoft extensions.

Select one of five warning levels with the /w{0-4} option. The five levels are as follows:

- /w0: Displays no warnings. Use this level only if you are tired of seeing the same warning messages over and over; it is dangerous to ignore every possible warning.

- /w1: Displays only the most severe warnings that are nearly sure to show up as bugs.

- /w2: Displays warnings for most common problems, including some that might safely be ignored. This is the default warning level.

- /w3: Adds warnings for methods with no declared return type, missing return statements, and type conversions that might cause a loss of data or precision.

- /w4: Displays as many warnings as possible. Before debugging, it is useful to compile the program with this highest warning level.

NOTE

To compile many source code files with a single command, use a wildcard specification, as in the command jvc *.java. To compile numerous files by their individual names, insert each filename into a text file and reference it with the @ character using a command such as jvc @files.txt.

Jview Application Viewer

The `Jview.exe` utility is Java's application viewer. The program runs stand-alone applications in `.class` files created by `Jvc.exe` (or by another Java compiler). Normally, the results of running a program this way appear in a DOS prompt (also called a console window).

Jview's syntax is

```
jview [options] <classname> [arguments]
```

Pass any of the following as `options`. The `classname` is a file ending with `.class`, containing an application with a `main()` method. You do not have to type the `.class` filename extension. (Jview cannot run an applet that doesn't have a `main()` method.) Optionally, pass one or more `arguments` to be used by the program. Jview's options are as follows:

- `/cp <classpath>`: Sets the `CLASSPATH` variable indicating where Jview looks for any class files it needs to run the program—such as the files containing classes imported by the program's modules, for example.

- `/cp:a <path>`: Adds a semicolon and the specified path to the end of the current `CLASSPATH` setting.

- `/cp:p <path>`: Inserts the specified path and a semicolon ahead of the current `CLASSPATH` setting. (Technically, the p is short for "prepend," but let's use a real word and pretend it means "preface.")

- `/p`: Pauses if an error occurs in the application. Press a key such as Esc to exit the program and return to DOS.

- `/v`: Verifies method calls as the VM does for remotely loaded classes. Use this option to ensure that your application's classes will pass the security watchdogs on a user's system.

- `/d:<name>=<value>`: Defines a system property, consisting of an identifying name and a value. Use `System.getProperty()` to import the property setting into an application. This option is relatively new, and it might not be available with all versions of Jview.

Wjview Windowed Application Viewer

One problem you may encounter when running applications with Jview is that a DOS prompt window is always created, even when using the Start button's Run command. Wjview is the solution—it runs an application just as Jview does, but does not require a DOS prompt window. (You may, however, run Wjview from a DOS prompt, as you do Jview.)

Wjview lacks standard console input and output, and it therefore ignores any `System.out.println()` or other input and output statements. When running code with Wjview, it is the application's responsibility to create a Frame window and provide graphical input and output methods.

Wjview's options are a subset of those recognized by Jview. You may use the /cp, /cp:a, /cp:p, and /v options with Wjview, but the program does not recognize the /? option that normally displays instructions.

> **NOTE**
>
> Frankly, Visual J++ and Java are not yet up to snuff when it comes to creating stand-alone Windows applications, but this will probably change in future releases. Meanwhile, Wjview is a reasonable, if temporary, solution to the problem of writing and running stand-alone Java applications under Windows.

Listing 19.1, AppWindow.java, illustrates the kind of application intended for running with Wjview. The sample program also shows how to write a stand-alone Java application that creates a Frame window without the services of an applet viewer or browser such as Internet Explorer. After the listing, I'll explain how to use Wjview to run the program.

Listing 19.1. AppWindow.java (Demonstrates graphical windows in stand-alone applications).

```
import java.io.*;
import java.awt.*;

//=============================================================
// Extend Frame class so it can close itself
//=============================================================

class MyFrame extends Frame {
 // Constructor
 MyFrame(String title) {
  super(title);
 }
 // Handle events
 public boolean handleEvent(Event evt) {
  // Displays events if run via jview
  // Displays nothing if run via wjview
  System.out.println(evt.toString());
  // Catch destroy notification event
  if (evt.id == Event.WINDOW_DESTROY) {
   dispose();        // Close window
   System.exit(0);   // Stop Java VM
   return true;      // Event handled
  } else {
   // Handle other events
   return super.handleEvent(evt);
  }
 }
}

//=============================================================
// Main program class
//=============================================================
```

continues

Listing 19.1. continued

```
class AppWindow {
 public static void main(String args[]) {
  // Display instructions, which are seen only
  // if program is run via jview, not wjview
  System.out.println("Creating application window...");
  // Create, size, and show graphics window
  Frame f = new MyFrame("Application Frame Window");
  f.resize(250,200);
  f.show();
 }
}
```

The key to creating a stand-alone graphical application in a window is to extend the Frame class. The sample program does this by declaring and implementing MyClass. In that class, the handleEvent() method watches for an event id field equal to Event.WINDOW_DESTROY. When this event occurs—as a result of you closing the Frame window—the method destroys the window object by executing this code:

```
if (evt.id == Event.WINDOW_DESTROY) {
 this.dispose();
 System.exit(0);
 return true;
}
```

Calling dispose() destroys the window object, after which exit() terminates the VM session. Together, the two statements close the window and exit Wjview, or whatever other interpreter is running the code.

To create and display the graphical window, the application constructs an object of the MyFrame class:

```
Frame f = new MyFrame("Application Frame Window");
```

After this, you can size the window and display it using these statements:

```
f.resize(250,200);
f.show();
```

Of course, you will want to add additional code to display graphics using a paint() method, and to add components, animate bitmaps, and use other graphics techniques explained in this book. The purpose of this demonstration, however, is to show how to *run* such an application.

The first method demonstrates why Jview is not suitable for this task. Get to a DOS prompt, and then compile and run the program by typing these commands:

```
jvc appwindow
jview appwindow
```

When the graphical window appears, move the mouse into its interior, and watch the DOS prompt window. You will receive a report of all events that occur for the window—a useful trick for debugging, by the way. Close the window as you normally do. (Click the close button, use the system menu, or press Alt+F4.) This issues the WINDOW_DESTROY event and disposes of the window by executing the statement

```
this.dispose();
```

The this standard variable refers to the current Frame object for which handleEvent() was called. In addition to closing the window, the program must also halt the Java VM and, in doing that, also exit Jview. These steps are performed by the System class's exit() method, called here with

```
System.exit(0);
```

The zero argument is a value passed back to the operating system—a holdover from DOS, and of no importance to Windows. (Debuggers display this value, however, which might provide a useful tag indicating a problem—but the value's definition is up to you.)

If you don't exit the VM by calling System.exit(), Jview continues running after the window closes. To close Jview in that case, you must return to the DOS prompt window and press Ctrl+C. You've probably had this trouble with various sample applications.

Now, run the same program again, but this time use Wjview. Enter this command at the DOS prompt:

```
wjview appwindow
```

The same graphical window appears, but you do not see any event debugging information in the DOS window. This is because Wjview does not support standard console I/O, and the program's System.out.println() statements are ignored. Any input statements would also be ignored. In fact, if you look closely at the DOS display, you'll see that Wjview exits *before* the applet begins to run. Close the applet window as you did before.

Although this technique is useful, it still requires users to open a DOS prompt window to run the application. A simple solution to that problem is to use the Start button's Run command: Enter wjview appwindow (assuming both Wjview.exe and Appwindow.class are on the system path or in the same directory) to run the program. With this approach, no DOS window appears, and the program runs the same as any other Windows application.

> **NOTE**
>
> Another, and perhaps superior, method for running stand-alone graphics applications is to convert them to .exe code files using the Jexegen.exe utility described in this chapter. Unfortunately, however, this attaches a Jview-like stub to the output, which causes a DOS window to open and enables standard I/O. To prevent this and run the program without a DOS window, you must attach your own stub as demonstrated by the SDK's Samples\Jexegen sample application and files. This requires using a C++ compiler to create the stub. I suspect that it will soon be much easier to create stand-alone Java applications—perhaps as soon as you read these words. If so, you can still use the sample AppWindow application in this section to get started creating stand-alone windowed programs.

Applet Viewer

If you have compiled and run the sample applets in this book's chapters (mostly in Part III), you are probably well aware that it takes a distressingly long time for Developer Studio or Studio 97 to open the Internet Explorer, start the VM, load the applet's HTML file, and finally, load and run the applet's code.

A faster way to view applets is to use the SDK's AppletViewer utility. You normally run this program from a DOS prompt, but you may also run it using the Start button's Run command. The target file must be an HTML document that loads an applet with an `<applet>` tag. AppletViewer is not a fully fledged browser, and it cannot display any HTML documents—only those with an `<applet>` tag. The program's syntax is

```
appletviewer url¦file
```

You may specify an URL or an `.html` filename. You must type the `.html` filename extension. For example, get to a DOS prompt, and change to the `Part3\ColorScroll` directory on this book's CD-ROM. To run the compiled applet, enter the command

```
appletviewer colorscroll.html
```

This causes the applet to appear in a graphical window far faster than when loaded into the full browser. Figure 19.1 shows the AppletViewer's display of the ColorScroll applet. The program provides several helpful commands in an *Applet* menu that you can use to obtain information about the applet and its properties, to clone the applet, to reload it, and to restart its code. Select the *Applet|Close* or *Applet|Quit* commands to end the applet. (It's not clear why there are two commands for this; they seem to do the same job.) AppletViewer has no command-line options.

Figure 19.1.

The AppletViewer utility can run any applet such as the ColorScroll demonstration from Part III shown here.

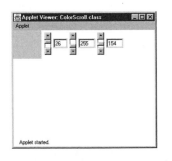

> **TIP**
>
> After you tire of typing `appletviewer` a few thousand times, do as I did—rename its file to `av.exe`.

Class Viewer

The `ClassVue.exe` utility is a show-all-and-tell-all program that will tell you more than you ever wanted to know about compiled `.class` files. All software companies have these kinds of utilities; fortunately, Microsoft decided to make this one available for investigating the Java compiler's byte-code output.

ClassVue's output is voluminous, and a lot of it will take careful study to understand. Nevertheless, you can find lots of interesting information about your compiled programs (or anyone else's) by feeding them to this tool. For example, open a DOS prompt window, and change to the `Part3\ColorScroll` directory. Enter a command such as

```
classvue colorscroll.class
```

to disassemble the class file's byte codes. As you see if you are following along, most of the text scrolls offscreen before you can read it, so you'll usually save the output in a file with a redirection command such as

```
classvue colorscroll.class >info.txt
```

Alternatively, use the `/Cvue` option to create a text file ending with the filename extension `.Cvue` and named the same as the disassembled class:

```
classvue /Cvue colorscroll.class
```

After this, you can load `Info.txt`—or, if you're using the alternate method, `ColorScroll.cvue`—into a text editor for reading and printing.

> **NOTE**
>
> Programmers are notoriously poor spellers, which might account for the Vue in ClassVue. I'm no better than most, but after I typed ClassView incorrectly a few times, I renamed the program `Cv.exe` and was a much happier camper.

ClassVue's syntax is

```
ClassVue [options] <classname>
```

You must enter the `.class` filename extension when specifying the `classname` file to disassemble. ClassVue's options are as follows:

- `/D?`: Displays brief descriptions of D levels selected by other options. (More on D levels and their meanings later.)
- `/min`: Writes only minimal level D1 ("Class/Interface Overview") information to the output.
- `/ltd`: Writes limited amounts of information (levels D1, D2, and D3) to the output.

- /v: Writes all possible (verbose) information to the output at all seven D levels. If you can't find what you're looking for with this option, it's not there.

- /cpno: Disables output of the constant pool information.

- /tables: Formats some information in tabular form.

- /ivmal: Disassembles method byte codes, showing their Virtual Machine Assembly Language (VMAL) mnemonics.

- /Cvue: Writes output to a text file named the same as the .class file, but ending with the filename extension .cvue. This option creates or overwrites the output file.

- /README: Displays a table that defines some of the terms and abbreviations used in ClassVue's output. Table 19.1 lists this information for reference, formatted and edited here and there for clarity and spelling.

- /q: This option, an abbreviation for "quiet mode," is supposed to suppress the program's identifying banner, but it doesn't seem to do anything.

Some of ClassVue's options select varying degrees of information. These are called D levels (probably short for Debug). The seven levels are as follows:

- D1: Class and interface overview, showing the class name, size in bytes, compiled version number, and other sundry facts and figures.

- D2: Class and interface methods, fields, and classes, including methods interfaced, fields accessed or modified, declared methods, declared fields, and classes accessed.

- D3: Class and interface root data structures, giving their offsets, bytes, field names, and descriptions.

- D4: Class and interface constant pool showing the offsets, bytes, field name, and description of all constant data.

- D5: Class and interface fields pool, showing all fields, their offsets, bytes, and descriptions.

- D6: Class and interface methods pool, showing a breakdown of the descriptors for each method in the class.

- D7: Attributes pool, which shows basic information such as the filename, length, and attribute (SourceFile, for example, if created from a .java text file). As with other D-level information, this section gives the offsets, bytes, and descriptions of each piece of information.

It will take a lot of time and patience to decipher the information that ClassVue generates. Processing even a small example produces hundreds of lines of data. For example, ClassVue reports the following variables and values for the ColorScroll sample applet. If this is all the information you need, specify the /min (level D1) option. This level provides the following overview:

```
Variable Name          Value Reported
~~~~~~~~~~~~~~~~~~~     ~~~~~~~~~~~~~~~~~~
Class Name             ColorScroll
Size                   1319 bytes
```

```
Version                 45.03
Access Flags            public
Super Class Name        java.applet.Applet
Interface(s)            * None Defined *
Source Filename         ColorScroll.java
Debug Information        YES
ActiveX Controls        NO
```

The meaning of some items is open to interpretation. For instance, the `size` variable is apparently equal to the `.class` file size, but the version seems to be the same for every file I disassembled. This is probably an internal version number related to the Jvc compiler's output—it's not your program's version.

Another portion of ClassVue's report tells you which methods are invoked. You might use this list to weed out old methods that your code no longer calls. For example, here's a portion of the method-invocation list for ColorScroll:

```
Methods (Invoked)
~~~~~~~~~~~~~~~~~~~~~~~~~~~~~~~~~~~~~~~~~~~~~~~~~~~
void ColorScrollbar.<init>(Applet)
void ColorScrollbar.updateText()
void java.applet.Applet.<init>()
void java.applet.Applet.resize(int,int)
...
void java.awt.Graphics.setColor(Color)
int java.awt.Scrollbar.getValue()
```

Notice that methods in the program's own classes and in system package classes such as AWT are listed. If a package isn't listed anywhere, you might use this information to delete an unnecessary `import` statement. Yet another portion of the report shows fields accessed or modified:

```
Fields (Accessed and/or Modified)
~~~~~~~~~~~~~~~~~~~~~~~~~~~~~~~~~~~~~~
ColorScrollbar ColorScroll.bluScroll
ColorScrollbar ColorScroll.grnScroll
ColorScrollbar ColorScroll.redScroll
int java.awt.Event.id
Object java.awt.Event.target
```

I could go on—the report continues for page after page, but I'll stop here. To interpret a full ClassVue report, you'll need to study the output carefully. As a useful guide, Table 19.1 lists various terms you might encounter in a class report. You can obtain a similar table onscreen by issuing the command `classvue /README`.

Table 19.1. ClassVue report terms.

Term or Abbreviation	Meaning or Synonym
DISPATCH	class java.lang.Object
In, _Out, _InOut	Describes a ptr2data, JString, or Jarray Param object

continues

Table 19.1. continued

Term or Abbreviation	Meaning or Synonym
ThreadAutoMarshal, ThreadNoMarshal	Threading model
void	No return value
s8bit, s16bit, s32bit, s64bit	Signed 1, 2, 4, and 8 byte values
u8bit, u16bit, u32bit, u64bit	Unsigned 1, 2, 4, and 8 byte values
f32bit, f64bit	float and double values respectively
CY	long. To obtain original value, divide by 10,000
DATE	double
ptr2data	A 32-bit linear address
byValStruct	A by-value structure or array
Iunknown	An IUnknown* derivative
Interface	com.ms.com.Iuknown
Jstring	Direct pointer to String[buffer]
BSTR	class java.lang.String
Jarray	Direct pointer to an array of primitives
Variant	Parameter passed either by value or by reference
class	com.ms.com.Variant

AWT Enhancements

Microsoft's Java SDK provides extended classes for writing system-dependent Windows applets and applications. When using these classes, be aware that your users must have Windows 95 or NT to run your code. They also must install the extended VM supplied with the SDK.

In this section, I'll explain how to use two sets of extended classes, one for accessing Windows fonts, and the other for creating and using Windows menus. The classes are located in the com.ms.awt package and are identified by a capital X somewhere in their names. For example, the MenuItemX class creates an extended menu item object. If you installed the SDK's source code, you'll find the complete .java files source files for all extended classes in the path C:\Windows\Java\Classes\com.

Using Windows Fonts

Java's AWT package supports only a limited subset of fonts, and while this limitation might seem severe, it ensures that applets and applications can run under any Java-aware browser. To use standard font techniques, which you should do in any code placed on the Internet, see

Chapter 17, "Graphics, Animation, and Multimedia," under the sections titled "The Font Class" and "The FontMetrics Class."

If you are absolutely, positively, certain beyond all shadow of a doubt that your code will run under Windows 95 and NT, then you'll probably want to access the variety of TrueType fonts available for these operating systems. You can also select embedded, strikeout, underline, and outline styles in addition to the standard plain, bold, and italic styles in the Font class. In Java, these are called *extended fonts*, which you can create using the SDK's FontX class, shown in Listing 19.2.

Listing 19.2. The FontX class.

```
public class FontX extends Font {
// Fields:
 public static final int EMBEDDED;
 public static final int STRIKEOUT;
 public static final int UNDERLINE;
 public static final int OUTLINE;
// Constructors:
 public FontX(String name, int style, int size);
 public FontX(String name, int style, int size, boolean bEmbed);
 public FontX(String name, int style, int size, int xFlags);
// Public methods:
 public boolean isTypeable(int language);
 public int getFlags();
 public boolean equals(Object obj);
 public String toString();
 public static String[] getFontList();
 public static FontX ChooseFont(Component c);
 public static FontX ChooseFont(Component c, FontX f);
}
```

Because FontX extends the standard AWT Font class, you can pass an instance of FontX to any method that declares a Font parameter. This means you can use extended fonts just as you do standard ones. However, the target system must have the extended VM installed, which among other characteristics, uses the extended GraphicsX class. You probably won't use GraphicsX directly, so I won't list it here. (It's included with the SDK.) However, with the extended VM installed, when you call a method such as Component.setFont() to select a font, it is the extended setFont() code that actually handles the task—a good example of how object-oriented programming permits inserting new code without affecting existing code, but also a good example of how OOP allows a language's system independence to be broken as easily as an egg dropped on the kitchen floor.

There are three ways to create an extended FontX object. The first method is similar to how you create a standard Font. Use a statement such as

```
FontX font = new FontX(name, style, size);
```

where name is a string representing the font's family name; style is the logical-OR combination of static fields such as Font.BOLD and Font.ITALIC; and size is the font's size in points.

535

Programs that use extended fonts need to import the `FontX` class from the SDK's `com.ms.awt` package. If the program is an applet, it will probably also bring in the standard `applet` and AWT packages. In general, to use extended fonts, insert these `import` statements into your applet's module:

```
import java.applet.*;
import java.awt.*;
import com.ms.awt.*;
```

To try extended fonts, create a test applet and import the `com.ms.awt` package. Insert the following `paint()` method into the program:

```
public void paint(Graphics g) {
 FontX font = new FontX("Arial", Font.BOLD, 24);
 g.setFont(font);
 g.drawString("AbCdEfG 1234 !@#$", 5, 20);
}
```

The method creates a `FontX` object and passes it to `Graphics.setFont()`. In this example, the specified TrueType font is named Arial, and its style is set to `Font.BOLD`. This style can be any combination of the `Font` class fields: `PLAIN`, `BOLD`, and `ITALIC`. Do *not* pass `FontX` styles in this parameter. The final argument, 24, indicates the font size in points. Calling `setFont()` for this `FontX` object prepares the `Graphics` context for displaying text in that font. Behind the scenes, however, the `GraphicsX.setFont()` method, supported only by the extended SDK VM, installs the extended font object. To draw text using the extended font, call `g.drawString()` as you normally do to display text in a window.

> **WARNING**
>
> Exactly what happens if you use this code on a system that does not support the extended VM is unclear. With luck, the font will default to a standard one, but it's conceivable that an exception will be thrown and the program halted.

A second way to construct a `FontX` object is to add a `boolean` argument that indicates whether the font is embedded. You can insert this statement into the preceding `paint()` method:

```
FontX font = new FontX("Arial", FontX.BOLD, 24, true);
```

The SDK documentation is fuzzy about when you might need to do this. Apparently, it's necessary only to indicate that a font was loaded by a non-Java piece of code. You probably don't need to create `FontX` objects this way in applications.

The third and final way to construct a `FontX` object is to pass one or more of the extended styles `STRIKEOUT`, `UNDERLINE`, and `OUTLINE`. Most fonts support the first two styles, but only some fonts can be outlined. A fourth "style" is `EMBEDDED`, which is apparently included in `FontX` so that you can indicate an embedded font along with other styles. However, I've yet to find any practical use for this style setting.

To try extended styles, insert the following `paint()` method in a test applet:

```
public void paint(Graphics g) {
 FontX font = new FontX("Britannic Bold",
  Font.BOLD, 24, FontX.OUTLINE);
 g.setFont(font);
 char[] chars = ("Outline".toString()).toCharArray();
 g.drawChars(chars, 0, 7, 5, 20);
}
```

Substitute a different font name if your system doesn't have Britannic Bold. Notice that the standard and extended font styles are selected separately, and are *not* logically ORed together. This is unfortunately messy, but (we can only hope) it will prevent a future clash if the Font class is modified.

After creating the extended font object, prepare an array of characters with the text to display in outline mode:

```
char[] chars = ("Outline".toString()).toCharArray();
```

This is necessary because Graphics.drawString() cannot display outlined text. To do that, you must call drawChars(), which draws each character individually:

```
g.drawChars(chars, 0, 7, 5, 20);
```

If output speed is unacceptable—drawChars() can be ponderously slow—use the offscreen graphics techniques explained in Chapter 17, under the section titled "Offscreen Images," to render the outlines to an in-memory bitmap. To display the outlined text, copy the finished image to the display.

The SDK's sample FontTest applet demonstrates some other aspects of using extended fonts. Figure 19.2 shows the program's display. Click inside the outlined text area, and type characters to display in the selected font.

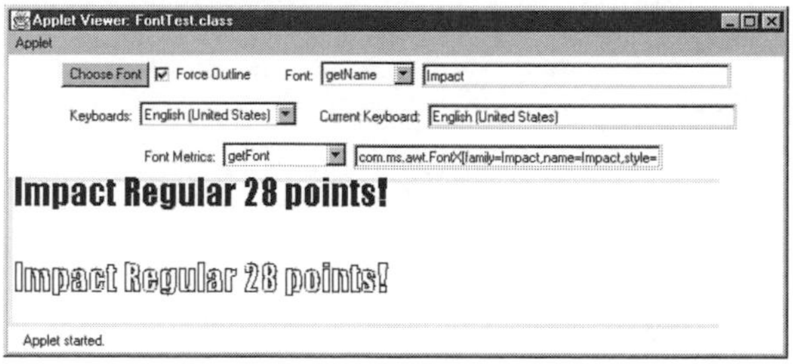

Figure 19.2.
The SDK's FontTest program demonstrates how to use TrueType and other fonts in Java programs.

The FontTest program makes use of the extended FontMetricsX class in Listing 19.3. This class extends the Win32Metrics class, which is defined in the sun.awt.win32 package. Because this class simply extends the standard FontMetrics class methods covered in Chapter 17, I don't list Win32Metrics here.

Listing 19.3. The `FontMetricsX` class.

```
public class FontMetricsX extends Win32FontMetrics {
// Constructor:
 public FontMetricsX(Font font);
// Public methods:
 public String getFace();
 public boolean canDrawOutline();
}
```

The extended `FontMetricsX` class adds only two methods to its inherited methods. Call `getFace()` for the font's name *after* it has been selected into a `Graphics` context. This might differ from the requested name. Call `canDrawOutline()` if the selected font has an outline mode—only some fonts do, even if created with the `FontX.OUTLINE` style.

Although it is simpler than the SDK sample applet, `FontXDemo.java` in Listing 19.4 shows the basic steps for creating and using a `FontX` extended font object. The program also shows how to prompt for extended fonts using a standard font-selection dialog. Figure 19.3 shows the program running in the SDK's AppletViewer utility after I selected the Algerian font in 48 points. (Hint: Use the viewer's *Applet\Restart* command to select other fonts.)

Figure 19.3.

The FontXDemo displays the name of a selected font using that font.

Listing 19.4 `FontXDemo.java` (Demonstrates the `FontX` and `FontMetricsX` classes).

```
import java.applet.*;
import java.awt.*;
import com.ms.awt.*;

public class FontXDemo extends Applet
{
 FontX font;   // Extended font object
 int height;   // Height obtained from extended metrics

 // Initialize applet
 public void init() {
  // Size window
  resize(320, 240);
  // Display font-selection dialog
  font = FontX.ChooseFont(this);
  if (font == null)
   throw new RuntimeException("No font selected");
  // Construct extended font from selection
  FontMetricsX metrics = new FontMetricsX(font);
  height = metrics.getHeight();
 }

 // Paint window contents
 public void paint(Graphics g) {
  g.setFont(font);
```

```
    g.drawString(font.getName(), 5, height);
  }
}
```

The FontXDemo sample applet declares a `FontX` object and an integer to represent the height of a line of text:

```
FontX font;
int height;
```

Method `init()` initializes the two variables. To obtain an extended font, the program displays a Windows font-selection dialog, using the following code:

```
font = FontX.ChooseFont(this);
if (font == null)
  throw new RuntimeException("No font selected");
```

`ChooseFont()` displays a standard Windows dialog. Pass the `Component` object (which can be your applet class object represented by `this`) that is to own the dialog. If this is the only argument, the dialog is not initialized to any specific font. To initialize the dialog to show a starting font—so that users can change its style, for example—pass an existing `FontX` object to `ChooseFont()` with a statement such as

```
font = FontX.ChooseFont(this, oldFont);
```

If the user cancels the font-selection dialog, `ChooseFont()` returns `null`. Always check for this and take appropriate action. The sample program throws a `RuntimeException` object to halt the applet, but of course, you are free to take whatever evasive maneuvers make sense for your program.

> **NOTE**
>
> Although Java is religious about not capitalizing method names, the Microsoft SDK breaks this rule with methods such as `ChooseFont()`. So much for consistency.

To properly display the selected text, the sample FontXDemo applet obtains the average height of most characters in the selected font. Because it uses an extended font, the program creates a `FontMetricsX` object to find the height. The following statements construct a `FontMetricsX` object for the extended font object:

```
FontMetricsX metrics = new FontMetricsX(font);
height = metrics.getHeight();
```

Because `FontMetricsX` is extended from the standard `FontMetrics` class (by way of the `Win32Metrics`, as I mentioned), you can use it in the same way as explained in Chapter 17. For example, the sample applet calls `getHeight()` to set the `height` variable.

The prepared `font` and `height` variables are next used in `paint()` to select the font into the `Graphics` context and display a line of text. Just for interest, I pass the name of the font to `drawString()` by calling the `getName()` method inherited by `FontX`:

```
g.setFont(font);
g.drawString(font.getName(), 5, height);
```

The SDK's FontTest sample applet has some additional code that you might find useful in your programs. For example, to determine whether an object is a standard Font or an extended FontX object, use instanceof in code like this:

```
if(font instanceof com.ms.awt.FontX)
 fontX = FontX.ChooseFont(this, (FontX)font);
else
 fontX = FontX.ChooseFont(this);
```

This code fragment passes a FontX object to ChooseFont() only if it is an instance of the FontX class. Otherwise, the code presents an uninitialized font-selection dialog.

Another useful trick demonstrates how to modify the style of an existing FontX object by calling Font methods. The following statement adds the extended FontX.OUTLINE style to an existing extended font object:

```
font = new FontX(font.getName(), font.getStyle(), font.getSize(),
 font.getFlags() | FontX.OUTLINE);
```

Using Windows Menus

Another SDK sample application, Menux, demonstrates how to use the SDK's extended menu classes to create Windows menus. The program's source code is a bit cumbersome, but it illustrates a variety of techniques for creating and using true Windows menus in Java applications.

To ease into the subject a little more smoothly, I developed a simpler example that will help you get started using the SDK's extended menu classes. The sample program shows every necessary technique for creating, displaying, and using true Windows menu bars in Java applications, but the SDK sample adds additional code for developing menus from HTML parameters and with some other methods I'll explain a bit later. After you study the sample code in this chapter, you will find the SDK's example easier to fathom.

At present, the SDK's extended menu classes are still in development, and comments throughout the SDK source files refer to bugs and unfinished business. For example, nested submenus are not yet supported. Even so, the end results are very close to what you can achieve using other Windows development systems such as C++. We will undoubtedly see additional improvements as the SDK is refined, so be sure you are using the latest version.

Advantages of the SDK's extended menu classes include the ability to underline menu hot keys so that users can press Alt and the designated character keys to open menus using the keyboard. You can also insert tab characters into menu strings to display a control key label aligned to the right of the menu command string. (However, responding to that keypress is not automatic and requires separate handleEvent() code.) You can also display a checkmark to the left of any menu command, and you can draw horizontal separators to categorize lengthy menus—but these capabilities are available in Java's standard menus as well.

The only major disadvantage of using extended menu classes is that, as with other SDK classes, users must have Windows 95 or NT to run your programs. They also must install the SDK's extended VM. If you're not concerned about these restrictions, then by all means use the techniques described here. Don't, however, put extended-class code on the Internet without proper warning!

Listing 19.5, `MenuXDemo.java`, demonstrates how to use the SDK's extended menu classes. I wrote the program as a stand-alone application, which is the most likely candidate for a Windows menu bar. You can use the extended menu classes in applets, but there are few good reasons for doing so. After explaining the listing, I'll cover each extended menu class in detail. Compile and run the program using `Jvc.exe` and `Jview.exe` (or `Wjview.exe`). This brings up a window with a Windows menu bar. Select any command to see a message box reflecting your choice. Click this box's OK button to return to the sample application window. Figure 19.4 shows the program's two windows after I selected *Edit\Properties*. The only command that actually works is *File\Exit*. Choose it to end the demonstration.

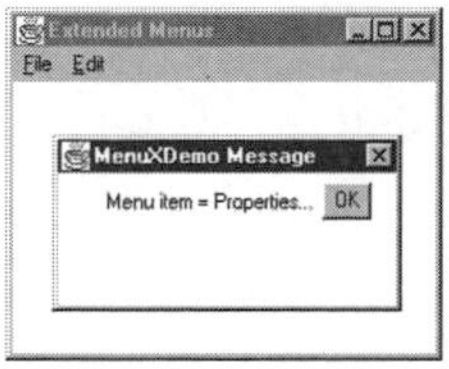

Figure 19.4.

MenuXDemo displays an application window with a true Windows menu bar.

Listing 19.5. `MenuXDemo.java` (Demonstrates extended menus).

```java
import java.io.*;
import java.awt.*;
import com.ms.awt.*;

//===============================================================
// MessageBox class
//===============================================================
class MessageBox extends Dialog {
 // Constructor
 public MessageBox(Frame parent, String message) {
  // Call superclass constructor
  super(parent, "MenuXDemo Message", true);
  resize(200, 100);  // Size window
  // Add label and button components
  Label caption = new Label(message, Label.CENTER);
  Button ok = new Button("OK");
  setLayout(new FlowLayout(FlowLayout.CENTER));
  add(caption);
  add(ok);
  // Prevent resizing and show window
  setResizable(false);
  show();
 }
 // Respond to MessageBox button selection
 public boolean action(Event evt, Object obj) {
```

continues

Listing 19.5. continued

```java
  if(obj instanceof String) {
   String s = (String)obj;
   if(s.equals("OK"))
    dispose();
  }
  return false;
 }
}


//============================================================
// MenuFrame class for extended menu bar window
//============================================================
class MenuFrame extends Frame
 implements MenuXConstants {

// Menu constant identifiers
public final int FILE_OPEN  = 1;
public final int FILE_CLOSE = 2;
public final int FILE_EXIT  = 3;
public final int EDIT_CUT   = 6 ;
public final int EDIT_COPY  = 7 ;
public final int EDIT_PASTE = 8 ;
public final int EDIT_DEL   = 9 ;
public final int EDIT_PROPS = 10;

// Array of extended menu item objects
MenuItemX items[] = {
 new MenuItemX("&File",          0,           POPUP),
 new MenuItemX("&Open...",       FILE_OPEN,   0),
 new MenuItemX("&Close",         FILE_CLOSE,  SEPARATOR_NEXT),
 new MenuItemX("E&xit",          FILE_EXIT,   ENDMENU),
 new MenuItemX("&Edit",          0,           POPUP),
 new MenuItemX("Cu&t\tCtrl+X",   EDIT_CUT,    0),
 new MenuItemX("&Copy\tCtrl+C",  EDIT_COPY,   0),
 new MenuItemX("&Paste\tCtrl+V", EDIT_PASTE,  0),
 new MenuItemX("&Delete\tDel",   EDIT_DEL,    SEPARATOR_NEXT),
 new MenuItemX("Pr&operties...", EDIT_PROPS,  ENDMENU)
};

 // Constructor
 MenuFrame(String title) {
  super(title);  // Call superclass constructor
 }
 // Create menu for frame
 public void createMenu() {
  MenuBarX mbx = new MenuBarX(items, items.length);
  setMenuBar(mbx);
 }
 // Handle events (window destruction only)
 public boolean handleEvent(Event evt) {
  if (evt.id == Event.WINDOW_DESTROY) {
   dispose();        // Close window
   System.exit(0);   // Stop Java VM
   return true;      // Event handled
  } else {
   return super.handleEvent(evt);
  }
```

```
  }
  // Handle menu item selections
  public boolean action(Event evt, Object obj) {
   if (evt.target instanceof MenuItemX) {
    // Get menu item id and initialize string
    MenuItemX mix = (MenuItemX)evt.target;
    int id = mix.getID();
    String itemName = "Unknown command";
    // Stubs for selected menu items. Insert
    // code in case statements to respond to
    // specific menu selections.
    switch (id) {
    case FILE_OPEN:
     itemName = "Open...";
     break;
    case FILE_CLOSE:
     itemName = "Close";
     break;
    case FILE_EXIT:
     // Code for File¦Exit (this one works!)
     postEvent(new Event(this,
      Event.WINDOW_DESTROY, null));
     return true;
    case EDIT_CUT:
     itemName = "Cut";
     break;
    case EDIT_COPY:
     itemName = "Copy";
     break;
    case EDIT_PASTE:
     itemName = "Paste";
     break;
    case EDIT_DEL:
     itemName = "Delete";
     break;
    case EDIT_PROPS:
     itemName = "Properties...";
     break;
    }
    // Display message box showing selected item
    new MessageBox(this,
      "Menu item = " + itemName);
   }
   return super.action(evt, obj);
  }
}


//================================================================
// Main program class
//================================================================
class MenuXDemo {
 public static void main(String args[]) {
  MenuFrame f = new MenuFrame("Extended Menus");
  f.resize(250,200);
  f.createMenu();
  f.show();
 }
}
```

Be sure to import the extended menu classes with a command such as the following:

```
import com.ms.awt.*;
```

You can then use the `MenuX`, `MenuItemX`, and `MenuBarX` classes, and the `MenuXConstants` interface class. The sample program uses all of these classes except `MenuX`, which is employed internally by `MenuBarX`.

Before examining the sample program's extended menu techniques, take a quick look at the `MessageBox` class, which extends Java's standard `Dialog`. This class, similar to a more extensive version in the SDK's menu demonstration, is handy for displaying quick messages and for debugging. You can cut `MessageBox` out of this listing, and insert it into any of your own programs. Be sure to import the `Dialog` class, or import `java.awt.*` as in the sample. Also, if you store `MessageBox` in a separate module, preface its class declaration with the keyword `public`. (Java prohibits declaring multiple `public` classes in the same file, and in the sample, `MessageBox` is friendly and is therefore available only to code in the module.) Use `MessageBox` by creating an object with a statement such as

```
new MessageBox(this, "Fan mail from a flounder!");
```

That might look fishy, but you don't have to save the object. To display a message dialog, just create the object on the fly. After the statement's code block exits, Java automatically deletes the `MessageBox` object. As the first argument, pass the `Frame` object that is to own the dialog window. As the second argument, pass the string to display in the window.

Getting back to the menu demonstration, following the `MessageBox` class is the program's extended `Frame` class, `MenuFrame`. This class is responsible for displaying and managing the application's graphical window, and of course, its menu bar. In addition to extending `Frame`, the `MenuFrame` class also implements the `MenuXConstants` interface. This makes some constants such as `POPUP` and `CHECKED` available for creating popup menus, menu items, and separators.

The extended menu techniques demonstrated here are not sacrosanct, but are probably easiest for most purposes. In your `Frame` class, declare public constant integers, one per menu command. For example, the two statements

```
public final int FILE_OPEN  = 1;
public final int FILE_CLOSE = 2;
```

arbitrarily assign 1 and 2 to identify the *File|Open* and *File|Close* commands, represented programmatically as `FILE_OPEN` and `FILE_CLOSE`. These constants provide handy means for determining which menu item a user selects. Because they are constants, I wrote them in all uppercase, but this isn't required. Their values are completely arbitrary. (Hint: Number by tens to make insertions easier and avoid renumbering existing constants.)

Next, declare an array of `MenuXItem` objects, one for each popup menu *and* menu command. Each `MenuXItem` object is created using this general form:

```
new MenuItemX("Title", id, type)
```

This is not a separate statement, and it has no ending semicolon. Instead, the expression goes along with others into a list of objects to be inserted in the array. The title string is the name of the popup menu or command, and it may have an ampersand character to underline a following letter as in `"&File"`, and a tab control code to label a hot key as in `"&Copy\tCtrl+C"`. The `id` value can be `0` for no identifier (usually only for a top-level menu such as File or Edit, which can't be selected), or one of the `Frame` class's declared menu constants such as `FILE_OPEN`. The `type` is the logical-OR combination of any constant from the `MenuXContants` interface.

Declare the array of `MenuItemX` objects as follows, using a pair of braces for the initializing values:

```
MenuItemX items[] = {
...
};
```

In place of the ellipsis, insert as many `MenuItemX` object expressions as you need, separating each with a comma. For example, these lines construct the program's File menu objects:

```
new MenuItemX("&File",     0,          POPUP),
new MenuItemX("&Open...", FILE_OPEN, 0),
new MenuItemX("&Close",    FILE_CLOSE, SEPARATOR_NEXT),
new MenuItemX("E&xit",     FILE_EXIT,  ENDMENU),
```

The File top-level menu can't be selected, so its identifying value is set to zero. The `POPUP` constant in that expression designates this object as a popup menu. The sample program's menu constants, `FILE_OPEN`, `FILE_CLOSE`, and `FILE_EXIT`, identify the File menu's other commands. `FILE_OPEN` requires no special configuration, so its type is set to zero. Use the `SEPARATOR_NEXT` constant to draw a horizontal separator under a menu item. Indicate the end of the popup menu with the `ENDMENU` constant.

> **TIP**
>
> If a popup menu fails to appear in the window, the cause is probably a missing `ENDMENU` type designator.

Combine multiple constants using the logical `OR` operator. For example, the statement

```
new MenuItemX("&Command", MENU_CMD, CHECKED | SEPARATOR_NEXT),
```

creates a menu item with a checkmark and draws a separator line under its text.

Continue as in the sample listing with as many popup menus and commands as you need. The final item must include the `ENDMENU` constant as in the sample program's last menu object, created with the statement

```
new MenuItemX("Pr&operties...", EDIT_PROPS, ENDMENU)
```

This final line does not end with any punctuation because it is the last item in the list of `MenuItemX` array initializers.

The preceding steps complete the construction of the raw menu item objects, but they don't form the actual Windows menu. To do that, we need additional code that inserts each item into an extended menu bar. We also need code to respond to menu item selections. Method createMenu() shows how simple it is to satisfy the first goal and create an extended menu bar. These statements construct a new MenuBarX object:

```
MenuBarX mbx = new MenuBarX(items, items.length);
setMenuBar(mbx);
```

The first argument is the items array of MenuItemX objects defined in the extended Frame class. The second argument is the number of items in that array. (The SDK's sample code uses a variable for this value, but it's far safer to use the array's length attribute as shown here.) Call setMenuBar() to attach the MenuBarX object to the Frame. This method is inherited from the Frame class, and it is a good example of solid object-oriented programming. Because extended menu classes are derived from Java's standard menus, you may pass the MenuBarX object mbx to setMenuBar(), which declares a parameter of the MenuBar class—the superclass from which MenuBarX extends.

To respond to menu selections, the extended Frame class overrides its inherited action() method. Inside that method, the first step is to determine whether the action that caused the method to be called was a menu selection. The statement

```
if (evt.target instanceof MenuItemX) ...
```

executes its statement block only if the Event object's target field is an instance of the MenuItemX class—one of our menu item objects, for example, from the items array. To determine which menu item was selected, obtain its identifying value by calling getID():

```
MenuItemX mix = (MenuItemX)evt.target;
int id = mix.getID();
```

The first line isn't strictly necessary, but it's clear at this point that target is a MenuItemX object, and for ease of use, I like to create a separate reference to it. Using that reference (named mix here), call getID() defined in the MenuItemX class to find the selected item's identifying value. This is one of the constants such as FILE_OPEN declared in the Frame class and used to construct the array of MenuItemX objects. The sample program uses the identifying value in a switch statement to select an appropriate action for each menu selection. If you are using the listing as a shell, insert your menu command statements where indicated by comments. Only one command is actually implemented—File|Exit, which posts a shutdown event to close the application window:

```
postEvent(new Event(this,
 Event.WINDOW_DESTROY, null));
return true;
```

This piece of code returns true from action() immediately to prevent any further processing after giving the order to shut down the program's window. Method handleEvent() intercepts and responds to the WINDOW_DESTROY message in the usual way. In that method, two statements destroy the window and exit the VM:

```
dispose();
System.exit(0);
```

Because most of the sample program's activity takes place in the extended Frame class, the application's main() method has little to do. Four statements create and display the program's window, and initialize its menu bar:

```
MenuFrame f = new MenuFrame("Extended Menus");
f.resize(250,200);
f.createMenu();
f.show();
```

The first line constructs an object of the extended MenuFrame class. After sizing the window, the program calls createMenu() to construct the frame's menu bar using the declarations in MenuFrame. Finally, show() brings the window into full view.

The MenuXConstants Class

Listing 19.6 shows the declaration for the MenuXConstants interface class. The class has no methods—it is entirely composed of public constants.

Listing 19.6. The MenuXConstants class.

```
public interface MenuXConstants {
// Miscellaneous constants:
 public final int UNCHECKED;
 public final int BY_COMMAND;
// MenuItemX constructor arguments:
 public final int POPUP;
 public final int CHECKED;
 public final int ENDMENU;
 public final int SEPARATOR_NEXT;
 public final int BY_POSITION;
}
```

Implement the MenuXConstants interface in any class—most often, an extended Frame class to serve as the application's graphical window. For example, declare the class as

```
class MenuFrame extends Frame
 implements MenuXConstants {
...
}
```

All methods in the class may now refer to MenuXConstants declarations without preceding them with a class name. In other words, you can simply use CHECKED and POPUP; you don't have to use expressions such as MenuXConstants.CHECKED and MenuXConstants.POPUP, although these longer forms are also correct.

The MenuXConstants interface class declares the following constants:

- int UNCHECKED: Used internally by the MenuX class's CheckMenuItem() methods. This value is of no practical use to applications.

- int BY_COMMAND: Used internally by MenuX to determine whether a menu item is identified by a command string rather than integer ID (which is the preferred method in most cases). This value is also of no importance to applications.

- int POPUP: This and the next four constants are bit flags that you can pass to the MenuItemX constructor's i2 integer parameter. You may combine these five constants using the logical OR operator, ¦. This constant identifies a MenuItemX as a popup menu—File or Edit, for example.

- int CHECKED: Displays a checkmark to the left of the menu item.

- int ENDMENU: Indicates that it is the last item in a popup menu.

- int SEPARATOR_NEXT: Draws a horizontal separator line below this MenuItemX object.

- int BY_POSITION: Indicates that the menu item is to be identified by its relative position rather than a constant identifying value.

The MenuItemX Class

Listing 19.7 shows the MenuItemX class declaration. Each popup menu and each command in that menu is represented as a separate object of this class.

Listing 19.7. The MenuItemX class.

```
public class MenuItemX extends CheckboxMenuItem {
// Constructor:
 public MenuItemX(String s, int i1, int i2);
// Public methods:
 public void Check(boolean val);
 public boolean isChecked();
 public int getID();
 public void setState(boolean t);
 public synchronized void addNotify();
}
```

As the MenuXDemo sample application in this chapter shows, the easiest way to use the MenuItemX class is to construct an array of objects and pass it to MenuBarX. Each object in the array represents one popup menu or an item in that menu. Pass the menu's or command's name to the MenuItemX constructor's String parameter. Pass an optional identifying value to the first integer parameter. Pass any logical-OR combination of the MenuXConstants interface constants to the final parameter. For example, the following lines create a simple array of two MenuItemX objects:

```
MenuItemX items[] = {
 new MenuItemX("&File", 0, POPUP),
```

```
 new MenuItemX("E&xit", 999, ENDMENU)
}
```

The resulting Frame window will have a menu bar with a File popup menu, and a single command File|Exit, identified by the integer 999. I use a similar menu in test programs; in a commercial application, each menu item is best identified by a constant such as FILE_OPEN as in the MenuXDemo application. Notice the ampersands in the menu strings. Because of these characters, users can press Alt+F to open the File menu and Alt+F+X to exit the program—standard hot keys in most Windows programs. Standard Java menus do not support Alt key selection.

MenuItemX extends from Java's standard CheckboxMenuItem, which is a subclass of the MenuItem, MenuComponent, and Object classes. Be sure to research all of these classes for the full set of methods you can call. MenuItemX provides the following public methods:

- void Check(boolean val): Sets the checkmark state of this menu item to display a checkmark (val = true) or remove it (val = false).

- boolean isChecked(): Returns true if the menu item has a checkmark; otherwise, returns false.

- int getID(): Returns the assigned identifying value for this menu item as passed to the MenuItemX constructor's i1 integer parameter.

- void setState(boolean t): For reasons that are unclear, this method *disables* the setState() method inherited from CheckBoxMenuItem. Consequently, you must call Check() to set the item's checkmark state. From the SDK's source code for the MenuItemX class, the overridden setState() method simply returns and ignores its parameter value.

- void addNotify(): As with other similarly named methods, this one attaches the menu item to its peer class—and in that way, connects the object to a Windows menu item. There's no good reason to call this method in an application.

The MenuBarX Class

Listing 19.8 shows the MenuBarX class declaration. Use the class to construct a true Windows menu bar composed of items represented by MenuItemX objects.

Listing 19.8. The MenuBarX class.

```
public class MenuBarX extends MenuBar
 implements MenuXConstants {
// Constructors:
 public MenuBarX(MenuItemX items[], int nItems);
 public MenuBarX(MenuItemX items[], int nItems, Applet theApp, String param);
 public MenuBarX(MenuItemX items[], int nItems, String params[]);
// Public method:
 public int getItemID(String s);
}
```

There are three ways to construct a MenuBarX object. The first, and most commonly used, technique requires an array of MenuItemX objects and an integer indicating how many items to use from that array. Pass the resulting MenuBarX object to the Frame class's setMenuBar() method. For example, this chapter's sample MenuXDemo application constructs its menu bar using these statements:

```
MenuBarX mbx = new MenuBarX(items, items.length);
setMenuBar(mbx);
```

Use the second constructor to read in menu items from an applet's HTML parameters. In this case, if the String param is null, each item's label in the MenuItemX array represents a parameter name rather than, as usual, a popup menu or item name. The MenuBarX constructor *changes* each label to the parameter in the HTML document, using the Applet class's getParameter() method to load the parameter value. If String param is not null, the MenuItemX object labels are ignored, and each parameter is loaded using constructed identifiers. For example, the statement

```
MenuBarX mbx =
 new MenuBarX(items, items.length, this, "MenuItem");
```

attempts to load HTML parameters MenuItem0, MenuItem1, MenuItem2, ..., MenuItem*num-1* for the applet object identified by this. Each MenuItemX object label in the items array is replaced by the loaded parameters. If any parameters are not found, the original labels are not modified, and no error is reported.

The third and final way to construct a MenuBarX object is convenient if you want to store your menu names in an array of strings rather than use individual literal strings as in the sample MenuXDemo application. The SDK's extended menu demonstration program appears to have some of the necessary code in place, but the technique isn't actually used. Apparently, this is an omission in the official demonstration, but it's not hard to figure out how to write the rest of the missing code. For example, you might declare a String array such as

```
public String menuStrings[] = {
 "File", "About", "Open", "Exit",
 "Edit", "Cut", "Copy", "Paste" , "Delete"
};
```

Next, construct a MenuItemX array in the usual way, but pass null instead of the menu title strings:

```
MenuItemX items[] = {
 new MenuItemX(null, 0, POPUP),
 new MenuItemX(null, 1, 0),
 new MenuItemX(null, 2, 0),
 new MenuItemX(null, 3, ENDMENU),
 new MenuItemX(null, 4, POPUP),
 new MenuItemX(null, 5, 0),
 new MenuItemX(null, 6, 0),
 new MenuItemX(null, 7, 0),
 new MenuItemX(null, 8, ENDMENU)
};
```

This creates a generic array of nameless menu items, with the first popup menu having space for three commands, and the second having space for four. For simplicity, I identified each item using literal integers, but you will probably want to define and use constants such as FILE_EXIT for better clarity.

To construct the menu bar, pass the items and menuStrings arrays to the MenuBarX constructor, and call setMenuBar() using code such as

```
MenuBarX mbx =
 new MenuBarX(items, items.length, menuStrings);
setMenuBar(mbx);
```

All this does is replace the null menu item labels with the strings in the menuStrings array. This works, but it isn't clear to me what advantage is gained; perhaps you'll find a practical use for this alternate technique. For my money, I'll stick with the methods outlined in the sample MenuXDemo application.

The MenuBarX class extends from MenuBar, which extends from MenuComponent, and of course, Object. The MenuBar class also implements the MenuContainer interface, so be sure to research all of these classes for the full set of available methods. MenuBarX declares only a single public method:

- int getItemID(String s): Call this method to obtain a menu item's integer identifier, given that item's string name. This might be useful, for example, when using the alternate technique of creating an array of string parameters. You can obtain each parameter's identifying value by using this method. The method returns -1 if the specified string is not found.

The MenuX Class

Listing 19.9 shows the last of the extended menu class declarations, MenuX. Objects of this class represent a popup menu of menu items.

Listing 19.9. The MenuX class.

```
public class MenuX extends Menu
 implements MenuXConstants {
// Constructor:
 public MenuX(String theLabel);
// Public methods:
 public boolean CheckMenuItem(int i, int flags);
 public boolean CheckMenuItem(String s, int flags);
 public int getItemID(String s);
}
```

When using the techniques in this chapter to create Windows menus, you don't need the MenuX class. MenuBarX uses it internally to construct individual popup menus, each element of which is represented by an object of the MenuItemX class. However, if you want to devise other ways to create Windows menus—certainly, there are many possibilities—you may need to use this class. It has only one constructor, which you can use in a statement such as

```
MenuX menu = new MenuX("&File");
```

This creates a menu object for a popup menu labeled File. However, the SDK extended classes don't provide any useful way to use the resulting object. You might attempt to construct a MenuItemX object and add it to the popup menu, and then add the result to a MenuBarX object to be passed to the Frame's setMenuBar() method. But practically speaking, the only use you'll have for MenuX is if you want to rewrite the MenuBarX class to suit your own purposes. Scan the source code for that class to see how MenuX is used.

In addition to its inherited methods, MenuX declares these public methods:

- **boolean CheckMenuItem(int i, int flags):** Adds or removes a checkmark from a menu item. The integer parameter may represent a menu item identifier or its relative position (specify BY_POSITION in flags). To display a checkmark, add the CHECKED bit flag to flags; otherwise, the checkmark, if present, is removed. If successful, the method returns true. The method returns false if the item is not an extended MenuItemX object.

- **boolean CheckMenuItem(String s, int flags):** This is the same as the preceding method, but it identifies a menu item by its string label. To add a checkmark to the item, pass CHECKED in flags; otherwise, the checkmark, if present, is removed. If successful, the method returns true. The method returns false if the item is not an extended MenuItemX object. Specifying BY_POSITION in flags is an error and causes this method to return false. (When identifying menu items by name, they cannot also be identified by position.)

- **int getItemID(String s):** Returns a menu item's integer identifier given that item's string name. The method returns -1 if the specified string is not found.

Summary

- This chapter introduced the Microsoft Java SDK and explained where to get it, what's in it, and how to install and use it.
- Tools in the SDK include the latest versions of the command-line Java compiler, Jvc.exe, and the application viewer, Jview.exe.
- The SDK also provides several useful utility programs such as AppletViewer, ClassVue, and others.
- Use the SDK's Jexegen program to convert any stand-alone Java application to a Windows .exe code file that users can run just as they do any other Windows program.

- Other SDK contents include the CAB developer's kit, documentation, DirectX and COM support, and various sample applications.
- The SDK's extended font classes provide access to Windows TrueType fonts in Java applications.
- The extended menu classes provide the means to create and use true Windows menu bars.
- The primary disadvantage of the Microsoft SDK is that users must run Windows 95 or NT, and they must install the extended VM supplied with the SDK. However, if you are certain that your programs will run under Windows, the SDK provides a wealth of useful classes and tools.

What's Next?

To the casual observer, Java and C++ might seem closely related, but there are many differences between the two languages that are not obvious. If you know C++, the next chapter will help you to learn Java quickly. You can also use the next chapter's comparison of Java and C++ as a guide for converting C++ source files to Java.

20

Java for C++ Programmers

Will Java replace C++? Which language is better, and which should you use? How can you convert C++ code to Java? Why would you want to do that—and why not? These and other questions about Java are hot topics among C++ programmers everywhere.

If you are a C++ programmer, you'll smooth the transition to Java by knowing as much as possible about both languages. I don't mean to suggest that you need to abandon one language for the other. Each has unique advantages, strengths, and weaknesses, and only by intelligently comparing Java and C++ can you make the right choice for a given project.

This chapter's comparisons of Java and C++ will help you make that choice. You can also use this chapter as a guide to converting C++ code to Java. To help you along that thorny path, this chapter lists numerous complete sample programs and code snippets written in the two languages. Finally, this chapter's comparisons of Java and C++ data types will help you to write code using both languages, and also to share data between Java and C++ applications.

> **NOTE**
>
> Many of the C and C++ sample listings and code fragments in this chapter are taken from my books, *Mastering Borland C++ 4.5* and *Mastering Borland C++ 5*. The only changes I made to the original files were to rename those ending in `.c` to `.cpp`, and to update comments at the beginning of each module. For the widest applicability, I selected only examples that conform to ANSI C++ specifications, and you should be able to use any C++ compiler of recent vintage to compile the programs listed here.

In This Chapter

This chapter covers the following fundamental comparisons of Java and C++:

- Strengths and weaknesses of Java and C++
- Fundamental constructions in the two languages
- Classes and object-oriented techniques in the two languages, including inheritance, virtual functions, and abstract classes
- Other comparisons of Java and C++ strings, keywords, and class libraries

Strengths and Weaknesses

Thoroughly studying a language's talents and shortcomings is the best way to envision how you will write a program's code. For example, if you expect your code to rely heavily on arrays, Java is a good choice because of its easy-to-use, dynamic array capabilities. But if linked lists figure prominently in your plans, Java's lack of pointers probably makes C++ the wiser selection. Programmers who fail to consider these types of issues are the ones who moan and groan on the network forums about a language's "bugs" and its lack of support for critical features.

The following notes about strengths and weaknesses in Java and C++ will help you determine which language is right for your project. Of course, the information reflects my personal opinion, which may differ from yours. For example, if your program needs pointers, you probably will not agree with me that Java's lack of pointers is an advantage.

Java: Strengths and Weaknesses

The following are Java's main strengths:

- *Fully object-oriented:* All code and data in a Java program are encapsulated in one or more classes. However, Java is not a pure object-oriented language. For example, variables of native data types such as int and float are not class objects, although wrapper classes are provided for all native types. This makes Java probably the most practical of all object-oriented programming languages ever invented.

- *Yes, we have no pointers:* Most programmers agree that by not supporting the concept of a pointer, Java code is far simpler, less bug-prone, and easier to maintain than equivalent C++ programming. Because Java does not have pointers, objects are easily cloned without risking duplicate address references in copied class member pointers, one of the more fertile breeding grounds for bugs in C++ code. The lack of pointers also simplifies references to data; there is never any need to dereference a pointer in Java, and you never have to ponder the intricacies of double indirection, another well-known bug producer in C++.

- *Simple classes and objects:* Java's classes and its implementation of object-oriented programming concepts are simpler and easier to use than in C++. All declared classes are superclasses of the standard Object class, and thus all objects in a Java program are related. Every piece of code and data in a Java program must be inside of a class declaration. Member functions are implemented directly in their classes, not separately as in C++. This is made possible in part by the importation of compiled .class files, which eliminates the need for class and other declarations in C++ header files. In Java, all objects are created similarly by using the new operator. Classes within a programming unit (a source file) have "friendly" access to one another's members, a simple but effective improvement over the more complex access specifier rules and friend classes j6557C++.

- *Automatic garbage collection:* It is never necessary for a Java program to dispose or delete variables and objects. When a variable or object goes out of scope, it is automatically deleted as necessary to provide room for other data. Java completely manages the use of memory through the services of an automatic garbage collector, which in most installations of the VM runs in the background as a separate thread process.

- *Interface classes:* Similar to an abstract C++ class, a Java interface class is a highly effective tool for specifying common protocols. Other classes can implement one or more interfaces to conform to the protocol's specifications and, therefore, guarantee compatibility with other code. For example, an interface class could define a set of database functions. By implementing the interface, another class ensures that its objects can be passed to method parameters that need access to data.

- *Strictly defined data types:* Java defines the bit and byte sizes of all native data types such as int, float, and double. This means that, on all Java installations, an int variable is *guaranteed* to be 32 bits in size. The Java char data type is 16 bits in length and can hold any Unicode character. Again, this is true for all Java installations.

- String *objects:* Java literal and variable strings are represented as objects of the String class. This makes string handling in Java consistent and robust. Java does not directly support null-terminated strings, although it is possible to create and use byte arrays for strings of ASCII characters, as in C++. It is also possible to convert String objects to and from character and byte arrays. Characters in String objects are represented as 16-bit Unicode values, which can hold text in any written language.

- *Dynamic arrays:* Java arrays are constructed at runtime, and they provide a length attribute that equals their size in elements. This is a tremendous advantage over C++, which, without additional and usually tricky programming, supports only fixed-size arrays. In Java, for example, an integer variable can be used to create an array of a calculated size. Accessing the resulting array outside of its defined boundaries throws an exception, eliminating another common source of C++ bugs—the infamous off-by-one boundary array index problem, which any C++ programmer knows all too well.

- *Standard packages:* Libraries of related Java classes are provided in packages that are easily imported into programs. Classes are imported from their compiled .class byte-code files, which eliminates the need to declare classes in header files as is necessary in C++. You can also write your own packages and share their classes among multiple programs. Package names are intimately related to their directory paths—an interesting concept that is surprisingly successful given the differences in disk operating systems. Standard package classes are stored and loaded directly from compressed ZIP archive files.

- *Applet and application generation:* Java is probably best known for its ability to create applets that can be embedded in HTML documents on the World Wide Web. Java-aware Internet browsers automatically download and execute applet code, adding a fresh element of interactive software to otherwise static information in HTML documents. However, although Java is great for developing applets, it is also perfectly suitable for large-scale application development. Applets are prohibited from performing file input and output operations, an understandable and necessary restriction that provides a high level of network security. Applications have no restrictions on I/O.

The following are Java's main weaknesses:

- *Interpreted code:* A Java compiler produces byte codes—also known as P codes—that represent instructions for a hypothetical, pseudo-processor. To run a program, the Java Virtual Machine (VM) interprets the program's compiled byte codes. This makes Java code run slower than equivalent native code produced by an optimizing C++ compiler. It also requires users to install the VM on their system. Most Internet browsers are Java-aware, so this limitation is not too severe. However, to run a stand-alone application, users still must install the VM through the services of a utility such as Jview.exe. The Microsoft Java SDK (covered in Chapter 19) provides the Jexegen utility that can convert Java stand-alone programs into Windows executable code files. The resulting program, however, still requires the VM interpreter; it merely eliminates the need to run a separate program such as Jview. I'll take a wild guess and predict that future releases of Visual J++ (perhaps as early as when you read this) *might* be able to compile programs directly to native 80x86 and Pentium processor instructions. This, however, will reduce Java's appeal as a system-independent development language, and it is not clear whether such a capability would be welcome or even practically possible.

- *Poor low-level access:* Java has no pointers, and it is therefore virtually incapable of accessing a computer system on a low level. This makes Java unsuitable for system software that performs such operations as calling BIOS and DOS subroutines, and responding to interrupts. Java is not a good choice for writing operating systems, device drivers, and other low-level code.

- *No multiple inheritance:* The Java class supports only single inheritance. Unlike C++, in which classes may be derived from multiple base classes, a Java subclass can be extended from only one superclass. On the other hand, a limited form of multiple inheritance is possible by using Java interface classes, though this is by no means equivalent to the more sophisticated concept of multiple inheritance in C++.

- *No value, variable, and reference parameters:* It is not possible to elect to pass parameters by value or by address (Java has no pointers). All Java method parameters are declared as though they were passed by value in C++. Simple variables such as integers are actually passed by value. Arrays and class objects, however, are passed by reference, and any change to array or object data passed to a method affects the original values. This is less clear, and somewhat less versatile, than in C++ where parameter passing rules are explicitly programmed, except for arrays, which are passed by reference in both languages. For example, in Java, a method must clone a class object parameter to protect the original object from modification. (The class itself can be made to do this—as does the String class, for example, which though passed by reference to a method does not permit the original String object argument to be changed in the method).

- *No ANSI specification:* Java does not yet have the backing of an ANSI specification, and individual software companies are free to modify the language and its class libraries at will. However, this same dangerous situation once existed for C and C++, and it was only the strong, collective voice of the programming community that kept these languages from disintegrating into chaos. (At one point not long ago, a half dozen or more C++ compilers were available for MS-DOS systems, but none could compile the other's code without modification. The stamp of ANSI adoption helped ensure that today's C++ compilers are a great deal more, if not perfectly, compatible.) Perhaps these same forces in the marketplace will maintain Java's integrity until an ANSI specification can be developed—a lengthy and uncertain process. Meanwhile, if you are developing software using Java, a real concern is what might happen to the language in the future, and whether the code you write using Visual J++ today will be compatible with another vendor's system tomorrow.

C++: Strengths and Weaknesses

The following are C++'s main strengths:

- *Standard libraries:* Standard C++ function and template libraries differ only in their implementations. Code based on the standard libraries is almost certain to compile unchanged (or with very little modification) on any ANSI C++ system. Although Java's packages are standardized, they do not provide the full range of algorithms and containers in the C++ standard template library (STL). Java does not have templates, but I would not be surprised to find them along with a version of the STL added to the language in a future release.

- *Based on C:* I was tempted to list this C++ attribute under weaknesses, but in many cases, being able to write C code and translate it with a C++ compiler is a plus. Also, backward support for C means that software can be upgraded gradually to C++. Contrast this with the job of converting C++ code to Java—the entire program must be rewritten from scratch. On the other hand, because C++ is based on C, certain constructions remain that might otherwise have been deleted. For example, C++ has a goto operator, which originated in C. Java does not yet have goto. Let's pray it never does.

- *Rich archives:* More code has been written and published for C and C++ than for any other programming language. Extensive archives of source code on the network, on CD-ROMs, in journals, and in books are available. Many programming problems are easily solved by researching published C and C++ code. Of course, there's a lot of Cobol code out there as well, and the existence of published programs in any language may not be important to all programmers.

- *Low-level access:* Many programmers consider C to be a medium-level language, higher in abstraction than assembly, but closer to the machine than Pascal or BASIC. C and C++ are therefore well-suited for writing operating system software, device drivers and interrupt service routines. Most C++ compilers also permit a mix of C, C++, and inline assembly language. Without a doubt, if you need access to low-level BIOS and DOS subroutines or to hardware ports, unless you are willing to use assembly language, C++ is the better choice.

- *Native code output:* C++ compilers generate native code for a specific processor. This makes programs written with C++ faster, on the average, than the equivalent code written in Java, which produces interpreted byte-codes. However, compatibility among C++ programs is on the source-code level; compatibility among Java programs is on the byte-code interpreted level.

- *Multiple inheritance:* C++ classes can be derived from one or more base classes, a concept known as multiple inheritance. Although this complicates programming with classes—and the benefits of the technique have always been controversial—multiple inheritance is useful for building versatile class hierarchies. A mistake in design—a forgotten protocol, for example—is temporarily repaired with little rearranging simply by inheriting a lower-level C++ class. In Java, which supports only single inheritance, a similar flaw might mean a complete reshuffling of class relationships. (Interface classes can be used in Java to partially simulate multiple inheritance in C++.)

- *Templates:* A C++ template is a super abstraction—a kind of ultimate schematic—from which the compiler creates classes tailored for specific use. For example, a sorting template can mold itself to any type of data that needs sorting. The standard ANSI C++ template library provides numerous templates and algorithms for processing all kinds of data objects. Java has nothing similar to C++ templates.

- *Inline functions:* A C++ program can specify that a function be compiled inline rather than called as a subroutine. This provides programmers with an optimization technique at the source-code level, which can have a great impact on a program's runtime speed. Java does not support inline functions, nor any other source-level optimizations. The Java compiler, however, supports some code optimizations—these are not language related, however.

- *Overloaded operator functions:* Again, I debated whether to include this on the list of C++ strengths, but overloaded operators are not a C++ liability, so I suppose they belong here. For some kinds of programming, and especially for I/O streams, declaring a function operator rather than a plain callable function simplifies the use of that code. For example, rather than call a function `add(a, b)` to sum two objects, you can overload the plus operator with an `operator+()` function, and use an expression `(a + b)` to call that code. This clarifies the source code, especially in programs using complex expressions. In practice, I find little use for overloaded operators, but if your code uses them extensively, you'll find them only in C++.

- *I/O streams:* The << and >> operators in C++ are used to stream data in and out of a program. They improve on standard I/O techniques by putting an object-oriented spin on a program's input and output. These operators can be overloaded in classes to provide I/O for any data in a consistent, easy-to-use fashion. Java does not have I/O streams, nor does it support the stream operators, although many capable I/O classes are available in the `java.io` package.

- *Value, variable, and reference parameters:* C++ function parameters are, under the programmer's control, passed by value, by address (variable), or by reference (the same as by address, but without using an explicit pointer). However, arrays, including null-terminated strings, are always passed by reference. Being able to specify how a variable is passed to a function parameter makes C++ more versatile than Java in this respect. For example, in C++, a `double` variable can be passed to a function by address. The function can modify that original value, perhaps to initialize it, simply by dereferencing the parameter pointer. To do the same in Java requires using either a function return result, or encapsulating the data in a class and passing it as an object to the function. (Java class objects are passed by reference.)

- *Variable numbers of parameters:* C++ supports functions with a variable number of parameters. It is also possible to create parameters that default to specified values. Java has no similar capabilities; methods can have no parameters or a fixed number of parameters. (With a little ingenuity, however, a set of extended classes, each with different instance variables, might be used to simulate variable numbers of parameters. Pass a subclass object to a method parameter of the superclass, and use `instanceof` to determine which object the method actually received.)

- *ANSI specification:* The ANSI C and ANSI C++ specifications rigorously define these languages. In theory, any ANSI-compatible compiler can translate a C++ program; however, in the real world, C++ development systems support proprietary keywords and provide class libraries that compile only with a specific vendor's product. Even so, ANSI specification is a powerful comfort to developers who spend months and years developing software. Java's lack of an official specification rightly makes developers nervous about whether the code they write today will run tomorrow.

The following are C++'s main weaknesses:

- *Pointers:* Okay, I'll join the fray and list pointers as a C++ weakness. But, if you've gotta use them, you've gotta have them, and I don't mean to suggest that there's anything wrong with pointers *per se*. In general, however, pointers cause many programmers more grief than comfort, especially for some kinds of work—database programming or text processing, for example. For these and other relatively high-level types of applications, pointers just get in the way. Programmers with only moderate experience have trouble understanding pointers, and those programmers might be better advised to use Java and stay out of trouble. Debugging code that uses pointers can be difficult. Personally, I think pointers are just great, but there's no accounting for taste. (I also like spicy hot food and anchovies.)

- *Multiple string types:* Although ANSI C++ now has a `string` template, string handling in C and C++ is a minefield that has caused numerous programs to self-destruct. Actually, C++ has no strings—but it supports various operations on character arrays, which are expected to end with a null byte indicating the end of the string data. Woe to the programmer who deletes a string's terminating null! The standard function library has numerous operations for processing null-terminated strings. Add Unicode characters and strings, and their associated and incompatible functions, along with the necessity for C++ compilers to provide backwards support for C, and it's easy to understand why string handling in C and C++ code is such a mess. Java's `String` class wins this one hands down.

- *Partially object-oriented:* Again, this might be an advantage if you wish to use a mix of standard and object-oriented techniques. However, it's fair to say that C++ is not as well object-oriented as Java. This is because classes and objects were added to C in order to create C++. Java did not have to struggle with its orientation; it began life object oriented, and so it will always remain. This is one reason classes are easier to use in Java than in C++. For example, arrays of objects in C++ require explicit programming so that constructors and destructors are called. There is no such concern in Java.

- *Memory management:* Objects in C++ are created and destroyed under program control. When a C++ function creates an object addressed by a pointer, that function must delete the data or, when the function returns, it becomes a dangling object that hangs around uselessly in memory until the program ends. The use of pointers in C++ also complicates memory management. For example, when cloning an object, a real concern is whether data addressed by member pointers should also be copied, and thus prevent a disaster if the program accidentally attempts to delete the addressed information more than once. Java's automatic garbage collection, and also its lack of pointers, greatly simplifies memory management. In Java, you simply create objects; they are deleted automatically as necessary. However, memory management in C++ is advantageous in one respect: It gives programmers control over the program's use of memory. If you need this kind of low-level access, C++ might be a better choice.

- *No dynamic arrays:* An array in C and C++ is fixed in place like a concrete block. There is no support for dynamic arrays that are sized at runtime, although this can be simulated by creating an array class or a container. Yes, it is possible to break the rules and create an array of any size at runtime, but the point is that C++ does not *define* a way of performing such magic. One reason this is so is because, in C++, arrays are actually pointers—there is no internal difference between the two. (Any pointer can be used as an array to elements of its data type.) Java's dynamic arrays are sensible and easy to use. They also eliminate the common error of indexing beyond an array's declared size, one of the most prevalent bug producers in C and C++ code.

Shared Features

The following are main features that Java and C++ share, though not perfectly in all cases:

- *Case-sensitivity:* Java and C++ are both case-sensitive, meaning that the identifiers `MyCounter` and `mycounter` are considered to be different objects. Case-sensitivity is a benefit because it forces programmers to use a consistent style. Also, conventions such as beginning all functions with lowercase letters and defining uppercase constants help make code more readable.

- *Identical comments:* Java and C++ use the same comment brackets. In either language, surround comments using `/*` and `*/`, or insert `//` to begin a comment from there to the end of the current line. Java adds a documentation comment `/** text */`, which C++ does not support. This comment, however, is not actually a part of the language, but it is employed by a separate tool to prepare documentation from the program's source code. Similar tools could easily be developed for C++.

- *Exceptions:* Java and C++ use exceptions in much the same ways. In both languages, to execute code that might throw an exception, insert statements in a `try` block, and trap any exceptions using `catch` statements. Exceptions are also thrown with the `throw` keyword, using similar techniques. One major difference in the languages' exception handling is that C++ can throw any object—an integer variable or a string, for example. Java exceptions must be objects of classes extended from the standard `Throwable` class. This makes Java's exception handling more rigorous but C++'s implementation more versatile. In C++, for instance, an exception object can be viewed simply as an alternate function-return mechanism—a way of returning different kinds of data from a function.

- *Strong type checking:* Both Java and C++ require assigned data to be compatible with the target object's type. Java is a little stronger in its type checking rules than C++, which does not define the sizes of native types such as `int`. In both languages, you can circumvent type checking by using a type-cast expression, which is simply a data type in parentheses. For example, if `obj` is a function parameter of the `Object` class, the expression `(String)obj` tells the compiler to consider `obj` as an object of the `String` class. Java's `instanceof` operator, which is not available in C++, goes a long way toward preventing bugs caused by irresponsible type-casting. For example, a Java program can use a statement such as `if (obj instanceof String)` to test whether it is appropriate to apply a `String` type-cast expression to `obj`. In C++, you can use RTTI (runtime type information) to perform similar checks.

- *Operators, expressions, and statements:* Most operators, expressions, and statements are similar in form in Java and C++. However, this superficial similarity is not always an advantage, because it is sometimes difficult in the middle of a listing to know whether you are reading C++ or Java source code.

- *Similar data types:* Both languages have similar native data types such as `int`, `double`, `float`, `char`, and so on. Only Java, however, defines the bit and byte sizes of variables of these native types. The sizes of C++ data types are not defined, although certain rules—such as the one stating that an `int` must be no larger than a `long`—are well defined in ANSI C++.

- *Similar object-orientation:* The fundamental concepts of object-oriented programming are implemented similarly in both languages. There are important differences, however—the fact that all classes are related to `Object` in Java, for example, and that C++ supports multiple inheritance. On the other hand, if you are comfortable with object-oriented programming in C++, you will be able to use what you know in Java programs. One major difference is that all Java methods are virtual. Member functions in C++ must be explicitly stated as being virtual.

- *Multithreading:* Both languages provide support for multithreaded programming. However, Java's support is system-independent and is controlled through the VM. This means that compiled Java programs, even those that use threads, can potentially run on any multitasking operating system. Multithreaded C++ code is, by contrast, system-dependent.

Fundamental Constructions

In the following sections, I list and explain sample programs written in Java and C++. In each case, I started with a C++ program that I converted to Java. The results are not perfect—in some cases, for example, output is not formatted exactly the same in each version—but this does not detract from illustrating specific comparisons between the two languages. In addition to helping you learn Java, the listings can also serve as a guide to converting C++ applications to Java.

A complete comparison of Java and C++ would fill a book, so I concentrate in this chapter only on topics that are likely to give you the most trouble.

> **TIP**
>
> For practice, I highly recommend that you attempt to convert each C++ listing to Java, and then compare your results with mine.

Variables

C++ and Java share most common data types, but their sizes and ranges can differ. For example, C++ does not define the size of an `int`, which is typically 16 or 32 bits long. In Java, an `int` variable is always 32 bits.

Listing 20.1, `Variable.cpp`, demonstrates common variables and data types in C++. Listing 20.2, `Variable.java`, shows the same program converted to Java. These and other listings in this chapter are intended to be compiled and run from a DOS prompt. To compile the C++ listing, if you have Borland C++, enter the command `bcc32 variable`, and run the program by typing its name. To compile and run the Java version, enter a command such as `jvc variable` followed by `jview variable`. Compile and run other listings in this chapter similarly.

> **NOTE**
>
> Some C++ compilers do not support long filenames, and therefore, all C++ listing filenames in this section are in 8.3 style (eight-character-maximum filenames and a three-character extension). Directories are named the same as their main source files. For example, the `DateTime.cpp` and `DateTime.java` files in this section are in the `Part4\DateTime` directory on the CD-ROM.

Listing 20.1. `Variable.cpp` (Demonstrates common variables).

```
//================================================================
// Variable.cpp - From Mastering Borland C++ 4.5, chapter 5
// Copyright (c) 1997 by Tom Swan. All rights reserved.
//================================================================

#include <stdio.h>

main()
{
  char slash = '/';
  short month = 4;
  int year = 2001;
  long population = 308700000L;
  float pi = 3.14159;
  double velocity = 186281.7;
  long double lightYear = 5.88e12;

  printf("Date = %02d%c%d\n", month, slash, year);
  printf("Population of the U.S.A. = %ld\n", population);
  printf("Pi = %f\n", pi);
  printf("Velocity of light =%12.2f miles/sec\n", velocity);
  printf("One light year = %.0Lf miles\n", lightYear);
  return 0;
}
```

Listing 20.2. `Variable.java` (Demonstrates common variables).

```
//================================================================
// Variable.java - Converted from Variable.cpp
// Copyright (c) 1997 by Tom Swan. All rights reserved.
//================================================================

import java.io.*;

class Variable {
 public static void main(String args[]) {
  char slash = '/';
  short month = 4;
  int year = 2001;
  long population = 308700000L;
  float pi = 3.14159f;
  double velocity = 186281.7;
  double lightYear = 5.88e12;

  System.out.println("Date = " + month + slash + year);
  System.out.println("Population of the U.S.A. = "
   + population);
  System.out.println("Pi = " + pi);
  System.out.println(
   "Velocity of light = " + velocity + " miles/sec");
  System.out.println("One light year = "
   + lightYear + " miles");
  System.exit(0);  // Not required
 }
}
```

Here are the key differences between `Variable.cpp` and `Variable.java`:

- An `import` statement replaces `#include`. However, these are not one-for-one substitutions because Java packages differ greatly from C++ standard function and template libraries.

- In Java, all variables and code are in a class. Because this is a stand-alone application, the program's main class, `Variable`, is the same as its filename.

- In the Java program's main class, the `main()` method's parameters are declared differently than in C++. However, `main()` serves the same purpose—it is where the program begins running. Java's `main()` method is declared `public` so that it can be called from outside of its class, and declared `static` so that it can be called in reference to the `Variable` class without creating an object of that class. The VM automatically calls `main()` to start the program.

- The `float` literal ends with the letter `f` because, in Java, floating-point literal values are of type `double` by default. In Java, type conversion from `double` to `float` is not automatic because this might cause a loss of precision.

- The `long double` declaration in C++ is replaced by `double` in the Java code. Because Java is a 32-bit compiler by definition, it does not have or need `long` data types.

- C++ `printf()` output statements are replaced by `System.out.println()`. This is an imperfect match. For example, Java's output is relatively simple and does not support embedded formatting commands available with `printf()`. To achieve the same level of formatting in Java requires a great deal more work, and I did not include the programming here. For example, you might need to write subroutines that build strings with leading zeros attached to numeric values.

- The C++ `return` statement that exits `main()` and returns a value to the operating system is replaced by an equivalent call to `System.exit()` in the Java code. However, this is not necessary, and Java's `main()` function can simply end without returning any value. This is the only example in the chapter that replaces `main()`'s return with `System.exit()`.

When converting C++ code to Java, in addition to variables, you will probably have to deal with global data. Because all code and data in a Java program must be inside a class, Java does not support global data. It can be approximated, however, as shown in Listing 20.3, `Global.cpp`, and Listing 20.4, `Global.java`.

Listing 20.3. `Global.cpp` (Demonstrates global variables).

```
//=============================================================
// Global.cpp - From Mastering Borland C++ 4.5, chapter 5
// Copyright (c) 1997 by Tom Swan. All rights reserved.
//=============================================================
```

continues

Listing 20.3. continued

```c
#include <stdio.h>

int value;

main()
{
  value = 1234;
  printf("Value = %d\n", value);
  return 0;
}
```

Listing 20.4. `Global.java` (Demonstrates pseudo-global variables).

```java
//==============================================================
// Global.java - Converted from Global.cpp
// Copyright (c) 1997 by Tom Swan. All rights reserved.    ·
//==============================================================

import java.io.*;

class Global {
 public static int value;
 public static void main(String args[]) {
  value = 1234;
  System.out.println("Value = " + value);
 }
}
```

Here are the key differences between `Global.cpp` and `Global.java`:

- The global `value` declaration in the C++ listing is moved into the Java program's main `Global` class. Note especially that, unlike in `Variable.java`, the integer declaration is *not* inside the program's `main()` method.

- The global declaration is prefaced with `public static`. The `public` designation makes the data available to other classes (which a more complex program would probably have) using the expression `Global.value`. The `static` designation permits accessing `value` without instantiating the `Global` class as an object.

Structured Data Types

The `struct` data type originated in C and is used as the basis of the C++ `class`. Java does not have a `struct` data type, but it is easily simulated by a class. Listing 20.5, `DateTime.cpp`, and Listing 20.6, `DateTime.java`, show how a Java program can use classes in place of C++ `struct` declarations.

Listing 20.5. `DateTime.cpp` (Demonstrates C and C++ structs).

```
//================================================================
// DateTime.cpp - From Mastering Borland C++ 4.5, chapter 8
// Copyright (c) 1997 by Tom Swan. All rights reserved.
//================================================================

#include <stdio.h>

typedef struct dateStruct {
  char month;   /* 0 == no date */
  char day;
  unsigned year;
} DateStruct;

typedef struct timeStruct {
  char hour;
  char minute;
  char second;
} TimeStruct;

typedef struct dateTime {
  DateStruct theDate;
  TimeStruct theTime;
} DateTime;

main()
{
  DateTime dt;

  printf("Date and time test\n");
  dt.theDate.month = 5;
  dt.theDate.day = 16;
  dt.theDate.year = 1972;
  dt.theTime.hour = 6;
  dt.theTime.minute = 15;
  dt.theTime.second = 0;
  printf("The date is: %02d/%02d/%04d\n",
    dt.theDate.month, dt.theDate.day, dt.theDate.year);
  printf("The time is: %02d:%02d:%02d\n",
    dt.theTime.hour, dt.theTime.minute, dt.theTime.second);
  return 0;
}
```

Listing 20.6. `DateTime.java` (Demonstrates classes used as `struct`s).

```
//================================================================
// DateTime.java - Converted from DateTime.cpp
// Copyright (c) 1997 by Tom Swan. All rights reserved.
//================================================================

import java.io.*;
```

continues

Listing 20.6. continued

```java
class dateStruct {
 public byte month;   // 0 == no date
 public byte day;
 public short year;
}

class timeStruct {
 public byte hour;
 public byte minute;
 public byte second;
}

class dateTimeStruct {        // Note name change!
 public dateStruct theDate;
 public timeStruct theTime;
 dateTimeStruct() {
  theDate = new dateStruct();
  theTime = new timeStruct();
 }
}

class DateTime {
 public static void main(String args[]) {
  dateTimeStruct dt = new dateTimeStruct();

  System.out.println("Date and time test");
  dt.theDate.month = 5;
  dt.theDate.day = 16;
  dt.theDate.year = 1972;
  dt.theTime.hour = 6;
  dt.theTime.minute = 15;
  dt.theTime.second = 0;
  System.out.println("The date is: " +
    dt.theDate.month + '/' + dt.theDate.day
    + '/' + dt.theDate.year);
  System.out.println("The time is: " +
   dt.theTime.hour + ':' + dt.theTime.minute
   + ':' + dt.theTime.second);
 }
}
```

NOTE

The `DateTime.java` listing merely illustrates how to use classes in place of C++ `structs`. For a better example of date and time handling in Java, see the `Part2\DateDemo` sample application on the CD-ROM, which demonstrates the standard Java `Date` class.

Here are the key differences between `DateTime.cpp` and `DateTime.java`:

- The `typedef struct` keywords in C and C++ (which can be reduced to `struct` in C++) are replaced with `class` in the Java code.

- In Java, instance variables such as `month`, `day`, and `year` are prefaced by `public`. This makes the instance variables available to statements outside of the class. However, because they are not declared `static`, references must be to objects of the class. This most closely resembles the way `struct` fields are used in C and C++.

- The C++ `char` type, which in this sample is used simply to create an 8-byte variable, is replaced in Java by `byte`. Java's `char` data type is 16 bits in length, and represents Unicode character values. The C++ `char` data type covers a multitude of sins—it can represent 8-bit bytes, ASCII characters, and true or false `boolean` values—and is a source of much trouble in C++ code. (The relatively new ANSI C++ `bool` type is nearly equivalent to Java's `boolean`, with one difference: Java's `boolean` values can be only `true` or `false`, which are not equated with integer values as they are in C++, where `false` equals zero and `true` is nonzero.)

- The C++ `unsigned` data type is replaced with `short`. This is not a one-for-one replacement. However, in this example, because Java defines `short` as a 16-bit signed entity, variables of this type are appropriate for holding the year component of a date.

- The C++ `dateTime` struct is renamed `dateTimeStruct` in Java. This is necessary because `DateTime` doubles as the main class name and its module's filename. Although the uncapitalized `dateTime` and the capitalized `DateTime` identifiers differ in case, their output file, `DateTime.class`, is *not* case-sensitive, a situation that causes a subtle but fatal runtime conflict. Such naming problems are rare, but they can show up as very strange bugs when converting C++ code to Java. As a rule, make sure your Java's main class is the only identifier named the same as its filename, and never use case to distinguish between two identifiers. Change one of them as I did here to avoid a conflict.

- The nested `dateTimeStruct` class in the Java listing must have a default constructor that initializes the class's instance variables by constructing the `dateStruct` and `timeStruct` objects. Without this constructor, the two objects are automatically set to `null`, causing the program to halt with a runtime `NullPointerException` error when it attempts to assign values to fields in the member objects. In C++, nested structures are *contained* by their host structure, and they are therefore created automatically.

- In the Java listing, the `dateTimeStruct` variable, `dt`, is instantiated with the `new` operator as an object rather than simply declared as a local variable as in the C++ code. (Note: As a result of this instantiation, `dateTimeStruct`'s constructor initializes its nested objects.)

- Except for output statements, the rest of the Java program is similar to the C++ version. However, I did not include the necessary code to format output strings exactly the same. For example, the C++ program displays a sample date as 05/16/72; the Java code shows this as 5/16/72, without a leading zero for the month.

> **NOTE**
>
> Java does not have the union structure of C and C++, in which data members are overlaid at the same addresses. There is apparently no way to simulate unions in Java, although you might be able to do this by declaring separate classes and using type-cast expressions to force the compiler to use an object as one class or the other.

Input and Output

Neither Java nor C++ have any built-in input or output capabilities. I/O in both languages is handled entirely by library functions or classes. For a discussion of input and output methods, including file-handling techniques, see Chapter 18, "Input and Output."

Java's I/O stream classes are not as versatile as the equivalent C++ classes. In particular, Java does not have overloaded operators, and as a result, the << and >> C++ operators are not available to Java programmers. This results in a lot of work converting C++ code that uses I/O streams. In fact, some conversions might not be worth the effort—if numerous classes, for example, overload operator<<() and operator>>() member functions to provide for input and output of class object data. There is no simple way to duplicate such code in Java.

However, in relatively simple cases, you can replace C++ I/O stream statements with calls to System.out.println() and System.in.read(). Listing 20.7, GetStr.cpp, and Listing 20.8, GetStr.java, demonstrate how to do this to read a string entered at the keyboard and display it onscreen.

Listing 20.7. `GetStr.cpp` (Inputs a string using I/O streams).

```
//==============================================================
// GetStr.cpp -- From Mastering Borland C++ 5, chapter 3
// Copyright (c) 1997 by Tom Swan. All rights reserved.
//==============================================================

#include <iostream.h>

void main()
{
  char s[25];
  char c;
```

```
  cout << "Enter a 24-char string safely: \n";
  cin.get(s, 25, '\n');
  cout << "You entered: " << s << endl;
  if (cin.get(c) && c != '\n')
    cout << "Maximum line length reached\n";
}
```

Listing 20.8. `GetStr.java` (Inputs a string using standard System input).

```
//===============================================================
// GetStr.java -- Converted from GetStr.cpp
// Copyright (c) 1997 by Tom Swan. All rights reserved.
//===============================================================

import java.io.*;

class GetStr {
 public static void main(String args[]) {
  try {
   StringBuffer s = new StringBuffer();
   char c;
   System.out.println("Enter a string safely:");
   while ((c = (char)System.in.read()) != '\n')
    s.append(c);   // Build string using c
   System.out.println("You entered: " + s);
  } catch (IOException e) {              // Trap exception
   System.out.println(e.toString());     // Display error
  }
 }
}
```

Here are the key differences between `GetStr.cpp` and `GetStr.java`:

- The null-terminated `char` array, typically used in C and C++ to hold string data, is replaced by an instance of the `StringBuffer` class. Because a `StringBuffer` object can be modified after its creation, this is the usual way to convert C and C++ strings. However, for representing strings that remain unchanged during the program—error messages, for example—you can instead use the Java `String` class.

- All I/O statements in Java programs are best executed in a `try` block, followed by a `catch` statement that traps any `IOException` errors. This is required in any code that calls an input method such as `System.in.read()`. In such cases, the method must either indicate that it can throw this exception, or it must execute the code in a `try` block as shown in `GetStr.java`.

- It is not necessary to be concerned about overwriting the end of the character array as you must in the C++ code. The `StringBuffer` object, coupled with the program's exception handling, fully protects against all possible memory and input and output errors.

Command-Line Arguments

Java and C++ stand-alone programs can obtain optional arguments entered at the command line or passed by some other method—through a debugger option, for example, or by the Windows 95 Start button's Run command. (Java applets can additionally read HTML-document parameters, as explained in Chapter 13, "Applets," under the section titled "Parameters.")

Listing 20.9, `CmdLine.cpp`, and Listing 20.10, `CmdLine.java`, show the differences between command-line parameters in C++ and in Java.

Listing 20.9. `CmdLine.cpp` (Demonstrates command-line arguments).

```cpp
//===============================================================
// CmdLine.cpp - From Mastering Borland C++ 4.5, chapter 9
// Copyright (c) 1997 by Tom Swan. All rights reserved.
//===============================================================

#include <stdio.h>

main(int argc, char *argv[])
{
  if (argc <= 1) {
    puts("");
    puts("CMDLINE by Tom Swan");
    puts("Enter CMDLINE [x[y][z]] to test");
    puts("command-line arguments.");
  } else
  while (--argc > 0)
    puts(*++argv);
  return 0;
}
```

Listing 20.10. `CmdLine.java` (Demonstrates command-line arguments).

```java
//===============================================================
// CmdLine.java - Converted from CmdLine.cpp
// Copyright (c) 1997 by Tom Swan. All rights reserved.
//===============================================================

import java.io.*;

class CmdLine {
 public static void main(String args[]) {
  int argc = args.length;
  if (argc == 0) {
    System.out.println("");
    System.out.println("CMDLINE by Tom Swan");
    System.out.println("Enter CMDLINE [x[y][z]] to test");
```

```
      System.out.println("command-line arguments.");
   } else {
    for (int i = 0; i < argc; i++)
     System.out.println(args[i]);
   }
  }
}
```

Here are the key differences between `CmdLine.cpp` and `CmdLine.java`:

- Java's `main()` method string-array parameter, `String args[]`, replaces the C++ pointer-to-string-pointer array parameter, `char *argv[]`. You might also see this declared using the equivalent double-indirection expression, `char **argv`. At first glance, you might not think the Java `char args[]` and C++ `char **argv` expressions are equivalent, but in Java, an object is internally a *reference* to an object. Thus, `char args[]` is technically a reference to an array of `String`-object references—which is fundamentally, if not physically, the same as the C++ `char **argv` double-indirection expression.

- Java's `main()` method parameter is required, even if it is not used. In C and C++, `main()`'s two parameters are optional. By the way, the main reason for this difference is that, in C and C++, a subroutine's caller is responsible for removing function arguments from the stack; thus, a function is free to ignore, or not even declare, values passed to the function's parameters. Variable numbers of parameters are also easily accommodated. In Java, it is the called subroutine's responsibility to remove arguments before returning to its caller; thus, any parameters must be declared explicitly in the method, and variable numbers of parameters are more difficult to implement (Java doesn't allow them).

- In Java, the expression `args.length`, which equals the number of elements in the `args[]` string array, replaces the `int argc` parameter in the C++ program. For clarity, in the Java code, I declared and assigned `args.length` to an `int` variable named `argc`; however, you can also replace all instances of `argc` with `args.length`. (Note: In Java, *all* arrays have a built-in `length` attribute that equals the number of elements in the array. C++ arrays have no equivalent attribute, although it is possible to compute this value by dividing the array size in bytes by the size of a single element.)

- In Java, the first string in `args[]` does not equal the program's path, as it does in C++. For this reason, I replaced the `if`-statement expression (`argc <= 1`) with (`argc == 0`). These expressions are each true in their respective programs if the user enters no arguments.

- Java command-line arguments are stored in the `args[]` string array in the order they are entered. Command-line arguments in C++ are stored in the opposite order. To accommodate this difference, I changed the C++ `while` loop (probably the most typical way of accessing arguments in the order entered) with a more straightforward `for` loop.

Strings and Text Files

In part because of its allegiance to C, C++ string handling is a mishmash of null-terminated `char` arrays and objects. In Java, strings are more sensibly programmed as objects of the `StringBuffer` and `String` classes, which makes string-handling one of Java's key strengths. For more information about Java's `StringBuffer` and `String` classes, see Chapter 6, "Strings and Characters."

The standard template library in ANSI C++ now provides a `string` template, which also goes a long way to standardizing string handling. You can probably replace many uses of the C++ `string` template with Java's `String` or `StringBuffer` classes—the classes are similar, though not perfect matches. However, despite the availability of a `string` template, many C++ programmers continue to use `char` arrays and `char*` pointers to address null-terminated strings. (Traditions die hard among programmers.)

Using the ANSI C++ `string` template, processing text files is far simpler than in Java. Although Java's I/O stream classes are intelligently designed, as the following sample programs demonstrate, they require a lot more effort to use. Listing 20.11, `RStrings.cpp`, and Listing 20.12, `RStrings.java`, show how to read a text file in C++ and in Java using the C++ `string` template and the Java `String` class.

Listing 20.11. `RStrings.cpp` (Reads a text file).

```
//===============================================================
// Rstrings.cpp -- From Mastering Borland C++ 5, chapter 11
// Copyright (c) 1997 by Tom Swan. All rights reserved.
//===============================================================

#include <iostream>
#include <fstream>
#include <string>

using namespace std;

void main()
{
  string s;

  ifstream ifs("Rstrings.cpp", ios::in);
  while (ifs.good()) {
    getline(ifs, s, '\n');
    cout << s << endl;
  }
}
```

Listing 20.12. `RStrings.java` (Reads a text file).

```
//===============================================================
// RStrings.java - Converted from RStrings.cpp
// Copyright (c) 1997 by Tom Swan. All rights reserved.
//===============================================================

import java.io.*;

class RStrings {
 public static void main(String args[]) {
  try {
   File fi = new File("RStrings.cpp");
   FileInputStream fin = new FileInputStream(fi);
   BufferedInputStream bin = new BufferedInputStream(fin);
   DataInputStream din = new DataInputStream(bin);
   String s = din.readLine();
   while (s != null) {
    System.out.println(s);
    s = din.readLine();
   }
  } catch (IOException e) {
   System.err.println(e.toString());
  }
 }
}
```

Here are the key differences between `RStrings.cpp` and `RStrings.java`:

- The C++ code is far simpler, made so by the use of the overloaded << operator and the input stream object's `getline()` function.

- The Java code, while more complex, is superior in its `try` and `catch` exception error handling. The C++ `ifs.good()` input-stream error-checking function is a poor substitute for exceptions, and this represents one of the most unpopular aspects of C++ I/O stream classes.

- Java's I/O stream classes are intelligently designed, but they require more effort to use. For example, the Java file objects are constructed in three stages, starting with a plain file input stream, adding buffered input, and finally arriving at the typed-data input stream object used to read the text file one line at a time. (See Chapter 18 for more information and additional examples of Java file handling and I/O stream classes.)

- The `while` loop in the Java code requires an initial call to `din.readLine()` before entering the loop. This takes care of the possibility that the text file is empty. The C++ program does not require this extra step. This is a minor difference, and I could have converted the code in other ways—using a `do-while` loop, for example. However, be aware that the action of reading past the end of the file is treated differently in C++

and Java, and its result is not always consistent in either language. For example, when reading text data, reading past the end of the file causes `readLine()` to return `null`. However, reading past the end of other types of files throws an `EOFException` object. When converting file-handling code from C++ to Java, be sure to thoroughly research the return values and any possible exceptions thrown by the Java I/O methods you call.

Arrays

As I mentioned, Java's arrays are far superior to arrays in C++. Actually, in C++, an array and a pointer are one and the same; any pointer, for example, can be used to address an array of objects of the pointer's element type. The C++ expressions `char* x` and `char x[]` are exactly equivalent.

Java arrays are dynamically created at runtime, which among other advantages, means their sizes are variable. Of course, Java does not have a pointer data type—but you can often use Java arrays in place of C++ pointers. For example, the C++ variable `int* p` can be represented in Java as an array of integers, `int p[]`. The results are not exactly the same, but with some elbow grease, you can make them close enough to convert many uses of C++ pointers into Java arrays.

Java arrays also provide a `length` attribute equal to the number of elements in the array. C++ arrays do not have this attribute, although as I mentioned, a common C++ trick is to divide the size of the array in bytes by the size of one element. For example, in C++, you might find the code

```
int iArray[100];
int numElements = sizeof(iArray) / sizeof(int);
```

This sets `numElements` equal to the number of elements in `iArray`. In Java, this code becomes

```
int iArray[] = new int[100];
int numElements = iArray.length;
```

Of course, you may as well use `iArray.length` directly; you don't have to assign it to a separate variable.

Although they are created differently, arrays in both languages are used similarly. In Java, however, any attempt to access elements outside of the array's boundaries throws a runtime exception of the `IndexOutOfBoundsException` class. The results of array boundary errors in C++ are undefined, and the effects depend in part on the operating system. For example, in a protected memory environment, a fatal exception might be thrown, but when executed by a simpler operating system, the program might simply fail to work properly.

A typical example of arrays is a program that sorts a series of object values. In addition to demonstrating arrays in C++ and Java, Listing 20.13, `Sorter.cpp`, and Listing 20.14, `Sorter.java`, also show C++ and Java random number generation and function recursion.

Listing 20.13. `Sorter.cpp` (Sorts an array of data).

```
//===============================================================
// Sorter.cpp -- From Mastering Borland C++ 4.5, chapter 8
// Copyright (c) 1997 by Tom Swan. All rights reserved.
//===============================================================

#include <stdio.h>
#include <stdlib.h>
#include <time.h>

#define ARRAYSIZE 100

void FillArray(void);
void DisplayArray(void);
void Quicksort(int left, int right);
void SortArray(int n);

int array[ARRAYSIZE];   /* Array of integers */

main()
{
  FillArray();
  DisplayArray();
  SortArray(ARRAYSIZE);
  DisplayArray();
  return 0;
}

/* Fill global array with values taken at random */
void FillArray(void)
{
  int i;

  srand((unsigned)time(NULL));       /* Randomize */
  for (i = 0; i < ARRAYSIZE; i++)     /* Fill array */
    array[i] = rand();
}

/* Display contents of array before and after sorting */
void DisplayArray(void)
{
  int i;

  puts("");   /* Start new display line */
  for (i = 0; i < ARRAYSIZE; i++)
    printf("%8d", array[i]);
}

/* Quicksort algorithm by C. A. R. Hoare */
void Quicksort(int left, int right)
{
  int i = left;
  int j = right;
  register int test = array[(left + right) / 2];
  int swap;
```

continues

579

Listing 20.13. continued

```
  do {
    while (array[i] < test) i++;
    while (test < array[j]) j--;
    if (i <= j) {
      swap = array[i];
      array[i] = array[j];
      array[j] = swap;
      i++;
      j--;
    }
  } while (i <= j);
  if (left < j) Quicksort(left, j);
  if (i < right) Quicksort(i, right);
}

/* Sort n elements in global array */
void SortArray(int n)
{
  if (n > 1) Quicksort(0, n - 1);
}
```

Listing 20.14. Sorter.java (Sorts an array of data).

```
//==============================================================
// Sorter.java - Converted from Sorter.cpp
// Copyright (c) 1997 by Tom Swan. All rights reserved.
//==============================================================

import java.io.*;
import java.util.Random;

class Sorter {
 public static int ARRAYSIZE = 100;
 public static int array[];  // Array of integers

 // Fill global array with values taken at random
 public static void FillArray()
 {
  int i;
  Random gen = new Random();        // Randomize
  for (i = 0; i < ARRAYSIZE; i++)  // Fill array
   array[i] = Math.abs(gen.nextInt());
 }

 // Display contents of array before and after sorting
 public static void DisplayArray()
 {
  int i;
  System.out.println();  // Start new display line
  for (i = 0; i < ARRAYSIZE; i++)
   System.out.print(array[i] + "    ");
  System.out.println();
 }
```

```
// Quicksort algorithm by C. A. R. Hoare
public static void Quicksort(int left, int right)
{
 int i = left;
 int j = right;
 int test = array[(left + right) / 2];
 int swap;

 do {
  while (array[i] < test) i++;
  while (test < array[j]) j--;
  if (i <= j) {
   swap = array[i];
   array[i] = array[j];
   array[j] = swap;
   i++;
   j--;
  }
 } while (i <= j);
 if (left < j) Quicksort(left, j);
 if (i < right) Quicksort(i, right);
}

// Sort n elements in global array
public static void SortArray(int n)
{
 if (n > 1) Quicksort(0, n - 1);
}

public static void main(String args[]) {
 array = new int[ARRAYSIZE];
 FillArray();
 DisplayArray();
 SortArray(ARRAYSIZE);
 DisplayArray();
}
}
```

Here are the key differences between Sorter.cpp and Sorter.java:

- For random-sequence generation, the Java program imports the Random class from the java.util package. C++ programs typically call a function such as rand() to produce random sequences, or they implement a local function. The rand() function is not standard, and it may be named something else on your system. It might also return floating-point values instead of integers, as in the sample C++ code, which I wrote using Borland's C++ compiler. Java's Random class standardizes random sequence generation—and furthermore, the *same* random sequences are guaranteed for equal seed values across all Java installations. For simpler applications, you can call the Math class's random() method, which returns type double. However, I prefer to use the Random class as demonstrated here.

- In C and C++, #define is used to create pseudo-constants, which are more correctly described as text macros that are preprocessed in advance of compilation. Java does

581

not have text macros. As a rough equivalent, you can usually replace `#define` statements with `public static` variables, as I did here for the `ARRAYSIZE` constant. C and C++ text macros can be exceedingly complex—they employ a language akin to ancient Greek—and in the worst case, macros can interact with one another in ways that only their authors can possibly understand. This makes the lack of `#define` advantageous in Java—unless, that is, you have to convert numerous complex C++ macros to Java `static` declarations. In that event, it's hard to recommend a safe course of action, but you might try running the C++ source code through a preprocessor. This will provide numerous clues about the uses of any mysterious text macros. Most C++ development systems provide a preprocessor for this purpose. For example, the Borland C++ preprocessors are `Cpp.exe` and `Cpp32.exe`.

- The C++ program defines a global, fixed-size, array of integers directly in the source code. The Java program creates the array with a statement in `main()` at runtime.

- The global functions in the C++ program are converted to methods and moved inside the Java program's main class. Each method is declared and implemented inline; in Java, functions are never declared and implemented separately as they are in C and C++.

- Arrays are used in largely the same way in both languages. The `[]` operator accesses an array element as shown in methods `FillArray()`, `DisplayArray()`, `QuickSort()`, and `SortArray()`. After you convert the code that declares and constructs an array, chances are good that few modifications will be needed in their uses. I made very few changes to these functions.

- A good example of the compatibility of array use in C++ and Java is the `QuickSort()` method. Except for the addition of `public` and `static` to the Java method, the function is identical in both listings. This also shows that recursion works the same in Java and C++. The `QuickSort()` method calls itself to partition the integer array, arranging each partition until all elements are ordered in sequence. (Note: The reason the program also has a `SortArray()` method is to prevent sorting empty arrays or those with only one element. As designed here, the recursive `QuickSort()` method requires its data array to have two or more elements.)

- Except for creating the dynamic array at runtime, the Java program's `main()` method is same as the `main()` function in the C++ code. However, as I mentioned, Java's `main()` method must declare its string array parameter even though it is unused.

Classes and Objects

This book's numerous listings show practically all aspects of classes, objects, and object-oriented programming in Java. To convert an object-oriented C++ program's classes to Java, you'll need to study this book's sample programs and read most of the chapters, especially those in Part II. The following sections are therefore not intended to be a complete comparison between C++ and Java classes. However, I cover several vital areas that are likely to trip you up.

Class Concepts

The following listings implement a class that can set, reset, and test individual bits in a 16-bit variable. The first two C++ files—Listing 20.15, BitSet.h, and Listing 20.16, BitSet.cpp—declare and implement the TBitSet C++ class. The third file—Listing 20.17, TBitSet.cpp—tests the TBitSet class. After these C++ listings (three in all) are two more files—Listing 20.18, BitSet.java, and Listing 20.19, TBitSet.java—which implement and test a similar Java class, which I renamed BitSet due to file and class name conflicts.

Listing 20.15. BitSet.h (Declares the C++ TBitSet class).

```
//================================================================
// BitSet.h - From Mastering Borland C++ 5, chapter 5, answers
// Copyright (c) 1997 by Tom Swan. All rights reserved.
//================================================================

#ifndef __BITSET_H
#define __BITSET_H   // Prevent multiple #includes

typedef unsigned int WORD;   // Assumes 16-bit integers

class TBitSet {
private:
  WORD bitset;
protected:
  bool IndexOkay(char n)
    { if (n <= 15) return true; return false; }
public:
  TBitSet() { bitset = 0; }
  void Add(char n);
  void Delete(char n);
  bool HasBit(char n);
  char Extract(char n);
  void Display(void);
};

#endif  // __BITSET_H
```

Listing 20.16. BitSet.cpp (Implements the C++ TBitSet class).

```
//================================================================
// BitSet.cpp - From Mastering Borland C++ 5, chapter 5, answers
// Copyright (c) 1997 by Tom Swan. All rights reserved.
//================================================================

#include <iostream.h>
#include "bitset.h"

// Set nth bit in bitset to 1
void TBitSet::Add(char n)
{
```

continues

Listing 20.16. continued

```
  if (IndexOkay(n))
    bitset |= 1 << n;   // i.e. OR 1 shifted left n times
}

// Set nth bit in bitset to 0
void TBitSet::Delete(char n)
{
  if (IndexOkay(n))
    bitset &= ~(1 << n);   // i.e. AND NOT 1 shifted left n times
}

// Return TRUE if nth bit in bitset == 1
bool TBitSet::HasBit(char n)
{
  if (!IndexOkay(n))
    return false;
  if ((bitset & (1 << n)) != 0)
    return true;
  return false;
}

// Return nth bit in bitset (1 or 0; 9==error)
char TBitSet::Extract(char n)
{
  if (!IndexOkay(n))
    return 9;   // Indexing error
  if (HasBit(n))
    return 1;
  return 0;
}

// Display bitset as a binary value
void TBitSet::Display(void)
{
  for (int i = 15; i >= 0; i--) {
    if (((i + 1) % 4) == 0)
      cout << ' ';
    cout << (int)Extract(i);
  }
}
```

Listing 20.17. TBitSet.cpp (Tests the C++ TBitSet class).

```
//=============================================================
// TBitSet.cpp - From Mastering Borland C++ 5, chapter 5, answers
// Copyright (c) 1997 by Tom Swan. All rights reserved.
//=============================================================

#include <iostream.h>
#include "bitset.h"

void main()
{
  TBitSet bits;
```

```
    bits.Add(0);       // Set bits 0, 2, 4, and 15
    bits.Add(2);
    bits.Add(4);
    bits.Add(15);
    bits.Display();    // Display set as a binary value
    bits.Delete(2);    // Reset bit 2
    cout << endl;
    bits.Display();
}
```

Listing 20.18. `BitSet.java` (Declares and implements the Java `BitSet` class).

```java
//================================================================
// BitSet.java - Converted from BitSet.h and BitSet.cpp
// Copyright (c) 1997 by Tom Swan. All rights reserved.
//================================================================

public class BitSet {
 // Instance variable
 private int bitset;

 // Constructor
 public BitSet() {
  bitset = 0;
 }

 // Return true if index n is in range
 protected boolean IndexOkay(int n) {
  if (n <= 15)
   return true;
  return false;
 }

 // Set nth bit in bitset to 1
 public void Add(int n)
 {
  if (IndexOkay(n))
   bitset |= 1 << n;  // i.e. OR 1 shifted left n times
 }

 // Set nth bit in bitset to 0
 public void Delete(int n)
 {
  if (IndexOkay(n))
   bitset &= ~(1 << n);  // i.e. AND NOT 1 shifted left n times
 }

 // Return TRUE if nth bit in bitset == 1
 public boolean HasBit(int n)
 {
  if (!IndexOkay(n))
   return false;
  if ((bitset & (1 << n)) != 0)
   return true;
  return false;
 }
```

continues

585

Listing 20.18. continued

```
// Return nth bit in bitset (1 or 0; 9==error)
public int Extract(int n)
{
 if (!IndexOkay(n))
  return 9;  // Indexing error
 if (HasBit(n))
  return 1;
 return 0;
}

// Display bitset as a binary value
public void Display()
{
 for (int i = 15; i >= 0; i--) {
  if (((i + 1) % 4) == 0)
   System.out.print(' ');
  System.out.print(Extract(i));
 }
}
}
```

Listing 20.19. TBitSet.java (Tests the Java BitSet class).

```
//==============================================================
// TBitSet.java - Converted from TBitSet.cpp
// Copyright (c) 1997 by Tom Swan. All rights reserved.
//==============================================================

import java.io.*;
import BitSet;

class TBitSet {
 public static void main(String args[]) {
  BitSet bits = new BitSet();
  bits.Add(0);       // Set bits 0, 2, 4, and 15
  bits.Add(2);
  bits.Add(4);
  bits.Add(15);
  bits.Display();  // Display set as a binary value
  bits.Delete(2);  // Reset bit 2
  System.out.println();
  bits.Display();
 }
}
```

Here are the key differences between the Java and C++ TBitSet and BitSet classes and test programs:

- A header file with an .h filename extension declares the TBitSet class separately in C++. In the Java program, file BitSet.java declares and implements the separate class (renamed `BitSet` due to the naming conflict mentioned). Both programs could have been written using single files, but the slightly more complex arrangement shown here will help you sort out how C++ and Java differ in their multimodule capabilities.

- The Java `BitSet` class is declared `public` to make it available to other modules.

- The Java `BitSet` class constructor is made `public` so that other modules can import the class and construct objects from it.

- Other `BitSet` protected and public functions are nearly the same in both programs. However, in the Java code, the `public`, `private`, and `protected` access specifiers preface each declaration. In the C++ code, these specifiers, which are identical in purpose, precede groups of declarations.

- Separate class member functions in the C++ `TBitSet` class are implemented inline in the Java `BitSet` class. Inline functions, however, are not the same in the two languages. In Java, all methods are implemented inline, but internally, they are treated as callable subroutines. In C++, an inline function is an optimization technique used to inject code in place of function calls. Java does not have a similar inline injection capability.

- In Java, it is not necessary to declare member functions separately, nor is it necessary to create a header file for other modules to import those declarations. Java-compiled byte-code `.class` files contain all the information needed for other modules to import *and* to use the modules' classes.

- I made several changes to the program's data types—converting C++ `bool` to `boolean`, `WORD` (a `typedef` for `unsigned int`) to `short`, and `char` parameters to `int`. I could have used `byte` in place of `char`, but this would have required more work and would give no real advantage in this case.

- `System.out.print()` statements in the Java program replace C++ output stream statements.

- The Java test program uses `new` to construct an instance of the `BitSet` class. The C++ test program merely defines a local variable of its `TBitSet` class. Except for the next-to-last output statement, `main()`'s declaration format, and the fact that all data and code are encapsulated in the Java program's `TBitSet` class, the test programs are the same in both languages.

- The Java test program imports the `BitSet` class. Because no package names preface the class name, Java looks in the current directory for a `BitSet.class` file. Actually, the `import` statement isn't needed because, if a module uses a class that is not explicitly imported, Java automatically looks for its `.class` file in the current directory.

Other Concerns

The following are some other areas of concern when converting C++ classes and object-oriented programming to Java.

One key difference involves the way objects are created and destroyed. In Java, to construct an object of a class (I'll use a hypothetical `TAnyClass` for demonstration purposes), a statement calls new like this:

```
TAnyClass obj = new TAnyClass();
```

This calls the no-parameter, default constructor—which the Java class may or may not declare explicitly. If one is not declared, Java adds an implicit default constructor to the class. Constructors in Java classes may also have parameters. The statement

```
TAnyClass obj = new TAnyClass("String", 123);
```

constructs an object by calling a constructor that declares `String` and `int` parameters.

In C++, class objects can be defined the same way as other variables. For example, the C++ statement

```
TAnyClass obj;
```

constructs `obj` as an object of the `TAnyClass` class, and calls that class's default constructor. In Java, this becomes

```
TAnyClass obj = new TAnyClass();
```

because `obj` is a *reference* to an object, and as such, it must be initialized by new. The only exception to this rule is a Java `String` object, which can be initialized using either of these two equivalent statements:

```
String s1 = "Abcdefg";
String s2 = new String("Abcdefg");
```

Like Java, C++ adds an implicit no-parameter constructor if one is not explicitly declared. To construct an object from a C++ class constructor using parameters, a statement such as

```
TAnyClass obj("String", 123);
```

is comparable to the Java statement

```
TAnyClass obj = new TAnyClass("String", 123);
```

that calls a constructor with `String` and integer parameters.

C++ also has a new operator, but it is used to construct dynamic objects addressed by pointers. For example, in C++, you might declare a pointer p to a class object as

```
TAnyClass *p;
```

Then you could construct the object with the following statement:

```
p = new TAnyClass("String", 123);
```

Statements like that directly translate to Java, but without using a pointer. For example, these two statements in Java are equivalent to the preceding C++ code:

```
TAnyClass r;
r = new TAnyClass("String", 123);
```

Alternatively, you can use this single statement:

```
TAnyClass r = new TAnyClass("String", 123);
```

I used r in place of p to indicate that, in Java, dynamic objects are referenced, whereas in C++ they are addressed by pointers.

As these examples show, object creation and the use of constructors is not very different between Java and C++. Object destruction, however, differs greatly. For example, a C++ class can declare a destructor, as in the following class:

```
class TBase {
private:
 char *basep;  // Pointer to private string
public:
 TBase(const char *s) { basep = strdup(s); }
 ~TBase() { delete basep; }  // Destructor
 const char *GetStr(void) { return basep; }
};  // Semicolon required because this is a declaration
```

The C++ TBase class declares a private char pointer, which is intended to address a null-terminated string. Such a string is passed to the class's public constructor in the char pointer parameter s, which is assigned to basep by calling the standard function strdup(). This creates a duplicate string object in memory, which the class must be careful to eventually delete. To provide this code, a destructor—a no-parameter function named the same as the class and preceded with a tilde—deletes the string addressed by basep. This destructor is called automatically when a TBase object goes out of scope, and thus, the memory allocated by strdup() is safely deleted. The class also declares a public method, GetStr(), which returns a pointer to the privately addressed string.

The following is one version of an equivalent Java class:

```
public class TBase {
 private String s;
 public TBase(String s) { this.s = new String(s); }
 public void finalize() { }  // Nothing to do!
 public String GetStr() { return s; }
}  // No semicolon--this is an implementation, not a declaration
```

Compare the two class declarations line for line. The Java class is prefaced with public so that other modules can use it. (However, public is not allowed if the class is used inside a module containing other classes. But don't worry about this; the compiler gives an error if you use public incorrectly.) The closing brace in the C++ class needs a semicolon; the Java class properly has none. Each of the Java class's data and method declarations is prefaced with access specifiers, which in the C++ class, define groups of items with the indicated attributes. The Java class stores its private string data as an object of the String class. I changed the name of this instance variable from basep to s reflecting the fact that it is now an object reference, and not a pointer.

The Java TBase() constructor employs a useful trick that avoids conflicts between instance variables such as s and method parameters named the same. In the constructor body, the expression this.s refers to the object's instance variable; s alone refers to the constructor's parameter. To construct a copy of the parameter, the class uses new to construct a copy of the String object in place of the C++ call to the standard strdup() library function.

> **NOTE**
>
> Java does not have a const keyword, which in this example, indicates that the TBase constructor does not change the data addressed by the pointer. The word const is applied at compile time, and when converting Java code, you can delete it. Of course, you lose the safety of the compiler verifying that constant arguments are not changed in their receiving methods.

Java classes do not have destructors, but you may implement a finalize() method as shown in TBase to perform cleanup chores. However, because Java's memory management is automatic, there is nothing for finalize() to do. The private String object will be deleted if necessary to make room for other objects. However, and this is important, Java does not guarantee that finalize() will be called. If enough memory is available to the program, it's possible that no objects will be destroyed. If you need to perform a critical task for an unused object, you must add a method (typically named dispose()) and call it from a statement. The finalize() method is not a one-for-one replacement for a C++ class destructor.

Finally, in the sample Java TBase class, method GetStr() returns a String object. Notice that the parenthetical void in the C++ code, which indicates that GetStr() requires no arguments, is not permitted. In Java, no-parameter methods are declared with empty parentheses, as they are in C. (C and C++ compilers have inconsistently handled this minor detail, and you might see f() and f(void) in C++ listings. In either case, f() is the proper Java replacement.)

Internally, all Java objects are actually references, and functions may return objects as in TBase.GetStr() regardless of complexity and size. If this causes you to suspect that pointers exist in Java after all, you are right. A reference is actually a pointer, but it is not used as such, and it does not require dereferencing as do pointers in C and C++. On the other hand, there is no guarantee that Java references are implemented as machine addresses. Depending on how the VM is implemented on a given system, references could conceivably be represented as index values into an array of memory blocks or as handles to system memory allocations.

Inheritance is another area where Java and C++ part company in their object orientation. Even the terminology is different. A C++ base class is called a superclass in Java; a C++ derived class is equivalent to a Java subclass. You derive classes in C++; you extend them in Java.

A single C++ program may have multiple class hierarchies, stemming from distinct base classes. In Java, all classes are subclasses of the ultimate superclass, Object, even if not explicitly extended as such. This means that all Java class objects are related. One advantage of this is that, if a method declares an Object parameter, you may pass *any* object of *any* class as an argument to that parameter.

As I've mentioned, Java classes support only single inheritance. ANSI C++ classes support multiple inheritance. Of all differences between Java and C++, this might give you the most trouble, especially if you are converting a complex class library that relies heavily on multiple inheritance. It might be possible to use Java class interfaces. A single Java subclass may implement an unlimited number of interfaces, although it may extend from only one superclass. In practice, however, C++ code that relies on multiple inheritance will be difficult if not impossible to convert directly to Java.

As an example of inheritance (single only), consider how a C++ module might derive a new class from TBase:

```
class TDerived: public TBase {
private:
 char *uppercasep;
public:
 TDerived(const char *s);
 ~Tderived() { delete uppercasep; }
 const char *GetUStr(void) { return uppercasep; }
};
```

The purpose of this class is to store a separate uppercase version of the object's private string data. The constructor is implemented separately, usually in another source file:

```
TDerived::TDerived(const char *s)
 : TBase(s)  // Call base constructor
{
 uppercasep = strupr(strdup(s));  // Initialize TDerived data
}
```

Compare that code with the following Java version of the TDerived class. As in all Java classes, all methods are declared and implemented inline, and only one source file is needed:

```
public class TDerived extends TBase {
 private String uppers;
 public TDerived(String s) {
  super(s);  // Call superclass constructor
  uppers = new String(s).toUpperCase();
 }
 String GetUStr() { return uppers; }
}
```

Again, the class is declared public, but you would not do this unless you are exporting TDerived for use in other modules. To extend the Java class, the word extends replaces the C++ : operator. The method for calling the C++ base class constructor is replaced in the Java class with the expression super(s). In Java, calling the base class constructor is optional, but if you call super(), it must be the first statement in the constructor's body.

The second statement in the Java class constructor creates a new String object and then calls toUpperCase() to convert it to uppercase text. This might be replaced with the simpler statement

```
uppers = s.toUpperCase();
```

But there is an important difference. In the first instance, a new String object is guaranteed to be created. In the simpler statement, a new object is not created if the original string is already in all uppercase. Each technique is correct; the one to use depends on your intended use of the data.

I did not insert a finalize() method in the Java class because it has nothing to do, and therefore, a replacement for the C++ destructor isn't needed. The class method, GetUStr(), simply returns a reference to the extended class object's private string data.

Finally, let's discuss a subject that confuses many C++ programmers, and even some experts: virtual member functions. In C++ classes, member functions are static unless explicitly declared virtual. If a base class calls a static member function in a statement, that statement will always call that same subroutine even if a derived class overrides the function. However, if the member function is virtual, a base class's call to it is *replaced* with a call to the derived class function without having to recompile the original statement.

All methods in Java classes are virtual. Any calls to class methods are replaceable simply by extended the class and overriding the method.

A typical example of virtual member functions—and a good illustration of the object-oriented programming technique called *polymorphism*—is a graphics program that draws a number of different shapes. For example, in C++, you might declare a Shape class to serve as the basis for actual graphical objects to be implemented at a later time. In part, Shape might be declared as

```
class Shape {
public:
 // Various members
 virtual void Draw();
};
```

The Draw() method is not implemented—classes derived from Shape are expected to do that to draw actual shapes. This makes Shape an *abstract* class. It is an abstraction of what a shape needs and does, but it does not provide the actual implementation of these concepts.

> **NOTE**
>
> The Java sample code in the rest of this chapter is on disk in the Abstract.java file in the directory Part4\Abstract on the CD-ROM.

In Java, the word `virtual` isn't needed, and you could write the class as follows:

```
public abstract class Shape {
 public abstract void Draw();
}
```

However, you must precede the class and all unimplemented methods with the keyword `abstract`, indicating that an extended class will provide the implementation details. (Alternatively, you could declare `Shape` as an interface, in which case all methods are abstract by default.) I remind you again that `public` in the first line is allowed only if this class is to be exported for use in other modules. If the class is used in its own module only, delete `public`. The `Draw()` method, however, must remain `public` so that it can be called in reference to `Shape` class objects.

> **NOTE**
>
> For more information on abstract Java classes, see Chapter 8, "More About Classes and Objects," in the section titled "Abstract Classes."

Continuing with the example, having declared the abstract `Shape` class, the C++ program might define an array of shapes as one way to represent a picture. The statement

```
Shape *picture[100];
```

defines an array of 100 `Shape` pointers, each of which can address an object of a class derived from the abstract `Shape`. In Java, a similar array simply holds `Shape` references, and it is constructed at runtime with a statement such as

```
public static Shape picture[] = new Shape[100];
```

The `public` and `static` keywords are needed if this statement is in the program's main class, which is not instantiated. The keyword `static` is not needed if this statement is in another class for which the program will create an object.

Alternatively, in the Java program, you can declare the array separately (perhaps in the program's main class):

```
public static Shape picture[];
```

Then you can construct it—perhaps in the `main()` method—at runtime, using the statement

```
picture = new Shape[100];
```

Either way, this makes `picture` an array of 100 `Shape` objects. However, in the C++ and Java code, the `picture` array merely has the *potential* to refer to 100 `Shape` objects; the actual objects have not yet been constructed. For this reason, drawing the picture requires some careful programming. For example, the C++ program can use code like this:

```
int i = 0;
while (i < 100 && picture[i] != 0) {
 picture[i]->Draw();  // Draw the Shape object
 i++;
}
```

The C++ while loop cycles through the array of Shape objects up to, but not including, the first one equal to zero. A literal zero is the correct way in ANSI C++ to represent a null pointer, though you will sometimes see the word NULL used in this kind of code. (This is dangerous because some systems define NULL specially.) Inside the C++ while loop, the first statement calls the Draw() virtual method for each Shape object. This, of course, draws the picture by calling the methods in objects of classes derived from Shape.

The equivalent Java loop might be programmed as

```
int i = 0;
while (i < 100 && picture[i] != null) {
 picture[i].Draw();  // Draw the Shape object
 i++;
}
```

This is very close to the C++ version. In Java, null is a defined keyword, and it must be in lowercase. All uninitialized object references are equal to null. A second difference is the first statement in the while loop. In place of the C++ pointer dereference operator ->, a period indicates that the Java statement should call the Shape object's Draw() method.

But wait a minute! We haven't yet defined any Draw() methods to call—and this is the beauty of polymorphism. Because Draw() is virtual, it is expected to be implemented in a derived (in Java, an *extended*) class. The while loop calls the method associated with the type of Shape object. To say that another way, the object determines how it is to be drawn—it literally draws itself. For example, the C++ program might derive Circle and Line classes from Shape:

```
class Circle: public Shape {
public:
 virtual void Draw() {
   // Statements that draw a circle
 }
};

class Line: public Shape {
public:
 virtual void Draw() {
  // Statements that draw a line
 }
};
```

In Java, these classes might be written as

```
public class Circle extends Shape {
 public void Draw() {
  // Statements that draw a circle
 }
}

public class Line extends Shape {
 public void Draw() {
  // Statements that draw a line
 }
}
```

I'll leave the actual details of how to draw circles and lines up to you. Here's a hint: To try these examples, insert output statements such as

```
System.out.println("Inside Circle.Draw()");
```

I did this for you in the `Abstract.java` demonstration on the CD-ROM. Other code would also be needed to construct actual `Circle` and `Line` objects. For example, each class probably needs a constructor that specifies parameters for defining particular kinds of shapes, their colors and sizes, and other attributes.

To create a picture of `Shape` objects, the C++ program might use code such as

```
picture[0] = new Circle();
picture[1] = new Circle();
picture[2] = new Line();
picture[3] = new Circle();
picture[4] = new Line();
```

The Java code is identical. When either program executes the `while` loop that calls the virtual `Shape.Draw()`, it is the method in the derived or extended classes that is actually called. Though the implementation details differ, in this important aspect of object-oriented polymorphism, Java and C++ are in perfect harmony.

Summary

- Java and C++ share many similarities, but each language has strengths and weaknesses. Only by knowing these facts can you intelligently decide which language is appropriate for a given project.
- This chapter's example listings compare many aspects of Java and C++ programming. If you are a C++ programmer, the listings will help you learn Java quickly. You can also use the chapter as a guide to converting C++ code to Java, and for sharing data between programs written in both languages.

- Input and output programming techniques vary greatly between Java and C++. In both languages, I/O is provided externally—by standard functions and I/O stream classes in C+, and by I/O stream classes in Java. However, there are few similarities between these Java and C++ classes.

- Java's key strengths include its full object-orientation, lack of pointers, relatively simple classes and objects, dynamic arrays, automatic garbage collection, interfaces, and string classes. Java's weaknesses include interpreted code, poor low-level access, lack of multiple inheritance, and the absence of an ANSI specification.

- C++'s key strengths include standard function and template libraries, rich archives of published code, low-level access, native code output, multiple inheritance, templates, and the support of an ANSI specification. C++'s weaknesses include pointers (but you might consider them a strength), a mishmash of string formats, only partial object-orientation, the need for objects to carefully manage memory, and (without resorting to tricky programming) only fixed-size arrays.

- Java and C++ share many features, though not perfectly in all cases, such as case-sensitivity, comment styles, exception handling, strong type checking, similar data types, classes, and most operators, expressions, and statement formats.

- Java is more fully object-oriented than C++. Many of the concepts of object-oriented programming are similar in both languages; however, C++ has sophisticated features such as templates and multiple inheritance, which are not available in Java.

What's Next?

Although this is the end of the last chapter, I hope this is only the beginning of your experiences with Java. Please write to me in care of the publisher if you have any comments or suggestions for a future edition of this book. The next step is up to you. Good luck!

V

Appendixes

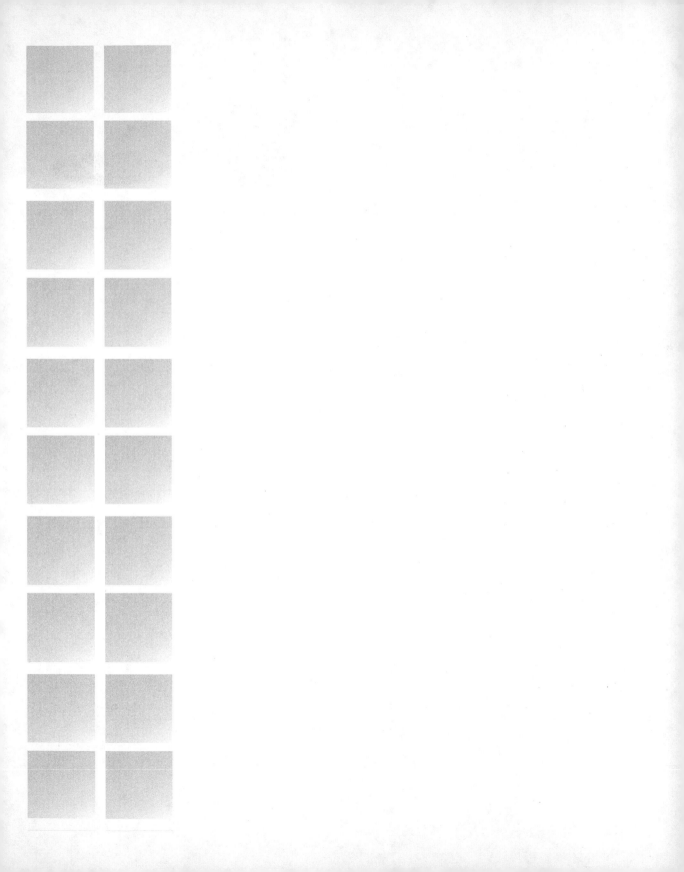

Operator Precedence and Associativity

Table A.1. Operator precedence.

Level	Operators
1(high)	() . []
2	++ -- ! ~ instanceof
3	* / %
4	+ -
5	<< >> >>>
6	< > <= >=
7	== !=
8	&
9	^
10	&&
11	¦¦
12	?:
13	= op=
14	,

B

Keywords

Table B.1. Visual J++ keywords.

abstract	int
boolean	interface
break	long
byte	native
byvalue	new
case	null
catch	package
char	private
class	protected
const	public
continue	return
default	short
do	static
double	super
else	switch
extends	synchronized
false	this
final	threadsafe
finally	throw
float	throws
for	transient
goto	true
if	try
implements	void
import	while
instanceof	

Answers to
Exercises

The following are answers to the exercises from the Java tutorial Chapters 4 to 11 in Part II. (Other chapters in other parts of this book do not have exercises.) Any listings are numbered *Ax.y*, where *x* is the chapter number, and *y* is the sequential listing number in this chapter's answer section. All listings are stored in named directories under the Answers directory on the CD-ROM.

Chapter 4

4.1

See Listing A4.1, TenNames.java.

Listing A4.1. TenNames.java.

```
class TenNames {
 public static void main(String args[]) {
  int count;  // Declare integer control variable
  for (count = 1; count <= 10; count++) {
   System.out.println(count +
     ": Tom Duck, Ugly Duckling Software, Inc.");
  }
 }
}
```

4.2

See Listing A4.2, NewWhileCount.java. Because postfix notation is used, the pre-incremented value of count is compared to 10 in the expression. Change the expression to ++count to see the difference.

Listing A4.2. NewWhileCount.java.

```
class NewWhileCount {
 public static void main(String args[]) {
  int count = 0;
  while (count++ < 10)
   System.out.println("Count = " + count);
 }
}
```

4.3

See Listing A4.3, ClearScreen.java. The program simply prints 50 new lines, which should be enough to scroll other text out of view.

Listing A4.3. `ClearScreen.java`.

```
class ClearScreen {
 public static void main(String args[]) {
  for (int i = 1; i < 50; i++)
   System.out.println("\n");
 }
}
```

4.4

See Listing A4.4, `BinOut.java`. This program uses the `StringBuffer` class, which is not yet introduced, to build an output string of `0` and `1` characters. Relevant to this chapter is the shift-left statement and the test for `k < 0`, which indicates that the high-order bit equals `1`. Shifting the integer left 32 times brings each bit into the high-order position for testing.

Listing A4.4. `BinOut.java`.

```
class BinOut {
 public static void main(String args[]) {
  int k = 0xFACE;  // decimal 64206
  StringBuffer s = new StringBuffer();
  System.out.println("k in decimal = " + k);
  for (int i = 0; i < 32; i++) {
   if (k < 0)
    s.append('1');
   else
    s.append('0');
   k = k << 1;
  }
  System.out.println("in binary, k = " + s);
 }
}
```

4.5

See Listing A4.5, `FpErrors.java`.

Listing A4.5. `FpErrors.java`.

```
class FpErrors {
 public static void main(String args[]) {
  double result;
  // Underflow
  result = 2.22507e-308;
  result--;
  System.out.println("Underflow result = " + result);
  // Overflow
  result = 1.79769e+308;
```

continues

Listing A4.5. continued

```
  result++;
  System.out.println("Overflow result = " + result);
  // Divide by zero
  result = 3.14159;
  result /= 0;
  System.out.println("Divide by zero result = " + result);
 }
}
```

Chapter 5

5.1

See Listing A5.1, DayOfWeek.java. The sample program merely prints the date as a string, which shows the day for any date from 1/1/70 on. An even better program might use a switch statement to extract only the day information from a Date object. For example, you could use code such as

```
String day;
Date d = new Date("5/6/86");
switch (d.getDay()) {
 case 0: day = "Sunday"; break;
 case 1: day = "Monday"; break;
 case 2: day = "Tuesday"; break;
 case 3: day = "Wednesday"; break;
 case 4: day = "Thursday"; break;
 case 5: day = "Friday"; break;
 case 6: day = "Saturday"; break;
}
```

Listing A5.1. DayOfWeek.java.

```
import java.io.*;
import java.util.*;
class DayOfWeek {
 public static void main(String args[]) {
  try {
   char ch;  // Keyboard input character
   StringBuffer str = new StringBuffer();  // Date as string
   System.out.println("Enter date (ex. 5/7/92");  // Prompt user
   while ((ch = (char)System.in.read()) != '\n') {
    str.append(ch);  // Construct string from keyboard
   }
   Date d = new Date(str.toString());  // Convert to date
   System.out.println(d.toString());   // Display full date
  } catch (IOException e) {  // Catch any input errors
   System.out.println("Input / output error");
  }
 }
}
```

5.2

Listing A5.2, `GetString.java`, implements a `getString()` method and shows how to use it to prompt users for a date. Call the method like this:

```
String str = getString("Enter something:");
```

Listing A5.2. GetString.java.

```
import java.io.*;
import java.util.*;
class GetString {
 // Prompt for and return a string from user
 public static String getString(String prompt) {
  char ch;  // Keyboard input character
  StringBuffer str = new StringBuffer();
  System.out.println(prompt);
  try {
   while ((ch = (char)System.in.read()) != '\n') {
    str.append(ch);
   }
  } catch (IOException e) {
   System.out.println(e.toString());
  }
  return str.toString();
 }
public static void main(String args[]) {
  String str = getString("Enter date (ex. 5/7/92)");
  Date d = new Date(str.toString());
  System.out.println(d.toString());
 }
}
```

5.3

Listing A5.3 shows one possible `yes()` method, extracted from the full answer, `GetYes.java`, on the CD-ROM. The method displays a prompt by calling `getString()` from the preceding exercise. It converts that string to lowercase, and then returns `true` if the first character equals y. Using this technique, users can enter Y, Yes, or even Ypsilanti as a "yes" response. The listing also demonstrates in `main()` how to call `yes()`.

Listing A5.3. GetYes.java (partial).

```
...
// Prompt for yes or no answer
public static boolean yes(String prompt) {
 String answer = getString(prompt).toLowerCase();
 return (answer.charAt(0) == 'y');
}
public static void main(String args[]) {
```

continues

Listing A5.3. continued

```
while (yes("Continue program?")) {
  System.out.println("Answer N next time to stop");
 }
}
...
```

5.4

Listing A5.4 shows one possible getSelection() method, extracted from the full listing, MenuDemo.java, on the CD-ROM. The sample code calls the getString() method from Listing A5.2 and returns the resulting string's first character in uppercase. The sample program, also shown here, demonstrates how to call the method.

Listing A5.4. MenuDemo.java (partial).

```
...
// Prompt for menu selection
public static char getSelection(String menu) {
 String answer = getString(menu).toUpperCase();
 return (answer.charAt(0));  // Return selection
}
public static void main(String args[]) {
 char ch;
 System.out.println("Enter selection from menu");
 while ((ch = getSelection("F-ile, D-ial, Q-uit")) != 'Q') {
  System.out.println("You selected " + ch);
 }
}
...
```

Chapter 6

6.1

See Listing A6.1, ParseFile.java. The main program demonstrates how to call the answer's getExtension() method to extract a possible filename extension, entered as a command-line argument. For example, run the program using a command such as

```
jview parsefile MyFile.txt
```

Listing A6.1. ParseFile.java.

```
class ParseFile {
 // Return filename extension or null if none
 public static String getExtension(String filename) {
  int index = filename.indexOf('.');
```

```
   if (index >= 0)
    return filename.substring(index, filename.length());
   else
    return "";
 }
public static void main(String args[]) {
  if (args.length == 0) {
   System.out.println("Enter a file name");
   System.out.println("ex. jview parsefile MyFile.txt");
  } else {
   String extension = getExtension(args[0]);
   System.out.println("extension = " + extension);
  }
 }
}
```

6.2

See Listing A6.2, ReturnSub.java. The answer calls toString() to convert the StringBuffer object s to a String object, and then calls the String class indexOf() method to find the substring's index.

Listing A6.2. ReturnSub.java.

```
class ReturnSub {
 // Return index of a substring
 public static int getSubIndex(StringBuffer s, String sub) {
  return s.toString().indexOf(sub);
 }
public static void main(String args[]) {
  StringBuffer buffer = new StringBuffer("Remember the Alamo");
  int index = getSubIndex(buffer, "Alamo");
  System.out.println("Index = " + index);
 }
}
```

6.3

See Listing A6.3, Palindrome.java. The method, isPalindrome(), returns true if its String argument is spelled the same backwards and forwards, ignoring punctuation. To run the program, enter a command such as the following examples, delimiting multiple-word arguments with quotes:

```
jview palindrome "Sex at noon taxes"
jview palindrome "Evil olive"
jview palindrome "Step on no pets"
jview palindrome "Never odd or even"
jview palindrome "Gnu dung"
jview palindrome "Senile felines"
```

The isPalindrome() method first removes any nonalphabetic characters from the String argument by using a for loop and the Character class isLetter() method. The resulting StringBuffer object, buffer, is then converted to a temporary String object, t1, and a reversed String, t2. The result of comparing these two String objects, ignoring case, is passed back as the method's return value. (There are numerous other ways to write this method, but I tried to use String, StringBuffer, and Character class methods exclusively in this answer, because these are the subjects of the chapter.)

Listing A6.3. Palindrome.java.

```java
class Palindrome {
 // Return true if argument is a palindrome, a string
 // that is spelled the same forward and back, ignoring
 // any punctuation.
 public static boolean isPalindrome(String s) {
  // Remove any non letters from string argument
  StringBuffer buffer = new StringBuffer();
  for (int i = 0; i < s.length(); i++)
   if (Character.isLetter(s.charAt(i)))
    buffer.append(s.charAt(i));
  // Convert buffer to String objects
  String t1 = new String(buffer);
  String t2 = new String(buffer.reverse());
  // Compare temporary strings, ignoring case
  return t1.equalsIgnoreCase(t2);
 }
public static void main(String args[]) {
  String str;
  if (args.length == 0)
   str = "Able was I ere I saw Elba";
  else
   str = args[0];
  System.out.println("The string: " + str);
  if (isPalindrome(str))
   System.out.println("... is a palindrome");
  else
   System.out.println("... is not a palindrome");
 }
}
```

6.4

Listing A6.4, CharMinMax.java, shows how to use the MIN_VALUE, MAX_VALUE, MIN_RADIX, and MAX_RADIX constants in the Character class. Because the _VALUE constants are type char, a typecast expression converts them to int. On my display, running the program shows the following text:

```
Minimum value = 0
Maximum value = 65535
Minimum radix = 2
Maximum radix = 36
```

Listing A6.4. CharMinMax.java.

```
class CharMinMax {
 public static void main(String args[]) {
  System.out.println(
    "Minimum value = " + (int)Character.MIN_VALUE);
  System.out.println(
    "Maximum value = " + (int)Character.MAX_VALUE);
  System.out.println(
    "Minimum radix = " + Character.MIN_RADIX);
  System.out.println(
    "Maximum radix = " + Character.MAX_RADIX);
 }
}
```

Chapter 7

7.1

See Listing A7.1, FpSum.java, which uses the Double wrapper class valueOf() and doubleValue() methods to parse command-line arguments, summing each in the double result variable.

Listing A7.1. FpSum.java.

```
class FpSum {
 public static void main(String args[]) {
  double result = 0.0;
  for (int i = 0; i < args.length; i++)
   result += Double.valueOf(args[i]).doubleValue();
  System.out.println("Result = " + result);
 }
}
```

7.2

See Listing A7.2, PowerOf.java.

Listing A7.2. PowerOf.java.

```
class PowerOf {
 public static void main(String args[]) {
  if (args.length < 2) {
   System.out.println("ex. jview powerof 2.5 8");
  } else {
   Double value = Double.valueOf(args[0]);
   Double exp = Double.valueOf(args[1]);
   double result =
    Math.pow(value.doubleValue(), exp.doubleValue());
```

continues

Listing A7.2. continued

```
    System.out.println(value.toString() + " to the "
     + exp.toString() + " power = " + result);
  }
 }
}
```

7.3

See Listing A7.3, `RandString.java`.

Listing A7.3. `RandString.java`.

```
import java.util.Random;
class RandString {
 // Declare random number generator
  public static Random generator;
 // Return randomized character (letter or digit)
 public static char getRandChar() {
  char ch;
  do {
   ch = (char)generator.nextInt();
  } while (!(Character.isLetterOrDigit(ch)));
  return ch;
 }
 // Return randomized string of len characters
 public static String getRandString(int len) {
  if (len <= 0) len = 1;     // Default minimum length
  if (len > 128) len = 128; // Default maximum length
  StringBuffer buffer = new StringBuffer(len);
  for (int i = 0; i < len; i++)
   buffer.append(getRandChar());
  return buffer.toString();
 }
 // Demonstrate preceding method
 public static void main(String args[]) {
  generator = new Random();  // Initialize generator
  String s;
  s = getRandString(8);
  System.out.println("s (len =  8) = " + s);
  s = getRandString(40);
  System.out.println("s (len = 40) = " + s);
  s = getRandString(72);
  System.out.println("s (len = 72) = " + s);
 }
}
```

7.4

See Listing A7.4, `IntToHexBin.java`.

Listing A7.4. IntToHexBin.java.

```
class IntToHexBin {
 public static void main(String args[]) {
  if (args.length < 1) {
   System.out.println("ex. jview inttohexbin 1234");
  } else {
   // Convert command-line argument to int value
   Integer intObject = new Integer(args[0]);
   int value = intObject.intValue();
   // Display in three formats using Integer wrapper
   System.out.println(
    "Decimal = " + Integer.toString(value, 10));
   System.out.println(
    "Hex     = " + Integer.toHexString(value));
   System.out.println(
    "Binary  = " + Integer.toBinaryString(value));
  }
 }
}
```

Chapter 8

8.1

Listing A8.1, ObjectCount.java, declares a static integer variable, count, in AnyClass. Because it is static, the variable exists for all objects of the class. To account for the number of objects created, the class constructor increments count.

Listing A8.1. ObjectCount.java.

```
class AnyClass {
 private static int count = 0;
 AnyClass() {
  count++;
 }
 public int getCount() {
  return count;
 }
}
class ObjectCount {
 public static void main(String args[]) {
  AnyClass object = new AnyClass();
  for (int i = 0; i < 10; i++)
    object = new AnyClass();
  System.out.println(
   "Objects created = " + object.getCount());
 }
}
```

8.2

The answer in Listing A8.2, ReadText.java, is a little different from the chapter's file I/O demonstration program. Arriving at the correct answer requires reading the documentation for class RandomAccessFile, which indicates that the readLine() method returns null—one of Java's built-in class variables, as explained in the chapter—instead of throwing an EOFException object. Consequently, rather than catching this object as in the chapter's file demo, the ReadText.java program loops until readLine() returns null.

Listing A8.2. ReadText.java.

```java
import java.io.*;
class ReadText {
 public static void main(String args[]) {
  String s;  // Holds each line of text from file
  try {
   // Open file for reading
   RandomAccessFile file =
    new RandomAccessFile("ReadText.java", "r");
   // Read text lines until end of file reached
   while ((s = file.readLine()) != null)
    System.out.println(s);
   // Close file
   file.close();
  } catch (IOException e) {
   System.out.println("Error: " + e.getMessage());
  }
 }
}
```

8.3

Listing A8.3 shows one way (not necessarily the best or only way) to declare a Point class that can hold an X,Y coordinate value. I purposely created the class to use all three access specifiers. The instance variables, x and y, are private. The class has a default and overloaded, parameterized constructor. A protected method, SetXY(), initializes the private instance variables and is called by both constructors, but it is not available to statements outside of the class or subclasses of Point. Four public methods—setX(), setY(), getX(), and getY()—provide controlled access paths to the class's instance variables. The main program demonstrates how to construct a Point object and use its data in a controlled, object-oriented fashion.

Listing A8.3. PointDemo.java.

```java
class Point {
 // Instance variables
 private int x, y;
 // Constructors
 Point() {
  setXY(0, 0);
```

```
 }
 Point(int xx, int yy) {
  setXY(xx, yy);
 }
 // Protected method
 protected void setXY(int xx, int yy) {
  setX(xx);
  setY(yy);
 }
 // Public methods
 public int getX() { return x; }
 public int getY() { return y; }
 public void setX(int n) { x = n; }
 public void setY(int n) { y = n; }
}
class PointDemo {
 // Display value of Point object p
 static void showPoint(Point p) {
  System.out.println("(" + p.getX() + "," + p.getY() + ")");
 }
 // Main program
 public static void main(String args[]) {
  Point p = new Point();     // Use default constructor
  showPoint(p);
  p.setX(123);                // Call data access methods
  p.setY(456);
  showPoint(p);
  p = new Point(654, 321);  // Use parameterized constructor
  showPoint(p);
 }
}
```

8.4

The Integer class is declared final, and as such, it cannot be extended into a subclass as this exercise suggests. Any attempt to do so with a declaration such as

```
class NewInteger extends Integer {  // ???
}
```

causes the compiler to issue the following error message:

```
X.java(6,26) : error J0048: Cannot extend final class 'Integer'
```

8.5

Listing A8.5 shows how to obtain the class name of any object. The first step is to write a method (which is static here for simplicity, but doesn't have to be) that receives an Object argument:

```
static void printClassName(Object obj) {...
```

Because all classes extend from Object, you can pass any object of any class to the method's obj parameter. Next, from the Object class's online documentation, you will discover a method named `getClass()`, which returns an object of the class, `Class`. This provides the key to the answer, because all classes in Java are actually represented as objects! Turning to the online documentation for `Class` reveals the method `getName()`, which returns type `String`. Thus to obtain the class name of any object, the program uses this expression:

```
obj.getClass().getName() ...
```

Listing A8.5. `ClassName.java`.

```
import java.util.Random;
class ClassName {
 // Display class name of any object
 static void printClassName(Object obj) {
  System.out.println(
    obj + " class is named " +
    obj.getClass().getName());
 }
 // Demonstrate preceding method
 public static void main(String args[]) {
  Random generator = new Random();
  printClassName(generator);
 }
}
```

Chapter 9

9.1

The answer in Listing A9.1, `FindFile.java`, constructs a `RandomAccessFile` object in a try block. Java's documentation states that this class's constructors throw an object of `IOException` if any problems are detected. The program catches this exception, which we assume means the specified file could not be found. If the file is found, the program merely reports this fact *immediately after constructing the file object.* This is an important concept. We simply *assume* that the construction works. If it doesn't, the `try` block jumps to an appropriate `catch` block, which reports the error.

Listing A9.1. `FindFile.java`.

```
import java.io.*;
class FindFile {
 public static void main(String args[]) {
  try {
   RandomAccessFile file = new RandomAccessFile(args[0], "r");
   System.out.println("File " + args[0] + " was found!");
   file.close();
  } catch (IOException e) {
   System.out.println("File not found: " + e.getMessage());
  } catch (ArrayIndexOutOfBoundsException e) {
   System.out.println("Enter a file name");
```

```
    System.out.println("ex. jview findfile findfile.java");
  }
 }
}
```

In addition to detecting whether a file exists, the `FindFile.java` program shows an alternate way to verify that users enter the correct number of arguments. In past examples, I did this using code such as

```
if (args.length < 1) { ...
```

Alternatively, you can use an exception handler that catches an object of the class `ArrayIndex-OutOfBoundsException`. In this way, an expression in the form args[*n*] (where *n* is out of range due to an improper number of arguments) throws the exception, which the sample code catches, and displays instructions. To see how this works, run the program with a command such as

```
jview FindFile
```

To verify that a file exists, use commands such as

```
jview FindFile FindFile.java
jview FindFile xxxx.yyyy
```

9.2

The answer in Listing A9.2, `CatchAll.java`, does not necessarily represent a good way to write `main()` methods. The technique, however, might be useful for tracing system problems during debugging. As listed, the program declares `main() throws Throwable`. This is necessary to avoid an error from the compiler due to the `throw` statement that rethrows an object of this type. Because all exception classes extend from `Throwable`, this code displays a stack trace for all possible exceptions. As mentioned in the chapter, however, application code is best written to catch `Exception` class objects rather than `Throwable`.

Listing A9.2. `CatchAll.java`.

```
class CatchAll {
 public static void f() {
  throw new OutOfMemoryError();  // For demonstration only!
 }
 public static void main(String args[])
  throws Throwable {
  try {
   f();
  } catch (Throwable e) {
   System.out.println("Error detected");
   e.printStackTrace();
   throw e;
  }
 }
}
```

9.3

Listing A9.3, NullObject.java, shows how to detect a null object argument (see method f()), and throw an exception of the NullPointerException class. Add the statement throw e; after the last println() statement to see how the system handles this error. Use the technique here to prevent programs from ending prematurely if a null object is passed as an argument to a method parameter, as main() purposely does for demonstration here.

Listing A9.3. NullObject.java.

```
// Sample class for creating a null object
class MyClass {
 MyClass() { }
}
// Main program class
class NullObject {
 // Throw an exception if argument is null
 public static void f(Object obj)
 throws NullPointerException {
  if (obj == null)
    throw new NullPointerException("Object obj in f() is null");
 }
 public static void main(String args[]) {
  MyClass obj = null;  // Uninitialized object
  try {
   f(obj);
  } catch (NullPointerException e) {
   System.out.println(e.getMessage());
  }
 }
}
```

9.4

The answer in Listing A9.4, Continue.java, might surprise you as being overly complex, but most of the programming involves prompting for and reading a response from the keyboard. (I "borrowed" most of this code from the Yes.java sample program also in the Answers directory on the CD-ROM.) The trick here is to use a while loop in main() that tries one or more statements. (The demonstration simply calls a method f() that purposely throws an exception.) On detecting any Throwable exception, the program repeats the while loop, which again tries to call f(), if the user answers yes to the prompt Continue (y/n)?. Here again is an example of a technique that is usually not recommended—catching Throwable class objects. Because main() rethrows the exception, however, this technique is perfectly harmless. Any exception that lives after main() ends will be passed along for proper handling to the Java virtual machine.

Listing A9.4. `Continue.java`.

```java
import java.io.*;
class Continue {
 // Test method throws exception
 public static void f() {
  throw new OutOfMemoryError("Out of memory");
 }
 // Prompt for and return a string from user
 public static String getString(String prompt) {
  char ch;  // Keyboard input character
  StringBuffer str = new StringBuffer();
  System.out.println(prompt);
  try {
   while ((ch = (char)System.in.read()) != '\n') {
    str.append(ch);
   }
  } catch (IOException e) {
   System.out.println(e.toString());
  }
  return str.toString();
 }
 // Prompt for yes or no answer
 public static boolean yes(String prompt) {
  String answer = getString(prompt).toLowerCase();
  return (answer.charAt(0) == 'y');
 }
 // Main method
 public static void main(String args[])
  throws Throwable {
  boolean okayToContinue = true;
  while (okayToContinue) {
   try {
    f();
   } catch (Throwable e) {
    System.out.println("Error detected: " + e.getMessage());
    if (!yes("Continue program (y/n)?"))
     throw e;
   }
  }
 }
}
```

Chapter 10

10.1

Listing A10.1 creates an array of unique integer values, and sorts the array using the Quick Sort algorithm. The `quickSort()` method is written in a general way and will work with any type of data stored in a common Java array.

Listing A10.1. SortArray.java.

```java
import java.util.Random;
class SortArray {
 // Declare integer array reference
 static int array[];
 // Return true if int n is in array
 static boolean inArray(int n) {
  for (int i = 0; i < array.length; i++)
   if (array[i] == n)
    return true;
  return false;
 }
 // Display contents of array
 static void showArray(String msg) {
  int n;  // Holds copy of each array value
  System.out.println("\n" + msg);
  for (int i = 0; i < array.length; i++) {
   n = array[i];
   if (n < 100) System.out.print(" ");
   if (n < 10 ) System.out.print(" ");
   System.out.print(array[i] + "   ");
  }
  System.out.println();
 }
 // Sort array using Quick Sort algorithm by C. A. R. Hoare
 static void quickSort(int left, int right) {
  int i = left;
  int j = right;
  int test = array[(left + right) / 2];
  int swap;
  do {
   while (array[i] < test) i++;
   while (test < array[j]) j--;
   if (i <= j) {
    swap = array[i];
    array[i] = array[j];
    array[j] = swap;
    i++;
    j--;
   }
  } while (i <= j);
  if (left < j) quickSort(left, j);
  if (i < right) quickSort(i, right);
 }
 // Main program
 public static void main(String args[]) {
  // Variables
  array = new int[100];        // Create array
  Random gen = new Random();   // Create a random number generator
  int n;                       // Miscellaneous integer
  // Fill array with unique values selected at random
  for (int i = 0; i < 100; i++) {
   do {
    n = Math.abs(gen.nextInt()) % 1000;
   } while (inArray(n));
   array[i] = n;
  }
  // Display array before and after sorting
   showArray("Before sorting:");
```

620

```
    quickSort(0, array.length - 1);
    showArray("After sorting:");
  }
}
```

10.2

Listing A10.2, CopyArgs.java, shows two ways to copy the array. Technique #1 is enabled; delete or comment it out, and remove the comment slashes from Technique #2 to test the alternate method, which calls System.arraycopy(). The first method uses a for loop, which is the simpler of the two methods.

Listing A10.2. CopyArgs.java.

```
class CopyArgs {
 // Display message and String array
 static void show(String msg, String[] sa) {
  System.out.println("\n" + msg);
  for (int i = 0; i < sa.length; i++)
   System.out.println("[" + i + "]=" + sa[i]);
 }
 public static void main(String args[]) {
  if (args.length == 0) {
   System.out.println("Enter command line arguments");
   return;
  }
  // Create array large enough to hold args[]
  String copy[] = new String[args.length];
  // Copy args into the new array
  // Technique #1 (simple):
  for (int i = 0; i < args.length; i++)
   copy[i] = new String(args[i]).toUpperCase();
  // Technique #2 (the hard way, but okay):
//  System.arraycopy(args, 0, copy, 0, args.length);
//  for (int i = 0; i < args.length; i++)
//   copy[i] = copy[i].toUpperCase();
  // Display original and copied arrays
  show("Original array", args);
  show("Copied array", copy);
 }
}
```

10.3

Listing A10.3, KeywordHash.java, demonstrates a good way to format an array of strings into a hash table container. First, the program declares the array of String values. It then calls Hashtable.put() to insert each string into the table, using the keyword as the key and value. This does not insert the words twice; keys are used only to compute a hash code—in this case, when put() calls String.hashcode(). You can use similar code to hash any set of strings and provide them as a fast-access lookup table.

621

Listing A10.3. `KeywordHash.java`.

```java
import java.util.Hashtable;
import java.util.HashtableEnumerator;
class KeyWordHash {
 public static void main(String args[]) throws Exception {
  String keywordArray[] = {
"abstract", "boolean", "break", "byte", "byvalue", "case",
"catch", "char", "class", "const", "continue", "default",
"do", "double", "else", "extends", "false", "final", "finally",
"float", "for", "goto", "if", "implements", "import", "instanceof",
"int", "interface", "long", "native", "new", "null", "package",
"private", "protected", "public", "return", "short", "static",
"super", "switch", "synchronized", "this", "threadsafe",
"throw", "transient", "true", "try", "void", "while" };
  // Construct hash table to hold keyword strings
  Hashtable keywordTable = new Hashtable();
  // Insert keywords into hash table
  // Note: Keys and values are the same! Because the key is
  // used merely to compute a hash code (by calling String.hashcode()
  // in this case), despite appearances, this does NOT store
  // duplicate words in the table.
  for (int i = 0; i < keywordArray.length; i++)
   keywordTable.put(keywordArray[i], keywordArray[i]);

  // Display keyword requested by user, or list table
  // if no command line arguments entered

  if (args.length == 0) {
   System.out.println("\nJava Keywords:");
   HashtableEnumerator enum =
    (HashtableEnumerator)keywordTable.elements();
   while (enum.hasMoreElements()) {
    String name = (String)enum.nextElement();
    System.out.print(name);
    for (int i = name.length(); i < 16; i++)
     System.out.print(" ");
   }
   System.out.println("\nEnter any keyword to search hash table");
   System.out.println("ex. jview keywordhash implements\n");
  } else {
   String keyword = (String)keywordTable.get(args[0]);
   if (keyword != null)
    System.out.println("\nFound keyword '" + keyword + "'\n");
   else
    System.out.println("\n'" + args[0] + "' not found\n");
  }
 }
}
```

10.4

Listing A10.4, `VectorDemo2.java`, shows the new method, `isSorted()`, added to the `VectorDemo.java` listing. (The complete listing is on disk in the `Answers\VectorDemo2` directory.) The `boolean` method calls the `Vector` `elementAt()` method to obtain each successive string.

To compare the strings and determine whether the array is in sorted order, the program calls the String.compareTo() method. In addition to the listing, the modified program calls isSorted() from its main body using the following code:

```
if (isSorted(array))
 System.out.println("\nArray is correctly sorted\n");
else
 System.out.println("\nError: Array is NOT sorted!\n");
```

Listing A10.4. VectorDemo2.java (partial).

```
static boolean isSorted(Vector va) {
 for (int i = 0; i < va.size() - 1; i++) {
  String a = (String)va.elementAt(i);
  String b = (String)va.elementAt(i + 1);
  if (a.compareTo(b) > 0) return false;
 }
 return true;
}
```

10.5

Listing A10.5, StackPlunk.java, shows one way to write a method that can remove an item from the middle of a Stack container without disturbing other values. The trick is to call Stack.search() to find the number of pops required to remove the target item. Pop that many objects, save them in a temporary Stack container, and then push them back to the original stack minus the item to be removed.

Listing A10.5. StackPlunk.java.

```
import java.util.Stack;
class StackPlunk {
 // Plunk out a string from the stack without
 // disturbing its other contents
 public static String plunk(String arg, Stack stack) {
  if (stack.empty()) return null;
  System.out.println("\nRemoving '" + arg + "'\n");
  int npops = stack.search(arg);
  if (npops == 0) return null;
  Stack temp = new Stack();
  while (npops > 0) {
   temp.push(stack.pop());
   npops--;
  }
  String returnValue = (String)temp.pop();
  while (!temp.empty())
   stack.push(temp.pop());
  return returnValue;
 }
 public static void main(String args[]) {
```

continues

Listing A10.5. continued

```
  String s;
  // Construct stack and push some strings onto it
  Stack fruit = new Stack();
  fruit.push("Apples");
  fruit.push("Banana");
  fruit.push("Cherry");
  fruit.push("Peaches");
  fruit.push("Pumpkin");
  fruit.push("Star fruit");
  // Remove string from middle of stack
  plunk("Peaches", fruit);
  // Display stack contents
  System.out.println("Stack contents:");
  while (!fruit.empty()) {
   s = (String)fruit.pop();
   System.out.println(s);
  }
 }
}
```

Chapter 11

11.1

Modify the main program as shown in Listing A11.1. (The full listing is in the Answers\ ThreadDemo2 directory on the CD-ROM.) You may set the priority level at any time, but it is convenient here to set it before calling start(). If you change MIN_PRIORITY to MAX_PRIORITY, you might have a long wait before the system recognizes your keypress to end the program— a better value would be MAX_PRIORITY - 1. Use the maximum priority level *only* for code that must have as much processor time as possible.

Listing A11.1. ThreadDemo2.java (partial).

```
background.setPriority(Thread.MIN_PRIORITY);
background.start();  // Start background thread
```

11.2

Listing A11.2 converts the Background class to one that implements Runnable rather than extending Thread. I've highlighted the significant changes in bold. In addition, the constructor no longer calls super(name), because Object has no such constructor. Also, the output statement references name instead of calling getName(), which was formerly inherited from Thread. The main program shows the correct way to create an object of the Background class and execute its run() method in a separate thread.

Listing A11.2. `ThreadDemo3.java`.

```java
// Extend Thread class and override the run() method
class Background implements Runnable {
 // Fields:
 long count;          // Number of loops in run()
 long trigger;        // Controls printing speed
 boolean finished;    // True when thread should die
 String name;
 // Constructor:
 Background(String name) {
  finished = false;    // Allows run() to continue
  trigger = 1000000;   // Increase to slow printing
  count = trigger / 2; // Makes first message appear sooner
  this.name = name;
 }
 // Override run() method (BUT DON'T CALL IT!)
 public void run() {
  try {
   while (!finished) {   // Note: loops "forever!"
    count++;
    if (count == trigger)
     System.out.println("\nHurry up!");
    else if (count == trigger * 2)
     System.out.println("\nWhat's taking you so long?");
    else if (count == trigger * 3) {
     System.out.println("\nC'mon, press that key!");
     count = 0;   // Reset count to repeat messages
    }
   }
  } catch (InterruptedException e) {
   halt();
  }
 }
 // Causes run() method to halt
 public void halt() {
  finished = true;
  System.out.println("Stopping thread " + name + "\n");
 }
}
// Main program demonstrates background processing
class ThreadDemo3 {
 public static void main(String args[]) throws Exception {
  Background background =
   new Background("Background process");
  System.out.println(
    "Starting thread. Press Enter to stop.");
  new Thread(background).start();
  while ((char)System.in.read() != '\n');  // Wait for key
  background.halt();   // Stop background thread
 }
}
```

11.3

Listing A11.3 shows the answer. (This code is for reference only and is not on disk.)

Listing A11.3. Reference only: not on disk.

```
public synchronized void inputString();
public synchronized void outputString();
```

Glossary

API: Application Programming Interface.

Applet: A Java program that runs inside a Web browser such as Internet Explorer.

Applet class: The standard Java class on which applets are based.

Application: A stand-alone Java program whose main class has a `main()` method.

AWT: The package of classes commonly known as "another window toolkit," but officially titled "abstract window toolkit" by at least one source.

Class: Java's fundamental object-oriented programming tool. Classes encapsulate data and code (methods), and all data and code in a Java program exists in one or more classes.

Class library: Java's class library consists of packages of classes that you can import, extend, and use in applets and applications.

Exception: An object that is thrown to indicate an exceptional condition, typically to report an error.

Hash code: A value that is generated for use as an index into a container of objects called a hash table.

Interface: A type of class that is purely abstract. Interface classes provide protocols that other Java classes may implement.

Interpreter: A program that runs compiled Java byte codes, also known as P codes.

Object: The class from which all classes are extended.

Package: A collection of related classes. Java provides numerous standard packages such as `java.awt` for graphics and window programming. You can also create your own packages.

SDK: Software Development Kit.

Thread: A Java class that can run a separate process. All Java programs are multithreaded—the automatic garbage collector, for example, executes in a separate thread.

Unicode: A 16-bit value that represents one character. Unicode characters can represent the text of most human, written languages.

Wrapper class: A class that provides object-orientation to a native data type. For example, an object of the `Integer` class can wrap an `int` value.

Bibliography

Anuff, Ed. *The Java Sourcebook,* John Wiley & Sons, Inc., 1996.

Davis, Stephen R. *Learn Java Now,* Microsoft Press, 1996.

Ritchey, Tim. *Java!,* New Riders Publishing, 1995.

Swan, Tom. *Mastering Borland C++ 5,* Sams, 1996.

INDEX

Index

I

A VIACOM SERVICE

The Information SuperLibrary™

Bookstore   **Search**   **What's New**   **Reference**   **Software**   **Newsletter**   **Company Overviews**

Yellow Pages   **Internet Starter Kit**   **HTML Workshop**   **Win a Free T-Shirt!**   **Macmillan Computer Publishing**   **Site Map**   **Talk to Us**

CHECK OUT THE BOOKS IN THIS LIBRARY.

You'll find thousands of shareware files and over 1600 computer books designed for both technowizards and technophobes. You can browse through 700 sample chapters, get the latest news on the Net, and find just about anything using our

We're open 24-hours a day, 365 days a year.

You don't need a card.

We don't charge fines.

And you can be as **LOUD** as you want.

MACMILLAN COMPUTER PUBLISHING USA

A VIACOM COMPANY

Technical ----- Support:

If you need assistance with the information in this book or with a CD/Disk accompanying the book, please access the Knowledge Base on our Web site at **http://www.superlibrary.com/general/support**. Our most Frequently Asked Questions are answered there. If you do not find the answer to your questions on our Web site, you may contact Macmillan Technical Support **(317) 581-3833** or e-mail us at **support@mcp.com**.

Teach Yourself Java in 21 Days, Professional Reference Edition

—*Laura Lemay & Michael Morrison*

Introducing the first, best, and most-detailed guide to developing applications with the hot new Java language from Sun Microsystems. This book provides detailed coverage of the hottest new technology on the World Wide Web. It shows readers how to develop applications using the Java language, and it also includes coverage of browsing Java applications with Netscape and other popular Web browsers. The book's CD-ROM includes the Java Developer's Kit.

$59.99 USA/$84.95 CDN   *Casual–Accomplished–Expert*
1-57521-183-1

Java Unleashed, Second Edition

—*Michael Morrison, et al.*

Java Unleashed, Second Edition is an expanded and updated version of the largest, most comprehensive Java book on the market. This book covers Java, Java APIs, JavaOS, just-in-time compilers, and more. The book's CD-ROM includes sample code, examples from the book, and bonus electronic books.

$49.99 USA/$70.95 CDN   *Intermediate–Advanced*
1-57521-197-1

Web Programming with Java

—*Harris & Jones*

This book puts readers on the road to developing robust, real-world Java applications. Various cutting-edge applications are presented, allowing the reader to quickly learn all aspects of programming Java for the Internet. The book's CD-ROM contains source code and powerful utilities. Readers learn to create live, interactive Web pages.

$39.99 USA/$56.95 CDN   *Accomplished–Expert*
1-57521-113-0

Developing Intranet Applications with Java

—*Jerry Ablan*

This book shows developers the intricacies of Java intranet development. It teaches how to create interactive databases, multimedia, animations, and sound for use on an intranet. Readers also learn how to add interactivity to Web databases. The book's CD-ROM includes source code from the book and powerful Java utilities.

$49.99 USA/$70.95 CDN   *Accomplished–Expert*
1-57521-166-1

Java Developer's Reference

—*Mike Cohn, et al.*

This is the information- and resource-packed development package for professional developers. It explains the components of the Java Development Kit (JDK) and the Java programming language. Everything needed to program Java is included within this comprehensive reference, making it the tool developers will turn to over and over again for timely accurate information on Java and the JDK. The book's CD-ROM contains source code from the book and powerful utilities. *Java Developer's Reference* also includes tips and tricks for getting the most from Java and your Java programs, and it contains complete descriptions of all the package classes and their individual methods.

$59.99 USA/$84.95 CDN   *Accomplished–Expert*
1-57521-129-7

Teach Yourself Visual J++ in 21 Days

—*Laura Lemay, Patrick Winters, & David Blankenbeckler*

Readers will learn how to use Visual J++, Microsoft's Windows version of Java, to design and create Java applets for the World Wide Web. Visual J++ includes many new Java features, including visual resource editing tools, source code control, syntax coloring, visual project management, and integrated bills. All of those tools are covered in detail, giving readers the information they need to write professional Java applets for the Web. This book includes information on the Java class libraries and how to use them to create specific applet effects, and it provides a detailed tutorial for developing applications with the new Java. The book's CD-ROM includes all the source code and all the examples from the book.

$39.99 USA/$56.95 CDN   *Casual–Accomplished*
1-57521-158-0

Web Programming with Visual J++

—*Cohn, Rutten, & Jort*

Readers get up to speed quickly with this comprehensive new reference on Microsoft's licensed Windows version of Java, Visual J++. This book discusses how to develop feature-rich Visual J++ applications, and it explores the advanced features of Visual J++. The book's CD-ROM includes various third-party tools, utilities, and demonstrations.

$39.99 USA/$56.95 CDN   *Accomplished–Expert*
1-57521-174-2

Visual J++ Unleashed

—*Bryan Morgan, et al.*

Java is the hottest programming language being learned today. And Microsoft's Windows version of Java, code-named Visual J++, might prove to be even hotter because Microsoft has added several new development features (such as graphic designing) to the Java language. *Visual J++ Unleashed* shows readers how to exploit the Java development potential of Visual J++. This book also teaches you how to add interactivity and Java applets to Web pages, and it details how the Windows enhancements to the Java environment can be exploited for "quick and easy" programming. The book's CD-ROM includes source code from the book and powerful utilities.

$49.99 USA/$70.95 CDN   *Accomplished–Expert*
1-57521-161-0

Add to Your Sams.net Library Today
with the Best Books for Internet Technologies

ISBN	Quantity	Description of Item	Unit Cost	Total Cost
1-57521-183-1		Teach Yourself Java in 21 Days, Professional Reference Edition (Book/CD-ROM)	$59.99	
1-57521-197-1		Java Unleashed, Second Edition (Book/CD-ROM)	$49.99	
1-57521-113-0		Web Programming with Java (Book/CD-ROM)	$39.99	
1-57521-166-1		Developing Intranet Applications with Java (Book/CD-ROM)	$49.99	
1-57521-129-7		Java Developer's Reference (Book/CD-ROM)	$59.99	
1-57521-158-0		Teach Yourself Visual J++ in 21 Days (Book/CD-ROM)	$39.99	
1-57521-174-2		Web Programming with Visual J++ (Book/CD-ROM)	$39.99	
1-57521-161-0		Visual J++ Unleashed (Book/CD-ROM)	$49.99	
		Shipping and Handling: See information below.		
		TOTAL		

Shipping and Handling: $4.00 for the first book, and $1.75 for each additional book. If you need to have it NOW, we can ship product to you in 24 hours for an additional charge of approximately $18.00, and you will receive your item overnight or in two days. Overseas shipping and handling adds $2.00. Prices subject to change. Call between 9:00 a.m. and 5:00 p.m. EST for availability and pricing information on latest editions.

201 W. 103rd Street, Indianapolis, Indiana 46290

1-800-428-5331 — Orders   1-800-835-3202 — FAX   1-800-858-7674 — Customer Service

Installing
the CD-ROM

The companion CD-ROM contains all the source code and project files developed by the authors, plus an assortment of evaluation versions of third-party products. To install, please follow these steps:

Windows 95/NT 4 Installation Instructions

1. Insert the CD-ROM into your CD-ROM drive.
2. From the Windows 95 or NT 4 desktop, double-click on the My Computer icon.
3. Double-click on the icon representing your CD-ROM drive.
4. Double-click on the icon titled `setup.exe` to run the CD-ROM installation program.

This program creates a Program group with the icons to run the programs on the CD-ROM. No files will be copied to your hard drive during this installation.

NOTE

If you have Windows 95 and the AutoPlay feature is enabled, the `setup.exe` program is executed automatically when the CD is inserted into the drive.

the date of receipt. Some states and jurisdictions do not allow limitations on duration of an implied warranty, so the above limitation may not apply to you. To the extent allowed by applicable law, implied warranties on the SOFTWARE PRODUCT and hardware, if any, are limited to ninety (90) days and one year, respectively.

CUSTOMER REMEDIES. Microsoft's and its suppliers' entire liability and your exclusive remedy shall be, at Microsoft's option, either (a) return of the price paid, or (b) repair or replacement of the SOFTWARE PRODUCT or hardware that does not meet Microsoft's Limited Warranty and which is returned to Microsoft with a copy of your receipt. This Limited Warranty is void if failure of the SOFTWARE PRODUCT or hardware has resulted from accident, abuse, or misapplication. Any replacement SOFTWARE PRODUCT or hardware will be warranted for the remainder of the original warranty period or thirty (30) days, whichever is longer. **Outside the United States, neither these remedies nor any product support services offered by Microsoft are available without proof of purchase from an authorized international source.**

NO OTHER WARRANTIES. To the maximum extent permitted by applicable law, Microsoft and its suppliers disclaim all other warranties, either express or implied, including, but not limited to, implied warranties of merchantability and fitness for a particular purpose, with regard to the SOFTWARE PRODUCT, and any accompanying hardware. This limited warranty gives you specific legal rights. You may have others, which vary from state/jurisdiction to state/ jurisdiction.

NO LIABILITY FOR CONSEQUENTIAL DAMAGES. TO THE MAXIMUM EXTENT PERMITTED BY APPLICABLE LAW, IN NO EVENT SHALL MICROSOFT OR ITS SUPPLIERS BE LIABLE.

FOR ANY SPECIAL, INCIDENTAL, INDIRECT, OR CONSEQUENTIAL DAMAGES WHATSOEVER (INCLUDING, WITHOUT LIMITATION, DAMAGES FOR LOSS OF BUSINESS PROFITS, BUSINESS INTERRUPTION, LOSS OF BUSINESS INFORMA- TION, OR ANY OTHER PECUNIARY LOSS) ARISING OUT OF THE USE OF OR INABILITY TO USE THE SOFTWARE PRODUCT, EVEN IF MICROSOFT HAS BEEN ADVISED OF THE POSSIBILITY OF SUCH DAMAGES. BECAUSE SOME STATES AND JURISDICTIONS DO NOT ALLOW THE EXCLUSION OR LIMITATION OF LIABILITY FOR CONSEQUENTIAL OR INCIDENTAL DAMAGES, THE ABOVE LIMITATION MAY NOT APPLY TO YOU.

8. **EXPORT RESTRICTIONS.** You agree that you will not export or re-export the SOFTWARE PRODUCT to any country, person, entity or end user subject to U.S.A. export restrictions. Restricted countries currently include, but are not necessarily limited to Cuba, Iran, Iraq, Libya, North Korea, Syria, and the Federal Republic of Yugoslavia (Serbia and Montenegro, U.N. Protected Areas and areas of Republic of Bosnia and Herzegovina under the control of Bosnian Serb forces). You warrant and represent that neither the U.S.A. Bureau of Export Administration nor any other federal agency has suspended, revoked or denied your export privileges.

9. **NOTE ON JAVA SUPPORT.** THE SOFTWARE PRODUCT CONTAINS SUPPORT FOR PROGRAMS WRITTEN IN JAVA. JAVA TECHNOLOGY IS NOT FAULT TOLERANT AND IS NOT DESIGNED, MANUFACTURED, OR INTENDED FOR USE OR RESALE AS ONLINE CONTROL EQUIPMENT IN HAZARDOUS ENVIRONMENTS REQUIRING FAIL-SAFE PERFORMANCE, SUCH AS IN THE OPERATION OF NUCLEAR FACILITIES, AIRCRAFT NAVIGATION OR COMMUNICATIONS SYSTEMS, AIR TRAFFIC CONTROL, DIRECT LIFE SUPPORT MACHINES, OR WEAPONS SYSTEMS, IN WHICH THE FAILURE OF JAVA TECHNOLOGY COULD LEAD DIRECTLY TO DEATH, PERSONAL INJURY, OR SEVERE PHYSICAL OR ENVIRONMENTAL DAMAGE.

MISCELLANEOUS

If you acquired this product in the United States, this EULA is governed by the laws of the State of Washington.

If you acquired this product in Canada, this EULA is governed by the laws of the Province of Ontario, Canada. Each of the parties hereto irrevocably attorns to the jurisdiction of the courts of the Province of Ontario and further agrees to commence any litigation which may arise hereunder in the courts located in the Judicial District of York, Province of Ontario.

If this product was acquired outside the United States, then local law may apply.

Should you have any questions concerning this EULA, or if you desire to contact Microsoft for any reason, please contact the Microsoft subsidiary serving your country, or write to Microsoft Sales Information Center/One Microsoft Way/Redmond, WA 98052-6399.

LIMITED WARRANTY. Except with respect to Microsoft Internet Explorer and the REDISTRIBUTABLES, which are provided "as is," without warranty of any kind, Microsoft warrants that (a) the SOFTWARE PRODUCT will perform substantially in accordance with the accompanying written materials for a period of ninety (90) days from the date of receipt, and (b) any hardware accompanying the SOFTWARE PRODUCT will be free from defects in materials and workmanship under normal use and service for a period of one (1) year from

any upgrades, this EULA, and, if applicable, the Certificate of Authenticity), and the recipient agrees to the terms of this EULA. If the SOFTWARE PRODUCT is an upgrade, any transfer must include all prior versions of the SOFTWARE PRODUCT. Notwithstanding the foregoing, you may permanently transfer all your rights under this EULA that pertain to the Microsoft Internet Explorer only in conjunction with a permanent transfer of your validly licensed copy of a Microsoft operating system product.

e. **Termination.** Without prejudice to any other rights, Microsoft may terminate this EULA if you fail to comply with the terms and conditions of this EULA. In such event, you must destroy all copies of the SOFTWARE PRODUCT. In addition, your rights under this EULA that pertain to the Microsoft Internet Explorer software shall terminate upon termination of your Microsoft operating system product EULA.

6. **REDISTRIBUTABLE COMPONENTS.**

a. **Redistributable Files.** In addition to the license granted in Section 1, Microsoft grants you a nonexclusive, royalty-free right to reproduce and distribute the object code version of those portions of the SOFTWARE designated in the SOFTWARE as: (i) the files identified in the REDISTRB.WRI file located in the \MSDev\Redist subdirectory on the "Microsoft Visual J++ version 1.00" CD-ROM (collectively, "REDISTRIBUTABLES"), *provided* you comply with Section 6.b.

b. **Redistribution Requirements.** If you redistribute the REDISTRIBUTABLES, you agree to: (i) distribute the REDISTRIBUTABLES in object code form only in conjunction with and as a part of your software application product which adds significant and primary functionality and which is designed, developed, and tested to operate in the Microsoft Windows and/or Windows NT environments; (ii) not use Microsoft's name, logo, or trademarks to market your software application product; (iii) include a valid copyright notice on your software product; (iv) indemnify, hold harmless, and defend Microsoft from and against any claims or lawsuits, including attorney's fees, that arise or result from the use or distribution of your software application product; and (v) not permit further distribution of the REDISTRIBUTABLES by your end user. Contact Microsoft for the applicable royalties due and other licensing terms for all other uses and/or distribution of the REDISTRIBUTABLES.

7. **U.S. GOVERNMENT RESTRICTED RIGHTS.** The SOFTWARE PRODUCT and documentation are provided with RESTRICTED RIGHTS. Use, duplication, or disclosure by the Government is subject to restrictions as set forth in subparagraph (c)(1)(ii) of the Rights in Technical Data and Computer Software clause at DFARS 252.227-7013 or subparagraphs (c)(1) and (2) of the Commercial Computer Software—Restricted Rights at 48 CFR 52.227-19, as applicable. Manufacturer is Microsoft Corporation/One Microsoft Way/Redmond, WA 98052-6399.

    b. You may use copies of the Microsoft Internet Explorer software only in conjunction with a validly licensed copy of Microsoft operating system products (e.g., Windows® 95 or Windows NT®). You may make copies of the SOFTWARE PRODUCT for use on all computers for which you have licensed Microsoft operating system products.

    c. Solely with respect to electronic documents included with the SOFTWARE, you may make an unlimited number of copies (either in hardcopy or electronic form), provided that such copies shall be used only for internal purposes and are not republished or distributed to any third party.

2. **UPGRADES.** If the SOFTWARE is an upgrade, whether from Microsoft or another supplier, you may use or transfer the SOFTWARE only in conjunction with upgraded product. If the SOFTWARE is an upgrade from a Microsoft product, you may now use that upgraded product only in accordance with this EULA.

3. **SUBSCRIPTION UPDATES.** If you have acquired the SOFTWARE PRODUCT as part of a subscription package, then you must treat as an upgrade any subsequent versions of SOFTWARE PRODUCT received as an update to your subscription package.

4. **COPYRIGHT.** All title and copyrights in and to the SOFTWARE PRODUCT (including but not limited to any images, photographs, animations, video, audio, music, text, and "applets" incorporated into the SOFTWARE PRODUCT), the accompanying printed materials, and any copies of the SOFTWARE PRODUCT are owned by Microsoft or its suppliers. The SOFTWARE PRODUCT is protected by copyright laws and international treaty provisions. Therefore, you must treat the SOFTWARE PRODUCT like any other copyrighted material except that you may either (a) make one copy of the SOFTWARE PRODUCT solely for backup or archival purposes or (b) install the SOFTWARE PRODUCT on a single computer provided you keep the original solely for backup or archival purposes. You may not copy the printed materials accompanying the SOFTWARE PRODUCT.

5. **DESCRIPTION OF OTHER RIGHTS AND LIMITATIONS.**

    a. Limitations on Reverse Engineering, Decompilation, and Disassembly. You may not reverse engineer, decompile, or disassemble the SOFTWARE PRODUCT, except and only to the extent that such activity is expressly permitted by applicable law notwithstanding this limitation.

    b. No Separation of Components. The SOFTWARE PRODUCT is licensed as a single product and neither the software programs making up the SOFTWARE PRODUCT nor any UPDATE may be separated for use by more than one user at a time.

    c. Rental. You may not rent or lease the SOFTWARE PRODUCT.

    d. Software Transfer. You may permanently transfer all of your rights under this EULA, provided that you retain no copies, you transfer all of the SOFTWARE PRODUCT (including all component parts, the media and printed materials,

END-USER LICENSE AGREEMENT FOR MICROSOFT SOFTWARE

MICROSOFT VISUAL J++, Publisher's Edition

IMPORTANT—READ CAREFULLY: This Microsoft End-User License Agreement ("EULA") is a legal agreement between you (either an individual or a single entity) and Microsoft Corporation for the Microsoft software product identified above and Microsoft Internet Explorer, which include computer software and associated media and printed materials, and may include "online" or electronic documentation (together, the "SOFTWARE PRODUCT" or "SOFTWARE"). By installing, copying, or otherwise using the SOFTWARE PRODUCT, you agree to be bound by the terms of this EULA. If you do not agree to the terms of this EULA, promptly return the unused SOFTWARE PRODUCT to the place from which you obtained it for a full refund.

SOFTWARE PRODUCT LICENSE

The SOFTWARE PRODUCT is protected by copyright laws and international copyright treaties, as well as other intellectual property laws and treaties. The SOFTWARE PRODUCT is licensed, not sold.

1. **GRANT OF LICENSE.** This EULA grants you the following rights:

    a. You may use one copy of the Microsoft Software Product identified above on a single computer. The SOFTWARE is in "use" on a computer when it is loaded into temporary memory (i.e., RAM) or installed into permanent memory (e.g., hard disk, CD-ROM, or other storage device) of that computer. However, installation on a network server for the sole purpose of internal distribution to one or more other computer(s) shall not constitute "use" for which a separate license is required, provided you have a separate license for each computer to which the SOFTWARE is distributed.